TERRORISM INFORMATICS

Knowledge Management and Data Mining for Homeland Security

INTEGRATED SERIES IN INFORMATION SYSTEMS

Series Editors

Professor Ramesh Sharda
Oklahoma State University

Prof. Dr. Stefan Voß
Universität Hamburg

Other published titles in the series:

TERRORISM INFORMATICS

Knowledge Management and Data Mining for Homeland Security

edited by
Hsinchun Chen
Edna Reid
Joshua Sinai
Andrew Silke
Boaz Ganor

 Sprin

Editors
Hsinchun Chen
University of Arizona
Tucson, AZ, USA

Edna Reid
Clarion University
Clarion, PA, USA

Joshua Sinai
The Analysis Corporation
McLean, VA, USA

Andrew Silke
University of East London
United Kingdom

Boaz Ganor
Lauder School of Government & Diplomacy
Herzliya, Israel

Series Editors
Ramesh Sharda
Oklahoma State University
Stillwater, Oklahoma, USA

Stefan Voß
Universität Hamburg
Germany

ISBN-13: 978-0-387-71612-1   e-ISBN-13: 978-0-387-71613-8

Library of Congress Control Number: 2008925539

Printed on acid-free paper.

9 8 7 6 5 4 3 2 1

springer.com

TABLE OF CONTENTS

UNIT I. METHODOLOGICAL ISSUES IN TERRORISM RESEARCH

Chapter 1. Domain Mapping of Contemporary Terrorism Research
Edna Reid and Hsinchun Chen

Chapter 2. Research on Terrorism: A Review of the Impact of 9/11 and the Global War on Terrorism
Andrew Silke

Chapter 6. A Quantitative Analysis of "Root Causes of Conflict"
Mihaela Bobeica, Jean-Paul Jéral, Teofilo Garcia, Clive Best

Chapter 7. Countering Terrorism with Knowledge
James O. Ellis III

Chapter 8. Toward a Target-specific Method of Threat Assessment
Yael Shahar

Chapter 9. Identifying and Exploiting Group Learning Patterns for Counterterrorism

Horacio R. Trujillo and Brian A. Jackson

Chapter 10. Homeland Insecurity: Data Mining, Privacy, Disclosure Limitation, and the Hunt for Terrorists

Stephen E. Fienberg

UNIT II.   TERRORISM INFORMATICS TO SUPPORT PREVENTION, DETECTION, AND RESPONSE

Chapter 11. Case Study of Jihad on the Web: A Web Mining Approach
Hsinchun Chen, Jialun Qin, Edna Reid, Yilu Zhou, and Marc Sageman

Chapter 12. Studying Global Extremist Organizations' Internet Presence Using the Dark Web Attribute System: A Three Region Comparison Study
Jialun Qin, Yilu Zhou, Edna Reid, and Hsinchun Chen

Chapter 13. Content Analysis of Jihadi Extremist Groups' Videos
Arab Salem, Edna Reid, and Hsinchun Chen

Chapter 14. Analysis of Affect Intensities in Extremist Group Forums
Ahmed Abbasi and Hsinchun Chen

Chapter 15. Document Selection for Extracting Entity and Relationship Instances of Terrorist Events
Zhen Sun, Ee-Peng Lim, Kuiyu Chang, Maggy Anastasia Suryanto, and Rohan Kumar Gunaratna

Chapter 16. Data Distortion Methods and Metrics in a Terrorist Analysis System
Shuting Xu and Jun Zhang

Chapter 17. Content-Based Detection of Terrorists Browsing the Web Using an Advanced Terror Detection System (ATDS)
Yuval Elovici, Bracha Shapira, Mark Last, Omer Zaafrany, Menahem Friedman, Moti Schneider, and Abraham Kandel

Chapter 18. Text Mining the Biomedical Literature for Identification of Potential Virus/Bacterium as Bio-terrorism Weapons
Xiaohua Hu, Xiaodan Zhang, Daniel Wu, Xiaohua Zhou, and Peter Rumm

Chapter 19. Leveraging One-Class SVM and Semantic Analysis to Detect Anomalous Content

Ozgur Yilmazel, Svetlana Symonenko, Niranjan Balasubramanian, and Elizabeth D. Liddy

Chapter 20. Individual and Collective Analysis of Anomalies in Message Traffic

D.B. Skillicorn

Chapter 24. Situational Awareness Technologies for Disaster Response
Naveen Ashish, Ronald Eguchi, Rajesh Hegde, Charles Huyck,
Dmitri Kalashnikov, Sharad Mehrotra, Padhraic Smyth,
and Nalini Venkatasubramanian

PREFACE

Terrorism informatics is defined as the application of advanced methodologies and information fusion and analysis techniques to acquire, integrate, process, analyze, and manage the diversity of terrorism-related information for national/international and homeland security-related applications. These techniques are derived from disciplines such as computer science, informatics, statistics, mathematics, linguistics, social sciences, and public policy. Because the study of terrorism involves copious amounts of information from multiple sources, data types, and languages, information fusion and analysis techniques such as data mining, data integration, language translation technologies, and image and video processing are playing key roles in the future prevention, detection, and remediation of terrorism[1]. Within the homeland security industry, information fusion is defined as the use of computer technology to acquire data from many sources, integrate this data into usable and accessible forms, and interpret the results[2]. Although there has been substantial investment and research in the application of computer technology to terrorism, much of the literature in this emerging area is fragmented and often narrowly focused within specific domains such as engineering, computer science, computer security, information systems, knowledge management, and biomedicine.

The goal of this edited volume is to present an interdisciplinary and understandable review of terrorism informatics work for homeland security along two dimensions: methodological issues in terrorism research, including information infusion techniques to support terrorism prevention, detection, and response; and legal, social, privacy, and data confidentiality challenges and approaches.

SCOPE AND ORGANIZATION

This book has been grouped into two units. Unit I focuses on the methodological issues in terrorism research including trends, achievements and failures in terrorism research, methodological challenges in terrorism, challenges in retrieving and sharing terrorism information resources, and root causes of terrorism and the implications for terrorism informatics. It

---

[1] National Research Council, 2003. Making the Nation Safer: the Roles of Science and Technology in Countering Terrorism, p11.
[2] Ibid, p. 166.

also attends to critical socio-technical topics relevant to information and knowledge management such as privacy, data confidentiality, and legal challenges. Unit I chapters address the following topics and concepts:

- Mapping the domain of terrorism research
- Identifying key terrorism researchers
- The impact on 9/11 on terrorism
- Primary sources for the study of terrorism
- Analyzing the root causes of terrorism
- The construction of information resources useful for the study of terrorism
- Threat assessment and analysis
- Methods to support counterterrorism
- Data mining and privacy concerns

Unit 2 presents current research, including case studies, on the application of terrorism informatics techniques (such as web mining, social network analysis, and multimodal event extraction and analysis) to the terrorism phenomenon. Unit 2 focuses on three major areas of terrorism research: prevention, detection, and response as identified by the National Research Council[3] and the U.S. White House's Office of Science and Technology Program (OSTP).[4] Unit III will present the critical sociotechnical topics relevant to information and knowledge management: social, privacy, data confidentiality, and legal challenges.

- Examining "Jihad" on the world wide web
- Comparing extremist groups websites across regions
- Analyzing extremist communications as manifested in web forums
- Terrorist analysis systems and detection
- Identification of potential bioterrorist weapons
- Detecting and analyzing anomalous content
- Examining "insider" threats
- Using web mining and social network analysis
- Video analysis and deception detection
- Situational awareness technologies for disaster response

---

[3] Ibid., p. 167.

[4] Zahn, M.A. and Strom, K.J., 2004, "Terrorism and the Federal Social Science Research Agenda". Edited by M. Deflem. In Terrorism and Counter-Terrorism: Criminological Perspectives. Elsevier p112.

CHAPTER STRUCTURE

Each chapter follows a consistent structure to ensure uniformity and ease of use:

- Title
- Authors and affiliations
- Introduction: introduces the relevance and significance of the topic
- Literature review/Overview of the field: a systematic review of related works in the topic area
- Case study/Methods/Examples: One or two detailed studies or examples of selected techniques, systems, implementations and evaluations
- Conclusion and discussion
- Acknowledgements
- References and notes
- Suggested readings
- Online resources
- Questions for discussion

The work is further enhanced by author and subject indexes at the back of the book, intended to facilitate ease of access to the contents./

INTENDED AUDIENCE

The audience of the book is intentionally broad. It is intended to bring useful knowledge to scientists, security professionals, counterterrorism experts, and policy makers. It is also intended to serve as reference material and as a textbook in graduate-level courses related to information security, information policy, information assurance, information systems, terrorism, and public policy. Readers will learn new concepts, technologies, and practices developed in terrorism informatics through the comprehensive reviews of recent work and detailed case studies presented in each chapter. Students and researchers will broaden their understanding and knowledge in these new research topics. Practitioners will be able to better evaluate and/or employ new and alternative technologies for their current projects and future work.

EDITOR BIOGRAPHIES

Dr. Hsinchun Chen is McClelland Professor of Management Information Systems at the University of Arizona and Andersen Consulting Professor of the Year (1999). He received the B.S. degree from the National Chiao-Tung University in Taiwan, the MBA degree from SUNY Buffalo, and the Ph.D. degree in Information Systems from the New York University. Dr. Chen is a Fellow of IEEE and AAAS. He received the IEEE Computer Society 2006 Technical Achievement Award. He is the author/editor of 15 books, 17 book chapters, and more than 150 SCI journal articles covering intelligence analysis, biomedical informatics, data/text/web mining, digital library, knowledge management, and Web computing. His recent books include: *Intelligence and Security Informatics for International Security: Information Sharing and Data Mining*, and *Digital Government: E-Government Research, Case Studies, and Implementationi* (Springer).

Dr. Chen was ranked eighth in publication productivity in Information Systems (CAIS 2005) and first in Digital Library research (IP&M 2005) in two recent bibliometric studies. He serves on ten editorial boards including: *ACM Transactions on Information System; ACM Journal on Educational Resources in Computing*; *IEEE Transactions on Intelligent Transportation Systems; IEEE Transactions on Systems, Man, and Cybernetics; Journal of the American Society for Information Science and Technology; Decision Support Systems;* and *International Journal on Digital Library*. Dr. Chen has served as a Scientific Counselor/Advisor to the National Library of Medicine (USA), Academia Sinica (Taiwan), and the National Library of China (China). He has been an advisor for major NSF, DOJ, NLM, DOD, DHS, and other international research programs in digital government, national security research, medical informatics, and digital library. Dr. Chen is the founding director of the Artificial Intelligence Lab and Hoffman E-Commerce Lab. The UA Artificial Intelligence Lab, which houses 25+ researchers, has received more than $20M in research funding from NSF, NIH, NLM, DOD, DOJ, CIA, DHS, and other agencies over the past 17 years. Dr. Chen is the (founding) conference co-chair of the IEEE International Conferences on Intelligence and Security Informatics (ISI) 2003-2007. The ISI conference, which has been sponsored by NSF, CIA, DHS, and NIJ, has become the premiere meeting for international and homeland security IT research. Dr. Chen's COPLINK system, which has been quoted as a national model for public safety information sharing and analysis, has been adopted in more than 550 jurisdictions nation-wide. COPLINK research had been featured in the *New York Times*, *Newsweek*, *Los Angeles Times*, *Washington Post*, *Boston Globe*, and ABC News, among others. The COPLINK project was selected as a finalist by the prestigious International Association of Chiefs of Police (IACP)/Motorola 2003 Weaver Seavey Award for Quality in Law Enforcement in 2003. COPLINK research has recently been expanded to border protection (BorderSafe), disease and bioagent surveillance (BioPortal), and terrorism informatics research (Dark Web), funded by NSF, CIA, and DHS. In collaboration with Customs and Border Protection (CBP), the BorderSafe project develops criminal network analysis and vehicle association mining research for border-crosser risk assessment. The BioPortal system supports interactive geospatial analysis and visualization, chief complaint classification, and phylogenetic analysis for public health and biodefense. In collaboration with selected international terrorism research centers and intelligence agencies, the Dark Web project has generated one of the largest databases in the world about extremist/terrorist-generated Internet contents (web sites, forums, and multimedia documents). Dark Web research supports link analysis, content analysis, web metrics analysis, multimedia analysis, sentiment analysis, and authorship analysis of international terrorism content. The project has been featured in the Associated Press, Fox News, National Public Radio (NPR), the British Broadcasting Corporation (BBC), the NSF Press, *Discover Magazine*, the *Arizona Republic*, and the *Toronto Star*, among others. Dr. Chen is the founder of the Knowledge Computing Corporation, a university spin-off company and a market leader in law enforcement and intelligence information sharing and data mining. Dr. Chen has also received numerous awards in information technology and knowledge management education and research including: AT&T Foundation Award, SAP Award, the Andersen Consulting Professor of the Year Award, the University of Arizona Technology Innovation Award, and the National Chaio-Tung University Distinguished Alumnus Award.

Dr. Edna Reid is an Associate Professor at Clarion University, Pennsylvania. Formerly, she was a senior research scientist and project manager in the Artificial Intelligence Laboratory at the University of Arizona, Tucson. She was an Associate Professor with Nanyang Business School, NTU, Singapore, and the president of the Society of Competitive Intelligence Professionals Singapore (SCIPSgp). Formerly, she was an entrepreneur with an Internet start-up in Malaysia. In 1993, she joined the Division of Information Studies, NTU. Prior to going to Asia, Edna was at the School of Communication, Information and Library Studies, Rutgers University. In 1990, she was a postdoctoral researcher at the University of California, Berkeley, where she conducted research in terrorism information services. She also served as a senior systems analyst and data analyst team leader at private enterprises in both Germany and northern Virginia in the U.S.. She has analytical and library sciences experience in the intelligence community. Her areas of specialization include competitive intelligence, web mining, and terrorism informatics. Her research focuses on web mining of extremist groups' digital artifacts (e.g., web sites, forums, multimedia). She has published in a number of journals, conference proceedings, and edited collections. She received a Certificate in Management Information Systems (MIS) from American University in 1984, and the DLS (Library Science) degree from the University of Southern California in 1983. She also holds a bachelors degree in Education from D.C. Teachers College and a Masters Degree in library science from the University of Maryland.

Dr. Joshua Sinai is a Program Manager for counter-terrorism studies & education at The Analysis Corporation (TAC) (www.theanalysiscorp.com), in McLean, VA. His government contracts range from a project to map the worldwide landscape of terrorism & counterterrorism studies to an assessment of tribalism in Iraq. He also assists in developing curriculum on counterterrorism analysis to TACLearn, TAC's internal distance learning educational program. Prior to joining TAC in June 2006, Dr. Sinai worked at Logos Technologies and ANSER (Analytical Services), from which for 18 months he was seconded to function as a government official in the Science & Technology Directorate, Department of Homeland Security, where he managed a project on the social and behavioral components of terrorism and its impact on society. As part of his duties, he co-chaired an interagency working group, under the White House Office of Science & Technology Policy, on how the social, behavioral and economic sciences can contribute to counterterrorism, which produced a report on this subject in April 2005. He also contributed to the formulation of the announcement for proposals to create the DHS center on terrorism studies and served on the evaluation committee to review all proposals. Dr. Sinai's publications include chapters in edited academic volumes, national security journals, and his column on Terrorism Books appears regularly in the Washington Times' book review section. He has also published newspaper articles on terrorists' use of the Internet and how the special operations community approaches counterterrorism. He is a frequent presenter at academic conferences on terrorism & counterterrorism. Dr. Sinai can be reached at: jsinai@theanalysiscorp.com.

Dr. Andrew Silke currently holds a Chair in Criminology at the University of East London where he is the Programme Director for Terrorism Studies. He has a background in forensic psychology and has worked both in academia and for government. His research and writings are published extensively in academic journals, books and the popular press. He is the author of over 100 articles and papers on subjects relating to terrorism, and has given numerous papers and invited lectures on these topics at conferences and universities across the world. In recent years, he has worked with a wide range of scientific, government and law enforcement agencies, including the U.S. Federal Bureau of Investigation, the United States Department of Justice, the United States Department of Homeland Security, NATO, the United States National Academy of Sciences, the Royal Society, the United Nations, the European Defence Agency, the European Commission, the Metropolitan Police and the House of Commons. He has also provided risk assessment and acted as an expert witness in several terrorism-related cases. Professor Silke serves by invitation on both the European Commission's Expert Group on Violent Radicalisation, and the United Nations Roster of Terrorism Experts. He is an Honorary Senior Research Associate of the renowned Centre for the Study of Terrorism and Political Violence at the University of St Andrews and is a Fellow of the University of Leicester. His work has taken him to Northern Ireland, the Middle East and Latin America.

Dr. Boaz Ganor is the associate dean of the Lauder School of Government, the founder and executive director of the International Policy Institute for Counter-Terrorism (ICT), and the head of the Homeland Security Studies program (Graduate degree, Executive program and Bachelor specialization) at the Interdisciplinary Center Herzliya, Israel. He is also the founder and Chairman of the International Counter Terrorism Academic Community (ICTAC). In addition, Dr. Ganor is a senior fellow of MIPT (The Memorial Institute for Prevention of Terrorism, Oklahoma City, USA) and a member of the International Advisory Council of the International Centre for Political Violence and Terrorism Research at the Institute of Defense and Strategic Studies (IDSS), Nanyang Technological University, The Republic of Singapore. Dr. Ganor is also a member of the board of directors of ICSR – The International Centre for the Study of Radicalization and Political Violence (a partnership of the University of Pennsylvania (U.S.A.), the Interdisciplinary Center (Israel), King's College (London, U.K.), and The Jordanian Institute of Diplomacy). Past positions for Dr. Ganor have included membership in the Israeli Delegation to the Trilateral (American-Palestinian-Israeli) Committee for Monitoring Incitement to Violence and Terrorism as well as the Israeli National Committee for Homeland Security Technologies. He has served as an advisor on counter-terrorism topics to the Israeli Ministry of Defense, the Israeli Counter-Terrorism Coordinator in the Prime Minister's office, Israel National Security Council, and the Israeli Transportation Ministry during the peace talks with Jordan. In addition, he advised Prime Minister Benjamin Nethanyahu on his book *Fighting Terrorism.* Dr. Ganor has been widely published and some of his key works have included *Israel's Counter-Terrorism Strategy – Efficacy versus Liberal–Democratic Values* (Political Science, The Hebrew University, Jerusalem, Israel, 2002), and *Terrorism and Public Opinion in Israel* (Tel-Aviv University, Israel, 1989). In addition, Dr. Ganor has written numerous articles on the topic of terrorism and counterterrorism. His latest book, *The Counter-Terrorism Puzzle – A guide for decision makers* (Transaction Publishers, 2005), is currently being used as a textbook is several universities. Dr. Ganor is also the editor of *Trends in International Terrorism* (2007), *Hypermedia Seduction for Terrorist Recruiting* (2007), and *Post Modern Terrorism* (2005).

AUTHOR BIOGRAPHIES

Ahmed Abbasi is a research associate at the Artificial Intelligence Lab and a doctoral student in the Management Information Systems department at the University of Arizona. He received his BS degree and MBA from Virginia Tech. His research interests include text mining, computer mediated communication, information visualization, and knowledge management.

Naveen Ashish is a Research Scientist and Research Faculty Member at the University of California, Irvine where he is affiliated with Calit2. He is the project leader of the SAMI project on situational awareness, within the larger (NSF funded) RESCUE project on advancing information technologies for disaster response. His research interests and expertise span various areas in data management and AI, including information integration, information extraction, and information semantics. He received his PhD in Computer Science from the University of Southern California in 2000 and worked at the NASA Ames Research Center before joining UCI.

Niranjan Balasubramanian is currently a doctoral student at the Center for Intelligent Information Retrieval (CIIR) in the Department of Computer Science at the University of Massachusetts, Amherst. His research interests include information retrieval, extraction, text classification and question answering. Prior to joining CIIR, Balasubramanian was a Software Engineer at the Center for Natural Language Processing where he participated in research and development of several natural language processing technologies and their applications.

Clive Best is a senior researcher within the "Support to External Security" Unit at the JRC's "Institute for the Protection and the Security of the Citizen" in Ispra, Italy. With a background in information technology, he is presently carrying our research on information processing, based on a media monitor system (Europe Media Monitor-EMM) developed at the Joint Research Centre. The Joint Research Centre (JRC) is one of the directorates general of the European Commission and it includes seven different research institutes located in several EU member states. The JRC's mission is to provide customer-driven scientific and technical support for the conception, development, implementation and monitoring of EU policies. It functions as a centre of science and technology reference for the EU independent of commercial and national interests. The JRC supports the policy-maker in addressing the concerns of the individual citizen, undertaking research in different fields such as security, health, agriculture, environment and energy.

Mihaela Bobeica has a background in language sciences and language technology. For the last few years her research focused on data processing and information systems for policy-making support, electronic governance and electronic democracy. She has worked as a researcher for several European research institutes, at international and national levels. She has several publications on data processing for policy-making support and electronic governance. Presently she is working at the Council of Europe in Strasbourg, France, on information systems and policy development for good governance in the Information Society.

Judee K. Burgoon is Professor of Communication, Family Studies and Human Development, at the University of Arizona, where she is Site Director for the Center for Identification Technology Research, Director of Research for the Center for the Management of Information, and Associate Director of the Media Interface Network Design Lab in the Eller College of Management, University of Arizona. Professor Burgoon has authored seven books and monographs and over 250 articles, chapters and reviews related to deception, nonverbal and relational communication, computer-mediated communication, research methods, and media use. A recent survey identified her as the most prolific female scholar in communication in the 20th century. She is the recipient of the National Communication Association's Distinguished Scholar Award, its highest award for a lifetime of scholarly achievement, and the International Communication Association's Steven H. Chaffee Career Productivity Award, also its highest award for scholarly achievement.

Dr. Kuiyu Chang joined the School of Computer Engineering of Nanyang Technological University in 2003 as an Assistant Professor in Information Systems. Prior to that, he served as Senior Risk Management Analyst for ClearCommerce (Texas). In 2001, he founded Mosuma (Texas). From 2000 to 2002 he was Member of Technical Staff at Interwoven (Texas). In 2000, he was also one of the core employees of the startup company Neonyoyo (Texas), which was acquired by Interwoven for US$70m. Kuiyu is a member of IEEE, ACM. He has served as program co-chair for Intelligence and Security Informatics workshops 2006 and 2007, publications chair for PAKDD2006, and Programme Committee member of several international conferences. He received his Ph.D. from the University of Texas at Austin, M.S. from the University of Hawaii at Manoa, and B.S. from National Taiwan University, all in Electrical Engineering.

Michael Chau is currently an Assistant Professor and the BBA(IS)/BEng(CS) Program Coordinator in the School of Business at the University of Hong Kong. He received his Ph.D. degree in Management Information Systems from the University of Arizona and a Bachelor degree in Computer Science (Information Systems) from the University of Hong Kong. When at Arizona, he was an active researcher in the Artificial Intelligence Lab, where he participated in several research projects funded by NSF, NIH, NIJ, and DARPA. His research has been published in such international journals as Communications of the ACM, ACM Transactions on Information Systems, IEEE Transactions on SMC, IEEE Computer, Decision Support Systems, and Journal of the American Society for Information Science and Technology.

Ronald Eguchi is President and CEO of ImageCat, Inc., a risk management company specializing in the development and use of advanced technologies for risk assessment and reduction. Mr. Eguchi has over 30 years of experience in risk analysis and risk management studies. He has directed major research and application studies in these areas for government agencies and private industry. He currently serves on several Editorial Boards including the *Natural Hazards Review* published by the American Society of Civil Engineers and the Natural Hazards Research and Applications Information Center, University of Colorado, and the *Journal on Uncertainties in Engineering Mechanics* published by Resonance Publications, Inc. He is also a past member of the Editorial Board of the Earthquake Engineering Research Institute's Journal *SPECTRA.* He is a past member of the Scientific Advisory Committee of the U.S. Geological Survey, a committee that reports to Congress on recommended research directions for the USGS in the area of earthquake hazard reduction. In 1997, he was awarded the ASCE C. Martin Duke Award for his contributions to the area of lifeline earthquake engineering. He still remains active in the ASCE Technical Council on Lifeline Earthquake Engineering serving on several committees and having chaired the Council's Executive Committee in 1991. In 1992, Mr. Eguchi was asked to chair a panel, established jointly by the Federal Emergency Management Agency and the National Institute of Standards and Technology, to develop a plan for assembling and adopting seismic design standards for public and private lifelines in the U.S. This effort has led to the formation of the American Lifeline Alliance, currently managed by the National Institute of Building Sciences. Mr. Eguchi currently serves on MCEER's (Multidisciplinary Center for Earthquake Engineering Research) Research Committee for Transportation Research. He is a member of the National Research Council's Disaster Roundtable. He is also a charter member of the Mayor's

Blue Ribbon Panel on Seismic Hazards for the City of Los Angeles. He has authored over 200 publications, many of them dealing with the seismic risk of utility lifeline systems.

James "Chip" O. Ellis III is the Research and Program Director for the Memorial Institute for the Prevention of Terrorism (MIPT), which he joined in March 2001. MIPT works to counter terrorism with knowledge and acts as a national point of contact for antiterrorism information sharing. MIPT is funded through the U.S. Department of Homeland Security. Chip completed his Master's of Letters in International Security Studies at the University of St Andrews in Scotland. His research program focused on terrorism and weapons of mass destruction. Chip also graduated summa cum laude from the University of Oklahoma with two Bachelor's of Arts degrees in political science and linguistics. Prior to MIPT, Chip served in the Response Division of the Oklahoma Department of Civil Emergency Management, where he developed plans and procedures for the State's terrorism program and revised the State Emergency Operations Plan to address Federal and State authorities during WMD events. Before this, he worked at the University of Oklahoma Police Department.

Yuval Elovici is a Senior Lecturer in the Department of Information Systems Engineering at Ben-Gurion University of the Negev and the Director of the University's Deutsche Telekom Laboratories. His research interests include information warfare, data mining, information retrieval, and detection of malicious code. He received his PhD in information systems from Tel-Aviv University. Contact him at DT Labs, Ben-Gurion Univ., PO Box 653, Beer- Sheva, Israel, 84105; elovici@inter.net.il.

Stephen E. Fienberg is Maurice Falk University Professor of Statistics and Social Science at Carnegie Mellon University, with appointments in the Department of Statistics, the Machine Learning, and Cylab. He has served as Dean of the College of Humanities and Social Sciences at Carnegie Mellon and as Vice President for Academic Affairs at York University, in Toronto, Canada, as well as on the faculties of the University of Chicago and the University of Minnesota. He was founding co-editor of Chance and served as the Coordinating and Applications Editor of the Journal of the American Statistical Association. He is currently one of the founding editors of the Annals of Applied Statistics and is co-founder of the new online Journal of Privacy and Confidentiality, based in Cylab. He has been Vice President of the American Statistical Association and President of the Institute of Mathematical Statistics and the International Society for Bayesian Analysis. His research includes the development of statistical methods, especially tools for categorical data analysis. His work on confidentiality and disclosure limitation addresses issues related to respondent privacy in both surveys and censuses and especially to categorical data analysis. Fienberg is the author or editor of over 20 books and 300 papers and related publications. His two books on categorical data analysis are Citation Classics. Fienberg is a prominent as an advisor to government agencies and to congress. He served two terms as Chair of the Committee on National Statistics at the National Research Council (NRC) during the 1980s. Recently, he chaired the NRC committee on the scientific validity of the polygraph and served as a member of the NRC panel on measuring discrimination. He currently serves on the NRC Committee on Technical and Privacy Dimensions of Information for Terrorism Prevention and Other National Goals, and is a member of the NAS-NRC Report Review Committee. He is a member of the U. S. National Academy of Sciences, and a fellow of the Royal Society of Canada, and the American Academy of Political and Social Science. He is also a longtime fellow of the American Association for the Advancement of Science, the American Statistical Association, and the Institute of Mathematical Statistics. He was the 1982 recipient of the Committee of Presidents of Statistical Societies Presidents' award as the Outstanding Statistician under the age of 40, and the 2002 recipient of the Samuel S. Wilks Award of the American Statistical Association recognizing his distinguished career in statistics.

Menahem Friedman, born in Jerusalem, Israel, received his M.Sc. in Mathematics from the Hebrew University in Jerusalem (1962) and his Ph.D. in Applied Mathematics from the Weizmann Institute of Science in Rehovot. From 1969 – 2005 he was a Senior Research Scientist at the Nuclear Research Center – Negev and in addition from 1969 – 1992 an Associate Professor at the Departments of Mathematics, Electrical Engineering and Computer Science teaching various courses in Applied Mathematics and Data Structure. Dr. Friedman has published numerous papers in the areas of Numerical Analysis and Fuzzy Mathematics, has contributed to several books in Numerical Analysis and Co-authored books in Numerical Analysis and Pattern Recognition. Since 2004 he is involved in designing mathematical models for detecting terrorist activity on the Internet.

Teofilo Garcia is a senior researcher within the "Support to External Security" Unit at the JRC's "Institute for the Protection and the Security of the Citizen" in Ispra, Italy. With a backgrounds in information technology, he is presently carrying our research on information processing, based on a media monitor system (Europe Media Monitor-EMM) developed at the JRC. Research results are meant to support EU policy-makers in the field of security and terrorism.

Dr. Rohan Gunaratna is Head of the International Centre for Political Violence and Terrorism Research, Singapore. A former senior fellow at the Combating Terrorism Centre, United States Military Academy at West Point, he is a senior fellow at the Jebsen Centre for Counter Terrorism Studies, Fletcher School for Law and Diplomacy and the National Memorial Institute for the Prevention of Terrorism, Okalahoma. He holds a masters degree in international peace studies from the University of Notre Dame, Indiana, US, and a doctorate in international relations from the University of St Andrews, Scotland, UK. He led the specialist team that designed the UN Database into the Mobility, Finance and Weapons of Al Qaeda, Taliban and their Entities. He was invited to testify before the 9-11 Commission.He is the author of 12 books including "Inside Al Qaeda: Global Network of Terror," Columbia University Press, New York. He serves on the editorial boards of "Studies in Conflict and Terrorism" and "Terrorism and Political Violence," leading counter-terrorism academic journals.

Dr. Rajesh M. Hegde graduated with a Ph.D (2005) in Computer Science and Engineering from the Indian Institute of Technology Madras (IIT-M), India. He is currently working as a Researcher at the California Institute of Telecommunication and Information Technology (CALIT2), at the University of California, San Diego. At CALIT2, he is involved in projects that highlight the interplay of multi-modal signal processing with wireless networking. His research interests include feature extraction for speech recognition, speaker identification, situation-aware ubiquitous computing, and multi-modal information fusion.

Dr. John Horgan is Senior Research Fellow at the Centre for the Study of Terrorism and Political Violence, University of St. Andrews, where is also Lecturer in International Relations. A Chartered Psychologist, his research interests relate to psychological aspects of political violence, with a particular focus on understanding how and why people become involved in, and disengage from, terrorism. Some of his previous research has examined political violence in Ireland, and the relationship between Irish Republican terrorism and organised crime, especially in the context of the group and organisational dynamics of terrorist movements. Dr Horgan's work is widely published. His books include *The Future of Terrorism* (2000, co-edited with Max Taylor) and *The Psychology of Terrorism* (2005). In July 2006, he was awarded an Airey Neave Trust Fellowship for an 18-month research project on how and why individuals disengage from terrorist movements. On the basis of this research, his new book *Walking Away*

From Terrorism: Accounts of Disengagement from Radical and Extremist Movements will be published by Routledge in 2008. It contains detailed first hand interviews he has conducted with members of 13 terrorist movements. Dr. Horgan is regularly invited to speak to a variety of government, police, and military audiences around the world, and since 2005, he has been a member of the European Commission Expert Group on Violent Radicalisation.

Dr. Xiaohua Hu is currently an assistant professor and founding director of the data mining and bioinformatics lab at the College of Information Science and Technology, Drexel University. His current research interests are in biomedical literature data mining, bioinformatics, text mining, semantic web mining and reasoning, rough set theory and application, information extraction and information retrieval. He has published more than 140 peer-reviewed research papers in various journals, conferences and books such as various IEEE/ACM Transactions, PR, JIS, KAIS, CI, DKE, IJBRA, SIG KDD, IEEE ICDM, IEEE ICDE, SIGIR, ACM CIKM, IEEE BIBE, IEEE CICBC etc, co-edited 8 books/proceedings. He has received a few prestigious awards including the 2005 National Science Foundation (NSF) Career award, the best paper award at the 2004 IEEE Symposium on Computational Intelligence in Bioinformatics and Computational Biology, the 2006 IEEE Granular Computing Outstanding Service Award, and the 2001 IEEE Data Mining Outstanding Service Award. He has also served as a program co-chair/conference co-chair of nine international conferences/ workshops and a program committee member in more than 50 international conferences in the above areas. He is the founding editor-in-chief of the International Journal of Data Mining and Bioinformatics, an associate editor/editorial board member of four international journals (KAIS, IJDWM, IJSOI and JCIB), and the founding advisory board member and secretary of the IEEE Granular Computing Task Force. His research projects are funded by the National Science Foundation (NSF), US Dept. of Education, and the PA Dept. of Health.

Charles K. Huyck is Senior Vice President of ImageCat, Inc., where he oversees a team of engineers, scientists, and programmers developing software tools and data processing algorithms for loss estimation and risk reduction. He has over 13 years of experience in GIS analysis and application development. He introduced GIS and Remote Sensing to EQE International, where he served as GIS Programmer Analyst on several loss estimation and research projects. With the emergence of GIS and remote sensing as vertical markets in insurance, he served as a key GIS and remote sensing technical advisor. At the California Governor's Office of

Emergency services, he was responsible for geographic and statistical analysis, database development, and mapping disaster information under intense time constraints. He also responded to the Northridge Earthquake, California Winter Storms, and California Fire Storms. He has contributed to the development of several GIS software programs for emergency management, real estate, and insurance industries, which include: the HAZUS flood module, EPEDAT, J-EPEDAT, EPEDAT-LA, USQuake, RAMP, U-RAMP, REDARS, Bridge Hunter/Bridge Doctor, VRS, VIEWS, INLET, GeoVideo, MIHEA, 3D-Cube, RT MapViewer and BETTER-DEMS. Application development environments used include: ArcObjects, MapObjects, ArcView/Avenue, MapInfo/MapBasic, ArcIMS, UMN MapServer, MapBasic, and ENVI/IDL. Databases used in a programming environment include SQL Server, DB2, Oracle and Access. Some of the specific projects for which Mr. Huyck has been the primary GIS or remote sensing analyst include: an advanced HAZUS-based risk analysis of the State of South Carolina, automated damage detection from satellite imagery following the Marama, Turkey (1999), Boumerdes, Algeria (2003), and Bam, Iran (2004) earthquakes; an assessment of the use of remote sensing and GIS after September 11th; various studies on the economic impacts of earthquakes on utility and transportation systems; and the extraction of GIS building inventories from optical and radar data. He has authored over 50 papers pertaining to GIS, remote sensing, and emergency management.

Brian A. Jackson is associate director of RAND's Homeland Security research program. His terrorism-focused research has examined tactical and operational learning by terrorist groups, terrorist groups' use of technology, projects developing approaches to assess the threat posed by potential terrorist use of specific weapons technologies, examination of the strategies to respond to terrorist targeting of national economies, development of terrorist attack scenarios to support policy analysis efforts, and a large-scale study emergency responder protection during responses to major disasters and terrorist attacks. Key publications in these areas include articles in *Studies in Conflict and Terrorism* and *Military Review* on technology adoption by terrorist organizations, terrorist organizational structures and behavior, and intelligence gathering for targeting terrorist and insurgent groups, as well as the RAND reports *Aptitude for Destruction, Volumes 1 & 2*, examining organizational learning in terrorist groups, *Breaching the Fortress Wall: Understanding Terrorist Efforts to Overcome Defensive Technologies*, and Volumes 1 and 3 of the RAND *Protecting Emergency Responders* series of publications. Brian holds a Ph.D. in bioinorganic chemistry from the California Institute of Technology and a Master's degree from George Washington University in Science, Technology, and Public

Policy.

Matthew Jensen is a post-doctoral researcher at the University of Arizona. He received his PhD from the University of Arizona. His research focuses on computer-aided decision making, knowledge-based systems, and automatic deception detection. He has published in IEEE Intelligent Systems, and in numerous conference proceedings.

Jean-Paul Jéral is a senior researcher within the "Support to External Security" Unit at the JRC's "Institute for the Protection and the Security of the Citizen" in Ispra, Italy. With a backgrounds in information technology, he is presently carrying our research on information processing, based on a media monitor system (Europe Media Monitor-EMM) developed at the JRC. Research results are meant to support EU policy-makers in the field of security and terrorism.

Dmitri V. Kalashnikov received his Ph.D. degree in computer science from Purdue University in 2003, and his diploma cum laude in applied mathematics and computer science from Moscow State University, Russia, in 1999. Currently, he is a research faculty member in the University of California at Irvine. He has received several scholarships, awards, and honors, including an Intel Ph.D. Fellowship and Intel Scholarship. His research interests are in several areas including large-scale data management, information quality and data cleaning, moving-object and spatio-temporal databases, and IT technology for crisis response management.

Abraham Kandel received a B.Sc. from the Technion – Israel Institute of Technology, a M.S. from the University of California, both in Electrical Engineering, and a Ph.D. in Electrical Engineering and Computer Science from the University of New Mexico. Dr. Kandel, a Distinguished University Research Professor and the Endowed Eminent Scholar in Computer Science and Engineering at the University of South Florida, is the Executive Director of the National Institute for Applied Computational Intelligence. He was the Chairman of the Computer Science and Engineering Department at the University of South Florida (1991-2003) and the Founding Chairman of the Computer Science Department at Florida State University (1978-1991). Dr. Kandel has published over 500 research papers for numerous professional publications in Computer Science and Engineering. He is also the author, co-author, editor or co-editor of 46 text books and research monographs in the field. Dr. Kandel is a Fellow of the ACM, Fellow of the IEEE, Fellow of the New York Academy of Sciences, Fellow of AAAS,

Fellow of IFSA, as well as a member of NAFIPS, IAPR, ASEE, and Sigma-Xi.

John Kruse is a Lead Information Systems Engineer with the MITRE Corporation. Previously he was the Director of Systems Development at the University of Arizona 's Center for the Management of Information. His primary field of interest is the development of collaborative systems for decision making. In pursuit of this, he has worked extensively in the field of military decision support and network-centric operations. Additionally, Dr. Kruse has been working to develop prototype systems for automated intent and deception detection. He has worked extensively with a wide range of educational, governmental and military groups to help develop group processes and software that support collaborative work.

Mark Last received his M.Sc. (1990) and Ph.D. (2000) degrees in Industrial Engineering from Tel Aviv University, Israel. He is currently a Senior Lecturer at the Department of Information Systems Engineering, Ben-Gurion University of the Negev, Israel. Mark Last has published over 110 papers and chapters in scientific journals, books, and refereed conferences. He has been a co-author of the monographs "Knowledge Discovery and Data Mining – The Info-Fuzzy Network (IFN) Methodology" (Kluwer 2000) and "Graph-Theoretic Techniques for Web Content Mining" (World Scientific, 2005) and a co-editor of six volumes including "Fighting Terror in Cyberspace" (World Scientific, 2005). His current research interests include data mining, text mining, and cyber intelligence. Mark Last is an Associate Editor of IEEE Transactions on Systems, Man, and Cybernetics - Part C and a Senior Member of the IEEE Computer Society.

Elizabeth Liddy is a Professor in the School of Information Studies at Syracuse University and Director of its Center for Natural Language Processing where she leads a team of researchers focused on developing human-like language-understanding software technologies. Liddy has successfully applied natural language processing to various information access technologies including information extraction, information retrieval, data-mining, question-answering, cross-language retrieval, 2-stage web-based retrieval and automatic metadata generation. Liddy's research agenda has been continuously supported by both government and corporate funders on a total of 65 projects.

Dr. Ee-Peng Lim received his Ph.D. from the University of Minnesota. He is currently the Head of Division of Information Systems in the School of Computer Engineering of the Nanyang Technological University. Dr Lim's research interests include information integration, data/text/web mining, digital libraries, and wireless intelligence. His papers appeared at ACM Transactions on Information Systems (TOIS), IEEE Transactions on Knowledge and Data Engineering (TKDE), Data and Knowledge Engineering (DKE), and other major journals. He is currently an Associate Editor of the ACM Transactions on Information Systems (TOIS), Journal of Web Engineering (JWE), International Journal of Digital Libraries (IJDL) and International Journal of Data Warehousing and Mining (IJDWM).

Sharad Mehrotra is a Professor of Computer Science at the University of California, Irvine. He is the Director of the 5-year NSF large-ITR project RESCUE on advancing information technologies for disaster response. His interests and expertise span many areas in data management and distributed systems. He received a PhD in Computer Science from the University of Texas at Austin in 1993.

Thomas O. Meservy is an Assistant Professor of Management Information Systems at the University of Memphis. He received his PhD from the University of Arizona. His research focuses on using technology to automatically detect deception in audio and video. He has published in IEEE Computer, IEEE Intelligent Systems, and a variety of conference proceedings.

Dr. Jay F. Nunamaker, Jr. is Regents and Soldwedel Professor of MIS, Computer Science and Communication and Director of the Center for the Management of Information at the University of Arizona, Tucson. Dr. Nunamaker received the LEO Award from the Association of Information Systems (AIS) at ICIS in Barcelona, Spain, December 2002 for a lifetime of exceptional achievement in information systems. He founded the MIS department at the University of Arizona, in 1974 and served as department head for 18 years. Dr. Nunamaker received his Ph.D. in systems engineering and operations research from Case Institute of Technology, an M.S. and B.S. in engineering from the University of Pittsburgh, and a B.S. from Carnegie Mellon University. He received his professional engineer's license in 1965.

Jialun Qin is an Assistant Professor in the Department of Management at University of Massachusetts Lowell. He received his Ph.D. degree in management information systems from the University of Arizona. His research interests include knowledge management, data and Web mining, digital libraries, and human computer interaction. His publications have appeared in Decision Support Systems, Journal of the American Society for Information Science and Technology, and IEEE Intelligent Systems.

Sam Raphael is a Teaching Fellow at the Defence Studies Department (DSD), which is part of the Joint Services Command and Staff College (JSCSC), Shrivenham, UK. Here, he delivers academic support to serving members of the UK armed forces on a wide variety subjects connected to 'security studies'. He is also a Visiting Lecturer at the University of East London (UEL), delivering lectures on the UK's only Master's-level degree course on terrorism studies. Sam is completing a doctoral thesis at the Department of War Studies, King's College London (KCL). His research is examining the 'knowledge' generated by key figures in the field of terrorism studies, in order to test the hypothesis that this body of work is politically biased.

Peter D. Rumm, M.D., M.P.H, F.A.C.P.M is a Deputy Director of the Division of General, Neurological and Restorative Devices for the Food and Drug Administration, US. DHHS. Dr. Rumm graduated from the Medical College of Georgia and received his MPH from the University of Washington, concentrating in health services administration. He is a Fellow of the American College of Preventive Medicine and was granted advanced standing in the American College of Physician Executives. Dr. Rumm's career was "profiled" in a workshop on career choices at the 2003 American College of Preventive Medicine Physicians Meeting "as an example to young physicians in this field". Dr Rumm was formerly a Chief Medical Officer and State Epidemiologist in the Wisconsin Division of Public Health. He worked in the broad area of chronic disease, terrorism prevention, patient safety, health promotion and health policy and directed a statewide committee on terrorism assessments and preparedness.

Marc Sageman is an independent researcher on terrorism and is the founder and principal of Sageman Consulting LLC in Rockville, Maryland. Dr. Sageman is a senior fellow at the Foreign Policy Research Institute in Philadelphia, Pennsylvania, and a senior associate at the Center for Strategic and International Studies in Washington, D.C. He graduated from Harvard University in 1973, and earned an M.D. and a Ph.D. in political sociology from New York University. He is the author of bestselling books including *Understanding Terror Networks* and *Leaderless Jihad.*

Arab Salem received his Masters in Science in Management Information Systems (2006) from the University of Arizona. His current research interests include content analysis, multimedia analysis and software design.

Dr. Moti Schneider received his Ph.D. in 1986 from the Florida State University. He is a member of the school of computer science at Netanya Academic college. His area of expertise include: Artificial Intelligence, Expert Systems, Data Mining, Fuzzy Logic, Nueral Networks, Image Processing, Pattern Recognition. He published over 120 refereed papers and books.

Young-Woo Seo received his B.S. in Computer Science from Konkuk University and M.S. in Computer Science from Seoul National University. He is currently a Ph.D. student at the Robotics Institute of Carnegie Mellon University. His research interests include statistical machine learning, multi-agents system, and behavior control for mobile robot. Before joining the PhD program, he worked on various research projects of developing intelligent software agents.

Yael Shahar heads the database project at Institute for Counter-Terrorism at the Interdisciplinary Center Herzliya. Her areas of expertise include technological trends in terrorism, terrorism informatics, datamining, and intelligence sharing She designed the ICT terrorist connections database and the terrorist incidents database, used for tracking links between terrorist individuals, front companies, and organizations. Ms. Shahar specializes in the study of technological trends as applied to terrorism and intelligence sharing. She lectures on terrorism trends, non-conventional terrorism, and threat assessment at the International Policy Institute for Counter Terrorism, Interdisciplinary Center Herzliya, as well as security conferences and seminars worldwide. Ms. Shahar's primarily responsibility is conducting open-source datamining in support of ICT research projects, as well as venue-specific threat assessments for ICT's commercial clients. Her background is in physics, database design, and security and installation protection. She served as a reservist in the IDF hostage rescue unit, and as a sniper in Israel's Border Guard "Matmid" units.

Dr. Bracha Shapira is currently a Senior Lecturer at the Department of Information Systems Engineering in Ben-Gurion University of the Negev in Israel. She holds an M.Sc. in computer science from the Hebrew University in Jerusalem and a Ph.D. in Information Systems from Ben-Gurion University. Bracha's research interests include Information Retrieval (IR) and Information Filtering (IF), privacy and user modeling. Bracha leads theoretical and empirical studies that make significant contribution in the mentioned domains. Bracha's numerous articles have been published in refereed Journals (such as JASSIST, DSS, IP&M, CACM). Her work was also presented at many professional conferences. Before turning to the academic world she gained professional experience while working as a system engineer and managing programming teams for telecommunication companies developing real-time applications.

David Skillicorn is a Professor in the School of Computing at Queen's University in Canada. His research is in smart information management, both the problems of extracting and sharing useful knowledge from data, and the problems of accessing and computing with large datasets that are geographically distributed. He has published extensively in high-performance computing and data mining. At present his focus is on understanding complex datasets in applications such as astrophysics, geochemistry, network intrusion, fraud detection, and counterterrorism. He has an undergraduate degree from the University of Sydney and a Ph.D. from the University of Manitoba.

Padhraic Smyth is a Professor in the School of Information and Computer Science, University of California, Irvine. He is currently also a member of the Institute for Mathematical Behavioral Sciences, the Institute for Genomics and Bioinformatics, and the Center for Biomedical Engineering (all at UC Irvine). Dr. Smyth's research interests include machine learning, data mining, statistical pattern recognition, applied statistics, and information theory. He was a recipient of best paper awards at the 2002 and 1997 ACM SIGKDD Conferences, an IBM Faculty Partnership Award in 2001, a National Science Foundation Faculty CAREER award in 1997 and the Lew Allen Award for Excellence in Research at JPL in 1993. He is co-author of *Modeling the Internet and the Web: Probabilistic Methods and Algorithms* (with Pierre Baldi and Paolo Frasconi), published by Wiley in 2003. He is also co-author of a graduate text in data mining, *Principles of Data Mining*, MIT Press, August 2001, with David Hand and Heikki Mannila. He was co-editor of *Advances in Knowledge Discovery and Data Mining*, published by MIT Press in 1996. He is currently an associate editor for the Journal of the American Statistical Association and, for the IEEE Transactions on Knowledge and Data Engineering, has served as an action editor for the *Machine Learning Journal*. He is also a founding associate editor for the *Journal of Data Mining and Knowledge Discovery*, and a founding editorial board member of the *Journal of Machine Learning Research*. He served as program chair for the 33rd Symposium on Computer Science and Statistics in 2001 and served as general chair for the Sixth International Workshop on AI and Statistics in 1997. He received a first class honors degree in Electronic

Engineering from University College Galway (National University of Ireland) in 1984, and the MSEE and PhD degrees from the Electrical Engineering Department at the California Institute of Technology in 1985 and 1988 respectively. From 1988 to 1996 he was a Technical Group Leader at the Jet Propulsion Laboratory, Pasadena, and has been on the faculty at UC Irvine since 1996.

Zhen Sun is a graduate student at the School of Computer Engineering, Nanyang Technological University. His research interests include information retrieval and data mining.

Maggy Anastasia Suryanto is a graduate student at the School of Computer Engineering, Nanyang Technological University. She is currently pursuing her PhD under the supervision of Dr Ee-Peng Lim. Her research interests include question answering and information retrieval.

Katia Sycara is a Professor in the Robotics Institute, School of Computer Science at Carnegie Mellon University and the Director of the Laboratory for Agents Technology and Semantic Web Technologies. She holds a B.S in Applied Mathematics from Brown University, M.S. in Electrical Engineering from the University of Wisconsin and PhD in Computer Science from Georgia Institute of Technology. She holds an Honorary Doctorate from the University of the Aegean (2004). She is a member of the Scientific Advisory Board of France Telecom, and a member of the Scientific Advisory Board of the Greek National Center of Scientific Research "Demokritos" Information Technology Division. She is a Fellow of the American Association for Artificial Intelligence (AAAI), Fellow of the IEEE and the recipient of the 2002 ACM/SIGART Agents Research Award. Prof. Sycara has served as General Chair and Program Chair of multiple conferences, has given numerous invited talks, has authored more than 300 technical papers dealing with Multiagent Systems, Negotiation, Software Agents, Agent Teams, Web Services, the Semantic Web, and Human-Agent-Robot Teams. She has led multimillion dollar research effort funded by DARPA, NASA, AFOSR, ONR, AFRL, NSF and industry. She is a founding member and member of the Board of Directors of the International Foundation of Multiagent Systems (IFMAS). She is a founding member of the Semantic Web Science Association, and serves as the US co-chair of the Semantic Web Services Initiative. She is a founding Editor-in-Chief of the journal "Autonomous Agents and Multiagent Systems" and is currently serving on the editorial board of 5 additional journals.

Svetlana Symonenko is a PhD candidate with the School of Information Studies at Syracuse University, New York. Her research interest is in the organization of Web-based information for better access. Symonenko's ongoing dissertation research explores indications of conventionalization in the observable structure of website content. Her dissertation proposal recently received the Thomson ISI Doctoral Dissertation Proposal in 2005. She works as a research assistant at the Center for Natural Language Processing at Syracuse University. Symonenko received her MLIS degree from St. John's University, New York.

Horacio R. Trujillo is a research fellow at the RAND Corporation and an adjunct professor in the Department of Diplomacy and World Affairs at Occidental College. At RAND, Horacio's work focuses on the intersection of international economics and security, spanning from research on the organizational dynamics of terrorist groups to efforts to adapt and develop various analytical methods to aid in the assessment and improvement of complex national economic and security strategies. Prior to joining RAND, Horacio worked with a number of national and multilateral institutions, including the U.S. Congress, the World Bank, and the United Nations. Horacio is a graduate of Georgetown University's School of Foreign Service, and holds advanced degrees from Oxford University's International Development Center and Stanford University's Graduate School of Business.

Nalini Venkatasubramanian received the M.S. and Ph.D. in Computer Science from the University of Illinois, Urbana-Champaign. She is an associate professor at the School of Information and Computer Science, University of California, Irvine. Her research interests include distributed and parallel systems, middleware, mobile environments, multimedia systems/applications and formal reasoning of distributed systems. She is specifically interested in developing safe and flexible middleware technology for highly dynamic environments. Nalini was a member of technical staff at Hewlett-Packard Laboratories in Palo Alto, California for several years where she worked on large scale distributed systems and interactive multimedia applications. She has also worked on various database management systems and on programming languages/compilers for high performance machines. She is a member of the IEEE and ACM.

Daniel D. Wu received the BS degree in Biochemistry from Xiamen University in China, MS in Physiology (1996) and MS in Computer Science (2001) from the Pennsylvania State University. He is currently pursuing the PhD degree in the College of Information Science and Technology at Drexel

University. His research interests are in data mining, bioinformatics, and biomolecular network analysis.

Jennifer J. Xu is an assistant professor of Computer Information Systems at Bentley College. She received her PhD in Management Information Systems from the University of Arizona in 2005. Her current research interests include knowledge management, social network analysis, virtual community, human-computer interaction, and information visualization. Her papers have appeared in Communications of the ACM, ACM Transactions on Information Systems, and Annual Review of Information Science and Technology.

Shuting Xu received her Ph.D. in Computer Science from The University of Kentucky in 2005. She is presently an Assistant Professor in the Department of Computer Information Systems at the Virginia State University. Her research interests include data mining and information retrieval, information security, database systems, parallel and distributed computing.

Ozgur Yilmazel is an Assistant Research Professor in the School of Information Studies at Syracuse University and the Chief Software Engineer of its Center for Natural Language Processing, research center. His research interests include machine learning applications for natural language processing, question answering and the use of complex linguistic features for text applications such as text categorization and information retrieval. Yilmazel received his Ph.D. and M.Sc. from Syracuse University, Electrical Engineering in 2006 and 2002.

Omer Zaafrany received his B.Sc. degree in Information Systems Engineering from Ben-Gurion University of the Negev in 2002. He is currently a Master's student in the same department. Omer has about 10 publications in professional journals and conferences. His current research interests include data mining, information retrieval, and information warfare.

Jun Zhang received his Ph.D. from The George Washington University in 1997. He is a Professor of Computer Science and Director of the Laboratory for High Performance Scientific Computing & Computer Simulation and Laboratory for Computational Medical Imaging & Data Analysis at the University of Kentucky. His research interests include computational neuroinformatics, data mining and information retrieval, large scale parallel and scientific computing, numerical simulation, iterative and preconditioning techniques for large scale matrix computation. Dr. Zhang is an associate editor and on the editorial boards of five international journals, and is on the program committees of a few international conferences. His research work has been funded by the National Science Foundation, Department of Energy, Kentucky Science and Engineering Foundation, and Alzheimer's Association. He is recipient of the U.S. National Science Foundation CAREER Award and several other awards.

Xiaodan Zhang, PhD student at College of Information Science and Technology, Drexel University, USA. He has a master degree in computer science and a bachelor degree in library and information science. He has been working on graph-based, model-based and semantic based text data mining.

Xiaohua Zhou is a PhD student at College of Information Science and Technology, Drexel University, USA. His current research interests are in information retrieval and text mining. He is the author or co-authros of 17 peer-reviewed publications in various journal, conference and books.

Dr. Yilu Zhou is an assistant professor in the Department of Information Systems and Technology Management at George Washington University. Her current research interests include multilingual knowledge discovery, Web mining, text mining and human computer interaction. She received her Ph.D. in Management Information Systems from the University of Arizona, where she was also a research associate at the Artificial Intelligence Lab. She received a B.S. in Computer Science from Shanghai Jiaotong University. She has published in *IEEE Intelligent Systems*, *Decision Support Systems*, and *Journal of the American Society for Information Science and Technology*.

Unit 1

METHODOLOGICAL ISSUES
IN TERRORISM RESEARCH

1

DOMAIN MAPPING OF CONTEMPORARY TERRORISM RESEARCH

Edna Reid[1] and Hsinchun Chen[2]

[1]Department of Library Science, Clarion University, Clarion, Pennsylvania, U.S.A.(ereid@clarion.edu); [2]MIS Department, University of Arizona, Tucson, Arizona, U.S.A.(hchen@eller.arizona.edu)

CHAPTER OVERVIEW

Mapping a domain involves mining, analyzing, charting, and visualizing a research area according to experts, institutions, topics, publications, and social networks. This chapter presents an overview of contemporary terrorism research by applying domain visualization techniques to the literature and author citation data from the years 1965 to 2003. The data were gathered from ten databases such as the ISI Web of Science then analyzed using an integrated knowledge mapping framework that includes selected techniques such as self-organizing map (SOM), content map analysis, and co-citation analysis. The analysis revealed (1) 42 key terrorism researchers and their institutional affiliations; (2) their influential publications; (3) a shift from focusing on terrorism as a low-intensity conflict to an emphasis on it as a strategic threat to world powers with increased focus on Osama Bin Laden; and (4) clusters of terrorism researchers who work in similar research areas as identified by co-citation and block-modeling maps.

1.   INTRODUCTION

Contemporary terrorism is a form of political violence that evolved in the 1960s and characterized by an increase in terrorist attacks across international boundaries [36].   The recent escalation of contemporary terrorism has attracted many new and non-traditional research communities such as information science and human factors, whose scholars have a desire to do research in this area.   This raises questions for new terrorism researchers as they try to adapt to the challenges in this domain "Who are the leading researchers in terrorism?" "What are their relevant publications?" "What are the dominant topics because I want to know if my ideas have already been explored?"   "What types of data are used?" "Who should I work with?"

The task of responding to these questions is difficult because of the explosive growth in the volume of terrorism publications, the interdisciplinary and international nature of the field, and the lack of a professional association to nurture the terrorism research area and provide a platform for organizing and providing systematic access to terrorism studies [15;27].   For example, terrorism information is spread across many electronic databases, government and research center's websites, and a large number of journals that deal with various specialized aspects of the phenomenon [16].

This work extends a prior effort using a manually-driven bibliometric approach to examine terrorism research and offers another view of the intellectual field of terrorism [26]. Bibliometrics is the quantitative study of the literature and scholarly communication processes in a field [3].   With the interest in terrorism increasing, the findings of this study will be immensely useful in understanding the contributions of key terrorism authors in guiding terrorism-related research.

This paper presents a brief review of analytical techniques and framework for knowledge mapping. Subsequent sections will describe the research design and results of our contemporary terrorism literature mapping with three types of analysis: basic analysis, content map analysis, and co-citation network analysis. The final section will provide conclusion.

2.   RELATED WORK

There is extensive literature on knowledge mapping of scholarly literature and patents to analyze the structure, the dynamics, social networks, and development of a field such as medical informatics and information science [5;14;17;33].   Mapping refers to an evolving interdisciplinary area of science aimed at the process of charting, mining, analyzing, sorting, enabling navigation of, and displaying knowledge [32]. Although it is useful to the subject expert for validation of perceptions and means to investigate trends, it provides an entry point into the domain and answers to domain-specific research questions for the non-expert [5].

2.1   Citation Data

Maps and snapshots of a field's intellectual space have been generated as a result of the pioneering work of Garfield and Small who stimulated widespread interest in using aggregated citation data to chart the evolution of scientific specialties [10]. By aggregating citation data, it is possible to identify the relative impact of individual authors, publications, institutions, and highlight emerging specialties, new technologies and the structure of a field [13].

The advent of citation databases such as the Institute for Scientific Information (ISI) Social Sciences Citation Index (SSCI) and Science Citation Index (SCI), which track how frequently papers are cited in a publication, and by whom, have created tools for indicating the impact of research papers, institutions, and authors [13]. The web-version of SSCI, SCI, and the Arts and Humanities Citation Index is the Web of Science (WoS). Web-based tools such as Google and ResearchIndex (formerly CiteSeer) have been created to harness the similarities between citation linking and hyperlinking [10;30]. Searching the digital citation indexes have resulted in enormous amounts of citation data that are difficult to analyze, extract meaningful results, and display using traditional techniques.

This was illustrated in earlier citation network studies of terrorism researchers in which Reid [26;27;28] used authors, institutions, and documents as units of analysis and the ISI databases to identify the invisible colleges (informal social networks) of terrorism researchers, key research institutions, and their knowledge discovery patterns. This manual process was labor-intensive and relied on citation data. While there are limitations in using the ISI citation data such as they are 'lagging indicators' of research that has already been completed and passed through the peer review cycle [13], they are widely used in visualization studies and are the basis for identifying key terrorism researchers, influential publications, and subgroups of terrorism researchers in this study.

2.2   Visualization Techniques

Recent developments in the field of domain visualization attempt to alleviate this "citation information overload problem" by applying information visualization techniques to interact with large-scale citation data [11]. Several techniques have been applied to citation visualization such as Pathfinder network scaling [7], social network analysis, and author co-citation analysis [33;4] which is particularly suited to investigation of intellectual structure because they provide the capability to interact with data and display it from different perspectives. Author co-citation map identifies interrelation among authors by analyzing the counts of the number of articles that cite pairs of authors jointly [34].

Content, or 'semantic', analysis is an important branch of domain analysis which relies on natural language processing techniques to analyze large corpora of literature [11]. The content map analysis technique produces content maps of large-scale text collections. The technique uses simple lexical statistics, key phrase co-occurrence analysis, and semantic and linguistic relation parsing. For example, Huang, et.al. [17] uses self-organizing map (SOM) algorithm to generate content maps for visualizing the major technical concepts appearing in the nanotechnology patents and their evolution over time.

Another visualization technique is block-modeling which seeks to cluster units that have substantially similar patterns of relationships with others [12]. It has been applied in criminal network analysis to identify interaction patterns between subgroups of gang members [8]. The application of visualization techniques to citation, content analysis, and author co-citation data provides a foundation for knowledge mapping. The techniques support the users' visual exploration of a domain to identify emerging topics, key researchers, communities, and other implicit knowledge that is presently known only to domain experts [32]. For example, the Namebase [25], mines names and organizations from terrorism books and periodicals included in its database and links names in a social network. Figure 1-1 provides an example of a terrorism social network for Brian M. Jenkins (name listed in the center in red), founder of terrorism research at Rand Corporation. It is based on the number of times a name is listed on the same page with Jenkins.

Although the Namebase visualization does not indicate whether there is a relationship between Jenkins and the other names listed on the page or the context of their relationships, it is the only web-based tool readily available for visualizing social networks of terrorism researchers. Additionally, no systematic study has been conducted that uses citation network, content map analysis, and author co-citation analysis for automatically mapping the terrorism research domain.

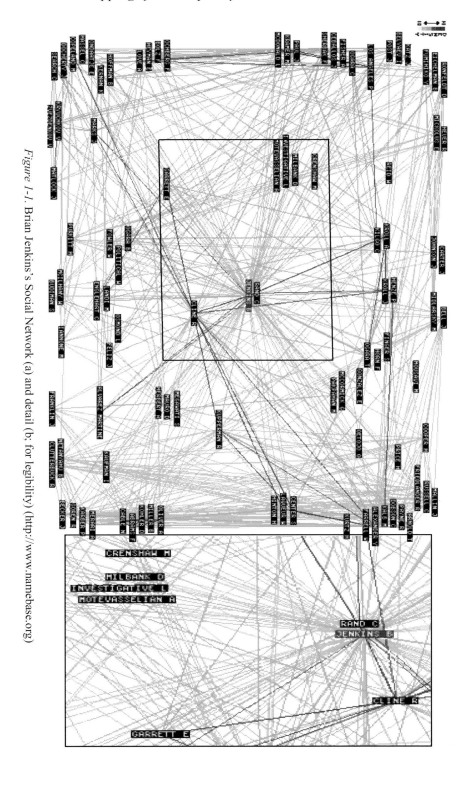

Figure 1-1. Brian Jenkins's Social Network (a) and detail (b; for legibility) (http://www.namebase.org)

3.   RESEARCH DESIGN

This study purports to provide empirically based answers to the research questions (RQs) listed in Table 1-1. It adopts the integrated knowledge mapping framework proposed by Huang [17] for patent analysis and used in Eggers study of medical informatics [11]. The framework includes three types of analysis: basic analysis, content map analysis, and citation network analysis to provide a multifaceted analysis of a research domain.

For the basic analysis, we analyze scientific output measures such as productivity (number of publications produced by a terrorism researcher) and impact (citation counts which allows one to find out how often a publication is cited). By analyzing documents and citation information, we identify key researchers, their influential terrorism publications, and research communities. The content map analysis visualizes the major subtopics and emerging concepts appearing in the publications while the co-citation map measures linkages and similarities among pairs of terrorism researchers as identified by citers. The co-citation data were also used in block-modeling to identify interaction patterns between subgroups of researchers within the terrorism scientific paradigms.

Table 1-1. Knowledge Mapping Framework and Research Questions

Type of Analysis	Unit of Analysis	Measure	Research Questions (RQs)
Basic analysis	▪ Authors ▪ Publications ▪ Publication's citations	Productivity Impact	▪ Who are key terrorism researchers? ▪ What institutions are they affiliated with? ▪ What are their influential terrorism publications? ▪ What are their collaboration patterns?
Content analysis	▪ Documents ▪ Words	Coverage	▪ What are the dominant terrorism topics? ▪ What are the new areas of research?
Co-citation analysis	▪ Author's co-citations	Linkage	▪ What groups of authors have papers with related content? ▪ What are the communities of researchers?

3.1   Basic Analysis

For the basic analysis, the initial step is to identify a set of key terrorism authors. We compiled a list of authors from several sources: terrorism publications [31;28], active terrorism experts identified by the KnowNet

<u>virtual community</u> (organized by the Sandia National Laboratories), and <u>terrorism research center portals</u> identified on the Internet. A total of 131 unique names were identified. Names are for researchers primarily from think tanks, academic institutions, and governments located in 13 countries including UK (18), Israel (7), and France (5). Sixty-four percent are from the United States.

The second step in the basic analysis is to identify the researchers' terrorism publications. A bibliography of English-language terrorism publications was compiled for each researcher using commercial databases. The publications include journal articles, books, book chapters, reviews, notes, newspaper articles, conferences papers, and reports. Table 1-2 lists the ten commercial databases that were searched using author's name and terrorism-related keywords such as terrorism, hijacking, bombing, political violence, or bombing. The commercial databases were selected because of subject coverage and availability through the University of Arizona (UA) Library.

Bibliographical data and abstracts were downloaded, parsed and imported into a database for additional processing. After purging duplicate records, 2,148 bibliographic records were manually reviewed to identify other records that may be duplicates (non-obvious) or non-terrorism publications. Database searches for 22 researchers failed to retrieve any terrorism-related publications while no English publications were retrieved for 21 other recommended researchers. As a result, terrorism publications (bibliographic data and abstracts) were retrieved for only 88 researchers.

Table 1-2. Databases Used to Compile Bibliographies

Database	Discipline	Records Exported
ABI/Inform	Business, management, information sciences	164
Academic Search Premier (ASP)	Multi-disciplinary	496
Expanded Academic ASAP (EA)	Multi-disciplinary	439
International Biblographie der Zeitschriften Literature (IBZ)	International, European	161
ISI Web of Science	Social sciences, science, arts & humanities	360
PAIS International	Public affairs, business, social studies, international relations, economics	588
Political Science Abstracts (PSA)	Political science, international, politics	539
Science Direct	Science, technology, medicine	9
Sociological Abstracts	Sociology, family studies	279
WorldCat (materials cataloged by libraries around the world)	Multi-disciplinary	1,154
Total		**4,129**

The third step is to identify key terrorism researchers from the group of 88 researchers. The publications of the 88 terrorism researchers were analyzed using basic citation analysis to identify how frequently these are cited in the literature. Basic citation counts for each terrorism-related publication for each terrorism researcher were collected from the ISI Web of Science. Citations to each publication from any other article in the ISI dataset are counted, and each indexed author is credited with the full tally of citations to that article [20]. If an author's total number of citations for a publication in our collection is four or more then he is considered a key terrorism researcher. After an author is identified as a key researcher, his terrorism-related publication with the highest citation count is considered as his influential publication

In addition, a coauthorship network was created to identify the collaboration patterns among the authors. The network covered the years 1965-2003. A hierarchical clustering algorithm was used to partition the core researchers who are connected if they coauthored a paper [37]. This allows for visualization of collaboration, research teams, and institutions.

3.2   Content Map Analysis

The influential terrorism researchers' bibliographic data and abstracts were used in a content map analysis to identify the dominating themes and terrorism topics in 1965-2003. Since we want to examine more than simple frequency counts, we applied our previous research in large-scale text analysis and visualization for content map technology to identify and visualize major research topics. The key algorithm of our content mapping program was the self-organizing map (SOM) algorithm developed in our lab [Huang]. It takes the terrorism titles and abstracts as inputs and provides the hierarchical grouping of the publications, labels of the groups, and regions of the terrorism document groups in the content map. Conceptual closeness was derived from the co-occurrence patterns of the terrorism topics. The sizes of the topic regions also generally corresponded to the number of documents assigned to the topics [23].

3.3   Co-citation Analysis

Author co-citation analysis was used to visualize the similarities among the researchers and their intellectual influence on other authors. It uses authors as the units of analysis and the co-citations of pairs of author (the number of times they are cited together by a third party) as the variable that indicates their distances from each other [1]. It was conducted based on co-citation frequencies for the key terrorism researchers, for the period 1965-

2003. The co-citation map was created using a GIS algorithm developed in our lab.

We conducted terrorism keyword searches in the Web of Science to retrieve records related to the topic of terrorism. The records were used to create a terrorism citation collection and included bibliographic records for 7,590 terrorism-related articles that were downloaded. Results were parsed and loaded into a database which was used for the co-citation analysis. Table 1-3 summarizes the data sets used for this study.

Table 1-3. Data Sets Summary

Data	Web of Science (terrorism keyword searches)	10 Bibliographic Databases (author & keyword searches)
Publications	7,590	4,129
Authors	6,090	1,168
Cited References	67,453	Not retrieved
Cited Authors	32,037	Not retrieved

Co-citation counts for each key terrorism researchers were derived using a program created by our lab. The program searched the citation field of each bibliographic record and counted the number of times two authors (or author pairs) were cited together. The result was the basis of the co-citation analysis portion of this study and offered a mapping of the field of terrorism research and the intellectual influence of the core researchers. Visualization of the relationships among researchers was displayed in a two-dimensional map that identifies their similarities, communities (clusters), and influence on emerging authors.

The co-citation data were also used in block-modeling to identify researchers' roles and positions in the terrorism research network. We used co-occurrence weight to measure the relational strength between two authors by computing how frequently they were identified in the same citing article [7]. We also calculated centrality measures to detect key members in each subgroup, such as the leaders [8]. The block-modeling algorithm is part of the social network analysis program developed in our lab.

4. RESULTS

4.1 Basic Analysis

The basic analysis provides responses to the initial set of questions identified in Table 1-1 such as who are the key terrorism researchers. Forty-two authors were identified as key terrorism researchers. A total of 284 researchers (including coauthors) and their 882 publications made up the sample for this study.

Table 1-4 lists the 42 key researchers, the number of terrorism publications in our dataset, and the number of times the researchers' publications were cited in the ISI databases. They are mainly affiliated with academic institutions (23), think tanks (15), media organizations (3), and the government (1). Their bases of operation are located in nine countries including the US (29), UK (4), and Ireland (1).

Table 1-4. Forty-two Key Terrorism Researchers (based on citation score in ISI)

Author Name	# of Pubs*	# Times Cited	Author Name	# of Pubs*	# Times Cited
1. Wilkinson, Paul	87	229	22. Lesser, Ian O.	5	23
2. Gurr, T.R.	51	214	23. Bassiouni, M.C.	8	22
3. Laqueur, Walter	37	191	24. Carlton, David	1	21
4. Alexander, Yonah	88	169	25. Chalk, Peter	17	20
5. Bell, J.B.	47	138	26. Freedman, Lawrence	14	20
6. Stohl, M.	30	136	27. Merari, Ariel	25	19
7. Hoffman, Bruce	121	100	28. Post, Jerrold	12	18
8. Jenkins, Brian M.	38	96	29. Evans, Ernest H.	3	17
9. Ronfeldt, David	20	95	30. Bergen, Peter	10	16
10. Crenshaw, Martha	40	90	31. Gunaratna, Rohan	14	16
11. Arquilla, John	20	75	32. Cline, R.S.	8	15
12. Mickolus, Edward F.	25	73	33. Friedlander, R.A.	4	14
13. Crelinsten, Ronald	19	62	34. Paust, Jordon J.	11	13
14. Schmid, Alex P.	6	59	35. Ranstorp, Magnus	8	13
15. Wardlaw, G.	25	49	36. Flynn, Stephen E	4	12
16. Hacker, F.J.	3	38	37. Cooper, H.H.A	10	11
17. Rapoport, David	26	37	38. Wolf, J.B	7	11
18. Sloan, Stephen R	31	30	39. Horgan, John	13	10
19. Dobson, C.	6	25	40. Sterling, C.	5	10
20. Kepel, Gilles	6	25	41. McCauley, Clark	4	8
21. Stern, Jessica E	21	25	42. Merkl, Peter	6	6

* number of publications in our dataset

The Appendix lists the most influential publication for each researcher which is based on the number of times cited in the ISI Web of Science.

Table 1-5 lists the 12 most influential publications because they were cited more than twenty-five times in ISI databases.

Table 1-5. Most Influential Terrorism Publications

Publication	# Times cited	Topic	Author	Organization
1. *Why men rebel*, 1970	145	political violence	Gurr, Ted	Univ Maryland
2. *Terrorism*, 1977	75	terrorism historical aspects	Laqueur, Walter	Center for Strategic & Intl Studies (CSIS)
3. *Terrorism & liberal state*, 1977	66	terrorism prevention	Wilkinson, Paul	Univ Aberdeen (formerly), CSTPV
4. *Inside terrorism*, 1998	47	terrorism religious aspects	Hoffman, Bruce	Rand Corporation
5. *Trans. Terrorism, a chronology*, 1980	41	terrorism incidents	Mickolus, E.	CIA (formerly)
6. *Crusaders, criminals*, 1976	34	terrorism case study	Hacker, F.J. (deceased)	USC Medical & Law Schools
7. *Time of terror*, 1978	33	terrorism responses	Bell, J.B. (deceased)	Columbia Univ
8. *State as terrorist*, 1984	32	state sponsored terrorism	Stohl, M.	Purdue Univ
9. *Political terrorism theory, tactics*, 1982	31	terrorism prevention	Wardlaw, G	Australian Institute of Criminology
10. *Intl. terrorism national regional*, 1976	30	terrorism anthology	Alexander, Y.	CSIS; SUNY
11. *Political terrorism a new guide*, 1988	29	terrorism directory	Schmid, Alex P.	Royal Netherlands Academy of Arts & Science
12. *Intl. Terrorism a new mode*, 1975	27	terrorism	Jenkins, Brian M.	Rand Corporation

An investigation of the coauthorship patterns provides an understanding of the researchers' social network patterns. Figure 1-2 exhibits the coauthorship network of key researchers in scientific collaboration networks. The nodes represent researchers who coauthored papers.

In the lower right corner of Figure 1-2, the Rand research teams led by Jenkins and Hoffman is one of the most active clusters.   Except for Gunaratna, all of the researchers in the cluster are Rand's employees. Gunaratna coauthored publications with Chalk and Hoffman, his PhD advisor at St. Andrews University, Scotland, and founded the terrorism research center at the Institute of Defence and Strategic Studies, Singapore.

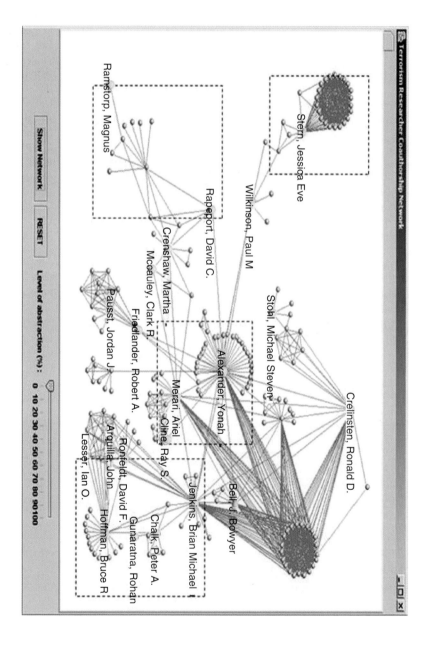

Figure 1-2. Key Terrorism Researchers' Coauthorship Network

Hoffman founded St. Andrews' Centre for the Study of Terrorism and Political Violence (CSTPV) and created the Rand-St. Andrews terrorism incident database which provides data for their studies [18].

For the cluster in the lower left corner that includes Ranstorp from CSTPV, it is sparse and shares few coauthorships. As chairman of the Advisory Board for CSTPV, Wilkinson has a few collaborations with Alexander but none with researchers at CSTPV who are in this sample. Another cluster includes researchers such as Alexander and Cline at the Center for Strategic and International Studies (CSIS). Since Alexander has 82 coauthors, this cluster displays a pattern of one to many coauthors. We found that coauthorships do not seem to be sustainable because many authors produce only a single publication with Alexander and did not publish with other terrorism researchers in this sample.

4.2   Content Map Analysis

Regarding the next set of questions identified in Table 1-1, several dominating terrorism topics have been identified for 1965-2003. Figure 1-3 displays the contemporary terrorism content map that was generated based on the title and abstracts of the 882 terrorism-related publications in our dataset. The topic map interface contains two components, a folder tree display on the left-hand side and a hierarchical content map on the right-hand side [17]. The terrorism publications are organized under topics that are represented as nodes in the folder tree and colored regions in the content map. These topics were labeled by representative noun phrases identified by our programs. The number of terrorism publications that were assigned to the first-level topics is displayed in parenthesis after the topic labels.

Major terrorism topics (large regions with depth in the content map) include "low intensity conflicts," "rand corporation paper series," "osama bin,' "political violence," "rand st andrews chronology," and "irish republican army". The topics "rand corporation paper series" and "rand st andrews chronology" highlight the major roles that Brian Jenkins, one of the pioneers of modern terrorism studies [36], and Paul Wilkinson, Chairman of the St. Andrews' Centre for the Study of Terrorism and Political Violence (CSTPV), Scotland, played. They established terrorism research centers, created databases of terrorism incidents, secured funding for terrorism research projects, produced terrorism studies, and supervised student's research on terrorism [27].

Several interesting shifts in the cognitive structure of contemporary terrorism research are identified. A traditional terrorism topic, "low intensity conflicts," first appeared in 1991 and appeared seven other times in the 1990s but only one time in 2000s. Prior to 11th September, the conventional wisdom was that the use of terrorism was endemic in low intensity conflict but that it rarely, if ever, posed a strategic threat to the security of major international powers [36].   After 1997, there was an increasing appearance of the topic "osama bin" which first emerged in our dataset in 1998 as the subject of an article by Peter Bergen [2].   "Osama bin' referring to Osama Bin Laden is a new topic of interest.

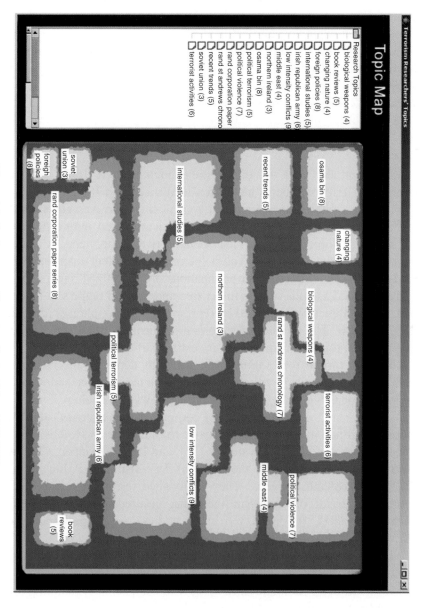

Figure 1-3. Contemporary Terrorism Content Map: 1965-2003

4.3   Co-citation Analysis

For the final set of questions identified in Table 1-1, the author co-citation analysis is used to visualize the closeness of research interests among the key terrorism researchers and their intellectual influences on others. The raw co-citation data derived from keyword searches of the ISI Web of Science were used for the analysis conducted in this part of the study. We created author co-citation networks to identify which key researchers in terrorism are often cited together.

Figure 1-4 shows a sample of pairs of authors (researchers) linked by co-citation counts of 1-3.

Authorship nodes are represented either by a square or circle followed by the last name of the first author, publication source, and year. The square node identifies a publication that cites the key terrorism researchers (circular nodes). The width of the arrows connecting authorship nodes have been made proportionate to their co-citation counts in size. The narrow arrow width reflects a count of one co-citation link while a thick one reflects a count of at least two co-citation links.

To illustrate the findings represented through the author co-citation map, boundaries were drawn around clusters of researchers. Figure 1-4 illustrates four groupings of author co-citation patterns.

The groupings provide a way of clustering pairs of researchers who share areas of interests. For example, publications cited in Group A focuses on terrorism and foreign policy (based on terms from the titles and abstracts of their publications). In Group A, Wardlaw's article on terror as an instrument of foreign-policy is citing several of the most frequent co-cited pairs. The most frequently appearing author co-cited pairs are Laqueur and Wardlaw (13 times), Stohl and Wardlaw (12 times), and Cline and Stohl (12 times). Cline and Stohl specialized in state sponsored terrorism.

Group B emphasizes the organizational perspectives of terrorism. It includes Oots' publication entitled "Organizational Perspectives on the Formation and Disintegration of Terrorist Groups". Oots cites seven of the key researchers and identifies almost fifty author co-citation pairs. Group C's subject deals with historical aspects while that of Group D is legal aspects of terrorism.

Another way of viewing subgroups and key members in contemporary terrorism research is to analyze their interaction patterns to identify the roles and positions that they play. It was found that, as Figure 1-5 shows, 18 terrorism researchers from the resulting network were co-cited in ISI.

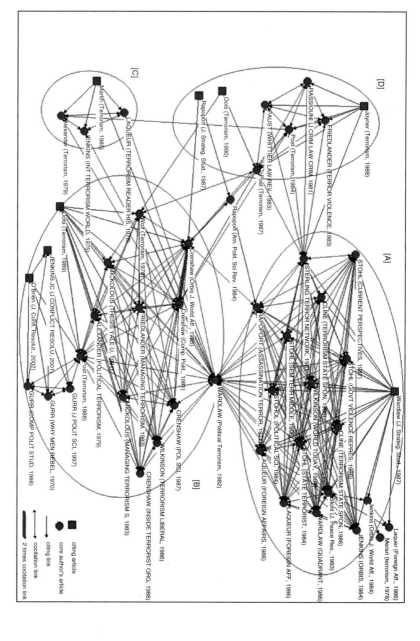

Figure 1-4. Key Terrorism Researchers' Co-citation Network

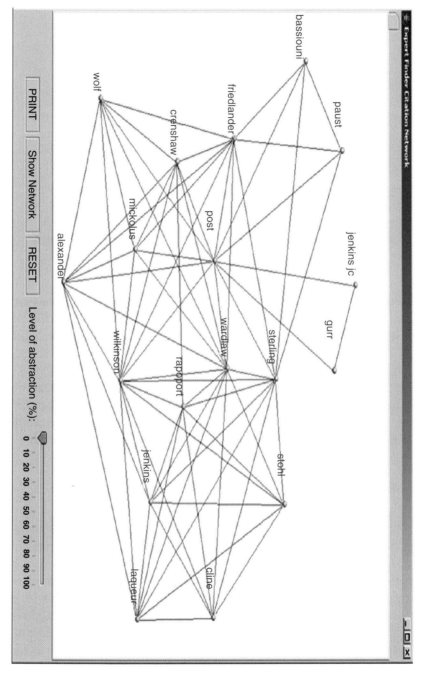

Figure 1-5. The 18 Key Terrorism Researchers Who Were Co-cited in ISI

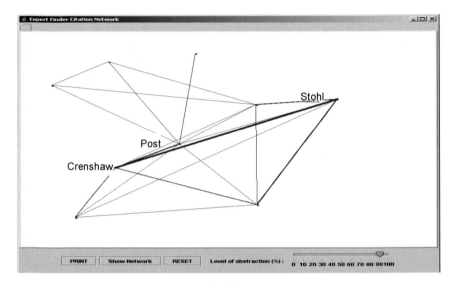

Figure 1-6. Subgroups of Co-cited Authors and Tagged with Leaders' Names

Figure 1-6 shows the subgroups identified by the system. They have the labels of their leaders' names (Crenshaw, Post, and Stohl). The thickness of the straight lines indicates the strength of relationships between subgroups.

For example, Crenshaw's group consists of Mickolous (cited with Crenshaw eight times), Post (cited with Crenshaw six times), Wolf (cited with Crenshaw six times), etc. Those familiar with terrorism research would not be surprised with the close co-cited relationship between Crenshaw and Post because they focus on the psychological aspects of terrorism with Crenshaw positing that there is no profile of the typical terrorist.

5.   CONCLUSION

The mapping of contemporary terrorism research provides a perspective that heretofore has not been afforded. As such, the tools such as content map analysis and co-citation analysis can help individuals visualize scholarly development within the field. For instance, while those familiar with terrorism will already know that, say, Stohl and Cline worked in similar areas and are often cited together, those who are not well oriented with the field, particularly new researchers could find such information relevant.

Although there are benefits of using visualization techniques, visualization is not a substitute for extensive reading and detailed content analysis for understanding the development of a field. For new researchers, it provides an alternative approach for understanding quickly the structure and development of a field. Thus, the knowledge mapping framework and tools provided here, could allow the expanding group of non-traditional terrorism researchers to conduct systematic exploitation of the terrorism field and identify trends and research gaps in a short period of time. This approach helps identify influential researchers in a field, the amount they are cited, the topics that are being investigated, and the frequency of co-citation with other terrorism authors who perhaps work in similar subject areas. With the current challenges in the interdisciplinary and international field of terrorism, new researchers must understand the intellectual structure of the field and how they can better frame their research questions.

We intend to supplement this work with other studies that will use time-series topic maps to present the development trends in terrorism across various periods to further examine the recent evolution and topic changes in the field. We will also include author content map analysis to group individual researchers based on their common research interests. In addition, we will use the results to develop a terrorism expert finder application that supports domain visualization and field test it with new and experienced terrorism researchers.

6. ACKNOWLEDGEMENTS

This research was funded by the National Science Foundation (NSF), ITR grant (Coplink Center for Intelligence and Security Informatics Research). Authors wish to thank Zhi-Kai Chen, Jennifer Jie Xu, the KnowNet Community, Dr. Jerold Post, and Dr. Marc Sageman for their support and assistance.

REFERENCES

1. Andrews, J.E., Author Co-citation Analysis of Medical Informatics. Journal of the Medical Library Association, 2003. 91(1): p. 47-56.
2. Bergen, P., Holy War, Inc.: Inside the Secret World of Osama Bin Laden. 2001, New York: Free Press.
3. Borgman, C.L. and J. Furner, Scholarly Communication and Bibliometrics, in Annual Review of Information Science and Technology (ARIST). 2002, ASIST.
4. Boyack, K.W. and K. Borner, Indicator-assisted Evaluation and Funding of Research: Visualizing the Influence of Grants on the Number and Citation Counts of Research Paper. Journal of the American Society of Information Science and Technology (JASIST), 2002.
5. Boyack, K.W., Mapping Knowledge Domains: Characterizing PNAS. Arthur M. Sackler Colloquium of the National Academy of Sciences, 2003, NAS: Irvine.
6. Brandes, U. and T. Willhalm. Visualization of Bibliographic Networks with a Reshaped Landscape Metaphor. In International Conference on Information Visualization. 2002: Konstanzer Schriften in Mathematik und Informatik.

7.   Chen, C. and R.J. Paul, Visualizing a Knowledge Domain's Intellectual Structure. IEEE Computer Society, 2001. 34(3): p. 65-71.

8.   Chen, H., et al., Crime Data Mining: a General Framework and Some Examples. IEEE Computer Society, 2004: p. 50-56.

9.   Chua, C., et al., Measuring Researcher-Production in Information Systems. Journal of the Association for Information Systems, 2002. 2: p. 146-215.

10. Cronin, B., High-Fidelity Mapping of Intellectual Space: Early and Recent Insights from Information Science, in Spaces, Spatiality and Technology Workshop. 2002, Napier University, Edinburgh Scotland: Edinburgh.

11. Eggers, S., et al., Mapping Medical Informatics Research. In Medical Informatics: Knowledge Management and Data Mining in Biomedicine, Springer Science, 2006.

12. Ferligoj, A., P. Doreian, and V. Batagelj, Optimizational Approach to Blockmodeling, 1992.

13. Garfield, E. and Welljams-Dorof, Citation Data: their Use as Quantitative Indicators for Science and Technology Evaluation and Policy-making. Science & Public Policy, 1992. 19(5): p. 321-327.

14. Garfield, E., A.I. Pudovkin, and V.S. Istomin, Algorithmic Citation-Linked Historiography: Mapping the Literature of Science, in ASIST 2002 Contributed Paper. 2002.

15. Gordon, A., Terrorism Dissertations and the Evolution of a Specialty: an Analysis of Meta-Information. Terrorism and Political Violence, 1999. 11(2): p. 141-150.

16. Gordon, A., Effect of Database and Website Inconstancy on the Terrorism Field's Delineation. Studies in Conflict & Terrorism, 2004. 27: p. 79-88.

17. Huang, Z., et al., International Nanotechnology Development in 2003: Country, Institution, and Technology Field Analysis Based on USPTO Patent Database. 2003.

18. Hughes, G., Analyze This, The Age. 2003.

19. Incites, Citation Thresholds. 2003, Institute for Scientific Information (ISI): Philadelphia.

20. ISI, How Does ISI identify Highly Cited Researchers? 2003, Institute for Scientific Information (ISI): Philadephia.

21. Kennedy, L.W. and C.M. Lum, Developing a Foundation for Policy Relevant Terrorism Research in Criminology. 2003, Rutgers University: New Brunswick.

22. Krebs, V.E., Uncloaking Terrorist Networks. First Monday, 2002. 7(4).

23. Lin, X., H.D. White, and J. Buzydlowski. AuthorLink: Instant Author Co-citation Mapping for Online Searching. in National Online Proceedings 2001. 2001. New York City: Information Today.

24. McCain, K.W., Mapping Authors in Intellectual Space: a Technical Overview. Journal of the American Society of Information Science, 1990. 41(6).

25. NameBase, Public Information Research, Inc.: San Antonio. http://www.namebase.org

26. Reid, E.O.F. and H. Chen, Contemporary Terrorism Researchers' Patterns of Collaboration and Influence. (unpublished).

27. Reid, E.O.F., Analysis of Terrorism Literature: a Bibliometric and Content Analysis Study. 1983, University of Southern California: Los Angeles.

28. Reid, E.O.F., Evolution of a Body of Knowledge: an Analysis of Terrorism Research. Information Processing & Management, 1997. 33(1): p. 91-106.

29. Reid, E., et al. Terrorism Knowledge Discovery Project: a Knowledge Discovery Approach to Addressing the Threats of Terrorism. In Second Symposium on Intelligence and Security Informatics, ISI 2004, June 2004 Proceedings. 2004. Tucson, Arizona: Springer-Verlag.

30. Reid, E.O.F. Identifying a Company's Non-Customer Online Communities. In Proceedings of the 36th International Conference on Systems Sciences (HICSS). 2004. Hawaii: HICSS.

31. Schmid, A. and A. Jongman, Political Terrorism: A New Guide to Actors, Authors, Concepts, Data Bases, Theories and Literature. 1988, Oxford: North Holland.
32. Shiffrin, R.M. and K. Borner, Mapping Knowledge Domains, in Arthur M. Sackler Colloquium of the National Academy of Sciences. Held May 9-11, 2003, at the Arnold & Mabel Beckman Center of the National Academies of Sciences & Engineering, Irvine, CA, NAS: Washington, D.C.
33. White, H.D. and K.W. McCain, Visualizing a Discipline: an Author Co-citation Analysis of Information Science 1972-1995. Journal of the American Society of Information Science, 1998. 49(4): p. 327-355.
34. White, H.D., X. Lin, and J. Buzydlowski. Co-cited Author Maps as Real-time Interfaces for Web-based Document Retrieval in the Humanities. In Joint International Conference o the Association for Computers and the Humanities and the Association for Literary and Linguistics Computing (ALLC). 2001. New York City: ACH/ALLC.
35. White, H.D., X. Lin, and J. Buzydlowski, Associative Information Visualizer, in Paper for InfoVis 2004 Contest. 2004.
36. Wilkinson, P. Terrorism: Implications for World Peace. In General Meeting Preparing for Peace Initiative. 2003. United Kingdom: Westermorland.
37. Xu, J., E. Reid, and H. Chen, Finding Communities in Related Networks. (unpublished paper)

APPENDIX: LIST OF 42 INFLUENTIAL TERRORISM RESEARCHERS (AS OF DEC. 2003)

Table 1-6. List of 42 influential terrorism researchers (as of December 2003)

Author Name	# of Pubs.	Active Years	# times cited for pubs in collection	Most Frequently Cited Terrorism Publication	Date	# times cited
1. Alexander, Yonah	88	32	**169**	Intl. terrorism national regional	1976	30
2. Arquilla, John	20	30	75	Cyberwar is coming	1993	18
3. Bassiouni, M.C.	8	17	22	Intl. terrorism & political …	1975	16
4. Bell, J.B.	47	35	**138**	Time of terror	1978	33
5. Bergen, Peter	10	7	16	Holy war inc	2001	15
6. Carlton, David	1	2	21	Terrorism theory & practice	1979	21
7. Chalk, Peter	17	26	20	West Euro-pean terrorism	1996	7
8. Cline, R.S.	8	14	15	Terrorism: The Soviet Conn-ection	1984	14

Author Name	# of Pubs.	Active Years	# times cited for pubs in collection	Most Frequently Cited Terrorism Publication	Date	# times cited
9. Cooper, H.H.A	10	25	11	Chapter in Terrorism Interdiscip.	1977	7
10. Crelinsten, Ronald	19	28	62	Political terrorism a research guide	1993	22
11. Crenshaw, Martha	40	35	**90**	Why violence spreads	1980	23
12. Dobson, C.	6	14	25	Black September	1974	8
13. Evans, Ernest H.	3	4	17	Calling a truce	1979	17
14. Flynn, Stephen E	4	4	12	Beyond border	2000	8
15. Freedman, Lawrence Z.	14	21	20	Terrorism & Intl Order	1986	7
16. Friedlander, R.A.	4	10	14	Terror violence Terrorism documents	1983 1979	7 7
17. Gunaratna, Rohan	14	8	16	Inside al qaeda	2002	14
18. Gurr, T.R.	51	41	**214**	Why men rebel	1970	145
19. Hacker, F.J.	3	5	38	Crusaders, criminals	1976	34
20. Hoffman, Bruce	121	27	**100**	Inside terrorism	1998	45
21. Horgan, John	13	18	10	Technology vs terrorism	1986	5
22. Jenkins, Brian M.	38	30	**96**	Intl. terrorism new mode	1975	27
23. Kepel, Gilles	6	4	25	Jihad expansion	2000	16
24. Laqueur, Walter	37	28	**191**	Terrorism	1977	75
25. Lesser, Ian O.	5	30	23	Intl. terrorism a chronology	1975	13
26. McCauley, Clark	4	12	8	Terrorism research & public	1991	8

Author Name	# of Pubs.	Active Years	# times cited for pubs in collection	Most Frequently Cited Terrorism Publication	Date	# times cited
27. Merari, Ariel	25	26	19	Readiness to kill & die	1990	8
28. Merkl, Peter	6	18	6	Political violence & terror	1986	6
29. Mickolus, Edward F.	25	28	73	Trans. terrorism, a chronology	1980	41
30. Paust, Jordon J.	11	30	13	Federal jurisdiction over …	1983	11
31. Post, Jerrold	12	19	18	Terrorist psycho logic	1990	12
32. Ranstorp, Magnus	8	13	13	Hizb'allah in …	1997	7
33. Rapoport, David	26	33	37	Assassination & terrorism	1971	20
34. Ronfeldt, David	20	30	**95**	Cyberway is coming	1993	18
				Networks & netwars	2001	18
35. Schmid, Alex P.	6	7	59	Political terrorism a new guide	1988	29
36. Sloan, Stephen R	31	34	30	Simulating terrorism	1981	10
37. Sterling, C.	5	7	10	Terror network	1981	10
38. Stern, Jessica E	21	13	25	Prospects of domestic bioterrorism	1999	12
39. Stohl, M.	30	28	**136**	State as terrorist	1984	32
40. Wardlaw, G.	25	23	49	Political terrorism theory, tactics	1982	31
41. Wilkinson, Paul	87	32	**229**	Terrorism & liberal state	1977	66
42. Wolf, J.B	7	16	11	Fear of fear	1981	5

Bold indicates most influential publications

SUGGESTED READINGS

- Boyack, K.W. *Mapping Knowledge Domains: Characterizing PNAS.* Arthur M. Sackler Colloquium of the National Academy of Sciences, 2003, NAS: Irvine.
- Eggers, S., et al. "Mapping Medical Informatics Research." In *Medical Informatics: Knowledge Management and Data Mining in Biomedicine,* ed. by H. Chen, et al. Springer Science, 2006.
- McCain, K.W. "Mapping Authors in Intellectual Space: a Technical Overview." *Journal of the American Society of Information Science,* 1990. 41(6).

ONLINE RESOURCES

- Börner, K., Chen, C., Boyack, K. Visualizing Knowledge Domains. *Annual Review of Information Science & Technology*, vol. 37. ASIST, 2003. Available at http://www.cs.sandia.gov/projects/VxInsight/pubs/arist03.pdf
- *Mapping Knowledge Domains.* Arthur M. Sackler Colloquium. National Academy of Sciences (NAS), May 9-11, 2003. Available at http://www.bmn.com/

DISCUSSION QUESTIONS

1. What are some advantages of using a knowledge domain framework and tools?
2. What are some of the challenges in using knowledge domain tools?
3. How can you overcome some of the challenges in using knowledge domain tools in emerging fields?
4. Since organizations such as the National Academy of Science (NAS) have started to focus on knowledge mapping, what are some research implications for the terrorism domain? What are some implications for other domains?

2

RESEARCH ON TERRORISM

A Review of the Impact of 9/11 and the Global War on Terrorism

Andrew Silke
School of Law, University of East London, London, U.K.(a.silke@uel.ac.uk)

CHAPTER OVERVIEW

This survey of terrorism research focused on research studies published in the first five years after the 9/11 attacks. It highlights a number of positive trends which can be seen in this initial period after 9/11. To begin with, it is clear that more researchers are working on the subject than before and there has been a real increase in collaborative studies. This allows studies to be more ambitious in both data-collection and data analysis, though there has only been a very small shift away from literature review-based research. There has, however, been a much more promising increase in the use of descriptive and inferential statistical analysis. The use of inferential statistics on terrorism data in particular has more than trebled since 9/11, a trend which can only help improve the reliability and validity of the conclusions being reached by researchers. Admittedly, this is an increase starting from an extremely low level indeed (and still compares poorly to core journals in other areas) but it is unquestionably a major step in the right direction.

1.   INTRODUCTION

Research on terrorism and terrorism-related issues has increased dramatically in the wake of the 9/11 attacks. This is not surprising. 9/11 witnessed the most destructive terrorist assaults in recorded history, and the attacks led to far bloodier conflicts as part of the subsequent war on terror. Terrorism has become the defining issue of international politics of the first decade of the 21st century. It would be remarkable if such prominence was not matched by a significant increase in research interest in this area. In 1988, Schmid and Jongman noted that 90 percent of the literature on terrorism had been written since 1969. If current trends continue, however, within two or three years we will certainly be able to say that over 90 percent of the entire literature on terrorism will have been written since 9/11. Indeed, we may already have passed that milestone. This is not to say that the literature before was sparse, but rather to emphasize the sheer volume of material now being produced in the area.

The scale of this new literature is difficult to grasp. Speaking in September 2002, Yonah Alexander commented that the previous year had seen roughly three new books on terrorism being published each week. This had sounded a considerable number at the time but as Figure 2-1 shows below it actually grossly underestimated the number of new books being published. Indeed, that level of publication was already reached in 2000 when some 150 books on terrorism were published. In contrast, in 2001 this figure jumped massively to 1108 titles, with naturally almost all of these being published in the final three months of the year. 2002 saw an even greater number of titles released with a staggering 1767 titles published (34 new books each week). Each of the following years has seen well over 1000 new books added to the literature. Indeed, the five years since 9/11 have probably seen more books published on terrorism than appeared in the previous 50 years. Currently, one new book on terrorism is being published every six hours. And this is just English-language titles (1).

The number of articles on terrorism in the academic journals has also increased hugely (though not to quite the same shocking level as with books). The journal *Studies in Conflict & Terrorism* brought out four issues per year prior to 9/11. Now it publishes on a monthly basis. Beyond the core terrorism studies journals, articles on the subject in other journals have also increased hugely across the board.(2) The ability to maintain an up-to-date understanding of the literature was already seriously stretched in the 1990s. Now, it is unquestionably impossible for one person to do so, and this can be seen in the growing number of research reviews being published both as articles and as books. In the final decades there were perhaps two or three such books published each decade. Today, that has changed to at least two or three published each year (with the volume you hold in your hand being of course another addition), though the sheer amount of new books detailed in Figure 2-1 suggests that even this level may be far too low an estimate.

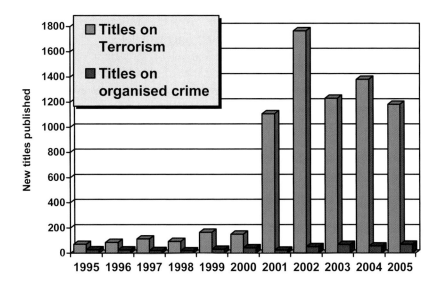

Figure 2-1. Books published on terrorism 1995 – 2005 (Organized crime books shown for comparison)

The rise in such reviews and surveys of the research literature reflects both the massive increase in volume and more significantly the massive increase in interest. For most of its history the study of terrorism has been conducted in the cracks and crevices which lie between the established academic disciplines. Few researchers devoted most of their scholarly activity to the area – for most it was a brief fling before returning to more traditional interests. But all this seems to be changing. The money available for research has increased markedly and a growing number of younger (and older) researchers are beginning to shift the bulk of their research activity to this area. We appear to be entering a renaissance age for terrorism studies and with so many students and scholars fresh to the field, the need for up-to-date and well informed reviews of the research has never been greater.

Yet gaining a good understanding of the existing knowledge base on terrorism is intimidating. The potential literature is vast and growing rapidly. In an effort to help provide a framework for understanding the literature, this chapter represents the latest in a series of articles by the author which have reviewed some aspects of research on terrorism.(3)

The first set of these papers focused on research carried out in the 1990s. That initial review found that many of the traditional problems associated with research on terrorism continued to eat away at the field's foundations during the 1990s. Early reviews such as Schmid and Jongman's famous work in 1988 had long appreciated that despite the fact that a very sizable body of literature had accumulated on terrorism, the substance of this writing was often very poor indeed. As Schmid and Jongman noted:

"Much of the writing in the crucial areas of terrorism research ... is impressionistic, superficial, and at the same time often also pretentious, venturing far-reaching generalizations on the basis of episodal evidence" (4).

This was an observation certainly shared by Ariel Merari who writing a few years later commentated that:

"There are few social scientists who specialize in this study area. Most contributions in this field are ephemeral. Precise and extensive factual knowledge is still grossly lacking. Much effort must still be invested in the very first stage of scientific inquiry with regard to terrorism -- the collection of data" (5).

In examining the quality of research on terrorism, Schmid and Jongman noted that "there are probably few areas in the social science literature on which so much is written on the basis of so little research". They estimated that "as much as 80 percent of the literature is not research-based in any rigorous sense; instead, it is too often narrative, condemnatory, and prescriptive" (6).

My first review showed that this pessimistic state of affairs was largely unchanged (7). During the 1990s, 68 percent of the research was found to be based on the literature-type reviews criticised by Schmid and Jongman. Further, the related long-running shortage of terrorism researchers also continued to weaken the area. While the backgrounds of researchers may be relatively diverse, there has in general been a consistent lack of researchers to carry out investigative work in the area. Since it emerged as a clear and substantial topic of study, terrorism has suffered from a near-chronic deficiency of active researchers. The 1990s review found that terrorism studies had 40 percent fewer authors contributing to articles compared to fields such as criminology (where many of the same research issues and limitations also apply). The lack of researchers meant that less expensive (in terms of time and effort) data gathering and data-analysis methods were being used with consequent concerns over the quality and reliability of the findings.

The next review added analysis of research in the first three years following 9/11 (8). While this showed some distinct changes had taken place in the field, the old problems were still very much present. That said, three years is a very short space of time in research terms. A survey by Garvey,

Lin and Tomita (1979), for example, found that on average it took researchers 13 months to complete a study and write up the results for submission to a journal (9). Once submitted, it took on average another 15 months before the article actually appeared in print. The result is that it can often take nearly two and half years between research starting and the findings actually making it into print in a journal. Thus the previous review arguably really only assessed the initial wave of research started in the direct aftermath of 9/11, and it is perhaps not terribly surprising that the old, long-running problems were still very much in evidence. Many of the major funding initiatives only became active after this period, and a review now – five years on – provides a somewhat better opportunity to assess the impact of the post-9/11 environment on the nature of research.

Arguably the best way to identify trends and patterns in research efforts is to examine the published literature produced by active researchers. While the literature on terrorism is relatively young in academic terms - existing in a meaningful sense since only the late 1960s – Schmid and Jongman noted that by the time of their review it had nonetheless grown far beyond the scope "of one single researcher [to] survey the field alone". Indeed, the two Netherlands-based writers pulled in the assistance of over fifty other researchers in order to complete their review.

As already indicated, the situation today is considerably more intimidating. The sheer volume of material being published is staggering and even five years after the dramatic events of 9/11 the current flood of books and articles shows no sign of abating. The result is that any effort to review the field faces increasingly difficult decisions in terms of what to review. Hundreds of academic journals have published at least one article relating to some aspect of terrorism in the past ten years. A review which incorporated every such journal would be a formidable undertaking. Fortunately, the presence of two long-established journals which have an explicit and primary focus on terrorism research provides an accessible medium to gauge the state of research. These journals are *Terrorism and Political Violence* (TPV) and *Studies in Conflict & Terrorism* (SICAT). Taken together, and bearing in mind their different publishers, separate editorial teams and largely separate editorial boards (though there is some overlap on this last) the two journals can be regarded as providing a reasonably balanced impression of the research activity and interests in the field.

However, it is important to note that many active researchers have not published in these two journals and have instead preferred to publish elsewhere. It would be a mistake to assume that all of the key researchers publish in these journals or that the journals reliably represent the nature of most research on the subject. Some other reviews of the field have tried to address this issue by incorporating a wider range of journals. Increasing the quantity of journals however is not necessarily a guarantee of increasing the reliability of a review. Czwarno (2006) for example, reviewed 12 journals in her survey (10). These included both SICAT and TPV but also included other journals which only rarely published terrorism related pieces. Czwarno reported that from 1993 – 2001 in most of the journals she reviewed only 1% to 3% of the articles were on terrorism. Such a very low rate does raise question marks over the merits of examining these journals to begin with and raises concerns over how representative the journals were. Czwarno focused primarily on international relations type journals but there would certainly be journals in other disciplines such as psychology and criminology which could also have provided a 1% publication rate. It is churlish however to be too critical. Clearly, there are different benefits to casting a wider net, but the essential point is that it is extremely difficult to be truly representative in reviewing an interdisciplinary area such as terrorism studies. The approach adopted here is to review only those journals which publish primarily and consistently on terrorism (and for both TPV and SICAT the clear majority of their articles are routinely focused on terrorism-related subjects).

Consequently, this paper presents the results of a review of the published output of the primary journals in the area from 1990 to October 2006. As with the previous reviews, it is hoped that a review of this nature can be both of interest and of practical value to other writers and researchers on the topic, and that it may also help to establish the broader context in which individual research efforts occur and help illustrate how the field is evolving in the aftermath of 9/11 and the advent of the so-called 'global war on terror'.

2.   THE NATURE OF THIS REVIEW

Academic journals have a surprisingly diverse range of content. For the two journals under consideration here, this includes articles, research notes, editorials, book reviews, conference reports, review essays, database reports, and official documents and reports. The most immediate question facing a surveyor is how much of this material should be considered? In deciding this, the main criteria has to be which items are consistently the best indicators of significant research activity and effort? This review follows the lead of the UK's RAE, which has judged that peer-reviewed journal articles provide a good measure of the broad quality of research work. As a result the following review focuses solely on articles published in the journals during the time period.

This is a relatively stringent criteria and other reviewers may be willing to be more inclusive. For example, there is case to consider that research notes should be included in a review such as this. They have not been included here however because of the considerable variation displayed in the items so classed in the journals. While some research notes were significant documents – both in terms of length and content – most were extremely brief and cursory. Indeed, it is something of a mystery as to why some papers were classed as research notes when they seemed in every respect to be comparable to articles published elsewhere in the same issue. It would be invidious however for one reviewer to subjectively select from among the other categories what he or she regards as equivalent to article standard. Rather than attempt this, this review simply excludes entirely from consideration all items which were labelled or described as other than an article. While this inevitably means that a few significant works are not considered, it means that overall the review is focused on what can be considered to be consistently the substantial research outputs of a nearly seventeen year period (11).

3.   TRENDS IN DATA-GATHERING AND ANALYSIS

One of the most serious problems facing research on terrorism has been the long running shortage of experienced researchers. As a field, terrorism studies has struggled to attract new researchers and then hold onto them. The review of research in the 1990s clearly showed that compared to other academic areas such as criminology (which presents many similar challenges to the study of terrorism), research on terrorism was depending on the work of far fewer researchers. In a review of leading criminology journals it was found that 497 articles had been written by a total of 665 authors. For the terrorism journals in the 1990s, 490 articles were written but this was the output of just 403 authors. This was a far lower level compared to the criminology journals and highlighted the dependence on a small pool of active researchers. The figure also highlighted the lack of collaborative research. As Figure 2-2 shows, less than 10 percent of articles published before 9/11 were the work of two or more researchers. The vast majority of studies were being carried out by individual researchers working alone.

This relative isolation emphasised the lack of research funding available in the area. Collaborative research is more dependent on research grants. Without funding, researchers are much more restricted in what they can aspire to and are much more likely to have to squeeze the research effort in between other activity. There are knock-on consequences of such a situation: limited resources mean that research which involves more time and effort will be avoided. Instead, researchers will focus on quicker and cheaper approaches. Quick and cheap is fine to a certain extent, but inevitably if a field is very heavily dependent on such work, serious questions about the reliability and validity of any findings must emerge.

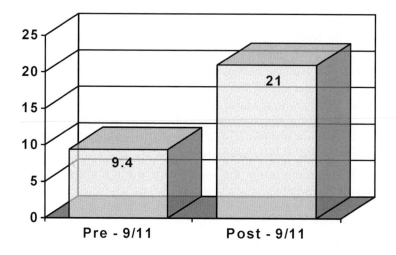

Figure 2-2. Collaborative Research

Following 9/11, however, there has been a major increase in collaborative work. This reflects the increased interest among researchers (new and old) for the area and also reflects the increased availability for funding on the subject. As Figure 2-2 shows, collaborative work has more than doubled. The field still lags well behind other applied disciplines such as criminology and forensic psychology, but it is certainly a step in the right direction.

The natural following issue is whether the increasing number of researchers and increased funding has led to any improvements in data gathering and analysis. Figure 2-3 presents a somewhat disappointing picture in this regard. An old failing of the field has been the very heavy reliance on literature review methods. Schmid and Jongman were very critical of the paucity of fresh data which researchers were producing. In the 1990s this problem continued with 68 percent of the research essentially taking the form of a literature review and not adding any data which was previously unavailable to the field. The influx of additional researchers since 9/11 does not seem to have improved this situation much. As Figure 2-3 shows, 65 percent of articles are still essentially reviews. While this represents a small improvement on the 1990s, it is only a small one. One feels that a great deal more needs to be done before research is consistently building on past work rather than merely rehashing old data.

While Figure 2-3 might present a dispiriting picture, there is somewhat more encouragement to be taken from Figure 2-4. While the data gathering methods appear to be more or less the same as before, the way in which this data is analysed does seem to be shifting a little faster.

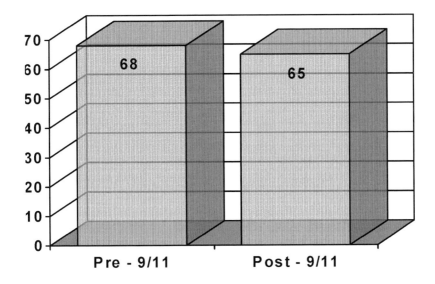

Figure 2-3. Literature review-based research

Since the 1950s, all of the social science disciplines have experienced a rapid increase in the use of statistics. People are extremely complex, and their behavior and thoughts are the result of a confusing interaction of emotions, motivations, learned behaviors and genetically determined traits. Consequently, social science researchers typically have to work with very 'noisy' data where there are potentially a vast number of factors exerting an influence on any one behavior, event or trend. Statistical analysis has emerged as a way for researchers to determine which factors genuinely are important and which are not. Descriptive statistics enable the researcher to summarize and organize data in an effective and meaningful way. Inferential statistics allow the researcher to make decisions or inferences by interpreting data patterns. Inferential statistics are regarded as particularly valuable as they introduce an element of control into research which can help to compensate if relatively weak data collection methods were used. In experimental designs control is normally achieved by randomly assigning research subjects to experimental and control groups. However, this can often be very difficult to achieve in real world research and consequently the lack of control throws doubt on any association between variables which the research claims to find. Inferential statistics though can help to introduce a recognized element of control, so that there is less doubt and more confidence over the veracity of any findings (12).

It is no coincidence that some of the most significant and influential books published on terrorism since 9/11 have been ones which have made extensive use of statistics to support the authors' arguments. Such key works include Marc Sageman's *Understanding Terror Networks*, Robert Pape's *Dying to Win* and Ronald Clarke and Graeme Newman's *Outsmarting the Terrorists* (13). While many might disagree with some elements of these books, there can be no denying that each has had a tremendous impact both in the research communities and (even more importantly) among policy-makers and other practitioners. It is highly unlikely that these texts could have been as influential if they had not provided and relied heavily on statistical evidence to support the arguments being made.

Figure 2-4 shows that these books are unusual within terrorism research. Only a small minority of studies included either descriptive or inferential statistics prior to 9/11. Just 19 percent of articles had such analysis to support any arguments. This is not surprising given the heavy reliance on literature review methods in the field. There has been a definite improvement in the situation since 9/11, with 28 percent of articles now using statistics. This is a definite step in the right direction and the big increase in inferential analysis in particular (going from 3 percent to 10 percent of articles) is an important shift.

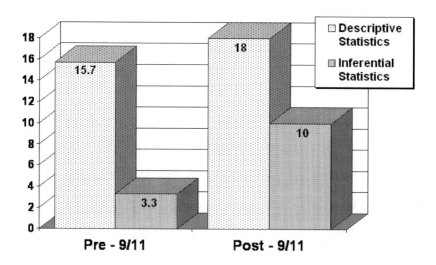

Figure 2-4. Statistical Analysis in Terrorism Research

It is important to stress here that this chapter is not arguing that statistical analysis should be a feature of *every* research study on terrorism. On the contrary, much valuable research can be conducted which does not involve the use of statistics. However, terrorism research clearly suffers from a serious imbalance and the argument here is that more effort should be made to address this imbalance. Statistics alone are not the way forward, but neither is avoiding their use to the degree that the terrorism research community currently does.

The extent of the imbalance is starkly illustrated in Figure 2-5. This compares the use of statistics in journal publications in two other areas of research with the terrorism journals: forensic psychology; and, criminology (14). The reason for choosing these particular areas is that the research backgrounds of both these disciplines have a number of similarities with research conducted on terrorism. The subject matter published in journals in these areas focus on the various actors and activities involved in the criminal justice system and in the commissioning of crime.

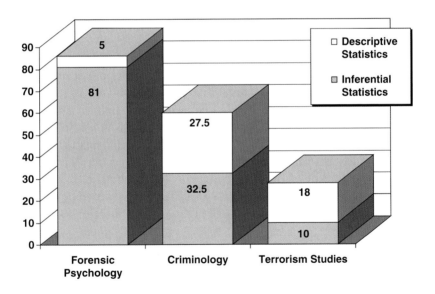

Figure 2-5. Comparing statistical analysis across three research areas

As a result, the subject matter often shares comparable similarities with terrorism in terms of difficult research populations, real world relevance as well as considerable concerns with human suffering and injustice. Thus when compared to other areas within the social sciences, such journals do seem to offer some legitimate comparison with the terrorism journals However, despite the similarities, the manner in which researchers in these two areas treat data is very different to how it is treated by terrorism researchers. 86% of research papers in forensic psychology and 60% of papers in criminology contain at least some form of statistical analysis. In both cases, inferential statistics account for the majority of this analysis. In both disciplines, the use of statistics is seen as an important and accepted way in which to ensure that the claims made by researchers meet recognized quality controls. Despite the improvements since 9/11, terrorism articles still lag well behind these other applied areas, and concerns must remain over the validity and reliability of many of the conclusions being made in the field.

4.   RESEARCH ON TERRORIST GROUPS

One of the most notable findings in the previous reviews of the research literature was just how little research was focused on al-Qaeda in the ten years prior to 9/11. Al-Qaeda was an active and growing organisation in this period and was responsible for several high profile terrorist attacks including the highly destructive bombings of US embassies in Africa in 1998 and the well publicised attack against the USS Cole in 2000. Yet despite what in hindsight seems quite a significant trajectory, the group attracted almost no research attention. As Figure 2-6 shows, in the twelve years prior to 9/11, al-Qaeda was the subject of only 0.5 percent of research articles. In the core journals this represented only two articles (al-Qaeda was mentioned briefly in other articles but in only two was the organisation a major focus for the research) (15).

This failure to notice the growing significance of al-Qaeda has been noticed by other reviewers and most especially by Monica Czwarno who found that the lack of attention paid to the organisation was mirrored across a wide range of journals and was not simply a failing of the two core specialist journals (16).

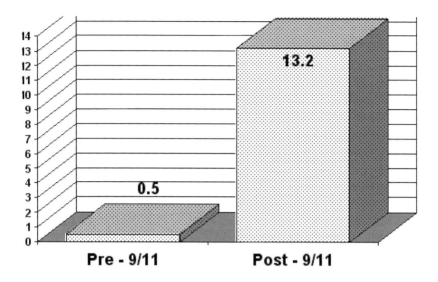

Figure 2-6. Research on al-Qaeda

As figure 2-6 emphasises the neglect preceding 9/11 has been replaced by a surfeit of interest in the five years after that date. Currently, out of every seven articles published in the core journals one is focused on al-Qaeda. It is rare indeed for any of the issues published in the last five years to not contain at least one article which is substantially devoted to at least some aspect of the group.

Figure 2-7 underlines this transformation in research attention. Since 9/11 there have been 30 research articles in the core journals focused on al-Qaeda (compared to just two in the preceding twelve years). Interest in other groups has remained broadly similar. The most studied terrorist group prior to 9/11, the Irish Republican Army (IRA) still attracts considerable attention. Indeed, the Irish group actually attracts slightly more attention now than it did in the 1990s which is remarkable given the group has been on cease-fire for many years. There have been perhaps more significant increases in attention on groups like Hezbollah and Earth liberation Front which are interesting.

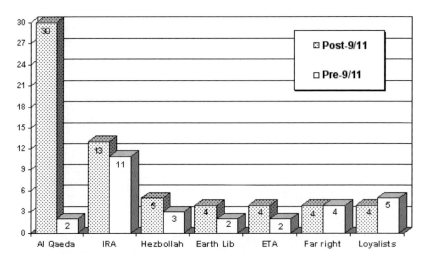

Figure 2-7. Most studied organisations post-9/11

The increased attention on Hezbollah is especially intriguing as this preceded the 2006 Israeli invasion of Lebanon in an effort to defeat the organisation and cannot be seen as a reaction to such events. On the contrary, it may be a sign that the research literature was showing awareness of the growing significance of the movement.

While the research literature clearly missed the growing significance of al-Qaeda, it would be unfair to say that the community was entirely unaware of the growing importance of Islamist terrorism. Figure 2-8 shows very clearly that research on Islamist terrorist groups has been steadily increasing over the past seventeen years. In the first half of the 1990s 14 percent of articles were focused on some aspect of Islamist terrorism. This included groups such as al-Qaeda, Hamas, Islamic Jihad and Hezbollah. This rose to over 23 percent in the latter half of the 1990s representing a significant increase in research attention on this area. Since 9/11, however, Islamist terrorism has completely dominated the field. Nearly 63 percent of the literature is on this subject (almost two out of every three articles). In the past forty years there has never been such a heavy focus on one category of group in the literature.

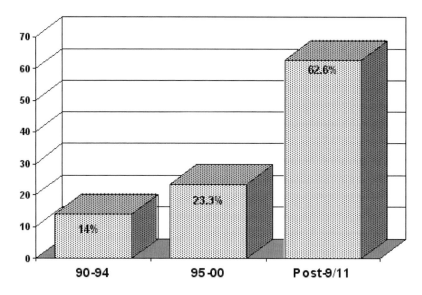

Figure 2-8. Research on Islamist Terrorist Groups

While it is understandable that the field would show such a heavy bias in this direction in the aftermath of 9/11 and the war on terror, any objective analysis must still regard the current state of the literature as extremely skewed. If it continues like this for much longer there is a serious risk that terrorism studies as an area will effectively become *Islamist* terrorist studies with all other types of organisations relegated to only peripheral interest.

5. RESEARCH ON TERRORIST TACTICS

Suicide terrorism is not a new phenomenon but prior to 9/11 it was certainly relatively ignored by terrorism researchers, considered more of a curiosity than a major subject for analysis. Figure 2-9 shows that only a tiny proportion of articles looked at this issue - only 0.5% of articles - a bare handful. That however changed in the aftermath of 9/11 the most devastating terrorist attacks of all time, and accomplished through the use of suicide tactics. Since 9/11, the amount of research work being focused on this phenomenon has increased enormously. For every one study carried out prior to 9/11, 20 are being carried out now. One article in ten published on terrorism since 9/11 has been focused particularly on suicide terrorism. So intense has been the growth of research on this one aspect of terrorism, that some researchers are now pushing for the creation of a sub-discipline of suicide terrorism studies. How realistic (or necessary) such ambitions are is questionable but the debate does at least emphasise the enormous growth of activity on an aspect of terrorism which traditionally was grossly under-explored.

The increased work being focused on suicide terrorism is arguably both overdue and useful. However, increased research is also being focused on other aspects of terrorism which are less obviously of growing importance. Of particular concern is the growing amount of research investigating the (potential) use of Chemical, Biological, Radiological and Nuclear weapons (CBRN) – also often referred to as weapons of mass destruction (WMDs) - by terrorists. Figure 2-10 shows that the amount of research being focused on CBRN terrorism has doubled since 9/11. The first review on research after 9/11 showed an even higher proportion of articles looking at this issue, though this seems to have declined slightly since then (17).

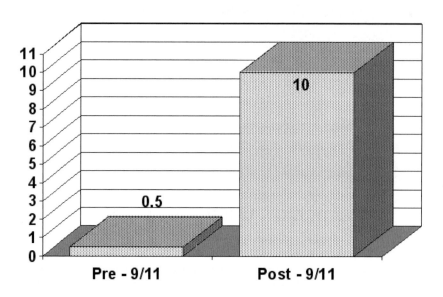

Figure 2-9. Research on Suicide Terrorism

As with the previous review, a key question here continues to be why is there this increased interest in terrorism using CBRN weapons? After all, 9/11 was not a CBRN attack. 3000 people may have been killed but the hijackers did not use a nuclear bomb to cause the carnage, they did not spray poisonous chemicals into the atmosphere or release deadly viruses. They used box-cutters. Nevertheless, CBRN research has experienced major growth in the aftermath. Is this increase justified?

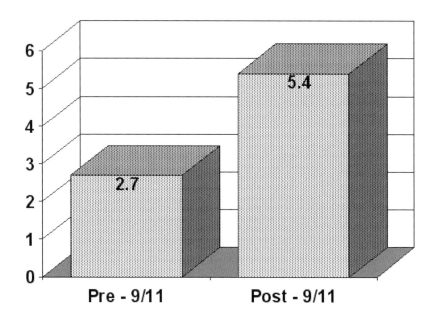

Figure 2-10. Research on CBRN Terrorism

The short answer is probably not, but then CBRN research has always probably been over-subscribed. Prior to 9/11, nearly six times more research was being conducted on CBRN terrorist tactics than on suicide tactics. Indeed, no other terrorist tactic (from car-bombings, hijackings, assassinations, etc.) received anywhere near as much research attention in the run up to 9/11 as CBRN. If the relatively low amount of research attention which was given to al-Qaeda is judged to be the most serious failing of terrorism research in the years prior to 9/11, the relatively high amount of research focused on the terrorist use of CBRN must inevitably be seen as the next biggest blunder.

To date, in the few cases where terrorists have attempted to develop CBRN weapons they have almost always failed. In the handful of instances where they have actually managed to develop and use such weapons, the highest number of individuals they have ever been able to kill is 12 people. In the list of the 300 most destructive terrorist attacks of the past twenty years, not a single one involved the use of CBRN weapons. Yet somehow one impact of the 9/11 attacks is that CBRN research - already the most studied terrorist tactic during the 1990s - has actually managed to attract even more research attention and funding - doubling the proportion of articles focused on CBRN in the journals.

If the articles were focused on mass casualty terrorism that would be more understandable. 9/11 was certainly a *mass casualty* terrorist attack, and indeed there have been a few studies which have looked at mass casualty terrorism since 2001 (18). However, the research is not taking such an approach and instead is very much focused on terrorist use of chemical, biological, radiological or nuclear weapons (CBRN). This relative (but increasing) obsession with CBRN is disturbing for a number of reasons. First, it detracts attention from more lethal tactics which terrorists frequently and routinely use. Consider the lack of attention given to suicide tactics in the 1990s. Well over 1000 people were killed by suicide terrorism in the 1990s. In the same period, attacks using CBRN weapons killed just 19 people. Yet it was CBRN which attracted six times more research energy than suicide terrorism.

A degree of research looking at CBRN terrorism is justified. Instances such as the 1995 Tokyo subway attack and the post-9/11 anthrax letters show that CBRN attacks *can* happen (albeit only rarely). Such attacks have never caused mass fatalities however and the popular acronym of Weapons of Mass Destruction (WMD) in describing CBRN weapons is desperately misleading. Despite the rarity - and the extreme unlikelihood of terrorists being able to accomplish a truly devastating attack using these weapons – CBRN remains a popular topic for government and funding bodies. They will award research grants for work on this topic when other far more common and consistently far more deadly terrorist tactics are ignored.

Those who had hoped that 9/11 - a stunning example of how non-CBRN weapons can be used to kill thousands of people - might then have heralded at least a modest shift away from CBRN research will be disappointed. Ultimately, the central lesson of 9/11 in this regard has been profoundly missed.

6.   SOME CONCEPTUAL ISSUES

Terrorism has a very long history, one that can be comfortably traced back thousands of years (19). Yet, it would be difficult to appreciate this based on the literature published in the core journals in the past two decades. As Figure 2-11 shows very little research explores past terrorist conflicts. Before 9/11, only one article in 26 looked at historical conflicts. Since 9/11, interest in historical cases has collapsed and now only one article in 46 is focused away from current events.

It is natural and reasonable that in the years immediately after the most destructive terrorist attacks in recorded history, that the research field should focusing on the now, on current issues, actors and events. Such a strong focus on contemporary issues, however, runs the real risk of losing an understanding of the broader context of terrorist conflicts, patterns and trends and without such awareness important lessons can be missed.

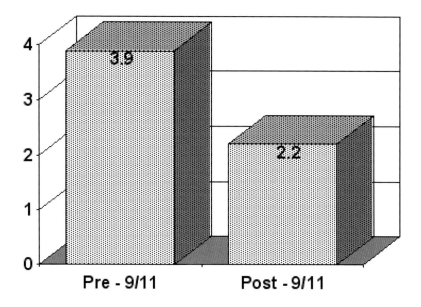

Figure 2-11. Research with a historical focus

An example I have used previously is that many observers treat the current US military involvement in Iraq as a strictly modern issue linked only to the previous Iraq war and the more recent Global War on Terror. There is no awareness that this is not the first time that the US military has faced an insurgency in an occupied country where the insurgents frequently use suicide tactics to attack technologically superior American forces. Yet, this was exactly the circumstances faced by US forces at the start of the 20th century as they fought insurgents in the Philippines. Beginning in 1900, US control of the Southern islands of the Philippines was contested by native Moro tribes. The US forces typically won overwhelming victories in all their conventional battles with the Moros, but then faced increasing attacks from individual *amoks* and *juramentados*, Moro warriors who attacked US positions and personnel in suicidal efforts armed often only with swords and spears (20). It took nearly 13 years of fighting before Moro resistance to the US presence finally receded. Yet the lessons from this bitter and painful conflict are being ignored. A closer inspection of such historical cases may help prevent the current conflict in Iraq enduring 13 years. Ignoring such experiences however seems unlikely to improve the odds of a more successful campaign.

Yet terrorism research has never been especially good at exploring the past. Prior to 9/11, only 3.9% of articles examined non-contemporary terrorism and less than half of these looked at terrorism prior to 1960. We know that terrorism is not a recent phenomenon and that it has been occurring in some form or another for over two thousand years. Yet this wider context is almost entirely ignored as terrorism research is increasingly driven by a need to provide a short-term, immediate assessment of current groups and threats. Efforts to establish more contextualised and stable guiding principles have been almost entirely side-lined. This is a serious cause for concern and the dramatic decline in historical research since 9/11 is deeply troubling.

7.   CONCLUSIONS

Prior to 9/11, the study of terrorism was carried out on the periphery of academia. The funding available for researchers was extremely limited and the number of researchers prepared to focus a substantial element of their careers on the subject was paltry. In most cases it was harmful to an academic or research career to follow such interests and most of those who were genuinely interested in the subject found that they had to incorporate other issues into their work in order to remain professionally viable. 9/11 has brought much greater interest in the subject of terrorism and for the first time the possibility of an expanded core of dedicated researchers exists. It is likely that the field and the amount of research being conducted will continue to grow over the coming years. It is not certain however whether this growth will be sustained or even if the gains made in the first years since the New York and Washington attacks will not be eroded over the coming decade.

In considering the focus of research on terrorism since 9/11, there are some worrying trends. The increased attention to CBRN threats is unjustified and it is disturbing that even more research activity is now being devoted to this area. The relatively heavy focus on CBRN prior to 9/11 was misplaced to begin with and produced research which was worthless with regard to what al-Qaeda did then and subsequently. The concern with CBRN is ultimately built on the premise of the fears and nightmares of politicians and policy-makers. The link to reality is often tenacious at best.

The diminishing place for historical analysis in terrorism research is also a cause for concern, but it is probably wise not to place excessive emphasis on this trend at this stage. The 9/11 attacks were the most destructive terrorist attacks in recorded history and many of the key factors relating to the event were notoriously under-studied (e.g. al-Qaeda, suicide terrorism, etc.). It is only natural that the field should now devote serious and substantial effort to improving our knowledge base and understanding of these subjects. Terrorism research, however, does have a legacy of missing important trends. The research of the 1990s would not have flagged to an interested reader that al-Qaeda would be universally regarded as the most important and prominent terrorist group of the 2000s. One wonders what other significant trends are now being dangerously overlooked?

Yet, this survey of research has not reached entirely negative conclusions and it is important to highlight a number of positive trends which can be seen in this initial period after 9/11. To begin with, it is clear that more researchers are working on the subject than before and there has been a real increase in collaborative studies. This allows studies to be more ambitious in both data-collection and data analysis and while there has only been a very small shift away from literature review-based research, there has been a much more promising increase in the use of descriptive and inferential statistical analysis. The use of inferential statistics on terrorism data in particular has more than trebled since 9/11, a trend which can only help improve the reliability and validity of the conclusions being reached by researchers. Admittedly, this is an increase starting from an extremely low level indeed (and still compares poorly to core journals in other areas) but it is unquestionably a major step in the right direction.

Ultimately, it is still very early to judge what the overall impact 9/11 and the new world order will have on terrorism research. This review was based on the research studies published in the first five years after the attacks. As discussed earlier, within research timeframes this is a short period of time. It will probably be another two or three years before a full and reliable assessment of the impact of the 9/11 on terrorism research will be possible. To date, we have seen that the field has become even more concerned with contemporary issues than before. This is probably unhealthy if it lasts but is hardly surprising given the issues which were missed prior to 9/11.

It is worth recognising as well that the field is showing signs of generally moving in the right direction when comparisons are made with the results of the first review carried out three years after 9/11. Compared to this chapter, that earlier review found a higher level of CBRN research, less historical research, less collaborative work, less variety in research methods, and less use of statistical analysis. In short on almost all of the key issues considered here, the first three years were less satisfactory than a review which includes the full five years after 9/11. The differences between these two reviews in most cases are small, but they exist nonetheless. The hope is that they represent a swing in positive directions, a change of direction which can be maintained and built upon.

REFERENCES

1. These figures are based on statistics provided by Amazon.com. The statistics relate to non-fiction titles on the subject of terrorism published in a given year. The figures may not include every relevant title published in a year, but should be seen as broadly representative. The statistics were accessed on August 1, 2006.
2. See, for example, Monica Czwarno (2006). Misjudging Islamic Terrorism: The academic community's failure to predict 9/11. *Studies in Conflict and Terrorism*, 29/7, pp.657-694.
3. The findings from the previous reviews were published in the following papers: (1) Andrew Silke (2001). The Devil You Know: Continuing Problems with Research on Terrorism, *Terrorism and Political Violence*, 13/4, pp.1-14; (2) Andrew Silke, (2004). The Road Less Traveled: Recent Trends in Terrorism Research. In A. Silke (Ed.), *Research on Terrorism: Trends, Achievements and Failures* (pp.186-213). London: Frank Cass; and, (3) Andrew Silke (2006). The Impact of 9/11 on Research on Terrorism. In Magnus Ranstorp (Ed.) Mapping Terrorism Research. Oxford: Routledge.
4. Alex Schmid and Albert Jongman (1988). *Political Terrorism: A New Guide to Actors, Authors, Concepts, Databases, Theories an Literature* (Amsterdam: North Holland Publishing Company), p.177.
5. Ibid.
6. Ibid., p.179.
7. See Andrew Silke (2001) note 3, and Silke (2004) note 3.
8. Andrew Silke (2006) note 3.
9. Garvey, W., Lin, N., & Tomita, K. (1979). Research studies in patterns of scientific communications: III, Information-exchange processes associated with the production of journal articles. In W. Garvey (Ed.), *Communication: The essence of science* (pp.202-224). Oxford, England: Pergamon Press.
10. Monica Czwarno (2006). Misjudging Islamic Terrorism: The academic community's failure to predict 9/11. *Studies in Conflict and Terrorism*, 29/7, pp.657-694.
11. Each article which was published in the review period was entered into a database based on eleven separate features. Coding was made for each author of each article on the following features:
    a. Author name
    b. Whether first, second or third author
    c. Journal title
    d. Journal Volume details
    e. Year of Publication
    f. Country where the author is based
    g. Occupation/background of the author
    h. Geographic focus of the article
    i. Temporal focus of the article
    j. Terrorist Group focus of the article
    k. Terrorist Tactic focus of the article
    l. Conceptual focus of the article
    m. Data-gathering methods used
    n. Statistical analysis methods used

12. Chava Frankfort-Nachmias and David Nachmias, *Research Methods in the Social Sciences (5th edition)* (London: Arnold, 1996) pp.427-428.
13. Marc Sageman (2004). *Understanding Terror Networks*. Philadelphia: University of Pennsylvania Press; Robert Pape (2005). *Dying to Win: The Strategic Logic of Suicide Terrorism*. New York: Random House; Ronald Clarke and Graeme Newman (2006). *Outsmarting the Terrorists*. London: Praeger Security International.
14. Two journals from both disciplines were reviewed. In all the cases the review period stretched from 1995 to 1999 and a random selection of eight issues from each journal title were reviewed.
15. The criteria used when judging the focus of an article was that the paper had to be primarily about one or at most two groups. It was not sufficient that a group was briefly mentioned or received discussion of a page or two. There had to be substantial evidence that the group was a major focus of the article.
16. Monica Czwarno (note 2).
17. See Andrew Silke (note 7).
18. For example the valuable contributions made by Chris Quillen: Chris Quillen, 'A historical analysis of mass casualty bombers', *Studies in Conflict and Terrorism* 25/5 (2002) pp.279-292; and, Chris Quillen, 'Mass casualty bombings chronology', *Studies in Conflict and Terrorism* 25/5 (2002) pp.293-302.
19. For an excellent introduction to this subject see Robert Asprey, *War in the Shadows* (London: Little Brown, 1994).
20. For more on this campaign see D. Woolman, 'Fighting Islam's fierce Moro warriors', *Military History*, 9/1 (2002) pp.34-40.

SUGGESTED READINGS

- Ranstorp, M. (2006). *Mapping Terrorism Research*. London: Routledge.
- Schmid, A. and Jongman, A. (1988). *Political Terrorism: A New Guide to Actors, Authors, Concepts, Databases, Theories and Literature* (Amsterdam: North Holland Publishing Company),
- Silke, A. (2004). *Research on Terrorism: Trends, Achievements and Failures*. London: Routledge.

DISCUSSION QUESTIONS

1. Very little research was carried out on al-Qaeda prior to 9/11. Can you assess why this happened? (It might be helpful to consider the terrorist groups which were receiving most of the research attention.)
2. Research on terrorism can be biased in a number of ways. Try and identify some potential biases and assess how they may affect the way research is conducted.
3. Does the wider interest in CBRN weapons help or harm terrorism studies?

4. Based on the material in this chapter, what do you think are the most
   serious problems facing research on terrorism today?

3

WHO ARE THE KEY FIGURES IN 'TERRORISM STUDIES'?

Sam Raphael
King's College, London (KCL), U.K. (sam.raphael@kcl.ac.uk)

CHAPTER OVERVIEW

The first part of this chapter constructs a analytical framework to enable the key figures in the field of terrorism studies to be identified. Use of this framework by future studies will ensure that their analysis of terrorism studies is based on a sample of authors and works which have been selected with sufficient methodological rigour. To have impact, such studies – which may interrogate the quality of research on terrorism, or examine the relationship between terrorism 'knowledge' and power, or attempt to reveal the existence of an 'invisible college' – must be able to show that they apply to the core (or, at least, *a core*) of terrorism studies, and that the selection of this core was achieved in a rigorous and explicit manner. The second part of this chapter employs this framework in order to identify three 'pools' of researchers: a *periphery pool* of over 300 authors, a *central pool* of 140 authors, and a *core pool* of just 31 authors.

1.   INTRODUCTION

This chapter describes one possible answer to a question which will be of interest to those examining 'the state of the field' of terrorism studies: *who are the key figures in the field of terrorism studies?* The results obtained from this research question can be used for a variety of further projects: once identified, the key figures themselves could be subjected to greater analysis (examining, for instance, their institutional affiliation, or their relationship to government); alternatively, their published works could be the subject of further inquiry (1). These second-order questions are not considered here. Rather, the chapter's primary concerns are twofold: to construct a framework within which people can think about how to identify the key figures in a way which displays sufficient methodological rigour; and to make an initial attempt at employing this framework, in order to generate a sample pool of key figures.

As will become clear, the results obtained depend very much on several choices made regarding research design; choices which *must* be made, and made explicitly, if the results are to stand up to scrutiny on methodological grounds. First, when is the time period considered by the study? Second, how is 'terrorism studies' to be defined, and delineated from other fields of academic study? Third, given that expertise is not an objective quality held independent of social context, whose opinion is to be privileged when deciding who within the field is considered key? Fourth, how is this opinion to be measured, from the wide range of possible scales that exist? Finally, what threshold will be applied in obtaining a specific pool of researchers? In other words, how stringent should the selection criteria be, where higher thresholds will produce a smaller results set? This chapter examines the significance of these research design choices, which ultimately ensure that each separate attempt to ascertain the key figures of terrorism studies is likely to identify a different pool of researchers.

By making its own choices in this regard, the chapter will also identify its own pool of key figures in terrorism studies. With one eye on the research design choices made by this study – the methodology employed – its results can be compared with others that have addressed the same research question (2). In particular, this study identifies three pools of researchers, each of a different size and with various degrees of centrality to the particular community which is taken to represent 'terrorism studies'. Thus, it finds that there is a *periphery* pool (with 312 members); a *central* pool (a subset of the periphery pool, with 140 members); and a *core* pool (a subset of the central pool, with 31 members). This final, core pool can be taken to include those researchers who are the key figures of terrorism studies. And although other studies, by virtue of their different research designs, will identify a non-identical set of researchers as key, the results obtained here display a high degree of *intuitive plausibility*. That is, despite the inclusion of some unexpected authors, and the surprise omission of others (a feature to be expected as a result of all studies which do not simply set down a subjective list of who is considered key by the author), the results obtained here broadly correlate to those which would be 'expected' by many who are familiar with the field (3).

2. CONSTRUCTING THE FRAMEWORK
The Multiplicity of 'Terrorism Studies', the Role of the Audience, and the Importance of Methodological Rigour

When establishing the parameters of terrorism studies, as well as when identifying the key figures within the field, the question of methodology is fundamental. Absent an explicit and rigorous process through which either is determined, a study is open to the charge of selecting, by stealth, both the field and the key figures within it in order to verify pre-existing assumptions. These assumptions may be to do with the nature of the field of terrorism studies, the identities of the pre-eminent experts working within this field, or the characteristics of the work produced by these key figures (4).

For a study to be rigorous in this sense, it needs to resolve five issues: *when* the relevant time period for study is; *which* actual research community is being examined; *who* the relevant 'expert-determining' audience is; *how* the opinion of that audience is to be measured; and *what* the threshold of that measurement is, above or beyond which would signify a key position within the research community (and in particular, whether that threshold is an absolute or relative quality).

As with other academic fields, determining the boundaries of 'terrorism studies' is problematic. This ambiguity is a function of both the lack of consensus regarding the definition of core concepts (i.e., what exactly is the 'terrorism' which 'terrorism studies' is studying?), and of the sheer number of those writing about terrorism. Given the myriad of perspectives employed by the literally thousands of academics who have published on the subject, and the varying degrees of commitment *to sustained research* on terrorism, an all-inclusive pool of terrorism researchers would consist of authors with little in common (5). Indeed, some argue that talk of a 'terrorism studies', as if it exists as a coherent field at all, is misleading, whilst proactive attempts to forge a independent identity for the 'science of terror', by pulling it out from 'the cracks and crevices which lie between the large academic disciplines', are misguided (6). Regardless of the desirability or otherwise of forming a distinct field, it is clear that a *singular, easily-identifiable* 'terrorism studies' does not exist; it is therefore impossible to speak of 'key figures within terrorism studies' without further qualification.

However, it may be possible to conceive of several 'research communities' which contribute, to a greater or lesser extent, to the study of terrorism. These communities can be seen as the analytical units which, in a loose sense, combine to form the field. Rather than mutually-exclusive sub-fields which allow for the neat division of the study of terrorism, they should be considered a multitude of independent, yet overlapping, *aspects* of a field which itself is amorphous and ill-defined, but which at the level of individual community can be made concrete, defined exactly, and subjected to rigorous analysis.

For example, one might make the case for researchers clustered around a particular institution (e.g., RAND) to be considered a viable research community. Alternatively, those who publish in a certain set of outlets (e.g., a collection of particular journals) about a specific subject (e.g., nonstate terrorism, or religious terrorism), could be considered a viable research community. The term 'viable' is of interest here, as the degree to which the centrality of that community to the idea of a 'terrorism studies' can be defended will determine the degree to which the results obtained are considered relevant to the study of 'terrorism studies'. In other words, if one does not accept a proposed community (say, everyone who contributes to a particular website) as reflecting a central aspect of one's broad conception of the field, then one will not consider the results of the proposed study as particularly significant.

In this way, despite the problems associated with the identification of key figures with terrorism studies *per se*, it becomes possible to speak of key figures *within a certain research community*. Shifting the focus in this way affects the universal applicability of the results obtained. Indeed, acknowledging that any research into 'terrorism studies' is actually research into one particular community amongst many reveals the possibility that two studies, each claiming to analyse the characteristics of 'terrorism studies', will arrive at very different conclusions *by virtue of the fact that they are analysing distinct communities*.

Not only is the idea of a coherent field of 'terrorism studies' a problematic one; the notion of 'expertise' also requires further exploration. Expertise is an intersubjective quality (7). Rigour can therefore only be obtained by treating expertise in relation to a particular *audience*; a social or political grouping that, in a collective sense, invests the quality of expertise in a certain set of actors. Therefore, once the research community is identified each study has a second choice to make: which audience will be put centre-stage; the opinions of which group of people will be privileged, with regards to who in any particular research community is key? Examples of choices which can be made regarding research community and audience, as well as time-scale, measurement scale and threshold, are provided in Table 3-1:

Table 3-1.

Study	**When** the relevant time period is	**Which** research community is being examined	**Who** the relevant audience is	**How** the audience's opinion is to be measured	**What** the threshold of that measurement is
A	1968-2003	That based around panels on terrorism in the five most relevant conferences	US Media	No. of interviews in top-ten US newspapers	All those interviewed more than ten times
B	1979-present	That based around posts as 'terrorism experts' in the ten biggest think-tanks	US Military	Award of DOD contracts	All those awarded more than £50k
C	1991-9/11	That based around the publication of terrorism articles in the top-20 IR journals	European General Public	High-street book sales across Europe	The top 20 biggest sellers
D	9/11-present	That based around posts as 'terrorism experts' in the top-100 universities, who are ex-government employees	British Counterterr or officials	Questionnaires	All those receiving more than three mentions

Within each of these hypothetical studies, there is no pre-determined link between any of the five design choices: Study A could legitimately decide to measure the key figures in its research community (based around the conference circuit) by reference to the general public, and could choose to focus on the post-9/11 years. Likewise, one could decide to measure general public opinion using opinion polls instead of book sales, or could choose to establish an absolute, rather than relative, threshold of the book-sales measurement (e.g., all those selling more than 20,000 copies, rather than the top 20 biggest sellers, will be considered 'key figures').

Of obvious significance here, every study which is ostensibly examining the same subject ('terrorism studies') could potentially arrive at a different understanding of who is key, given the very different choices made regarding research community, audience, measurement, and threshold. Even studies *of the same research community* will potentially produce a very different set of results.

Moreover, each of these five choices has an *inescapable political function*. By either foregrounding certain audiences or research communities over others, or by ensuring that the choices are made so as to generate results which conform to pre-existing assumptions and overarching political agendas, they privilege certain social and political perspectives over others. However, by ensuring that a study makes its methodology explicit, its *results* can then be gathered *in an impartial, objective sense*, can be fully justified by reference to the choices, and can be re-generated at will by others.

3. EMPLOYING THE FRAMEWORK
Selecting the Time Period; Constructing the Research Community

As a specific phenomenon, contemporary terrorism is generally considered to have emerged during the late 1960s (8). The birth of the academic consideration of this phenomenon can also be charted back to this time (9). However, in employing the framework described above, this study excludes the first decade of considerable research, restricting the analysis to a shorter timeframe: the twenty-five years between September 1979 and September 2004. This choice ensures that the results more accurately reflect the period during which a core community within terrorism studies has operated in a *unified and coherent* manner. It therefore excludes the initial period of flux, beginning instead when research on terrorism had 'stabilised' after its initial take-off period (10). This stabilisation at the end of the 1970s, and the consequent emergence of a concrete research community (as opposed to a collection of disparate researchers), can be seen in the establishment of the two core journals of the time: *Terrorism* (first published in 1977) and *Conflict* (first published in 1978). As will be seen, the management of, and the output from, core academic journals will be taken as a significant criteria when establishing the key figures of the research community.

This study will focus on two research communities, both of which are central to any viable conception of a 'terrorism studies'. The first community consists of the approximately 200 people identified by Schmid and Jongman in their major survey of the field as representing 'a good cross section of the field', plus the extra individuals identified by this group via Schmid and Jongman's questionnaire. Together, the community consists of around 400 individuals (11). Although one may question the basis upon which Schmid and Jongman selected the original 200 authors (were they *really* a good cross-section of the field? According to which measure?), the success of their effort can be measured by the subsequent approval bestowed upon it by the wider research community (12), as well as by the extent to which their results have been used by others who attempt to research characteristics of the field of terrorism studies (13).

However, despite the wide acceptance of Schmid and Jongman's methodology, and the continued use of their results by others, the data are now more than twenty years old (the questionnaires were sent out in 1985). For current analyses to remain relevant, it must be supplemented by the consideration of an additional research community. This is particularly true if the study is interested in the key figures in terrorism studies over the entire 1979-2004 period; Schmid and Jongman's research provides a fascinating snapshot of a research community as it existed during the mid-1980s, but is not necessarily applicable outside of this context.

Given that the sheer size of today's field makes it 'unlikely that anyone would happily attempt to replicate Schmid and Jongman's review' (14), and that identifying a new 'good cross-section of the field' begs the question of what constitutes the field, this study will identify a second, separate research community which will fulfil this supplementary function: that which is clustered around *the core journals of the field*. The 'core' is taken to be those journals which have a large proportion of their content dedicated to terrorism.

In line with the findings of others, this study identifies two current core journals (*Terrorism and Political Violence (TPV)*, and *Studies in Conflict and Terrorism (SCT)*), and four in total over the 1979-2004 time period (*Conflict* and *Terrorism* amalgamated in 1992 to form *SCT*). Gordon has found that 27% of all journal publications on the subject of terrorism between 1988 and 1998 were concentrated in *TPV*, *SCT* and their predecessors. This concentration 'constitutes the nucleus of publications in the field, and the journals in the nucleus are core journals' (15). Likewise, Silke finds that the two current core journals 'exist as the primary publishing outlets for research on terrorism', and that, taken together, they 'can be regarded as providing a reasonably balanced impression of the research activity and interests in the field' (16). These findings are confirmed by a survey of a sample of academic journals, designed to establish the number of terrorism articles published between 1979 and 2004 (17). Table 3-2 lists the results obtained from a search of one of the largest social science bibliographic databases (18):

Table 3-2.

Journal	Number of 'Terror' Articles (1979-2004)	Total Number of Articles (1979-2004)	% Total Focused on 'Terror'
Terrorism and Political Violence	485	808	60
Terrorism	37	52	60
Studies in Conflict and Terrorism	213	553	39
Conflict	5	65	8
Contemporary Security Policy	39	567	7
Survival	83	1333	6
Washington Quarterly	59	1140	5
International Security	23	632	4
International Affairs	82	3449	2
Foreign Affairs	64	2915	2
Israel Affairs	6	494	1
Journal of Strategic Studies	6	814	<1
International Peacekeeping	5	648	<1
Security Studies	2	240	<1
Total number in IBSS (1979-2004)	8293		

As this survey shows, the 'core' output of *SCT*, *TPV*, *Terrorism* and *Conflict* represents a far lower proportion of overall journal output on terrorism than that found by Gordon: together, terrorism articles in the four core journals constituted just 9% of the total number of terrorism articles indexed by IBSS during the period 1979-2004 (740 out of 8293). This figure contrasts with the 27% found by Gordon. As well as resulting from the use of different databases, this lower figure is likely to be a consequence of the different timescales in each survey. In particular, the period since 9/11 has seen a vast proliferation of terrorism articles (19), published in a bewildering array of academic journals (20).

However, it is also clear from the survey that a far higher proportion of the output of *SCT*, *TPV*, and *Terrorism* concerns terrorism, as compared to this particular set of other journals in the wider field of international security and international relations. Moreover, it seems likely that these figures have been deflated by the fact that articles appearing in journals dedicated to the study of terrorism may not include the keywords 'terror', 'terrorism', etc. (assuming as they would that the focus on terrorism is self-evident).

A word is also needed about the journal *Conflict*. Given that it appears to have published just a handful of articles on terrorism, representing a fraction of its total output, the inclusion of the journal as part of the focus of the research community may be puzzling. However, its history as one of the two predecessors of *SCT*, which is certainly a core journal, qualifies it for inclusion, and potentially demonstrates the limitation of this superficial bibliographic database search. The significance of this history is attested by the fact that 12 out of the 17 people on the editorial board of *Conflict* during its final volume (i.e., 70%) moved over to the board of *SCT*, where they made up 60% of the new board (12 out of 20 editors).

So in attempting to identify the key figures in terrorism studies 1979-2004, this study will examine two specific research communities: that clustered around Schmid and Jongman's extensive survey of the field in 1985; and that clustered around the four core journals. And although neither of these communities encompasses the entire field of what may be called 'terrorism studies', the fact that the results generated here have an intuitive plausibility suggests that they are both central to any viable conception of the field.

4. CONSTRUCTING THE AUDIENCE

Although the research community and the audience are analytically distinct categories, this particular study will equate the two. In other words, rather than asking 'who does the media consider to be key from the two research communities identified?', the study will ask 'who do the two research communities identified consider to be key from within their own ranks?' In this way, the study takes as significant *peer assessment*; it is the *peer community* that is granted the voice over who should be considered key. Just as peer judgement forms the key indicator of the value of academic *research*, it will be considered the key indicator of the expertise of individual *researchers*.

This follows the lead of past studies which ask similar questions. For instance, the questionnaires sent by Schmid and Jongman to the approximately 200 people who represented '*a good cross section of the field*' asked the question: 'Who are the leading authors in the field?' These authors mentioned 166 individual names, 35 of which had three or more citations, and were therefore considered 'leading authors in the field of terrorism' (21). This list of 35 leading authors is clearly generated *by reference to the peer community*. Indeed, the rationale provided by Reid when using this list of 35 as the basis for her own research community was that it represented a viable expression of peer assessment, and 'the selection of experts is considered most relevant when done by peers who share common research interests and expertise' (22).

It is worth noting that one could potentially interpret the 'peer community audience' widely, and as non-equivalent to the research communities under examination. For example, a study could take the relevant peer audience to be the *entire academic community*. Peer assessment on this scale could be measured via a citation database such as *Web of Knowledge* (23). Here, a cited reference search could determine which authors within the two research communities have had the greatest impact on subsequent academic work (perhaps with results sufficiently weighted to reflect the varying lengths of time each work has existed in the public domain).

Such a study would generate very different results from the present one, as the academic community *as a whole* will not have the same view regarding the key figures in these research communities. As one example of the potential differences in opinion, one can look at the treatment of scholars such as Noam Chomsky and Edward Herman. Both of these form part of the first research community (in that they were identified by Schmid and Jongman as part of the 'good cross section of the field', or were identified by someone within that 'good cross section' as a key person, or an author of a valuable work). Both of these authors (Chomsky in particular) are cited copiously by many academics *as experts on terrorism*. However, both are ignored by the specific audience consisting of members of the two research communities themselves (i.e., those representing 'terrorism studies'). This will be seen in the fact they do not appear as key figures in the results generated here; it can also be seen in the silence regarding their work by those who *are* identified as key (24).

5.   MEASURING THE OPINIONS OF THE RELEVANT AUDIENCE
What does the Peer Research Community Think?

For this study, the assessment of this 'peer research community' regarding who is key within the communities will be measured according to three scales. First, by reference to the proactive judgements of the 'good cross-section of the field', as gathered by Schmid and Jongman in 1985 (in other words, the response given by the 'good cross section' to the question: 'Who are the leading authors in the field?'). The second and third scales relate to the core journals in the field. As the key institutions of peer assessment (founded upon, and underpinned by, peer review), academic journals are the primary source for measuring the opinion of the peer-audience. The assessment will be measured by reference to both the appointments to the editorial boards of these journals (the second scale), and the peer-reviewed inclusion of articles in those core journals (the third scale).

Results from the first scale were gathered simply by the list of 166 names given by responses to Schmid and Jongman's questionnaire. Results from the second and third scales were gathered by an analysis of each of the four core journals throughout the period September 1979 – September 2004. Table 3-3 sets out the range of issues of each journal included in the study, so as to match as closely as possible the 25-year timeframe:

Table 3-3.

Journal	Start Issue	End Issue
Conflict	vol. 1, no. 3 (1979)	vol. 11, no. 4 (1991)
Terrorism	vol. 3, no. 1 (1979)	vol. 14, no. 4 (1991)
SCT	vol. 15, no. 1 (1991)	vol. 27, no. 4 (Jun-Jul, 2004)
TPV	vol. 1, no. 1 (1989)	vol. 16, no. 2 (Summer, 2004)

To determine the members of the editorial boards (the second scale), the study examined the first issue in each included volume, and noted all names which appeared. In this way, if someone joined the board for less than one year, it is possible that their name escaped the survey. This does not seem problematic, however, as such a short tenure could not be presented as evidence of their serious participation within the field.

The study also surveyed the authorship of all named publications which appeared in the four journals within this period (the third scale). Rather than restrict the survey solely to article-length pieces, it included introductions, forewords, conference papers and reports, review articles, research notes, and the odd letter and reply, *assuming that these pieces were credited with an individual authorship.* Pieces with no credited authorship (such as anonymous conference reports) were excluded, as were pieces authored by organisations (such as the State Department). Finally, book reviews were excluded from the survey (although, as previously stated, review articles were included).

Although including such 'minor' pieces as letters and forewords does not give a balanced assessment of who has authored the substantial research, a wider scope does provide a more indicative assessment of *active participation* in the institutions of peer review. In other words, it is not the case that letters or research notes from every source are published; peer review (even if only in the form of editorial selection) is crucial, ensuring that a measure of peer assessment is present even in the case of 'minor' pieces. One potential danger of this method is that someone could be selected as a key figure purely on the basis of their writing lots of letters, but not authoring any substantial peer-reviewed work. The final results should therefore be double-checked to ensure that such anomalies do not occur. In general, however, one can always envisage a range of anomalous results generated by any particular methodology. This points to the importance of a *triangulation of methods* in determining the key figures in terrorism studies; a strategy which is explored and employed below.

6.   ESTABLISHING THE THRESHOLD
Exactly *What* Determines an Expert as Key?

Now that the method by which this study will *measure* the assessment of the peer community as to who is key in the field has been resolved, a final question remains to be answered before results can be generated: what is the threshold of these measurements, above which signifies inclusion within a 'pool' of key researchers? In other words, how many pieces in a core journal must an individual have authored in order to be considered key? Is this a relative value (e.g., the ten most prolific authors), or an absolute value (e.g., all those authoring more than five pieces)?

Rather than setting the threshold at one level, in order to generate just one pool of experts, this study will set it at three separate levels. This results in the creation of three pools: a periphery pool (with 312 members); a central pool (a subset of the periphery pool, with 140 members); and a core pool (a subset of the central pool, with 31 members).

6.1   The First Threshold: Identifying the Periphery Pool

This study assumes that a scholar is considered at least a periphery part of the research community if they: appear on Schmid and Jongman's overall list, generated by their questionnaire; or have appeared on the editorial board of the four core journals at any point between September 1979 and September 2004; or have published more than one piece in one or more of the four core journals, during the same period. Those publishing just one piece during this period are not considered part of the community in any meaningful sense, as such a record potentially signifies only a passing interest in the subject of terrorism.

As a reminder, Schmid and Jongman's questionnaire generated 166 names in response to the question: 'Who are the leading authors in the field?' Meanwhile, Table 3-4 presents the results from the survey of editorial board membership:

Table 3-4.

Journal	No. Editors, Sept 1979 – Sept 2004
Conflict	22
Terrorism	77 (incl. the International Editorial Advisory Board)
SCT	37
TPV	29
TOTAL	**165**

Bearing in mind the criteria for which pieces of work to include in the survey of journal contents, Table 3-5 presents the number of pieces in each journal during the relevant time period:

Table 3-5.

Journal	No. Pieces, Sept 1979 – Sept 2004
Conflict:	154
Terrorism:	347
SCT:	269
TPV:	522
TOTAL:	**1292**

In other words, throughout the 25-year time period from September 1979 until September 2004, the four core journals in the field of terrorism studies published 1292 separate pieces which were accredited to specific authors (either writing singularly, or with others). This figure, as mentioned, does not include the extensive number of book reviews.

Together, these pieces were authored by 921 individuals. In other words, almost one thousand people contributed, in some form or another, to the output of one of these journals during the time period. Of these, more than three-quarters (706) published, or co-published, only one piece throughout the 25-year period. This confirms the oft-repeated observation that, despite the massive volume of work produced within the field of terrorism studies, 'a huge proportion of the literature is the work of fleeting visitors: individuals who are often poorly aware of what has already been done and naïve in their methods and conclusions' (25). This has consequences for the proportion of journal authors to be considered even as just a periphery part of the community, as highlighted in Table 3-6:

Table 3-6.

No. of publications	No. authors
1	706
>1	215
TOTAL	**921**

Combining all these results, Table 3-7 gives an indication of the size of the periphery pool of researchers:

Table 3-7.

Measurement	No. of names
Schmid and Jongman's list	166
Repeat authors list	215
Editorial board membership list	165
Overall list	546
Total (with duplicates removed)	**312**

As can be seen from the difference between the size of the 'overall list' and the 'total' in Table 3-7, there are many names which appear on more than one of these lists. As one example, Paul Wilkinson appears on all three lists: on Schmid and Jongman's list (as very highly-rated by peers, with 20-25 citations); on the repeat authors list (with 18 pieces authored or co-authored); and on the editorial board membership list (as an editor of *SCT* from 1995-2004, of *TPV* from 1989-2004, and of *Terrorism* from 1979-1988). Indeed, this overlap is to be both expected and welcomed, as a sign that the methodology employed is identifying those central to the research communities (and to the field of terrorism studies in general), who would be expected to be rated by peers in a questionnaire, as well as to write for, and serve on the editorial board of, the core journals in the field. Once duplicates have been removed, the periphery of the community consists of 312 individual authors. For brevity's sake, these names are not provided here.

6.2   The Second Threshold: Identifying the Central Pool

By raising the threshold levels, the study can identify a *central pool* of researchers amongst those considered to have only a periphery relationship with the field. This study will take it that a scholar is considered a central part of the research community if they: appear on Schmid and Jongman's list as *having received three or more citations* from their questionnaire; or have appeared on the editorial board of one of the core journals *for at least five years* (26); or have published *four or more pieces* for one or more of the core journals. This higher threshold, it is argued, results in removing those who show more than a passing interest in the subject, but who do not necessarily have an ongoing professional dedication to the academic study of terrorism.

Those having received three or more citations from the questionnaire are essentially those 35 people considered 'leading authors in the field of terrorism' by Schmid and Jongman (27). Table 3-8 gives the results of those on the editorial board of one or more core journal for at least five years:

Table 3-8.

Journal	No. editors, 5+ years
Conflict	17
Terrorism	40 (incl. the International Editorial Advisory Board)
SCT	28
TPV	22
TOTAL	**107**

Of the 215 authors responsible for two or more pieces in the core journals, only 58 published more than three pieces in the core journals between September 1979 and September 2004. Given these figures, Table 3-9 provides the overall numbers considered central to the community:

Table 3-9.

Measurement	No. names
Schmid and Jongman's list	35
Editorial board membership list	107
Prolific authors list	58
Overall list	200
Total (with duplicates removed)	**140**

Once duplicates are removed, the list has 140 individual names on it, each of which had done *at least* one of the following: appeared on Schmid and Jongman's select list; served on the editorial board for one or more of the four core journals for at least five years; authored, or co-authored, at least four pieces for one or more of the core journals. This pool of central figures is under half (45%) of the total research community of 312. Again, for brevity's sake, these names are not provided here.

6.3 The Third Threshold: Identifying the Core Pool

By employing a strategy of triangulation with the threshold levels for the central pool, a *core pool* of researchers can be identified. Core figures are those who surpass at least two of the three measurement thresholds for the central threshold. In other words, they have authored more than three pieces *and* are on Schmid and Jongman's list, or they have authored more than three pieces *and* have been on an editorial board for five or more years, or they have been on an editorial board for five or more years *and* are on Schmid and Jongman's list.

This triangulation should ensure that several possible anomalies are removed from the results. These could include those who may have appeared on Schmid and Jongman's list due to several people citing them as key in 1985 *due to their activities in the 1970s or earlier*, but who have not been active in the community during the 1979-2004 timeframe. It should also remove anyone cited by Schmid and Jongman's sample, but who otherwise has no substantial connection with others in the community. Hannah Arendt, present in the central community (she received 5-9 citations as a result of Schmid and Jongman's questionnaire), is probably an anomaly on both of these counts. Triangulation will also remove those figures asked to join the editorial board of a core journal not because of their perceived centrality to the field, but because of their wider reputation in international affairs (thus lending the terrorism journal greater credence). Bernard Lewis is a potential anomaly in this regard. Finally, this strategy will remove those who may appear on the list of authors who have published four or more pieces, but only do so due to writing relatively minor pieces (such as letters to a journal), or as clear second authors for multi-authored articles. Moreover, not all articles in the core journals are properly considered articles on the subject of terrorism. Indeed, in the IBSS search discussed above, 40% of both *TPV* and *Terrorism* articles, 61% of *SCT* articles, and 92% of *Conflict* articles do not relate to the keywords 'terror', 'terrorism', 'terrorist', etc. This is not to suggest that *none* of these are terrorism-related, but it is certainly the case that the core journals carry articles which would generally be taken to be outside the remit of terrorism studies. Given this, an author may make it on to the above list of central figures through the authorship of four or more articles not directly related to terrorism. Triangulation should identify and remove such anomalies, as a prolific author who is *also* on the editorial board, or is *also* considered key by respondents to Schmid and Jongman's questionnaire, is much more likely to have authored pieces on terrorism.

It is important to note that the triangulation method employed to generate the core community does not *just* remove anomalies. By setting the threshold levels higher, it also distinguishes those more central to the field from those less central. In other words, authors who appear on the central list, but not on the core list, are not all anomalous results; most are simply those who are properly considered terrorism experts, but who are just not as central as those who surpass at least two of the three measurement thresholds. Table 3-10 (at the end of this chapter) displays the results of this higher threshold, which form the core community.

Of the 31 core figures in terrorism studies, 16 appear on Schmid and Jongman's list from data collected in 1985, all but one (Livingstone) was an editor for five or more years, and 25 have authored four or more pieces for the core journals. Nine individuals appear on all three lists.

To recall, there is complete flexibility over where the exact position of each threshold is set. Another study may set even more stringent criteria, thus forming a smaller pool of key figures. For example, a study could decide that, in order to qualify for the core pool, authors must have had at least five citations in Schmid and Jongman's survey (17 individuals), or been on the editorial boards of *at least two core journals* for five or more years (12 individuals), or have authored 10+ pieces for the core journals (11 individuals) (28). Or, even more stringently, the study could triangulate these three thresholds, and ask for an author to be considered key they must have surpassed at least two of these thresholds (eight authors) (29), or even all three (three authors) (30).

However, the higher the threshold is set, the more the resulting pool loses its group-like characteristics, and begins to resemble no more than the sum of the individuals within it. Consequently, any further analysis would have less to say about the core figures *as a group* (e.g., how they sustain each other's position at the core by uncritical referencing of each other's work), and be more restricted to commentary on an individual level only. This may not be an issue, but could potentially be detrimental to a wider project that seeks to analyse this group level. This is especially true if other filters are going to be applied to this pool to further reduce its size.

7.   CONCLUSION

These 31 individuals have been identified as key figures in terrorism studies, using an explicit and rigorous methodology which is clear about all the research design choices made. There are no grounds to believe that this pool should *necessarily* be privileged over others, created according to alternative design choices within this overall framework. However, the high degree of *intuitive plausibility* associated with this particular list (these 31 include most that one would suspect, and no real surprises) suggests that the choices made here will hold their own against most alternative studies.

In and of themselves, these results will be of no more than minor interest to most researchers. However, their true significance is revealed as soon as one attempts any further analysis of the field of terrorism studies: before interrogating the quality of research on terrorism, and perhaps questioning the grounds upon which terrorism 'knowledge' is based; before examining the relationship between terrorism researchers and those in positions of power; before attempting to reveal the ways in which terrorism authors operate as if in an 'invisible college' (31); before all of this, if such further analysis is to have any impact, it must be able to show both that it applies to the core (or, at least, *a core*) of terrorism studies, and that the selection of this core was achieved in a rigorous and explicit manner.

As one example of potential further research using the data gathered here, the doctoral thesis from which this study is drawn examines the relationship between terrorism experts and the US Government. It has often been claimed that this relationship is particularly close and that, further, this ensures that the output from the experts is politically biased. Verifying or refuting this claim depends firstly on establishing the identities of the terrorism experts, before examining the relationship between this pool and government, and then investigating the neutrality of their output. Once the identities have been ascertained (as described in this chapter), this wider project finds that the close relationship *does* exist, as measured by who has testified in front of US Congress, or given evidence to at least one of several US national commissions on terrorism. 36% of the *central pool* have these sort of links (i.e., 50 out of the 140); a proportion which rises to 58% when considering the *core pool* (i.e., 18 out of the 31). In other words, more than half of the core figures in terrorism studies have provided intellectual services to the US Government. The thesis is then able to examine the political neutrality (i.e., objectivity) of these researchers' publications, *and argue that the results obtained are significant for the field of terrorism studies as a whole, given the 'core' status of the sample* (32). This is only possible given the framework constructed and employed here.

Table 3-10.

No.	Name	S&J List	5+ years on editorial board	4+ pieces for core journals
1	Alexander, Yonah	•	•	•
2	Barkun, Michael		•	•
3	Bell, J Bowyer	•	•	•
4	Chalk, Peter		•	•
5	Cline, Ray S.	•	•	
6	Clutterbuck, Richard	•	•	•
7	Crelinsten, Ronald		•	•
8	Crenshaw, Martha	•	•	•
9	Ferracuti, Franco	•	•	
10	Gurr, Ted	•	•	
11	Hoffman, Bruce		•	•
12	Jamieson, Alison		•	•
13	Jenkins, Brian M.	•	•	•
14	Kupperman, Robert	•	•	
15	Laqueur, Walter Z.	•	•	
16	Livingstone, Neil	•		•
17	Merari, Ariel	•	•	•
18	Miller, Abraham H.	•	•	•
19	Murphy, John F.		•	•
20	Pluchinsky, Dennis A.		•	•
21	Post, Jerrold M.		•	•
22	Ranstorp, Magnus		•	•
23	Rapoport, David C.		•	•
24	Raufer, Xavier		•	•

No.	Name	S&J List	5+ years on editorial board	4+ pieces for core journals
25	Schmid, Alex	•	•	•
26	Schultz, Richard		•	•
27	Smith, Michael L.R.		•	•
28	Sprinzak, Ehud		•	•
29	Wardlaw, Grant	•	•	
30	Weinberg, Leonard		•	•
31	Wilkinson, Paul	•	•	•

REFERENCES AND FOOTNOTES

1. Indeed, the results obtained here are used by the author as part of his doctoral project, which is designed to analyse the publications of a set of key terrorism experts, in order to test the hypothesis that their work is politically biased. See Sam Raphael, *Embedded Expertise? Bias in the Study of Terrorism*, unfinished PhD thesis, Department of War Studies, King's College London, forthcoming. This claim has been made by many over the years, although it has yet to be supported by a sufficiently rigorous investigation. A necessary precursor to this is, of course, to determine the identities of the key experts; a requirement which drives the current investigation.

2. See, for instance, Reid and Chen, "Domain Mapping of Contemporary Terrorism Research," in this volume.

3. This is a necessarily unscientific statement to make, although intuition certainly plays a role in rigorous research. For instance, if this study had resulted in a list of twenty unheard-of names, it would lead to questions over not only the prior knowledge of the researcher, but also the applicability of the research design.

4. In this respect, a charge may be levelled against Herman and O'Sullivan's *The Terrorism Industry*, which selects its sample of 'pre-eminent terrorism experts' using less than rigorous methods. Although not necessarily the objective of the authors, it is hard to escape the conclusion that their selection was made so as to verify the author's thesis that pre-eminent terrorism experts 'rarely if ever depart from the official Western model and line on terrorism'. Edward S. Herman and Gerry O'Sullivan, *The 'Terrorism' Industry: The Experts and Institutions That Shape Our View of Terror* (New York: Pantheon Books, 1989), pp. 142-145. For further discussion of the methodological weaknesses of this key work, see Sam Raphael, *Embedded Expertise?*

5. See below for evidence that, even in the core academic journals, the majority of authors are 'one-timers', entering into the field only briefly.

6. For the characterisation of the field as traditionally located in the cracks and crevices, see Andrew Silke, "An Introduction to Terrorism Research," in Andrew Silke (ed.), *Research on Terrorism: Trends, Achievements and Failures* (London: Frank Cass, 2004), p. 1. Scholars keen to forge this separate identity include Avishag Gordon, "Terrorism as an Academic Subject After 9/11: Searching the Internet Reveals a Stockholm Syndrome Trend," *Studies in Conflict and Terrorism* 28(1) (January/February 2005); those more cautious include John Horgan, "Understanding Terrorism: Old Assumptions, New Assertions and Challenges for Research", conference paper, *Is it Time for a Critical Terrorism Studies?*, University of Manchester, 27-28 October 2006. A separate field, it can be argued, could lead to

analysis which is decontextualised from the wider political and social milieu; by focusing only on the terroristic elements of a conflict, much relevant analysis is lost.

7.   For a description of the meaning of 'intersubjective', see Buzan *et al*'s treatment of the concept of 'security': it is neither objective, nor 'held in subjective and isolated minds; it is a social quality, a part of a discursive, socially constituted, intersubjective realm'. Thus, specific expression of the idea, as with all politics, 'ultimately rests neither with the objects nor with the subjects but *among* the subjects'. Barry Buzan, Ole Waever, and Jaap de Wilde, *Security: A New Framework for Analysis* (London: Lynne Rienner, 1998), p. 31.

8.   Although an argument can be made that this claim has attained the status of a myth in the terrorism literature, which works to privilege certain actors in international politics over others. For example, by focusing on Palestinian hijacking as one strategy which signified the birth of international terror, the literature ignores the Israeli violence which preceded and provoked such acts, thus casting the Palestinian people as aggressor, and the State of Israel as defender. For an in-depth discussion of the political consequences of this myth, see Sam Raphael, *Embedded Expertise?*

9.   For example, the first incident recorded in the RAND Terrorism Chronology Database took place on 9 February 1968 (see http://www.tkb.org/Incident.jsp?incID=6, accessed 21 November 2006). Reid has found that the systematic study of contemporary terrorism 'took-off' in the period 1970-1978, with only 'a sprinkling of terrorism studies' before this time. Edna O.F. Reid, "Terrorism Research and the Diffusion of Ideas," *Knowledge and Policy* 6(1), (Spring 1993), p. 22.

10.   Ibid.

11.   The original 200 people (or, at least, the 58 of these who responded) provided a list of 166 separate names, approximately 10 percent of which were in the original sample (leaving around 150 new names). They also provided a list of 156 valuable works, whose authors are included in this community. See Alex P. Schmid and Albert J. Jongman (eds.), *Political Terrorism: A New Guide to Actors, Authors, Concepts, Data Bases, Theories and Literature*, 2nd edn. (North-Holland: Amsterdam, 1988), p. xii, note 1; and pp. 186-199.

12.   See, for instance, later comments on the quality of their survey by other terrorism scholars: it is cited as 'the most important review of research and researchers into terrorism to date' by Andrew Silke, "The Devil You Know: Continuing Problems with Research on Terrorism," *Terrorism and Political Violence* 13(4) (Winter 2001), p. 3, and as a 'magisterial survey' by Bruce Hoffman, *Inside Terrorism* (New York: Columbia University Press, 1998), p. 39.

13.   E.g., Herman and O'Sullivan, *The Terrorism Industry*, Reid, "Terrorism Research and the Diffusion of Ideas," and Edna O.F. Reid, "Evolution of a Body of Knowledge: An Analysis of Terrorism Research," *Information Processing and Management* 33(1) (1997).

14.   Andrew Silke, "The Road Less Travelled: Recent Trends in Terrorism Research," in Andrew Silke (ed.), *Research on Terrorism: Trends, Achievements and Failures* (London: Frank Cass, 2004), p. 186.

15.   Avishag Gordon, "The Spread of Terrorism Publications: A Database Analysis," *Terrorism and Political Violence* 10(4) (Winter 1998), p. 191. See, also: Avishag Gordon, "Terrorism and Knowledge Growth: A Databases and Internet Analysis," in Andrew Silke (ed.), *Research on Terrorism: Trends, Achievements and Failures* (London: Frank Cass, 2004), p. 113.

16. Silke, "The Road Less Travelled", p. 187.
17. This is actually a slightly wider timeframe than the study in general (26 years), given that the database used only searches full calendar years (and so could not be set for a September-September limit). Potentially, a better search would be for the 25 years from 1980-2004, although in practice this would not affect the main findings.
18. The International Bibliography of the Social Sciences (IBSS), which was searched, by journal, for the number of articles returning the keyword 'terror' as a truncated term (i.e., 'terror', 'terrorise', 'terrorism', 'terrorist', etc.). Search conducted 30 November 2006.
19. Indeed, of the more than 8000 articles found by IBSS in the 26-year period 1979-2004, over half were published in the three years 2002-2004!
20. Examples of journals from other fields carrying special 'terrorism issues' after 9/11 include *International Migration Review* 36(1) (March 2002), *Political Psychology* 23(3) (September 2002), *History and Technology* 19(1) (March 2003), and *Qualitative Inquiry* 8(2) (April 2002). That terrorism as a subject of inquiry now transcends the boundaries of any sort of 'terrorism studies', and even the broad field of international politics, can be seen by the publication in the following journals of these terrorism articles: Anthony Yanxiang Gu and Michael Schinski, "Patriotic Stock Repurchases: The Two Weeks Following the 9-11 Attack," *Review of Quantitative Finance and Accounting* 20(3) (May 2003); H. V. Savitch, "Does 9-11 Portend a New Paradigm for Cities?," *Urban Affairs Review* 39(1) (September 2003); and David M. Walker, "9/11: The Implications for Public Sector Management", *Public Administration Review* 62 (September 2002). All of these articles appear amongst the 8293 total found by IBSS between 1979-2004.
21. Schmid and Jongman, *Political Terrorism*, pp. 180-181.
22. Reid, "Terrorism Research and the Diffusion of Ideas," p. 20; Reid, "Evolution of a Body of Knowledge," p. 94.
23. Accessed at: http://wok.mimas.ac.uk.
24. For the very few occasions that these authors are mentioned by the key figures identified in this study, it is, as a rule, only in order to ridicule their research. See Raphael, *Embedded Expertise?*
25. Silke, "An Introduction to Terrorism Research," p. 1. For similar remarks, see Ariel Merari, "Academic Research and Government Policy on Terrorism," *Terrorism and Political Violence* 3(1) (Spring 1991), p. 92; Walter Z. Laqueur, *No End to War: Terrorism in the Twenty-First Century* (New York: Continuum, 2003), p. 139, note 53.
26. This includes anyone who spent two or three years on the board of *Terrorism* or *Conflict*, during the late 1980s and early 1990s, and then two or three years on the board of SCT after these two titles had amalgamated.
27. Schmid and Jongman, *Political Terrorism*, p. 181.
28. With duplicates removed, this would give a community of 29 people, as opposed to the 140 in this study.
29. As opposed to the 31 in this study. The eight are: Alexander, Bell, Crenshaw, Hoffman, Jenkins, Post, Schmid and Wilkinson.
30. In other words, there are three authors (J. Bowyer Bell, Brian Jenkins and Paul Wilkinson) who, between 1979 and 2004, received five or more citations from the Schmid and Jongman survey, *and* have been on the editorial board of at least two core journals for five years or more, *and* have authored at least 10 pieces for the core journals.

31. See Reid, "Terrorism Research and the Diffusion of Ideas"; Reid, "Evolution of a Body of Knowledge".
31. The exact figure depends on exactly how one measures this.
32. See Raphael, *Embedded Expertise?* for a full explanation of the links with US Government, and the degree of political neutrality displayed by the publications.

SUGGESTED READINGS

- Herman, Edward S., and O'Sullivan, Gerry (1989), *The 'Terrorism' Industry: The Experts and Institutions That Shape Our View of Terror.* New York: Pantheon Books.
- Reid, Edna O.F. (1993), 'Terrorism Research and the Diffusion of Ideas', *Knowledge and Policy*, 6(1).
- Reid, Edna O.F. (1997), 'Evolution of a Body of Knowledge: An Analysis of Terrorism Research', *Information Processing and Management*, 33(1).
- Schmid, Alex P., and Jongman, Albert J., eds. (1988), *Political Terrorism: A New Guide to Actors, Authors, Concepts, Data Bases, Theories and Literature*, 2nd ed. Amsterdam: North-Holland.
- Silke, Andrew, ed. (2004), *Research on Terrorism: Trends, Achievements and Failures*. London: Frank Cass.

DISCUSSION QUESTIONS

1. What problems are associated with identifying the parameters of a field of 'terrorism studies'?
2. Why is the ability to identify 'key figures' in terrorism studies important? What does it allow the researcher to achieve?
3. Employing the framework described in this chapter, what alternative sets of 'key figures' can be generated?
4. In what ways do the choices made regarding research design have a *political function*? Is there any way to avoid this?

4

INTERVIEWING TERRORISTS
A Case for Primary Research[1]

John Horgan
Centre for the Study of Terrorism and Political Violence, University of St. Andrews, Fife, Scotland (jh91@st-andrews.ac.uk)

CHAPTER OVERVIEW

While the events of 11 September 2001 have catalysed a significant upsurge in terrorism research, social science efforts to systematically research terrorist behaviour have yet to convincingly demonstrate their greater potential, particularly in relation to not only how existing theoretical frameworks might be tested with data, but on a broader level in terms of how data-driven evidence can lead to the formulation of a more solid basis for the development of counter-terrorism initiatives. It is unfortunate that much academic research on terrorism, despite (or perhaps because of) its often prescriptive nature, remains often misinformed, skewed in nature but perhaps most significantly, often unsupported by empirical enquiry. Reasons for this include a general reluctance to admit that our analyses (however plausible) remain limited in part by our perceptions both of the concept and phenomenon of terrorism, this is turn markedly influenced by our reluctance to engage in first hand research with people who are, or have been, involved in terrorist violence – the very prospect still remains unpalatable to many. This Chapter presents a short descriptive attempt to address a variety of practical issues for consideration in the hope that it may ultimately help lead to an increased acceptance that field research on terrorist behaviour is not only viable, but represents a research tool which we need to seriously exploit and subject to comparative analysis (e.g. of individual researchers' experiences to begin with). A case study of the author's experiences in Ireland conducting PhD research illustrates a variety of themes, but seek to assert that exciting data with subsequent extensive

[1] This article is a revised version of a Chapter that appeared in A. Silke (ed.). *Researching Terrorism: Trends, Achievements, Failures*. London: Frank Cass and Co. (2004).

hypothesis testing and theory formation will become an inevitable implication of employing such methodologies. Given the perennial problems highlighted by scholars of political violence, the space to vocally develop such avenues deserves support and researchers should be encouraged to disclose and discuss their experiences of primary research.

1.   INTRODUCTION

Francis Bacon is credited with saying that "if we are to achieve results never before accomplished, we must employ methods never before attempted". His comments appear particularly appropriate to discussions about evaluating the progress of terrorism studies. Despite the multidisciplinary label attributed to terrorism studies, it remains the case that conceptual development, serious interdisciplinary discussion, and exploration of intra-disciplinary aspirations to 'ownership' of aspects of the terrorism process remain limited, and in some cases, non-existent. Psychological approaches to terrorism remain especially fraught and theoretically underdeveloped. While a variety of factors contribute to this, a continuing problem that plagues existing efforts results from an almost total reliance on secondary and tertiary source material to both to inform, but more pressingly, to serve as a basis to test theoretical formulation and development. Although the argument is sometimes inappropriately perceived as an assault on non-primary source terrorism studies, it is fair to say that, to echo Crenshaw (2001, p.416), terrorism studies continues to lack an empirical foundation of "primary data based on interviews and life histories" of those engaged in terrorism.

However, and despite it being easy to identify the limitations of terrorism research on paper, to say that terrorism does not easily lend itself to reliable, valid and systematic research from any discipline is an understatement (see Merari, 1991, p.88; Merari and Friedland, 1985, p.196). It is in such light that one common issue emerges from discussions of terrorism research – a reluctance for researchers to enter the violent field (Horgan, 1997; 1999; White, 2000), even, depressingly, after the conflict has largely ended. Terrorism may be a social and political process, but it is essentially psychological factors that drive individual motivation, action, and decisional processes: consequently, it remains inevitable that if one is to effectively study terrorism and terrorists from criminological and psychological perspectives, one must meet with and speak to individuals who are, or who have been directly involved with a terrorist organisation (Horgan, 2005; Taylor and Quayle, 1994).

The primary purpose of this Chapter is to contribute to the argument that primary, or first-hand research involving direct contact with terrorists is, despite its difficulties, quite possible. Furthermore, there exists the possibility that if we collectively acknowledge the benefits from pursuing such approaches in informing our theoretical and conceptual development, this may open the possibility of comparative analysis of researchers' experiences.

2. PROCURING INTERVIEWS

A small but growing number of scholars have engaged in primary source research, in particular, interviews involving direct contact with either active and/or former terrorists. Some of these include the work of Alonso (2006), Bloom (2005), Bowyer-Bell (1998, 2000), Bruce (1992), Coogan (1995a, 1995b), Crawford (2003), della Porta (1995), Hoffman (2006), Horgan (2005), Jamieson (1989), Reinares (2004), Speckhard and Akhmedova (2005), Schweitzer and Goldstein Ferber (2005), Stern (2003), Taylor (1988, 1991), Taylor and Quayle (1994), and White (1993, 2000). No consensus exists regarding both procedures to procure and undertake interviews, with perceptions of researchers differing considerably regarding its assumed practical difficulty (Bowyer-Bell, 1998; Horgan, 1997; Taylor and Quayle, 1994). The prevailing but informal consensus is that interviews are sparse, and it seems that more often than not, it may be some more 'unconventional' elements such as personal contacts that tends to facilitate access to such interviews. Brief perusal of 'Acknowledgements' pages quickly reveals the nature of author contacts (e.g. Coogan, 1995a, pp.ix-x; 1995b, p.xi). Before the research process adopted by the present author for Irish-based research is described, it is first necessary to introduce some of the issues relating to terrorism research from this 'hands-on' perspective.

From the outset, it would be wise to reassert what might seem obvious - communication is a central feature of almost everything that a terrorist movement does. In going some way towards explaining his own success in accessing PIRA members, Bowyer-Bell (1998, p.xv) writes:

> "Everyone likes to talk about him or herself, none more than the saved. And talking is much easier when your arrival somehow validates the seriousness of the local armed struggle...Such investigation based on access - achieved after an endless vigil in some largely uninhabited hotel at the back of the beyond - often assures that the orthodox assume sympathy with the rebel."

Once researchers contemplate access options, routes do not take long to emerge. An obvious avenue is to contact imprisoned terrorists: many terrorist groups have support structures within prisons and it is sometimes useful to direct an interview request through a designated political representative outside. In Northern Ireland, where there was always a great deal of contempt by prisoners towards the prison authorities, it would have been perhaps futile for a researcher to attempt to arrange an interview through the prison authorities. However, in the case of a terrorist who may be isolated in a foreign country then the full co-operation between the researcher and prison authorities may be essential in facilitating access. Therefore, effort spent producing carefully drafted letters, fully stating the researcher's intentions, background and motive, can be well worth the time when communicating with either or both prisoner or prison official, depending on the context.

If on the other hand, meetings are arranged by a higher 'legitimate' source within the terrorist movement itself, perhaps for example via the movement's political wing, then there is more often than not a set course of procedures to be followed. Organizations such as Sinn Fein continuously receive requests mostly from journalists seeking interviews. It may be required that lists of questions to be asked be handed over in advance of the proposed interview. Of course, this approach assumes some familiarity with the potential interviewee, even if through media exposure - i.e. the researcher has identified one particular individual whom the researcher feels important to the work. This is not a prerequisite for those researchers who, rather than attempt to approach known individuals, simply "seek an interview or comment" per se. It is similarly possible to approach the political wing of a terrorist group and ask to speak with, for example "activists", in order to ascertain answers to a particular research question, which might include why people joined the movement, how they explain their behavior, etc. This will be returned to in more detail, but let us acknowledge that there are several easily identifiable avenues of approach.

These aside, valuable open sources exist – websites, newspapers, newsletters etc., with which one may identify at least potential 'gatekeepers'. Details of public meetings held by supporters or political wings of the terrorist movement can be especially useful for a researcher to attend: introductions can be made to potential interviewee in such non-threatening environments, and if successful, researchers have much potential gain in establishing first steps on the interview ladder, given the numbers of individuals present at such meetings and their inter-familiarity with each other.

Informally approaching former terrorists represents another avenue, assuming perhaps some familiarity, if only at an intermediary level through a third party - broad types of potential interviewee that emerge at this point might include the retired terrorist who has renounced his/her involvement (an increasing number of whom occupy a visible presence on the television and print media as 'experts' on terrorism) and the retired terrorist who has not renounced involvement: an important element of such research can relate to the 'location' of the researcher, and how that might relate to ease of access: it is likely to be the case that a locally-based (i.e. where the conflict is primarily located) researcher would have potentially more useful information at hand than a researcher who comes to the region 'cold', i.e. without at least some local contacts to facilitate access to knowledge. By this knowledge, this refers to an aspect of large terrorist organisations that may appear surprising to many: terrorist movements (and involvement in them) is not as clandestine as may be assumed (though this will certainly be a function of the kind of terrorist movement in question). Certainly in the case of ethno-nationalist movements, including the IRA in Northern Ireland, the Basque ETA, or the Sri Lankan Tamil Tigers, if one has even the most basic of local knowledge it is not difficult to discover who the local personnel are and how/where an interview request may be directed. 'Outsiders' may encounter difficulties, naturally, but if one is sensible and does some basic research, it is not difficult to know where well-known figures may at the very least, be contacted. And importantly, researcher nationality does not appear to be a problem. Indeed it appears to be the case that 'outsiders' are greeted with less suspicion than local researchers, and it is likely that following initial contact, a terrorist movement or its members may be more welcoming of a foreign researcher. A safe assumption, in the eyes of the movement and its personnel, is that the outsider is more easily manipulable in terms of either the a) particular 'story' that is being portrayed or b) the overall image of the group, and vulnerability to perceptions of sympathy that the movement assumes of a 'naïve' outsider.

It would be remiss to not explore the perceptions that the terrorists have of those who research them. Joe Bowyer-Bell (1979, 1998) whose outstanding work on the IRA remains the cornerstone research on the movement, was granted permission by the IRA leadership to write his book on the history of the movement. The leadership appears to have facilitated his access on the basis that an account of the movement's history should (from their own perspective) portray them in as best a light as possible. As above, there is no doubt that terrorist figures assume a level of naivety in outsiders to be firmly exploited for international audiences.

The academic discipline of the researcher may bring its own baggage regarding how the researcher may be perceived. A psychologist's request for interviews may indeed be perceived as an attempt at clinical diagnosis (Crenshaw, 1990, p.248) or be the source of particular interest or curiosity. When the present author first began to interview members of the IRA for doctoral research a number of years ago, the response from an IRA member when asked about what background I have (psychology) was: "Oh Christ, you're definitely in the right place so! There's a lot of mad fellas here!" But more specifically, and in the context of beginning a research project that will ultimately entail primary contact, the nature of any research needs consideration as to how it ought to be communicated to the terrorist movement or its individual members: obviously, it would appear to wise not to attempt to engage in discussion on what might be seen as sensitive or dangerous issues. These could be matters, which from the perspective of the terrorist group might have potential intelligence usage to the security forces. Again, common sense ought to prevail. For a researcher to place him or herself in a potentially compromising position is probably best avoided in the first place rather than mulling over subsequent ethical or moral dilemmas.   Moreover, if a particular discussion occasionally drifts into revelations of sensitive material, what is always implied by the terrorist movement of course is the threat of violence (although frequently overstated) a threat of which few interviewers who value their safety will be unaware (Sluka, 1989, p.22).

There is a multitude of issues embedded in the preceding points, and there is simply not the space to explore them all, but a few are worth considering. It should be pointed out as a result of the assertions made above that by highlighting the valuable possibilities offered by first-hand data sources, it is not to say that researchers should ever exceed their ethical and legal boundaries. Bob White (2000, p.102) describes how Joe Bowyer-Bell was preparing to interview IRA members in a house while IRA bombs were actually being prepared, which raises a separate set of concerns altogether.

On another level, the novice researcher needs to realise that terrorist organisations are fully appreciative of how academic research may be exploited for their own purposes. The present author interviewed a former Director of Intelligence of the Official IRA who mentioned that it was common practice to have his own intelligence officers read scholarly work on terrorism and counter-terrorism. Equally, on page 21 of the IRA's Green Book (its training manual), Bowyer-Bell's (1979) "The Secret Army" is listed as recommended reading for the recruit's "frame of reference" (page 11) in appreciating Republican history!

Following a necessary discussion of the some of the factors influencing how researchers study terrorism, the present author has chosen briefly to illustrate the complexity of some of the methodological research issues in the study of terrorism primarily by reference to the Provisional IRA. This is so as it is the first organisation with which the author began engaging in primary research, as a PhD student, and it is a movement whose members have regularly engaged with many researchers over the years of its campaign (and especially since then). Obviously, there can be no sweeping statements on "doing" primary source terrorism research, and the issues raised in this Chapter cannot possibly be exhaustive.

Time will tell if there are any patterns to be found between researchers' experiences of the kinds of 'issues' raised here. This section outlines, in narrative form, some practical issues around the research process that the author adopted for researching terrorism in Ireland as a postgraduate student at University College, Cork.

3.   A CASE ILLUSTRATION: INTERVIEWS WITH THE IRA

Between late-1995 and 2000, I engaged in PhD research on the activities of the Provisional IRA, the largest of all Irish paramilitary groups, through a number of research avenues. These include more than one type of participant-observation, library and case study research, but above all, extensive structured and unstructured interviewing with 301 individuals lasting a total of 948 hours. Those interviewed included alleged members of four Republican terrorist groups and their political affiliates, but of these primarily members of the main Republican terrorist grouping and its political wing - Sinn Fein and the IRA. The accounts presented in the doctoral thesis of the author (Horgan, 2000) also derive from interviews and communication with security forces and police personnel from various countries, a number of experienced journalists and others closely connected to Irish terrorism affairs (including academic researchers and a small number of non-Republican politicians).

The principal focus of the thesis was a conceptual and theoretical critique of the literature on the psychology of terrorist behaviour, incorporating two extensive case studies conducted by the author – namely, the Provisional IRA's command and functional structure, as well as their fundraising activities – in order to illustrate the nature and importance of incorporating organisational themes within a comprehensive psychology of terrorist behaviour.

When I began to formulate research questions specific to the doctoral thesis that emerged as the end product of the research, it became clear very quickly, that even if I would be granted access to members of the security forces that I would probably achieve somewhat of, as Bowyer-Bell (1998) and White (1993) recognised, a synoptic view of the IRA. On the other hand, if I was to rely solely on what research efforts I would produce through attempted fieldwork, I would potentially (as with Bowyer-Bell and White) achieve a great deal of information about certain matters and maybe little or none about other, even more valuable matters. From speaking to IRA members, I felt that I could probably gather a great deal of information on how relationships work, and with luck, I might have been able to arrive at a picture of how the IRA's command and functional structure is constructed (and with even greater luck understand how it operates in practice, as well as the factors that direct, control, and hinder this). On fundraising activities in particular, at the time I began the research, the most I expected to was to simply gain a glimpse of how the IRA themselves place their involvement in crime into some organisational context. Conversely, if I would eventually be successful (both formally, and informally I hoped) in gaining similar access to members of the security forces, it would be likely that I might, even if only briefly, have access to a potential goldmine of data on individuals or perhaps some aspect of their organisation. Either way, I realised at the time that I would not feel comfortable with what would surely amount to a skewed focus as a result of reliance on one type of source.

At the time, I also became quickly concerned that even if I were to produce an empirical piece of work, and certainly one assessed within a social science context, that despite the clear reasoning in going to the "source", in contrast to most other research efforts, there was a possibility that much external doubt could be cast upon my use of sources, and the reliability of the information they imparted to me during the research process. I was in no doubt that if I were to have some communication with both police and terrorists, I would probably be given some private information, which (even at that point, regardless of its reliability and validity) I could use in a very constricted way anyway for ethical reasons (even if only to prevent the possible identification of individuals). Looking back on this period now, and having had the benefit of conducting similar research with members of other movements, I remain firm in the belief that it is absolutely critical that such issues need acknowledgement – at the planning stages of my original research in Ireland, and given that some terrorism research does not easily lend itself to criticism from peers anyway, I was extremely mindful that any attempt to disguise the almost overwhelmingly real and practical research issues would only be self-defeating, particularly if I were to at least have some success by the end of the research process. With these concerns in mind, the interview attempts began.

4.   FINDING AND 'COLLECTING' PARTICIPANTS

This research proper began in late 1995, when I made a formal approach to the Sinn Fein National Headquarters, in 44 Parnell Square, Dublin. I had sent a letter, which followed several telephone calls, to the head of the

Prisoner of War (POW) Department, explaining that I was a student of psychology who wanted to meet with and speak to people who had been involved in political violence. I identified this person through the Republican newspaper, *An Phoblacht*. As the weeks went by however, I received no reply and my calls were not being returned. Having received no answer to my letter either, I decided to telephone again to ask for a meeting. I asked to speak to the Head of the POW Department. She informed me that she had been too busy to ring me back. However, she said that if I came to Dublin to meet with her, she would be there and would listen to what I was looking for, for the purposes of my research.

I travelled to Dublin a few days later and met with this person. After explaining to her that I wanted to speak to people in Sinn Fein and the IRA about "people involved in the armed struggle", I was told that there were two men I should speak to. She gave me the details of both of these men: one based in Dublin and the other in Belfast, both described to me as members of Sinn Fein. With them, I was told I would at the very least become aware of a means of approaching potential participants.

After leaving the Sinn Fein National Headquarters (HQ), I visited the Dublin man who asked me to give great detail in explaining my research. I did so, and told him that there were some sensitive questions I wanted to ask (relating to fundraising – the subject of a then recent publication), at which point he told me that I would not get "much help on that". On hearing this, and mindful of the now real prospect of undermining what progress I had apparently already made, I decided to focus on the issues posed by involvement in the Republican movement, and kept the focus of the discussion (as far as my research was concerned) strictly on wishing to examine the experiences of members, specifically, "why people joined the Republican movement" and "what life is like as a member of the Republican movement". In no way was this deception, but simply represented a move towards expressing my interests in perhaps different language. I began to express what I wanted to ask members about in this more general form before I would even identify the more specific questions. All the while, I emphasised my concerns about wanting to gain direct access to people who were, or are, directly involved in paramilitary activity. When I asked this man about being able to speak to Republican prisoners, I was told that prison visits to interview Republican inmates would be extremely difficult. In a telephone call a week later to this man, he then told me that it would be completely out of the question. Apparently, my timing was not fortunate. I was referred to a case in which, during the weeks before I had made my request for interviewees, a journalist had interviewed one particular *Republican prisoner*. The journalist, according to this man, had directly misinterpreted comments made by the prisoner. Upon the 'misquoted' comments being published, there was, seemingly, uproar in Republican circles. "Everyone knew", according to my contact, that "she had been deliberately misquoted" about the treatment of prisoners in the Republic. There were now some immediate measures to ensure that such 'misquoting' would not happen again – an informal embargo on outsiders being allowed to interview *Republican inmates*. My request immediately became insignificant. The contact recommended however that I attend meetings at which recently released prisoners would be in attendance to discuss various matters. The meetings, he told me, would not be in the public forum but he told me that he did not see any problem in me attending them if I "wanted to":

> "...It's a good place to go up and introduce yourself, to say that you were talking to me and you're going to have to explain what you're doing, and ah...chances are that they're probably going to talk to you. I can't say for definite you know, it all...ah...depends on the day, y'know, but I know that...[name of a then recently released prisoner] is going to be there on Tuesday, and she would I'm sure talk to you about what you're asking..."

These meetings would take place in anterooms of the Sinn Fein Headquarters in Parnell Street, Dublin. He then recommended that I speak to one woman in particular, who become a senior Sinn Fein member in the years following her release from prison. This was the first clear indicator to me that I was going to be 'given' to someone. As White (1993, 2000) notes, with every research method there is the possibility that respondents will tailor what they say, for a number of reasons, including making themselves and/or their political movement look good. For this reason, and as White has advocated, prolonged interaction in the field, carefully constructed questions, and carefully selected respondents provide more valuable insights, and potentially more valid data.

This contact kept responding to all subsequent telephone calls I had made to him, and he appeared very co-operative and facilitative, in so far as he knew what "kinds of questions" I was going to be asking, and to whom they were going to be addressed. He told me over the telephone that he could personally arrange "three or four" Republicans to meet me and speak about their involvement and experiences as IRA members. These interviews would take place both in Northern Ireland and in the Republic. He asked me to send him lists of all of the questions and topics I wanted to discuss with them. I did this and, bearing in mind my conversation in Dublin, phrased several general questions relating to broad themes. With luck, I reasoned that they would allow me to open more detailed discussion with respect to the main themes that were to be explored.

As above, following this initial meeting and upon leaving Dublin, I realised from speaking to this man that any respondents through this channel were going to be selectively chosen, articulate individuals, and probably with experience in discussing 'sensitive' issues as much as more general ones. I had made it clear from the outset that I was a student of psychology, and that I wanted to discuss issues of motivation and "various aspects" of Republicanism, later including those matters of what Republicans describe as "black propaganda" (i.e. fundraising). During these early stages of the research, and before I realised just how selected people were probably going to be 'given to me', I was still generally surprised at the level of cooperation and welcome I received from Sinn Fein and the IRA.

I also asked the Dublin man by telephone, about one week after our meeting, if there was a possibility of being able to speak with someone who was *actively* involved in IRA operations. He hesitated for a short time, and replied that it would "probably take a long time, and it would probably be very difficult." I later did not resume contact with this man as my perception that he was reluctant to have questions relating to fundraising addressed, was later confirmed in a conversation with other Republicans and a subsequent telephone conversation with between us. It emerged in late 1999 that this man had actually made subsequent efforts to block any interviews with Republicans that he felt I might procure without his knowledge or assistance, but the exact details remained unclear until I discovered years later from a fellow researcher that as a result of some of the questions I wanted to ask, I had "muddied the water".

During this initial phase however, and while making efforts to establish a grounding in speaking to Republicans about issues relating to their activities, I was aware that a good technique to broaden my participant base (and therefore, in accordance with White's (1993) experiences, and to help myself to become more selective with potential respondents) would be through the use of 'snowballing' or snowball sampling. This research method is useful in dangerous field research, or when issues of trust and apprehension at the levels described in the present context come into play, and can be vital to establishing contacts and building on previous efforts (for good examples in similar contexts, see Bowyer-Bell, 1998; Knowles, 1996; White, 1993). Essentially the procedure involves asking interviewees to recommend other potential interviewees, and so on, until a network begins to form.

At about the same time, I simultaneously began to initiate contact with members of the Irish security forces. Through a friend of my family who had been working as a Garda (police officer) in Cork (whom I had never approached formally in such a context before), with his help, and subsequent assistance of those Gardai met through this man, I soon built up what was to be a surprisingly good (and relatively large) informal network of Gardai who worked across several levels of the organisation, including the anti-terrorism branches of An Garda Síochána. Informal cooperation from the Gardai in participating in interviews was exceptionally good, as was the very high level of assistance from individual members in helping me gain access to 'other members'.

Across both terrorists and security services, it is possible to clarify the nature of participants with respect to eliciting information from them. Participant types can be epitomised by the following "categories", as initially described by Swanson, Chamelin and Territo (1988) in the context of general interviewee types: Honest and co-operative; "Hear nothing, say nothing", Reluctant/suspicious interviewees, Hostile/deceitful interviewees, timid interviewees, boastful interviewees, and the slightly common "under the influence" interviewees.   This last category aptly describes many Republican sympathisers who, when not interviewed in participant-observation contexts such as republican fundraiser parties, which I began to attend as my research progressed, attempted to become "friendly" with me and also became anxious that I account for the finer points of Republican history as correctly as they would have it. It is important to state, however, that such categorisation of interviewees and potential participants equally applied to members of the security forces that I interviewed. The similarity in the dynamics as far as creating and building a network of likely participants between the IRA and Irish security forces was remarkable – the power of the snowball sampling method was very quickly apparent to me, but the overall conclusion I arrived at throughout my experiences then was that informal enquiries and informal attempts at access proved much more fruitful than official attempts at accessing individuals (given the bureaucratic nature of both aspects of the security services and indeed the terrorists and their political wings).

Another quickly learned lesson at the time was the realisation that my approach to interviewing would have to be flexible enough to vary with each of the 'types' of interviewees I would encounter, some of whom were reluctant to discuss or impart any comment relating to fundraising. Although I had planned to ask questions in a systematic, semi-formal fashion, this initially proved difficult in practice and quite an amount of flexibility had to be employed with most interviewees. It was only when details about two specific case studies on fundraising came to light that I was able to begin to purposively target specifically relevant individuals, and with specifically organised and relevant questioning about those case studies.

Following my initial experiences with Sinn Fein members in Dublin, I realised that I should begin preparing to initiate two other research outlets, and to explore the possibility of exploiting them as best as possible in order to procure a level of access to members of IRA and Sinn Fein. Also it was clear that this would have to be done as quickly as possible, should the initial attempt at making contacts fail due to some aspect of me which my Dublin contact felt should warrant a dismissal of my request (through an active effort being made not to answer my questions for instance, I thought, or through simply giving me an outright "no", which was always a possibility). Through local knowledge, media reports and the assistance of a number of helpful journalists, and informal interviewing of both Gardai and Sinn Fein sources, I soon began to build a picture of localised Sinn Fein and IRA membership in various locations around Ireland. An example of one interview will be presented to help illustrate how such localised knowledge (as I described earlier) can materialise into a more fruitful eventuality, and consequently led to the establishment of an 'IRA participant base'.

5.   A CASE EXAMPLE: INTERVIEWING A TERRORIST

In early 1996, I contacted a person (to be referred to as "Peter") whom I had known about through the Irish media (in connection with a paramilitary crime for which Peter had been charged). I knew roughly where Peter lived, but knew from media reports that he worked in a certain named pub in a named town. I telephoned the pub asking to speak with Peter but instead spoke to a man that described himself as "a friend of Peter's". I asked him to deliver a message to Peter - simply stating my name that I was a student from University College, Cork (UCC) and that I would call back. A few days later I called back and spoke to Peter himself. I introduced myself to him as a student of psychology from UCC, and requested that Peter help me get in touch with one of Peter's colleagues, a well- known IRA man who had frequently appeared both on television and in the print media as a result of several allegations of IRA membership and paramilitary offences. Peter told me that if I wrote a letter to this man, addressing it to Peter, describing my background and intentions regarding the 'interview', that he would pass the letter on to my targeted participant. The participant was, to the Gardai, a well-known IRA activist whom they alleged was then a member of the IRA's Army Council, and this has been alleged through several television and print media sources. I thanked Peter for his help and told him that he would receive the letter within a few days. I wrote the letter to 'Michael', and sent it care of Peter at his address.

About five weeks later, I received a telephone call from a man identifying himself as a colleague of Peter's saying that "a meeting" could be arranged "no problem". It was specified that I would meet Michael. I was told that he had received the letter and that "he'll talk to you alright".

Peter's colleague said that he would arrange the interview and would communicate again when a time and place would be confirmed with Michael.

Through a telephone call a few days after this, this "second" intermediary, Peter's contact, called me and told me that the interview with Michael "definitely" was "on", and that I was to come to a specific location for an interview with him. Peter's colleague told me that Michael would arrive to meet me two days from the moment of the phone call, early in the morning, to discuss a "few things" in the letter I wrote to him. Peter's colleague told me that he himself would pick me up at the train station and that I would stay in his house for the night before travelling onto the town in which Peter's pub was located. His closing remark was, "y'know this man now wouldn't have time for people who call him a terrorist". I said that I understood. I knew that I did not have a lot of time. I had been told on Thursday evening that Michael would meet me in Peter's pub on the following Saturday morning. On Friday morning, I travelled by train to a town where after waiting about 10 minutes, was picked up in a car by Peter's friend.

I stayed in Peter's friend's house on that Friday night where he called Peter on the telephone (in my presence) to check that Michael was still coming. Their conversation was very short, lasting less than a minute. The man then told me: "Yeah, it's on, tomorrow morning, at 10 o'clock". The next morning, the man drove me for about 35 minutes to the interview location, Peter's pub, where the interviewee would meet me.   A barman (himself a convicted IRA gunman) waved from inside a window, gesturing us around to the side of the building. He greeted us both as he let us enter through a back door, as the pub had not yet opened for business. Michael had not arrived and the barman said that he would "be along in a few minutes", following which he and my 'chauffeur' engaged in conversation about business in the pub.   After about five minutes, a tall, middle-aged slightly greying man walked in with a newspaper under his arm.   I recognised Michael immediately through pictures I had seen of him in books and on television, and introduced myself to. I was surprised to find a quiet, very soft-spoken man. With a sense of urgency, Michael said, "where do you want to go?" referring to a place to hold the interview. The barman intervened, saying there was an unused room upstairs in the pub and that we could use it. We ascended a long flight of stairs and entered a small stuffy and dusty room, a lounge section of the bar under renovation. There were 4 or 5 tables in the room, and I suggested that we sit down at the middle one. I sat with my back to a wall and Michael sat directly opposite me across a narrow table. I placed my briefcase on the table and took out a notepad, reiterating some points made in the letter about confidentiality as I began to describe my background and intentions for research. I had said that I had just begun to speak with Republicans previous to our meeting and that I had also just begun to seek and gain interviews and meetings with members of the security forces. I emphasised that there was no co-operation or collusion with them, and that for all of the interviews I had conducted and would in the future be seeking to conduct, identifiable features of interview materials and discussions were not and would not be retained or communicated in any way to any other participant or otherwise. Michael nodded his head as I emphasised these points, but said nothing. I thought to myself, that he would have doubtless known about me anyway through the meeting organiser (Peter and his friend downstairs) and it would have been ensured that no collaboration would have existed, or at the very least, I was just a student perceived as posing no threat whatsoever to Michael.

I then asked Michael if he would mind that I used a tape-recorder. In the same breath I said that not only would it facilitate the "quality of the research", but also that I would give him my guarantee that the tapes would be transcribed and destroyed "within 24 hours". Michael nodded and said "yeah, that's all right...I'll take your word for it".

The tape-recorder was switched on and the interview began. A number of themes were addressed, but I began the interview by asking Michael very general questions about his involvement in the Republican movement. I asked him about his reasons for joining the movement as well as his involvement in actions for which he had been convicted. I did not ask about activities for which Michael was not charged for having committed. As the interview progressed, I began to attempt to guide the discussion onto more specific issues relating to the IRA's organisational structure and involvement in criminal activities for the purpose of fundraising. As noted already, the practice of asking general questions to interviewees before more specific ones is one practiced by the few researchers who speak to terrorists first hand. This practice also applied to how questions were asked to security sources and other participants: security sources were asked general questions such as: "Is the IRA involved in criminal activities to raise funds?" before more specific ones were posed (e.g. "Does the IRA make use of professional expertise in the private business sector to facilitate money laundering?").

Michael's responses to all of my questions were without hesitation, even with respect to the 'sensitive' questions when I began to ask him about the IRA's involvement in criminal activities. He was very forthright and direct at all times, and for each question I asked him. I got the feeling that I could have asked him anything about the IRA and at least I would have been answered directly. This was a factor that contributed to the compelling nature of what he had to say, and how he was saying it. This was very far removed from the more traditional republican "rhetoric" on nationalism which is so evident in what terrorists say about themselves (and from the rhetoric repeated ad nauseam at Republican meetings, which I frequently attended North and South to reach other participants), as he began to describe his activities, making no excuses for what he had done as a member of the IRA, nor did he try to excuse the present IRA for any atrocious acts since then.

The interview with Michael lasted about 50 minutes, and because this was one of the very first interviews I conducted, at the time I felt that I had some "good" material – a solid starting point for building my picture of the IRA's command structure, as well as some valuable commentary (from a significant source) on what the IRA thinks of criminal activities. I switched off the tape-recorder and thanked him for coming to meet and for speaking so openly to me. He said it was "no problem" and said, "I wish you luck with whatever it is you're doing". I then realised that this was probably one of hundreds of such interviews Michael had conducted, none necessarily of great consequence other than him being assured of creating a sense of cooperation with the "outsiders", the non-Republican observers, including the media, academics and others.

We left the room while I asked him: "do you know of some other members that would be willing to talk to me?" He said that there would be many people who would be willing to talk to me and that: "if ever you want to be put in touch with someone, give me a ring. I'm usually fairly busy, but leave a message and I'll get back to you if I'm not there". This I did, and it proved to be very useful in acquiring the participation of several further Republicans.

Following the interview, I listened to the tape recording and began taking notes of what had happened in the interview, and soon after began 'processing' the transcript of the interview, making sure that it did not bear any marks of recognition, i.e. names, dates, places etc, a wise step to avoid accidentally compromising the identity of any individual. I subsequently began to examine the transcript to ascertain its 'value', with respect to those research questions I wanted to attempt to answer. It was only about a week after my interview with Michael, and having read and re-read the transcript, that I began to realise just how irrelevant most of the material was that I had gained from what I initially thought was a very fruitful interview. I later reasoned however, that these very initial experiences in interviewing people such as Michael helped provide a solid foundation upon which later experiences and interview efforts could subsequently be improved. I certainly had felt nervous in interviewing him, and this probably was reflected more so given that he is alleged to be an IRA Army Council member, but also that he is also a well-known Sinn Fein member in his local area (in the vicinity of the pub). I was thus exposed to some prior perception of him, and although my concerns about the meeting were quickly allayed by his demeanour with me, my initial nervousness was reflected in the way in which I probably failed to guide the interview more effectively from the outset.

I chose this interview example (and frequently use it as a case study for teaching) for a number of reasons. It was one of the very first interviews I had conducted with an actual 'terrorist', and is thus very memorable in a personal sense in the first year of my study as well as being a valuable learning experience for me in gaining some initial 'hands-on' experience. However, I feel that it also illustrated a variety of issues that can arise for a would-be researcher. It is also particularly memorable for me at the time of my doctoral research in that it demonstrated to me how writing a simple letter led to an interview with a significant IRA figure.

6. INTERVIEW CONSIDERATIONS

To meet with and talk to people who have been involved in terrorist activities requires considerable planning, patience and knowledge that what is expected throughout the course of any such meeting may not actually happen. Interviews can take weeks, often months, to arrange, be cancelled at the last minute for various reasons such as security considerations or perhaps "cold feet", and a wasted journey, sometimes of considerable length is not an uncommon feature in these investigations. There are many practical lessons that a researcher can only learn through experience with talking to any individuals involved in violence.

An important (and not always obvious, even in academic circles) lesson to be learned for the researcher who will speaking to either a retired or currently active terrorist for the first time, is that the caricatured image of the fanatic does not emerge when meetings are finally established: to seasoned interviewers, this point may appear trite, but its significance for the novice cannot be underestimated. A striking feature of many of the terrorists interviewed for the research presented in the research is their apparent 'normality' (or perhaps, more appropriately, their lack of outright distinctiveness), conviction of belief, and ability to place accounts of their behaviour within some form of ideological context (a quality of prolonged membership in a terrorist movement). Hoffman (1998, p.7) relates a personal experience:

"I have been studying terrorists and terrorism for more than twenty years. Yet I am still always struck by how disturbingly 'normal' most terrorists seem when one actually sits down and talks to them. Rather than the wild-eyed fanatics or crazed killers that we have been conditioned to expect, many are in fact highly articulate and extremely thoughtful individuals for whom terrorism is (or was) an entirely rational choice, often reluctantly embraced and then only after considerable reflection and debate."

During my interview experiences in Ireland, the process of gaining interviews with police and intelligence personnel operated more or less along the same lines as I employed for the Republican respondents, although the snowballing procedure seemed to operate much faster, as were the responses for being granted or denied interviews. Across both camps, there were some refusals to participate, but encouragingly, not as many as I had initially expected. I received approximately double the amount of refusals from the IRA and Sinn Fein as I did from security forces. Many IRA members to whom I had sent letters never replied through any channel at all, while others simply sent a short and polite message of refusal to me. Several Sinn Fein members referred me to Sinn Fein "publicity" officers, whom they said would take responsibility for arranging such interviews. Many Gardai in the Republic of Ireland also refused to grant me an interview with them, but this was (in formal cases) responded to with a letter (or message) of declination, often stating that due to time constrictions, or operational reasons, that interviews could not be granted at that time. When I did formally approach (i.e. without relying on the informal nature of the snowballing technique) specialised divisions (including the anti-terrorism branch) of An Garda Síochána with letters, telephone calls, and "references" from other Gardai, I received extremely little help. The snowballing sample method and informal 'vetting' from important figures I believe was responsible for the level of success in accessing participants to the extent I did.

At the time, I felt surprised (although less so now having interviewed members from a variety of different movements) I received very little intimidation from IRA members; indeed the most disconcerting incident arose when being overtly chastised by some members of the Gardai. As far as intimidation from the IRA is concerned, presumably this was lacking because in no way did I represent a realistic threat or nuisance to either the security and well being of those participants I succeeded in interviewing, or to the organisation to which they belong. On one occasion, again, in the early stages of my interviews, I did call into question my personal motivation for conducting the research. One former IRA member followed a friend of mine and I into a public restaurant one evening. He sat at our table and proceeded to explain what would happen to me if he discovered that I had given the police information about him that might in some way incriminate him. It later emerged that the Gardai had raided his house on suspicion that he was in possession of a weapon. This raid, unfortunately for me, had taken place about 2-3 days after I had spoken with the man in an interview he granted me. He was quick to let me know what the situation was: "It's like this. You asked me to talk to you about my involvement in the Republican movement and the next thing, the cops are breaking down my door. The bastards only found the [1916] Proclamation [of Independence] hanging on the wall. So now where does that leave us?" I assured him that I did not disclose any information to the police, but he continuously interrupted my attempts to placate him. He referred to his being "fed up" with people like me, and that "y'know, something will have to be done if you're trying to screw me". I obviously was getting extremely uncomfortable at his comments, not to mention my friend who suggested that she leave. The IRA man stopped her, apologising for his interruption, and left just as quickly as he appeared at our table. The next day, I attempted to contact him again to explain that I did not do what he implied. He then apologised and said that he behaved out of character, and that he realised when he had cooled down that there was nothing to suggest that I had been in collusion with the police. I was obviously relieved, but was not too enthusiastic about interviewing for a few weeks to come.

There are similar examples of accounts from others who have conducted research in Northern Ireland (e.g. Burton, 1978; Elliot and Hickie, 1971; Sluka, 1989; Taylor, 1988; Taylor and Quayle, 1994; White, 1993, 2000) but the consensus by and large appears to be one of danger-free experiences. Obviously however, it might only takes one serious incident to change the common view for a considerable time. Anderson (1996, p.5), an American journalist and researcher, came to Belfast in 1986 and several times after, illustrates how he, also in researching fundraising, encountered a similar, although more explicit, issue. He described how he met a senior IRA member in Belfast, whom he appears to have been "accepted" by:

> "With each new secret I shared, I was being held that much more accountable by the hard men. This became bluntly clear to me on a spring night in 1998, when I was taken to a heavily fortified row house just off the Falls Road to meet a man whom I will call Martin, a senior commander in the Provisional IRA. "Do you know what the most dangerous thing to possess in Northern Ireland is?" Martin asked me. "Knowledge. People run into trouble here for knowing things they're not supposed to...What you are looking into, the money aspects, no one in Belfast talks about – it's a death sentence. If you ever identify me in any way, I will be destroyed. If that happens, you will be destroyed. This is not a threat; it's simply a new fact in your life."

James Adams (1986, p.275) described IRA financing as "extremely difficult to research on the ground" due to the sensitive, and particularly secretive nature of this element of terrorist activity, something I came to agree upon with him very quickly. He adds that: "various British journalists have attempted to write about the subject, and all have been threatened by different terrorist groups" (ibid.).   Adams himself notes that he received warnings not to travel to specific cities while researching for his book on terrorist finances (p.x) and again highlighted the particular sensitivities in researching the topic. In many ways then it appears that I was fortunate at the time in the context of my own research. Although not all those Republicans approached agreed to meet me on the basis that I was asking "sensitive questions", with "questionable motivation" (according to one Sinn Fein publicity officer), not only was it possible to describe detailed examples of IRA fundraising operations, but also it was possible to construct a detailed description of the IRA's command and functional structure.   Although nothing dramatic happened to me during the research activities themselves, I received a telephone call from an interviewee during the writing of the thesis (August, 1999), who commented that: "...no-one's doing what you're doing. They've all been doing the other stuff to death, hundreds of times over, but no-one's looked at the money side of things. And the reason is because they're afraid of being killed. No-one's done anything detailed since [the mid-1980s]...and you can be sure that if you pose a threat in any way you're going to be executed."

Not posing a threat therefore would perhaps be an obvious guiding principle to such research. Fortunately for me, I received no direct threat or injury, but this and other examples like it serve as a reminder to always be careful, engage in extensive preparation and when in doubt, adopt plain common-sense in such approaches.

Another approach at that time that I took in obtaining such information relevant to the research questions was in a brief period of what might constitute a form of participant observation in a number of pubs (hosting Republican fundraisers) and graveyards (hosting Republican commemorations). Although I remember viewing it as a very unusual experience at the time, graveyards provided me with the perfect location not only to observe one of the most important and sacred traditions of Republicans - honouring their dead - but provided me with ample opportunity to introduce myself, either to graveside orators (in the hope of using my snowballing technique) or to Sinn Fein/IRA members in the 'congregation' whom I recognised from media sources. This technique in particular proved very valuable during the Republicans' Easter Commemorations (to honour the leaders of the 1916 IRA Easter Rising in Dublin) in one county in the Republic, and represented a valuable first step in procuring several subsequent interviews.

The information gained across all interviews during my doctoral research ranged from detailed, and highly technical information (for example, particularly from former IRA members and security force personnel in the context of detailing the IRA's command structures and its related terminology) in interviews lasting from literally five minutes to five and a half hours. The former interview involved a Sinn Fein member leaving the interview when I began to ask questions relating to IRA fundraising (questions which he had earlier been informed about through a telephone call), and the latter interview, which incorporated several breaks, took place in the Republic when a senior member of the Irish anti-terrorist police agreed to meet and discuss the veracity of the description I had constructed on the IRA's command structure, having already interviewed this valuable participant twice before.

As such, detailed accounts of the information presented in subsequent research papers that have emerged from those early efforts ranged from what could be seen as single points, sentences or assertions, to accounts and descriptions of the command structure as one paper summarised (Horgan and Taylor, 1997; also see Horgan and Taylor, 1999 and 2003). While many participants agreed to have their comments quoted verbatim, many others did not, insisting that their comments be paraphrased or used simply to help build a level of knowledge about the IRA. It must be said that no interview was a waste of time, that is excluding the 16 interview meetings for which my respondents did not show (4 of these were journalists, 5 were Gardai, and 7 were alleged IRA members), after having made commitments to be present. They did not make any subsequent attempt to explain why they did not come, nor did they actually make any subsequent contact.

Three interviews in particular were of very special value, in that a member of the security forces provided me with a copy of the IRA's Green Book, a IRA interviewee provided me with a copy of a short 'minimanual' (more perhaps a collection of personal notes by an IRA member shot dead in 1988) and a different man again provided me with a copy of the OIRA intelligence manual (the "Reporter's Guide to Ireland"). All of these were given to me in similar circumstances, in that there seems to have been a gesture of "good will", at least that is certainly the way in which these gestures appeared. The security force detective who provided me with the Green Book asked me after I interviewed him for his views on IRA fundraising, "do you have the Green Book?" When I said no, he left the room (the interview took place in an empty debriefing room of a police station) for about 20 minutes and came back to say that he had photocopied his 'version' for me.

Although I have highlighted the reasons why no participant in such research is without value, I began to realise early that some of the interviewees were clearly appearing more valuable than others, particularly with respect to my attempts at narrowing 'gaps' in the then emerging fundraising and command structure accounts, but also regarding their length of experience and the value of their long-term views of the topics under examination. In particular, I interviewed three men who had each been an IRA leader at very different stages of the conflict – one during the 1950s until the split in 1969 (who was later to become the Official IRA's Director of Intelligence and prominent Army Council member), another in the post-split and turbulent 1970s and early 80s, while the last (a member of the IRA's Army Council) oversaw the transition of the IRA since the 1994 ceasefire through, and beyond, the peace process.

7.   ISSUES OF VALIDITY AND RELIABILITY

It might appear to be both premature and extraneous to begin a commentary on issues of validity and reliability when the challenges posed by the practical issues in interviewing seem so overwhelming. Despite the relative novelty of first-hand research with terrorists, we must not ignore its limitations, regardless of the differential value that different disciplines might place on the nature of that data (perhaps a particular issue for psychological research). White (1993) outlined several important issues that may proceed to hamper the validity of those accounts gained through intensive interviewing in such circumstances. Such 'biases' according to him, include interviewer/respondent interaction and recall and memory distortion.

During my research on Northern Ireland, factual details from respondents, particularly in relation to fundraising operations, were checked with 11 journalists (out of 24 interviewed in total) with close knowledge and extensive experience of the Northern Ireland problem. While other details (especially those relating to the IRA's command structure and some issues relating to fundraising) were checked and verified with some terrorist sources and sources from the above media agencies with expertise and long experience in covering Northern Ireland terrorism, I did not go beyond this and adopt the same practice that Bruce, for example, employed while researching his book. Bruce (1992) actually gave drafts of his book "The Red Hand" to "a number of well-informed loyalists", and reports them having made "helpful suggestions" (p.vii). Given the sensitive nature of the particular subjects being discussed in my dissertation, I felt that from the outset, that this would be ill advised and rather pointless. The nearest I came to this method is described at the end of the description of the command structure of the IRA, when I discussed the 'final product' of the description with a small number of select Republicans, whom I felt had the necessary experience and level of knowledge to be able to comment about the strength and weaknesses of any such account. It is important to realise therefore that, in accordance with White's further important assertion, the conclusions reached in the dissertation are "not solely based" on the accounts given by participants in the interviews (White, 1993, p.186). As per White's recommendation, I also searched the data for "patterns and for accounts that negated respondents – and my own – interpretations" (p.186), not least with experienced and respected terrorism analysts from well-established academic contexts, but also with several of the most experienced journalists who have covered Northern Irish terrorism for many years. As with White's research, this practice not only reinforced the veracity of the final accounts, but also "allowed the discovery" (White, 1993, p.186) of influential factors in the accounts of the fundraising activities and the command structure that were "not necessarily apparent" (p.186) to any or all of the participants in this study, particularly given that I relied on what results were produced ultimately by the snowball sampling methodology.

White's model discusses the problem of memory error in such research and it is an issue deserving of inclusion here also. Memory error in interviewing contexts is a potential problem that would not sit easily within the rigorous demands of academic investigation, and fuels the kinds of issues raised by Merari (1991) about how psychologists and others perhaps because of their own fault often do not contribute worthy pieces of work (or often misconstrue, through a variety of reasons, the relevance of their contributions). However, and given that where appropriate, my note-taking was at the very least effective in capturing major details, White (1993, p.187) says, "instead of rejecting all recall data as invalid, reconstructive accounts may be treated as working hypotheses", which can then be verified (also see Swanson, Chamelin and Territo, 1998, pp.136-138).

That I chose not to describe my sources by name I realised would render my original research vulnerable to yet further criticism. Where possible however, a researcher would do well to adopt the same practice as Adams did in his 1986 study of the financing of terrorism, by supporting relevant points or assertions with verifiable references (from newspaper reports and other sources – particularly so to make my accounts of the IRA command structure and initial discussion of IRA fundraising as valid as possible in the context of some (although few in number and variable in quality) existing attempts to describe the same areas of study).

A final point to assert here is that despite the constrictions preventing research efforts in the study of terrorism using traditional psychological methodologies (Horgan, 1997; Merari, 1991), case studies offer distinct advantages over experimental methodologies and other methods of investigation.   Case studies, put simply, represent an intensive, detailed investigation of a single case (Elmes, Kantowitz and Roediger, 1992, p.57). Given the nature and direction of the literature on this area, detailed case studies obviously appear to be a welcome respite from the types of generalised and increasingly ill-informed accounts that have plagued terrorism research, and have not allowed for the basis of meaningful interventions to be developed (to identify but one consequence).   On the whole, the generalisability of principles from case studies is fraught with difficulty, but case studies are extremely important because they allow necessary avenues of exploration "when one desires simply to gain some idea as to the breadth and range of the problem of interest" (Elmes, Kantowitz, and Roediger, 1992, p.59).   Thus, while case studies may not appear to have universal appeal within mainstream psychology (given their essentially descriptive nature), it is clear that they offer substantial contributions to particular areas   (Elmes, Kantowitz and Roediger, 1992, p.59) – having reviewed the terrorism literature, such a sentiment might seem to apply especially in terrorism research.

8.   CONCLUSIONS

Whatever the short to medium term future of terrorism studies brings, there is a need to both encourage primary research involving access to (and interviews with) terrorists as well as to encourage a systematic discussion and dissection of issues that emerge for a terrorism researcher, perhaps via comparative analyses. That so few commentaries on interview issues have emerged in recent times on the one hand represents an encouraging step in the right direction, but in critical surveys of the literature, Silke (2001, 2004) has on more than one occasion correctly pointed to an apparent continued reluctance to engage in primary research activity. The author of this Chapter chose to highlight a variety of early personal experiences to attempt to support greater transparency in what many assume to be a necessarily secretive approach whenever first-hand research is even contemplated. As researchers we ought to know better - that terrorism research findings often do not lend easily themselves towards criticism from peers should not disallow us from discussing methodological issues more openly and rigorously in line with mainstream disciplines. Finally, the points raised here may well typify *sui generis* claims, and that is perfectly fine. It would be pointless to attempt to present assertive conclusions or falsify hypotheses in the literature which might emerge from some of the methodological issues (and experiences of them) described here, if only for the simple reason that no comparative attempt has yet been made to identify common themes or experiences between those who have approached the study of terrorism in this way. This now reflects a gap in our analyses, and consequently, any form of primary research on terrorist behaviour might be seen (for some) to warrant no justification. We should resist this, and instead encourage researchers in the field to discuss their experiences of primary research so that we may progress on this front.

POST-SCRIPT

In mid-2006, John Horgan began a comparative analysis of the experiences of former terrorists (based on interviews) from over a dozen terrorist movements around the world. The results of this study will be published in *Walking Away from Terrorism: Accounts of Disengagement from Radical and Extremist Movements* (Routledge).

REFERENCES

Adams, J. (1986). The Financing of Terrorism. London: New English Library.

Alonso, R. (2006). The IRA and Armed Struggle. London: Routledge.

Anderson, S. (1996, February 1). Making a killing. Harper's Magazine, 288, Retrieved on 8th July, 1996 from the World Wide Web: http://www.elibrary.com.

Bloom, M. (2005). Dying to Kill: The Allure of Suicide Terror. New York: Columbia University Press.

Bowyer-Bell, J. (1979). The Secret Army: The IRA 1916-1979. Dublin: Academy Press.

Bowyer-Bell, J. (2000). The IRA 1968-2000: An Analysis of a Secret Army. London: Frank Cass and Co.

Bowyer-Bell, J. (1998). The Dynamics of the Armed Struggle. London: Frank Cass and Co.

Bruce, S. (1992). The Red Hand: Protestant paramilitaries in Northern Ireland. Oxford: Oxford University Press.

Burton, F. (1978). The Politics of Legitimacy: Struggles in a Belfast community. London: Routledge and Kegan Paul.

Coogan, T.P. (1995a). The IRA. London: HarperCollins.

Coogan, T.P. (1995b). The Troubles: Ireland's Ordeal 1966-1995 and the Search for Peace. London: Hutchinson.

Crawford, C. (2003). Inside the UDA: Volunteers and Violence. Dublin: Pluto Press.Crenshaw, M. (1990). Questions to be answered, research to be done, knowledge to be applied. In W. Reich (Ed.) Origins of Terrorism: Psychologies, Ideologies, Theologies, States of Mind (pp.247-260). New York: Cambridge University Press.

Crenshaw, M. (2001). The psychology of terrorism: an agenda for the 21st century. Political Psychology, 21 (2), 405-420.

della Porta, D. (1995). Social Movements, Political Violence and the State. Cambridge: Cambridge University Press.

Elliot, R.S.P. and Hickie, J. (1971). Ulster: A Case Study of Conflict Theory. London: Longman.

Elmes, D.G., Kantowitz, B.H., and Roediger, H.L. (1992). Research Methods in Psychology (4th Edition). St. Paul, MN: West Publishing Company.

Horgan, J. (1997). Issues in Terrorism Research. The Police Journal, 50 (3), 193-202.

Horgan, J. (1999). Psychology and Terrorism Research. Paper presented at the Psychological Society of Ireland 30th Annual Conference, Cork. 11-14th November.

Horgan, J. (2000). Terrorism and Political Violence: A Psychological Perspective. PhD dissertation. Department of Applied Psychology, University College, Cork.

Horgan, J. & M. Taylor. (1997). The Provisional Irish Republican Army: command and functional structure. Terrorism and Political Violence, 9 (3), 1-32.

Horgan, J. & M. Taylor. (1999). Playing the green card: financing the Provisional IRA – part 1. Terrorism and Political Violence, 11 (2), 1-38.

Horgan, J. and Taylor, M. (2001). The Making of a Terrorist. Jane's Intelligence Review,13 (12), 16-18.

Jamieson, A. (1989). The Heart Attacked: Terrorism and Conflict in the Italian state. London: Marian Boyers.

Knowles, G.J. (1996, July). Dealing Crack Cocaine: A View from the Streets of Honolulu. FBI Law Enforcement Bulletin. Retrieved on 22nd January, 1997 from the World Wide Web: http://www.fbi.gov/library/leb/july961.txt

Merari, A. (1991). Academic Research and Government Policy on Terrorism. Terrorism and Political Violence, 3 (1), 88-102.

Merari, A., & N. Friedland. (1985). Social psychological aspects of political terrorism. In S. Oskamp (Ed.) Applied Social Psychology Annual (Vol. 6): International Conflict and National Public Policy Issues (pp.185-205). London: Sage.

Reinares, F. (2004). Who Are The Terrorists? Analysing Changes in Sociological Profile Among Members of ETA. Studies in Conflict and Terrorism, 27 (6), 465-488.

Schweitzer, Y. and Goldstein Ferber, S. (2005). Al-Qaida and the Internationalisation of Suicide Terrorism. Tel Aviv: Jaffee Centre for Strategic Studies.

Silke, A. (2001). The Devil You Know: Continuing Problems with Research on Terrorism. Terrorism and Political Violence, 13 (4), 1-14.

Silke, A. (Ed.) (2004). Researching Terrorism: Trends, Achievements, Failures. London: Frank Cass and Co.

Sluka, J. (1989). Hearts and Minds, Water and Fish: Support for the IRA and INLA in a Northern Irish Ghetto. Greenwich, CT: JAI Press.

Speckhard, A. and Akhmedova, K. (2005). Talking to Terrorists. Journal of Psychohistory (Fall).

Stern, J. (2003). Terror in the Name of God: Why Religious Militants Kill. New York: Ecco.

Swanson, C.R., Chamelin, N.C., and Territo, L. (1988). Criminal Investigation (4th Edition). New York: McGraw Hill.

Taylor, M. (1988) The Terrorist. London: Brassey's.

Taylor, M. (1991). The Fanatics: A Behavioural Approach to Political Violence. London: Brassey's.

Taylor, M. and Horgan, J. (2001). The Psychological and Behavioural Bases of Islamic Fundamentalism. Terrorism and Political Violence, 13 (4), 37-71.

Taylor, M. and Quayle, E. (1994) Terrorist Lives. London: Brassey's.

White, R. (1993). Provisional Irish Republicans: An Oral and Interpretive History. Westport, CT: Greenwood Press.

White, R. (2000). Issues in the study of political violence: understanding the motives of participants in small group political violence. Terrorism and Political Violence, 12 (1), 95-108.

SUGGESTED READINGS

- Crenshaw, M. (2000). "The Psychology of Terrorism: An Agenda for the 21st Century." *Political Psychology* (21): 405-420.
- *Political Psychology*, 21 (2), 405-420.
- Horgan, J. (2005). *The Psychology of Terrorism*. London: Routledge.
- Merari, A. (1991). Academic Research and Government Policy on Terrorism. *Terrorism and Political Violence*, 3 (1), 88-102.
- Silke, A. (2001). The Devil You Know: Continuing Problems with Research on Terrorism. *Terrorism and Political Violence*, 13 (4), 1-14.

DISCUSSION QUESTIONS

1. Is primary research on terrorism (e.g. interviewing) a realistic exercise?
2. Is interviewing terrorists and former terrorists ethical?
3. What type of ethical problems might confront a researcher who wants to interview terrorists? Are there ways to try to resolve these problems?
4. Should we believe everything terrorists and former terrorists tell us in interviews?
5. Do any of the issues involved in interviewing terrorists, also apply to research interviews with counter-terrorism professionals (e.g. law enforcement, military, etc.)?

5

RESOLVING A TERRORIST INSURGENCY BY ADDRESSING ITS ROOT CAUSES

Joshua Sinai
The Analysis Corporation (jsinai@the-analysis-corp.com)

CHAPTER OVERVIEW

To effectively resolve a terrorist insurgency against a state, it is crucial to map the root causes underlying the conflict because terrorism does not emerge in a political, socio-economic, religious or even psychological vacuum. Root causes form the initial components driving the terrorist life cycle (TLC), e.g., why terrorist groups are formed, how they are led and organized, the nature of their grievances, motivations, strategies and demands and their relations with their constituency, while the terrorist attack cycle (TAC) refers to how they conduct a spectrum of operations, ranging from non-violent to violent activities, and their choice of weaponry and targeting. Once these underlying causes are mapped, then it would be possible to formulate appropriate response measures, although some terrorist insurgencies can be resolved through conciliatory measures, some by means of a mix of coercion and conciliation, whereas others may only be resolved by defeating the terrorists militarily.

1.   INTRODUCTION

To effectively resolve the violent threats posed by terrorist (1) groups to the security and well-being of their state adversaries, it is crucial to develop an appropriate understanding of the root causes underlying such conflicts because terrorist insurgencies do not emerge in a political, socio-economic, religious or even psychological vacuum. (2). It could be argued, in fact, that the root causes underlying an insurgency are the initial components driving the terrorist life cycle (TLC) and the terrorist attack cycle (TAC). The TLC refers to why and how terrorist groups are formed, led and organized, the nature of their grievances, motivations, strategies and demands vis-a-vis their adversaries, and the linkages that terrorist groups form with their supporting constituency. These components of the TLC, in turn, affect the TAC—a group's modus operandi, how they conduct the spectrum of operations, ranging from non-violent to violent activities, and their choice of weaponry and targeting.

To understand the context in which root causes relate to the TLC and TAC, it is necessary to conduct a comprehensive study of the magnitude of the warfare threat posed by a terrorist group against its adversary. The manifestations of the threat would then be 'drilled down' into their component warfare elements, such as conventional low impact (CLI) (e.g., warfare in which a few persons will be killed in a single attack involving conventional weapons warfare, such as explosives or shootings), conventional high impact (CHI) (e.g,, warfare in which conventional means are used to cause hundreds or thousands of fatalities), or warfare employing chemical, biological, radiological or nuclear (CBRN) (e.g., utilizing 'unconventional' means to inflict catastrophic damages). It is here, for example, where the latest advances in social science conceptual approaches, such as social network theory, would be applied to model how terrorist groups organize themselves, plan attacks, conduct recruitment, develop operational capabilities, link up with counterparts, etc. (3). Other components of the TLC and TAC also would need to be addressed, such as why certain groups choose to embark on 'martyrdom'-driven suicide terrorism, as opposed to other forms of warfare where operatives seek to stay alive and escape from the scene of the incident.

Once the magnitude of the terrorist threat is identified and outlined (i.e., whether conventional low impact, conventional high impact, CBRN or a combination of the three), then one could begin the process of trying to understand the underlying conditions, or root causes, for why such warfare is being waged against a specific adversary (or adversaries). Thus, to attain the capability to anticipate and, in the most ideal cases preemptively contain or defeat on-going or emerging terrorist insurgencies, understanding the root causes underlying such conflicts must constitute the first line of analysis in a government's combating terrorism campaign's strategies and programs.

To resolve terrorist insurgencies it is essential to research and systematically map the spectrum of root causes underlying a rebellion's origins, grievances and demands.

2.   WHY ROOT CAUSES ARE SIGNIFICANT

Terrorists, whether operating as small or large groups, are generally driven to commit acts of terrorism due to a variety of factors, whether rational or irrational, in which extreme forms of violence are utilized to express and redress specific grievances and demands. Root causes are the factors and circumstances underlying insurgencies that radicalize and drive terrorists – whether they are consciously or unconsciously aware of these root causes – into carrying out their violent actions (4). Root causes consist of multiple combinations of factors and circumstances, ranging from general to specific, global, regional or local, governmental-regime, societal or individual levels, structural or psychological, dynamic or static, facilitating or triggering, or other possible variations, some of which may be more important and fundamental than others (5).

Root causes are not the product of a single causal factor, but generally a confluence or convergence of a multitude of interrelated factors and causes, with such causes varying from one conflict to another. It is important to analyze these underlying factors because, at least by definition, addressing such factors would solve problems that have identifiable root causes. Uproot the cause and the problem is solved. By contrast, leave the roots intact and the problem will persist.

Root causes are not static, but dynamic and constantly changing. In fact, even when a government begins to address a root cause, it is always possible for the terrorist group to claim that another, yet unresolved, root cause needs to be resoled. Thus, to attain a complete picture of the underlying causes driving an insurgency it is crucial to examine them at levels that are general and specific, including at the individual, group, societal and governmental levels. They also need to be examined and synthesized from the divergent points of view of the insurgents, the targeted governments, and academic researchers.

Various theories, whether general or specific, developed by social science are especially relevant to understanding the origins of terrorism (6). Structural theories, for example, "focus on social conditions ('structures') that affect group access to services, equal rights, civil protections, freedom, or other quality-of-life measures" (7). Examples of structural factors include government policies and bureaucracies, the geographic location of the insurgent group, the actions of security forces, and access by a local population to social institutions (8). The state or government is the key focus in structural theories of terrorism because of its role in serving as the precipitating factor for a terrorist uprising. According to this theory, societal injustice, popular discontent, the alienation of elites, and a sense of societal crisis are key ingredients for a terrorist eruption in society (9).

Unlike structural theories which focus on the central role of the state and its instruments of power in causing terrorist rebellions, relative deprivation (RD) theory, which was developed by Ted Robert Gurr, focuses on the relationship between frustration and aggression (10). As applied to the terrorism milieu, according to Gurr, feelings of frustration and anger underlie individual decisions to engage in collective action against the perceived source of their frustration and constitute one of the necessary conditions for joining a terrorist group. Their motive for engaging in political violence is their perception that they are *relatively* deprived, vis-à-vis other groups, in an unjust social order. When rising expectations are met by governmental resistance in the form of sustained political repression, low ranking socio-economic or political status, or lack of educational opportunities, a group is likely to turn to political violence.

As a corollary to relative deprivation, absolute deprivation theory holds that when a group has been deprived of the basic necessities for survival by a government or social order, such as physical abuse, poverty or starvation, it turns to political violence (11). Thus, the difference between relative and absolute deprivation is based on the degree of discrepancy experienced by an individual or group between what people have and what they need for daily sustenance, as opposed to what they have and what they believe they deserve vis-à-vis others in society. Both types of deprivation are capable of driving those believing themselves to be aggrieved into carrying out acts of political violence.

Moving from these general theories to more specific indicators of terrorist outbreaks, the social sciences have also studied factors at the societal, group, and individual levels. At the societal level, countries experiencing economic and social inequality, poverty, low levels of social services, a lack of political or civil rights, low literacy rates and a lack of education, and ethnic conflict are likely to serve as springboards for terrorism, or at least some manifestation of active discontent that may fall below the threshold of violence. The group level of analysis intervenes between the societal and individual levels. Thus, at the group level, agents of mobilization, such as charismatic leaders, radical movements and their political and religious ideologies, serve as causal factors for terrorist outbreaks. At the individual level, susceptibility to radicalization and actual recruitment into terrorist organizations are additional causal factors. According to Arie Kruglanski, extremist ideology is appealing to individuals experiencing psychological uncertainty because such ideologies are "formulated in clear-cut, definitive terms" and provide "cognitive closure" (12). The ecological framework or springboard for terrorist insurgencies are therefore comprised of at least three levels—individual, group and societal, with additional explanatory value provided by theories at more general levels.

As demonstrated by these approaches, no single theory or factor provides a sufficient explanation for terrorism. Links between poverty, lack of education and other socio-economic variables, including the clash between tradition and modernity, and terrorism, are complex, as are the links between state repression, lack of political opportunities and terrorism. Other political factors may also contribute to terrorism, such as the ability of terrorist groups to exploit political disorder or a lack of political order in weak or failed states. At other times, however, groups may actually receive political support from governments (such as support by the Iranian government of the Lebanese Hizballah). Theories or models for understanding terrorism therefore need to focus on the causal mechanisms or processes in which multiple factors, working together in specific social and other contexts, influence and drive terrorist uprisings.

Applying these theories to explain the causes underlying a terrorist rebellion, however, still need to overcome what Marc Sageman calls the "problem of specificity" (13). Thus, while it may be possible to identify some of the necessary conditions for such rebellions, Sageman argues that "such an approach is overly broad and leads to the fundamental problem of specificity. Many people share the identified characteristics of such an analysis, but very few become terrorists. What accounts for this vast difference?" (14).

Once these theoretical and empirical issues are resolved, these conceptual frameworks can then be applied to investigating the underlying conditions, or root causes of specific conflicts, including the factors driving them to attack a specific adversary (or adversaries). The underlying causes would then be hierarchically decomposed, itemized, categorized (e.g., poverty, political inequality, foreign subjugation, religious extremism, nihilism, etc.) and codified (e.g., short-, medium-, or long-term, 1st order root cause, 2nd order root cause, etc.) (15).

Another important consideration in understanding a rebellion's underlying root causes is to identify them from the varying perspectives of the insurgents, the threatened governments, and independent academic experts (who are likely to disagree among themselves) because these three general perspectives are likely to differ and, in some cases, even clash. Thus, for example, what the insurgents consider to be the underlying causes to their rebellion may be perceived entirely differently by the challenged government, which may deny the existence of such underlying factors. For example, while both Palestinians and Israelis agree that the central root cause underlying their conflict is the contention by two peoples over the same territory, there is disagreement over other possible root causes. To the Palestinian insurgents, the continued presence and expansion of Israeli settlements in the heart of the West Bank is claimed to constitute one of the primary root causes of their rebellion, whereas certain factions in the Israeli government may claim that such settlements should remain and are not an obstacle to reaching a peace accord. Independent academic experts may agree that such settlements may in fact represent an important root cause driving the conflict, because of the refusal by a minority of Israelis, in the form of the Jewish settlers, to give up their idea of a "Greater Israel" and live within the pre-June 1967 War confines of the Jewish state. At the same time, academic experts may find that the Palestinian insurgents engage in subterfuge on this issue because even if the settlements were evacuated many Palestinians would still refuse to ever recognize the legitimacy of Israeli rights to a homeland in a re-partitioned historical Palestine. Moreover, the Israeli government and academic experts, but not the Palestinian insurgents, may argue that an important root cause is the unresolved generational conflict among the Palestinians, with the younger generation, such as the leaders of Hamas, who are much more militant and extremist than their elders, desiring to impose an Islamic theocracy over Palestinian society and reject any negotiated compromise with Israel.

To bridge the different interpretations between a government and its insurgent adversary, it is necessary for academic experts, who, as pointed out earlier, may even disagree among themselves, to provide as independent, impartial and objective as possible assessments of a conflict's root causes in order to assist the two adversaries to better understand the underlying problems that require resolution of their conflict.

In another important step, identifying and categorizing a conflict's underlying root causes will make it possible to hypothesize whether or not it may be possible to influence or resolve them so that long-term insurgency termination may take hold.

3.   HOW TO RESOLVE A CONFLICT'S ROOT CAUSES

In ideal cases, it is hoped that such mapping of root causes will then produce the knowledge and insight on the part of governments to formulate appropriate responses that would be most effective in terminating a terrorist insurgency (16), whether peacefully, militarily, by law enforcement, or through a combination of these measures. By incorporating such an understanding of a conflict's underlying root causes into a government's combating terrorism (17) campaign, such response strategies and tactics could be effectively calibrated to address their specific challenges and threats. It is this paper's objective to provide an analytic framework to enable the combating terrorism community, whether in government or the academic sectors, to develop the conceptual capability and tools to resolve terrorist insurgencies using the most appropriate mix of coercive and conciliatory measures that address the general and specific root causes and other underlying factors that give rise to such insurgencies. Without understanding how to utilize such a root causes-based conceptual capability and tools, combating terrorism campaigns are likely to be ineffectual and terrorist insurgencies will become, due to lack of effective resolution, increasingly protracted and lethal in their warfare.

Addressing a conflict's underlying root causes may not necessarily automatically lead to conflict termination. First, there may not be a direct correlation in every case between a specific root cause and a terrorist rebellion because of the myriad of alternative forms of action, ranging from non-violent to violent, that may be available to a group to express the underlying grievances and demands driving their group. In fact, a terrorist rebellion is likely to occur only when certain significant propitious circumstances in the form of political, economic, social, military, and other underlying trends coincide and coalesce, but even these trends may not be sufficient to launch such rebellions unless they are buttressed by the availability of effective leaders, organizational formations, including a willing cadre, access to particular types of weaponry and the logistical and other covert capabilities to carry out an operation against its adversary. Second, root causes should not be viewed as necessarily static, with some of the root causes that might play a significant role in the initial phase of a conflict becoming peripheral later on, while other root causes may emerge as paramount at a later phase in a conflict.

Thus, it is important to understand and map the spectrum of root causes underlying all phases in a terrorist rebellion because of their impact on future directions, including influencing a group's choice of targeting and degree of lethality in its warfare. In fact, the intensity of how a group perceives its adversary and the strategies that it believes are required to redress the grievances against it, will affect the types of tactics and weaponry it will employ in the warfare against its stronger adversary. This is particularly the case in determining whether a group's warfare proclivity will be characterized by conventional low impact, conventional high impact, or

CBRN warfare, with the latter form of warfare exponentially escalating the lethality threshold of casualties.

Once the spectrum of a conflict's underlying root causes are mapped and identified—initially, as in most cases, at the academic level, and then at the governmental level, it will be up to governments and their security and military organizations to formulate the appropriate combating terrorism response measures to resolve these underlying problems. For the underlying factors to be resolved, however, it is also up to the insurgents to incorporate into their demands grievances and other objectives that are amenable to the 'give and take' of compromise and negotiations because otherwise even addressing a conflict's root causes may not succeed in terminating the insurgency.

In this analytic approach, a government's combating terrorism campaign against an insurgent movement that utilizes terrorist tactics in order to overthrow that government, punish it for alleged transgressions, or seek independence against foreign rule, must be comprehensive and holistic in scope. This is because resolving terrorist insurgencies requires a much more thoroughgoing response than the narrower military or law enforcement orientations of most counter-guerrilla or counter-terrorist operations, which generally do not include crucial political, diplomatic, and socio-economic dimensions that are required to resolve a conflict's underling root causes.

The objective of the government's combating terrorism campaign therefore is to employ a mix of coercive (e.g., military or law enforcement) and conciliatory (e.g., political, diplomatic, or socio-economic) measures that either will militarily defeat the insurgents on the battlefield or peacefully terminate the insurgency by resolving the root causes and conditions that may prolong the conflict.

A successful combating terrorism campaign that seeks to address a conflict's underlying root causes must be based on the following three measures:

First, governments need to map, identify and prioritize what they consider to be the most significant underlying root causes driving the terrorist insurgency threatening them. To conduct such an assessment combating terrorism planners need to take into account their own perspectives, those of the insurgents, and academic experts. Once such a prioritized assessment is finalized, then the most appropriate measures need to be formulated on how these discrete root causes can be influenced and resolved. In fact, in determining the root causes associated with a terrorist insurgency, it is crucial to map all possible root causes, not just a select few that may be perceived as most likely. Such a comprehensive mapping effort will then generate the basis from which one could select those root causes whose resolution might yield the greatest benefit to eventual conflict termination. In this process, all perceived underlying root causes in a conflict would be itemized, categorized and codified (18).

Second, governments then need to formulate a clear definition in their directives and policies about the combating terrorism campaign's short-, medium- and long-term strategic objectives, including, as the final component, formulating a methodology to measure the effectiveness of their responses to the underlying root causes driving the terrorist insurgency. This involves formulating a mission area assessment that provides a roadmap for how strategic objectives can be implemented tactically on the ground for insurgency resolution to take place.

Third, the combating terrorism campaign must be coordinated and integrated at all levels of government, especially among the political, diplomatic, law enforcement, intelligence, and military establishments, resulting in a 'unity of effort.'

In ideal cases, when such a three-pronged combating terrorism campaign is implemented, in situations where an insurgent conflict is caused by political or socio-economic deprivations or disparities that are exploited by the insurgents, a government's conciliatory policies that address and resolve that conflict's root causes is likely to succeed in peacefully winning the affected populations 'hearts and minds.' Also in ideal cases where a foreign power controls a territory that is inhabited by a hostile population, a combating campaign's conciliatory components is likely succeed in terminating the insurgency by providing autonomy or independence to that territory, following a consensual peace accord between the government and the insurgents.

Thus, a conflict resolution-based combating terrorism strategy is likely to be the most effective way to resolve a protracted terrorist-based insurgency where the insurgents represent 'genuine' grievances that succeed in mobilizing the local population to support their cause. This does not imply that coercive measures are not necessary as an initial governmental response to nip the insurgency in the bud. In fact, during the initial phase, coercive measures are required to counteract the insurgency's violent threats to the maintenance of law and order. These coercive measures will likely take the form of military, police, and intelligence operations against the insurgent forces; governments will insist that no concessions be made to insurgent demands, which they perceive as illegitimate because violent means are used to express them; insurgent movements will be declared illegal; a state of emergency accompanied by prevention of terrorism laws will be imposed, particularly in insurgent areas; and diplomatic pressure will be exerted on the external patrons or supporters of the insurgency to cease such support.

While these coercive measures may be necessary in the initial stages of an insurgency, there are limits to the degree of coercion that democratic governments will employ in their combating terrorism campaign. Thus, for example, democratic governments, such as Israel, will refrain from employing crushing military force to wipe out civilian populations that provide the insurgents with support because of the damage that such devastation would inflict on their own democratic constitutional nature. This is the situation currently confronting Israel in its response to the al-Aqsa Intifada, where even the deployment of massive Israeli military force in Spring 2002 against Palestinian cities and towns in response to devastating Palestinian suicide terrorism against Israelis was not intended to massacre Palestinian civilians, but to ensure that terrorists, their operational handlers, and infrastructures were uprooted and destroyed so that a political settlement might be possible when conditions were considered ripe.

Moreover, even during the initial coercive phase of their response, democratic governments are likely to include certain limited conciliatory measures. These conciliatory measures will be restricted in scope, and will likely consist of limited degrees of political, legal, and socio-economic reforms, including permitting human rights groups to monitor the impact of the combating terrorism campaign on the affected population.

Authoritarian governments, on the other hand, are less inclined to act with such restraint against civilian supporters of an insurgency, as demonstrated by the crushing by Syrian forces of the Muslim Brotherhood insurgents in Hama in 1982, the Iraqi use of chemical weapons against the Kurdish villagers in early 1988, the 1998 bombardment by Serbian forces against the rebellious ethnic Albanian villagers in Kosovo, and Russia's military campaign against the Chechnyan terrorist separatists.

However, when an insurgency, even when it employs terrorism to achieve its objectives, succeeds in gaining the support of a significant segment of the population to its cause and in protracting the insurgency, and the government's coercive measures, accompanied by limited conciliation, are unable either to decisively defeat the insurgents on the battlefield or to resolve the insurgency peacefully, then a new combating terrorism strategy is required to resolve the conflict. Based on my research, I believe that in a situation of a protracted 'hurting stalemate' that is damaging to both sides, in which there is no military solution to end the insurgency, long-term resolution can only come about when governments begin to address the conflict's underlying root causes – but only when the insurgents' grievances are considered legitimate and grounded in some aspects of international law.

This recommendation does not imply that resolving a conflict's root causes will automatically terminate the insurgency peacefully. Some insurgent movements are inherently extremist and not interested in compromising their demands, such as militant religious fundamentalists who are intent on establishing highly authoritarian theocratic states (e.g., in

Algeria, Egypt, Jordan and Lebanon (19)), or are filled with unrelenting rage against a superpower (e.g., Usama bin Laden's al-Qaida's group and its network of affiliates), while other insurgents may be use narcotrafficking means to fund their political activities (e.g., the FARC in Colombia). Thus, in such cases no peaceful accommodation may be possible between governments and insurgents even when governments are willing to resolve a conflict's 'root causes,' such as socio-economic and political inequalities.

One way to determine whether it is possible for governments and insurgents to arrive at a negotiated compromise is by distinguishing between insurgents' legitimate and illegitimate grievances. Legitimate grievances may be defined as those that are anchored in international law, particularly in the areas of constitutionalism and human rights, and are politically, legally, economically, and geographically equitable to all relevant parties affected by the conflict. Illegitimate grievances, on the other hand, generally are based on anti-democratic, theocratic, religiously exclusionary, or criminal principles and objectives, as well as desiring the destruction or annihilation of the adversary.

4.   CONCLUSION

Because of the different responses that are necessary to address legitimate and illegitimate demands being espoused by terrorist groups, employing conciliation to resolve a terrorist rebellion can be applied to certain types of insurgencies, but not others. In the case of the insurgency mounted by al-Qaida, for example, there may be no alternative but to pursue a full-scale military campaign, backed by intelligence and law enforcement measures, to round up as many of their insurgents as possible, because of their operatives' single-minded pursuit of causing as much catastrophic damage to their adversaries as possible, regardless of the consequences to their own societies. In fact, even under these circumstances, it is still possible to address the underlying conditions that facilitate recruitment and support for al-Qaida (such as the prevalence of Arab regimes that stifle opportunities for educated youths to attain socio-economic and political advancement) without giving in to al-Qaida's demands or long-term goals (20).

Similarly, for Israel, while it may be difficult to negotiate with insurgents such as Hamas (which came to power in the Palestinian Authority in March 2006), the Palestinian Islamic Jihad and Fatah's armed militias, because of their determination to sabotage all efforts at a peace process by launching wave upon wave of suicide bombers and other conventional tactics to achieve their goal of a theocratic Palestinian state in all of historical

Palestine, the underlying conditions that perpetuate that conflict still need to be addressed. Thus, in spite of extremist demands by its terrorist adversaries, Israeli counterterrorism planners must map that conflict's root causes in order to generate responses that will effectively terminate or mitigate that insurgency. For example, if the presence of Jewish settlers in the heart of Palestinian territories in the West Bank and Gaza Strip is considered to constitute one of the underlying root causes for continued Palestinian hostility, then evacuating and resettling those settlers in Israel 'proper' may prove to be a solution to addressing those Palestinian demands that may be judged to be 'legitimate. In fact, there is a substantial segment of the Israeli leadership that supports the notion of 'unilateral disengagement' from such territories, even without a negotiating process with a counterpart Palestinian peace partner. Fortunately, such a conciliatory approach began to take shape in 2005 when the Israeli government uprooted its Jewish settlers in the Gaza Strip which set the stage in 2006 for further evacuations of Israeli settlements in the West Bank. Although conciliation by the Israeli government was not matched by the Hamas-led Palestinian government, which demonstrated that even a government's best intentions may not succeed in resolving the underlying causes when faced by an extremist adversary, even such an imperfect approach to conflict resolution at least recognizes that certain underlying problem areas can be resolved without appeasing the insurgents' extremist demands. Here, as in other cases, intransigence by insurgents should not preclude the need for the threatened governments facing protracted insurgencies to strive to resolve their conflicts' underlying problems by using as many creative and 'out of the box' measures as possible, because the alternative is continued suffering for all contending sides.

REFERENCES AND FOOTNOTES

1. In this framework, terrorism is defined as "a form or tactic of warfare characterized by the deliberate acts of violence, such as killing persons and causing physical damage, perpetrated by sub-state or non-state groups against all citizens of a state, whether civilian or military, to achieve a myriad of objectives." This definition is not intended to demonize a group that uses violence to achieve its goals or to delegitimize its grievances and demands, but to highlight its chosen form of tactical warfare, which is distinguished from guerrilla warfare, which deploys different sets of tactics and objectives, such as using paramilitary forces against government forces to increase territory under insurgent control.

2. In the academic literature on terrorism, several important studies have been published on the need to understand the root causes of terrorism. These include Ted Robert Gurr's *Why Men Rebel* (Princeton, NJ: Princeton University Press, 1970); Walter Reich, ed., *Origins of Terrorism: Psychologies, Ideologies, Theologies, States of Mind* (Baltimore:

The Johns Hopkins University Press, 1998); Neil J. Smelser and Faith Mitchel, eds., *Terrorism: Perspectives from the Behavioral and Social Sciences* (Washington, DC: The National Academies Press, 2002), and Tore Bjorgo, editor, *Root Causes of Terrorism* (New York: Routledge, 2005).

3. For an example of how social network theory can be applied to excavating how terrorist groups such as al-Qaida and its affiliates are organized and led, see Marc Sageman, *Understanding Terror Networks* (Philadelphia: University of Pennsylvania Press, 2004).

4. See Bjorgo, "Conceptual Framework," in Tore Bjorgo, *Root Causes of Terrorism*.

5. *Ibid.*

6. For initial examinations of root causes, see Reich, editor, *Origins of Terrorism: Psychologies, Ideologies, Theologies, States of Mind*; and Bjorgo, editor, *Root Causes of Terrorism*.

7. Gus Martin, *Understanding Terrorism: Challenges, Perspectives, and Issues* (Thousand Oaks, CA: SAGE Publications, 2003), p. 67. Martin based his analysis on the works of Steven E. Barkan and Lynne L. Snowden, *Collective Violence* (Boston: Allyn & Bacon, 2001) and Jack A. Goldstone, "Introduction: The Comparative and Historical Study of Revolutions," in Jack A. Goldstone, editor, *Revolutions: Theoretical, Comparative, and Historical Studies* (San Diego, CA: Harcourt Brace Jovanovich, 1986).

8. Martin, *Understanding Terrorism: Challenges, Perspectives, and Issues*, p. 67.

9. Ibid., p. 68.

10. Gurr, *Why Men Rebel*.

11. See Charles Y. Glock, "The Role of Deprivation in the Origin and Evolution of Religious Groups," in Religion and Social Conflict , R. Lee and M. E. Marty, editors (New York: Oxford University Press, 1964), pp. 24-36

12. Arie Kruglianski, "Inside the Terrorist Mind," paper presented to the National Academy of Science annual meeting, Washington, DC, April 29, 2002.

13. Marc Sageman, "Threat Convergence: The Future of Terrorism Research" [unpublished paper prepared for the workshop on "Threat Convergence: Possible New Pathways to Proliferation – Terrorism, Weapons of Mass Destruction, and Weak and Failing States, April 7, 2006, Washington, DC; cited by permission].

14. *Ibid.*

15. For an analysis of how a root causes tool developed for the engineering milieu can be applied to terrorism studies, see Robert J. Latino, "The Application of PROACT RCA to Terrorism/Counter-Terrorism Related Events," pages 579-589 in Paul Kantor, et al, editors, Intelligence and Security Informatics, ISI 2005 (IEEE International Conference on Intelligence Security Informatics, ISI 2005, Atlanta, GA, USA, May 19-20, 2005 Proceedings] (Berlin: Springer, 2005).

16. The term 'terrorist insurgency' is used because incidents of terrorism are not single or isolated acts but are part of a protracted rebellion that employs terrorist tactics against its stronger adversary.

17. Combating terrorism (CbT) is an umbrella concept incorporating anti-terrorism, which is defensively oriented, and counter-terrorism, which is offensively oriented.

18. This approach is based on Robert J. Latino and Kenneth C. Latino, *Root Cause Analysis: Improving Performance for Bottom-Line Results* (Boca Raton, FL: CRC Press, 2002).

19. In the case of Lebanon, Hizballah's political party is part of the country's confessional democratic political system, but a major intangible element is whether at some point it will seek to overthrow the political system and impose an Iranian-based theocracy over the country.

20. This insight was suggested by Bjorgo, editor, *Root Causes of Terrorism*, in correspondence with the author.

SUGGESTED READINGS

- Bjorgo, Tore, editor, *Root Causes of Terrorism*. New York: Routledge, 2005.
- Gurr, Ted Robert, *Why Men Rebel*. Princeton, NJ: Princeton University Press, 1970.
- Latino, Robert J. and Latino, Kenneth C., *Root Cause Analysis: Improving Performance for Bottom-Line Results*. Boca Raton, FL: CRC Press, 2002.
- Reich, Walter, ed., *Origins of Terrorism: Psychologies, Ideologies, Theologies, States of Mind.* Baltimore: The Johns Hopkins University Press, 1998.

ONLINE RESOURCES

- Root Causes of Terrorism? International Expert Meeting, Organized by the Norwegian Institute of International Affairs, Oslo June 9-11, 2003. http://www.nupi.no/IPS/filestore/Root_Causes_Summaries.pdf

DISCUSSION QUESTIONS

1. Choose a particular terrorist rebellion and begin hierarchically decomposing it into its component root causes.
2. What are the manifestations of the conflict (e.g., type of warfare)?
3. What are the underlying causes from the perspectives of the insurgents, the threatened governments, and academic experts?
4. What are its general, specific, long-term and short-term underlying causes?
5. Have these underlying causes changed over the years?
6. Has the threatened government attempted to address any of these underlying causes?
7. Which of these underlying causes, in your view, are amenable to compromise, and which are not?

6

A QUANTITATIVE ANALYSIS OF "ROOT CAUSES OF CONFLICT"

Mihaela Bobeica[1], Jean-Paul Jéral[2], Teofilo Garcia[2], and Clive Best[2]

[1]University of Nice, CRDL, Bureau 411, BP 3209, 98 Bvd. Herriot, 06204 Nice Cedex, France (mihaela.bobeica@wanadoo.fr); [2]IPSC, Joint Research Centre, European Commission, I-21020 Ispra, Italy ({jean-paul.jeral, teofilo.garcia, clive.best}@jrc.it)

CHAPTER OVERVIEW

This chapter describes a method for the measurement of root causes of conflicts, as defined in a checklist drawn up by the European Commission's External Relations Directorate General (DG RELEX) for monitoring and early warning. Our approach uses Latent Semantic Analysis to measure these conflict indicators on a corpus composed of news articles extracted from the archive of a media monitoring system, Europe Media Monitor (EMM), designed at the European Commission's Joint Research Center (JRC). Latent Semantic Analysis is a statistical technique based on the analysis of the semantic similarity between words distributed across a corpus of documents. By taking a purely numerical approach to estimating these conflict indicators in news data, we have produced results that could be further used in foreign policy analysis and conflict assessment tasks and could provide timely alerts to policy-makers and analysts.

1.   INTRODUCTION

Organizing and classifying pre-conflict information into meaningful categories indicating threat context and levels turns out to be a real challenge for those involved in preventive policy and early warning, due to information overload and diversity.

Automatic information processing has become the key instrument for law enforcement agencies' investigations and information retrieval, for threat assessment and for general situation monitoring. It is being applied to many other areas, such as disaster and crisis early warning, disease outbreak detection, counter-terrorism studies, and regional conflict assessment studies.

The European Union Common Foreign and Security policy needs worldwide monitoring of warning indicators for conflicts. A methodology to derive conflict assessment indicators from long term news monitoring can support desk officers and give regular situation updates. The challenge is to automatically extract these indicators.

The European Commission's External Relations Directorate General (DG RELEX) has defined a methodology for assessing the risks of conflict within a given country using eight identified problem areas. These assessments are known as Country Conflict Assessments (CCAs) and are based on a questionnaire filled in by experts and country desk officers. Each problem area is further broken down into two or three sub-topics. The assessing officer gauges the seriousness of each of these topics by marking an indicator value between 0 (no problems) and 4 (very serious). The CCAs are a valuable source both for detecting long-term trends (improving or worsening situation) and for maintaining a current watch list of countries assessed as being at high risk of conflict. A weakness of this methodology is that it depends on the qualitative judgment of the assessor and opinions can differ, especially over long time periods. Thus, variations can be expected between countries assessed by different experts and for the same country over time.

Using a statistical technique called Latent Semantic Analysis, our study offers results that could be used to alleviate conflict assessment officers' analysis burdens and generate assessments as objectively as possible. Latent Semantic Analysis is a modern IR technique that allows for the calculation of the semantic similarity between words and between documents, each represented as a normalized vector in a semantic space. We have automatically analyzed a high number of news articles extracted from the EMM archive, in order to calculate the normalized vectors for each article. We have also generated the LSA signature for each root of conflict indicator, following their definition in the European Commission's checklist for root causes of conflict. Subsequently, we have computed the semantic similarity between articles, on the one hand, and root causes of conflicts, on the other hand. Thus, we generated graphs showing the importance of each root cause of conflict per country. These statistics can further be used for policy-making support and conflict assessment tasks for preventive policy.

In the next sections we present other systems for automatic analysis of conflict indicators (Section 2), a detailed description of our data source (EMM) and the methodology we used (Section 3), our results together with a study case based on African countries (Section 4), and conclusions and perspectives (Section 5). The appendix contains several figures and tables to illustrate the results.

2. CONFLICT INDICATORS AND AUTOMATIC DATA ANALYSIS FOR EARLY WARNING

Monitoring of conflicts encompasses more than early warning systems, since it can be defined as "any initiative that focuses on systematic data collection, analysis and/or formulation of recommendations, including risk assessment and information sharing, regardless of topic, whether they are quantitative, qualitative or a blend of both" (Austin 2003). An early warning system to be included in a continuous process of conflict monitoring has to achieve three main goals: (a) identify the causes of conflict, (b) predict the outbreak of conflict and, (c) mitigate that conflict (Austin 2003). Six mechanisms are associated with these goals: (i) data collection (quantitative and/or qualitative) and (ii) data analysis; (iii) assessment for warning or identification of different scenarios; (iv) formulate an action proposal, (v) transmit recommendations and (vi) assess the early response.

Our study focuses on the first goal and respectively on the first two mechanisms. The identification of root causes of conflicts requires data collection and analysis. These data represent figures or groups of figures that, when monitored over time, tell about changes in political and economic conditions of a country and are used in forecasting. These figures or groups of figures are called indicators. They can point to political, economic, social, religious, military, security or judicial issues. There are three categories of indicators: systemic - general underlying, structural, deep-rooted (e.g. economic disparity, historic oppression, high military expenditure); proximate - specific situational circumstances (e.g. increasing insecurity on streets, frequency of political arrests); triggers - electoral fraud, political assassination, new & enforced discriminatory policies (Schmid 1998). Depending on the method of collection, the indicators can be qualitative, key criteria to be taken into account in the mapping of a conflict, and quantitative, statistics-based, measurable data on given countries and situations.

We describe below two systems for event data collection and analysis. Following Austin's classification, early warning systems can be qualitative (FAST), quantitative (KEDS) or both (FAST). Qualitative systems rely on field-based analysts and use qualitative indicators, which are key dimensions in the understanding of the outbreak of a conflict. The European Commission checklist for root causes of conflicts is composed of qualitative indicators. Quantitative systems are based on the systematic collection and processing of empirical information, following given criteria.

News media have a tremendous impact on the prediction and assessment of country conflict and crisis. Event data extracted from news sources are used in quantitative analysis by reducing journalists' reports to categorical data that can be analyzed statistically (Schrodt and al. 1994). Kansas Event Data System (KEDS), developed within the department of Political Science, at the University of Kansas, is a fully operational machine coding system for generating event data from English language news reports. KEDS data is subsequently used to develop quantitative early warning indicators of political change. KEDS, which uses the Nexis database as its data source, does pattern recognition and simple linguistic parsing on the news reports in English and it identifies actors and compound syntagms in texts, associating actors and agents. Although machine coding with KEDS gave good results in comparison with a human-coded dataset (Schrodt & Gerner 1994), the system relies on the extensive use of dictionaries of proper nouns and verb phrases that need to be optimized for particular analyses, which could be time-consuming. Moreover, the KEDS system analyzes only texts in English, which could represent a drawback for a multilingual data system, such as EMM.

The FAST (early recognition of tension and fact-finding) early warning system (Schmeidl 2001), a project of the Swiss Peace Foundation, combines both qualitative (field monitoring, fact finding and expert analysis) and quantitative approaches (event data analysis). FAST's specificity is the use of event data analysis, automatic processing of data divided into "single cooperative and conflictive events" and the distinction between root causes, proximate causes and positive/negative intervention. The events collected are entered into a web-based software tool using the IDEA coding scheme (Integrated Data for Event Analysis), which is based on the WEIS (World Interaction Survey) coding scheme (Schrodt and Gerner 2000). By assigning a certain numeric value to each event according to a distinct conflict scale, FAST produces Country Risk Profiles, which are graphs representing the evolutions over time of listed indicators. Since the methods of data collection and the mathematical processing of data are highly standardized, the weak point of such a methodology lies in the bias notable in the data collection and in the process of granting a rating to a specific event.

In order to overcome the shortcomings concerning language independence and bias of the data collection, we have based our own approach on a purely numerical technique, the processing criteria being a set of qualitative indicators as defined above.

Latent Semantic Analysis is a statistical technique based on the analysis of word distributions across a corpus of documents. Latent Semantic Analysis can be thought of as representing "the meaning of a word as a kind of average of the meanings of all the passages in which it appears, and the meaning of a passage as a kind of average of the meaning of all the words it contains" (Landauer and Dumais 1997). It builds a semantic space where words and passages are represented as vectors. LSA is based on Singular Value Decomposition (SVD), a mathematical technique that causes the semantic space to be arranged so as to reflect the major associative patterns in the data.

Each document is represented as a vector within a normalized vector space derived from the eigenvectors of the initial dataset (i.e. training data). The base vectors of the space are determined by a vector algebra technique called Singular Value Decomposition (SVD) derived from the co-occurrences represented by a matrix of terms by documents.

The key point is that, for a given term or document, the information is now concentrated in the first components of the associated vector and, progressively, the later components indicate only noise and can be dropped, resulting in information compression and noise removal. It has been shown that the resulting dimensions of the description of documents and terms are analogous to the semantic features often postulated as the basis of word meaning.

The novel idea of LSA is to apply SVD to co-occurrences of words in texts, these texts being considered as "bags of words," to extract the hidden (latent) semantic content. The LSA literature indicates that it is best to keep between 200 and 300 first components. The dimensionality of the resulting vector space is of high importance. Reducing the dimensionality (i.e. the number of component vectors) of the observed data from the number of initial contexts to a much smaller number will often produce much better results.

Each document can be referenced as a 200-component vector in the semantic space. Likewise, individual keywords become linear combinations of the new component vectors. The semantics of a document or a word then becomes a direction within the new space. Documents or words pointing approximately in the same direction then are semantically related, and this will be true for a new document if it does not contain too many unknown terms.

The use of Latent Semantic Analysis offers several advantages that are of high importance for our task. LSA is a fully automatic technique, widely applicable on a variety of texts in any language. Given that the EMM corpus is highly multilingual, LSA proved most suitable for our task, as it allows for cross-language querying without the need for previous query translation.

LSA is perfectly suitable for processing very large corpora. It uses no humanly constructed dictionaries, knowledge bases, semantic networks, grammars, syntactic parsers, or morphologies, and takes as its input only raw text parsed into words defined as unique character strings and separated into meaningful passages or samples such as sentences or paragraphs. LSA uses as its initial data not just contiguous co-occurrences of words, but detailed patterns of occurrences of many words over very large numbers of meaning-bearing contexts. It ignores word order, to capture only how differences in word choice and differences in passage meanings are related.

With no human aid, LSA performs a powerful and correct induction of knowledge, by accommodating a very large number of local co-occurrence relations simultaneously in a space of the right dimensionality, hypothetically one in which there is a match of dimensionality between the semantic space of the source (i.e. training data) and that of the representation in which it is reconstructed, thereby extracting much indirect information from the multitude of entailments latently contained in the data.

3.   LSA APPLIED TO ENGLISH ARTICLES IN EMM

3.1   Europe Media Monitor

The Europe Media Monitor is the European Commission's electronic media monitoring system, which runs 24/7 scanning about 600 news web sites in 30 languages and 15 news agencies. EMM detects new articles as they are published in the world's media. Each article is retrieved and scanned against 8,000 multilingual keywords in order to classify an article into zero, one or more "Alerts." An alert consists of either weighted lists of keywords or Boolean combinations of keywords or both. About 35,000 articles are processed every day against some 600 alerts. All open source article texts are analyzed and the alerts they triggered are recorded. EMM has processed about 10 Million articles spanning over 30 months of news. In addition, hourly statistics are kept on the flux of articles for each alert and a separate Breaking News detection system monitors keywords to look for sudden increases in usage or the appearance of new keywords. EMM also provides an early warning service through email or SMS.

The block diagram below describes the basic processing chain in EMM: Scraper goes off to 1000 web sites and converts the headline pages to RSS. The alert system detects new entries in the RSS file for each news source. It then goes to the article and extracts just the textual content of the page. The text is filtered across 10,000 keywords defined in 600 alerts in 100 msec. An RSS "topic" file is maintained in real time for all the alerts. These are displayed in NewsBrief. All articles are indexed and can be searched on NewsBrief. A Breaking News system then statistically identifies the top stories in each language based on occurrences of current keywords in the news.

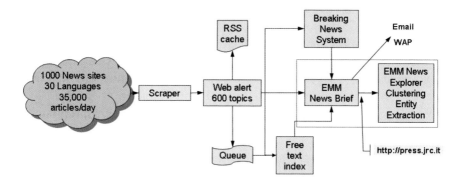

Figure 6-1. EMM processing chain

3.2 Software and System Training

When proceeding to LSA on large text collections one is faced with the need to perform the SVD of very large terms by documents' co-occurrence matrixes. To be able to process them one stores only the nonzero elements (typically 0.5 percent of the total). To perform the SVD on a matrix stored in this way hence requires specialized algorithms.

The Latent Semantic Analysis "gtp"- General Text Parser software - from the University of Tennessee, Knoxville (UTK) was obtained. To run the analysis on news articles from EMM, most of the default settings were used. Minimum length of a word was set to 2 characters. The words used in the analysis must occur at least twice in the same document (in order to be relevant) and in at least two documents (to be useful).

The reference run was performed on 18,451 articles scraped by EMM during March, April and June 2002 representing 55,900 different terms. The run provided vectors of 212 components. As this was done on news covering a wide range of topics; all of these "flash shots" together should be a comprehensive picture of the world.

Several programs (terminal-interactive and then web-based) were written which read the "terms" output of the gtp program and calculated the angular distance between two terms or the sorted n-nearest neighbors terms of a term or new text.

3.3   Artificial Topic Creation

In order to be able to measure the presence of each conflict indicator, as defined by the European Commission, in each EMM article, we have decided to represent each root cause of conflict as a vector in the LSA space. We have therefore created "artificial topics" corresponding to lists of semantically similar words, each list being associated to a root cause of conflict.

The lists of words representing the topic space (or semantic space) for each cause of conflict have been derived by using two LSA-based systems: "LSA applications" developed by the Science and Applications of Latent Semantic Analysis Group at the University of Colorado at Boulder - the system allows the selection of the topic space which is more appropriate for the input; and the system trained at the JRC, specifically on a corpus extracted from EMM.

The application used to derive the lists was "nearest neighbors." It allows for the selection of a set of n-nearest neighbor terms based on a submitted term or piece of text. The terms returned are those that are nearest the submitted term or terms, within the chosen semantic space. Every term, every text, and every novel combination of terms has a high dimensional vector representation. Comparing two terms equals comparing the cosine of the angle between the vectors representing the terms. This comparison occurs within the semantic space.

The root causes of conflicts as defined by the European Commission' DG RELEX are organized in eight main themes, each split in several sub-themes (Table 6-1). The eight main themes are: legitimacy of the state, rule of law, respect for fundamental rights, civil society and media, relations between communities and dispute-solving mechanisms, sound economic management, social and regional inequalities, geopolitical situation. The definition of each root cause of conflict represented the input for the two LSA systems. The output consisted of a list of the n terms most semantically similar to the input terms, within the given topic space (example list Appendix 2). Figure 2 shows the creation of the topic spaces. The output lists included a number of named entities (names of places, including country names, people, organizations), which were subsequently eliminated from the list, in order to avoid time and location dependency.

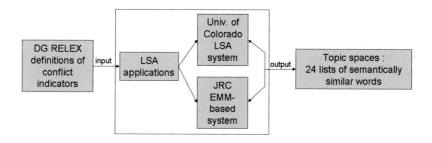

Figure 6-2. Topic space creation

Twenty-four word lists, corresponding to the twenty-four sub-themes, have been generated, each containing several hundred words. The initially generated lists were longer, but they were cut when the word relevance became fuzzy. The subsequent identification of the root causes of conflicts as they can be measured from the EMM news articles is based on the measurement of the semantic similarity that exists between these artificially created topics and the text of each new article. An example of the word list used for "External Threats" is given in the Appendix.

Table 6-1. The 8 themes and associated 24 sub-themes

Theme	Category	Category	Category	Category
Geopolitical Instability	External Threat	Regional Instability		
Legitimacy Deficit	Rejection of State Authority	Widespread Corruption	Checks & Balances	Exclusive Power
Poor Economic Management	Economic Dependence	Macroeco-nomic Instability	Environmental Degradation	
Rule of Law	Unlawful State Violence	Weak Judicial System	Uncontrolled Security Forces	Widespread Organized Crime
Socio-economic and Regional Inequality	Neglected Social Welfare	Regional Disparities	Social Inequalities	
Tension between Communities	Public Arbitration	Tension between Groups	Migration generates tension	
Violations of Fundamental Rights	Religious & Cultural Rights	Civil & Political Freedom	Basic Rights	
Weak Civil Society	Press Freedom	Ineffective Civil Society		

3.4   EMM Article Signature

The signature of an English article is defined as its 212 dimensional vector in the normalized vector space identified in the LSA analysis described above. The texts of close to 300,000 English articles in the EMM archive from mid-March until the end of May 2004 have been analyzed to calculate the component vectors for each article.

The signatures for each root cause of conflict indicator have likewise been identified with 212 component vectors, calculated using the keyword lists shown in the Appendix. Therefore each indicator represents a unique direction in the LSA space.

3.5   Similarity Calculation

The article indicator proximity value is defined as the vector DOT product between a given article-normalized vector and the indicator-normalized vector. The DOT product is simply the cosine of the angle between the two vectors (in the 212 dimension space).

The defined angle cosine cutoff has been studied by varying the cutoff between 0.5, 0.6 and 0.7 and then manually comparing the resultant article relevancy to the indicator concerned. A value of 0.5 gave 70% relevance, 0.6 gave 80% relevance and 0.7 gave 95% relevance. A cutoff of 0.7 (95% relevance) is used for the results presented here.

For each indicator the articles were further divided by country alert. Countries mentioned most with respect to a given root cause of conflict will score higher. Some countries like the USA are always in the news. Therefore a normalized indicator was calculated in addition to simple article counts. The normalized indicator is simply the number of articles in a given indicator divided by the total number of articles in any indicator. This reflects the relative importance of a particular indicator for that country.

A few indicators were rejected because the population of articles was too low, with the 0.7 cutoff. For an indicator to be significant, at least 3 countries had to have more than 5 articles each. The indicators "Basic Rights," "Ineffective Civil Society," "Migration Generates Tension," "Neglected Social Welfare," "Social Inequalities," "Unlawful State Violence," and "Widespread Organized Crime" were excluded for this reason.

4.   RESULTS AND DISCUSSION

The results for the conflict indicators can be presented in three ways.

The first is simply the numbers of articles detected for each country falling into each of the twelve categories. However, this overemphasizes countries that are always in the news such as the USA. Given that the results of this data processing are subsequently meant to be used by policy-makers for decisions in the field of security, the results of our analysis have been normalized in different ways. This normalization produced two kinds of statistical indicators, which are described below. Other different indicators could be calculated, according to the needs and requirements of policy-makers and foreign policy specialists.

The first statistical indicator – Irel – was calculated to show the relative importance of a given conflict indicator with regard to all the other indicators for a given country. Let Ni be the number of articles for a given country in category I and Na be the total number for that country in any of the categories. The first indicator Irel is defined as the fraction Ni/Na which measures the relative weight (importance) for category I for the given country.

For the second indicator – Iabs - the normalization takes into account the overall reporting level for that country. If Ntot is the total number of articles published during the period on any subject but referring to the given country, then this indicator Iabs is defined as (Ni/Ntot)*1000. For practical reasons, the indicator is scaled by 1000 to give results near to unity. Therefore numbers greater than one correspond to more than one article in a thousand, which shows the importance of that particular indicator.

Table 6-2 gives example values for the Irel and Table 6-3 gives example values for Iabs. All countries in the world with more than five articles in at least one category are listed in each table. These lists of countries are entirely generated by statistics, and there is no manual selection.

The results for some indicators are displayed graphically in Figures 6-3 to 6-8. For each indicator both the numbers of articles per country AND the normalized indicator importance per country are displayed. The total number of articles represents a measure of the media coverage for that country regarding the relevant indicator, whereas the index represents the relative importance of the indicator for that country with respect to all other indicators.

The advantage of the LSA analysis is that it is a fully automatic method to identify countries at risk of conflict. This enables cross-country comparisons. Some clear patterns are visible in the results. The importance of root cause indicators in conflict areas in the Middle East and Africa are rather different. The Middle East emphasizes the Religious and Group tensions, whereas Africa emphasizes the Economic and External Threats (Figures 6-9 to 6-12 in Appendix 1).

4.1   A Study Case: High-risk African Countries

The results concerning some African countries - the Democratic Republic of Congo, Chad, Sudan, Rwanda, Uganda, Burundi, Benin – reveal interesting facts. We have analyzed these results and tried to relate them to the facts and data described in risk assessments reports corresponding to these countries for the given period (April-May 2004).

- Central and East Africa is a region of serious concern, as armed conflicts involving the Democratic Republic of Congo and the Republic of Congo, as well as Sudan, Chad, Burundi, Rwanda and Uganda have destabilized the region, due to the large number of refugees and the increased military spending. Our results (Tables 6-2 and Figures 6-3 and 6-4) show that Burundi and Uganda have high scores for External Threat and Rejection of State Authority.
- **Geopolitical instability** - Rwandan troops briefly entered Burundi on April 22nd to chase DRC-based Hutu rebels. The Sudanese refugees regard Chad as a sanctuary. Many armed conflicts have reportedly taken place between the Rwandan rebels and the DRC troops in April and May 2004.
- Burundi, Rwanda and Uganda on the one hand and the Democratic Republic of Congo, Congo and Sudan on the other hand, all have a high risk overall assessment, as, following the reports, they all had high or very high risk composite scores for history of armed conflict and governance and political instability.

Table 6-2. Irel and Iabs for Burundi and Uganda

Conflict Indicator	External Threat		Rejection of State Authority	
Country	Burundi	Uganda	Burundi	Uganda
Irel	0.407	0.129	0.852	0.355
Iabs	6.88	1.18	14.38	3.24

- **Rejection of state authority** – our figures show high scoring for Burundi, Uganda and Tanzania. As reported in the news, the Burundi Hutu FNL rebel group offered on April 22nd, 2004 to cease attacks on government forces and enter into negotiations, hoping for international community support. But the government later clashed with FNL and the conflict worsened. In Uganda, President Museveni offered a ceasefire to Lords Resistance Army (LRA) rebels on April 15th, 2004 if they agreed to peace talks - but said military strikes against LRA would continue until such agreement.

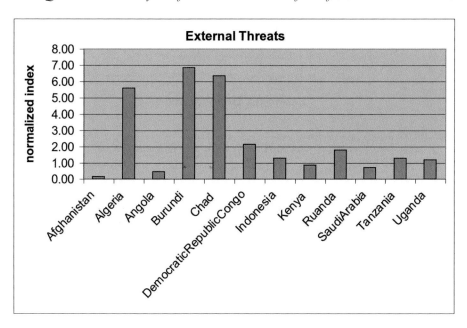

Figure 6-3. The countries with the largest "External Threats" absolute indexes

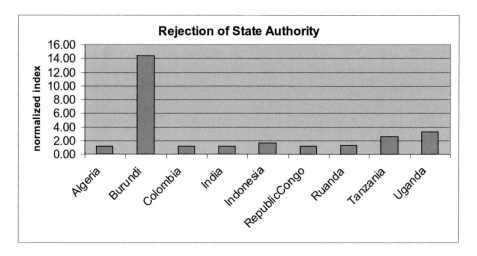

Figure 6-4. Countries with the largest absolute indicator for "Rejection of State Authority"

- **Economic dependence** - Figure 6-5 shows that Burkina Faso scored highly for economic dependence. Benin, Kenya and Chad also had scores ranging from medium to high overall risk, partly due to poor and unequal economic development.

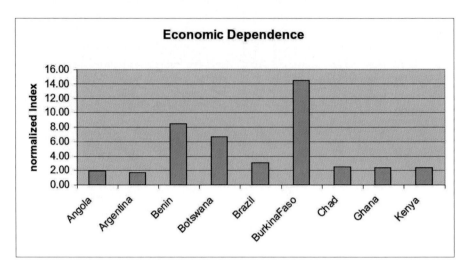

Figure 6-5. Countries with the highest absolute value of the indicator "Economic Dependence"

With a poor infrastructure and widespread poverty, Burkina Faso's economy is extremely fragile. As a result Burkina Faso (which scored 14.38 in the Iabs table) has accrued a heavy external current account deficit and is extremely dependent on external assistance. The economy of Benin (8.46 for Iabs) remains underdeveloped and dependent on subsistence agriculture. The country has a high amount of demographic and environmental stress and poor economic performance. Kenya and Chad scored less than the previous two (Kenya – 2.36 and Chad – 2.42): Kenya is on an improving trend for GDT per capita and inflation although the exchange rates are worsening and Chad has been sited as one of the poorest economies in the world, but progress in the oil sector is changing this position.

Table 6-3. Iabs for "Economic Dependence" for some African countries

	Iabs
Burkina Faso	14.38
Benin	8.46
Chad	2.42
Kenya	2.36

- **Weak judicial system** – Figure 6-6 shows that Tanzania and Zambia scored highly for weak judiciary (2.17 and 2.22). In Tanzania, the major risks to investments arise from incidents of corruption in the judiciary; lawbreakers see little risk of getting caught and punished, while much of the appropriate legislation essential to combating transnational organized crime has not yet been passed or is ineffective. In Zambia, the judicial system lacks the capacity to cope competently with the proliferation of litigation and cases and is constrained by a diminishing physical capacity in terms of courtroom space and a critical shortage of judges and magistrates to expeditiously dispense justice.

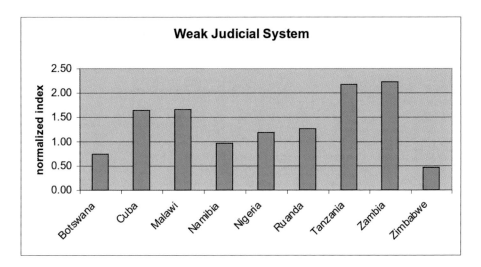

Figure 6-6. Countries with the highest absolute value for the indicator "Weak Judicial System"

One question is why ongoing conflicts like Iraq are not scoring higher for the absolute normalized index. The reason for this is that there is a much larger volume of news in general mentioning Iraq, and the normalization suppresses ongoing conflicts. The index tends to enhance other countries at risk, rather than the well known ones. It would be possible to redress this by plotting article numbers. Figures 6-7 and 6-8 show raw article distributions for External Threats and Tension between Groups.

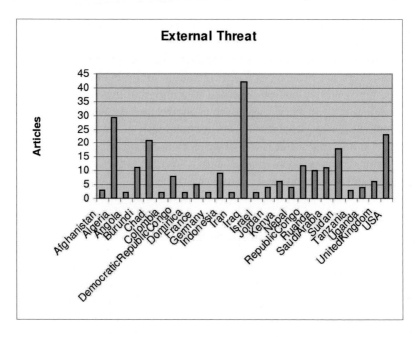

Figure 6-7. Raw article numbers for "External Threat." Note that here both Iraq and USA score high, but not in the absolute normalized indexes.

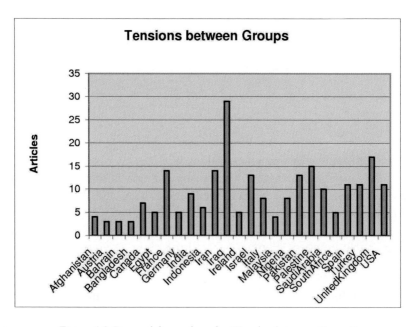

Figure 6-8. Raw article numbers for "Tension between Groups"

5.   CONCLUSIONS AND FUTURE WORK

In this paper we have used a statistical method – Latent Semantic Analysis – to measure conflict indicators – as defined by RELEX and Carleton University – in news articles extracted from EMM. Artificial topics have represented the starting point for the procedure; the identification of the indicators was based on the measurement of the semantic similarity that exists between the artificially created topics and the text of each news article. We have listed the results obtained and have shown, through a study case, that the figures concerning conflict-prone countries could be mapped to the data that can be found in risk assessment reports from a variety of national and international research organizations.

Nevertheless, work remains to be done with regards to the accuracy of the method and the language and news sources coverage, which would allow for a more balanced and accurate distribution of results across countries and themes. It is also important to note that country coverage is essential for the usefulness of the analysis, as data collections may mirror the perception that journalists from countries with developed media production capabilities have of the situation. We can suspect that more precise artificial topic definitions would score more valuable results (e.g. a clearer distinction between internal and external threats and, more generally, clearer differentiation between the levels of conflict risk for given countries).

This initial LSA study is only in English and therefore it could be argued that a fairer comparison would cover all languages. Work is currently underway to generalize the LSA analysis to work in any language. Similar articles on any subject will point in the same direction even in languages the reader cannot understand. Therefore a large improvement in statistics and viewpoint coverage can be expected.

This work has identified countries with high normalized values for each of the main root cause of conflict indicators. This analysis assumes that news reports in English reflect the real situation in each of the countries and that the relative importance depends on the relative numbers of articles as a fraction of the total in each category.

This initial study used a very tight criteria for article similarity to each of the conflict indicators, namely cosine >0.7 giving high accuracy but few articles. Loosening the criteria to 0.6 will result in many more articles, but more or less the same overall picture. EMM will soon have an operational LSA analysis running in all languages. Therefore this analysis can be automated in the future to give near continuous monitoring of these conflict indicators and other general purpose indicators.

REFERENCES

Austin, A. (2003). "Early Warning and The Field: A Cargo Cult Science?" Berghof Research Center for Constructive Conflict Management.

Best, C.; van der Goot, Erik; de Paola, Monica; Garcia, Teofilo; & Horby, David (2002). "Europe Media Monitor – EMM." *JRC Technical Note* No. I.02.88. http://press.jrc.it/NewsBrief/

Carleton University, Country Indicators for Foreign Policy, http://www.carleton.ca/cifp/about.htm

Carment, D. (2001). "Assessing Country Risk: Creating an Index of Severity," Background Discussion Paper prepared for CIFP Risk Assessment Template, Carleton University.

Coplin, W.D. and O'Leary, M, editors (1994). *The Handbook of Country and Political Risk Analysis.* 2nd ed., East Syracuse, NY: Political Risk Services.

Delany C., Varga, S. (2002). Country Risk Assessment Report. Sub-Sahara Africa, Risk Assessments, Country Indicators for Foreign Policy, Carleton University.

European Commission CheckList for Root Causes of Conflict, available at http://europa.eu.int/comm/external_relations/cpcm/cp/list.htm

Fischer, M. and Wils, O. (2003). "Ploughing Through the Field: An Introduction to the PCIA Handbook Debate," in A. Austin, M. Fischer and O. Wils (ed.), *Peace and Conflict Impact Assessment. Critical Views on Theory and Practice*, Berghof Handbook.

Gerner, D. and Schrodt, Philip A. (1998). "The Effects of Media Coverage on Crisis Assessment and Early Warning in the Middle East," *in* Schmeidl, Susanne; Adelman, Howard, *Early Warning and Early Response*. New York: Columbia International Affairs Online, 1998.

Gotoh,Y. and Renals, S. (1997.) "Document Space Models Using Latent Semantic Analysis." In *Proc. Eurospeech*, pages 1443-1446, Rhodes, 1997.

Landauer T K, & Dumais, S T (1997) A Solution to Plato's Problem: The Latent Semantic Analysis Theory of the Acquisition, Induction, and Representation of Knowledge. *Psychological Review*, 104, 211-240.

Landauer T K, Foltz, P W, & Laham, D (1998) Introduction to Latent Semantic Analysis. *Discourse Processes*, 25, 259-284

Schmeidl S (2001) Early Warning and Integrated Response Development (Paper prepared for the Inter-regional Forum on Coping with Crises and Conflicts, Bucharest)

Schmid A (1998) Thesaurus and glossary of early warning and conflict prevention terms, (abridged version). London, Fewer. Available at: www.womenwarpeace.org/issues/prevention/docs/thes.pdf

Schrodt, Philip A. and Deborah J. Gerner (2000). *Analyzing International Event Data: A Handbook of Computer Based Techniques.*

Schrodt, Philip A., Shannon G. Davis and Judith L. Weddle (1994). "Political Science: KEDS – A Program for the Machine Coding of Event Data," *Social Science Computer Review* 12,3: 561-588

Schrodt, Philip A. and Deborah J. Gerner (1994). "Validity Assessment of a Machine-Coded Event Data Set for the Middle East, 1982-1992," *American Journal of Political Science* 38:825-854

University of Colorado at Boulder, "Latent Semantic Analysis @ CU Boulder," available at http://lsa.colorado.edu

University of Tennessee, Department of Computer Science, "General Text Parser," available at http://www.cs.utk.edu/~lsi/

SUGGESTED READINGS

- William D. Coplin and Michael K. O'Leary, editors (1994). *The Handbook of Country and Political Risk Analysis*. Second Edition, East Syracuse, NY: Political Risk Services
- *Berghof Handbook for Conflict Transformation*: http://www.berghof-handbook.net/general_intro.htm
- Landauer, T. K., Foltz, P. W., & Laham, D. (1998). "Introduction to Latent Semantic Analysis." *Discourse Processes*, 25, 259-284

ONLINE RESOURCES

- Europe Media:
  http://press.jrc.it/NewsBrief
- Early warning program:
  http://www.swisspeace.org/fast/default.htm
- International Crisis Group:
  http://www.icg.org/home/index.cfm
- Country Risk Assessment:
  http://www.times-publications.com/risk-assesment/risk-assesment.html
- SIPRI Early Warning Indicators Database:
  http://www.sipri.org/contents/it/db/db2/
- Country indicators for foreign policy: briefs and reports:
  http://www.carleton.ca/cifp/risk.htm:
- Latent Semantic Analysis @ CU Boulder, USA:
  http://lsa.colorado.edu

DISCUSSION QUESTIONS

1. Discuss quantitative and qualitative indicators with respect to objectivity and subjectivity.
2. Can manual filtering of the word lists improve results? To what extent?
3. Please comment on the importance of the word lists and how their length can influence the results.
4. How would you describe the importance of bias in news reports from Western countries? Discuss news sources and language coverage.
5. Discuss how the choice of indicators used for analysis influences or has an effect on the realistic description of the situation in countries at risk. Your discussion should include the following subtopics: importance of historic, present and future indicators; indicators reflective only of the

current phase of the conflict; and the indicators' importance in terms of facts and perceptions.

APPENDICES

APPENDIX 1: TABLES

Table 6-4. Irel Results. This measures the relative significance for each country of the named root cause of conflict

Country	Econ. Depend.	External Threat	Regional Instability	Rejection of State Authority	Tension between Groups	Weak Judicial System
Afghanistan	0.000	0.070	0.023	0.000	0.093	0.000
Algeria	0.000	0.518	0.000	0.107	0.000	0.000
Angola	0.500	0.125	0.000	0.000	0.000	0.000
Antarctica	0.000	0.000	0.000	0.000	0.000	0.000
Azerbaijan	0.000	0.000	0.000	0.000	0.000	0.000
Bahrain	0.000	0.000	0.000	0.000	0.600	0.200
Bangladesh	0.000	0.000	0.000	0.000	0.107	0.000
Benin	0.846	0.000	0.000	0.000	0.000	0.000
Botswana	0.643	0.000	0.000	0.000	0.000	0.071
BurkinaFaso	0.920	0.000	0.000	0.040	0.000	0.000
Burundi	0.000	0.407	0.000	0.852	0.000	0.000
Cameroon	0.000	0.000	0.000	0.000	0.000	0.000
Central African Rep.	0.000	0.000	0.000	0.000	0.000	0.000
Chad	0.242	0.636	0.000	0.000	0.000	0.000
China	0.297	0.000	0.000	0.021	0.000	0.007
Colombia	0.250	0.100	0.000	0.250	0.000	0.000
Comoros	0.000	0.000	0.000	0.000	0.000	0.000
Costa Rica	0.000	0.000	0.000	0.000	0.000	0.000
Cuba	0.000	0.000	0.000	0.000	0.000	0.333
Dem. Rep. Congo	0.172	0.276	0.000	0.103	0.000	0.000
Eritrea	0.000	0.000	0.000	0.000	0.000	0.000
Ghana	0.538	0.000	0.000	0.000	0.000	0.000
Greenland	0.000	0.000	0.000	0.000	0.000	0.000
Guam	0.000	0.000	0.000	0.000	0.000	0.000
Guinea	0.000	0.000	0.000	0.125	0.000	0.000
India	0.194	0.000	0.000	0.184	0.087	0.039
Iran	0.100	0.040	0.040	0.020	0.280	0.000
Iraq	0.000	0.307	0.029	0.007	0.212	0.095
Israel	0.000	0.063	0.000	0.000	0.406	0.000
IvoryCoast	0.000	0.000	0.000	0.286	0.000	0.000
Kenya	0.459	0.162	0.000	0.000	0.000	0.000
Kuwait	0.000	0.000	0.286	0.000	0.000	0.000

Country	Econ. Depend.	External Threat	Regional Instability	Rejection of State Authority	Tension between Groups	Weak Judicial System
Lebanon	0.000	0.000	0.000	0.000	0.000	0.000
Malaysia	0.000	0.000	0.000	0.063	0.250	0.000
Namibia	0.000	0.000	0.000	0.000	0.000	0.051
Nepal	0.000	0.087	0.000	0.826	0.000	0.000
Nigeria	0.000	0.000	0.000	0.011	0.088	0.143
Pakistan	0.000	0.000	0.000	0.250	0.271	0.063
Palestine	0.000	0.000	0.000	0.000	0.556	0.000
Republic of Congo	0.000	0.316	0.000	0.184	0.000	0.000
Ruanda	0.000	0.345	0.000	0.241	0.000	0.241
Russia	0.000	0.000	0.000	0.014	0.000	0.000
SaudiArabia	0.000	0.289	0.053	0.000	0.263	0.000
SouthAfrica	0.000	0.000	0.000	0.000	0.034	0.034
Sudan	0.000	0.750	0.000	0.042	0.000	0.000
Syria	0.000	0.000	0.273	0.000	0.000	0.000
Tanzania	0.000	0.115	0.000	0.231	0.000	0.192
Uganda	0.000	0.129	0.000	0.355	0.000	0.000
USA	0.000	0.087	0.019	0.015	0.042	0.034
Yemen	0.000	0.000	0.000	0.000	0.000	0.063
Zambia	0.000	0.000	0.000	0.000	0.000	0.111

Table 6-5. Iabs Results. This measures the absolute significance of the named root cause of conflict. Values greater than 1.0 mean that more than 1 article per thousand articles on any subject strongly (LSA similarity>0.7) concerns that category

Country	Econ. Depend.	External Threat	Regional Instability	Rejection of State Authority	Tension between Groups	Weak Judicial System
Afghanistan	0.00	0.13	0.04	0.00	0.17	0.00
Algeria	0.00	5.58	0.00	1.15	0.00	0.00
Angola	1.86	0.47	0.00	0.00	0.00	0.00
Azerbaijan	0.00	0.00	0.00	0.00	0.00	0.00
Bahrain	0.00	0.00	0.00	0.00	0.71	0.24
Bangladesh	0.00	0.00	0.00	0.00	1.15	0.00
Benin	8.46	0.00	0.00	0.00	0.00	0.00
Botswana	6.67	0.00	0.00	0.00	0.00	0.74
Burkina Faso	14.38	0.00	0.00	0.63	0.00	0.00
Burundi	0.00	6.88	0.00	14.38	0.00	0.00
Cameroon	0.00	0.00	0.00	0.00	0.00	0.00
Central African Rep.	0.00	0.00	0.00	0.00	0.00	0.00
Chad	2.42	6.36	0.00	0.00	0.00	0.00
China	1.30	0.00	0.00	0.09	0.00	0.03
Colombia	1.14	0.45	0.00	1.14	0.00	0.00
Comoros	0.00	0.00	0.00	0.00	0.00	0.00
Costa Rica	0.00	0.00	0.00	0.00	0.00	0.00
Cuba	0.00	0.00	0.00	0.00	0.00	1.64

Country	Econ. Depend.	External Threat	Regional Instability	Rejection of State Authority	Tension between Groups	Weak Judicial System
Dem. Rep. Congo	1.35	2.16	0.00	0.81	0.00	0.00
Eritrea	0.00	0.00	0.00	0.00	0.00	0.00
Ghana	2.41	0.00	0.00	0.00	0.00	0.00
Greenland	0.00	0.00	0.00	0.00	0.00	0.00
Guam	0.00	0.00	0.00	0.00	0.00	0.00
Guinea	0.00	0.00	0.00	0.48	0.00	0.00
India	1.18	0.00	0.00	1.12	0.53	0.24
Iran	0.26	0.11	0.11	0.05	0.74	0.00
Iraq	0.00	0.26	0.03	0.01	0.18	0.08
Israel	0.00	0.06	0.00	0.00	0.38	0.00
Ivory Coast	0.00	0.00	0.00	0.63	0.00	0.00
Kenya	2.36	0.83	0.00	0.00	0.00	0.00
Kuwait	0.00	0.00	0.29	0.00	0.00	0.00
Lebanon	0.00	0.00	0.00	0.00	0.00	0.00
Malaysia	0.00	0.00	0.00	0.18	0.71	0.00
Namibia	0.00	0.00	0.00	0.00	0.00	0.95
Nepal	0.00	2.50	0.00	23.75	0.00	0.00
Nigeria	0.00	0.00	0.00	0.09	0.73	1.18
Pakistan	0.00	0.00	0.00	0.75	0.81	0.19
Palestine	0.00	0.00	0.00	0.00	0.94	0.00
Republic Congo	0.00	2.00	0.00	1.17	0.00	0.00
Rwanda	0.00	1.82	0.00	1.27	0.00	1.27
Russia	0.00	0.00	0.00	0.02	0.00	0.00
Saudi Arabia	0.00	0.71	0.13	0.00	0.65	0.00
South Africa	0.00	0.00	0.00	0.00	0.27	0.27
Sudan	0.00	3.00	0.00	0.17	0.00	0.00
Syria	0.00	0.00	0.46	0.00	0.00	0.00
Tanzania	0.00	1.30	0.00	2.61	0.00	2.17
Uganda	0.00	1.18	0.00	3.24	0.00	0.00
USA	0.00	0.19	0.04	0.03	0.09	0.08
Yemen	0.00	0.00	0.00	0.00	0.00	0.24
Zambia	0.00	0.00	0.00	0.00	0.00	2.22
Zimbabwe	0.00	0.00	0.00	0.00	0.00	0.47

APPENDIX 2: CONFLICT INDICATORS

1. Civil and Political
2. Economic Dependence
3. Environment Degradation
4. External Threat
5. Macroeconomic Stability
6. Press Freedom

6. Public Arbitration
7. Regional Instability
8. Rejection of State Authority
9. Religious and Cultural Rights
10. Tension between Groups
11. Weak Judicial System

APPENDIX 3: FIGURES

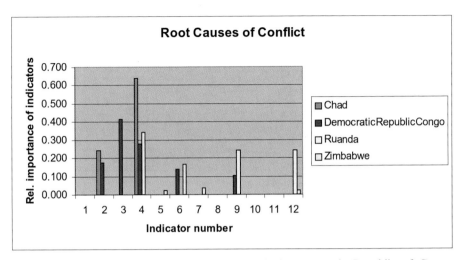

Figure 6-9. Relative importance of indicators: Chad, Democratic Republic of Congo, Rwanda, Zimbabwe

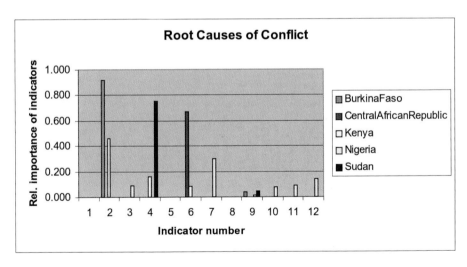

Figure 6-10. Relative importance of indicators: Burkina Faso, Central African Republic, Kenya, Nigeria, Sudan

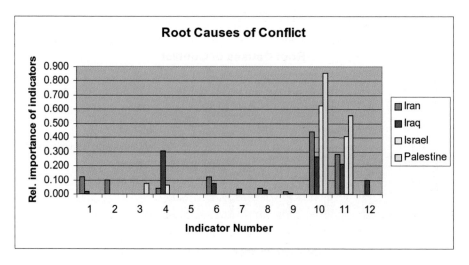

Figure 6-11. Relative importance of indicators: Iran, Iraq, Israel, Palestine

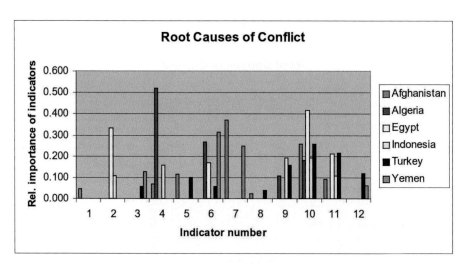

Figure 6-12. Relative importance of indicators: other Islamic countries

APPENDIX 4: WORD LISTS

An example of the word lists used to define each root cause of conflict indicator. This is a partial word list for "External Threats." It was developed using LSA itself as described in the text.

abuse	compromise	force	oust
abused	conspiracy	forces	ouster
abuses	conspirators	foreign	perpetrate
abusive	conspiration	front	perpetrated
aggressor	conspire	fuel	political
aggressors	contrary	fuelled	politicizes
ammunition	counter	government	predate
arm	countered	governments	predated
armed	coup	grenades	propaganda
arming	coups	guerrillas	punitive
arms	damage	gun	rebel
army	damaged	guns	rebellion
artillery	defeat	hostile	rebels
assassinate	defeated	hostilities	regime
assassinated	defence	illegal	regimes
assassination	defensive	illegitimacy	reject
assassinations	destabilize	illegitimate	rejection
atrocities	destabilized	illicit	revolution
atrocity	destabilizes	imposed	revolutionary
attack	diplomatic	impunity	right
attacked	disloyal	income	rights
attacks	disloyalty	independence	rival
baffle	dissent	inquisitive	rivals
baffles	dissenter	insurgency	rulers
barrages	dissidents	insurgents	salvation
beheaded	enclave	massacre	separatism
billet	enclaves	massacres	separatist
billeted	ethnic	mercenaries	separatists
blacklisted	execute	militants	soldier
bombing	executed	militarized	soldiers
bomb	execution	military	strategic
bombs	external	militia	strategically
casualties	extortion	militias	tactics
casualty	extremism	mines	target
cell	extremist	munition	targets
cells	extremists	munitions	territorial
civil	faction	neighbor	terror
civilian	factions	neighbors	terrorism
civilians	fiefdoms	opponent	terrorist
coalition	finance	opponents	terrorists
combatant	financed	oppose	threat
combatants	financial	opposed	threats
command	flee	opposing	thwart
commanders	follower	opposition	thwart

7

COUNTERING TERRORISM WITH KNOWLEDGE

James O. Ellis III
Memorial Institute for the Prevention of Terrorism, Oklahoma City, Oklahoma, U.S.A.
(ellis@mipt.org)

CHAPTER OVERVIEW

The study of terrorism is beset by many problems, ranging from the broad and dynamic nature of the phenomenon, the arrested development of applied research, and the disconnected databases covering the subject. The Memorial Institute for the Prevention of Terrorism (MIPT) seeks to enable better research on terrorism by developing and sharing pioneering information resources, including its Terrorism Knowledge Base. MIPT acts as a living memorial to the victims, survivors, rescuers, and family members of the bombing of the Alfred P. Murrah Federal Building in Oklahoma City on April 19, 1995. Serving the needs of emergency responders, counterterrorism practitioners, policymakers, and the public, MIPT conducts research into the social and political causes and effects of terrorism, and its mission is to expand and share knowledge to prevent terrorism or mitigate its effects.

1.   INTRODUCTION

In the information age, fighting terrorism means sharing knowledge. Simply sharing information is not enough; researchers must take stock of what we already know, build upon it, and develop credible and relevant policy recommendations to help manage the threat. Despite nearly four decades of research on terrorism, only now is the stage being set to help move this field of study into a more rigorous and revelatory discipline within the modern social sciences. Why do terrorism studies appear to have lagged behind other scholarly pursuits? A great deal of this arrested development stems from the problematic nature of the subject itself and the slow manner in which the field has evolved.

2.   PROBLEMS IN RESEARCHING TERRORISM

Terrorism is a difficult research subject. It is not a "homogenous activity;" the associated actors and activities vary widely over time and across the globe [17]. There is no universally accepted definition of terrorism and even when people agree on a definition, they sometimes disagree about whether or not the definition fits a particular incident or group. Placing terrorist activity within its larger political context can be challenging, as it often appears amongst other forms of violence during times of interstate war, rebellion, civil war, occupation, and military intervention [15]. Collecting data on terrorism can be trying, and the information is often imperfect. Determining who has perpetrated an act, whether a claim is credible, and if the attributed motives qualify it as a terrorist incident often bedevil even the most earnest of investigators [3, 10]. Likewise, the impact of these threats and violence usually go well beyond the immediate victims, nations, and regions in which they occur [2]. Terrorists typically do not control territory, wear uniforms, carry their weapons openly, function in discernable formations, or maintain permanent bases. Clearly, terrorism is not "a simple phenomenon with easy explanations and direct solutions" [17].

Changes in the nature of terrorism over the last fifteen years have made observing it more complex. In the heyday of the 1970s and 1980s, terrorist organizations consisted of a core, elite vanguard that conducted the violence, a more moderate, political wing, and a wider support network of fundraisers, volunteers, front groups, and safe house suppliers. Terrorist groups learned that it is easy to disable groups formed into corporate-style organizations with discernable power structures. Many groups now depend less on formal leadership and no longer maintain traditional hierarchies. This, in turn, requires less frequent communications and makes them much more difficult to spot, track, and intercept. Claims of responsibility for terrorist acts have also declined sharply [15]. Though traditional terrorist organizations still commit the majority of terrorist attacks using the standard tactics of bombing, assassination, armed assault, kidnapping, hostage-taking, and hijackings, other groups and individuals are increasingly responsible for terrorist violence and innovations. The classic conceptual model of recognizable, restrained, tightly-knit, professional, political organizations with clear aims appears to be breaking down in favor of groups and individuals with more varied and hazy objectives, shorter life spans, and a greater interest in violence for its own sake. Terrorism is increasingly perpetrated by amateurs and splinter groups, deemphasizing the organizational and ideological aspects of terrorism in favor of short-term interests and planning.

Terrorist organizations have changed in size and structure. Though the number of groups has risen sharply, the number of members per group has dropped. The cost-effective nature of free-floating cells has rendered formal state support unnecessary. Many groups have moved toward a networked organizational structure, opting for highly decentralized decision-making and more local initiative and autonomy. Networks can be much more difficult to visualize, because they have fluid organization and infrastructure. When fighting a terrorist network, usually only small portions can be revealed and confronted at one time, presenting itself as a group of more or less autonomous, dispersed entities linked by advanced communications and perhaps nothing more than a common purpose. A network may simply absorb a number of attacks on its distributed nodes, leading observers to believe it has been harmed and rendered inoperable when, in fact, it remains viable and is seeking new opportunities for tactical surprise. Analytically, it is difficult to predict the proliferation of amateur terrorists and ad hoc cells of like-minded individuals seeking to conduct do-it-yourself warfare, briefly joining forces for come-as-you-are attacks and then disbanding.

The shrinking size and organizational self-sufficiency of non-state terrorist groups limit their financial traces and the size of their footprint. The plans, motivations, and preferred targets of small terrorist organizations are less transparent than those with an established reputation and constituency. Lone zealots do not offer communications to intercept nor co-conspirators to capture for information about upcoming operations. Experts across academia, business, and government sectors have indicated that terrorism is becoming more amorphous, more complex, more sporadic, more amateurish, more difficult to predict, more difficult to trace, and more difficult to observe and analyze. Researchers and analysts require new methods and tools to help them make sense of such a complex threat environment.

3.   PROBLEMS IN TERRORISM RESEARCH

Terrorism studies was born an academic orphan with no midwife. It grew up in the "cracks and crevices which lie between the large academic disciplines" [17]; its foster parents were the schools of political science, history, psychology, sociology, anthropology, communications, criminology, law, economics, philosophy, and military science [18]. This interdisciplinary background has pushed terrorism research beyond the bounds of a single discipline, but it has also bred theoretical confusion [6]. With little consensus on concepts and typologies, there has been no clear home for terrorism studies in the academic literature. The literature of terrorism comprises dispersed and uncoordinated publications, with little distinction between the popular and the scientific, and evidence of "a very small core and a very large periphery" [4]. The absence of a large body of dedicated researchers has led to a lack of rigorous analysis and a focus on simple and seismic fluctuations in the phenomenon on terrorism. Several have noted that much of the published literature comes from transients – "researchers out for a once-off publication and who have no real interest in making a substantial contribution to the field" [16]. This is aided and abetted by the "aperiodic increase in attention paid to terrorism by the media, educators, and policymakers" [10].

Though the field of terrorism studies has roots back to the late 1960s, it has not matured as rapidly as it should have, due to a lack of data access, inhibited empiricism, and inadequate analytical tools. Terrorist organizations are notoriously difficult research subjects, as they usually operate covertly and are averse to exposing their organizational inner workings and leadership structure. Terrorists are rarely accessible for social scientific research on their group and individual dynamics, and data on their organizations is often classified [6]. Consequently, one of the best remaining options for studying these organizations and activities is by examining their exploits in the press and government reports. However, this has led to an over-reliance on secondary and state-produced material.

Prior to the 1970s, most terrorism research presented case studies on particular groups and individuals. Unlike modern social scientists, most terrorism scholars still shy away from statistical and comparative research, opting for qualitative rather than quantitative analyses. Some have observed that the "majority of research on terrorism has been marked by theoretical generalizations based upon a lack of hard data" [8]. The majority of researchers depend entirely on data produced by others [16]. Part of this is because the cost of compiling and acquiring data is prohibitive. Still, many investigators are reluctant to share data, and most researchers try to "exhaust the utility of their datasets... and publish as much as possible from them until they make them public if they do so at all" [13].

Much of the earliest scholarship and data collection on terrorism, especially within the United States, focused almost exclusively on international terrorism – terrorism involving the citizens of more than one country. However, international terrorism only accounts for about one tenth of all recorded terrorist incidents [15]. This means much of the study of terrorism has blinded itself to up to ninety percent of its occurrence in the world. It is highly questionable to attempt to generalize about all terrorist behavior from trends seen in international incidents [10]. Indeed, the much described decline in the incidence of international terrorism over the last two decades does not appear to hold true when one combines this with domestic terrorism [15]. This type of international terrorism myopia often makes for unusual situations, such as when the National Counterterrorism Center was forced to count one of two Russian suicide plane bombings (simply because the flight included an Israeli citizen) but not the other.

Since 9/11, terrorism research has increased dramatically but it often appears ahistorical, ignoring the literature and data from previous decades. Little research has looked at actual terrorist events [17]. Much of the current policy, research, and debate on terrorism does not examine what terrorists have actually been doing over the last four decades. While it is healthy and necessary to question pre-9/11 scholarship, perhaps even "wip[ing] the slate clean of the conventional wisdom on terrorists and terrorism" [5], we do ourselves a disservice by ignoring our intellectual forebears. Furthermore, we must work to supply a burgeoning crop of new terrorism specialists and counterterrorism professionals with the data and tools they need to understand this subject as never before.

4. PROBLEMS IN TERRORISM DATABASES

In most social sciences, data is the coin of the realm. Since the 1950s, these disciplines have substantially increased their use of statistics and quantitative analysis [16]. Collaborative research, improved research methods, and shared databases have nurtured this growth in empiricism. The effective maintenance of databases in particular is crucial, since "databases can be used:
A. As extended memory for the analyst;
B. To discover underlying patterns of terrorism;
C. To facilitate trend analysis;
D. To compare terrorist campaigns cross-nationally and over time;
E. To generate probability estimates of future terrorist activities;

F. To make statistical correlations with other phenomena that might be the causes, concomitants or consequences of terrorism;

G. To evaluate the success of counter-terrorist policies" [15].

The primary advantage of using databases is "the ability to look at many factors simultaneously in a coherent fashion" [2]. Databases help researchers find answers to many questions. In terrorism research, datasets usually establish "who did what to whom and when" [2], though they are not as good at covering the why and how of terrorist events [17]. Despite the clear advantages that databases convey, many terrorism analyses have been largely "data impoverished" and, at times, "fact free" for several decades. While the ultimate goal is to develop monitoring and forecasting tools to better estimate trends in terrorist behavior [2], current databases can only give a general view of this behavior and should not be expected to predict that "the next attack will occur at site X in country Y next Tuesday at 11 a.m." [10].

There are natural limits and tensions in building and maintaining terrorism databases. Data collectors invariably must balance "the desire for comprehensiveness with the necessity for rigor and relevance of the data" [3]. Due to the difficulties in tracking terrorism, many databases are drawn from media accounts, which may be affected by selective reporting coverage and gaps. By focusing on terrorists and their acts, many databases seem "generally detached from the overall political conflict situation in which the terrorist group is often only one of several actors" [15]. By attempting to exclude certain kinds of acts and actors, researchers must assume a certain amount of systematic bias, though this may be desirable [3]. Most terrorism databases are events databases, built upon previous chronologies. For the most part, terrorism databases are more like census databases (which attempt to collect data on every person) and less like public opinion polls (which generally select a specially defined 'sample' of individuals that represent a larger universe), meaning sampling methods are usually not used and missing incidents have been accidentally omitted [3]. This orientation means that most data collectors are bound to miss some, perhaps many, incidents in compiling their databases. The consistent application of a realistic working definition over time can also be very difficult to achieve [15], and most struggle in applying their definitions to specific cases [6]. The need for considerable resources and constant vigilance usually overtakes most data collection. As a result, there are frequent gaps and other discontinuities, because quite often a single researcher has been responsible for maintaining a database [15].

There are considerable differences between the various databases in existence. Some of these differences are to be expected, since many databases have been developed to meet the needs of particular missions or applications [3]. They often employ uniquely derived definitions and methodologies. However, this usually results in considerable differences of opinion as to what constitutes terrorism and significant variance in the numbers of incidents [15]. Much of this stems from questions of intercoder reliability and individual judgment. As Alex Schmid has noted, with regard to explaining these differences, "it is not only a question of who is counting, but also of what is counted and how" [15]. Most long-running databases have been maintained primarily by government agencies, research centers, and international organizations. Government data, in particular, is used quite frequently, though it is "inevitably influenced by political considerations" [6]. However, there may be greater neutrality and growing intellectual honesty in government reporting on terrorism. For example, the National Counterterrorism Center released data showing over 11,000 terrorist incidents in 2005, which averages to more than one attack per hour [11]. This is a far cry from the few hundreds of "significant" international terrorist incidents released in previous years by the U.S. State Department. Likewise, the British and French governments have also begun releasing compiled lists of terrorist attacks or databases. However, these data are usually rather limited in how they can be studied and manipulated, and many other databases provide information only in chronological order with little or no search engine capabilities [1]. Furthermore, terrorism databases are often cloistered, isolated, inaccessible, or languishing in obsolete computer programs. It is clear that unifying forces must coalesce if the field of terrorism studies is to overcome its state of arrested development and enjoy a research renaissance.

5.   MIPT AS AN INFORMATION CLEARINGHOUSE

The Memorial Institute for the Prevention of Terrorism (MIPT) is focused on expanding and sharing knowledge to prevent terrorism or mitigate its effects. The United States Congress directed MIPT to conduct "research into the social and political causes and effects of terrorism" and to "serve as a national point of contact for antiterrorism information sharing among Federal, State and local preparedness agencies, as well as private and public organizations dealing with these issues." MIPT firmly believes that the accurate dissemination of knowledge on terrorism is a critical ingredient for combating it. We realized early on that a high priority need for terrorism research is the creation of authoritative and accessible databases. Therefore, some of the first research projects undertaken by MIPT were to create and maintain comprehensive electronic databases on terrorism-related subjects.

To this end, MIPT partnered with the RAND Corporation to improve the nation's awareness of the history of and emerging trends in terrorism. By learning lessons from past incidents and grasping current trends, policymakers and scholars can better understand the nature of future threats and how to protect against them. MIPT serves the terrorism research community by offering access to a wealth of information resources including its terrorism databases, websites, and library collection.

As there was no authoritative, central source of unclassified information on terrorism, MIPT worked to develop a world class collection of unclassified resources on terrorism, antiterrorism, and counterterrorism. With information and research on terrorism developing almost daily, creating and maintaining a comprehensive repository of that knowledge and data is a difficult task, which has become more daunting following the September 11th attacks. MIPT's physical library houses thousands of books, videos, reports, articles, and pamphlets on terrorism and related subjects. It collects more than two dozen journals and bulletins, with complete sets of the two most influential journals in the terrorism field – Terrorism and Political Violence running since 1989 and Studies in Conflict & Terrorism dating back to 1977. MIPT also holds complete sets of the two most important U.S. government chronicles of international and domestic terrorism – the State Department's "Patterns of Global Terrorism" (which has been replaced by "Country Reports on Terrorism") and the Justice Department's "Terrorism in the United States." These have been made available electronically in their entirety for the first time through the MIPT website. The MIPT Terrorism Information Center employs numerous electronic resources like the Open Source Center (formerly the Foreign Broadcast Information Service), the Open Source Information System (OSIS), Nexis, and the Thompson/Gale E-encyclopedias. The library staff monitors approximately twenty-five listservs dealing with terrorism, first responders, emergency management, and weapons of mass destruction. MIPT also offers free access to an EBSCO database containing over 750,000 full text reports, articles and documents on terrorism and homeland security. Part of the OCLC interlibrary loan network, the Terrorism Information Center also provides an individual book lending program. Patrons can simply request an item by email, and it will be sent directly to the requestor with return postage included. Ultimately, MIPT intends to acquire all available English language material on terrorism and related subjects for on-site study by researchers, response practitioners, government agencies, and the public at large. A special effort is also underway to house scholarly archival collections from major terrorism experts. Some of the most valuable MIPT resources are a number of unique terrorism databases.

6.   MIPT-FUNDED TERRORISM DATABASES

In 2000, MIPT began collaboration with RAND to create open, online databases that capture domestic and international acts of terrorism. This venture encompassed two databases – the RAND Terrorism Chronology and the RAND-MIPT Incident Database. The RAND Terrorism Chronology (also known as the RAND-St. Andrews Chronology) represents thirty years of research on international terrorism that RAND collected and maintained from 1968 to 1997. By working with MIPT, RAND has opened this large, proprietary database to the public for the first time.   Though several excellent chronologies of terrorist events exist, other systems are limited in their ability to let users manipulate the data, drawing out, for example, only terrorism involving certain kinds of weapons, or certain groups or places, or any combination thereof. The RAND-MIPT Incident Database covers both international and domestic terrorism incidents worldwide from 1998 to the present day. These incident databases contain data from open sources and publications, collected by RAND.   This collection process has been conducted in accordance with the same definition and vetting standards established at the beginning of the RAND Terrorism Chronology.   An independent survey of terrorism databases by the Federal Research Division of the Library of Congress found these two databases "represent a very comprehensive and valuable resource of information on incidents of terrorism in the United States and abroad" [1].   In conjunction with the databases, RAND has produced biannual reports containing articles by subject matter experts, who draw heavily upon these databases.   These publications offer contemporary analysis and insights, probe cross-cutting issues, and describe the terrorist threat environment. They are also intended to inspire others to take advantage of these tools in order to develop further knowledge. By keeping these databases open, objective, and online, MIPT affords researchers unparalleled access to a useful resource.

MIPT also funds and hosts a robust database focused on terrorism-related trials in the U.S.   Headed by the University of Arkansas, the MIPT Indictment Database compiles records related to federal criminal cases as a result of official FBI terrorism investigations under the Attorney General Guidelines from 1980 to present.   The project provides a powerful quantitative dataset for researchers.   The Indictment database includes information on nearly 500 suspected terrorists from about 60 groups indicted for over 6,000 federal criminal counts over the last 25 years. Approximately 75 variables can be analyzed, including: (1) demographic descriptions of indicted and convicted persons; (2) group type, affiliation, and ideology; (3) case and count outcomes (conviction, plea, acquittal, etc.); (4) and sentencing information. Analyses can be conducted on any combination of these variables, and the source court records are also made available as Acrobat PDF documents. This material is invaluable in looking for pre-incident indicators or discovering more historical information about specific groups and incidents within the United States. It will also aid in the development of practical recommendations regarding the investigation, prosecution, and sanctioning of persons indicted for terrorism-related crimes. This data is being merged with powerful mapping tools to enable temporal-spatial research on the planning, preparation, and execution of terrorist attacks, and MIPT hopes to provide this information to the public in the coming years.

7.   MIPT TERRORISM KNOWLEDGE BASE

In 2004, MIPT released the new Terrorism Knowledge Base (TKB) – www.tkb.org – to act as one-stop resource for comprehensive research and analysis on global terrorist incidents, terrorist organizations, and terrorism-related trials. By combining its databases, library materials, and other resources into an in-depth, interactive system, MIPT has put the facts concerning global terrorism at the fingertips of policymakers, professionals, and the public. TKB covers the history, affiliations, locations, and tactics of terrorist groups operating across the world, with nearly 40 years of terrorism incident data and more than a thousand group and leader profiles. This system represents the most advanced, web-based tool of its kind. Users can search using directories, keywords, and more. Country profiles provide thorough background information, and group profiles describe bases of operations, founding philosophies, and current goals. They also contain Quick Facts, offering a snapshot of vital data and a "baseball card" of statistics for side-by-side comparisons. Key leader profiles display brief biographies, legal cases, and photographs where available. Most importantly, TKB offers highly interactive maps and sophisticated analytical tools that can create custom graphs and tables. The system provides remarkable analytical capabilities across a single, integrated knowledge base, including statistical summaries and trend graphing. Researchers can create all manner of graphs and charts examining incidents by region, by target, by tactic, by weapon, by group, by court case, and more. For less experienced users, the system includes a quick reference guide and a graphing wizard to walk them through the process of creating their own specialized tables, graphs, and maps. No other terrorism website provides such user-friendly features for free. The site has become very popular; at the time of this writing, the TKB was within the top ten websites for a Google search on "terrorism."

8. BETTER KNOWING WHAT WE KNOW ABOUT TERRORISM

Some believe that after more than three decades of study, "we simply should know more about terrorism than we currently do" [16]. While I share this frustration, I believe we know more about terrorism than we realize, but we have hidden this knowledge away in disparate databases and disconnected research centers. Enabling open access to this knowledge is the most efficient way to redress the current problems and to attract more researchers. We must strive to support the "invisible college" that has attempted empirical inquiry with more data [7]. The vast majority of terrorism research is still conducted alone, with limited resources, by and for non-academicians [18]. Therefore, the research community should recognize terrorism data as a public good, like economic data, to be shared, debated, and dissected. Until now, statistical information on terrorism has been "generally unavailable to the public, inaccurate, dated, or limited to international or transnational events" [13]. By democratizing data and integrating both qualitative and quantitative information, we can develop new knowledge and bring greater empiricism to this field of study. Along with centralizing the published literature, institutes and government agencies should focus on sharing databases. Indeed, some believe that aggregating data on terrorist groups is probably the most useful way to test macro-theories about terrorism [12], and large databases can provide rigorous tests of the conventional wisdom [9].

As Alex Schmid states, "incident databases have, especially when compared to each other, much to say about the phenomenon of terrorism" [15]. Comparing databases may even help to uncover a common conception of terrorism. After all, though the definition debate has raged for decades, researchers have recorded tens of thousands of incidents. Wouldn't it help us describe terrorism to compare and contrast what we have been counting all these years? We should work to reduce duplication of effort if possible, since it appears that "everyone seems to be collecting the same data over and over again" [3]. Twenty-five years ago, it was apparent that the increasing number of terrorism databases did "not necessarily reflect a substantial increase in the amount of information available about terrorism" [3]. All databases die or undergo changes in who maintains them and how they gather data as time passes and new technologies emerge. Without intervention, many datasets end up being integrated, becoming unavailable, or disappearing altogether. Some believe "a reliable master or comprehensive database could be created, one that integrates the MIPT data set with those that are linked to country-specific collection efforts" [14]. In this way, the Terrorism Knowledge Base could serve as a database repository of sorts and encourage complementary rather than competitive collection efforts. Perhaps this could assuage the concern that "as long as the world of violence portrayed by one data set differs from the worlds of violence described by other data sets it is difficult to gain credibility outside the academic area" [15].

The terrorism research community should build upon existing consortia and databases, drawing together institutions based on their regional or functional specialties. MIPT prides itself on its ability to serve as a bridge linking like-minded institutions. In this endeavor, we should engage the Inter-University Consortium for Political and Social Research (ICPSR), the International Counter-Terrorism Academic Community (ICTAC), the International Relations and Security Network (ISN), and the Department of Homeland Security's newly created University-Based Centers of Excellence. We should try to draw together past and present databases such as:

- University of Maryland's Global Terrorism Database (GTD);
- International Terrorism: Attributes of Terrorist Events (ITERATE);
- International Policy Institute for Counter-Terrorism/Merari database;
- Monterey Institute's WMD Terrorism database;
- Int'l. Centre for Political Violence & Terrorism Research database;
- Jan Engene's Terrorism in Western Europe: Event Data (TWEED);
- Jeffrey Ian Ross' Attributes of Terrorism in Canada (ATIC) database;
- Christopher Hewitt's Domestic Terrorism database;
- Marc Sageman's Al-Qaeda database;
- Robert Pape's Suicide Terrorism database;
- Robert Leiken's Nixon Center Jihadi database; and
- University of Auburn and Pennsylvania's Eco-terrorism database

Many other datasets should be added to this list. The Interuniversity Consortium for Political and Social Research offers a useful model, by preserving and providing access to an archive of social science data. However, terrorism data must serve a large body of non-academic researchers and analysts that are not affiliated with universities.

Regardless of whether it is MIPT, ICPSR, the National Counterterrorism Center, or some other organization, someone needs to take the initiative in uniting these divided efforts. As a whole, we must become better at sharing information and share better information. Ultimately, the community must aim for the creation of new knowledge and enhanced understanding, so as to predict the emergence of similar events in the future [16]. We can ill-afford new intellectual blind spots like those that appeared before 9/11. The Terrorism Knowledge Base may provide a vehicle for improving the skills and awareness of the next generation of terrorism scholars and observers. It is incumbent upon us to take stock of the research that has gone before and to ensure its evolution going forward.

9.   ACKNOWLEDGEMENTS

The Terrorism Knowledge Base is supported under Award Number MIPT-2003D-C-001, Terrorism Knowledge Base, from the Memorial Institute for the Prevention of Terrorism (MIPT) and the Office of Grants & Training, U.S. Department of Homeland Security.   Points of view in this paper are those of the author and do not necessarily represent the official position of the U.S. Department of Homeland Security or MIPT.

REFERENCES

1. Buchalter AR, Curtis GE (2003) Inventory and assessment of databases relevant for social science research on terrorism. Federal Research Division, Library of Congress
2. Fowler WW (1980) An agenda for quantitative research on terrorism. Rand Corporation, Santa Monica, CA
3. Fowler WW (1981) Terrorism data bases: a comparison of missions methods, and systems. Rand Corporation, Santa Monica, CA
4. Gordon A (2004) Terrorism and knowledge growth: a databases and internet analysis. In: Silke A (ed) Research on terrorism: trends, achievements and failures. Frank Cass, London, pp 104-118
5. Hoffman B (2004) Foreword. In: Silke A (ed) Research on terrorism: trends, achievements and failures. Frank Cass, London, pp xvii-xix
6. LaFree G, Dugan L (2004) How does studying terrorism compare to studying crime? Law and Deviance, vol 5: 53-74
7. Mickolus EF (1977) Statistical approaches to the study of terrorism. In: Alexander Y, Finger SM (eds) Terrorism: interdisciplinary perspectives. John Jay Press, New York
8. Mickolus EF (1981) Combating international terrorism: a quantitative analysis. Ph.D. dissertation, Yale University
9. Mickolus EF (1987) Comment – terrorists, governments, and numbers: counting things versus things that count. Journal of conflict resolution, vol 31, no 1: 54-62
10. Mickolus EF (2002) How do we know we're winning the war against terrorists? issues in measurement. Studies in Conflict & Terrorism, vol 25, issue 3: 151-160
11. National Counterterrorism Center (2006) Country reports on terrorism 2005, statistical annex.
12. Ross JI (1988) An events data base on political terrorism in canada: some conceptual and methodological problems. Conflict Quarterly, vol III, no 2: 47-65
13. Ross JI (2004) Taking stock of research methods and analysis on oppositional political terrorism. The American Sociologist, Summer: 26-37
14. Ross JI (2006) Political terrorism: an interdisciplinary approach. Peter Lang Publishing, New York
15. Schmid AP (2004) Statistics on terrorism: the challenge of measuring trends in global terrorism. Forum on Crime and Society, vol. 4, nos 1 and 2: 49-69
16. Silke A (2001) The devil you know: continuing problems with research on terrorism. Terrorism and Political Violence, vol 13, no 4: 1-14
17. Silke A (2004) An introduction to terrorism research. In: Silke A (ed) Research on terrorism: trends, achievements and failures. Frank Cass, London, pp 1-29

18. Silke A (2004) The road less travelled: recent trends in terrorism research. In: Silke A (ed) Research on terrorism: trends, achievements and failures. Frank Cass, London, pp 186-213

SUGGESTED READINGS

- Jeffrey Ian Ross (2006). *Political terrorism: an interdisciplinary approach.* Peter Lang Publishing, New York.
- Alex P. Schmid and Albert J. Jongman (2005*). Political terrorism: a new guide to actors, authors, concepts, data bases, theories, & literature.* Transaction Publishers, New Brunswick, New Jersey.
- Andrew Silke (ed) (2004). *Research on terrorism: trends, achievements and failures.* Frank Cass, London.

ONLINE RESOURCES

- MIPT Terrorism Knowledge Base
  www.tkb.org
- Centre for the Study of Terrorism and Political Violence
  http://www.st-andrews.ac.uk/academic/intrel/research/cstpv/
- International Centre for Political Violence and Terrorism Research
  http://www.pvtr.org/
- International Policy Institute for Counter-Terrorism
  http://www.ict.org.il
- Jane's Terrorism and Insurgency Centre
  http://jtic.janes.com
- Monterey Institute Center for Nonproliferation Studies
  http://cns.miis.edu/dbinfo/about.htm
- National Consortium for the Study of Terrorism & Responses to Terrorism
  http://www.start.umd.edu/
- South Asia Terrorism Portal
  http://www.satp.org
- Terrorism Research Center
  http://www.terrorism.com
- Worldwide Incidents Tracking System
  http://wits.nctc.gov

DISCUSSION QUESTIONS

1. Is historical information of little use to understanding the current terrorist threat?
2. Do perceptions of the amount and intensity of global terrorism match empirical data?
3. Where do you seek objective and comprehensive coverage of the subject of terrorism?
4. How can one present a fair picture of the current state of terrorism?
5. What types of data inform you most without hyping the threat?

8

TOWARD A TARGET-SPECIFIC METHOD OF THREAT ASSESSMENT

Yael Shahar
Institute for Counter-Terrorism, Interdisciplinary Center, Herzliya, Israel
(yaelradlauer@yahoo.com)

CHAPTER OVERVIEW

This chapter describes a threat assessment model used at ICT to estimate the "attractiveness" of specific facilities to terrorist organizations. The model uses on-site evaluations of vulnerabilities to build a portfolio of possible attack scenarios. The scenarios are then analyzed using known or estimated sensitivities and target-assessment criteria for the different organizations. The results provide a means of rating the different scenarios according to their attractiveness to different types of terrorist groups. This will enable decision-makers to concentrate resources on the most the probable scenarios, rather than on worst-case scenarios. The model has provided credible results for actual venues.

1.   INTRODUCTION

An accurate estimation of the threat posed by terrorism is of the utmost importance in deciding whether – and how much – to enhance security at a given venue. The stages in preparing an operational counter-terrorism plan are: first, to identify those groups or individuals that are both *motivated and capable* of attacking the facility under consideration (threat assessment); and second, to review existing security precautions in light of this knowledge, based on the known vulnerabilities of the venue (risk analysis).

The overall process of threat assessment is particularly complex in that the threat posed by any given terrorist organization will reflect its estimate of the venue's attraction as a target and the ease of attacking it. In other words, the threat assessment depends on the risk analysis as much as the risk analysis depends on the threat assessment.

In reality, this interdependence is rarely taken into account; practical, political, and economical circumstances generally bring about a fragmentation of effort, with threat assessments carried out at a national or regional level, without any consideration of the characteristics of the venue under consideration. Likewise, risk analyses are generally not based upon the same considerations as the threat assessment. In effect, the two procedures often appear to be based on totally different sets of assumptions.

The venue-specific risk assessment model discussed here is designed to integrate these two aspects of security planning. This model estimates the "attractiveness" of specific facilities to specific terrorist organizations. Its utility lies in its ability to help security planners categorize possible attacks in terms of most probable vs. most damaging. In the absence of empirical data on threats, planners and pundits often fall back on "worst case" scenarios. However, this has often meant the over-allocation of resources to some of the least likely attack scenarios. Preparing for the "low risk / high consequence" attack is not the only (or even the best) approach. Scarce resources can be better exploited if a way is found to classify threats according to likelihood, and not just according to the severity of consequences.

2.   METHODOLOGY

The probability of a terror attack on a particular target is dependant not only on the characteristics of the target—its symbolic or strategic value and its vulnerabilities—but also on the ambition, capabilities, and sensitivities of the relevant terrorist organizations.

In the sections that follow, I'll present an overview of a statistical method for evaluating the threat presented by different types of terrorist groups to particular venues. The method builds on input regarding the known characteristics of the terrorist groups active in the region in question, combined with the characteristics of each potential *modus operandi*. The goal is not so much to give a precise prediction of who, how, and where; but rather to provide a better basis for deciding how best to allocate finite counter-terrorism resources.

The stages used in the proposed model are:

1. *Determination of Organization-specific factors* – We determine which organizations present the greatest threat to the venue in question, based on the motivations, capabilities, and ideologies of the organizations. Each organization is given a Risk Score, based on the relative score of each index applied to that organization. The analysts running the model determine the threshold above which organizations will be included in the model.

2. *Determination of Venue-specific factors* – An exhaustive analysis of the vulnerabilities of the venue in question is carried out by a professional security team. For most high-profile venues, this analysis will already have been performed by the installation's security personnel as part of their routine duties. Care must be taken to examine the vulnerabilities of the venue in question from the point of view of the potential attacker— seeking weaknesses that might be exploited to carry out an attack.

3. *Scenario building* – the information on venue vulnerabilities is combined with data on potential scenarios. In our model, the list of scenarios is taken from a database of hundreds of potential terror attacks, chosen in accordance with the vulnerabilities of the venue in question. Each scenario will be given a score based on the difficulty of carrying it out and the potential damage of a successful attack.

4. *Numerical synthesis* – Combining the results of the last three stages, we arrive at a numerical evaluation of the likelihood that any particular type of attack will be carried out by a particular terrorist organization. We do this by categorizing the various scenarios according to the target-selection methods of the different organizations: for example, the difficulty of successfully perpetrating the attack and the desirability of the outcome of the attack from the point of view of the terrorist organization. For each terrorist organization, we include factors to weigh the terrorists' sensitivity to these attack-specific factors. The result is a score that indicates the net "attractiveness" of a particular type of attack to a particular type of organization. For example, some organizations may be more deterred by physical difficulty or by attacks requiring years of planning, while others would be undeterred by these factors. Some may see achieving maximal casualties as a central goal, while others may be

unwilling to risk causing high casualties.

Naturally, the resulting numbers are only as good as the information that goes into the model. In effect, the model should be viewed as merely a template for better organizing our knowledge; without that knowledge, the template is empty of all content. However, when based on reliable information, the model is a very useful tool for data visualization and risk assessment.

3.   ORGANIZATION-SPECIFIC INDICATORS

For the purposes of illustration, we will base the following example on a tourist venue in the United States. An analysis of organizations in the ICT database and their characteristics leads us to believe that the greatest threat to tourist sites in the United States is likely to be posed by groups or cells having the following characteristics:

3.1   Structure and Reach

- *Supported by a state or sub-state entity.* The stronger such support, the greater the resources at the disposal of the group, and the more ambitious a potential attack is likely to be.
- *Loose network affiliated with other like-minded cells or groups around the world.* Such international connections are particularly useful in the planning stages of an attack, and facilitate the escape of those directly involved in supervising and perpetrating the attack. Groups posing the greatest danger are those with a broad-based support system around the world. Such a support system often consists of fundraising and political activists living outside the group's normal sphere of operations.
- *Is able to blend in with immigrant groups in the target country.* Because of the need for extensive planning and pre-operational intelligence, the members of a potential attack cell would be required to spend long periods under cover inside the target country. Connections with a particular ethnic group within that country could greatly facilitate the existence of "sleeper" cells.

3.1.1   Motivation

- *Motivated by religion or quasi-religious ideology.* This entails a preference for mass-casualty attacks, as well as the potential to carry out suicide attacks. Such organizations may share some of the characteristics of apocalyptic cults.

- *Shows past history of hatred of the target country/countries.* Most terrorist groups are fairly vocal about their agenda, in order to recruit like-minded individuals to their camp. Although not all vocally anti-Western groups pose a threat, it is probable that those that do pose a threat will make no secret of their intentions.
- *Has been, or expects to be, targeted by the country under consideration..* Potentially the most dangerous groups to our venue are likely to be those directly affected by the policies of the country under consideration. In the past, this meant that the groups to worry about would be those adversely affected in some way by the target country's foreign policy. However, in light of the U.S.-led campaigns in Afghanistan and in Iraq, we can expect the circle of those with an axe to grind against the U.S. and its allies to have grown considerably wider. Because of the inter-relatedness of the threat, the potential risk is spread out among dozens of semi-autonomous organizations in a number of countries. Many of these countries are not themselves in any way directly affected by the U.S. campaign.

3.1.2   Characteristics of Past Attacks

- *Has carried out attacks outside its local sphere of influence.* Often, this is a function of how much assistance the group receives from a state or sub-state sponsor. Those foreign-based organizations that have demonstrated capability to act far from their home ground are naturally to be considered of greater threat.
- *Has carried out attacks against similar targets.* For example, an organization that has singled out tourism targets for attack is one whose goals generally include inflicting economic damage on the target country. This is true of some domestic groups, such as ETA, as well as of international terrorist groups. However, organizations that single out tourist sites popular with international travelers generally have a more globe-spanning goal. International tourism-related targets are often chosen because they represent the antithesis of the terrorists' own worldview: they stand for openness, diversity, and globalization.
- *Has carried out attacks against targets or interests belonging to the country under consideration.* For example, a history of attacks on American targets indicates not only a pre-existing enmity toward the United States, but more importantly, a readiness to transform this enmity into action.

These indicators of potential threat will be given a relative weight according to the proportional contribution to a given organization's potential to attack similar targets in the target country. Table 8-1 shows one example of how these indicators might be chosen in the case of a tourism-related venue.

Table 8-1. Organization-specific indications of potential threat

Indicator	Relative Weight
Structure and Reach	
Supported by a state or sub-state entity.	20
Part of international network of groups or cells.	15
Ability to blend in with immigrant groups in the United States.	10
	Max: 45
Attack History	
Past history of attacks outside its own sphere of influence.	15
Past history of attacks against similar targets	10
Past history of attacks against American interests	5
	Max: 30
Motivation	
Motivated by religion or quasi-religious ideology.	15
Has threatened to attack American interests.	5
Has been, or expects to be, targeted by the target country.	5
	Max: 25

The values of the variables chosen here are not necessarily the values that would be used for an actual threat assessment. Since we have not specified a real venue, we are using these values as an example only. The exact values of the variables would be determined by the researchers according to the nature of the venue under consideration. The total of all the variables should equal to 100.

3.2   Example of Organization Input

Table 8-2. Gama'ah al-Islamiya: Relative risk from analysis of indicators

Structure and Reach

0	*Supported by a state or a sub-state entity*
	The Egyptian Government believes that Iran, Bin Ladin, and Afghan militant groups have all provided financial support to the Gama`ah al-Islamiyya. However, the group does not benefit from significant state-sponsorship.
	Part of an international network of like-minded groups and cells
5	The Gama`ah al-Islamiyya operates mainly in southern Egypt, and in urban centers. However, the group has been indirectly involved in international terror, through 'Arab-Afghans' (Egyptian citizens who trained in the Mujahideen camps after the end of the war) who operate as individuals within autonomous Islamic terrorist cells abroad. Such cells exist in Sudan, the United Kingdom, Afghanistan, Austria, and Yemen.
	Ability to blend in with immigrant groups in the United States
5	Other than a small group of radicals, the Islamic Group has only a limited presence in the United States. However, the group has been known to run fundraising operations in the U.S. and in Canada.

Attack History		
15	*International terrorist activity*	
	From 1993 until the cease-fire, al-Gama`ah carried out attacks on tourists in Egypt, most notably the attack at Luxor that killed 58 foreign tourists.	
	The Egyptian organizations, predominantly Al-Gama`ah al-Islamiya, were indirectly involved in international terror, through 'Arab-Afghans' operating as individuals within autonomous Islamic terrorist cells abroad. Attacks carried out, or claimed by these cells, include a suicide bomb attack against the police station in Rijeka, Croatia (October 1995) and the attempted assassination of Hosni Mubarak during his visit to Ethiopia (June 1995).	
	The Gama`ah has never specifically attacked U.S. citizens or facilities, and has not conducted an attack inside Egypt or abroad since August 1998.	
10	*Attacks against tourism-related interests*	
	Until the ceasefire, GIA was known for its attacks on tourism in Egypt. However, the organization has not attacked tourist targets outside of Egypt.	
2	*Attacks against American Targets*	
	American tourists were attacked in Egypt, along with nationals of other countries.	

Motivation		
	Motivated by religious ideology	
15	The Islamic Group was greatly influenced by the militant ideology of Sayyid Qutb. The blind Egyptian cleric, Sheikh Omar Abdel Rahman, the supreme spiritual authority of Al-Gama`ah al-Islamiya and the Egyptian 'Jihad,' issued a fatwa sanctioning terrorist activity.	
	Has expressed willingness to attack Western interests	
5	The group has sided with Osama bin Ladin in the past, including signing his 1998 fatwa calling for attacks on U.S. civilians. While the Gama`ah's traditional goal was the overthrow of the Egyptian Government, Taha Musa's faction has expressed an interest in attacking U.S. and Israeli interests.	
	Targeted by U.S. anti-terrorism campaign	
5	The U.S.-led campaign may have cut off some of the group's funding, and driven Musa Taha, the leader of the radical faction, out of Afghanistan. The US treasury has added the GI to the list of groups targeted by economic sanctions.	

Overall relative risk: 62

A similar analysis would be carried out for each organization deemed to present a potential threat. Those having the highest overall risk score would be those used in the analysis that follows. The organization above would most likely not be one of those included in the analysis, due to its relatively low risk score.

3.3   Venue-specific factors affecting target selection

In order to evaluate the net "attractiveness" of a particular type of attack to a particular type of organization, each type of attack receives a combined

Difficulty score, as well as three separate Impact scores, as shown below in Table 8-3:

Table 8-3. Attack-type parameters

Parameters	Relative Weight
Difficulty, based on:	
Planning time required	33
Resources required	33
Physical difficulty	33
Impact, based on:	
Physical/economic damage	33
Casualties	33
Symbolic value (includes psychological impact)	33

3.4   Example scenarios

The following scenarios illustrate how these factors are applied to particular scenarios. Since we are not dealing with a particular venue in these examples, these samples are very general in nature. An actual threat assessment would require that the specific vulnerabilities of the venue be factored into the scenario rating.

Remotely detonated bomb

This is the simplest type of attack and requires only moderate investment. However, in order for this type of attack to be successful, the organization must carry out at least minimal pre-operational intelligence to determine the best time and location for bomb placement. For example, if the intention is to inflict casualties, the bomb will need to be set in an area with heavy traffic and time to go off during working hours. On the other hand, if the aim is to gain media attention without causing casualties, then the bomb might be placed in the same area at midnight.

Bomb in public area

Leave bomb package in lobby or in garbage container.	A bomb placed in a travel bag or plastic bag is left in a public area or in a garbage container. The bomb can then be activated by timer or remote control mechanism.	Planning time: 20 Resources: 10 Difficulty: 10
	Result: Possible large damage to property; Disruption of operations for short while; Possible moderate number of casualties	Physical/Economic Damage: 25 Casualties: 20 Symbolic: 25

Suicide attacks

The human bomb is extremely motivated either by ideological and/or religious impulses. His/Her main aim is mass killing and destruction, without regard for his or her own life or the lives of others.

Spiritually, these people are ready to die, and as a result they are usually calm and determined. Until they get to the specific spot where they will operate the explosives, only a highly trained eye would notice anything suspicious.

Such a human bomb can approach any public facility—particularly a crowded place such as a bar or restaurant—and operate a charge of a few dozen kilograms. Such charges are usually stuffed with nails and shrapnel, in order to maximize casualties and loss of limbs.

The effects of this type of bombing are generally limited by the amount of explosives that the attacker can carry into the target zone. However, unlike a static charge, the attack can choose both the time and the place of detonation, thus maximizing damage and casualties.

Suicide bomb

Suicide bomber	A suicide bomber conceals the explosives on his body or in a bag and manually activates the device.	Planning time: 20 Resources: 15 Difficulty: 15
	Result: Possible large number of casualties; Closure of facility for several days / weeks	Physical/Economic Damage: 25 Casualties: 25 Symbolic: 25

Carbomb attack on main entrance or external walls

An additional and potentially even more devastating kind of attack would be to break into the lobby of a public building with a carbomb. We've seen the effects of such an attack at the American embassy in Beirut, in some Israeli official facilities in Lebanon and the bombings of the American embassies in Kenya and Tanzania, not to mention the more recent attacks on the Marriot Hotel in Jakarta and the Taba Hilton Hotel in the Sinai.

Such a vehicle can carry a few hundred kilograms of explosives. Operating such a charge at the center of the building will cause many casualties and large-scale damage to the structure.

Terrorists are well aware of the potential impact of this type of attack; it is exactly the sort of outcome they aim for. The fall of the World Trade Center towers in NYC illustrates the possible result far better any other description.

Suicide Car bomb attack on lobby / external wall

Explosives-laden vehicle attack on public building.	Drive a car or truck filled with explosives into the entrance or lobby. (This was the method used in the attack on the Hilton Hotel in Taba in October 2004.)	Planning time: 20 Resources: 20 Difficulty: 15
	Result:Possible large number of casualties; Closure of building for several weeks / months	Physical/Economic Damage: 30 Casualties: 28 Symbolic: 25

More "professional" terrorists could carry out a carbomb attack by crashing the vehicle into the lobby through the main entrance, leaping out of the vehicle (an action requiring no more than 30 seconds) and escaping through a secondary entrance while everyone in the vicinity is in shock. The explosives can be detonated a few minutes later by timer or remote control.

Carbomb in underground parking lot

One of the most vulnerable and crucial weak points of many public building is the underground parking lot. In many cases, these parking lots are open to the public, and there is no control whatsoever over who parks there. Some of the cars may be parked in the lot on a permanent basis, either daily or periodically. It would be extremely easy for hostile elements to park a vehicle packed with a few hundred kilograms of explosives, which could be timed to detonate after the perpetrators have left the country.

In quite a few cases, the layout of underground parking lots allows a vehicle to be parked near the main load-bearing pillars of the building. A very large charge detonated in such a place could cause major damage, many casualties, and at the very least, disruption of operations for a long time. Structural damage could be serious enough to lead to the complete closing of the facility, if not to even worse consequences.

A regular sedan type car is capable of carrying a few hundreds kilo of explosives. Such a charge can be operated by timer or remote control mechanism. A blast of a few hundred Kilos will shock the entire building. There is no doubt that the blast wave will impact the entire building. Depending on the exact location of the blast, it is possible that a section of the building will collapse as well.

Car bomb – underground car park

Place car or small truck loaded with high explosives or a gas container in car park – detonate by timer or remote control.	One or more vehicles are bought, hired, or stolen. The vehicles are packed with explosives or gas tanks and parked in the underground parking, in a location designed to cause maximum structural damage. The vehicles are detonated using remote control devices or timers.	Planning time: 25 Resources: 25 Difficulty: 28
	Result: Possible large number of casualties; Possible major/total structural damage; Disruption/ cessation of operations	Physical/Economic Damage: 33 Casualties: 33 Symbolic: 33

Indiscriminate shooting attacks

Indiscriminate shooting attacks aim to kill as many people as possible, regardless of who they are. Such a method can be executed in a number of ways, among them, entering the building and opening fire, shooting from a moving vehicle, etc.

One of the main problems facing security authorities in many countries is the fact that they are not allowed to carry weapons themselves. This means that in the case of a shooting attack, the chances of effective return fire are slim. The security staff can only attempt to minimize the damage by preventive measures and by damage control after the attack is over. In such a scenario, time lost equates to lives lost. Since the security staff cannot respond, the attackers will have a free hand to continue the attack; civilians are similarly unarmed and will thus not be able to stop the attack. Any emergency plan should include a response to such an attack, including evacuation of wounded and direction of people to a shelter.

Shooting attack in public building (eg. Shopping Mall)

Use automatic weapons and explosive in crowded public area.	Terrorists enter the building with weapons concealed in bags or under coats. The gunmen open fire and throw grenades. A hostage scenario can evolve from here, or the operation can be a suicide attack, ending with a firefight with the authorities and the eventual death of the attackers. If the building has entrances to other public areas, it would be easy to move from one location to the other.	Planning time: 5 Resources: 10 Difficulty: 15
	Result: Possible large number of casualties; Closure of the facility for several hours / days; Creation of an incident in which security personnel may shoot at each other.	Physical/Economic Damage: 15 Casualties: 20 Symbolic: 15

Obviously, the list of potential scenarios is huge. It is the job of the on-site investigative team to come up with as many potential attacks as possible based on the venue's vulnerabilities.

3.5 Evaluation of organizational sensitivities

Each category of terrorist organization receives four "sensitivity" scores, as shown in Table 8-4. These scores will be combined with each attack-type's Difficulty and Impact factors to determine the importance of these factors to the organization type. When the resulting "Weighted Difficulty" is subtracted from the resulting "Weighted Impact," the result is the "Attractiveness" of that attack to that organization type.

Table 8-4. Sensitivity parameters (Negative interest indicates aversion to causing this type of damage.)

Parameters	Range
Sensitivity to difficulty	0 – 100%
Interest in causing physical/economic damage	-100% – 100%
Interest in causing casualties	-100% – 100%

As mentioned above, the organizations selected for analysis will be those having the highest overall threat score, estimated in Stage 1. Based on our familiarity with the characteristics of these organizations, we can estimate their sensitivities. Table 8-5 below shows a sample of such a categorization; since we have not specified a venue, we will use group types, rather than actual organizations, for the analysis. Note that this table is based only on a generic analysis; in order to be truly effective, it would require far more parameters than those shown — an analysis that is beyond the scope of this paper.

Table 8-5. Organization-type sensitivities

	Al-Qaida "Central"	Local Islamists	Ad hoc Groups
Sensitivity to Difficulty	25%	60%	90%
Interest in Physical / Economic Damage	100%	60%	95%
Interest in Casualties	100%	80%	-70%
Interest in Symbolic Value of Targets	100%	100%	90%

4. SYNTHESIS

Putting all these factors together, we can derive the following numerical breakdown, indicating the attractiveness of specific types of attack to the groups discussed above.

Table 8-6. Numerical Synthesis

Attack Type	Al-Qaida Central	Local Extremist Groups	Ad hoc Groups
Open Space Bomb	60	32	8
Restaurant Bomb	58	25	-8
Suicide Bomb	63	30	-3
Suicide Car Bomb	69	32	-3
Static Car Bomb	54	16	-20
Car-Park Bomb	80	32	-13
Open Space Shooting Spree	43	22	-4
Mortar/Missile Attack	16	-9	-29
Food Poisoning	23	0	-15
Bio-Agent in Food	34	-1	-32
Explosive Bio-Device	57	16	-24
Pressurized Bio-Device	55	13	-28
Bio-Agent in A/C	53	7	-36
Bio-Agent in Fire Sprinklers	52	4	-40
Suicide Bio-Aerosol	54	15	-16
Leave Radioactive Substance	40	6	-25
Radioactive in A/C	33	-11	-47
Crash Private Plane	27	1	-11
Arson	20	7	1

A graph of this information provides a more visually satisfying view of the data:

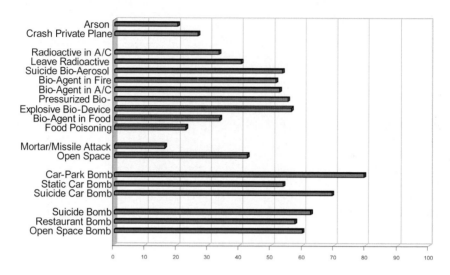

Figure 8-1. Attacks attractive to al-Qaida "Central"

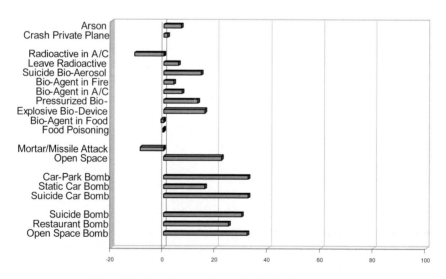

Figure 8-2. Attacks attractive to local Islamist extremists

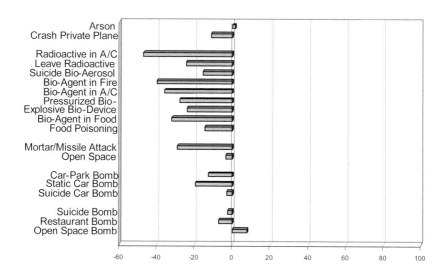

Figure 8-3. Attacks attractive to al hoc groups

5. SUMMARY: SCENARIOS MOST LIKELY TO BE CARRIED OUT BY RELEVANT TERRORIST GROUPS

As described above, we have attempted to establish criteria for judging which attack scenarios might prove "attractive" to the various categories of terrorist groups that might be interested in attacking the venue in question. As our judgments regarding the affinities and sensitivities of these groups are necessarily approximate, and our judgments as to the difficulties and impact of the various forms of attack are not necessarily the same as the judgments made by the terrorists themselves, the specific numbers and rankings should be taken only as a general guide.

Nonetheless, we can draw some conclusions from the analysis:

The most "attractive" types of attack for al-Qaida and its associates are "high quality" explosive attacks—particularly car-park bombings aimed at destroying or severely damaging the entire facility. Many other types of attack are reasonably "attractive" as well, but there is no pressing reason for these organizations to use non-conventional weapons where explosives will serve well enough.

Local extremist groups are likely to select from a smaller menu of attack types; they are most likely to carry out bombings or shooting attacks, but may also attempt a low-level non-conventional attack.

Ad hoc groups, on the other hand, should not find a tourist venue to be all that attractive a target. As most of the attack scenarios we envision involve significant casualties, and input data was based on the assumption that these groups generally prefer to avoid killing many people, it would seem that the venue should not be high on their list of targets. However, should one of these groups nevertheless choose our venue as a target, certain types of attack are likely to be more attractive than others. For example, they may elect to perform bombings with warnings phoned in before the explosives detonate, in order to cause large-scale damage while minimizing casualties. As such an attack has in fact occurred at tourist venues in the past, we must assume that it can happen again.

Further Enhancements – Advanced Data-Mining Capabilities

This method can be further enhanced to include data-mining abilities using open source information and building on the ICT database of terrorist incidents. This raw data would provide the basis for a continual reevaluation of the organizational factors that enter into the equation, as well as the availability of resources that could be used in the perpetration of certain types of attack. The result will be a dynamic threat assessment apparatus which could be programmed to "flag" certain types of incidents and organization when the relevant threat indices reach a critical level.

This enhancement would build on current data-mining technologies and off-the shelf database tools. The end product would be applicable to governments, installation security, public transport officials, and a host of other sectors that could be targeted by terrorists.

The enhancement of the model to include advanced data-mining technologies will enable the model to become self-adjusting to changes in terrorist organization make-up, local circumstances, and political realities.

6.   CONCLUSION

The value of the model discussed here lies not in its ability to reveal new information, but rather in its usefulness as a planning and pedagogical aid: a means to visualize data so that trends may be readily apparent where they might otherwise have been lost in a sea of data. Such data-visualization tools are important in helping us better manage our resources.

While the model's methodology is quite general, the particular target characteristics generate very specific risk vs. impact numbers for that target. We have used this model for evaluating threat / impact risks for tourist and transportation facilities with credible results. The end goal is to turn this model into a computational apparatus that can be used by those responsible for installation security, who may not have extensive knowledge of the terrorist groups most likely to target their facility. This will require extensive data-mining capabilities to allow the model to "self-adapt" and "learn" from open source material.

However, any such model, and the intelligence on which it is based, should be seen as only one component in the fight against terrorism. We must never forget that terrorism is psychological warfare and that its real target is not one venue or another, but the targeted society as a whole. Thus, a significant portion of our resources must go toward thwarting the effectiveness of terrorism as a whole.

Terrorism works somewhat like a virus; by hijacking society's own means of communication—the news media—terrorism succeeds in disseminating its own messages. In a sense, the media plays a multi-level role in the chain of terrorism effectiveness—it carries scenes of death and destruction into the homes of every member of society, while at the same time carrying the fears and anxieties of society to the ears of the terrorists. By telling the terrorists what we are most afraid of, we play an active role in their selection of targets and modes of attack.

We can weaken the effectiveness of terrorism as a tool for policy-making by informing the public of the real extent of the threat. In helping citizens understand what terrorists can and cannot do, and what the individual can do to defend his or her society, we undermine the efficacy of terrorism while strengthening the ability of our society to withstand the threat of terrorism. It is up to us to see that this information reaches both the media and the citizenry.

SUGGESTED READINGS

- Ganor, Boaz (2005). *The Counter-Terrorism Puzzle: A Guide for Decision Makers.* Transaction Publishers.
- Hoffman, Bruce (2006). *Through Our Enemies' Eyes: Osama Bin Laden, Radical Islam, And the Future of America.* Potomac Books; Revised edition.
- Cragin, Kim (2004). "The Dynamic Terrorist Threat an Assessment of Group Motivations and Capabilities in a Changing World." RAND Corporation
- Jackson, Brian A. et al. (2005). "Aptitude for Destruction: Organizational Learning in Terrorist Groups and Its Implications for Combating Terrorism." RAND Corporation
- Sageman, Marc (2004). *Understanding Terror Networks.* University of Pennsylvania Press

ONLINE RESOURCES

- Memorial Institute for the Prevention of Terrorism (MIPT). Terrorism Knowledge Base (TKB). TKB provides in-depth information and tools on terrorist incidents, groups, and trials.
  http://www.tkb.org
- Terrorism Threat Assessment Resources, Intelligence Resource Program, Federation of American Scientists.
  ttp://www.fas.org/irp/threat/terror.htm
- LaFree, G., Dugan, L., Fogg, H.V., Scott, J. (2006). Building a Global Terrorism Database. The report provides an analysis of several terrorism databases. PDF file, 209 pages.
  http://www.ncjrs.gov/pdffiles1/nij/grants/214260.pdf

DISCUSSION QUESTIONS

1. How would one go about testing the model described in this chapter?
2. What are the risks inherent in relying solely on models such as the one discussed here? How might these risks be minimized?
3. To what degree does the model discussed here depend on the expertise and knowledge of the analyst? Which inputs could be deemed "objective" and free of the personal opinions of the analyst and which are by nature subjective?
4. Might there be a way of "automating" the model so that it could be used by laymen? What risks would this pose to the accuracy of the resultant conclusions?
5. How might the organization-specific factors change if we were dealing with threats from domestic groups rather than international ones?

9

IDENTIFYING AND EXPLOITING GROUP LEARNING PATTERNS FOR COUNTERTERRORISM

Horacio R. Trujillo[1] and Brian A. Jackson[2]
[1]*Research Fellow, RAND Corporation, Santa Monica, California, U.S.A. (trujillo@rand.org);*
[2]*Associate Director, Homeland Security Program, RAND Corporation, Arlington, Virginia,*
U.S.A. (bjackson@rand.org)

CHAPTER OVERVIEW

In this chapter, we describe a model for analyzing organizational learning in terrorist groups and suggest ways in which such a model can support counterterrorism analysis within the law enforcement and intelligence communities. Specifically, we discuss how such a model can contribute to the design of terrorism informatics and data analysis efforts.

1.   INTRODUCTION

Terrorist groups operate under largely hostile and unstable conditions, in which their ability to adapt to their circumstances is critical not only to their effectiveness but also their very survival.[1] Successful adaptation, however, does not occur automatically. Instead, the ability of terrorist groups to adapt successfully is dependent on their ability to learn.[2]

When a terrorist group can learn, it can purposefully adapt to improve its effectiveness. A terrorist organization that is adept at learning can alter its behavior to better evade detection, modify its tactics to inflict more damage in its attacks, recruit more aggressively without increasing its risk of infiltration, and even alter its portfolio of operations to realize its strategic agenda. This learning can range from incremental efforts by a group to continuously improve its capabilities, such as the ongoing development of improvised explosive devices (IEDs), to more dramatic efforts to bring about a discontinuous transformation of the group's capabilities and strategy, such as a shift from simple explosives to biological weapons or a shift from targeting local security forces to targeting civilian populations abroad. The greater a group's capacity for learning, the more resilient it can be to pressures from law enforcement and intelligence agencies, and the greater the threat it poses to its adversaries.

Simply acknowledging that terrorist groups can and do learn, however, does not automatically help law enforcement and intelligence organizations seeking to prevent terrorism. While noting that terrorist groups adapt to their environment and efforts to defeat them can help to explain why counterterrorism activities are not always effective, this acknowledgement alone provides little guidance as to how to anticipate terrorist groups' adaptations before they happen or how to disrupt these groups' efforts to improve their survivability or destructive capability. To do this, the *process* by which these groups learn and change over time must be understood.

In this chapter, we introduce a model for analyzing the process of organizational learning in terrorist groups and suggest ways in which such a model can support counterterrorism analysis, including the exploitation of informatics tools and strategies, within the law enforcement and intelligence communities. An understanding of the organizational learning process can contribute to counterterrorism informatics efforts in two complementary ways. First, an appreciation of how groups learn can help ensure that information collection and analysis systems capture this facet of terrorist behavior and therefore contribute most effectively to efforts to combat terrorism. Conversely, terrorism informatics may also have much to contribute to efforts to understand how these groups learn and adapt. Building a detailed understanding of groups' learning efforts can require the integration and analysis of a variety of data, potentially drawn from many independent sources. Appropriate information and simulation systems could potentially play critical roles in the process of bringing together that data, developing and validating models of group learning efforts, and contributing more broadly to the understanding of how these organizations learn and adapt over time.

In the remainder of the paper, we introduce the theory of organizational learning and a variety of concepts to describe different facets of groups learning efforts. As part of this discussion, we include a model of organizational learning as a four-stage process, which we have used in our past work to examine groups' learning activities. In the second section, we discuss how organizational learning models and theory can inform the design of terrorism informatics systems intended to contribute to efforts to combat terrorism.

2. ORGANIZATIONAL LEARNING

Before introducing a model for the analysis of organizational learning in terrorist groups, it is important to be clear on what is meant by organizational learning. We define organizational learning as the process through which the members of a group develop new knowledge about their activities and the outcomes they are generating, share it among group members, incorporate the new knowledge into the routines of the group, and preserve this knowledge in collective memory.[3]

Defined in this manner, organizational learning is a function of the learning activities of a group's members, but it is more than the sum of the individual learning of those members.[4] The unique attributes of organizational as opposed to individual learning provide groups with critical advantages in their generation and exploitation of knowledge. One of the most important of these advantages is that an organization is not capable of learning completely independently from all individual learning, but an organization can learn independently from any one particular individual. This resiliency advantage is complemented by a production advantage, in that organizations have been identified as also being more effective than individuals at continually building new knowledge or absorbing it from external sources. Organizational learning, unlike that of individuals, can both persist in the absence of any one person and grow more rapidly and broadly than that of any single group member alone.

However, the potential of organizational learning should also not be overstated. At the most basic level it is important not to overlook the critical role of individuals to an organization's learning process by either anthropomorphizing organizations or analyzing organizations as a unified, rather than collective and fragmented, entity. As Garratt (1987) and others have pointed out, in reality a relatively small number of a group's members usually have the most significant control or influence over the strategic decisions and direction of an organization. Because of the relative influence of such individuals within in an organization, what and how they learn may provide significant insight as to how their organization will learn and adapt to the environment. In this respect, the organization is viewed as a system that shapes and maintains the results of individuals learning efforts, but is still also dependent upon the learning of individuals.

Organizational learning of terrorist groups, thus, is both an important and complex process. And, as such, if we are to incorporate the assessment of organizational learning into counterterrorism analysis efforts, we need a model that can help us understand how terrorist groups learn and what factors affect this learning.

3.   A FOUR STAGE MODEL OF ORGANIZATIONAL LEARNING

A number of models of how organizations learn have been described in the literature, each seeking to break down the general concept of "learning" into specific sub-processes that are more analytically useful. In our work, we have used a model of organizational learning as a four-stage information process. We consider this model to be particularly appropriate for counterterrorism analysis because it breaks down organizational learning into four distinct stages – acquisition, distribution, interpretation and storage – which can make the analysis both more tractable. [5] The following sections describe each of the four components of the learning process.

3.1   Acquisition

The acquisition of information occurs in four ways, which we refer to as congenital or inherited knowledge, direct experience, vicarious experience and strategic learning actions. *Inherited knowledge* is the knowledge that the founding members, and especially leaders, bring to the group. The capabilities that were available to many Islamic fundamentalist groups by their individual members' prior experience in the Afghanistan resistance against the Soviets is one example of inherited knowledge; similar concerns have been cited about the potential knowledge individuals with experience in Iraq could bring to future terrorist groups and activities. Another is the experience that the original members of the Provisional Irish Republican

Army brought the group from their earlier experiences as part of the Republican movement. Inherited knowledge is most critical to newer terrorist groups and will decline in importance as the organization matures and acquires additional knowledge required for its survival and effectiveness.

Direct experience can be acquired in two ways – through experiments or through "learning-by-doing." While some terrorist groups might engage in intentional experiments to develop new knowledge, it is more likely that new knowledge is acquired unintentionally and unsystematically as groups carry out their activities. The challenge of learning-by-doing, not surprisingly, is thus the further processing of this new knowledge in a systematic fashion, as discussed below. In terms of intentional direct experience, experiments or other "learning actions" can take various forms, ranging from regularly executed activities aimed at uncovering new opportunities, such as uncovering new weaknesses in security systems, to more complex and unproven demonstration projects designed to test new ideas. A range of terrorist organizations have carried out such experimentation and innovation efforts in their development and improvement of explosives devices and other weapons systems.

Groups also capture by watching what other similar groups are doing, which we refer to as *vicarious experience*. While such observation might appear to be an obvious and even simple route to acquire new information, it can be difficult for groups to truly benefit from what they see. Terrorists can gain insight from other terrorist groups' activities either by actively monitoring other groups or passively becoming aware of other groups' activities through public reports. At the same time, however, terrorist groups, like other organizations, will frequently not be able to simply translate the insights they gain into actionable knowledge without some, potentially significant, effort.

Problems in applying new knowledge frequently come from the different between *explicit knowledge*, which is knowledge captured in writing or in a physical object like a piece of technology that can be easily transferred to a group, and *tacit knowledge*, the expertise needed to use the explicit knowledge effectively. Simply put, the knowledge involved in much terrorist activity can be characterized as explicit knowledge. Examples of the acquisition of explicit knowledge include the acquisition of basic tactical concepts by groups that they could employ explosives strapped to persons or airplanes as missiles from sources such as manuals or Internet knowledge sources, or even the actual acquisition of new weapons. However, the actual execution of new activities or the use of novel weapons will depend heavily upon tacit knowledge of how to utilize this explicit knowledge effectively. Tacit knowledge includes the expertise needed to use technologies or execute tactics well, elements frequently not transferred to the group when they acquire new explicit knowledge or technology. In reality, although explicit knowledge can be more readily obtained vicariously, it is often necessary for groups to actually develop the tacit knowledge needed to exploit their vicarious experience on their own through direct experience or experimentation. Finally, because of the need for terrorist groups to protect themselves from detection or infiltration, it is likely that they would be particularly resistant to importing tacit knowledge, which could require the introduction of foreign elements into their organizations, and would thus depend even more so intentional experimentation/training or learning-by-doing to develop this know-how.[6]   Nevertheless, if an organization is able to learn vicariously, it would not be limited to learning from other terrorist groups, but could also learn from organized crime, transnational businesses, or even counterterrorism agencies themselves. Examples of groups that have learned by observing counterterrorism operations, include the Provisional Irish Republican Army, Hezbollah in Lebanon, or the Tamil Tigers in Sri Lanka.[7]

Finally, terrorist groups can also acquire information by engaging in *strategic learning actions*, which include internal research and development, technology acquisition, and seeking to transfer knowledge from other entities. One of the most noteworthy examples of independent research and development by a terrorist group is Aum Shinryko's work on the development of biological and chemical weapons.[8] A similarly noteworthy example of inter-group cooperation is the reported training of members of the Revolutionary Armed Forces of Colombia (FARC) by the Provisional Irish Republican Army (PIRA).[9]

3.2   Distribution

While the acquisition of new information is an obvious necessary step in the organizational learning process, once new information is obtained it must also be distributed, interpreted and stored for organizational learning to occur. Distribution advances the learning process in that the more widely information can be distributed within an organization the more likely it is that it will be interpreted and exploited effectively. Distribution is also important for the storage of information, since the possession of knowledge by many group members reduces the chance the organizations' capabilities will deteriorate over time as members leave or are lost. Finally, the more broadly information can be distributed within an organization the more likely it is that the information will be available for use when it is needed.

Terrorist groups utilize a variety of distribution modes to disseminate information among their members, from training activities that impart knowledge first-hand, to documents that are either written and passed on by hand or published electronically and distributed and stored, openly or hidden, on the internet. In spite of the various alternatives, training activities, such as Islamic groups' use of camps in Afghanistan for many years, continue to be an especially critical means of distributing knowledge, both operational and strategic, to group members who can then disperse throughout a group's area of operations.

3.3 Interpretation

Interpretation is the assessment of information in the context of an organization's goals, capabilities and environment. Without interpretation, the information an organization collects cannot be meaningfully exploited to further the groups' goals. Factors that influence a group's ability to effectively interpret information include: how widely the information is distributed within the group,; the capabilities of and richness of the group's internal communication modes; and the extent to which different members of groups share common frames of reference to assess the information In its fullest sense, interpretation encompasses the values and criteria a group uses to judge the effectiveness of its current operations, the methods by which the group assesses how its environment or needs may be changing and how it might need to change in response, and the process that the group employs to decide whether to pursue new opportunities or activities.

Time can also be a critical factor in the interpretation process. In a high-pressure environment, a group must make judgments about new information and how to respond quickly enough to be effective. A group that makes the right decision, but does so too late, may damage rather than advance its interests. For example, terrorist groups' requirement to safeguard their knowledge from organizations seeking to combat terrorism is an important constraint on their abilities to distribute and thus interpret new information. If groups cannot maintain their security without bottlenecking critical information, their ability to learn will be degraded.[10]

Finally, beyond assessing new information and translating this information into new behaviors, a key element of groups' interpretation efforts is *unlearning*, or the discarding of ineffective or outmoded organizational dynamics.[11] Such unlearning can be especially important to terrorist groups as their evasion of counterterrorism and law enforcement activities, which are frequently based on the recognition of patterns in a group's past activities, is dependent on their ability to discard those modes of operation that have already been identified.

3.4   Storage

The fourth component of the organizational learning process is the storage of information so that the group can effectively access this information again in the future, either to use it as already interpreted or to be reinterpreted in light of newly added information. Most often, learning is captured almost exclusively in the memories of individual members of group, and as a result is largely a function of the distribution of the information. Not surprisingly, this is a rather limited approach to maintaining information and is potentially fragile and subject to deterioration – particularly for terrorist groups where the loss of members is a not unexpected, and occasionally inevitable, outcome of their activities (Carley, 1992; and Kim, 1993). Not surprisingly, this is the mode of storage most used by newly established groups. Significant amounts of information are stored by terrorist groups in this manner through in-person training. Beyond a reliance on its individual members, an organization can store its information in the fabric of the organization, including in the language employed by its members, in routine group activities or rituals, in group symbols and other forms of group culture, and even in the structure of the organization itself. Of course, information can also be stored in written manuals or in other physical media, such as in computers, on the Internet, or in physical storage repositories. As demonstrated by the range of terrorist training materials that have been captured by intelligence organizations or posted on the Internet websites demonstrate, these groups have often chosen combinations of these approaches to store information in written and readily transferable resources.

4.   PATHS OF ORGANIZATIONAL LEARNING

Not all organizational learning is of the same significance to terrorist groups. These groups, like others, can experience both incremental learning and transformational learning, with very different consequences.[12] Incremental learning is the changing of repetitive routines, such as the tracking and correction of errors in specific activities, within the existing boundaries, rules, and norms of the group. In other words, incremental learning is what groups experience as they learn to carry out even more effectively those activities in which they already engaged. Incremental learning generally focus on process improvement: a good example of such a process is the improvement of the Provisional Irish Republican Army of its explosive initiation devices in response to deployment of countermeasures by the British military or, in a more recent example, in the Iraqi insurgents' improvisation of new explosive devices and roadblock strategies.[13]

In comparison, transformational learning involves the innovation of entirely new processes, objectives or organizational structures that can usually be recognized in more dramatic departure from a group's current activities. As examples, terrorist groups experience transformational learning when they redefine their strategic goals, abandon a regularly employed tactic, or adopt an entirely new mode of attack. While transformational learning can result from adaptations to remedy errors in specific activities, the source of most incremental learning, transformational learning entails the philosophical and/or strategic re-evaluation of the of the group's raison d'etre rather than simply its tactical or operational activities. The focus of transformational learning is not to do a previously identified activity more effectively, but to reconsider which activities to engage in and why, with an appreciation of the effects of any change on the long-term mission of the group. As such, transformational change occurs in most cases when a group experiences significant shifts in its environment that threaten its survival or present a unique opportunity for a dramatic step forward towards the realization of its overall organizational goal. Both Al Qaeda's choices in designing its organization as an international network of loosely coupled cells and its use of airplanes as bombs are examples of transformational learning (Arquilla and Ronfeldt, 2001). Importantly, the distinction between incremental and transformational learning should not be interpreted as absolute, as incremental learning over time can result in the transformational adaptation of a group.[14]

5. DETERMINANTS OF ORGANIZATIONAL LEARNING

Even though all groups learn to some extent, the ability to do so can differ considerably from group to group. Researchers have identified a wide variety of organizational characteristics that influence a group's ability to learn effectively.[15] We focus on four groups of factors that are key influences in a group's capacity to learn – group structure, culture, resources, and environment.

5.1 Structure

The structure of authority and communication within an organization can be a major shaping force of its learning ability. We focus on two aspects of structure that we consider to be particularly strong influences on a group's learning capacity – (1) the extent of hierarchy or centralization of organizational command and control processes, and (2) the robustness of organizational communications systems. First, a range of studies have identified learning problems associated with hierarchical organizational structures since information can be lost as it is transmitted from level to level within the group.[16] This implies that less structured terrorist operations might be more capable of effective learning. On the other hand, this passing of information through a hierarchy can serve as an institutional mechanism for the redundant storage of information, which makes the more structured organization more resilient to deterioration of accumulated knowledge. Similarly, because of their formally defined communications paths, more hierarchically structured or centralized organizations can be less susceptible to information distribution failures.

Of course, organizations do not have to be either fully centralized or decentralized, and as such groups can blend strengths and weaknesses of these different structures depending on where they position themselves along the spectrum of network organizational types.[17] The most well-known example of this phenomenon is al Qaeda, which has seemingly been able to benefit from both forms of organizational structure, in accumulating and diffusing knowledge while also promoting rapid experimentation by local cells. While there is some benefit that can be gained from blending these different organizational structures, these so-called hybrid organizations can also be more difficult to control.

The communications structure within an organization can also facilitate or impede the group's ability to learn and adapt. In this context, communications should be understood broadly, including training of group members, manuals circulated in the group that codify organizational values and practices, operating routines and tactics that are shared informally among group members, and formal and informal meetings of members, in addition to the actual technical infrastructure set-up for group communications (i.e. fixed and mobile telephony, radios, Internet systems). The more robust a group's communications systems, the more capable the organization can be in carrying out the four phases of group learning.

5.2   Culture

Because organizational culture is difficult to define, studies of its effect of the learning capacity of groups have focused on specific group dynamics that can influence learning. We focus first on two of these factors – (1) the organizational interest in learning, and (2) the organizational tolerance for risk-taking. Organizational interest in learning, is driven primarily by the group's leadership and the emphasis it places on seeking out new capabilities and opportunities, including undertaking intentional efforts to acquire and distribute new knowledge. An organization's tolerance for risk, characterized by the prevailing attitude of a group's membership toward experimenting with new and even unproven practices, is also influence significantly by group leadership. The more willing a group and particularly its leaders are to taking risks, the greater the chance the organization will be to both purse new opportunities (which involve the risk of failure and other potentially negative consequences) and to avoid emerging threats to the group. For example, a terrorist organization that won't try new things – transition from placed bombs to mortars, for example – would lose its ability to carry out attacks if security measures were put in place to defend against its preferred attack mode. In comparison, if a group were willing to experiment, even though this might result in a number of less than successful operations as its members gained proficiency with a new weapon, might eventually overcome the new hardening measures and continue to pose a meaningful threat against the target.

Organizations also suffer from "learning disturbances" – elements of an organization's culture that get in the way of learning, such as role constraints, situational and fragmented learning, and opportunistic learning. Role constraints arise from rigid organizational assignments that limit the individual group members' ability to acquire, distribute, interpret or store information. In cases of situational and fragmented learning, new knowledge gained by individual members is not distributed or stored in such a way that it can be readily accessed and exploited by the full membership that could benefit from it to enhance the capabilities of the organization. Finally, opportunistic learning occurs when there are appropriate mechanisms in place for storing and distributing organizational knowledge, but a group's culture may motivate members not to use them. In such cases, individuals intentionally bypass organizational learning processes that they perceive as inadequate or not in their individual interests, which prevents the organization from learning along with the individual.

5.3   Resources

Third, the learning potential of organizations depends on what we call knowledge resources – its access to external sources of information and the absorptive capacity embodied in its members. First, the greater the degree to which an organization is connected to similar organizations and other sources of information relevant to its environment and operations, the higher the learning potential of the group. Second, an organization's absorptive capacity, or the degree to which it is capable of acquiring and interpreting new information, is related to the skills and especially the subject-area or technology-specific expertise of its members. As such, groups that already possess similar or complementary tacit or explicit knowledge to that which they are obtaining anew can more readily absorb and exploit this new information.   Any terrorist group that thus lacks an adequate level of absorptive capacity will be limited in its capacity to learn, regardless of its raw rate of information acquisition, distribution or storage.

5.4   Environment

Finally, an organization's environment will also shape its learning ability. Changes in groups' environment can provide incentives for learning or even force groups to experiment in ways they might not otherwise. A number of researchers have identified the level of uncertainty and the rate of change in an organization's environment as factors that can provide both incentives and disincentives for learning (Dodgson, 1993; and Garvin, 1993).   For example, Bron Taylor links the founding of Earth First!, whose members splintered from other less violent elements of the environmental movement, with the significant changes that were made in environmental policies during the Reagan Administration, and the Earth Liberation Front's initiation of major fire bombings with shifts in federal logging policy.[18]

More general environmental factors can also directly affect a groups' learning capability.   Some environmental characteristics – such as the proximity of knowledge sources or a particularly permissive security environment – can facilitate learning for groups that attempt it by making it easier to access needed resources and providing the freedom of action needed to experiment with and explore new operational concepts or technologies.   These factors are key reasons why terrorist access to safe havens – areas or nations where they are insulated from counterterrorist pressures – are worrisome from an innovation perspective. Although strong security pressure can provide a potent incentive for learning – as described previously – it can also make learning more difficult by depriving groups of the access to resources and liberty to learn.

6.   HOW AN ORGANIZATIONAL LEARNING MODEL CAN INFORM THE DESIGN OF TERRORISM INFORMATICS SYSTEMS

Although it is important to recognize that terrorist groups learn, simply noting that such adaptation is occurring does not provide sufficient guidance or insight to meaningfully improve counterterrorism analysis. Greater detail and specificity is needed to make such awareness *actionable* – that is, counterterrorist analysts need to understand not just that terrorist groups learn but *how* they learn in order to appropriately monitor and assess their learning activities and outcomes. The model of terrorist learning described above moves toward that needed understanding: by breaking down the composite and complex process of "learning" into discrete pieces, the information process model helps frame specific and actionable questions about how individual terrorist groups learn. Such actionable questions – questions of sufficient specificity that they suggest both the data necessary to answer them and how that data might be collected – can similarly help to link information systems and informatics tools to efforts to detect and understand terrorist group behavior. For the purposes of highlighting how a model of organizational learning can inform the design of terrorism informatics, we will examine the utility of the model in ensuring the right intelligence is collected to understand terrorist efforts to innovate, how those data are filtered, and that the data can be properly interpreted.[19]

6.1   Collecting the Right Information

For an intelligence analyst to be able to detect and understand terrorist learning efforts, the right information must be available. Because successful organizational learning requires a terrorist group to carry out all four of the component processes described previously (acquisition, distribution, interpretation and storage), information regarding a group's progress along all four dimensions is necessary to piece together a complete picture of the group's learning. In the absence of information on any of the steps – if there are "blind spots" where intelligence data are not available – the analyst cannot be expected to understand what a group is doing or the likely consequences of its learning activities. By providing a clear delineation of what information must be collected to have a complete picture of a terrorists' group learning, the model that we have described can help to ensure that blind spots do not go unnoticed and can instead be filled. As such, a model of organizational learning can help to guide the design of information systems and the collection of data to populate them and, once gathered, ensure that it is managed in a way that ensures it will be available and appropriately evaluated to increase understanding of how groups are changing over time.

6.2   Filtering Collected Data

Because of the nature of intelligence collection, much more data is invariably collected than can be analyzed effectively. In a deep stream of incoming intelligence, there is always therefore the risk that key pieces of information will slip by unnoticed. Pieces of data that are clearly important are not likely to be overlooked. As a result, large transformational changes in a group are generally obvious – its operations have changed direction in major ways or it has adopted entirely new weapons and tactics than it did so before. Such shifts are likely to be noticed and will therefore be pulled out of the intelligence stream for additional attention. More subtle changes, such as those associated with incremental learning may be less obvious, however, as the immediate outputs of incremental change will generally be harder to recognize and the larger effects of incremental change emerge over time. In their incremental learning, terrorist groups may also exploit different acquisition, interpretation, distribution, and storage practices than when pursuing more transformative learning. As discussed previously, ignoring the succession of incremental changes over time could set the stage for not being able to detect any subsequent transformative shift in capabilities or strategies.

In order to make use of the massive amounts of intelligence that can be collected each day, analysts must rely on analytical frameworks to contextualize this information and make judgments about the relative importance of individual pieces of data.[20] In the absence of analytical frameworks describing group learning, relevant data indicating that a group is attempting to innovate or change its operational practices may not be identified as important and could therefore slip by unnoticed. By dissecting group learning processes in more detail and defining a broader range of processes and characteristics relevant to adaptive behaviors, models of group learning can provide an analytical framework to help ensure relevant intelligence is detected and examined. Such frameworks could be built into informatics systems to help the analyst continually scan and analyze data on various critical indicators of organizational learning, shifts in which could suggest that a group is attempting to or has been able to enhance their capabilities or shift targets. These type of automated filters or analysis tools could potentially be used to cue analysts attention to data relevant to understanding learning activities – provided appropriate cues can be devised that can help to identify potentially useful data out of the background of other data. Some such cues could be based on the outputs of learning – use of new tactics, significant changes in apparent group skill or performance, etc. but, such filters only suggest to the analyst that learning has occurred, not how or why. Models that drill inside the process could help develop tools that can cue attention toward less obvious data and apparent group activities to lead the analyst to recognize the learning process before it is complete and its effects realized.

6.3   Analyzing Intelligence Data

The analysis of intelligence data relating to learning can be seen as attempting to achieve two goals: (1) detect group learning efforts before they are complete and (2) once detected, anticipate whether or not the group will be successful in its attempt to learn. Models of group learning can contribute to achieving both goals – and to the design of informatics systems to help analysts do so.

Frameworks to Help Detect Group Learning. The process of intelligence analysis is one of ascertaining meaning from fragmentary, deceptive, and otherwise imperfect data. Just as analytical frameworks help to identify what pieces of data are important and merit attention, similar frameworks or "analytical lenses" help to make sense of individual pieces of information in light of what is otherwise known about the group. That is, they help to determine what a newly detected piece of information means in light of current understandings of the group's strategy, the behavior of its leadership, its internal dynamics, and so on.[21]

The assumed meaning ascribed to a group recruiting members in a new geographical area can be heavily dependent on framework. In a framework focused on the group's strategic goals, such an act might be interpreted as an expansion of violent activities into the new country. In a framework assessing behavior with respect to the psychology and internal dynamics of an organization, the same act might be interpreted as reflecting the group's need to appear dynamic to support the morale of its current membership. Without an analytical framework that captures a terrorist group's learning activities, an analyst may not be able to appreciate the learning implications of the group's actions. From a learning perspective, such activity might indicate that the group is gathering information or knowledge for the purpose of expanding its capabilities.

Similarly, specific attacks that do not make sense from a strategic perspective may be perfectly reasonable from a learning perspective. For example, if a terrorist group attacks a target that seems to have low priority or is outside its usual areas of operation, an analysis focused on strategy might conclude that the group has been forced away from its favored targets or has shifted its goals. But from a learning perspective, such an attack could be seen quite differently, perhaps as an important "dress rehearsal" to help the group learn what it needs to do to carry out a higher-profile operation in the future. Similarly, individual operations that appear detrimental to a terrorist group's interests from a strategic or psychological perspective may have very different implications when viewed from the perspective of the group's learning goals.

While analytic lenses and frameworks will be always applied "manually" by analysts as part of their interaction and examination of intelligence data, appropriately designed informatics tools and expert systems could play a part in doing so as well. Informatics tools, incorporating models of group learning, could help analysts examine group activities through all such lenses – helping to suggest hypotheses about the meaning of different group activities to ensure that activities are not misinterpreted and their importance overlooked.

Tools to Help Anticipate Whether Terrorist Learning Efforts Will Be Successful. Even after they have been identified, the analyst must assess whether or not the effort will be successful. Even if a terrorist organization *wants* to do something new, if it cannot do it successfully its desire to do so poses little or no threat. Trying to anticipate whether or not a group will be successful in its learning efforts is a problem of projection – based on what we know about the group and its past learning efforts, what are the chances that it will succeed at what it is trying to do now? Even if it will succeed, will it be easy or hard? How much will doing so cost the group in time, money, or other resources that have to be devoted to the learning effort?

Because learning is the link between a group's intentions and its ability to bring together the information and resources to actually realize these intentions, understanding how terrorist groups learn can directly contribute to anticipating whether their learning actions will be successful and, accordingly, to determine the level of threat they pose. Because of the range of characteristics that have been identified as relevant to assessing learning performance, informatics tools could provide critical support to intelligence analysts in making these assessments. Data and analytical systems that tabulate available data on groups in relevant ways are a simple example. At a more sophisticated level, given the complexities of group learning processes and the heterogeneity among groups that make it difficult to draw unambiguous conclusions about learning ability, systems that enable comparison of different models, theories, data, and analytical approaches could be very important for assessing the sensitivity of conclusions to particular assumptions – and the potential consequences if those assumptions turn out to be wrong.

7.   CONCLUSIONS AND DISCUSSION

Understanding and detecting terrorist group learning and adaptation is largely a question of data – collecting the right information, identifying the right pieces of data for subsequent attention, and interpreting the data to provide insight as to its implications for about terrorist motivations and capabilities. Success in this process means the intelligence analyst can deny the terrorist the advantage of surprise and may gain the opportunity to disrupt the group's future plans. Failure by a security organization means success for the terrorist, and the need for security organizations once again to respond and "catch up" to the new security environment.

Informatics systems can play an important role in this ongoing competition. Unambiguous and easy indicators of terrorist groups' learning – new weapons used, new skills applied, new strategic targets hit – are readily available to counterterrorism analysts only after the terrorists' learning efforts are complete and most opportunities for prevention or disruption are already past. Detecting learning earlier requires bringing together data from disparate sources and seeking out clues to learning efforts still underway – indicators of terrorists'' information gathering, assessments of their current operations or future opportunities, their distribution of information, and their ability to store and recall lessons from their experiences. Though much more difficult, if law enforcement and intelligence agents can develop and employ well-crafted informatics tools to detect such signatures, a much broader range of options for prevention and disruption could be available and could meaningfully increase the capacity of security organizations for defending against the terrorist threat.

8. ACKNOWLEDGEMENTS

This chapter draws on research supported in part by Grant No. 2003-IJ-CX-1022, awarded by the National Institute of Justice, Office of Justice Programs, U.S. Department of Justice. Points of view in this document are those of the authors and do not necessarily represent the official position or policies of the RAND Corporation or the U.S. Department of Justice. Portions of this chapter draw on the project reports of that study, whose full bibliographic information is cited in the suggested readings at the conclusion of the chapter.

We would like to thank the many individuals at RAND, the National Institute of Justice and elsewhere who contributed to and supported the original RAND study on organizational learning in terrorist groups. In particular, we would like to acknowledge and express our gratitude to John C. Baker, Kim Cragin, John Parachini and Peter Chalk, our colleagues and coauthors of our original study. Finally, we would like to thank our colleagues Barbara Raymond and Mike Wermuth for their helpful suggestions for improving the manuscript.

NOTES

[1] For detailed discussions of the adaptability of terrorist groups, see K. Cragin and S. Daly, *The Dynamic Terrorist Threat: An Assessment of Group Motivations and Capabilities in a Changing World*, Santa Monica: RAND, 2004; M. Crenshaw, "Innovation: Decision Points in the Trajectory of Terrorism," presented at the Conference on Trajectories of Terrorist Violence in Europe, Minda de Gunzburg Center for European Studies, Harvard University, Cambridge, MA, March 9–11, 2001; S. Gerwehr and R. Glenn, *Unweaving the Web: Deception and Adaptation in Future Urban Operations*, Santa Monica: RAND, 2003. pp. 49-53; "Change and Continuity in Terrorism," *Studies in Conflict and Terrorism*, Vol. 24, 2001, pp. 417–428.; B. Jackson, et al, *Aptitude for Destruction*, Volumes 1 and 2, Santa Monica: RAND, 2005; J. Kitfield, "Osama's Learning Curve," *National Journal*, Vol. 33, No. 45, 2001, pp. 3506–3511; C. Lutes,, "Al-Qaida in Action and Learning: A Systems Approach," December 2001, http://www.au.af.mil/ au/awc/awcgate/ readings/ al_qaida2.htm; Stern, Jessica, "The Protean Enemy," *Foreign Affairs*, Vol. 82, No. 4, 2003, pp. 27–40; and Thomas, Troy S., and William D. Casebeer, *Violent Systems: Defeating Terrorists, Insurgents, and Other Non-State Adversaries*, Colorado Springs, CO: United States Air Force Academy, United States Air Force Institute for National Security Studies, 2004, pp. 35–38.

[2] While change in the way a group carries out its activities is frequently indicative of learning, change alone is not sufficient to indicate that organizational learning has occurred. All change is not necessarily intentional; some change can be unintentional or be a byproduct of other group behavior. As such, in this discussion, we consider learning to be the sustained change of organizational behavior that arises from intentional action by or within a group, such as one or more of the following: the intentional search for new knowledge or skills; intentional evaluation of group behaviors, new or old, that leads to efforts to retain valuable behaviors and discard others; and intentional dissemination of valued knowledge within a group or among groups.

[3] This definition is a composite of others that can be found in the organizational learning literature. Ours draws in particular from that of Barnett (C. Barnett, n.d., "Rethinking organizational learning theories: A review and synthesis of the primary literature," Unpublished manuscript, University of New Hampshire, Whittemore School of Business and Economics) cited by Lipshitz et al (2002) which defines organizational learning as: "an experience-based process through which knowledge about action-outcome relationships develops, is encoded in routines, is embedded in organizational memory and changes collective behavior" (p.82).

[4] Two brief citations from the literature on organizational learning distill the argument of recognizing organizational learning as distinct from individual learning. The first, from Romme and Dillen (1997), emphasizes the nature of organizational learning as focusing on the change of shared beliefs and collective behaviors of members of a group: "Organizations do not have brains but do have cognitive systems and memories at their disposal, through which certain modes of behavior, mental models, norms and values are retained." The second, from Easterby-Smith et al (2000), emphasizes the supra-individual character of organizational learning: "Members [of an organization] come and go, and leadership changes, but organizations' memories preserve certain behaviors, mental maps, norms and values over time."

[5] Romme and Dillen (1997) present a brief but detailed treatment of organizational learning as an information process from which some of this material has been adapted.

[6] See K.K. Jones "Competing to learn in Japan," *McKinsey Quarterly* 1, 1991 pp.45-57.

[7] See discussion in B.A. Jackson, et al, *Aptitude for Destruction, Volume 2: Case Studies of Organizational Learning in Five Terrorist Groups*, Santa Monica, CA: RAND Corporation, 2005

[8] J. Parachini, "Aum Shinrikyo," in *Aptitude for Destruction, Volume 2: Case Studies of Organizational Learning in Five Terrorist Groups*, Santa Monica: RAND Corporation, 2005.

[9] A. Ward, "The IRA's Foreign Links," *IISS Strategic Comments* 9:5, July, 2003

[10] See R.L. Daft and R.H. Lengal, "Organizational Information Requirements: Media richness and structural design," *Management Science* 32, pp. 554-571, 1986.

[11] It should be noted that some researchers use the term unlearning to refer to the maladaptation of organizations that results in unwanted or less effective outcomes (see Crossan et al, 1995). We have chosen not to adopt this convention since it is our belief that defining learning as a positive process, and unlearning as simply a mode of learning, simplifies the analysis. From the perspective adopted in this paper, maladaptive learning, rather than unlearning, would be the result of a group attempting to learn but doing it very poorly.

[12] We utilize incremental and transformational learning as roughly equivalent to "single-loop" and "double-loop" learning as discussed in the academic literature on organizational learning. We believe that the distinction originally drawn by Argyris and Schön (1978) is a valuable one, which we borrow from.

[13] See Hoffman, B. "Terrorism Trends and Prospects," in *Countering the New Terrorism*, I.O. Lesser et al, Santa Monica:RAND,1999, pp.7-38, on the IRA,, and Scarborough, R., "Iraqi guerrillas devise new tactics as Americans fine tune techniques" *The Washington Times*, 31 July 2003, on the Iraqi insurgents.

[14] Both Argyris and Schön (1978) and Senge (1990) note that most organizations do reasonably well with incremental learning but not with transformational learning.

[15] See, B. Jackson et al., *Aptitude for Destruction*, Volumes 1 and 2 (2005), and references therein, for a more complete discussion on the determinants on organizational learning in terrorist groups.

[16] See D.M. Schweiger,, T. Atamar and R. Calori, "Transnational project teams and networks: making the multinational organization more effective," *Journal of World Business* 38, pp.127-140, 2003

[17] For a review of network forms of organization, including a discussion of the classification of more structured hierarchies and more loosely organized groups as forms of networks, see J. Podolny and K. Page, "Network Forms of Organization." *Annual Review of Sociology*, 24, pp.57-76, 1998. See also, B.A. Jackson, "Groups, Networks or Movements," *Studies in Conflict and Terrorism*, 29:3, April-May 2006, pp.241-262, for a discussion of command and control linkages in groups as distinct from the group structure defined by those linkages

[18] B. Taylor, "Religion, Violence and Radical Environmentalism: From Earth First! to the Unabomber to the Earth Liberation Front," *Terrorism and Political Violence*, 10/4, pp. 1-42, 1998. Also, for a discussion of organizational in the radical environmentalist movement, see H. Trujillo "The Radical Environmentalist Movement," in *Aptitude for Destruction, Volume 2: Case Studies of Organizational Learning in Five Terrorist Groups*, Santa Monica: RAND Corporation, 2005, pp. 141-172.

[19] For readers interested in a comprehensive discussion of applications of organizational learning in efforts to combat terrorism, see Jackson et al, 2006a.

[20] See M. Libicki and S. Pfleeger, *Collecting the Dots*, Santa Monica: RAND, January 2004

[21] See, for example, McCormick, Gordon H., "Terrorist Decision Making," *Annual Review of Political Science*, Vol. 6, 2003, pp. 473-507.

REFERENCES

Argyris, C. and D. Schön, *Organizational Learning: A Theory of Action Perspective*, Reading: Addison-Wesley, 1978.

Argyris, C. and D. Schön, *Organizational Learning II: Theory, Method and Practice*, Reading: Addison-Wesley, 1996.

Carley, K. "Organizational Learning and Personnel Turnover," *Organization Science* 3, pp. 20-46, 1992.

Crossan, M.M., Lane, H.W., White, R.E. and Djurfeldt, L. (1995), "Organizational learning: dimensions for a theory", *The International Journal of Organizational Analysis*, Vol. 3, No. 4, (October), pp.337-360.

Cyert, R.M. and J. G. March, *A Behavioral Theory of the Firm*, Englewood Cliffs: Prentice Hall, 1963.

Dodgson, M. "Organizational Learning: A review of some literature," *Organizational Studies* 14, 1993, pp. 375-394.

Easterby-Smith, M., and M. Crossan and D. Nicolini, "Organizational Learning: Debates Past, Present and Future," *Journal of Management Studies* 37:6, September 2000.

Fiol, C.M., and M.A. Lyles, Organizational Learning," *Academy of Management Review* 10, pp. 803-813, 1985.

Garratt, R., *The Learning Organization*, London: Fontana: Collins, 1987.

Garvin, D.A., "Building a Learning Organization," *Harvard Business Review* 71, July-August, 1993, pp.78-91.

Hedberg, B. "How Organizations Learn and Unlearn" in *Handbook of Organizational Design*, Volume 1, P.C. Nyström and W.H. Starbuck, editors, Oxford: Oxford University Press, pp. 3-27, 1981.

Huber, G.P., Organizational Learning: "The contributing process and the literatures," *Organizational Science* 2, pp. 88-115.

Kim, D.H., "The link between individual and organizational learning," *Sloan Management Review*, Fall 1993, pp. 37-50.

Lipshitz, R. M. Popper, and V. Friedman, "A Multifacet Model of Organizational Learning," *The Journal of Applied Behavioral Science*, 38:1, March 2002

McGill, M.E., and J.W. Slocum, Jr., "Unlearning the Organization," *Organization Dynamics* 22, pp. 67-79, Autumn 1993.

March, J.G. and J.P. Olsen, "The uncertainty of the past: Organizational learning under ambiguity," *European Journal of Policy Review* 3:2, pp. 147-171, 1975.

Miller, D., "A preliminary topology of organizational learning: Synthesizing the literature," *Journal of Management*, 22:3, pp. 485-505,

Romme, G., and R. Dillen, "Mapping the Landscape of Organizational Learning," *European Management Journal* 15:1, 1997.

Senge, P. *The Fifth Discipline: The art and practice of the learning organization*, New York:Doubleday, 1990.

Shrivastava, P. "A Typology of Organizational Learning Systems," *Journal of Management Studies* 20, pp. 7-28, 1983.

SUGGESTED READINGS

- B.A. Jackson, et al, *Aptitude for Destruction, Volume 1: Organizational Learning in Terrorist Groups and its Implications for Combating Terrorism*, Santa Monica, CA: RAND Corporation, 2005.
- B.A. Jackson, et al, *Aptitude for Destruction, Volume 2: Case Studies of Organizational Learning in Five Terrorist Groups*, Santa Monica, CA: RAND Corporation, 2005.
- J. Arquilla and D. Ronfeldt, *Networks and Netwars: The Future of Terror, Crime and Militancy*, Santa Monica, CA: RAND Corporation, 2001.
- M. Libicki, and S. Pfleeger, *Collecting the Dots*, Santa Monica: RAND, January 2004.
- I.O. Lesser et al, *Countering the New Terrorism*, Santa Monica: RAND, 1999, pp.7-38.

ONLINE RESOURCES

- RAND Corporation
  www.rand.org
- National Memorial Institute for the Prevention of Terrorism (MIPT)
  www.mipt.org
- National Institute of Justice
  www.ojp.usdoj.gov/nij

DISCUSSION QUESTIONS

1. What is the role of models or analytical frameworks in counterterrorism analysis? What value does an appreciation of organizational learning add to counterterrorism analysis and especially terrorism informatics?
2. Structure, culture, resources and environment are introduced as general categories of factors that influence the capacity of an organization to learn. Identify specific examples of how each of these determinants might be considered to have influenced the adaptive behavior of one or more terrorist groups. What lessons do these examples suggest for the design of terrorism informatics systems?
3. In thinking about designing information systems to help detect group learning efforts, what type of information should be collected and input into the system? What indicators or signatures might be valuable to look

for in the data? What ways could groups adapt their behaviors to obscure or remove those signatures?

4. The model of organizational learning presented here is considered to apply to all organizations. However, terrorist groups are different from other organizations in important ways. What adjustments in data collection and interpretation do these differences make necessary to properly assess the organizational learning of terrorist groups?

5. How do terrorist organizations' need to maintain their security affect their ability to learn and adapt?

6. Provide specific examples of the incremental learning and transformational learning of a terrorist group. What characterizes the one type of learning from the other? If one group adapts its behavior in a way that is incremental for that group, does the same adaptation have to be considered incremental for all other groups that make the same change in behavior? How can counterterrorism analysis systems, and especially terrorism informatics systems, be designed to provide appropriate detection and warning of incremental and transformational learning?

7. In recent years, there has been significant focus on violent organizations that have adopted loosely controlled network structures where individual units may not know about the existence of other units and make all their own decisions about the activities their unit undertakes. What are the strengths and weaknesses of this model from a group learning perspective?

8. In the chapter, the example of a group recruiting members in a new area was used to illustrate how a "learning-focused analytical lens" could suggest a different interpretation for a piece of intelligence data. What alternative meanings might be ascribed to the detection of a large explosion in a suspected terrorist safehouse through the different analytical lenses described in the text?

10

HOMELAND INSECURITY
Data Mining, Privacy, Disclosure Limitation, and the Hunt for Terrorists

Stephen E. Fienberg
Department of Statistics, Machine Learning Department, and Cylab, Carnegie Mellon University, Pittsburgh, Pennsylvania, U.S.A. (fienberg@stat.cmu.edu)

CHAPTER OVERVIEW

Following the events of September 11, 2001, there has been heightened attention in the United States and elsewhere to the use of multiple government and private databases for the identification of possible perpetrators of future attacks, as well as an unprecedented expansion of federal government data mining activities, many involving databases containing personal information. There have also been claims that prospective datamining could be used to find the "signature" of terrorist cells embedded in larger networks. We present an overview of why the public has concerns about such activities and describe some proposals for the search of multiple databases which supposedly do not compromise possible pledges of confidentiality to the individuals whose data are included. We also explore their link to the related literatures on privacy-preserving data mining. In particular, we focus on the matching problem across databases and the concept of "selective revelation" and their confidentiality implications.

1.   INTRODUCTION

The events of September 11, 2001 changed our lives in irrevocable ways. They have also changed the focus of US government activities, both at home and abroad. You would have to have been in hibernation for the past five years to miss the fact that the U.S. government is engaged in a hunt for terrorists. While the government has often used data collected for administrative and other purposes as part of security efforts, after 9/11 the effort has intensified and shifted in some surprising ways, raising questions about the appropriate uses of data mining tools, privacy, and the protection of individual information.

Where and how does the government look for terrorists? Multiple government organizations are involved in these security efforts, beginning with the National Security Agency (NSA), and including a variety of other agencies such as the Central Intelligence Agency (CIA), Federal Bureau of Investigation (FBI), and those within the Department of Homeland Security (DHS). Clearly there are many sources of information that government officials tap into in this regard. Many believe that if we sift through the data available from a wide array of sources using the latest data mining techniques we'll find the clues to prevent the next terrorist attack. Some of these people believe that every database and every source of information is fair game—airline and other transportation records, telephone call logs, responses to surveys, credit card purchases, census data, etc.—irrespective of promises of protection, legal and otherwise.

If data mining of existing data bases is such a good thing, why are civil libertarian and public watch-dog groups like the American Civil Liberties Union (ACLU) so upset over its use?   One of the problems is that many of the databases that are targets for data mining contain personal information that we have long believed was not subject to such data snooping such as our telephone and library records and especially those data back up by legal pledges of confidentiality. Thus there is a public issue as to whether or at least the extent to which we should trade our privacy for the protection against terrorist attacks that data mining might afford us.

There's one further problem: We don't know what form the next attack will take, but we can look for clues about potential terrorists we have seen in the past. This is why Congress, in its wisdom as part of the USA Patriot Act, rescinded the confidentiality provision for data from the National Center of Educational Statistics (NCES) to allow government access to identifiable individual information. This still might sound strange to you until you realize that NCES data files include information on individuals enrolling in flight schools and we know that several of the 9/11 hijackers spent time at a flight school in Florida prior to their coordinated attack!

Moreover, the 20 attackers showed up in a variety of other "unprotected" non-confidential databases once they had been identified. And the price for this kind of "retrodiction" is the potential loss of privacy, especially when we look at the sources of the data the advocates of data mining want to exploit. As the Patriot Act came up for renewal this past summer, some in Congress attempted to force the government to disclose its use of data mining techniques in tracking suspects in terrorism cases, an effort that the Bush administration strongly resisted. Advocates for controls believe the public has the right to know what databases are being searched and with what data mining algorithms.

As pernicious as the USA Patriot Act provision rescinding the confidentiality provision of NCES was to many, perhaps the biggest threat to privacy in the hunt for terrorists comes from data warehouse operations that draw on all databases, public and private, confidential and not. Companies such as Acxiom, ChoicePoint and LexisNexis use their data to perform background check on prospective applicants to employers, insurers, and credit providers. The recent security lapses at these and other large organizations, such at Bank of America, have been regular news items over the past couple of years and they point to serious security vulnerabilities. Someone recently observed that the security lapses at these companies confirm the maxim that "a company can have information security without privacy but not privacy without information security."

The data warehouses also participate in the hunt for terrorists. They merge and match data on individuals, impervious to error and inaccuracies, and then repackage the data for sale to other private enterprises and government programs, at both the federal and state level. The ACLU website includes a "flash movie" of a telephone pizza order[1] that triggers a series of data retrievals from some gigantic integrated data base that includes medical records, travel information, magazine subscriptions, clothing purchases, and seemingly instantaneously linked local area crime reports. It represents the public's worst fears regarding the invasion of privacy that has come from e-commerce and growth and spread of data-warehousing. The website warns that "Government programs such as MATRIX and Carnivore are destroying our privacy. We live in a democratic society and government-controlled data systems are a dangerous step toward establishing a 24-hour surveillance society." What are these programs? Is the pizza movie myth or reality?

The remainder of this chapter is organized as follows: In the next section we briefly describe a related set of government data mining and data warehousing activities that came into the public eye following the terrorist attacks of September 11, 2001. One of the links with the more public e-commerce activities was MATRIX, referred to by the ACLU webpage but which has since been "publicly" abandoned. We then give an overview of record linkage and its use for merging large data files from diverse sources as well as its implications for the splitting of data bases for privacy protection, and following this we review some proposals that have surfaced for the search of multiple data bases without compromising possible pledges of confidentiality to the individuals whose data are included and their link to the related literature on privacy-preserving datamining. In particular, we focus on the concept of *selective revelation* and its confidentiality implications especially for the types of transaction data bases envisioned for incorporation into TIA. We relate these ideas to the recent statistical literature on disclosure limitation for confidential data bases and explain the problems with the privacy claims and we also discuss the utility of transactional data bases in the discovery of terrorist networks. We conclude with some observations regarding privacy protection, data warehousing, and data mining.

2.   HOMELAND SECURITY AND THE SEARCH FOR TERRORISTS

A recently issued report from the U.S. General Accounting Office (2004) notes that at least 52 agencies are using or are planning to use data mining, "factual data analysis," or "predictive analytics," in some 199 different efforts. Of these, at least 29 projects involve analyzing intelligence and detecting terrorist activities, or detecting criminal activities or patterns. Notable among the non-responders to the GAO inquiry were agencies like the CIA and the NSA.

Perhaps the most visible of these efforts was the *Total Information Awareness* (TIA) program initiated by the Defense Advanced Research Program (DARPA) in DARPA's Information Awareness Office (IAO), which was established in January 2002, in the aftermath of the September 11 terrorist attacks. The TIA research and development program was aimed at integrating information technologies into a prototype to provide tools to better detect, classify, and identify potential foreign terrorists. When it came under public scrutiny in 2003, TIA morphed into the *Terrorist Information Program* (still TIA) with essentially the same objectives although it too did not move forward into implementation. TIA served as the model, however, for the *Multistate Anti-terrorism Information Exchange* (MATRIX) system that was in use in seven states for a period of time during 2004 and 2005, and was intended to provide "the capability to store, analyze, and exchange sensitive terrorism-related information in MATRIX data bases among agencies, within a state, among states, and between state and federal agencies."

According to a recent report from the Congressional Research Service (Relyea and Seifert 2005) [footnotes omitted]:

The MATRIX project was initially developed in the days following the September 11, 2001, terrorist attacks by Seisint, a Florida-based information products company, in an effort to facilitate collaborative information sharing and factual data analysis. At the outset of the project, MATRIX included a component Seisint called the High Terrorist Factor (HTF), which was designed to identify individuals with high HTF scores, or so-called terrorism quotients, based on an analysis of demographic and behavioral data. Although the HTF scoring system appeared to attract the interest of officials, this feature was reportedly dropped from MATRIX because it relied on intelligence data not normally available to the law enforcement community and because of concerns about privacy abuses.

...The analytical core of the MATRIX pilot project is an application called Factual Analysis Criminal Threat Solution (FACTS), described as a "technological, investigative tool allowing query-based searches of available state and public records in the data reference repository." The FACTS application allows an authorized user to search "dynamically combined records from disparate datasets" based on partial information, and will "assemble" the results. The data reference repository used with FACTS represents the amalgamation of over 3.9 billion public records collected from thousands of sources. The data contained in FACTS include FAA pilot license and aircraft ownership records, property ownership records, information on vessels registered with the Coast Guard, state sexual offender lists, federal terrorist watch lists, corporation filings, Uniform Commercial Code filings, bankruptcy filings, state-issued professional license records, criminal history information, department of corrections information and photo images, driver's license information and photo images, motor vehicle registration information, and information from commercial sources that "are generally available to the public or legally permissible under federal law.

...To help address the privacy concerns associated with a centralized data repository, some officials have suggested switching to a distributed approach whereby each state would maintain possession of its data and control access according to its individual laws.

The data reference repository is said to exclude data from the following list of sources:

- telemarketing call lists,
- direct mail mailing lists,
- airline reservations or travel records,
- frequent flyer/hotel stay program membership information or activity,
- magazine subscription records,
- information about purchases made at retailers or over the Internet,
- telephone calling logs or records,
- credit or debit card numbers,
- mortgage or car payment information,
- bank account numbers or balance information,
- records of birth certificates, marriage licenses, and divorce decrees,
- utility bill payment information.

Nonetheless, MATRIX and its data records sound suspiciously like the ACLU Pizza Movie scenario! And in 2004, LexisNexis acquired Seisint and the security breaches were in the new Seisint subsidiary, the very same one that provides the data for MATRIX!

MATRIX was officially abandoned as a multi-state activity in April 2005 although individual states were allowed to continue with their parts of the program. For an assessment of the lack of privacy policies for MATRIX, see Privacy Office (2006). This does not mean the demise of the TIA effort, however, as there are other federal initiatives built on a similar model:

> *Analysis, Dissemination, Visualization, Insight, and Semantic Enhancement* (ADVISE), a research and development program within the Department of Homeland Security (DHS), part of its three-year-old "Threat and Vulnerability, Testing and Assessment" portfolio.[2]

> The *Information Awareness Prototype System* (IAPS), the core architecture that tied together numerous information extraction, analysis, and dissemination tools developed under TIA, including the privacy-protection technologies, was moved to the Advanced Research and Development Activity (ARDA), housed at NSA headquarters in Fort Meade, Md.[3]

In TIA, MATRIX, ADVISE, and IAPS, the idea is for the data miner to issue queries to the multiple linked data bases and receive responses that combine data on individuals across the data bases. The goal is the identification of terrorists or criminals in a way that would not be possible from the individual data bases. We distinguish between two aspects of this goal: (1) identification of known terrorists which is a form of retro- or postdiction, and (2) identification of potential future terrorists and profiling, which involves prediction. Prediction cannot be separated from uncertainty, postdiction might conceivably be. Most of the public outcry regarding TIA and MATRIX has focused on concerns regarding what Clarke (1988) described as "dataveillance" and terrorist profiling, i.e., concerns both about the use of data for purposes other than those for which they were collected without the consent of the individual, and about the quality and accuracy of the mined data and the likelihood that they may help falsely identify individuals as terrorists.

In the next two sections, we explore some issues related to the creation and the use of "linked" data bases for the privacy of the individuals whose confidential information in contained in them.

3.   MATCHING AND RECORD LINKAGE METHODS

More than 100 vendors offer record matching systems, some of which sell for thousands of dollars, but most of the underlying methodology for such systems is proprietary and few details are publicly available. Matches can occur at random. For example, consider a pair of files, A and B, containing n records on the same individuals. Then the probability of correctly matching exactly r individuals by picking a random permutation for file B and linking to file A is

$$\sum_{v=0}^{n-r} \frac{(-1)^{n-r}}{v!} / r!$$

Domingo-Ferrer and Torra (2003) derive this baseline and illustrate it numerically in an example with $n = 90$, where the expected number of correct matches is $O(10^{24})$. Working with actual data in the matching process can change this situation drastically.

Bilenko et al. (2003) provide an overview of the published literature on the topic noting that most methods rely on the existence of unique identifiers or use some variation of the algorithm presented in Fellegi and Sunter (1969). Fellegi and Sunter's approach is built on several key components for identifying matching pairs of records across two files:

- Represent every pair of records using a vector of features (variables) that describe similarity between individual record fields. Features can be Boolean (for example, last-namematches), discrete (for example, first n-characters-of-name-agree), or continuous (for example, string-edit-distance-between-first-names).
- Place feature vectors for record pairs into three classes: matches (M), non-matches (U), and possible matches. These correspond to "equivalent," "nonequivalent," and possibly equivalent (e.g., requiring human review) record pairs, respectively.

- Perform record-pair classification by calculating the ratio $P(\gamma|M)/(P(\gamma|U)$ for each candidate record pair, where γ is a feature vector for the pair and $P(\gamma|M)$ and $(P(\gamma|U)$ are the probabilities of observing that feature vector for a matched and nonmatched pair, respectively. Two thresholds based on desired error levels—T_μ and T_λ—optimally separate the ratio values for equivalent, possibly equivalent, and nonequivalent record pairs.
- When no training data in the form of duplicate and nonduplicate record pairs is available, matching can be unsupervised, where conditional probabilities for feature values are estimated using observed frequencies.
- Because most record pairs are clearly non-matches, we need not consider them for matching. The way to manage this is to "block" the data bases, e.g., based on geography or some other variable in both data bases, so that only records in comparable blocks are compared. Such a strategy significantly improves efficiency.

The first four components lay the groundwork for accuracy of record-pair matching using statistical techniques such as logistic regression, the EM algorithm, and Bayes networks (e.g., see Jaro 1995, Larson and Rubin 2001, and Winkler 2002). Accuracy is well-known to be high when there is a 1-1 match between records in the two systems and deteriorates as the overlap between the files decreases as well as with the extent of measurement error in the feature values. While the use of human review of possible matches has been an integral part of many statistical applications, it may well be infeasible for large-scale data warehousing. The fifth component provides for efficiently processing large data bases, but to the extent that blocking is approximate and possibly inaccurate its use decreases the accuracy of record pair matching.

There are three potential lessons associated with this literature on matching and the methods it has produced:

- If we are trying to protect against an intruder who would like to merge the data in a confidential data base with an external data base in his/her possession, then we need to assure ourselves and the intruder that the accuracy of matching is low and that individuals cannot be identified with high probability. We need to keep in mind that an intruder will have easy access to a host of identifiable public record systems. For example, as of September 7, 2005, *SearchSystems.net*[4] listed 34,035 free searchable public record data bases on its website!
- One strategy for protecting a data base against attack from an intruder is to split it into parts, perhaps overlapping, to decrease the likelihood of accurate matches. The parts should be immune from attack (with high probability) but of value for analytical purposes. For categorical data this might correspond to reporting lower-dimensional margins from a high-dimensional contingency table, c.f., Dobra and Fienberg (2001, 2003),

and Fienberg and Slavkovic (2004). For continuous data we might need to apply disclosure protection methods to the split components, e.g., see Duncan et al. (2001) and Fienberg (2005a) for overviews. It is the uncertainty associated with efforts to concatenate the separate pieces that provides the confidentiality protection in both instances. The higher the uncertainty the better the protection.

- Unless Choicepoint and other data warehousers are adding data into their files using unique identifiers such as Social Security numbers (and even Social Security numbers are not really unique!), or with highly accurate addresses and/or geography, some reasonable fraction of the data in their files will be the result of inaccurate and faulty matches. Data quality for data warehouses is an issue we all need to worry about, see Winkler (2005).

4.   ENCRYPTION, MULTI-PARTY COMPUTATION, AND PRIVACY-PRESERVING DATAMINING

If you search the WWW for "e-commerce" and "data privacy protection" you will find extensive discussion about firewalls, intrusion prevention (IPS) and intrusion detection (IDS) systems, and secure socket layer (SSL) encryption technology. Indeed, these technological tools are important for secure data transmission, statistical production, and offline data storage, c.f. Domingo-Ferrer et al. (2000). But encryption cannot protect the privacy of individuals whose data is available in online data bases!

Among the methods advocated to carry out such data mining exercises are those that are described as privacy-preserving data mining (PPDM). PPDM typically refers to data mining computations performed on the combined data sets of multiple parties without revealing each party's data to the other parties. The data consist of possibly overlapping sets of variables contained in the separate data bases of the parties and overlapping sets of individuals. When the parties have data for the same variables but different individuals the data are said to be horizontally partitioned, whereas when the individuals are the same but the variables are different the data are said to be vertically partitioned. Here we are concerned with the more complex case involving both overlapping variables *and* overlapping sets of individuals. PPDM research comes in two varieties. In the first, sometimes referred to as the construction of "privacy-preserving statistical databases," the data are altered prior to delivery for data mining, e.g., through the addition of random noise or some other form of perturbation. While these approaches share much in common with the methods in the literature on statistical disclosure limitation, they are of little use when it comes to the identification of terrorists. In the second variety, the problem is solved using what is known as "multi-party secure computation," where no party knows anything except its own input and the results. The literature typically presumes that data are included without error and thus could be matched perfectly if only there were no privacy concerns. The methods also focus largely on situations where the results are of some computation, such as a dot product or the description of an association rule. See the related discussion in Fienberg and Slavkovic (2005).

A major problem with the PPDM literature involving multi-party computation is that the so-called proofs of security are designed not to protect the individuals in the data base but rather the data base owners, as in the case of two companies sharing information but not wanting to reveal information about their customers to one another beyond that contained in the shared computation. Once the results of the data mining consist of linked extracts of the data themselves, however, the real question is whether one of the parties can use the extra information to infer something about the individuals in the other party's data that would otherwise not be available.

Secure computation is a technique for carrying out computations across multiple data bases without revealing any information about data elements found only in one data base. The technique consists of a protocol for exchanging messages. We assume the parties to be *semi-honest*—i.e., they correctly follow the protocol specification, yet attempt to learn additional information by analyzing the messages that are passed. For example, Agrawal et al. (2003) illustrate the secure computation notion via an approach to the matching problem for parties A and B. They introduce a pair of encryption functions E (known only to A) and E' (known only to B) such that for all x, $E(E'(x)) = E'(E(x))$. A's data base consists of a list $\mathbf{A}$ and B's consists of a list $\mathbf{B}$. A sends B the message $E(\mathbf{A})$; B computes $E'(E(\mathbf{A}))$ and then sends to A the two messages $E'(E(\mathbf{A}))$ and $E'(\mathbf{B})$. A then applies E to $E'(\mathbf{B})$, yielding $E'(E(\mathbf{A}))$ and $E'E(\mathbf{B}))$. A computes $E'(E(\mathbf{A}))\cap E'(E(\mathbf{B}))$. Since A knows the order of items in $\mathbf{A}$, A also knows the order of items in $E'(E(\mathbf{A}))$ and can quickly determine $\mathbf{A}\cap\mathbf{B}$. The main problems with this approach are (1) it is asymmetric, i.e., B must trust A to send $\mathbf{A}\cap\mathbf{B}$ back, and (2) it presumes semi-honest behavior.

Li et al. (2004) describe a variety of scenarios in which the Agrawal et al. protocol can easily be exploited by one party to obtain a great deal of information about the other's data base and they explain drawbacks of some other secure computation methods including the use of one-way hash-based schemes. As Dwork and Nissim (2004) note: "There is also a very large literature in secure multi-party computation. In secure multi-party computation, functionality is paramount, and privacy is only preserved to the extent that the function outcome itself does not reveal information about the individual inputs. In privacy-preserving statistical data bases, privacy is paramount." The problem with privacy-preserving data-mining methods for terrorist detection is that they seek the protection of the latter while revealing individual records using the functionality of the former. For more details on some of these and other issues, see Karr et al. (2005).

The U.S. Congress and various private foundations have taken up the issue of privacy protection from government datamining activities especially in the post-9/11 world. For example, in its recent report, the U.S. Department of Defense Technology and Privacy Advisory Committee (TAPAC) (2004) has stressed the existence of a broad array of government data mining programs, and "disjointed," "inconsistent," and "outdated" laws and regulations protecting privacy. TAPAC recommended broad new actions to protect privacy, both within the Department of Defense and across agencies of the federal government.

The long standing concern regarding surveillance of U.S. citizens and others by government agencies has been heightened during the war on terror, e.g., see Kreimer (2004) and especially most recently with the controversy over unauthorized domestic spying.[5]

5. SELECTIVE REVELATION, RISK-UTILITY TRADEOFF, AND DISCLOSURE LIMITATION ASSESSMENT

To get around the privacy problems associated with the development of the TIA and MATRIX systems Tygar (2003a, 2003b) and others have advocated the use of what has come to be called "selected revelation," involving something like the risk-utility tradeoff in statistical disclosure limitation. Sweeney (2005b) used the term to describe an approach to disclosure limitation that allows data to be shared for surveillance purposes "with a sliding scale of identifiability, where the level of anonymity matches scientific and evidentiary need." This corresponds to a monotonically increasing threshold for maximum tolerable risk in the R-U confidentiality map framework described in Duncan et al. (2001), Duncan and Stokes (2004) and Duncan, McNulty and Stokes (2004), as depicted in Figure 10-1. Figure 10-2 depicts the basic selective revelation scheme described in a committee report on TIA privacy methodology (ISAT:2002).

The TIA privacy report (ISAT, 2002) suggests that

Selective revelation works by putting a security barrier between the private data and the analyst, and controlling what information can flow

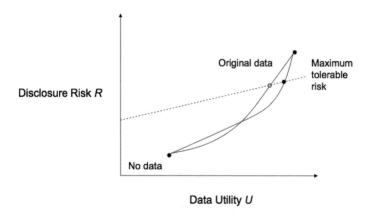

Data Utility *U*

Figure 10-1. R-U Confidentiality Maps For Two Different Disclosure Limitation Methods With Varying Parameter Settings. Adapted from Duncan and Stokes (2004)

across that barrier to the analyst. The analyst injects a query that uses the private data to determine a result, which is a high-level sanitized description of the query result. That result must not leak any private information to the analyst. Selective revelation must accommodate multiple data sources, all of which lie behind the (conceptual) security barrier. Private information is not made available directly to the analyst, but only through the security barrier.

One effort to implement this scheme was dubbed *privacy appliances* by Lunt (2003) and it was intended to be a stand-alone device that would sit between the analyst and the private data source so that private data stays in authorized hands. These privacy controls would also be independently operated to keep them isolated from the government. According to Lunt (2003) the device would provide:

- *Inference control* to prevent unauthorized individuals from completing queries that would allow identification of ordinary citizens.
- *Access control* to return sensitive identifying data only to authorized users.
- *Immutable audit trail* for accountability.

Implicit in the TIA Report and in the Lunt approach was the notion that linkages across data bases behind the security barrier would utilize identifiable records and thus some form of multi-party computation method involving encryption techniques. Popp and Poindexter (2006) give a similar account.

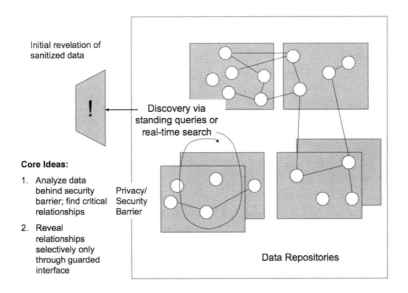

Figure 10-2. Idealized Selective Revelation Architecture. Adapted from ISAT (2002)

The real questions of interest in "inference control" are (1) What disclosure limitation methods should be used? (2) To which data bases should they be applied? and (3) How can the "inference control" approaches be combined with the multi-party computation methods? Here is what we know in the way of answers:

- Both Sweeney (2005b) and Lunt (2005) refer to Sweeney's version of micro-aggregation, known as k-anonymity, but with few details on how it could be used in this context. This methodology combines observations in groups of size k and reports either the sum or the average of the group for each unit. The groups may be identified by clustering or some other statistical approach. Left unsaid is what kinds of users might perform with such aggregated data. Further, neither k-anonymity nor any other confidentiality tool does anything to cope with the implications of the release of exactly-linked files requested by "authorized users."

- Much of the statistical and operations research literature on confidentiality fails to address the risk utility trade-off, largely by focusing primarily only on privacy, or on technical implementations without understanding how users wish to analyze a data base, e.g., see Gopal, Garfinkel and Goes (2002).

- A clear lesson from the statistical disclosure limitation literature is that privacy protection in the form of "safe releases" from separate data bases does not guarantee privacy protection for a merged data base. A figure in Lunt (2005) demonstrates recognition of this fact by showing privacy appliances applied for the individual data bases and then, again, independently for the combined data.

To date there have been a limited number of crosswalks between the statistical disclosure limitation literatures on multi-party computation and risk-utility tradeoff choices for disclosure limitation. Yang, Zhong, and Wright (2005) provide a starting point for discussions on *k*-anonymity. There are clearly a number of alternatives to *k*-anonymity, and ones which yield "anonymized" data bases of far greater statistical utility!

The hype associated with the TIA approach to protection has abated, but largely because TIA no longer exists as an official program. But similar programs continue to appear in different places in the federal government and no-one associated with any of them has publicly addressed the privacy concerns raised here regarding the TIA approach.

When the U.S. Congress stopped the funding for DARPA's TIA program in 2003, Lunt's research and development effort at PARC Research Center was an attendant casualty. Thus to date there have been no publicly-available prototypes of the privacy appliance, nor are there likely to be in the near future. The claims of privacy protection and selective revelation continue with MATRIX and other data warehouse systems, but without an attendant research program, and the federal government continues to plan for the use of data mining techniques in other federal initiatives such as the Computer Assisted Passenger Profiling System II (CAPPS II). Similar issues arise in the use of government, medical and private transactional data in bio-terrorism surveillance, e.g., see Fienberg and Shmueli (2005) and Sweeney (2005a).

6.   ANALYZING NETWORK DATA BASED ON TRANSACTIONS

Transactions can often be described in terms of networks, e.g., in the form of graphs $G(V,E)$ with vertices (nodes), V, corresponding to units or individuals and edges, E, corresponded to the transactions. If unit i sends something to unit j, then there is a directed edge connecting them. Much of the DARPA initiative linked to TIA was focused on *link mining* of transaction data bases, e.g., see the summary in Senator (2005). For discussion of related machine learning methodologies see the papers in the special issue of *SIGKDD Explorations* on link mining (Getoor and Diel, 2005).

This problem has been in the news very recently because of the controversy over the access by the National Security Agency to the telephone log records of millions of Americans (or attempted access). Clearly such log records can be represented in network form. The claim has been made that such data will be used to discover linkages among individuals in a terrorist cell. This can typically be done in one of two ways:

1. By looking at telephone links to and from known or suspected terrorists. *Issue*: how far out do we look for links, and how do we distinguish between terrorist links and links that represent everyday life–ordering take-out meals from a pizza parlor or calling neighbors or work colleagues at home.

2. By using a "template" or signature for a terrorist cell and sifting the entire data base of linkages looking for cliques that resemble the signature. *Issues*: One needs to discover one or more terrorist network templates, and distinguishing them from other sub-networks and cliques that present similar pattern.

Much has been made of efforts to retrospectively discover linkages among the 20 9-11 terrorists, using publicly available information from newspapers and the WWW, as well as from various transaction data bases. Krebs (2005) gives a detailed discussion of the use of publicly available data to construct the terrorist network reproduced here in Figure 10-3, but he also notes that he only needed to look at links between known individuals and retrospectively.

He provides little information on how many others there are to whom these twenty are linked in multiple transaction data bases and what one might do with those links if we didn't have definitive information on which individuals composed a terrorist cell. Krebs discusses how one might move towards this kind of prospective analysis, but much of what he suggests is speculation at best. See also the related discussions in the other papers that appear in the 2005 special issue of *Connections* on this topic, available online.[6]

Despite the extensive literature on link mining and social network analysis there seems to be limited progress at best in understanding how we can use transaction data bases to identify terrorist cells or networks. The size of the telephone log records data bases makes searching for "signatures" especially problematic.[7] Schneier (2006) has claimed: "Finding terrorism plots is not a problem that lends itself to data mining. It's a needle-in-a-haystack problem, and throwing more hay on the pile doesn't make that problem any easier." Viewed from the perspective of risk-utility tradeoff, the use of large-scale transaction data bases appears to have high privacy risk and low utility, at least given the current state of data mining and privacy-protection methodology.

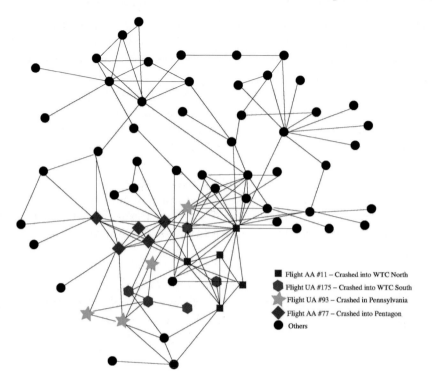

Figure 10-3. Network map of the 9-11 terrorist networks based on public information. The hijackers are coded by the flight they were on. The circle nodes are others who were reported to have had direct, or indirect, interactions with the hijackers. Source: Adapted from V. Krebs (2005). [8]

7.   CONCLUSIONS

Data privacy protection is a major issue for government administrative data bases, data collected by commercial organizations, especially for e-commerce. (Fienberg 2006). While solutions like SSL encryption may help companies with protection for confidential data transmission, the privacy pitfalls of data bases of all sorts are constantly in the news and at issue. In this paper, we have focused on both transaction data bases and on large-scale data warehousing in part because the repeated announcements of security breaches in systems operated by the major vendors such as Acxiom, ChoicePoint, and LexusNexus have filled our morning newspapers during the past several years. The public and civil rights groups have argued that this is just the tip of the privacy-violation iceberg and they have called for government intervention and legal restrictions on both public and private organizations with respect to data warehousing and data mining. The lessons from such privacy breaches extend easily to virtually all electronically accessible data bases. Companies need to take data security seriously and implement "best practices," and they need to rethink their policies on "data access" by others. As the recent "thefts" of 26.5 million records from the Department of Veterans Affairs[9] and of 1,500 records at a National Nuclear Security Administration center in Albuquerque[10] makes clear, government agencies are just as vulnerable (U.S. GAO 2006b).

The giant data warehouses described in this paper have been assembled through the aggregation of information from many separate data bases and transactional data systems. They depend heavily on matching and record linkage methods that intrinsically are statistical in nature, and whose accuracy deteriorates rapidly in the presence of serious measurement error. Data mining tools can't make up for bad data and poor matches, and someone beyond "wronged consumers" will soon begin to pay attention.

Should you worry about these data warehouses? With very high probability they contain data on you and your household, but you will never quite know what data or how accurate the information is. And soon the data may be matched into a government-sponsored terrorist search systems such as the one being set up by the Transportation Security Administration (TSA) to match passenger lists into a consolidated watch list of suspected terrorists. On September 19, 2005, the "Secure Flight" Working Group to the Transportation Security Administration (TSA) submitted a report questioning TSA's secrecy regarding what data it plans to use and how (Secure Flight Working Group 2005):

> The TSA is under a Congressional mandate to match domestic airline passenger lists against the consolidated terrorist watch list. TSA has failed to specify with consistency whether watch list matching is the only goal of Secure Flight at this stage....
>
> Will Secure Flight be linked to other TSA applications? ...
>
> How will commercial data sources be used? One of the most controversial elements of Secure Flight has been the possible uses of commercial data. TSA has never clearly defined two threshold issues: what it means by "commercial data;" and how it might use commercial data sources in the implementation of Secure Flight. TSA has never clearly distinguished among various possible uses of commercial data, which all have different implications.

The story continues, however, since a few months later it was revealed that TSA had purchased a database from ChoicePoint to be matched against the watch list.[11]

None of these comments nor the discussion in this paper is intended to imply that the government should not share data bases across agencies, either for statistical purposes or to support homeland security initiatives (U.S. GAO, 2006a). Rather we stress that such data sharing needs to be done with care and due attention to privacy and confidentiality concerns.

Finally, we want to stress the need for new computational and statistical technologies to protect linked multiple data bases from privacy protection in the face of commercial and government queries. Slogans like "selective revelation" are not enough without technical backup. This might be provided by the serious integration of research ideas emanating from the statistical disclosure and cryptography communities. The technologies that result from such collaborative research must be part of the public domain, because only then can we evaluate their adequacy.

8.   ACKNOWLEDGMENTS

The research reported here was supported in part by NSF grants EIA–9876619 and IIS–0131884 to the National Institute of Statistical Sciences and by Army contract DAAD19-02-1-3-0389 to CyLab at Carnegie Mellon University. This paper is based in part on an earlier and much shorter paper focusing on homeland security issues presented at the 2005 session of the International Statistical Institute and a related paper on e-commerce and security which appeared in *Statistical Science*, as well as an article in a Carnegie Mellon University publication, *Focus*, on the *Hunt for Terrorists*, and parts of those papers are reproduced here with permission. I have benefited from conversations with Chris Clifton, Cynthia Dwork, Alan Karr, and Latanya Sweeney about the material described here but they bear no responsibility for how I have represented their input.

NOTES

[1] http://www.aclu.org/pizza/
[2] Mark Clayton, "US Plans Massive Data Sweep," *Christian Science Monitor*, February 09, 2006. http://www.csmonitor.com/2006/0209/p01s02-uspo.html. c.f., U.S. Government Accountability Office (2007).
[3] Shane Harris, "TIA Lives On," *National Journal*, Thursday, Feb. 23, 2006.
[4] http://www.searchsystems.net/
[5] David Johnston and Neil A. Lewis, "Domestic surveillance: The White House; Defending Spy Program, Administration Cites Law," *New York Times*, December 23, 2005.
[6] http://www.insna.org/Connections-Web/Volume26-2/Cover26-2.htm
[7] Paitience Wait, "Too much for NSA to mine?" *Government Computer News*, May 22, 2006. http://appserv.gcn.com/cgi-bin/udt/im.display.printable?client.id=gcn&story.

id=40827

[8] http://www.orgnet.com/hijackers.html

[9] "Stolen VA Data Goes Beyond Initial Reports," *New York Times*, May 31, 2006. http://www.nytimes.com/aponline/us/AP-Vets-ID-Theft.html

[10] David Stout, "Data Theft at Nuclear Agency Went Unreported for 9 Months," New York Times, June 10, 2006. http://www.nytimes.com/2006/06/10/washington/10identity.html

[11] "TSA Chief Suspends Traveler Registry Plans," Associated Press, February 9, 2006.

REFERENCES

Agrawal R. Evfimievski A, and Srikant R (2003) Information sharing across private databases. In Proceedings of the 2003 ACM SIGMOD International Conference on Management of Data, San Diego, CA

Bilenko M, Mooney R, Cohen WW, Ravikumar P, Fienberg, SE (2003) Adaptive name-matching in information integration. IEEE Intelligent Systems 18: 16–23

Bishop YMM, Fienberg SE, Holland PW (1975) *Discrete Multivariate Analysis: Theory and Practice.* MIT Press, Cambridge MA. Reprinted by Springer-Verlag, 2007

Clarke R (1988) Information technology and dataveillance. Communications of the ACM 31:498–512

Dobra A, Fienberg SE (2001) Bounds for cell entries in contingency tables induced by fixed marginal totals. Statistical Journal of the United Nations ECE 18: 363–371

Dobra A, Fienberg SE (2003) Bounding entries in multi-way contingency tables given a set of marginal totals. In Y Haitovsky, HR Lerche, and Y Ritov, eds., *Foundations of Statistical Inference: Proceedings of the Shoresh Conference 2000,* Springer-Verlag, Berlin, 3–16

Domingo-Ferrer JM, Mateo-Sanz JM, and S\'anchez del Castillo, RX (2000). Cryptographic techniques in statistical data protection. *Proceedings of the Joint UN/ECE-Eurostat Work Session on Statistical Data Confidentiality*, Office for Official Publications of the European Communities, Luxembourg, 159–166

Domingo-Ferrer J, Torra V (2003) Statistical data protection in statistical microdata protection via advanced record linkage. Statistics and Computing 13: 343–354

Duncan GT (2001) Confidentiality and statistical disclosure limitation. *International Encyclopedia of Social & Behavioral Sciences*, Elsevier, Amsterdam, 2521–2525

Duncan GT, Fienberg SE, Krishnan R, Padman R, Roehrig SF (2001) Disclosure limitation methods and information loss for tabular data. In P Doyle, J Lane, J Theeuwes, and L Zayatz, eds., *Confidentiality, Disclosure and Data Access: Theory and Practical Applications for Statistical Agencies*, Elsevier, Amsterdam, 135–166

Duncan GT, Keller-McNulty SA, Stokes SL (2004) Database security and confidentiality: Examining disclosure risk vs. data utility through the R-U confidentiality map. Technical Report Number 142, National Institute of Statistical Sciences, March, 2004

Duncan GT, Stokes SL (2004) Disclosure risk vs. data utility: The R-U confidentiality map as applied to topcoding. Chance,17(No. 3): 16–20

Dwork C, Nissim K (2004) Privacy-preserving data mining in vertically partitioned databases. Proc. CRYPTO 2004, 24th International Conference on Cryptology, University of California, Santa Barbara

Fellegi IP, Sunter AB (1969) A theory for record linkage. Journal of the American Statistical Association, 64:1183–1210

Fienberg SE (2005a) Confidentiality and disclosure limitation. *Encyclopedia of Social Measurement*, Elsevier, Amsterdam, 463–469

Fienberg SE (2005b) Homeland insecurity: Datamining, terrorism detection, and confidentiality. Bulletin of the International Statistical Institute, 55th Session: Sydney 2005

Fienberg SE, Shmueli G (2005) Statistical issues and challenges associated with rapid detection of bio-terrorist attacks. Statistics in Medicine 24: 513–529

Fienberg SE, Slavkovic AB (2004) Making the release of confidential data from multi-way tables count. Chance 17(No. 3): 5–10

Fienberg SE, Slavkovic AB (2005) Preserving the confidentiality of categorical statistical data bases when releasing information for association rules. Data Mining and Knowledge Discovery 11:155–180

Getoor L, Diehl CP (2005) Introduction: Special issue on link mining. SIGKDD Explorations, 7(2):76–83

Gopal R, Garfinkel R, Goes P (2002) Confidentiality via camouflage. Operations Research 50:501–516

ISAT–Information Science and Technology Study Group on Security and Privacy (chair: JD Tygar) (2002) Security With Privacy. December 13, 2002 Briefing

Jaro MA (1995) Probabilistic linkage of large public health data files. Statistics in Medicine 14:491–498

Karr AF, Lin X, Sanil AP, Reiter, JP (2006) Secure statistical analysis of distributed databases. In D Olwell and AG Wilson, eds., *Statistical Methods in Counterterrorism*, Springer-Verlag, New York, in press

Krebs VE (2005) Mapping networks of terrorist cells. Connections 24(3): 43-52 http://www.insna.org/Connections-Web/Volume24-3/Valdis.Krebs.web.pdf

Kreimer SF (2004) Watching the watchers: Surveillance, transparency, and political freedom in the war on terror. Journal of Constitutional Law 7: 133–181

Larsen MD, Rubin DB (2001) Alternative automated record linkage using mixture models. Journal of the American Statistical Association 79: 32–41

Li Y, Tygar JD, Hellerstein JM (2005) Private matching. Chapter 3 in D. Lee, S. Shieh, and J.D. Tygar, eds., Computer Security in the 21st Century, Springer-Verlag, New York, 25–50

Lunt T (2003) Protecting privacy in terrorist tracking applications. Presentation to Department of Defense Technology and Privacy Advisory Committee, September 29, 2003 http://www.sainc.com/tapac/library/Sept29/LuntPresentation.pdf

Lunt T, Staddon J, Balfanz D, Durfee G, Uribe T, and others (2005) Protecting privacy in terrorist tracking applications. Powerpoint presentation. http://research.microsoft.com/projects/SWSecInstitute/five-minute/Balfanz5.ppt

Muralidhar KR, Parsa K, Sarathy R (2001) An improved security requirement for data perturbation with implications for e-commerce. Decision Sciences 32: 683–698

Popp, R, Poindexter, J (2006) Countering terrorism through information and privacy protection technologies. IEEE Security & Privacy, 4 (6): 18-27

Privacy Office (2006) Report to the Public Concerning the Multistate Anti-Terrorism Information Exchange (MATRIX) Pilot Project. U. S. Department of Homeland Security, December, 2006

Relyea HC, Seifert JW (2005) .Information Sharing for Homeland Security: A Brief Overview. Congressional Research Service, Library of Congress (Updated January 10, 2005)

Secure Flight Working Group (2005) Report of Secure Flight Working Group. Presented to the Transportation Security Administration, September 19, 2005

Schneier, B (2006) We're giving up privacy and getting little in return, Minneapolis Star Tribune, May 31, 2006, http://www.startribune.com/562/v-print/story/463348.html

Senator, TE (2005) Link mining applications: Progress and challenges. SIGKDD Explorations, 7(2): 76–83

Sweeney L (2005a) Privacy-preserving bio-terrorism surveillance. AAAI Spring Symposium, AI Technologies for Homeland Security

Sweeney L (2005b) Privacy-preserving surveillance using selective revelation. Carnegie Mellon University, LIDAP Working Paper 15, February 2005. (PDF)

Sweeney L (2005c) Privacy-enhanced linking. SIGKDD Explorations, 7(2): 72–75

Tygar JD (2003a) Privacy architectures. Presentation at Microsoft Research, June 18, 2003. http://research.microsoft.com/projects/SWSecInstitute/slides/Tygar.pdf

Tygar JD (2003b) Privacy in sensor webs and distributed information systems. In M Okada, B Pierce, A Scedrov, H Tokuda, A Yonezawa, eds., *Software Security*, Springer-Verlag, New York, 84–95

U.S. Department of Defense Technology and Privacy Advisory Committee (TAPAC) (2004) Safeguarding Privacy in the Fight Against Terrorism.

U.S. General Accounting Office (2004) Data Mining: Federal Efforts Cover A Wide Range of Uses. GAO-04-548, Report to the Ranking Minority Member, Subcommittee on Financial Management, the Budget, and International Security, Committee on Governmental Affairs, U.S. Senate, Washington, DC

U.S. Government Accountability Office (2006a) Information Sharing: The Federal Government Needs to Establish Policies and Processes for Sharing Terrorism-Related and Sensitive but Unclassified Information. GAO-06-385 March 17, 2006. U.S. Government Printing Office, Washington, DC

U.S. Government Accountability Office (2006b) Privacy: Preventing and Responding to Improper Disclosures of Personal Information. GAO-06-833T June 8, 2006. U.S. Government Printing Office, Washington, DC

U.S. Government Accountability Office (2007) Datamining: Early Attention to Privacy in Developing a Key DHS Program Could Reduce Risks. GAO-07-293 February 2007 U.S. Government Printing Office, Washington, DC

Winkler WE (2002) Record Linkage and Bayesian Networks. Proceedings of the Section on Survey Research Methods, American Statistical Association, CD-ROM

Winkler WE (2005) Data Quality in Data Warehouses. In J Wang, ed., *Encyclopedia of Data Warehousing and Data Mining*, Idea Group Publishing, Hershey, PA

Yang Z, Zhong S, Wright RN (2005) Privacy-Enhancing *k*-anonymization of customer data. 24th ACM SIGMOD International Conference on Management of Data/Principles of Database Systems (PODS 2005)

SUGGESTED READINGS

- Doyle P, Lane J, Theeuwes J, and Zayatz L, eds., (2001) Confidentiality, Disclosure and Data Access: Theory and Practical Applications for Statistical Agencies. Elsevier, Amsterdam

- Duncan GT, Jabine TB, and de Wolf VA (1993)   Private Lives and Public Policies: Confidentiality and Accessibility of Government Statistics. Panel on Confidentiality and Data Access, Washington DC: National Academy Press
- Vincent B, Kendall LS (2002) Social Netwoks and Trust.   Dordrecht: Kluwer
- Schneier B (2003) Beyond Fear: Thinking Sensibly about Security in an Uncertain World. New York: Copernicus Books
- Winkler WE (1995) Matching and Record Linkage, in B. G. Cox *et al.* (ed.) *Business Survey Methods*, New York: Wiley, 355-384

DISCUSSION QUESTIONS

1. Locate a copy of the Privacy Act of 1974.   To what extent are the provisions of the Act compatible with the use of data mining of large government and commercial data bases in the hunt for terrorists?
2. The United States Department of Homeland Security is attempting to create a consolidated database of biometric and biographic data for individuals who voluntarily exchange personally identifiable information in return for expedited transit at U.S. border entry points. How could such a data base be used in the hunt for terrorists?
3. Security expert Bruce Schneier (2006) has claimed: "Finding terrorism plots is not a problem that lends itself to data mining. It's a needle-in-a-haystack problem, and throwing more hay on the pile doesn't make that problem any easier. We'd be far better off putting people in charge of investigating potential plots and letting them direct the computers, instead of putting the computers in charge and letting them decide who should be investigated." Explain the reasoning here in the context of statistical models for networks.
4. Compile a list of government, commercial, and other data bases in which data on you or your family might be included. Can you access the information on you and verify its correctness?
5. How can encryption be used to protect privacy but at the same time allow linkage of data across databases?

Unit 2

Terrorism Informatics to Support Prevention, Detection, and Response

11

CASE STUDY OF JIHAD ON THE WEB
A Web Mining Approach

Hsinchun Chen[1], Jialun Qin[2], Edna Reid[3], Yilu Zhou[4], and Marc Sageman[5]

[1]*Management Information Systems, The University of Arizona, Tucson, Arizona, U.S.A. (hchen@eller.arizona.edu); [2]Department of Management, University of Massachusetts-Lowell, Lowell, Massachusetts, U.S.A.; (jialun_qin@uml.edu) [3]Department of Library Science, Clarion University, Clarion, Pennsylvania, U.S.A. (ereid@clarion.edu); [4]Information Systems & Technology Management Department, George Washington University, Washington D.C., U.S.A. (yzhou@gwu.edu); [5]Sageman Consulting, LLC, Rockville, Maryland, U.S.A. (sageman@post.harvard.edu)*

CHAPTER OVERVIEW

Terrorist and extremist groups and their sympathizers have found a cost-effective resource to advance their courses by posting high-impact Websites with short shelf-lives. Because of their evanescent nature, terrorism research communities require unrestrained access to digitally archived Websites to mine their contents and pursue various types of analyses. Organizations that specialize in capturing, archiving, and analyzing Jihad terrorist Websites employ different, manual-based analysis techniques that are 'hidden' from the research communities. This chapter proposes the development of automated or semi-automated procedures and systematic methodologies for capturing Jihad terrorist Website data and its subsequent analyses. By analyzing the content of hyperlinked terrorist Websites and constructing visual social network maps, our study is able to generate an integrated approach to the study of Jihad terrorism, their network structure, component clusters, and cluster affinity.

1.   INTRODUCTION

With weekly news coverage of excerpts from videos produced and webcasted by terrorists, it has become obvious that terrorists have further exploited the Internet beyond routine communication and propaganda operations to better influence the outside world. Some warn that the Internet allows terrorist groups to acquire sensitive intelligence information and control their operations [19] while others argue that terrorists use the Internet to develop a world-wide command, control, communication and intelligence system (C3I). Jenkins posited that terrorists have used the Internet as a broadcast platform for the "terrorist news network" [12], which is an effective tactic because they can reach a broad audience with relatively little chance of detection.

Although this alternate side of the Internet, referred to as the "Dark Web" has recently received extensive government and media attention, our systematic understanding of how terrorists use the Internet for their campaign of terror is limited. According to studies by the Institute for Security and Technology Studies (ISTS) at Dartmouth College [11] and Anderson [2], there is a need to address this under-researched issue. In this study, we explore an integrated approach for harvesting Jihad terrorist Websites to construct a high quality collection of Website data that can be used to validate a methodology for analyzing and visualizing how Jihad terrorists use the Internet, especially the World Wide Web, in their terror campaigns. Jihad terrorist Websites are Websites produced or maintained by Islamic extremist groups or their sympathizers.

In this study, we answer the following research questions: What are the most appropriate techniques for collecting high-quality Jihad terrorism Web pages? What are systematic approaches for analyzing and visualizing Jihad terrorist information on the Web so as to identify usage and relationships among groups? How does content analysis of the Jihad terrorists' collection help reveal the terrorist's ideology, propaganda, and communication patterns?

2.   PREVIOUS RESEARCH

2.1   Terrorist Websites

Information technology, especially the Internet, has heightened the whole spectrum of conflict by giving rise to networked forms of terrorism organizations, doctrines and strategies. Arquilla and Ronfeldt [3] described this trend as netwar, an emerging model of conflict in which the protagonists use network forms of organization and exploit information technology. Since networks can be diverse, redundant, and lack centralized control, terrorist groups with network structures create new challenges for governments and researchers to monitor, analyze, and counter.

Arquilla and Ronfeldt's research stimulated several investigations into terrorists' use of the Internet such as Elison [9], Tsfati and Weimann [21], ISTS [11], and Weimann [22]. All of them used terrorists' and their sympathizers' Websites as their primary data sources and provided brief descriptions of their methodologies. For example, Elison used search engines to identify the group's official Websites and manually analyzed its narratives, graphics, and hyperlinks. He also analyzed newsgroup messages to understand how the group may be affecting public opinion.

Although an increasing number of terrorists' Websites are posted on the Internet, they are also very dynamic and have short shelf-lives: they emerge overnight, disappear by changing their URLs, and are often shut down. To ensure controlled access to terrorist Websites for research and intelligence analyses, several organizations are collecting, archiving, and analyzing Jihad terrorist Websites. These organizations can be grouped into three areas: archive, research community, and vigilante group.

For the archive group, the Internet Archive has been spidering the Web and collecting Webpages every two months since 1996. However, it is not comprehensive and is technically limited by factors such as database access, password protection and Java script which inhibit its full capture capability [14]. The research community, the second group, includes the Project for Research of Islamist Movements, (PRISM) at the Interdisciplinary Center Herzliya, the Jihad and Terrorism Studies Project at the Middle East Research Institute (MEMRI), the Search for International Terrorist Entities (SITE Institute), and Professor Gabriel Weimann's collection at the University of Haifa, Israel [17]. Although all of them manually capture and analyze terrorist Websites to publish research reports, none publish their specific collection building and analytical approaches. The Internet Haganah is an example for the third group because it is made up of self-appointed volunteers who surf the Web to identify and download terrorist Websites for inclusion in their database of Jihad sites. Later, they contact authorities to report suspicious activities as they try to get Websites closed down. Except for using search engines to identify terrorist Websites, none of the organizations seem to use any other automated methodologies for capturing and analyzing terrorist Websites.

2.2 Web Harvesting Approaches

The first step towards studying the terrorism Web infrastructure is to harvest terrorist Websites back to a local repository for further analysis. Web harvesting is the process of gathering and organizing unstructured information from pages and data on the Web [13]. Previous studies have suggested 3 types of approaches to harvesting Web contents in specific domains: manual approach, automatic approach, and semiautomatic approach.

In order to build the September 11 and Election 2002 Web Archives [18], the Library of Congress' approach was to manually collect seed URLs for a given theme. The seeds and their close neighbors (distance 1) are then downloaded. The limitation of such a manual approach is that it is time-consuming and inefficient.

Albertsen [1] used an automatic approach in the "Paradigma" project. The goal of Paradigma is to archive Norwegian legal deposit documents on the Web. It employed a focused Web crawler, an automatic program that discovers and downloads Websites in particular domains by following Web links found in the HTML pages of a starting set of Web pages. Metadata was then extracted and used to rank the Websites in terms of relevance. The automatic approach is more efficient than the manual approach; however, due to the limitations of current focused crawling techniques, automatic approaches often introduce noise (off-topic Web pages) into the harvest results.

The "Political Communications Web Archiving" group employed a semiautomatic approach to harvesting domain-specific Websites [16]. Domain experts provided seed URLs as well as typologies for constructing metadata that can be used in the crawling process. Their project's goal is to develop a methodology for constructing an archive of broad-spectrum political communications over the Web. We believe that semiautomatic approach is the most suitable one for harvesting terrorism Websites because it combines the high accuracy and high efficiency of manual and automatic approaches.

2.3   Web Link and Content Analysis

Once the terrorist Websites are harvested, two types of analysis can be applied to study the terrorists' use of the Web: Hyperlink analysis and Web content analysis.

Hyperlink analysis has been previously used to discover hidden relationships among communities [10]. Borgman [4] defines two classes of web link analysis studies: relational and evaluative. Relational analysis gives insight into the strength of relations between Web entities, in particular Websites, while evaluative analysis reveals the popularity or quality level of a Web entity. In this study, we are more concerned with relational analysis as it may bring us insight into the nature of relations among terrorist Websites and, possibly, terrorist organizations. Gibson [10] describes a methodology for discerning Web communities on the WWW. His work is based on Hyperlink-Induced Topic Search (HITS), an algorithm that identifies for authoritative hypermedia on a broad topic. In contrast, we construct a Website topology from a high quality Jihad Terrorism collection. Reid [15] made use of hyperlink-based topologies to uncover companies' non-customer online communities. Our goal is to visualize and analyze hidden Jihad terrorism hyperlinked communities and inter-community relationships.

In order to reach an understanding of the various facets of Jihad terrorism Web usage and communications, a systematic analysis of the Websites' content is required. Researchers in the terrorism domain have traditionally ignored existing methodologies for conducting a systematic content analysis of Website data [21,11]. In Bunt's [5] overview of Jihadi movements' presence on the Web, he describes the reaction of the global Muslim community to the content of terrorist Websites. His assessment of the influence such content has on Muslims and Westerners is based on a qualitative analysis of extracts from Taliban and Al-Qaeda Websites. Tsfati and Weimann's [21] study of terrorism on the Internet acknowledges the value of conducting a systematic and objective investigation of the characteristics of terrorist groups' communications. Nevertheless, they claim that the small size of their collection and the descriptive nature of their research questions make a quantitative study infeasible. It may be unreasonable to conduct a quantitative analysis if only a small collection is available. Conversely, we believe Jihad terrorism content on the Web falls under the category of communicative contents and a quantitative analysis is critical for a study to be objective.

Demchak and Friis' [8] work provides a well-defined methodology for analyzing communicative content in government Websites. Their work focuses on measuring "openness" of government Websites. To achieve this goal they developed a Website Attribute System tool that is basically composed of a set of high level attributes such as transparency and interactivity. Each high level attribute is associated with a second layer of attributes at a more refined level of granularity. For example, the right "operational information" and "responses" on a given Webpage can induce an increase in the interactivity level of a government Website. This system is an example of a well-structured and systematic content analysis exercise. Demchak and Friis' work provides guidance for the present study.

3. PROPOSED APPROACH

We propose an integrated approach to the study of Jihad Terrorism Web infrastructure. We combine a sound semiautomatic methodology for harvesting and constructing a high quality Jihad terrorism collection, a hyperlink analysis and node clustering algorithm for the study of hyperlinked Jihad terrorism communities, and a systematic and deep content analysis of our dataset.

To achieve our goal, we have developed a three step process: first, we construct a high quality Jihad terrorism collection, and then conduct link analysis on the collection to induce a network of Jihadi Web communities. Finally, we perform a systematic content analysis of the Websites in the collection.

3.1   Jihad Collection Building Process

A systematic and sound methodology for collecting the Jihad terrorism Websites guarantees that our collection, which is the cornerstone of the study, is comprehensive and representative. Hence, we take a three step systematic approach to construct the collection:

1) Identify seed URLs of Jihad terrorism groups and perform backlink expansion: The first task is to find a small set of Jihad terrorism Websites. To identify terrorist groups, we completely relied on the US Department of State's list of foreign terrorist organizations. In particular, we only selected Middle-Eastern terrorist organizations from that list.   After identifying the terrorist groups in the Middle-East region we manually search major search engines (google.com, yahoo.com …etc) to find Websites of these groups. Our goal here is not to construct a comprehensive list of URLs. We are merely compiling a very small list of URLs that can serve as the seeds for backlink expansion. The backlink search is then automatically performed and a collection of Websites is automatically retrieved.

2) Manual filter of the collection: Because bogus or unrelated terrorist sites can make their way into our collection, we have developed a robust filtering process based on evidence and clues from the Websites. Aside from sites which explicitly identify themselves as the official sites of a terrorist organization or one of its members, a Website that contains even minor praise of or adopts ideologies espoused by a terrorist group is included in our collection. All other Websites are excluded.

3) Extend the search manually: To ensure the comprehensiveness of our collection we augment the collection by means of manual search. Based on the backlink search results, we construct a short lexicon of Jihad terrorism. The lexicon is then used to manually search major search engines. The Websites that are found are then filtered using the same rules used for filtering the backlink search results.

3.2 Hyperlink Analysis on Jihad Collection

Our goal here is to shed light on the infrastructure of Jihad Websites and to provide the necessary tools for further analysis of Jihad terrorist group relationships. We believe the exploration of hidden Jihadi communities over the Web can give insight into the nature of relationships between Websites of the same group as well as relationships between the Websites of different groups. Moreover, from these relationships we can conjecture the existence of real-world communication channels between terrorist groups themselves. In fact, as we will show later, the virtual hyperlinked communities and their interactions conform to the current geopolitical structure of Middle-Eastern terrorist groups as recognized by terrorism experts.

Uncovering hidden Web communities involves calculating a similarity measure between all pairs of Websites in our collection. We define similarity to be a real-valued multivariable function of the number of hyperlinks in Website "A" pointing to Website "B", and the number of hyperlinks in Website "B" pointing to Website "A." In addition, a hyperlink is weighted proportionally to how deep it appears in the Website hierarchy. For instance, a hyperlink appearing at the homepage of a Website is given a higher weight than hyperlinks appearing at a deeper level. The similarity matrix is then fed to a multidimensional scaling (MDS) algorithm which generates a two dimensional graph of the Websites. The proximity of nodes (Websites) in the graph reflects the similarity level.

3.3 Content Analysis on Jihad Collection

To better understand how Jihad terrorists use the Web to their own advantages, we propose a framework for analyzing the contents of Jihad Websites. The framework consists of 6 high level attributes, each of which is composed of multiple fine grained low level attributes. This approach is similar to what is presented in Demchak and Friis' study [8]. Table 11-1 shows the high level and associated low level attributes used in this study.

Table 11-1. Attributes used in the study

High Level Attribute	Low Level Attribute
Communications	Email
	Telephone
	Multimedia
	Online Feedback Form
	Documentation
Fundraising	External Aid Mentioned
	Fund Transfer
	Donation
	Charity

High Level Attribute	Low Level Attribute
	Support Groups
Sharing Ideology	Mission
	Doctrine
	Justification of the use of violence
	Pin-pointing enemies
Propaganda (insiders)	Slogans
	Dates
	Martyrs
	Leaders
	Banners and Seals
	Narratives of operations and Events
Propaganda (outsiders)	References to Western media coverage
	News reporting
Virtual Community	Listserv
	Text chat room
	Message board
	E-conferencing
	Web ring

We developed a set of coding schemes to identify the presence of each attribute in a Jihad Website. Using this coding scheme, human coders can easily identify whether or not the terrorists are using a Website for a particular purpose (e.g., fundraising, propaganda, etc) and to what extend they are using the Website for that purpose (by assigning a weight score to that attribute). Finally, the results of the content analysis are visualized using snowflake diagrams for easier understanding and comparison.

4.   ANALYSIS RESULTS

4.1   Collection of Jihad Websites

We identified three Websites: www.qudsway.com of the Palestinian Islamic Jihad, www.hizbollah.com of Hizbollah, and www.ezzedine.net which is a Website of the Izzedine-Al-Qassam, the military wing of Hamas. These Websites serve as seed URLs for the backlink search. Performing a one level deep backlink expansion using Google's backlink search tool, we obtained a total of 88 sites. Going through each of the URLs, we then carefully followed the set of rules for filtering out the unrelated Websites. The filtering process reduced the initial set of 88 by about a third (only 26 sites were retained).

Based on the 26 Websites we have identified in the previous step, we constructed a short lexicon of Jihad terrorism with the help of Arabic language speakers. Examples of highly relevant keywords included in the

lexicon are: "حرب صليبية" ("Crusader's War"), "المجاهدين" ("Moujahedin"),
"الكفار" ("Infidels") …etc. This lexicon is utilized to do the manual search.
The same rules used in the filtering process are used here to discern fake and
unrelated websites. The manual search resulted in 13 additional Websites. A
total of 39 Websites are classified by ideological affiliation (Table 11-2).

Table 11-2. Middle-Eastern Terrorist Groups and Their Supporters' Websites

Web Site No.	Terrorist Group Name	URL	Ideological Affiliation
Terrorist Groups' Web Sites			
1	Hizbollah	www.specialforce.net	Shi'a
2	Hamas	palestine-info-urdu.com	Sunni
3	Hizbollah	web.manartv.org	Shi'a
4	Islamic Jihad	www.abrarway.com	Sunni
5	Islamic Jihad	www.jimail.com	Sunni
6	Ezz-al-dine Al-Qassam	www.ezzedeen.net	Sunni
7	Hizbollah	www.hizbollah.tv	Shi'a
8	Hamas	www.infopalestina.com	Sunni
9	Al Aqsa Martyr's Brigades	www.kataebalaqsa.com	Secular
10	Chechen Rebels	www.kavkaz.org.uk	Sunni
11	Hizbollah	www.moqawama.tv	Shi'a
12	Hizbollah	www.nasrollah.org	Shi'a
13	Hamas & Islamic Jihad	www.b-alshohda.com	Sunni
14	Islamic Jihad	www.qudsway.com	Sunni
15	Hamas	www.rantisi.net	Sunni
16	Kahane Chai	www.kahane.org	Jewish
17	Mujahedin-e Khalq	www.iran.mojahedin.org	Secular
18	Mujahedin-e Khalq	www.iranncrfac.org	Secular
19	Mujahedin-e Khalq	www.siahkal.com	Secular
20	Mujahedin-e Khalq	www.fadai.org	Secular
21	Mujahedin-e Khalq	www.fadaian.org	Secular
22	Mujahedin-e Khalq	www.etehadefedaian.org	Secular
23	Revolutionary Peoples Liberation Army/Front	www.dhkc.net	Secular
24	Revolutionary Peoples Liberation Army/Front	www.dhkc.info	Secular
25	Lashkar-e Tayyiba	jorgevinhedo.sites.uol.com.br	Sunni
Supporters' Web sites			
26	Al Ansar	www.al-ansar.biz	Sunni
27	Alsakifah Forum	www.alsakifah.org	Sunni
28	Cihad	www.cihad.net	Sunni
29	Clear Guidance Forum	www.clearguidance.com	Sunni
30	Sheikh Hamid Bin	www.h-alali.net	Sunni

Web Site No.	Terrorist Group Name	URL	Ideological Affiliation
	Abdallah Al Ali		
31	Jihadunspun	www.jihadunspun.com	Sunni
32	Maktab-Al-Jihad	www.maktab-al-jihad.com	Sunni
33	Qoqaz	www.qoqaz.com	Sunni
34	Supporters of Shareeah	www.shareeah.org	Sunni
35	Moltaqa	www.almoltaqa.org	Sunni
36	Saraya	www.saraya.com	Sunni
37	Osama Bin Laden	1osamabinladen.5u.com	Sunni
38	Tawhed	www.tawhed.ws	Sunni

4.2 Jihad Collection Link Analysis Results

Following the procedure described in section 3.2 we have visualized the hidden hyperlinked communities in our collection (see Figure 11-1). Interestingly, domain experts recognized the existence of six clusters representing hyperlinked communities in the network. On the left side of the network resides the Hizbollah cluster. Hizbollah is a Lebanese militant organization. Established in 1982 during the Israeli invasion of Lebanon, the group routinely attacked Israeli military personnel until their pullout from south Lebanon in 2000. A cluster of Websites of Palestinian organizations inhabits the bottom left corner of the network: Hamas, Al-Aqsa Martyr's Brigades, and the Palestinian Islamic Jihad. An interesting observation here is the link between the Hizbollah community and the Palestinian militant groups' community. Hizbollah has traditionally sympathized with the Palestinian cause. In fact, it is widely believed that Hizbollah attempted to support Palestinian militant groups during the "Intifada". Hence, it is not surprising at all to see a link between the two virtual communities.

On the top left corner sits the Hizb-ut-Tahrir cluster. Hizb-ut-Tahrir is a political party with branches in many countries over the Middle-East and in Europe. Although the group was recently associated with Al-Qaeda, an apparent relation between the two groups has not been proven. In our network, Hizb-ut-Tahrir's Websites are isolated and have hyperlinks to two other Websites: the Jihadunspun (www.jihadunspun.com) and the Tanzeem-e-Islami (www.tanzeem.org). Tanzeem-e-Islami is also a political party based in Pakistan. Although the two groups espouse extreme Islamist ideologies both are not officially recognized as terrorist groups. Indeed, the representing clusters in the network seem to be relatively isolated with the exception of a link between Tanzeem-e-Islami and Hizbollah and two links to www.jihadunspun.com.

After investigating the nature of the link between Hizbollah and Tanzeem-e-Islami we found that only a single hyperlink pointing to Hizbollah's Website was posted on Tanzeem-e-Islami's site under a general

"Islamic Links" section. Looking at the bottom right corner one can see a cluster of Al-Qaeda affiliated sites. This cluster has links to two Websites of the radical Palestinian group Hamas. Al-Qaeda sympathizes with Palestinian groups. As well, some Palestinian Islamist groups like Hamas and Islamic Jihad share the same Salafi ideology with Al-Qaeda. In the top right hand corner, the Jihad Sympathizers Web community gathers Websites maintained by sympathizers of the Global Salafi movement. "kavkazcenter.net" and "clearguidance.com" are two Websites maintained by sympathizers of Chechen rebels [13]. "shareeah.com" is associated with Abu Hamza, a Muslim cleric who advocates extreme Salafi views. This community of Salafi sympathizers and supporters has links to three other major Sunni Web communities: the Al-Qaeda community, Palestinian extremists, and Hizb-ut-Tahrir communities. As expected the sympathizers community does not have any links to Hezbollah's community as they follow radically different ideologies.

Visualizing hyperlinked communities can lead to a better understanding of the underlying Jihad terrorism Web infrastructure. In addition, the visualization serves as a tool for showing the relationships among various hyperlinked communities. Furthermore, it helps foretell likely relationships between terrorist groups in the real world.

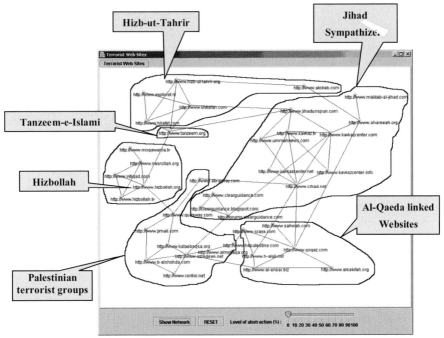

Figure 11-1. The Jihad terrorism network with automatically generated hyperlinked communities.

4.3   Jihad Collection Content Analysis Results

We asked our domain expert to go through each Website in our collection and record the presence of low-level attributes based on our coding schema mentioned in section 3.3. For instance, the Web page of www.al-ansar.biz shown in Figure 11-2 contains a recording of "Sheikh Usama Bin Laden". The presence of this recording contributes to the Website's richness in terms of media and subsequently to the "Propaganda directed towards insiders" attribute.

Figure 11-2. A Webpage from www.al-ansar.biz featuring a downloadable recording of Usama Bin Laden

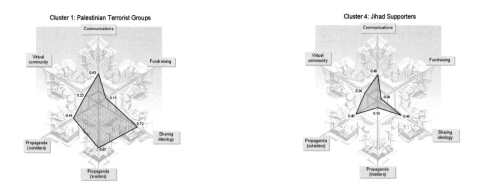

Figure 11-3. Snowflake Diagrams for Palestinian terrorist groups and Jihad Supporters Web Communities.

The manual coding of the attributes in a Website takes around 45 minutes of work. After completing the coding scheme for 32 Websites in the collection, we then compared the content of the clusters or hyperlinked communities in the network shown in Figure 11-1.

We aggregated data from all Websites belonging to a cluster and displayed the results in snowflake diagrams. Figure 11-3 shows two such diagrams.

An interesting observation in these snowflake diagrams is the discrepancy in the "propaganda towards insiders" attribute. Militant groups, in this case Palestinian groups, tend to use the Web for disseminating their ideas in their own communities. They utilize propaganda as an effective tool for influencing youth and possibly recruiting new members. Conversely, the sympathizers try to explain their views to outsiders (Westerners) and try to justify terrorist actions.

To ensure that the coding schema we developed for this analysis is reliable, we conducted an experiment to test the reliability of the coding schema. We asked 5 individual coders to perform content analysis on 4 randomly selected Jihad Websites using the coding schema. For each of the 4 Website, the 5 sets of content analysis results were compared and a reliability score (Cronbach's Alpha) were calculated. The results of the experiment are shown in Table 11-3.

Table 11-3. Reliability test results

Website:	al-ansar.net	ezzedeen.net	nasrollah.org	jihadunspun. com	Avg
Cronbach's Alpha:	0.816	0.899	0.759	0.740	0.8035

The high average Cronbach's Alpha of 0.8035 shows that our coding schema has high reliability.

5. DISCUSSION AND FUTURE WORK

We have developed an integrated approach to the study of the Jihad terrorism Web Infrastructure. Hyperlinked communities' analysis brings an overall view of the terror Web infrastructure. Visualizing hyperlinked communities facilitates the analysis of Web infrastructures and paves the way for more refined microscopic content analysis of the Websites. We then conducted a systematic content analysis of the Websites and compared the content of various clusters. As part of our future work, we envisage implementing feature extraction algorithms for automatically detecting attributes in Webpages. We believe that our methodology can be an effective

234 *Chapter 11. Chen et al.*

tool for analyzing Jihad terrorism on the Web. Moreover, it can be easily extended to analyze other Web contents.

REFERENCES

[1] K. Albertsen, "The Paradigma Web Harvesting Environment," 3rd ECDL Workshop on Web Archives, Trondheim, Norway, August 2003.
[2] A. Anderson, "Risk, Terrorism, and the Internet," Knowledge, Technology & Policy, 16:2, 24-33, Summer 2003.
[3] J. Arquilla, D.F. Ronfeldt, Advent of Netwar, Rand Report, 1996. http://www.rand.org/
[4] C. L. Borgman, J. Furner, "Scholarly Communication and Bibliometrics," Annual Review of Information Science and Technology, ed. B. Cronin. Information Today, Inc, 2002.
[5] G. R. Bunt, Islam In The Digital Age E-Jihad, Online Fatwas and Cyber Islamic Environments, Pluto Press, London, 2003.
[6] K. M. Carley, J. Reminga and N. Kamneva, "Destabilizing Terrorist Networks," NAACSOS Conference Proceedings, Pittsburgh, PA, 2003.
[7] Y. Carmon, "Assessing Islamist Web Site Reports Of Imminent Terror Attacks In The U.S.," MEMRI Inquiry & Analysis Series #156, 2003.
[8] C. C. Demchak, C. Friis, T. M. La Porte "Webbing Governance: National Differences in Constructing the Face of Public Organizations," Handbook of Public Information Systems, G. David Garson, ed., New York: Marcel Dekker Publishers, 2000.
[9] W. Elison, "Netwar: Studying Rebels on the Internet," The Social Studies, 91:127-131 May/June 2000.
[10] D. Gibson, J. Kleinberg, P. Raghavan, "Inferring Web Communities from Link Topology," Proceedings of the 9th ACM Conference on Hypertext and Hypermedia, ACM, 1998.
[11] Institute for Security Technology Studies, "Examining the Cyber Capabilities of Islamic Terrorist Groups." Report, ISTS, 2004. http://www.ists.dartmouth.edu/
[12] B.M. Jenkins, "World Becomes the Hostage of Media-Savvy Terrorists: Commentary," USA Today. August 22, 2004. http://www.rand.org/
[13] R. Kay, "Web Harvesting", Computerworld, June 21, 2004 http://www.computerworld.com.
[14] A.R. Kenney, N.Y. McGovern, P. Botticelli, R. Entlich, C. Lagoze, & S. Payette, "Preservation Risk Management for Web Resources: Virtual Remote Control in Cornell's Project Prism," D-Lib Magazine, 8:1, 2002.
[15] E. O. F. Reid, "Identifying a Company's Non-Customer Online Communities: a Proto-typology," Proceedings of the 36th Hawaii International Conference on System Sciences, 2003.
[16] B. Reilly, G. Tuchel, J. Simon, C. Palaima, K. Norsworthy, Leslie Myrick, "Political Communications Web Archiving: Addressing Typology and Timing for Selection, Preservation and Access," 3rd ECDL Workshop on Web Archives, Trondheim, Norway, August 2003.
[17] Research Community. PRISM. The Project for the Research of Islamist Movements. http://www.e-prism.org. MEMRI: Jihad and Terrorism Studies Project. The Middle East Research Institute (MEMRI). http://www.memri.org/jihad.html/ SITE Institute, http://www.siteinstitute.org/mission.html.
[18] S.M. Schneider, K. Foot, M. Kimpton, & G. Jones, "Building thematic web collections:

challenges and experiences from the September 11 Web Archive and the Election 2002 Web Archive," 3rd ECDL Workshop on Web Archives, Trondheim, Norway, August 2003.

[19] S. Tekwani, "Cyberterrorism: Threat and Response," Institute of Defence and Strategic Studies, Workshop on the New Dimensions of Terrorism, 21-22, Singapore, March 2002.

[20] The 9/11 commission report: http://www.gpoaccess.gov/911/

[21] Y. Tsfati, G. Weimann, "www.terrorism.com: Terror on the Internet," Studies in Conflict & Terrorism, 25:317-332, 2002.

[22] G. Weimann, "www.terrorism.net: How Modern Terrorism Uses the Internet," Special Report 116, U.S. Institute of Peace, 2004. http://usip.org/pubs/

SUGGESTED READINGS

- W. Elison, "Netwar: Studying Rebels on the Internet," *The Social Studies*, 91:127-131 May/June 2000.
- J. Arquilla, D.F. Ronfeldt, *Advent of Netwar*, Rand Report, 1996. http://www.rand.org/
- S.M. Schneider, K. Foot, M. Kimpton, & G. Jones, "Building thematic web collections: challenges and experiences from the September 11 Web Archive and the Election 2002 Web Archive," 3rd ECDL Workshop on Web Archives, Trondheim, Norway, August 2003.

ONLINE RESOURCES

- Terrorism Knowledge Base. Memorial Institute for the Prevention of Terrorism (MIPT). http://www.tkb.org.
- G. Weimann, "www.terrorism.net: How Modern Terrorism Uses the Internet," Special Report 116, U.S. Institute of Peace, 2004. http://usip.org/pubs/Questions

DISCUSSION QUESTIONS

1. How can analysts, researchers, and counterterrorism specialist use the social network maps of terrorist and extremist groups' online communities?
2. What do you think is the nature of the relationship between Hizb-ut-Tahrir and Al-Qaeda?
3. How can the different organizations that collect and analysis extremist groups' Websites collaborate and design a comprehensive database of groups' digital resources? What policies, incentives, and funding are needed?

12

STUDYING GLOBAL EXTREMIST ORGANIZATIONS' INTERNET PRESENCE USING THE DARK WEB ATTRIBUTE SYSTEM
A Three Region Comparison Study

Jialun Qin[1], Yilu Zhou[2], Edna Reid[3], and Hsinchun Chen[4]

[1]*Department of Management, University of Massachusetts-Lowell, Lowell, Massachusetts, U.S.A. (jialun_qin@uml.edu);* [2]*Information Systems and Technology Management, George Washington University, Washington, D.C., U.S.A.(yzhou@gwu.edu);* [3]*Department of Library Science, Clarion University, Clarion, Pennsylvania, U.S.A. (ereid@clarion.edu);* [4]*Department of Management Information Systems, The University of Arizona, Tucson, Arizona, U.S.A. (hchen@eller.arizona.edu)*

CHAPTER OVERVIEW

Nowadays, global extremist organizations are heavily utilizing Internet technologies to increase their abilities to influence the world. Studying those global extremist organizations' Internet presence would allow us to better understand extremist organizations' technical sophistication and their propaganda plans. However, due to the lack of efficient automatic methodologies, few previous researches have attempted to study the extremist organizations' online presence on a global scale. In this work, we explore an integrated approach for collecting and analyzing extremist online presence. We employed automatic Web crawling techniques to build a comprehensive extremist Web collection which contains around 1.7 million multimedia Web documents. We then used a systematic content analysis tool called the Dark Web Attribute System to study these extremist organizations' Internet usage from three perspectives: technical sophistication, content richness, and Web interactivity. We also conducted statistical analysis to cross-compare the technical sophistication and effectiveness of Web sites created by extremist groups from different regions. Our analysis results showed that all extremist organizations covered in this study demonstrated high level of technical sophistication in their Web presence but extremist organizations from different regions have different patterns in their Internet technology deployment and online content delivery. Our analysis results would help domain experts deepen their understanding on the global extremism movements and make better counter-extremism measures on the Internet.

1.   INTRODUCTION

Global extremist organizations, ranging from U.S. domestic racist and militia groups to Latin American guerrilla groups and Islamic military groups, have created thousands of Web sites that support psychological warfare, fundraising, recruitment, and distribution of propaganda materials. From those Web sites, supporters can download multimedia training materials, buy games, T-shirts, and music CDs, and access forums and chat services such as PalTalk (Bowers, 2004; Muriel, 2004; Weimann, 2004). Such Web sites are technically supported by those who are Internet Savvy to provide sophisticated propaganda images and videos via proxy servers to mask ownerships (Armstrong & Forde, 2003). As posited by Jenkins (2004), through operating their own Web sites and online forums, extremists have effectively created their sophisticated "terror news network."

Studying the sophistication of global extremist organizations' Web presence would allow us to better understand extremist organizations' technical sophistication, their access to information technology related resources, and their propaganda plans. However, due to the covert nature of the Dark Web and the lack of efficient automatic methodologies to monitor and analyze large amount of Web contents, few previous research have attempted to study the extremist organizations' Web sites on a global scale. Scope of existing Dark Web studies was often limited by the low efficiency of manual analysis approaches. Many basic questions about global Dark Web development remain unanswered. For example, do different organizations have different level of sophistications in terms of their Internet usage? How effective have they been using the Internet technologies in terms of supporting communications and propaganda activities?

In order to gain a more comprehensive understanding of the global Dark Web development, in this work, we explore an integrated approach for collecting and monitoring Dark Web contents. We employed automatic Web crawling techniques to build a comprehensive Dark Web collection which covers Web sites created by more than 200 domestic and international extremist organizations. We then applied a systematic content analysis methodology called the Dark Web Attribute System (Qin et al., forthcoming) to enable quantitative assessment of the technical sophistication and effectiveness of these extremist organizations' Internet usage. We already tested the DWAS in a study of the major Middle Eastern extremist organizations' Internet usage (Qin et al., forthcoming). The results demonstrated the effectiveness of the DWAS in studying organizations' Internet usage. Furthermore, the high level of automation in the DWAS leads to high efficiency, making the analysis of very large Web collection possible.

The rest of this paper is organized as follows. In Section 2, we briefly review previous works on extremists' use of the Web. In Section 3, we present our research questions and the proposed methodologies to study those questions. In Section 4, we describe the findings obtained from a case study of the analysis of technical sophistication, content richness, and Web interactivity features of major extremist organizations from three regions: North America, Latin American, and Middle Eastern countries. In the last section, we provide conclusions and discuss the future directions of this research.

2. LITERATURE REVIEW

2.1 Extremism on the Internet

Previous research showed that extremists mainly utilize the Internet to enhance their information operations surrounding propaganda, communication, and psychological warfare (Thomas, 2003; Denning, 2004; Weimann, 2004). According to Weimann (2004), almost all major extremist organizations in the world have established their presence on the Internet.

Islamic militant organizations, such as Al Quaeda, Hamas, Hezbollah, etc., have been intensively utilizing the Internet to disseminate their anti-Western, anti-Israel propaganda, provide training materials to their supporters, plan their operations, and raise funds by selling goods through their Web sites (9/11 Commission Report, 2004; Waldman, 2004). The level of technical sophistication of the Islamic extremist organizations' Web sites has been increasing according to Katz, who monitors Islamic fundamentalist Internet activities (Internet Haganah, 2005; SITE, 2004).

Latin American guerrilla groups are also among the Internet-savvy extremist organizations. Mexico's Zapatista guerrillas have been rallying support online since their 1994 uprising. Their Web site (http://www.ezln.org/) has long been a Lycos Web Points' (http://point.lycos.com/) top 5% WWW sites and serves a mouthpiece for the organization. Other major Latin American extremist groups such as the Revolutionary Armed Forces of Colombia (FARC) and the "Shining Path" in Peru also host their own Web sites containing scrolls of propaganda materials.

U.S. domestic extremist and hate groups have also exploited Internet technology to enhance their operations and were among the early adopters of computer bulletin boards that eventually evolved into the Internet (Gerstenfeld et al., 2002). Stormfront.org, a neo-Nazi's Website set up in 1995, is considered the first major domestic "hate site" on the World Wide

Web because of its depth of content and its presentation style which represented a new period for online right-wing extremism (Whine, 1997). The neo-Nazis groups share a hatred for Jews and other minorities, and a love for Adolf Hitler and Nazi Germany. A social network analysis of extremist Websites revealed that the Stormfornt.org served as a central node that occupied a prominent position within the White Supremacist network (Burris et al., 2000).

Extremist groups have sought to replicate or supplement the communication, fundraising, propaganda, recruitment, and training functions on the Web by building web sites with massive and dynamic online libraries of speeches, training manuals, and multimedia resources that are hyperlinked to other sites that share similar beliefs (Coll & Glasser, 2005; Weimann, 2004). The Web sites are designed to communicate with diverse global audiences of members, sympathizers, media, enemies, and the public (Weimann, 2004). Since extremist organizations are active on the Internet, studying their Web presence may help us develop a better understanding of the extremists themselves.

2.2   Existing Dark Web Studies and Research Gaps

In recent years, there have been studies on how extremist organizations use the Web to facilitate their activities (Zhou et al., 2005; Chen, et. al., 2004; ISTS, 2004; Thomas, 2003; Tsfati & Weimann, 2002; SITE, 2004; Weimann, 2004). For example, since the late 1990s, several organizations, such as SITE Institute, the Anti-Terrorism Coalition, and the Middle East Media Research Institute (MEMRI), started to monitor contents from extremist Web sites for research and intelligence purposes. However, due to the limitations of manual analysis approaches employed in those studies, the scopes of those studies have been limited to some selected groups. Table 2 lists some of the organizations that capture and analyze extremists' Web sites grouped into three functional categories: archive, research center, and vigilante community.

Table 12-1. Organizations that Capture and Analyze Extremists' Web Sites

Organization	Description	Access
Archive		
1. Internet Archive (IA)	1996-. Collect open access HTML pages (every 2 mths.)	Via http://www.archive.org
Research Centers		
2. Anti-terrorism Coalition (ATC)	2003-. Jihad Watch. Has 448 extremist Web sites & forums	Via http://www.atcoalition.net
3. Artificial Intelligence (AI)	2003-. Spidering (every 2	Via testbed portal called

Organization	Description	Access
Lab, University of Arizona	mos.) to collect extremist Web sites. Has 1000s Web sites: U.S. Domestic, Latin America, & Middle Eastern Web sites	Dark Web Portal
4. MEMRI	2003 -. Jihad & Terrorism Studies Project.	Access reports via http://www.memri.org
5. Site Institute	2003 -. Capture Web sites every 24 hrs. Extensive collection of 1000s of files.	Access reports & fee-based intelligence services http://siteinstitute.org
6. Weimann (Univ. Haifa, Israel)	1998 -. Capture Web sites daily. Extensive collection of 1000s of files.	Closed collection
Vigilante Community		
7. Internet Haganah	2001-. Confronting the Global Jihad Project. Has 100s links to Web sites.	Provides snapshots of terrorist Web sites http://haganah.us

Except for the Artificial Intelligence (AI) Lab, none of the enumerated organizations seem to use automated methodologies for both collection building and analysis of extremist Web sites. Due to the low efficiency of the manual collection and analysis approaches, comprehensiveness of their analyses has been limited. In order to gain deeper understanding on global extremists' use of the Internet, we believe it is important to analyze the technical sophistication, content richness, and Web interactivity of extremist Web sites on a global scale.

2.3   Dark Web Collection Building

The first step towards studying the extremist Web presence is to capture extremist Web sites and store them in a repository for further analysis. Previous studies have suggested three types of approaches to collecting Web contents in specific domains: manual approach, automatic approach, and semiautomatic approach. In order to build the September 11 and Election 2002 Web Archives (Schneider et al., 2003), the Library of Congress manually collected relevant seed URLs and downloaded their contents. The limitation of such a manual approach is that it is time-consuming and inefficient. To archive Norwegian legal deposit documents on the Web, Albertsen (2003) used an automatic approach in the "Paradigma" project. They employed a focused Web crawler (Kleinberg et al., 1999), an automatic program that discovers and downloads Web sites in particular domains by following Web links. The automatic approach is more efficient than the manual approach; however, due to the limitations of current focused crawling techniques, automatic approaches often introduce noise (off-topic Web pages) into the collection.

In order to ensure both quality and efficiency in collecting Dark Web contents, we proposed a semi-automatic Dark Web crawling approach which combined the accuracy of human experts and the efficiency of automatic Web crawlers (Zhou et al., 2004). The semi-automatic approach contains four major steps. First, a list of extremist organizations is identified from authoritative sources such as U.S. State Department report, FBI report, and UN security counsel. Then, URLs of Web sites created by these organizations are identified either directly from the same authoritative sources or by searching the Internet using those organizations' information (group name, leader names, jargons, etc.) as queries. The identified URLs form the initial seed URL set and this set are then further expanded through out-link and in-link expansion approaches. Last, the identified extremist Web sites are automatically downloaded using an intelligent Web crawler.

Using this approach, we successfully created a comprehensive Dark Web testbed containing more than 100 Web sites created by extremists. We believe that this semiautomatic approach is most suitable for creating the comprehensive Dark Web collection for this study.

2.4   Dark Web Content Analysis

In order to reach an understanding of the various facets of extremists' Web usage and communications, a systematic analysis of the Web sites' content is required. Researchers in the extremism domain have used observation and content analysis to analyze Web site data. In Bunt's (2003) overview of Jihadi movements' presence on the Web, he described the reaction of the global Muslim community to the content of extremist Web sites. His assessment of the influence such content had on Muslims and Westerners was based on a qualitative analysis of message contents extracted from Taliban and Al-Qaeda Web sites. Tsfati and Weimann (2002) conducted a content analysis of the characteristics of extremist groups' communications. They said that the small size of their collection and the descriptive nature of their research questions made a quantitative analysis infeasible.

In order to enable quantitative study, we proposed a systematic Dark Web content analysis approach called the Dark Web Attribute System (DWAS). The DWAS extracts the appearances of specific attributes from extremist Web sites and assigns each Web site three scores to indicate their levels of technical sophistication, content richness, and Web interactivity. The attributes used in DWAS were identified from literatures in e-

Commerce (Palmer & David, 1998), e-Government (Demchak & Friis, 2004), and e-Education (Cho, 2004) domains. Unlike most manual-based, qualitative content analysis approaches used in previous Dark Web studies, the DWAS employs programs to automatically identify the appearances of attributes and generate quantitative results. We successfully applied the DWAS to study the technical sophistication and effectiveness of Middle Eastern extremist organizations' Internet usage. We believe that the DWAS is also an effective tool to study the extremist's tactical use of the Internet on a global scale.

3. STUDYING GLOBAL EXTREMIST ORGANIZATIONS' INTERNET USAGE: A THREE-REGION EMPIRICAL STUDY

Studying the Dark Web helps us deepen our understandings on the global extremism movements. However, traditional manual based Web analysis approaches were not efficient enough to conduct comprehensive Dark Web studies on a global scale. To address this research gap, we propose a large scale empirical study on the technical sophistication and effectiveness of global extremist organizations' Internet usage. To ensure the comprehensiveness, our study covers Web sites created by major extremist organizations from three geographical regions across the world: US domestic racist and hate groups, Latin American guerrilla and separatist groups, as well as Middle Eastern Islamic extremist groups. We also conducted cross-compared Web sites of different types of extremist groups to reveal the differences in extremist organizations' online capabilities and strategies.

The research questions postulated in our study are:

- What design features and attributes are necessary to build a highly relevant and comprehensive global Dark Web collection for analysis purposes?
- For extremist Web sites, what are the levels of technical sophistication, content richness, and interactivity?
- What major differences exist between the characteristics of Web sites created by extremists from different regions with different ideologies?

To study the research questions, we propose to use the Dark Web analysis methodology proposed in Qin et al. (forthcoming) and expand the scope of the study to a global level. Both the semi-automatic collection build approach and the DWAS have been shown as effective tools in our previous studies on the Middle Eastern extremist organizations' Web presence (Qin et al., forthcoming).

3.1   Dark Web Collection Building

To ensure the quality of our collection, we propose to use a semi-automated approach to collecting Dark Web contents (Zhou et al., 2004). The collection used in this study was built in May 2006. The collection was built in the following 4 steps:

1. Identify extremist groups: We started the collection building process by identifying the groups that are considered by authoritative sources as extremist groups. The sources include government agency reports (e.g., U.S. State Department reports, FBI reports, etc.), authoritative organization reports (e.g., Counter-Terrorism Committee of the UN Security Council, etc.), and studies published by extremism research centers such as the Anti-Terrorism Coalition (ATC), the Middle East Media Research Institute (MEMRI), etc. From those sources, we identified around 200 U.S. domestic groups, and around 400 International groups. Information such as extremist group names, leader names, and extremist jargons are identified from the sources to create a extremism keyword lexicon for use in the next step.

2. Identify extremist group URLs: We manually identified a set of seed extremist group URLs from two sources. First, some extremist URLs were directly identified from the authoritative sources and literatures mentioned above. Second, we identified another set of extremist URLs by querying major search. The initial set of seed URLs was then expanded. The queries were issued in the corresponding extremist groups' native languages. For example, the queries we used when searching for Middle Eastern groups' URLs include extremist leaders' names such as "الشيخ المجاهد بن لادن" (Sheikh Mujahid bin Laden), extremist groups' names such as "ايران خلق" ("Khalq Iran"), and special words used by extremists such as "حرب صليبية" ("Crusader's War") and "الكفار" ("Infidels").

3. Expand extremist URL set through link and forum analysis: After identifying the seed URLs, We extracted out-links and in-links of the seed URLs using an automatic link-analysis programs. The out-links were extracted from the HTML contents of "favorite link" pages under the seed Web sites. The in-links were extracted from Google in-link search service through Google API. We also had language experts who browsed the contents of extremist supporting forums and extract the extremist URLs posted by extremism supporters. The expanded extremist URL set was them manually filtered by domain experts to ensure that irrelevant and bogus Web sites did not make way into our collection. After the filtering, a total of 224 extremist group URLs (92 U.S. domestic group URLs, 53 Latin American group URLs, and 79 Middle Eastern

group URLs) were included in our final URL set.

4. Download extremist Web site contents: The multimedia and multilingual contents of the identified extremist Web sites were automatically collected using a Web crawler developed by our group. Our Web crawler was designed to download not only the textual files (e.g., HTML, TXT, PDF, etc.) but also multimedia files (e.g., images, video, audio, etc.) and dynamically generated Web files (e.g., PHP, ASP, JSP, etc.). Moreover, because extremist organizations set up forums within their Web sites whose contents are of special value to research communities, our Web crawler also can automatically log into the forums and download the dynamic forum contents. The automatic Web crawling approach allows us to effectively build Dark Web collections with millions of documents. This would greatly increase the comprehensiveness of our Dark Web study.

Following the four steps described above, we built a global Dark Web collection contain around 1.7 million multimedia documents. Table 2 summarizes the detailed file type breakdown of the global Dark Web collection. The textual files make the large category in the Dark Web collection. Textual files include static textual files such as HTML files, PDF files, MS Word documents, as well as dynamic files such as PHP files, ASP files, and JSP files. Interestingly, more than half of the textual files in the Dark Web collection are dynamic files. In particular, dynamic files make up to 78% of all textual files. We conducted a preliminary analysis on the contents of these dynamic files and found that most dynamic files were forum postings. This indicates that online forums play an important role in extremists' Web usage, especially for Middle Eastern groups.

Other than textual files, multimedia files also make a significant presence in the extremist collection which indicates heavy use of multimedia technologies in extremist Web sites. The last two types of files, archive files and non-standard files, made up less than 5% of the collection. Archive files are compressed file packages such .zip files and .rar files. They could be password-protected. Non-standard files are files that cannot be recognized by the Windows operating system. These files may be of special interest of extremism researchers and experts because they could be encrypted information created by extremists. Further analysis is needed to study the contents of these two types of files.

Comparing documents created by groups from different regions, we found that the number of Web documents created by the Middle Eastern groups is much larger than those of the U.S. domestic groups and the Latin American groups. This indicates the Middle Eastern extremist organizations are making a more prominent presence on the Web. A more detailed analysis on the technical sophistication and effectiveness of the extremists' Internet presence will be described in the next section.

Table 12-2. Dark Web Collection File Type Breakdown

File Types	# of Files		
	U.S. Domestic	**Latin American**	**Middle Eastern**
Textual Files	312408	230977	804145
Static Files	154148	89150	176061
Dynamic Files	158260	141827	628084
Multimedia Files	96738	55618	225557
Image Files	91089	54422	216520
Audio Files	3769	941	1437
Video Files	1880	255	7600
Archive Files	327	852	1499
Non-Standard Files	1355	650	1537
Total	410828	288097	1032738

3.2   Dark Web Content Analysis Using the DWAS

We used the DWAS as our content analysis tool to generate quantitative indications of the technical sophistication and effectiveness of global extremists' use of the Internet. The DWAS contains three sets of attributes: 13 technical sophistication (TS) attributes, five content richness (CR) attributes (an extension of the traditional media richness attributes), and 11 Web interactivity (WI) attributes. Different weights were assigned to each technical sophistication and Web interactivity attribute to indicate their different levels of importance. A list of these attributes is summarized in Tables 3.

Table 12-3. Summary of DWAS Attributes and Weights

TS Attributes		Weights
Basic HTML Techniques	Use of Lists	1
	Use of Tables	2
	Use of Frames	2
	Use of Forms	1.5
Embedded Multimedia	Use of Background Image	1
	Use of Background Music	2
	Use of Stream Audio/Video	3.5
Advanced HTML	Use of DHTML/SHTML	2.5
	Use of Predefined Script Functions	2
	Use of Self-defined Script Functions	4.5
Dynamic Web Programming	Use of CGI	2.5
	Use of PHP	4.5
	Use of JSP/ASP	5.5

	CR Attributes	Scores
Hyperlink	# of hyperlinks	Hyperlink
File/Software Download	# of downloadable documents	File/Software Download
Image	# of images	Image
Audio Files	# of audio files	Audio Files
Video Files	# of video files	Video Files
WI Attributes		**Weights**
One-to-one Level Interactivity		
Email Feedback		1.75
Email List		2.25
Contact Address		1.25
Feedback Form		2.75
Guest Book		1.50
Community Level Interactivity		
Private Message		4.25
Online Forum		4.25
Chat Room		4.75
Transaction Level Interactivity		
Online Shop		4.00
Online Payment		4.00
Online Application Form		4.00

We developed strategies to efficiently and accurately identify the presence of the DWAS attributes from Dark Web sites. The TS and CR attributes are marked by HTML tags in page contents or file extension names in the page URL strings. For example, a URL string ending with ".jsp" indicates that the page utilizes JSP technology. We developed programs to automatically analyze Dark Web page contents and URL strings to extract the presence of the TS and CR attributes. Since there are no clear indications or rules that a program could follow to identify WI attributes from Dark Web contents with a high degree of accuracy, we developed a set of coding scheme to allow human coders to identify their presence in Dark Web sites. Technical sophistication, content richness, and Web interactivity scores are calculated for each Web site in the collection based on the presence of the attributes to indicate how advanced and effective the site is in terms of supporting communications and interactions.

3.3 Experimental Results

Following the DWAS approach, presence of the technical sophistication and media richness attributes was automatically extracted from the collections using programs. Presence of the Web interactivity attributes was extracted from each Web site by language experts based on the coding scheme in DWAS. Because of the time limitation, language experts only examined the top two level Web pages in each Web site. For each Web site in the global Dark Web collection, three scores (technical sophistication, content richness, and Web interactivity) were calculated based on the presence of the attributes and their corresponding weights in DWAS. Statistical analysis was conducted to cross-compare the advancement/effectiveness scores achieved by the Web sites of extremist organizations from the three different regions.

3.3.1   Comparison Results: Technical Sophistication

To learn whether there are differences in extremist organizations' level of sophistication, we used ANOVA analysis to compare the technical sophistication scores achieved by Web sites of extremist groups from different regions. Figures 12-1.a to 12-1.e show the ANOVA results of different technical sophistication levels.

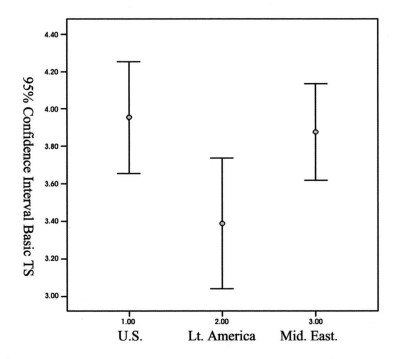

ANOVA Basic TS (Significance Level at 0.05)

F	p-Value	F crit
3.987669	0.019863**	3.035794

Figure 12-1.a. Basic HTML Technical Sophistication ANOVA Results

Figure 12-1.a shows that, in terms of applying basic HTML techniques, there are significant differences in the levels of technical sophistication between Web sites created by groups from the three regions. More specifically, the confidence interval plot shown in the upper side of Figure 12-1.a shows that U.S. domestic group Web sites and Middle Eastern group Web sites achieved similar level of basic technical sophistication and they are both significantly better than Latin American group Web sites.

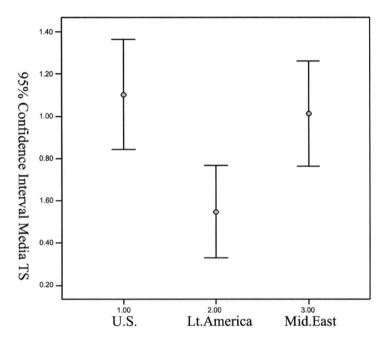

ANOVA Media TS (Significance Level at 0.05)		
F	p-Value	F crit
6.23225	0.00233**	3.036902

Figure 12-1.b. Embedded Media Technical Sophistication ANOVA Results

In terms of embedded media usage, as shown in Figure 12-1.b, the ANOVA result shows that there are significant differences (p-Value = 0.00233) in the levels of technical sophistication between Web sites created by groups from the three regions. The confidence interval plot further shows that the differences in embedded media usage between Web sites created by groups of the three regions follow the same pattern as the differences in basic HTML techniques: while U.S. groups and Middle Eastern groups are comparable; both of them are significantly better than Latin American groups.

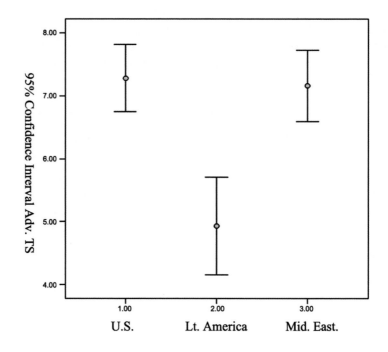

ANOVA Advanced TS (Significance Level at 0.05)		
F	p-Value	F crit
16.10481	2.97E-07**	3.036902

Figure 12-1.c. Advanced Technical Sophistication ANOVA Results

For advanced HTML technique usage, as shown in Figure 12-1.c, similar patterns were observed again. U.S. domestic group Web sites and Middle Eastern group Web sites performed comparably and they both significantly (p-Value < 0.00001) outperformed the Latin American Web sites.

For the use of dynamic Web programming languages such as PHP and JSP, a different pattern was observed. As shown in Figure 12-1.d, Middle Eastern groups are the most advanced ones in terms of applying dynamic Web programming techniques in their Web sites. They are significantly better (p-Value = 0.012885) than both U.S. domestic groups and Latin American groups. While the U.S. domestic groups performed better than the Latin American groups, the difference is not significant.

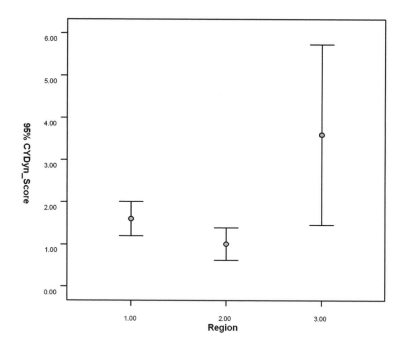

ANOVA Dynamic TS (Significance Level at 0.05)		
F	p-Value	F crit
4.438946	0.012885**	3.036902

Figure 12-1.d. Dynamic Web Programming Technical Sophistication ANOVA Results

When taking all four attributes of technical sophistication into consideration, as shown in Figure 12-1.e, Middle Easter groups are the best among all extremist groups across the world, although the difference between them and U.S. domestic groups is not significant. Latin American groups lag behind both Middle Eastern groups and U.S. domestic groups. The difference between Latin American groups and groups from the other two regions is significant (p-Value = 0.0000107).

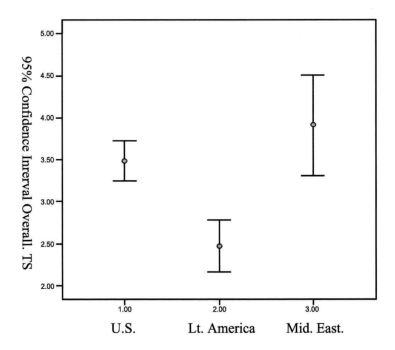

ANOVA Overall TS (Significance Level at 0.05)		
F	p-Value	F crit
12.06542	1.07E-05**	3.036902

Figure 12-1.e. Overall Technical Sophistication ANOVA Results

Technical sophistication of Web sites run by extremist organizations is a good indication of the level of IT expertise the organizations have as well as the level of investment the organizations have put on building their Internet presence. Considering the United State is the most IT savvy country in the world where Internet technologies and services are easily and cheaply available, it is not surprising to see U.S. domestic extremist organizations have achieved high level of technical sophistication in utilizing the Internet infrastructure. The Middle Eastern groups, on the other hand, are mostly rooted in countries where Internet technologies and infrastructure are much less developed. Nevertheless, they achieved a technical sophistication level that is even higher than that of the U.S. domestic groups. This indicates that the Internet has become a very important part of the Middle Easter extremist organizations' agenda and they have made the efforts to take advantages of the latest Internet technologies. The Latin American extremist groups seem to have a different attitude towards Internet. Their Web sites are significantly less sophisticated than groups from the other two regions, which indicates that they had less investment on Internet technologies. Furthermore, the Middle Eastern groups are significant more advanced in terms of utilizing dynamic Web programming techniques in their Web site than groups from the other two regions. Based on our preliminary studies, in extremist Web sites, dynamic Web programming techniques are usually used to support communication functionalities such as online forums and chat rooms. This high level usage of dynamic Web programming techniques in the Middle Easter group Web sites calls for further investigations.

3.3.2   Comparison Results: Content Richness

Content richness is an important criterion to measure the effectiveness of extremists' online propaganda plans. The richer the contents are on their Web sites, the more information can the extremist groups convey to their supporters, thus achieving better mobilization goals. To study the propaganda plans of different extremist groups, we conducted ANOVA analysis to compare the content richness of their Web sites.

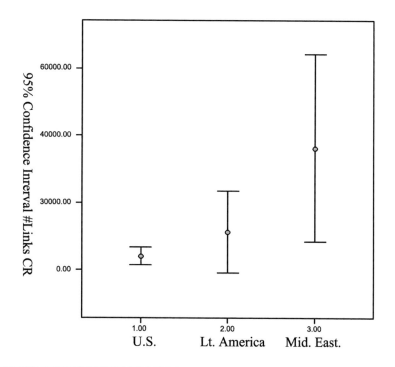

ANOVA # of Links CR (Significance Level is at 0.05)		
F	p-Value	F crit
3.037265	0.048818**	3.013056

Figure 12-2.a. Number of Links ANOVA Results

Figure 2.a shows the comparison results of average number of hyperlinks per Web site. As we can see from the confidence interval plot, the Middle Eastern groups Web sites contain significantly more hyperlinks than Web sites of the other two categories of groups (p-Value = 0.048818). Having more hyperlinks in their Web sites, the Middle Eastern groups provide their supporters with more opportunities to locate Web documents that they really want. Moreover, more hyperlinks between different groups Websites indicates that stronger real world relationships exist between those Middle Eastern extremist organizations.

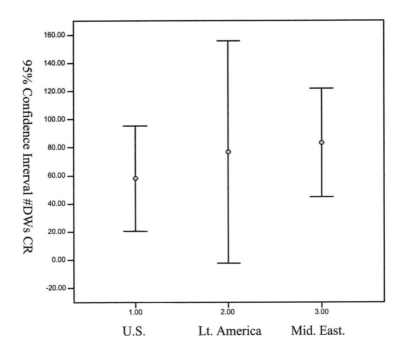

ANOVA # of Downloads (Significance Level is at 0.05)		
F	p-Value	F crit
0.226105	0.797729	3.016694

Figure 12-2.b. Number of Downloads ANOVA Results

Another important content richness attribute is the number of downloadable documents on a Web site. Downloadable documents include textual files (e.g., PDF files, MS Word Files, etc.) and archive files (e.g., ZIP files, RAR files, etc.). Previous studies (Bowers, 2004; Muriel, 2004;

Weimann, 2004; SITE, 2004) showed that providing downloadable documents on Web site has become a major means for extremists to disseminate their propaganda materials. From Figure 2.b, we can see that extremist groups from all three major regions provide similar amount of downloadable documents on their Web sites.

Multimedia documents, including images, audio files, and video files, are the most important vehicles to convey information to Web users. They are more attractive and tend to leave a stronger impression on people than pure textual contents. As shown in Figures 2.c-2.e, the Middle Easter groups posted significantly (p-Value = 0.001219) more images and video files on their Web sites than the U.S. domestic and Latin American groups. The U.S. Domestic groups posted more audio files than the Middle Eastern and Latin American groups; but the difference is not significant (p-Value = 0.135728).

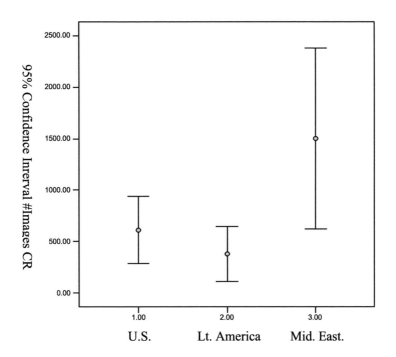

ANOVA # of Images (Significance Level is at 0.05)		
F	p-Value	F crit
4.218931	0.015325**	3.016602

Figure 12-2.c. Number of Images ANOVA Results

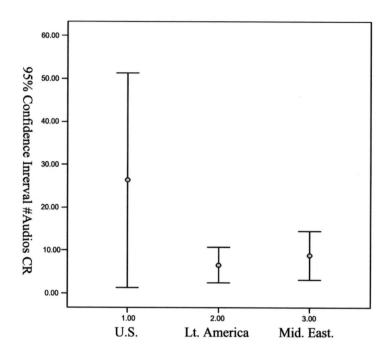

ANOVA # of Audio Files (Significance Level is at 0.05)		
F	p-Value	F crit
2.00641	0.135728	3.016694

Figure 12-2.d. Number of Audio Files ANOVA Results

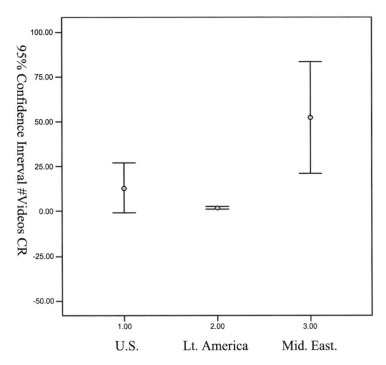

ANOVA # of Video Files (Significance Level is at 0.05)		
F	p-Value	F crit
6.816345	0.001219**	3.016893

Figure 12-2.e. Number of audio files ANOVA results

The large amount of multimedia content posted on the Middle Eastern groups Web sites is an indication that the Middle Eastern groups have very active propaganda strategies. Moreover, hosting large volume of multimedia contents usually requires Web servers with high stability and bandwidth. The Middle Eastern extremist groups succeeded in building such a stable online infrastructure to support their sophisticated online propaganda campaigns.

3.3.3   Comparison Results: Web Interactivity

Supporting the communications between their members and their supporters is one of the major goals of extremists' Internet exploitation. We conducted ANOVA analysis to compare the effectiveness of extremist groups' communications through their Web sites.

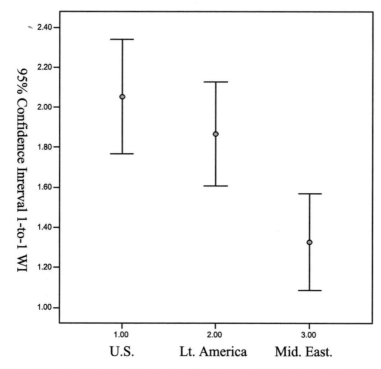

ANOVA 1-to-1 Interactivity (Significance Level is at 0.05)		
F	p-Value	F crit
9.027465	0.000181**	3.044505

Figure 12-3.a. 1-to-1 level interactivity ANOVA results

As shown in Figure 12-3.a, in terms of one-to-one level interactivity, both the U.S. domestic groups and Latin American groups performed significantly (p-Value = 0.000181) better than the Middle Eastern groups. One possible explanation for the low one-to-one interactivity support from the Middle Easter groups is that the Middle Eastern extremist groups are more radical and covert than the U.S. domestic and Latin American groups. Many of the Middle Eastern groups are currently under military suppression from the West. In many cases, they could not give out their address and other contact information to the public.

At the community level, as shown in Figure 12-3.b, the U.S. domestic groups and the Middle Eastern groups both performed better than the Latin American groups. The difference between the U.S. domestic and Latin American groups is significant (p-Value = 0.044895). The U.S. domestic extremist groups are among the earliest adopters of Internet forums.

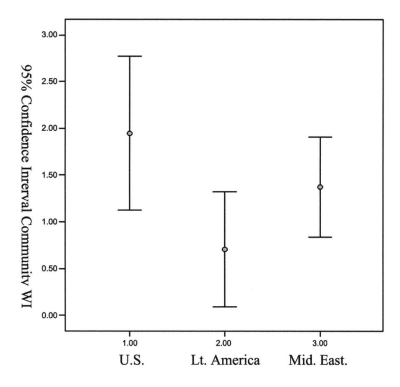

ANOVA Community Interactivity (Significance Level is at 0.05)		
F	p-Value	F crit
3.155795	0.044895**	3.044505

Figure 12-3.b. Community level interactivity ANOVA results

It is not surprising to see that they are still heavily utilizing Internet tools such as forums and chat rooms to support their communication with their supporters. The Middle Eastern groups are the newer adopters of such Internet-based communication tools, but they are also very active in terms of hosting and maintaining online forums and bulletin boards. Some of the Middle Eastern extremist group forums have grown very large in scale. For example, www.shawati.com has 31,894 registered forum members and 418,196 posts; www.kuwaitchat.net has 11,531 registered members and 624,694 posts. Not all of the forum members are extremism or extremists. Many of them are just supporters or sympathizers. Members of these large forums participate in daily discussions, express their support of the extremist groups, and reinforce each other's beliefs in the extremist groups' courses. They sometimes can get messages directly from active members of extremist groups. For example, messages from the Iraqi extremist leader, Abu Mus'ab Zarqawi can often be found in online forum www.islamic-f.net. These dynamic forums provide snapshots of extremist groups' activities, communications, ideologies, relationships, and evolutionary developments.

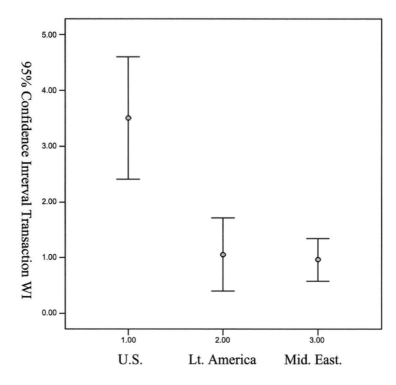

Figure 12-3.c. Transaction level interactivity ANOVA results

ANOVA Transaction Interactivity (Significance Level is at 0.05)		
F	p-Value	F crit
15.69915	5.01051E-07**	3.044505

   The transaction level interactivity is the most advanced level of interactivity that Web sites can support. At this level, as shown in Figure 12-3.c, the U.S. domestic groups significantly outperformed both the Latin American and Middle Eastern groups. Supporting transaction level interactivity requires high level of technical sophistication which the Latin American groups did not demonstrate based on our TS comparison results. That is one possible explanation for Latin American groups' low performance. On the other hand, transaction level interactivities usually involve the transfer of funds online. In order to perform such tasks, one is often required to provide their identity information (bank account member, billing address, contact information, etc.) to online service providers. It is difficult for the Middle Eastern groups to meet these requirements because they have to remain covert, which is a possible explanation for their low performance in supporting transaction level interactivity.

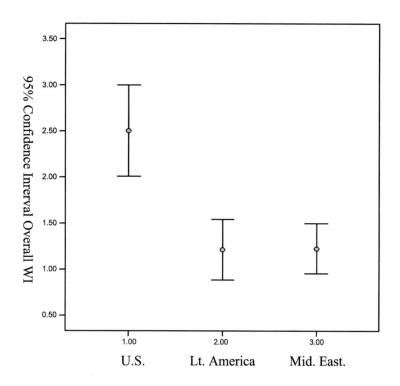

ANOVA Overall Interactivity (Significance Level is at 0.05)		
F	p-Value	F crit
15.7745	4.7E-07**	3.044505

Figure 12-3.d. Overall Web interactivity ANOVA results

When taking all three levels of Web interactivity into consideration, as shown in Figure 12-3.d, the U.S. domestic groups performed significantly better (p-Value < 0.0001) than both the Latin American and Middle Eastern groups.

4.   CONCLUSIONS AND FUTURE DIRECTIONS

In this paper, we discussed a large scale empirical study to explore the application of automatic Web crawling techniques and the Dark Web Attribute System in studying global extremist organizations' Internet presence. Using a semi-automatic crawling approach, we collected more than 1.7 million multimedia Web documents from around 224 Web sites created by major extremist organizations rooted in North America, Latin America, and Middle Eastern countries. We then used the Dark Web Attribute System to study these extremist organizations' Internet usage from three perspectives: technical sophistication, content richness, and Web interactivity. In order to gain a deeper understanding on different extremist organizations' IT capabilities, we also conducted statistical analysis to cross-compare the technical sophistication and effectiveness of Web sites created by extremist groups from different regions.

Our analysis results showed that, among groups from all three regions, the Middle Eastern extremist organizations are the most active exploiters of the Internet. They demonstrated the highest level of technical sophistication and provided the richest multimedia contents in their Web sites. However, due to their covert nature, they did not perform as well as the U.S. domestic extremist organizations in terms of supporting communications using Internet technologies. Because the U.S. domestic groups take full advantages of Internet technologies such as forums, chat rooms, and e-Commerce transactions, to facilitate their communication and interaction with their supporters. The Latin American groups, on the other hand, lagged behind groups from the other two regions in terms of exploiting the Internet. Their Web sites are not as sophisticated as those of their U.S. and Middle Eastern counterparts. They were also not as effective in terms of utilizing the Internet to support their communications.

The contribution of this study is twofold. First, this study further explored the high effectiveness and efficiency of automatic Web mining techniques in Dark Web studies. It expanded the scope of our previous Dark Web content analysis (Qin et al., forthcoming) and pushed the comprehensiveness of Dark Web studies to a new level. Second, the results of our empirical study help domain experts deepen their understanding on the global extremism movements and make better counter-extremism measures on the Internet.

We have several future research directions to pursue. First, we will further improve the Dark Web Attributes System by incorporating more accurate attributes into the system. We will also collaborate with more Internet technology experts to further fine tune the weights associated with the DWAS attributes. Second, we will explore more effective Web crawling techniques to further expand the coverage of our Dark Web study. Third, we will collaborate with more extremism domain experts to better interpret our findings. Last but not least, we will explore the application of the proposed automatic Web crawling and content analysis tools in other domains such as business intelligence and e-Government.

REFERENCES

Anderson, A., "Risk, Terrorism, and the Internet," Knowledge, Technology & Policy, 16:2, 24-33, Summer 2003.

Armstrong, H. L. and Forde, P. J., "Internet Anonymity Practices in Computer Crime," Information Management & Computer Security, 11(5), pp. 209-215, 2003.

Arquilla, J. and Ronfeldt, D., "Cyber War Is Coming!" Comparative Strategy, 12(2), 1993.

Becker, A. "Technology and Terror: the New Modus Operandi," Frontline, 2004, available at http://www.pbs.org/wgbh/pages/frontline/shows/front/special/tech.html

Bowers, F., "Terrorists spread their messages online," Christian Science Monitor, July 28, 2004, available at http://www.csmonitor.com/2004/0728/p03s01-usgn.htm.

Chakrabarti, S., van den Berg, M. and Dom, B., "Focused crawling: a new approach to topic-specific Web resource discovery," in Proc. of the 8th International World Wide Web Conference, Toronto, Canada, 1999.

Chen, H., Qin, J., Reid, E., Chung, W., Zhou, Y., Xi, W., Lai, G., Bonillas, A. A. and Sageman, M., "The Dark Web Portal: Collecting and Analyzing the Presence of Domestic and International Terrorist Groups on the Web," In Proc. of International IEEE Conference on Intelligent Transportation Systems, 2004.

Chou, C., "Interactivity and interactive functions in web-based learning systems: a technical framework for designers." British Journal of Educational Technology, 34(3), pp. 265-279, 2003.

Coll, S. and Glasser, S. B., "Terrorists Turn to the Web as Base of Operations," Washington Post, Aug 7, 2005.

Demchak, C., Friis, C., and La Porte, T. M., "Webbing Governance: National Differences in Constructing the Face of Public Organizations," Handbook of Public Information Systems. G. D. Garson. NYC, Marcel Dekker, 2001.

Denning, D. E., "Information Operations and Terrorism," Journal of Information Warfare (draft), 2004, available at http://www.jinfowar.com.

Elison, W., "Netwar: Studying Rebels on the Internet," The Social Studies, 91, pp. 127-131, 2000.

FBIS, "Arab Afghans Said to Launch Worldwide Terrorist War," Paris al-Watan al-'Arabi, December 1, 1995, pp.22-24, FBIS-TOT-96-010-L.

Hillman, D. C. A., Willis, D. J., and Gunawardena, C. N., "Learner-interface interaction in distance education: an extension of contemporary models and strategies for practitioners." The American Journal of Distance Education, 8(2), pp. 30-42, 1994.

Hoffman, D. L. and Novak, T. P., "Marketing in hypermedia computer-mediated environments: Conceptual foundation." Journal of Marketing, 60(3), pp. 50-68, 1996.

ISTS, "Examining the Cyber Capabilities of Islamic Terrorist Groups". Report, Institute for Security Technology Studies, 2004. http://www.ists.dartmouth.edu/

Internet Haganah, Internet Haganah report, 2005, available at http://en.wikipedia.org/wiki/Internet_Haganah.

Jenkins, B. M., International Terrorism, Crescent Publication, Los Angeles, 1975.

Jenkins, B. M., "World Becomes the Hostage of Media-Savvy Terrorists: Commentary", USA Today, August 22, 2004. http://www.rand.org/

Delio, M., "Al Qaeda Websites Refuses to Die," Wired, April 7, 2003, available at: http://

www.wired.com/news/infostructure/0,1377,583562,00.html?tw=wn_story_page_next1.

Jackson, Brian J. Technology Acquisition by Terrorist Groups: Threat Assessment Informed by Lessons from Private Sector Technology Adoption. Studies in Conflict & Terrorism, vol. 24, p183-213. 2001

Jesdanun, A., "WWW: Terror's Channel of Choice," CBS News, June 20, 2004.

Kelley, J., "Terror Groups Hide Behind Encryption," USA Today, Feb 5, 2001, available at http://www.usatoday.com/tech/news/2001-02-05-binladen.htm

Lawrence, S. and Giles, C. L., "Searching the World Wide Web." Science, 280(5360), 1998, pp. 98.

Lawrence, S. and Giles, C. L. "Accessibility of information on the Web." Nature, 400, 1999, pp. 107-109.

Lyman, P. and Varian, H.R., "How Much Information." published by the UC Berkeley School of Information Management and Systems, 2000.

McCallum, A., Nigamm, K., Rennie, J., and Seymore, K., "Building Domain-Specific Search Engines with Machine Learning Techniques" Proc. AAAI-99 Spring Symposium on Intelligent Agents in Cyberspace, 1999

Michalewicz, Z., Genetic algorithms + data structures = evolution programs. Berlin/Heidelberg: Springer-Verlag, 1992.

Muriel, D., "Terror Moves to the Virtual World," CNN News, April 8, 2004, available at http://edition.cnn.com/2004/TECH/04/08/internet.terror/.

Nunnelly, J., Psychometric theory. McGraw Hill, New York, 1978.

Palmer, J. W. and Griffith, D. A., "An Emerging Model of Web Site Design for Marketing," Communications of the ACM, 41(3), pp. 45-51, 1998.

Preece, J., Online Communities: Designing Usability, Supporting Socialability, 2000, New York City, Wiley.

Reid, E., Qin, J., Chung, W., Xu, J., Zhou, Y., Schumaker, R., Sageman, M., and Chen H., "Terrorism Knowledge Discovery Project: a Knowledge Discovery Approach to Addressing the Threats of Terrorism" in Proc. of 2nd Symposium on Intelligence and Security Informatics, ISI 2004, , Tucson, Arizona, 2004.

Rusay, C., "User-centered design for government portals," Digital Web Magazine, Jan 16, 2003, available at http://www.digital-web.com/articles/user_centered_design_for_large_government_portals/

Schneider, S. M., Foot, K., Kimpton, M., and Jones, G., "Building thematic web collections: challenges and experiences from the September 11 Web Archive and the Election 2002 Web Archive," in Proc. of the 3rd ECDL Workshop on Web Archives, Trondheim, Norway, August 2003.

Tekwani, S., "Cyberterrorism: Threat and Response," Institute of Defence and Strategic Studies, in Proc. of the Workshop on the New Dimensions of Terrorism, 21-22, Singapore, 2002.

Thomas, T. L., "Al Qaeda and the Internet: The Danger of 'Cyberplanning,'" Parameters, Spring 2003, pp. 112-23, available at http://carlisle-www.army.mil/usawc/Parameters /03spring/thomas.htm.

Tsfati, Y. and Weimann, G., "www.terrorism.com: Terror on the Internet," Studies in Conflict & Terrorism, 25, pp. 317-332, 2002.

Trevino, L. K., Lengel, R. H., and Daft, R. L., "Media symbolism, media richness, and media choice in organizations: A symbolic interactionist perspective." Communication Research, 14(5), pp. 553-574, 1987.

Qin, J., Zhou, Y., Reid, E., Lai, G. and Chen, H. (forthcoming). "Analyzing Terror Campaigns on the Internet: Technical Sophistication, Content Richness, and Web

Interactivity," International Journal on Human Computer Studies, accepted for publication, forthcoming.

Weimann, G., "www.terror.net: How Modern Terrorism Use the Internet," Special Report, U.S. Institute of Peace, 2004, Available at http://www.usip.org/pubs/specialreports/sr116.pdf.

Whine, M., "Cyberspace: A New Medium for Communication, Command and Control by Extremists," 1999, available at http://www.ict.org.il/articles/cyberspace.htm

Xu, J. and Croft, B., "Querying Expansion using Local and Global Document Analysis." in Proc. of the 19th Annual International ACM SIGIR Conference on Research and Development in Information Retrieval, Zurich, Switzerland, 1996.

Zhou, Y., Reid, E., Qin, J., Chen, H., and Lai, G., "U.S. Domestic Extremist Groups on the Web: Link and Content Analysis," IEEE Intelligent Systems Special Issue on Homeland Security, 20(5), pp. 44-51, 2005.

SUGGESTED READINGS

- Sageman, M., (2004) *Understanding Terror Network*, University of Pennsylvania Press. A book written by Al Qaeda expert Dr. Marc Sageman which provides great insights into the understanding of terrorist networks.

- Weimann, G., (2004) "www.terror.net: How Modern Terrorism Use the Internet," *Special Report*, U.S. Institute of Peace. A report published by the U.S. Institute of Peace on global terrorist organizations' Internet usage.

- Jenkins, B. M., (2004) "World Becomes the Hostage of Media-Savvy Terrorists: Commentary", USA Today, August 22, 2004. An article written by famous terrorism expert Brian M. Jenkins on terrorist organizations' online propaganda activities.

- ISTS, (2004) "Examining the Cyber Capabilities of Islamic Terrorist Groups". Report, Institute for Security Technology Studies. A report published by the Institute for Security Technology Studies at the Dartmouth College on Islamic terrorist organizations' online activities.

ONLINE RESOURCES

- The RAND organization website
  http://www.rand.org.
- The Institute for Counter-Terrorism website
  http://www.ict.org.il
- The SITE (Search for International Terrorist Entities) Institute website.
  http://www.siteinstitute.org/

DISCUSSION QUESTIONS

1. What other Web mining technologies can we use to detect and monitor terrorist organizations' online activities more efficiently?
2. How can we improve the general public's awareness and preparedness of the terror campaign in the cyber space?
3. What type of counter-terrorism measures should our government take in the cyber space?

13

CONTENT ANALYSIS OF JIHADI EXTREMIST GROUPS' VIDEOS

Arab Salem[1], Edna Reid[2], and Hsinchun Chen[3]

[1]*Private consultant (arabsalem@gmail.com);* [2]*Department of Library Science, Clarion University, Clarion, Pennsylvania, U.S.A. (reid@clarion.edu);* [3]*Management Information Systems Department, The University of Arizona, Tucson, Arizona U.S.A. (hchen@eller.arizona.edu)*

CHAPTER OVERVIEW

This paper presents an exploratory study of jihadi extremist groups' videos using content analysis and a multimedia coding tool to explore the types of video, groups' modus operandi, and production features that lend support to extremist groups. The videos convey messages powerful enough to mobilize members, sympathizers, and even new recruits to launch attacks that are once again captured (on video) and disseminated globally via the Internet. They communicate the effectiveness of the campaigns and have a much wider impact because they are media rich with nonverbal cues and vivid images of events that can evoke not only a multitude of psychological and emotional responses but also violent reactions. The videos are important for jihadi extremist groups' learning, training, and recruitment. In addition, the content collection and analysis of extremist groups' videos can help policy makers, intelligence analysts, and researchers better understand the extremist groups' terror campaigns and modus operandi, and help suggest counter-intelligence strategies and tactics for troop training.

1.   INTRODUCTION

Technological advances and the decreasing cost and size, ease of use, and sophistication of video capturing and editing technology have made Web-hosted audio and video clips a powerful and robust information platform and communication medium for terrorist/extremist groups (henceforth referred to as extremist groups). Extremist groups have become independent and prolific producers of multimedia artifacts that they feed not only to their own terrorist news network (Jenkins 2004) but to the legitimate global news networks, as well.

As reported in news articles (BBC 2002; Coll and Glasser 2005) and reports (Becker 2005; SITE 2004a; Weimann 2004), multimedia resources such as audios and videos are widely used by jihadi extremist groups, such as Tandhim al-Qa'ida fi Bilad al-Rafidayn (al-Qaeda's Organisation in Mesopotamia)[1] and Jaysh Ansar al-Sunna (Partisans of the Sunna Army), to spread and gain wider acceptance of their ideologies, justify their causes, raise funds, and show real results based on their view of justice. Many jihadi extremist groups' multimedia artifacts are in Arabic and often posted (momentarily) in numerous discussion forums and websites to avoid intelligence surveillance (Becker 2005).

For extremist groups, multimedia supports their resource mobilization strategy of using rich medium to visually communicate with audiences (e.g., their members, sympathizers, enemies, and the public). They create new knowledge in the form of multimedia to meet their strategic and tactical goals. From an organizational learning perspective, multimedia supports vicarious learning (learning by acquiring second-hand experience) for obtaining technical "know how" quickly (Huber 1991).

Because of the sheer volume of extremist groups' multimedia artifacts that are produced and disseminated via the Web, their evanescent nature, and cultural barriers, researchers expend substantial resources and effort to identify, monitor, translate, and analyze these video artifacts. This study is part of a larger effort called the Dark Web Portal research project that takes advantage of automatic methodologies for identifying, capturing, classifying, analyzing, and visualizing extremist groups' multimedia web-based artifacts to support the research communities.

This exploratory study analyzes extremist groups' Arabic videos and constructs a coding scheme for examining the types of video, groups' modus

---

[1] Formerly Jamaat al-Tawhid wal-Jihad (Monotheism and Jihad), is a radical Islamist terrorist group affiliated with al Qaeda (Boucher 2004; SITE 2004c) and previously led by Abu Musab al Zarqawi who was killed in a US operation in June 2006. Via jihadi websites, the group has claimed responsibility for videotaped executions of many civilians such as Nicholas Berg (Boucher 2004).

operandi, and production features, as well as the relevancy of the videos to the groups' goals. The remainder of this paper is organized as follows. Section 2 reviews the related literature. Section 3 describes the research questions, the content analysis methodology, and creation of the coding scheme. Section 4 presents the results of the content analysis of extremist groups' videos. The final section provides conclusions, implications, and directions for future research.

2. RELATED WORK

In this section, we review trends in jihadi groups' video usage, approaches for organizing and analyzing extremist videos, and video content analysis.

2.1 Jihadi Extremist Groups' Usage of Videos

The jihadi extremist groups' extensive use of the Web, technical sophistication, and media savvy have been described in several studies (Becker 2005; Chen et al. 2004; Weimann 2004; IntelCenter 2004). Their websites, blogs, and discussion forums provide hyperlinks to many video clips that vary in language (e.g., Arabic, English, French), size, format (e.g., wmv, ram), level of technical sophistication (e.g., amateur, professionally produced), and purpose (e.g., document attacks, boost morale, 9-11 anniversary commemoration).

Some of the videos are mirrored hundreds of times at different websites or forums within a matter of days (Terrorist 2004). The persuasive messages make videos an important resource, which supports the collective mobilization of members and sympathizers. The resource mobilization approach provides a framework for emphasizing the importance of resources such as knowledge, money, labor, and communication media for social movement organizations (Duijvelaar 1996; Gustavon and Sherkat 2004).

The extensive use of the Web, as described above, also supports extremist groups' ability to adapt, enhance their organizational learning, and succeed. As described by Huber (1991, p.90), Jackson, et al., (2005) and Lutes (2001), the organizational learning process includes knowledge acquisition, information distribution, information interpretation, and organizational memory. The Web provides opportunities for groups to produce, interpret, share (e.g., lessons from insurgency in Afghanistan), and disseminate information (e.g., videos of beheadings) that fits their cultures, learning styles, preferences, and goals.

In 2000, the Chechen rebels pioneered the creation of videos that capture their operations (Intelcenter 2005). Even if the attack against Russian soldiers was limited in scale, if the operation was filmed and then shown to the world the impact would be greater. Over the last few years, the filming of attacks, the sophistication of video production, quantity, and speed of video dissemination have become important operational and learning strategies for jihadi extremist groups around the world.

According to Berger's (2005) primer on terrorist videos, the vast majority of the web-based videos are simple, amateur productions filmed with handheld cameras or video cell-phones. Videos a) are a powerful and easy way to communicate messages quickly; b) are a cost-effective means to produce lots of information in a short amount of time; and c) can provide persuasive action, vivid images, and sound to reach viewer's emotions (APS 2006).

Professionally produced videos are released through the Al-Sahab Institute for Media Production (video production arm of al Qaeda) and appear frequently on the al-Jazeera channel as well as the Web (IntelCenter 2004). Videotaping extremist groups' operations resulted in a mimetic effect, which Gladwell (2002) refers to as an "infectious idea." Its multiplier effect among jihadi extremist groups emboldened them to produce more videos documenting their brazen attacks on soft targets (especially the beheadings of defenseless civilians), which are then disseminated via the Web. Extremist groups, such as al Qaeda and their avid sympathizers, have been incredibly successful in using videos to show their resolve (SITE 2004b), share messages (e.g., Osama Bin Laden's speeches), and provide training (IntelCenter 2005). The popular press' focus on video reporting (especially the beheadings) has gotten global attention (Robertson 2002; Coll and Glasser 2005), heightened the importance of the videos (Caught 2004), and may have unfortunately contributed to the increase of violence.

2.2   Collections of Extremist Videos

The mass production and dissemination of jihadi extremist groups' videos have prompted several organizations to identify, monitor, collect, translate, and analyze such videos. Table 13-1 identifies commercial companies that support the counter-terrorism communities, such as IntelCenter (2005), and research centers, such as the Middle East Media Research Institute (MEMRI), that focus primarily on systematic analysis. Most of the organizations manually collect and analyze the videos and generate reports; while the Artificial Intelligence (AI) Lab at the University of Arizona collects videos using a systematic web spidering approach and performs research using content and link analysis. Some organizations provide fee-based access to their video collections; while the AI Lab's Dark Web video collection is intended for systematic terrorism and intelligence studies.

Table 13-1. Companies and research centers that support the counter-terrorism communities

Organizations		Collections	# Videos	URLs
Commercial Companies	Global Terror Alert Director, E. Kohlmann	Clearinghouse on International Terrorism	134 titles	http://www.globalterror alert.com/archive.html
	IntelCenter Director, B. Venzke	Audio/Video	60 volumes	http://www.intelcenter .com
	Intelwire.com Editor, J.M. Berger	Jihad Videos Online Archive	208 titles	http://intelfiles.com/ (partial list of videos)
	Ogrish	Hostage Archives	26 titles	http://www.ogrish .com/archives/terrorism / hostage
Research Centers	AI Lab, Univ. Arizona Director, H. Chen	Dark Web Portal testbed	680 titles	http://ai.eller.arizona .edu/ (closed research collection)
	MEMRI	Jihad & Terrorism Studies Project	12 titles	http://www.memri.org/ jihad.html
	SITE Institute Director, R. Katz	Multimedia Catalog	400 titles	http://www.siteinstitute .org
	Total (estimate)		1460 titles	Note: some are duplicate videos

2.3   Content Analysis of Videos

As indicated in Table 13-1, there are thousands of jihadi extremist groups' videos. They contain massive amounts of information, including visual, text, and audio content (Dimitrova et al. 2002). The information are useful for analyzing the types of violence (Aikat 2004), violent trends in groups' operations (SITE 2004a), leadership styles (SITE 2004c), and insight into the different networks (Intelcenter 2004). There is a wealth of content analysis studies of violence in television programs, video games (Lachlan et al. 2003), and online music videos (DuRant et al. 1997; Makris 1999). Content analysis is a methodology for making inferences by objectively and systematically identifying specific characteristics of messages (Holsti 1969).

Since viewers can learn social norms and aggressive behavior through observing and cognitively processing violent scenes, video games and music video studies explore the levels and types of violence (e.g., number of violent acts, types of weapons used), and potential impacts of the videos (Lachlan et al. 2003; Aikat 2004). The studies used coding guidelines adapted from the National Television Violence Study (NTVS) and the Incident Classification and Analysis Form (ICAF) developed by the ABC Television Network and the Gerbner's Violence Index for media research (Lachlan et al. 2003; Makris 1999; Aikat 2004).

However, in-depth studies of the extremist groups' videos such as patterns of the groups involved, types of violence, modus operandi (e.g., types of attacks, weapons, targets), and sophistication of videos are not available. Furthermore, if researchers want to use the video content (e.g., bombing or kidnapping scenes) and the content-based metadata for integration with other information (e.g., group profiles, attack incidents, news stories) for advanced analysis such as triangulation, entity extraction, and social network analysis then automated content analysis approaches (MOCA 2005; Wactlar 2000) are needed to extract structural and semantic content from the videos.

This may require specialized tools such as terrorism ontologies (Guitouni, et al. 2002; Mannes and Golbeck 2005) be used in the content analysis process to untangle, map, and extract extremist groups' patterns, events, group actions, and actors captured in the video. The Movie Content Analysis (MOCA 2005) and the Informedia Digital Video Library (Wactlar 2000; Wactlar and Chen 2002) projects are examples of pioneering research to conduct content analysis of continuous data, especially videos, and automatic extraction and summarization of information and objects.

These types of automatic approaches are needed for a fine grained analysis and mining (e.g., identify similarities, patterns, anomalies) of videos which are primary source data generated by the groups. A systematic exploration of the content of the videos to enhance our understanding of how they are used to support extremist groups' operations is therefore in order. In addition, research communities need coding guidelines, schemes, and other tools to support investigation of the videos. This study is an initial attempt to fill that gap.

3.   METHODOLOGY

Researchers have identified several factors that influence groups' use of rich mediums such as videos. This study uses the resource mobilization (Duijvelaar 1996) framework to undertake a systematic content analysis of extremist groups' videos. We aim to answer the research questions listed below.

- What types of video, groups' modus operandi, and production features are identified in extremist groups' videos?
- How are the videos used by the jihadi extremist groups?

From a resource mobilization perspective, the use of the videos is viewed as a rational choice for enhancing the groups' communications, propaganda, and training resources necessary to publicize and diffuse their campaigns. For this content analysis study, the unit of analysis is a video. The content analysis process includes several steps: selection of the sample collection of videos, generation of a list of content categories and associated content features, assessment of coding reliability, design of a coding tool (Multimedia Coding Tool), coding the videos, and analysis of results.

3.1   Sample Collection

The initial step is to construct a high quality collection of videos from extremist groups and/or their sympathizers.   We used a collection development approach used by Zhou, et al. (2005) and Reid, et al. (2005, p.402) in their Dark Web portal project.   The Dark Web is the alternate (dark) side of the Web which is used by extremist groups to spread their ideas.

The approach involved identifying a set of seed URLs' for extremist groups' websites, manually searching major search engines using the group names as queries to find other websites, conducting in-link expansion from Google in-link search, filtering the collection, and automatically collecting the extremist groups' websites and content using a spider program.

The spider program harvests the websites and web files (e.g., html, php, pdf) including multimedia files. The files are harvested every 3-4 months with the latest collection (6th batch) downloaded in November 2005. Table 13-2 provides a summary of the 705 multimedia files that were downloaded.

Table 13-2. Dark Web Multimedia Collection for 6th Batch (as of Nov 2005)

# Videos	File Formats	Video Format	Audio Format	Duration (h :m :s)	Size (MB)	Avg. Size (MB)
357	asf	wmv	wma	68:09:36	3,934.36	11.02
291	real	real	real	69:06:00	2,907.10	9.99
21	asf	asf	wma	01:59:20	112.70	5.37
13	quicktime	quicktime	quicktime	00:19:44	136.16	10.47
11	asf	asf	asf	02:15:30	216.28	19.66
5	real	real	none	00:10:22	23.82	4.76
4	mpeg	mpeg	mp2	00:03:42	37.03	9.26
3	quicktime	mpeg4	quicktime	00:02:15	18.17	6.06
705				142:01:12	7,385.62	

From the Dark Web multimedia collection (6th batch), we identified Arabic videos that were produced by jihadi extremist groups or their sympathizers. Many of the videos were shot in Iraq. We previewed the videos and looked for clues such as natural backdrops (desert, palm trees), language used (Arabic), and extremist groups' name such as Tandhim al-Qa'ida fi Bilad al-Rafidayn. An arbitrary number of 20 videos was chosen for purposes of this exploratory study using a random number generator to select the sample.

3.2   Coding Tool and Scheme

We designed a Multimedia Coding Tool (MCT) that allows the coder to record his observations in a systematic and structured manner. The MCT stores both the coding scheme and the Arabic videos (e.g., wmv, rm) as well as supports database query. It supports the creation of new coding categories and direct coding of the videos.

The content of videos produced by jihadi extremist groups was coded following the scheme based on features of videos, terrorism ontologies (Guitonni et al., 2002; Mannes and Golbeck 2005), the Intelcenter's video categorization (2005), and the (narrowly scoped) domain of videos produced by jihadi extremist groups. The process of refining the scheme was incremental in nature.

Table 13-3 summarizes the coding scheme that is arranged into class, content category, content feature, and description. Although there are 5 classes, the first four focus on the types of video such as violent attacks (e.g., suicide bombing) and others (e.g., message such as leader statement), the content properties (e.g., date of attack, location), groups involved (e.g., extremist group), and expressions (e.g., quotation). Production is the last class, which includes the technical features (e.g., subtitle, logo) of the video. Each class is subdivided into content category and feature that capture specific aspects of the videos. For example, the attack content category has content features that describe the group's modus operandi such as planning, the target, and weapon used.

Table 13-3. Coding Scheme

Class	Content Category	Content Feature	Description
1.Types of Video	Violent Attacks		
	Attack	Planning; Statement; Target; Weapon used (e.g., bombing)	All kinds of attacks except hostage taking and suicide bombing
	Hostage Taking	Captive's name; Captive's nationality;	Person held against his/her will

Class	Content Category	Content Feature	Description
		Demand; Execution; Hostage ; Negotiation; Statement	
	Suicide Bombing	Method; Suicider's name; Suicider's nationality; Statement; Target	Bombing carried out by a person who does not hope to survive it
	Others		
	Message	Tribute; Leader Statement; Newsletter	Statement by prominent members of the extremist group (IntelCenter, 2005)
	Education	Instruction; Training	Instruction is for teaching specific skills, while training is for documenting activities
2. Content Properties	Victim	Number of person(s); Name(s); Nationality; Civilian/Military	Injury or loss of life
	Date of Attack	Hijri (Islamic) Calendar; Julian Calendar	Reported attack date in the video
	Location	City; County; District; Town; Country	Location of depicted event
	Target of threat	Person; Organization; Country	Threatened entity
3. Groups	Extremist group	Reported name ; Sub-group; Media agency	Group involved
4. Expression	Quotation	Religious quotation; Violent quotation	Quotation used
	Reference to Media	Arab Media; Western Media	Mention of media
5. Production	Production Feature	Title of the video; Sound; Visual (e.g., subtitle); URL; Multiclip	Video feature

Figure 13-1 displays the MCT interface for coding videos that identified extremist groups such as Tandhim al-Qa'ida fi Bilad al-Rafidayn. The group's names (e.g., Arabic and English), types of video, and other information were coded. A multiclip video file was coded as a single entry.

Four videos from our sample are coded independently by two domain specialists. The coding scheme is iteratively revised until a satisfactory level of agreement between the coders is reached. Category reliability is measured using Holsti's formula for computing reliability (Holsti 1969). The

percentage agreement between the two coders was higher than 0.80 for all
the content categories that were analyzed.

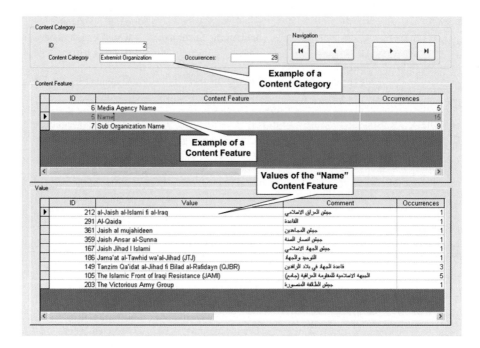

Figure 13-1. MCT Interface for Coding Extremist Group's Information

4.   RESULTS

Twenty Arabic videos were content analyzed. The average length of the
sample videos was 3 minutes and 6 seconds. Important content analysis
results indicate: types of video, names of extremist groups involved, groups'
modus operandi (e.g., targets, weapons, attack locations), and production
features (e.g., subtitles, logos) that lend support to extremist groups.

4.1   Types of Video

The types of video were organized into two categories: violent attacks
(e.g., suicide bombing) and others (e.g., message such as leader statement).
Table 13-4 provides the frequency count for the types of video identified.
The attack video (which includes all types of attacks except hostage taking

and suicide bombing) was the most frequently identified.

The videos are often filmed in real-time (show the attacks in action), instructive (takes the viewer inside the planning and attack execution processes including scenes of the different weapons, such as rocket propelled grenades, and skills required for their operations), and low budget (limited promotional costs as indicated by low quality of some videos and appeal to diverse audiences because of Arabic and English subtitles). The plots were simple (focus on a few goals such as to destroy the enemy's tankers), versatile (can be used for meetings, training, fundraising, motivational sessions), persuasive (display actors' emotions and dedication), succinct (quickly present the materials in short videos), and targeted (producers have complete control over the message and sequence of events). The videos also demonstrated rituals such as wearing a headdress that completely covers the face so only the eyes are visible.

Table 13-4. Types of Video

Types of Videos		Frequency
Violent Attacks	Attack	13
	Hostage Taking	1
	Suicide Bombing	4
	Subtotal	*18*
Others	Message	2
	Total	*20*

4.2 Groups Identified

Although 15 extremist groups were identified, there were only 9 unique groups that took credit for the videos. In 5 videos the groups did not identify themselves. Two groups, Al-Jabha al-Islamiya lil-Muqawama al-'Iraqiya (the Islamic Front of the Iraqi Resistance) (JAMI) and the Tandhim al-Qa'ida fi Bilad al-Rafidayn, produced a total of eight videos that were in our sample. Both represent insurgency groups in Iraq.

Among the groups identified, 7 were involved in violent attacks. Extremist groups, such as al Zarqawi's Tandhim al-Qa'ida fi Bilad al-Rafidayn, produced videos which include planning meetings (with maps, diagrams, and logistic preparations) before the suicide bombings. The videos stimulated solidarity because they made one feel a part of the campaign against the 'enemies.' They supported mental models of the group members' dedication, closeness, emotional rituals, and skills as they executed the attacks. Scenes provide emotional and spiritual support because of the hugging, greeting, and praying together.

4.3   Groups' Modus Operandi

Since many of the videos involve attacks in Iraq, the major targets are Western military humvees, cargo convoys, and other vehicles. Figure 13-2 provides a chart of the types of targets identified. Most of the videos explicitly mentioned locations of the depicted attacks. The locations are often mentioned in the subtitles and occasionally the narrator provides it.

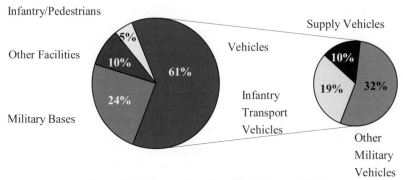

Figure 13-2. Target Sites Identified in Sample Videos

Figure 13-3. RPG Attack to Disrupt a Supply Line

These results are compatible with media reports on the Iraqi insurgency. Most attacks occur in the Sunni triangle, which includes: Balad, Dayali, Baghdad, Fallujah, and Abu-Ghraib. In addition, U.S. military installations in Mosul are frequently attacked, as reported in the international media.

Roadside bombs and RPGs (handheld antitank grenade-launchers) are the most common types of weapons utilized. They are more effective than machine guns in hit and run attacks. Figure 13-3 provides a snapshot of a video of someone shooting an RPG to disrupt a supply line.

The RPG is an inexpensive and single-shot weapon that is easy to operate with very little training but extremely effective (Military 2006). The RPG and mortar attacks can cause considerable damage without being in close-range engagements.

4.4 Production Features

Eleven sample videos had both Arabic or English subtitles and logos. A range of production quality patterns, from amateurish to professional, were identified. In addition, diverse visual production patterns were identified such as the use of subtitles (English or Arabic), the groups' logos, background hymns (with/without music), and excerpts of leaders' speeches.

Figure 13-4 provides a screenshot of a video with English subtitles by al Qaeda that shows Bin Laden giving a speech. Bin Laden messages are often directed towards a worldwide audience. Al Qaeda's media agency "Al-Sahab" produced the "Bin Laden interview excerpt" in our sample. This agrees with the SITE Institute (2004b) and Intelcenter's (2005) reports about al Qaeda's use of a production company to plan and produce high quality videos.

Figure 13-4. Video by al Qaeda with English subtitles

Thirteen videos had Arabic subtitles. Ideologies and customs identified in the videos were consistent with real-world activities. For example, hymns in Tandhim al-Qa'ida fi Bilad al-Rafidayn videos were not accompanied by musical instruments, abiding by the strict stance on the use of such instruments in Salafi jihad ideology[2].

In summary, the videos convey messages powerful enough to mobilize members, sympathizers, and even new recruits to launch attacks that are once again captured (on video) and disseminated globally via the Internet. They are important for the survival and growth of jihadi extremist groups' because they support propaganda, fundraising, learning, training, and recruitment.

5.   CONCLUSION

In this study, we conducted an exploratory analysis of 20 Arabic extremist groups' videos and designed a Multimedia Coding Tool (MCT) as well as a coding scheme for examining the content. We identified different types of videos, extremist groups, modus operandi (e.g., targets, weapons, attack locations), and video production features (e.g., subtitles, logos). Eighteen videos were violent attacks in which some included planning sessions with maps, diagrams, and logistic preparations. By creating their own training and operational videos, the extremist groups support organization learning in several ways such as the groups producing the video get first hand experience (learn by doing) and those viewing the video get second hand experience (learn by imitation).

Since jihadi extremist groups' multimedia collections will continue to increase, automatic extraction of structural (e.g., subtitles, images) and semantic content (e.g., weapons, target locations) can aide in the systematic analysis of the groups' modus operandi, violent events, learning styles, networks, and tactical operations. Therefore, we need to expand our efforts to analyze multimedia content by creating collaborations with research teams in the automated video content analysis domains.

The results of this research are relevant for our Dark Web project, in that it provided a glimpse into some of the challenges in analyzing Arabic extremist groups' videos. Because this study was limited to a sample of 20 Arabic video clips, future studies of this kind should endeavor to enlarge the sample and verify if similar results were found. Further research should also

---

[2] Salafi jihad ideology advocates the use of violence against any foreign or non-Muslim government or population (the "far enemy") to establish an Islamist state in a core Arab region (Sageman 2005).

be done to provide insights into extremist groups' operations, organizational learning styles, and diffusion of multimedia.

Finally, we plan to expand our efforts by collaborating with research teams in the automated video content analysis domains such as the Movie Content Analysis (MOCA 2005) and the Informedia Digital Video Library (Wactlar 2000) projects. Systematic extraction and analysis of videos would facilitate correlation and triangulation of information from different sources (e.g., groups' websites, news articles, incident chronologies, reports, discussion forums) as well as improve analytical capabilities.

6. ACKNOWLEDGEMENTS

This research has been supported in part by the following grants:
- DHS/CNRI, "BorderSafe Initiative," October 2003-March 2005.
- NSF/ITR, "COPLINK Center for Intelligence and Security Informatics – A Crime Data Mining Approach to Developing Border Safe Research," EIA-0326348, September 2003-August 2005.

We would like to thank all of the staff of the Artificial Intelligence Lab at the University of Arizona who have contributed to the project, in particular Wei Xi, Homa Atabakhsh, Catherine Larson, Chun-Ju Tseng, and Shing Ka Wu.

REFERENCES

Aikat, D. (2004) Streaming Violent Genres Online: Visual Images in Music Videos on BET.com, Country.com, MTV.com, VH1.com. Popular Music and Society 27.

APS (2006) 17 1/2 Advantages of Using Video. Fort Mill, APS.

BBC (2002) Video Shows al-Qaeda Terrorist Training. BBC.

Becker, A. (2005) Technology and Terror: the New Modus Operandi. Frontline. Washington, D.C., PBS.

Berger, J. M. (2005) Short Primer on Terrorist Videos. Intelfiles, Alexandria, Virginia. http://www.intelfiles.com

Boucher, R. (2004) Foreign Terrorist Organization: Designation of Jama'at al-Tawhid wa'al Jihad and Aliases. Press Statement. Washington, D.C., U.S. Department of State.

Caught on Tape: Video as a Terrorist's Weapon. (2004) ABC News Internet Ventures.

Qin, J., Zhou, Y., Lai, G., Reid, E., Sageman, M., and Chen, H. (2005) The Dark Web Portal Project: Collecting and Analyzing the Presence of Terrorist Groups on the Web. Proceedings of the IEEE International Conference on Intelligence and Security (ISI 2005), Atlanta, Georgia.

Coll, S. and S. Glasser (2005) Rifles and Laptops al-Qaeda's New Armoury. Washington Post. Washington, D.C.

Dimitrova N., Zhang H-J., Shahraray B., Sezan I., Huang T., Zakhor A. (2002) Applications of Video-content Analysis and Retrieval. IEEE Multimedia: 42-55.

Dominick, J. R. (1984) Videogames, Television Violence, and Agression in Teenagers. Journal of Communication 34: 136-147.

Duijvelaar, C. (1996) In the Books: Theoretical Outlines. Resource Movilization Approach. East-East Cooperation Among Environmental NGOs in Central and Eastern Europe. Budapest, Regional Environmental Center for Central and Eastern Europe.

DuRant R.H., Rich M., Emans S.J., Rome E.S., Allred E., Woods E.R.. (1997) Violence and Weapon Carrying in Music Videos: a Content Analysis. Arch Pediatr Adol Med 15(1): 443-338.

Fong, T. (2005) Indonesia: Terror Groups Spreading Video Bomb-making Guide. Jakarta Post. Jakarta.

Ghashghai, E. and R. Lewis (2002) Issues Affecting Internet Use in Afghanistan and Developing Countries in the Middle East. Issue Paper. R. Corporation, RAND Corporation.

Gladwell, M. (2002) Tipping Point: How Little Things Can Make a Big Difference, Little Brown & Company.

GlobalSecurity (2005) Jaish Ansar al-Sunna. Military, GlobalSecurity.org.

Gossett, S. (2006) al Qaeda Video is Green Light for an Attack: Analyst Warns. CNS News.

Gustavson, A.T. and D.E. Sherkat (2004) Elucidating the Web of Hate: the Ideological Structuring of Network Ties among Right Wing Hate Groups on the Internet. Annual Meetings of the American Sociological Association, (ASA)

Guitonni, A., A. Boury-Brisset, et al. (2002) Automatic Documents Analyzer and Classifier. 7th International Command and Control Research and Technology Symposium, Quebec.

Holsti, O. R. (1969) Content Analysis for the Social Sciences and Humanities. Reading, Addison-Wesley.

Huber, G. P. (1991) Organizational Learning: Contributing Processes and the Literatures. Organization Science 2(1): 88-114.

Intelcenter (2004) Al Qaeda Videos & 3rd 9-11 Anniversary v1.0. Intelcenter, Alexandria, Virginia.

Intelcenter (2005) Evolution of Jihad Video, v1.0. IntelCenter, Alexandria, Virginia.

Brian A. Jackson, John C. Baker, Peter Chalk, Kim Cragin, John V. Parachini, Horacio R. Trujillo (2005) Aptitude for Destruction: Organizational Learning in Terrorist Groups and its Implications for Combating Terrorism. RAND Corporation.

Jenkins, B. M. (2004) World Becomes the Hostage of Media-Savvy Terrorists: Commentary. USA Today.

Kelley, J. (2001) Militants Wire Web With Links to Jihad. USA Today.

Lachlan, KA, Smith, SL, Tamborini, R. (2003) Popular Video Games: Assessing the Amount and Context of Violence. Annual Meeting of the National Communication Association, Seattle, Washington.

Lutes, C. (2001) al Qaida in Action and Learning: a Systems Approach. . Fulfillment of Course   Requirements.   George   Washington   University. http://www.au.af.mil/au/awc/awcgate/readings/al_qaida2.htm

Makris, G. (1999) Searching for Violence on the Internet: an Exploratory Analysis of MTV Online Music Video Clips, North Caroline, Chapel Hill.

Mannes, A. and J. Golbeck (2005) Building a Terrorism Ontology. ISWC Workshop on Ontology Patterns for the Semantic Web,

Military Factor (2006) Rocket Propelled Grenade. MilitaryFactor.com. http://www.militaryfactor.com/smallarms/

MOCA (2005) Overview: Movie Content Analysis Project (MoCA) Univ. Mannheim. Mannheim.

Reid, E., J. Qin, et al. (2005) Collecting and Analyzing the Presence of Terrorists on the Web: a Case Study of Jihad Websites. Intelligence and Security Informatics: IEEE International Conference on Intelligence and Security Informatics, ISI 2005, May 2005, Atlanta, Georgia. Springer.

Robertson, N. (2002) Tapes Shed New Light on bin Laden's Network. cnn.com.

Sageman, Marc (2005) Undersanding Jihadi Networks. Strategic Insights, Volume IV(4) http://www.ccc.nps.navy.mil/si/2005/Apr/sagemanApr05.asp

SITE (2004a) Jaish Ansar al Sunah Insurgency Group in Iraq Issues a Clarification Statement and Video Regarding the Blessed Attack Against the American Base in Mosul. SITE Institute. Washington, D.C.

SITE (2004b) Manufacture of the Explosive Belt for Suicide Bombing Operations. SITE Institute. Washington, D.C.

SITE (2004c) Communique No. 11 Issued by Zarqawi's Attawhid Wal Jihad Group Military Department. SITE Publications. SITE Institute. Washington, D.C.

Smith, S. L., Wilson, B. J., Kunkel, D., Linz, D., Potter, W. J., Colvin, C. M., Donnerstein, E. (1998) National Television Violence Study: Vol. 3. Violence in television programming overall: University of California, Santa Barbara study (pp. 5-220). Newbury Park, CA: Sage.

Terrorists threaten more attacks on Britain. (2005) News from Russia.

Wactlar, H. (2000) Informedia: Search and Summarization in the Video Medium. Proceeedings of Imagina 2000 Conference, January 31-Februrary 2, 2000, Monaco, France.

Wactlar, H. and Chen, C. (2002) Enhanced Perspectives for Historical and Cultural Documentaries Using Informedia Technologies. Joint Conference on Digital Libraries (JCDL'02), July 13-17, 2002, Portland, Oregon.

Weimann (2004) www.terror.net How Modern Terrorist Uses the Internet. Washington, D.C., U.S. Institute of Peace.

Zhou, Y., Reid, E., Qin, J., Chen, H., Lai, G. (2005) U.S. Domestic Extremist Groups on the Web: Link and Content Analysis. IEEE Intelligent Systems: 44-51.

SUGGESTED READINGS

- Berger, J. M. (2005) Short Primer on Terrorist Videos. Intelfiles, Alexandria, Virginia. http://www.intelfiles.com
- Qin, J., Zhou, Y., Lai, G., Reid, E., Sageman, M., and Chen, H. (2005) The Dark Web Portal Project: Collecting and Analyzing the Presence of Terrorist Groups on the Web. Proceedings of the IEEE International Conference on Intelligence and Security (ISI 2005), Atlanta, Georgia.
- Weimann (2004) www.terror.net How Modern Terrorist Uses the Internet. Washington, D.C., U.S. Institute of Peace.

ONLINE RESOURCES

- Intelcenter (2004) Al Qaeda Videos & 3rd 9-11 Anniversary v1.0. Intelcenter, Alexandria, Virginia

http://www.intelcenter.com
- Intelcenter (2005) Evolution of Jihad Video, v1.0. IntelCenter, Alexandria, Virginia
  http://www.intelcenter.com
- Memorial Institute for the Prevention of Terrorism (MIPT). Terrorism Knowledge Base
  http://www.tkb.org
- Sageman, Marc (2005) Undersanding Jihadi Networks. Strategic Insights, Volume IV(4)
  http://www.ccc.nps.navy.mil/si/2005/Apr/sagemanApr05.asp
- Weimann (2004) www.terror.net How Modern Terrorist Uses the Internet. Washington, D.C., U.S. Institute of Peace
  http://www.institutepeace.org

DISCUSSION QUESTIONS

1. How are extremist groups using video technologies to support their campaigns?
2. How can officials use the videos to enhance their knowledge about the groups' operations and learning styles?
3. What other Internet technologies are being exploited by extremist groups?

14

ANALYSIS OF AFFECT INTENSITIES IN EXTREMIST GROUP FORUMS

Ahmed Abbasi and Hsinchun Chen
Management Information Systems Department, The University of Arizona, Tucson, Arizona, U.S.A.(aabbasi@email.arizona.edu, hchen@eller.arizona.edu}

CHAPTER OVERVIEW

Affects play an important role in influencing people's perceptions and decision making. Affect analysis is useful for measuring the presence of hate, violence, and the resulting propaganda dissemination across extremist groups. In this study we performed affect analysis of U.S. and Middle Eastern extremist group forum postings. We constructed an affect lexicon using a probabilistic disambiguation technique to measure and visualize usage of violence and hate affects. These techniques facilitate in depth analysis of multilingual content. The proposed approach was evaluated by applying it across 16 U.S. supremacist and Middle Eastern extremist group forums. Analysis across regions reveals that the Middle Eastern test bed forums have considerably greater violence intensity than the U.S. groups. There is also a strong linear relationship between the usage of hate and violence across the Middle Eastern messages.

1.   INTRODUCTION

The fast propagation of the Web has fueled the increased popularity of computer mediated communication. Computer mediated communication (CMC) research has become an important focus with areas of inquiry including analysis of social behavioral factors pertaining to online communities as well as some of the vices associated with web-based communication. In addition to misuse in the form of deception [1], software piracy [2] and pornography [3], the internet has also become a popular communication medium for extremist and hate groups. This aspect of the internet is often referred to as the Dark Web [4].

Stormfront, what many consider to be the first hate group web site [5], was created around 1996. Since then researchers and hate watch organizations have begun to focus their attention towards studying and monitoring such online groups [6]. Nevertheless, there has been limited evaluation of forum postings, with the majority of studies focusing on web sites. Burris et al. [7] acknowledged that there was a need to evaluate forum and chat room discussion content. Schafer [8] also stated that it was unclear as to how much and what kind of extremist forum activity was going on. Due to the lack of understanding and current ambiguity associated with the content of such groups' forum postings, analysis of extremist group forum archives is an important endeavor.

Sentiment analysis attempts to identify and analyze opinions and emotions. Hearst [9] originally proposed the idea of mining direction-based text (text containing opinions and emotions). Traditional forms of content analysis, such as topical analysis may not be effective for forums. Nigam and Hurst [10] found that only 3% of USENET sentences contained topical information. In contrast, web discourse is rich in sentiment and affects related information [11]. In recent years, sentiment analysis has been applied to various forms of web-based discourse [12]-[13]. Application to extremist group forums can provide insight into important discussion and trends.

Affect analysis is the category of sentiment analysis dealing with emotions/affects. Affects play an important role in influencing people's perceptions and decision making [14]. Consequently affect analysis is useful for measuring the presence of hate, violence, and the resulting propaganda dissemination in hate/extremist forums. In this study we perform affect analysis of extremist group forum postings. We constructed an affect lexicon using a probabilistic disambiguation technique to measure usage of violence and hate affects. Our analysis encompassed measuring and visualizing affect intensities and correlations across these forums. The results provide significant insight into the affect related content within and across regions.

The remainder of this paper is organized as follows. Section 2 presents a review of current research on hate/extremist groups on the web as well as an examination of existing literature pertaining to affect analysis. Section 3 describes research gaps, and questions while Section 4 outlines our proposed research design. Section 5 presents the system design used for implementing our affect analysis techniques and Section 6 presents a description of the evaluation methods and proposed hypotheses. Section 7 describes the experimental results and Section 8 concludes with closing remarks, limitations, and future directions.

2.   RELATED WORK

2.1   Analysis of Extremist Groups on the Web

There have been several studies analyzing the presence of hate/extremist groups on the web in recent years. Extremist groups often use the Internet to promote hatred and violence [15]. The Internet offers a ubiquitous, quick, inexpensive, and anonymous means of communication for extremist groups [16]. Consequently many believe that the internet acts as an ideal method for such groups to disseminate information and spread propaganda [17]-[18]. Schafer [8] performed an extensive analysis of the content of 132 White supremacist websites. Burris et al. [7] used social network analysis to evaluate white supremacist networks on the internet, based on 80 web sites. Their analysis included an evaluation of the level of interaction between the various groups (e.g., skinheads, neo-Nazis, KKK, militia, etc.) based on link densities. They found that there was considerable communication between certain web sites in terms of in and out links. Gerstenfeld et al. [19] performed a content analysis of 157 U.S. hate group web sites and also found considerable linkage between certain groups. Gustavson et al. [20] surmised that white supremacist factions used the internet as a means for ideological resource sharing. Zhou et al. [21] did an in depth analysis of U.S. hate group web sites and found significant evidence of fund raising, propaganda, and recruitment related content. Abbasi and Chen [22] also corroborated signs of the usage of the web as a medium for propaganda by U.S. supremacist and Middle Eastern extremist groups.

These findings provide insight into extremist group web usage tendencies and also suggest that there may be many usage similarities across regions. However the extent of those similarities is unclear due to limited work on non-U.S. groups. Furthermore, there has been little analysis of extremist group web forums. Burris et al. [7] acknowledged the need to evaluate forum and chat room discussion content. While Schafer [8] performed an extensive analysis of the content of White supremacist websites, he was also unclear as to how much and what kind of forum activity was going on with respect to extremist groups. The lack of previous analysis of these forums can be attributed to the large volumes of information contained in such archives combined with the predominantly manual analysis methods incorporated in previous studies [21]. Manual examination of thousands of messages can be an extremely tedious and labor intensive effort when applied across thousands of forum postings. With increasing usage of CMC, the need for automated text analysis techniques has grown in recent years. These include techniques for stylometric, topical, genre, and sentiment analysis. We focus primarily on sentiment analysis for two reasons. Firstly, web discourse is rich in opinion and emotion related content. Secondly, analysis of this type of text is highly relevant to propaganda usage on the web, which attempts to use opinionated content to create and exploit biases and stereotypes.

2.2   Sentiment Analysis

Sentiment analysis is concerned with analysis of direction-based text, i.e. text containing opinions and emotions. There are two basic types of sentiment analysis tasks: classification and content analysis. Sentiment content analysis uses features shown to provide effective sentiment discrimination for content analysis. Sentiment classification deals with classifying sentiments or affects. Sentiment content analysis is concerned with evaluation of sentiment related phenomenon such as sentiment and/or affects balance and temporal trends. Sentiment content analysis can be further divided into two categories: sentiment balance and affect analysis. We are concerned with applying affect analysis to extremist forums.

Sentiment balance and affect analysis have many similarities, including the techniques and application domains. The major difference is the underlying features used (sentiment polarity versus affect lexicons). Consequently, we review all previous sentiment content analysis research first, and then focus on affect analysis. Common sentiment content analysis characteristics include the tasks, techniques, and application domains. These are summarized in the taxonomy presented in Table 14-1.

Based on the proposed taxonomy, Table 14-2 shows previous studies dealing with sentiment content analysis. We discuss the taxonomy and related studies in detail below.

Table 14-1. A Taxonomy of Sentiment Content Analysis Research

Tasks

Category	Description	Label
Sentiment Balance	Classifying sentiment polarity	C1
Affect Analysis	Evaluating sentiment balance and temporal trends	C2

Techniques

Category	Examples	Label
Intensity Scores	Phrase pattern matching, affect intensity, etc.	T1
Visualization	Loom, radar charts, etc.	T2
Manual	Manual coding of affects/sentiments.	T3

Domains

Category	Description	Label
Reviews	Product, movie, and music reviews	D1
Web Discourse	Web forums and blogs	D2
News Articles	Online news articles and documents	D3

Table 14-2. Previous Studies in Sentiment Content Analysis

Study	Tasks		Temporal Analysis	Techniques			Domains			Multi-lingual
	C1	C2	Y/N	T1	T2	T3	D1	D2	D3	Y/N
Donnath et al., 1999		√	Yes	√				√		No
Subasic & Huetner, 2001		√	No	√	√				√	No
Tong, 2001	√		Yes	√	√		√			No
Morinaga et al., 2002	√		No	√	√		√			No
Liu et al., 2003		√	No	√	√			√		No
Nasukawa & Yi, 2003	√		No	√			√			No
Grefenstette et al., 2004		√	No	√				√		No
Henley et al., 2004		√	No		√				√	No
Glance et al., 2005	√		No	√	√		√			No
Liu et al., 2005	√		No	√	√		√			No
Robinson, 2005	√		Yes		√		√			Yes
Yi & Niback, 2005	√		No	√	√		√		√	No
Wiebe et al., 2005		√	No		√				√	No

2.2.1 Tasks

There are two common types of sentiment content analysis tasks: sentiment balance and affect analysis. Sentiment balance measures the breakdown of positive/negative sentiments across corpora [23]-[10]. Tong [24] generated sentiment timelines for move reviews which demonstrated how people perceived certain movies over time. Liu et al [25] developed the Opinion Observer tool to analyze and compare product sentiments.

A closely related area is affect analysis which attempts to analyze emotions instead of sentiments. Sample affect classes include happiness, sadness, anger, horror etc. [11]-[16]-[27]. Donath et al. [28] visualized a lexicon of anger related terms. They were able to infer that a large proportion of messages from a Greek USENET group had an angry tone. Subasic and Huettner [11] performed affect analysis of various categories including violence and anger while Mishne [27] performed affect analysis on web blogs. Henley et al. [29] evaluated the frequency of various violence referents in anti-gay attack news reports in two major newspapers. They found that the terms used reflected the views of the writers.

2.2.2 Sentiment Content Analysis Techniques

Previously used techniques for sentiment content analysis can be classified into three categories which include score-based approaches, visualization techniques, and manual coding methods. Visualization and automatically computed usage scores have been used most often.

Scores-based approaches have been used for measuring sentiment and affect intensity. Scores are generally determined based on feature summation or averaging. Summation approaches believe that the additional presence of features strengthens the sentiment or affect within a document. Averaging methods assume that a weak intensity feature coupled with a strong intensity feature will result in medium intensity since the weak feature offsets some of the strength of the high intensity term. Subasic and Huettner [11] measured affect intensity as the average of term intensities across a document. A popular summation based sentiment intensity approach is the phrase pattern matching technique [23]-[30]. This technique assigns each positive phrase "+1" and negative "-1". The overall message/document score can be used to determine the sentiment polarity and intensity (e.g., messages with a positive sum score have positive intensity). Henley et al. [29] used a summation approach for affect intensity where the message/document intensity is the summation of each feature's frequency multiplied by its affect weight.

Various *visualization techniques* have been used to view sentiment and affect trends. Timelines [24] visualizes sentiment balance over time for movie reviews. Loom [28] visualizes temporal usage patterns for different types of affects (e.g., angry, informative, etc.). Subasic and Huettner [11] used radar charts to visualize features relating to various affects (e.g., anger, violence, hate). Morinaga et al. [31] used principal component analysis to visualize the key sentiment features for various digital cameras based on product reviews.

Manual methods entail reading and coding every message. Henley et al. [29] manually coded newspaper articles for biases pertaining to violence related reports. Robinson [32] manually classified thousands of message sentiments relating to the war in Iraq across English, French, and Brazilian forums. Manual approaches have the advantage of being more accurate and reliable than automated techniques since they are not hindered by interpretation of ambiguous language. However, these techniques can be exhausting and time consuming.

2.2.3 Sentiment Analysis Domains

Sentiment analysis has been applied to numerous domains including reviews, web discourse, and news articles. *Reviews* include movie, product, and music reviews [31]-[33]-[34]. Sentiment analysis of movie reviews is considered to be challenging since movie reviewers often present lengthy plot summaries and also use complex literary devices such as rhetoric and sarcasm.

Web Discourse sentiment analysis includes evaluation of web forums, newsgroups, and blogs. These studies assess sentiments about specific issues/topics. Sentiment topics include abortion, gun control, and politics [12]-[13]. Robinson [32] evaluated sentiments about 9/11 in three forums in the United States, Brazil, and France. Donnath et al. [29] evaluated the USENET forum alt.soc.greek for sentiments relating to anger and aggression.

Sentiment analysis has also been applied to *news articles* [30]-[39]. Henley et al. [29] analyzed newspaper articles for biases pertaining to violence related reports. They found that there was a significant difference in between the manner in which the newspapers reported news stories with the reporting style reflecting newspaper sentiments.

Some general conclusions can be drawn from Table 14-2 and the literature review. Most previous studies have focused on English data, predominantly in the review domain, with lesser emphasis on forum discourse. Furthermore, there has been limited temporal analysis of sentiment related content.

2.3   Affect Lexicons

A central component of affect analysis is the affect lexicon. Affect lexicons are manually crafted lexicons with words/phrases for specific emotions [36]. Each term in the lexicon receives an intensity score [11]-[29] that is typically assigned manually. For example, "kill" is more intense than "hit" in a violence affect lexicon. An important assumption of the intensity assigned to an affect feature is that it is contingent upon the feature being used in the appropriate context. However, terms can have different meanings depending on the context. Such affect ambiguity is particularly evident for verbs. Even part-of-speech tagging can't help disambiguate the usage of "hang" in the example presented in the table below. Only two of the three sentences convey violent affect. In order to overcome this problem, several methods have been proposed to compensate for affect term/phrase ambiguity [11]-[37].

| "I'm going to hang elves on the tree." |
| "Hang those savages!" |
| "We should hang him for those crimes." |

Liu et al. [37] combined different NLP models with a real-world knowledge database (Common Sense Database). The rationale behind this approach is to use knowledge bases to alleviate this ambiguity. In contrast, Subasic and Huettner [11] devised an approach that embraces ambiguity rather than trying to remove it. Their Fuzzy Semantic Typing method assigns each feature to multiple affect categories with varying intensity scores depending upon the word and usage context. For example, the word "alarm" is assigned to the fear, warning, and excitement affect categories with different intensities. Although the accuracy for specific term affects may be inaccurate, the fuzzy logic approach is intended to capture the essence of a document's various affect intensities. While the two aforementioned disambiguation methods use automated techniques to reduce linguistic affect ambiguity, manual coding [29] avoids ambiguity altogether by reading through all the text.

3.   RESEARCH GAPS AND QUESTIONS

Based on our review of previous literature and conclusions we have identified several important research gaps. Firstly, there has been no previous analysis of affect intensity in extremist group forums. Secondly, there has only been a single multilingual sentiment content analysis study. Thirdly there has been little work on affect intensity relationships (interaction/correlation between affects). Finally, there has been no previous work on analysis of affect feature usage variation (across documents and over time).

3.1   Multilingual Extremist Group Forums

Most previous sentiment analysis of web discourse has focused on USENET and financial forums. Applying such methods to extremist forums is important in order to assess the presence of propaganda, anger, and hate. Furthermore there has been little evaluation in a multilingual context with the exception of Robinson [32] performing manual analysis of Brazilian and French forums. The global nature of the internet necessitates more multilingual analysis.

3.2   Affect Intensity and Relationships

There is a need to evaluate the intensity of terms relating to violence and racism/hate affects. These affects can provide a good indication of the level of animosity and aggression in these forums [32]. Furthermore, previous work has focused on the intensity of affects within a document or corpus, but there has been no work assessing the relationships between the usages of different affects across text. The relationship between affects is also important. Forums with elevated usage of violence and hate may have greater propaganda and violent intent.

3.3   Affect Usage Variation

Previous affect analysis has looked to evaluate the level of affect intensities at a given point in time. Temporal variation is a good indicator of how consistent a forum's content is over time. Dynamic forums may undergo greater variations based on current events or other external factors.

4.   RESEARCH QUESTIONS

We propose the following research questions:
1. How do extremist groups differ in terms of their violent and hateful affect intensities?
2. Is there any relationship between the occurrence of violent and hateful

affects across regions?

3. How do these groups' affect intensities vary over time?

5.   RESEARCH DESIGN

In order to address these research questions, we developed a generic affect analysis method that can be applied in a multilingual text setting. Our approach utilizes probabilistic disambiguation to overcome affect ambiguity in the lexicon creation phase. We also visualized affect intensities over time to evaluate trends.

Our affect lexicon creation phase involves overcoming ambiguity using *probabilistic disambiguation.* Other automated forms of disambiguation are either not applicable or infeasible in a multilingual setting. For example, knowledge databases such as the one used by Liu et al. [37] are not available in many languages. Furthermore, handling web forum discourse with such knowledge databases can be less effective due to the forum-specific terminology and challenges associated with free text (e.g., misspelling, grammatical mistakes, etc.). Similarly Fuzzy Logic may not be highly accurate, particularly for shorter messages with fewer affect features (as are commonly found in web discourse). This is because the fuzzy semantic typing approach relies on the cumulative effect of the usage of related vocabulary to effectively represent a document's affective content [11]. In contrast probabilistic models provide a simpler, more generic method for coping with ambiguity [38]. Our approach assigns each term/phrase a probability of being used in the proper context. This is done by selecting a sample number of occurrences of each affect feature and determining the number of times the feature appears in an unrelated/irrelevant context. For evaluation of intensity correlations, we propose the use of *linear regression analysis.* For temporal analysis of affect intensities, we propose the use of an information *visualization technique* specifically designed to illustrate affect usage intensities over time.

6.   SYSTEM DESIGN

Our system design has two major components: affect lexicon creation, and the analysis techniques that can be used to perform affect analysis. The affect lexicon creation component consists of several steps, including term list creation, intensity assignment, and probabilistic disambiguation. The analysis technique steps are affect parsing, intensity score computation, and affect intensity analysis, including intensity scores, correlation analysis, and intensity visualization. Figure 14-1 shows each of these steps in our affect analysis system design. Details of key steps are presented below.

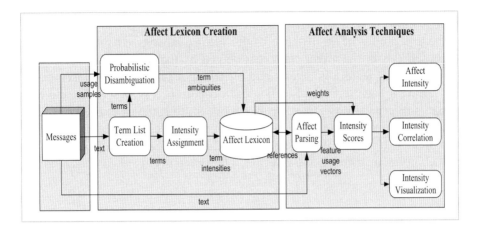

Figure 14-1. Affect Analysis System Design

6.1 Affect Lexicon Creation

6.1.1 Term List Creation

The affect term lists are manually created by inspecting messages using native speakers familiar with the forum content and web discourse terminology for each region. Such a manual term list creation approach has also been used in many previous studies [29]-[11]-[26]. Manual list creation is incorporated for a couple of reasons. Firstly, psycholinguistic databases such as those used by Anderson [39] only exist for English and do not feature many common racial and violent terms. Secondly, forums have their own terminology [40] which can be difficult to extract without manual evaluation of conversation text. This is particularly true for hate related terms, where a considerable amount of slang is involved. Hence, humans are better equipped to identify appropriate affect terms for web discourse.

6.1.2 Intensity Assignment

Coders assign each term/phrase an intensity score. The scores are assigned based on the word's degree of intensity or valence for its particular affect category. The intensity scores are on a scale of 1-20, with 20 signifying high intensity. This approach is consistent with the intensity score assignment methods incorporated in previous studies [29]-[11]-[26].

6.1.3 Probabilistic Disambiguation

Each affect feature is assigned an ambiguity score. The ambiguity score is the probability of an instance of the feature having semantic orientation congruence with the affect class represented by that feature. The ambiguity score for each feature is determined by taking a sample set of instances of the feature's occurrence and coding each occurrence as to whether the term usage is relevant to its affect. A maximum of 20 samples is used per term. Using more instances would be exhaustive and we observed that using a maximum sample of this size was sufficient to accurately capture the probability of an affect being relevant. The ambiguity score can be computed as follows:

$$A(f) = \frac{c_f}{s_f}$$

Equation 14-1

where:

$A(f)$	ambiguity score for affect feature f;
c_f	number of correctly appearing instances for affect feature f;
s_f	total number of sampled instances for affect feature f;

6.2   Affect Analysis Techniques

6.2.1 Affect Parser

The affect parser extracts the affect features from the message text. The parser is specifically designed for handling noisy text that appears in web discourse. It is able to detect and ignore duplicate posts, content forwarded multiple times and requoted messages. For Arabic, the parser also uses an elongation filter and an n-gram based morphological similarity detector (based on Dice's equation) for capturing certain inflected forms of an affect feature that may have been omitted during the feature list creation phase [22]. After accounting for noise, the parser performs stemming and word tokenization and generates affect feature vectors which are used as input for the affect intensity and variation analysis.

6.2.2 Affect Intensity Scores

The affect intensity score for an affect class across a set of messages can be computed as follows:

$$I(c) = \sum_{j=1}^{n} \frac{\sum_{f=1}^{k} I_f A_f x_{fj}}{n}$$

Equation 14-2

where:

$I(c)$	intensity score for affect class c;
I_f	intensity of affect feature f;
A_f	ambiguity score for affect feature f;
x_{fj}	occurrence frequency of feature f in message j;
k	total number of features in affect class c;
n	total number of messages;

We used an additive intensity score approach [29]-[30] over an averaging one such as that used by Subasic & Huettner [11]. We believe that additional occurrences of an affect feature strengthen the overall affect intensity, especially when applied to affect classes such as racism and violence. For example, we believe that the phrase "I am going to beat and stab you" is more intense than the phrase "I am going to stab you."

7. EVALUATION

In this section we describe the research hypotheses and proposed experiments. The experiments are intended to evaluate our hypotheses and also demonstrate the effectiveness of our affect analysis approach in a multilingual web discourse setting. We propose performing affect analysis of extremist forums using our approach to assess the presence and trends pertaining to violence and hate related affects. The multilingual nature of extremist forums provides a good test bed for evaluating the efficacy of our approach. Additionally, there is a need to assess extremist forums to better understand the content and propaganda dissemination within these online communities.

7.1 Hypotheses

For the affect intensity analysis, we wish to compare average affect intensity scores across forums and regions. For the intensity score comparison, we present the following hypothesis:

H1a: There is no difference between U.S. and Middle Eastern forums in terms of hate affect intensity.

H1b: There is no difference between U.S. and Middle Eastern forums in terms of violence affect intensity.

For the affect intensity correlation analysis, we wish to assess the correlation between the violence and hate affect intensities. For the affect intensity correlation, we present the following hypothesis:

H2a: There is no correlation between hate and violence affect usage in U.S forum messages.

H2b: There is no correlation between hate and violence affect usage in Middle Eastern forum messages.

For the affect variation analysis, we wish to compare the average variation scores for messages and over time. We present the following hypothesis:

H3a: There is no difference between U.S. and Middle Eastern forums in terms of hate affect usage over time.

H3b: There is no difference between U.S. and Middle Eastern forums in terms of violence affect usage over time.

7.2   Test Bed

Extremist group forums were collected and extracted as part of the Dark Web project in the Artificial Lab at the University of Arizona [4]. This project involves spidering the web and collecting web sites and forums relating to hateful and extremist groups. In order to ensure the integrity of the collection, extremist group URLs are gathered from reputable sources including government reports (e.g., United Nations, intelligence agencies), research centers, and domain experts. These URLs are then used to gather additional relevant forums and web sites [21].

The test bed consists of messages from 16 U.S. and Middle Eastern forums taken from the Dark Web collection (shown in Table 14-3). All forums were taken from Yahoo, which has taken some heat in recent years for hosting hate and supremacist group forums [41]-[42]. Forums from the same web site were used to offset content variations attributable to web site structures as well as site/forum specific usage dynamics. For example, the use of serial versus threaded message structures can impact content, and specifically sentiment. Agrawal et al. [12] observed that linked messages (ones referencing another) in USENET threads tended to contain antagonistic sentiments. Efron [13] observed the opposite phenomenon for several discourse web sites, where linked sites shared sentiments. This suggests that different web artifacts may have their own content and interaction dynamics.

Table 14-3. Extremist Group Forum Test Bed

U.S.			Middle Eastern		
Forum	Authors	Messages	Forum	Authors	Messages
Angelic Adolf	28	78	Azzamy	60	337
Aryan Nation	54	189	Friends	119	339
CCNU	2	229	Islamic Union	67	473
Neo-Nazi	98	632	Kataeb	66	229
NSM	289	2654	Kataeb Qassam	57	582
Smash Nazi	10	66	Taybah	63	290
White Knights	24	751	Osama Lover	42	173
World Knights	35	77	Wa Islamah	363	926
Total	540	4676	Total	837	3349

7.3   Affect Lexicons

The affect lexicon consisted of 4 affect term lists for violence and hate related terms in the U.S. and Middle Eastern forums. The total lexicon used was composed of over 200 unique entries reflecting different facets of the 2 affect classes selected in our analysis. The term lists for each affect class were generated manually and assigned intensities by coders familiar with the forum content. A pair of coders was used for each language and the intensity was taken as the average of the two coders' assigned scores.

Table 14-4. Violence Affect Lexicon Examples

Term	Description	Intensity	Ambiguity	Weight
hit	-	5.50	0.80	4.40
beat	-	8.00	0.67	5.34
stab	-	11.50	1.00	11.50
hang	-	16.00	0.65	10.40
kill	-	17.00	0.95	16.15
lynch	-	20.00	1.00	20.00
الدم	blood	4.00	0.90	3.60
قتل	kill	17.00	1.00	17.00
الذبح	slaughter	15.50	0.70	10.85
تفجير	detonation	18.00	0.85	15.30
العمليات الاستشهادية	martyrdom operation	20.00	1.00	20.00

8.   RESULTS

8.1   Affect Intensity Scores

The affect intensity scores were computed for each forum as well as across all messages within a region. Table 14-5 shows the intensity scores for the racism and violence affects. In our first hypothesis H1, we postulated that there would be no difference in violence and hate related affect intensities across the two regions.

The U.S forums have a significant amount of racism related content but less violence related affect intensity. Overall, the Middle Eastern forums' intensity of hate affect per message is close to the U.S. forums (p=0.178). However, there is much more violent affect intensity in the Middle Eastern forums (p<0.000).

With respect to individual forums Azzamy and Kataeb Qassam have the greatest occurrence of violent and racist affect. For the U.S. forums, White Knights has the highest occurrence of racism but less violence content while CCNU (Council of Conservative Citizens) features the greatest amount of violence affect but significantly less racist discussion. It is interesting to note that Azzamy and White Knights are the only two open forums in our collection, with the remainder requiring membership. It is possible that the greater bi-partisan discussion in these forums elevates the overall affect intensities as suggested by [12].

Table 14-5. Affect Intensity Scores

U.S.			Middle Eastern		
Forum	Racism	Violence	Forum	Racism	Violence
Angelic Adolf	5.513	0.962	Azzamy	**30.182**	**19.833**
Aryan Nation	9.921	5.683	Friends	2.076	6.238
CCNU	3.712	**14.546**	Deen Union	2.657	9.198
Neo-Nazi	5.458	5.614	Kataeb	2.610	6.605
NSM	10.740	10.740	Kataeb Qassam	25.203	18.670
Smash Nazi	12.424	10.591	Taybah	14.989	15.348
White Knights	**19.313**	6.353	Osama Lover	14.369	14.584
World Knights	2.468	2.234	Wa Islamah	4.075	9.193
All Forums	**10.988**	**6.902**	**All Forums**	**11.892**	**12.644**

8.2   Affect Intensity Relationships

Linear regression analysis was used to evaluate the relationship between violent and hate affect intensities for the U.S. and Middle Eastern forums. The analysis was performed at the individual message and forum level.

Figure 14-2 shows the plots of hate versus violence for all messages within each region.

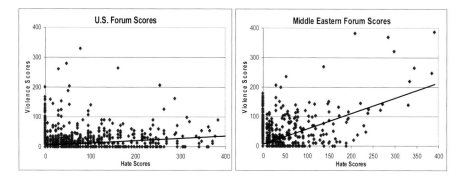

Figure 14-2. Message Affect Intensity Plots

The message level regression results are presented in Table 14-6. The test statistic and p-values for both regions indicate that there is a statistically significant linear relationship between the intensity scores for violence and hate affects. However, based on the slope coefficient b_1 and the coefficient of determination R^2, the relationship is fairly strong for the Middle Eastern forums and very weak for the U.S. messages.

Table 14-6. Message Level Regression Results for Hate versus Violence

Region	n	b_1	t stat	P-value	R^2
U.S.	4676	0.079	21.354	0.000	0.076
Middle Eastern	3349	0.682	48.265	0.000	0.486

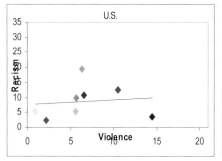
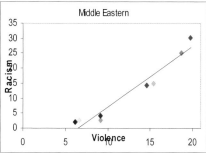

Figure 14-3. Forum Affect Intensity Plots

Figure 14-3 shows the forum level plots of violence versus hate. For the Middle Eastern forums, we can see four distinct clusters (two forums each)

ranging from minimal use of violence and hate affect to more escalated usage.

The forum level regression results are presented in Figure 14-7. The test statistic and p-values indicate that there is a statistically significant linear relationship between the intensity scores for the Middle Eastern forums but not the U.S. forums. Based on the coefficient of determination R^2, the relationship is very strong for the Middle Eastern forums with a slope coefficient b_1 of 0.471.

Table 14-7. Forum Level Regression Results for Hate versus Violence

Region	n	b_1	t stat	P-value	R^2
U.S.	8	0.347	1.760	0.139	0.383
Middle Eastern	8	0.471	10.306	0.000	0.947

8.3   Temporal Visualization of Affect Intensities

Figure 14-4 shows a visual representation of the violent affect usage across the U.S. and Middle Eastern forum postings.

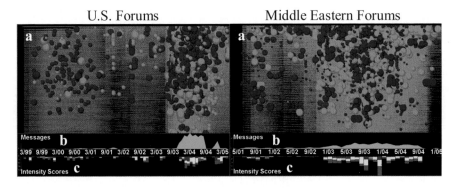

Figure 14-4. Violent Affect Visualization

The top view (a) uses a text overlay technique to show the violence related content usage over time. Each usage incident is represented by a circle of certain color (red, yellow, blue) and size. The colors represent the violent term's affect weight, which is the product of its intensity and ambiguity (blue indicates most severe terms), while the sizes are based on how common the terms are (larger circles signify less common terms). The U.S. forums have predominantly red circles signifying terms with lower affect weights. We can see that there is a great deal more violent content in the Middle Eastern forums in terms of the overall number of circles as well as the larger proportion of severe violence terms. The blue circles, which are more prevalent in the Middle Eastern forums, represent content such as killings, murder, rape, martyrdom operations, sniper shootings, bombings, and tank detonations.

The visualization also shows the number of messages posted per month (b). The message volume per month is displayed in green in the top half of the bottom panel. We can see a large spike in the amount of postings in the U.S. forums around September of 2003 (9/03). There is also a gradual increase in the amount of posting activity in the Middle Eastern forums, coinciding with the start of the war in Iraq (3/03).

The bottom half of this panel shows an inverted histogram presenting a breakdown of intensity scores per message over time (c). Each bar shows the overall intensity score per message broken down by term severity weights (red, yellow, blue). We can see that the violence intensities per message in the U.S. forums are relatively lower than in the Middle Eastern forums (based on the lower height of the bars). The intensity scores per message in both forums increase with the corresponding amplification in the number of messages posted observed in (b). This can be seen by the taller height of the histogram bars during this period. Much of this increased affect intensity is in the form of severe terms, as denoted by the blue portions of the bars. The rising violence intensity during this period could be attributable to the increased antagonism phenomenon that Agrawal et al. [12] also observed.

9. CONCLUSIONS

The research findings suggest that the Middle Eastern and U.S. forums in our test bed have similar levels of hate related affect. In contrast, the Middle Eastern test bed forums also have twice as much violence related intensity as the U.S. forums. The Middle Eastern forums also have a strong affect correlation between violence and racism across messages and forums. Forums with high usage of hate and violence affects (such as Azzamy and Kataeb) may be of greater interest to the research and intelligence communities. It is important to note that the results of this study are based on our test bed of U.S. and Middle Eastern forums. The significant variability in content and usage patterns across various web artifacts makes further investigation necessary. Furthermore, as with most sentiment analysis research, the accuracy of the results is contingent upon human judgment of the intensities of affect lexicon entries.

In this work we developed a new, holistic approach for affect analysis. Our techniques perform affect intensity, relationship, and temporal analysis to provide deeper insight into multilingual discourse affects usage trends. The technique uses probabilistic disambiguation for overcoming affect ambiguity. It also incorporates an affect intensity visualization technique for determining temporal affect variation. The visuals present forum usage trend snapshots. We believe the suggested affect analysis approach would also appropriate for further analysis of extremist group web discourse.

REFERENCES

1. J. Donath. "Identity and deception in the virtual community", *In Communities in Cyberspace*, London, Routledge Press, 1999.
2. T. Moores, and G. Dhillon. "Software piracy: A view from Hong Kong", Comm.of the ACM, vol. 43(12), pp. 88-93, 2000.
3. M. D. Mehta. "Pornography in usenet: a study of 9,800 randomly selected images", Cyberpsychology and Behavior, vol. 4(6), pp. 695-703, 2001.
4. H. Chen. *Intelligence and security informatics for international security: information sharing and data mining*, London, Springer Press, 2006.
5. J. Kaplan and L. Weinberg. *The Emergence of a Euro-American Radical Right*, New Brunswick, NJ: Rutgers University Press.
6. L. Leets. "Responses to internet hate sites: Is speech too free in cyberspace?", Comm. Law and Policy, vol. 6(2), pp. 287-317.
7. V. Burris, E. Smith, and A. Strahm. "White supremacist networks on the internet", Soc. Focus, vol. 33(2), pp. 215-235, 2000.
8. J. Schafer. "Spinning the web of hate: Web-based hate propagation by extremist organizations", J. Criminal Justice and Popular Culture, vol. 9(2), pp. 69-88, 2002.
9. M. A. Hearst. "Direction-based text interpretation as an information access refinement", In P. Jacobs (Ed.), *Text-Based Intelligent Systems: Current Research and Practice in Information Extraction and Retreival*. Mahwah, NJ: Lawrence Erlbaum Associates, 1992.
10. K. Nigam and M. Hurst. "Towards a robust metric of opinion", In Proceedings of the AAAI Spring Symposium on Exploring Attitude and Affect in Text, 2004.
11. P. Subasic, and A. Huettner. "Affect analysis of text using fuzzy semantic typing", IEEE Tran. Fuzzy Systems, vol. 9(4), pp. 483-496, 2001.
12. R. Agrawal, S. Rajagopalan, R. Srikant, & Y. Xu. "Mining newsgroups using networks arising from social behavior", In Proceedings of the 12th International World Wide Web Conference (WWW 2003), 2003.
13. M. Efron. "Cultural orientations: classifying subjective documents by cocitation analysis", In Proceedings of the AAAI Fall Symposium Series on Style and Meaning in Language, Art, Music, and Design (AAAI 2004), 2004.
14. R.W. Picard. *Affective Computing*. Cambridge, MA. MIT Press, 1997.
15. J. Glaser, J. Dixit, and D. P. Green. "Studying hate crime with the internet: what makes racists advocate racial violence?", J. of Soc. Iss., vol. 58(1), pp. 177-193, 2002.
16. K. Crilley. "Information warfare: new battle fields terrorists, propaganda, and the internet", In Proceedings of the Association for Information Management, vol. 53(7), pp. 250-264, 2001.
17. D. S. Hoffman. "The web of hate: Extremists exploit the internet", Anti-Defamation League, New york, NY, 1996.
18. M. Whine. "The governance of cyberspace: Politics, technology, and global restructuring", Routledge, London, U.K, 1997.

19. G. A.Gerstenfeld, D. R.Grant, C. P. Chiang. "Hate online: A content analysis of extremist internet sites", Anal. of Soc. Issues and Pub. Policy, vol. 3(1), pp. 29-44, 2003.

20. T. Gustavson, and D. E. Sherkat. "Elucidating the web of hate: The ideological structuring of network ties among white supremacist groups on the internet", Paper presented at Annual Meeting of American Sociological Association, 2004.

21. Y. Zhou, E. Reid, J. Qin, H. Chen, and G. Lai. "U.S. extremist groups on the web: Link and content analysis", IEEE Int. Sys., vol. 20(5), pp. 44-51, 2005.

22. Abbasi, and H. Chen. "Applying authorship analysis to extremist-group web forum messages", IEEE Int. Sys., vol. 20(5), pp. 67-75, 2005.

23. T. Nasukawa and J. Yi. "Sentiment analysis: Capturing favorability using natural language processing", In Proceedings of the 2nd International Conference on Knowledge Capture, 2003.

24. R. Tong. "An operational system for detecting and tracking opinions in on-line discussion", SIGIR 2001 Workshop on Operational Text Classification, 2001.

25. B. Liu, M. Hu, and J. Cheng. "Opinion observer: Analyzing and comparing opinions on the web", In Proceedings of the 14th International World Wide Web Conference (WWW 2005), 2005.

26. G. Grefenstette, Y. Qu, J. G. Shanahan, and D. A. Evans. "Coupling niche browsers and affect analysis for an opinion mining application", In 12th International Conference Recherche d'Information Assistee par Ordinateur (RIAO-2004), 2004.

27. G. Mishne. "Experiments with mood classification", In Proceedings of Stylistic Analysis of Text for Information Access Workshop (SIGIR, 2005), 2005.

28. J. Donath, K. Karahalio, and F. Viegas. "Visualizing conversation", In Proceedings of the 32nd Conference on Computer-Human Interaction (CHI' 02), Chicago, USA, 1999.

29. N. M. Henley, M. D. Miller, J. A. Beazley, D. N. Nguyen, D. Kaminsky, and R. Sanders. "Frequency and specificity of referents to violence in news reports of anti-gay attacks", Disc. & Soc., vol. 13(1), pp. 75-104, 2002.

30. J. Yi, R., Bunescu and W. Niblack. Sentiment analyzer: Extracting sentiments about a given topic using natural language processing techniques", In Proceedings of the 3rd In Proceedings of the 3rd IEEE Inter. Conf. on Data Mining (ICDM 2003), 2003.

31. S. Morinaga, K. Yamanishi, K. Tateishi, and T. Fukushima. "Mining product reputations on the web", In Proceedings of the Eighth ACM SIGKDD International Conference on Knowledge Discovery and Data Mining (SIGKDD 2002), 2002.

32. L. Robinson. "Debating the events of September 11th: Discursive and interactional dynamics in three online fora", J. Comp. Med. Comm., vol. 10(4).

33. B. Pang, L. Lee, and S. Vaithyanathain. "Thumbs up? Sentiment classification using machine learning techniques", In proceedings of the Empirical Methods in Natural Language Processing (EMNLP 2002), 2002.

34. P. D. Turney. "Thumbs up or thumbs down? Semantic orientation applied to unsupervised classification of reviews", In Proceedings of the 40th Annual Meetings of the Association for Computational Linguistics (ACL 2002), 2002.

35. T. Wilson, J. Wiebe, and P. Hoffman. "Recognizing contextual polarity in phrase-level sentiment analysis", In Proceedings of the Human Language Technology Conference and Conference on Empirical Methods in Natural Language Processing (HLT/EMNLP 2005), 2005.

36. Ortony, G. L. Clore, M. A. Foss. The referential structure of the affective lexicon. Cog. Science, vol. 11(3), pp. 341-364.

37. H. Liu, H. Lieberman, T. Selker. A model of textual affect sensing using real-world knowledge. In Proceedings of the 8th International conference on Intelligent user interfaces, Miami, Fl., 2003.

38. R. Weischedel, R. Schwartz, J. Palmucci, M. Meteer, and L. Ramshaw. "Coping with ambiguity and unknown words through probabilistic models", Comp. Ling., vol. 19(2), pp. 361-382, 1993.

39. W. Sack. "Conversation map: An interface for very large-scale conversations", J. Mgmt. Info. Sys., vol. 17(3), pp. 73-92, 2000.

40. Anti-Defamation League. ADL says Yahoo violates its own rules by hosting hate clubs. ADL Press Release. February 23, 2000.

41. J. Scheeres. Wired news: Helpful hints for hate haters. Wired News, June 20, 2001.

42. N. Glance, M. Hurst, K. Nigam, M. Siegler, R. Stockton, and T. Tomokiyo. "Analyzing online discussion for marketing intelligence", In Proceedings of the 14th International World Wide Web Conference (WWW 2005), 2005.

43. J. Yi, and W. Niblack. "Sentiment mining in WebFountain", In Proceedings of the 21st International Conference on Data Engineering (ICDE 2005), 2005.

44. J. Wiebe, T. Wilson, and C. Cardie. "Annotating expressions of opinions and emotions in language", Language Resources and Evaluation, vol. 1(2), 2005.

SUGGESTED READINGS

- Interesting affect analysis paper. P. Subasic, and A. Huettner. "Affect analysis of text using fuzzy semantic typing", IEEE Tran. Fuzzy Systems, vol. 9(4), pp. 483-496, 2001.
- Seminal book on affective computing. R.W. Picard. *Affective Computing.* Cambridge, MA. MIT Press, 1997.
- Book chapter describing the importance of analyzing direction-based text. M. A. Hearst. "Direction-based text interpretation as an information access refinement", In P. Jacobs (Ed.), *Text-Based Intelligent Systems: Current Research and Practice in Information Extraction and Retrieval.* Mahwah, NJ: Lawrence Erlbaum Associates, 1992.
- Work on classifying text into various emotion classes. G. Mishne. "Experiments with mood classification", In Proceedings of Stylistic Analysis of Text for Information Access Workshop (SIGIR, 2005), 2005.

ONLINE RESOURCES

- Machine Readable Dictionary (MRC) Psycholinguistic Database at the University of Western Australia
  http://www.psy.uwa.edu.au/mrcdatabase/uwa_mrc.htm
  This database contains many important psychological measures for various words which may be useful for affect analsyis.
- Affect Analysis Research Group at University of Pittsburgh.
  http://www.pitt.edu/~emotion/
  This world renowned research lab does work on multimodal affect

analysis, including the use of facial expressions and motion. Such analysis could be very useful if applied to multimedia content found in the Dark Web.

DISCUSSION QUESTIONS

1. What other affect sets/classes would be relevant for extremist group discourse analysis?
2. How might individual participant level affect analysis improve our understanding of the roles played by the various members of these online communities?
3. Do you think affect analysis can be used as a content filtering mechanism to isolate more extreme or propaganda related content?
4. In addition to intensity, correlation, and temporal evaluation, what other forms of affect analysis may beneficial to improving our understanding of extremist group forums?

15

DOCUMENT SELECTION FOR EXTRACTING ENTITY AND RELATIONSHIP INSTANCES OF TERRORIST EVENTS

Zhen Sun[1], Ee-Peng Lim[1], Kuiyu Chang[1], Maggy Anastasia Suryanto[1], and Rohan Kumar Gunaratna[2]

[1]*Centre for Advanced Information Systems, School of Computer Engineering, Nanyang Technological University, Singapore (sunz0001@ntu.edu.sg and aseplim@ntu.edu.sg);*
[2]*International Center for Political Violence and Terrorism Research Institute of Defence and Strategic StudiesNanyang Technological University, Singapore*

CHAPTER OVERVIEW

In this chapter, we study the problem of selecting documents so as to extract terrorist event information from a collection of documents. We represent an event by its entity and relation instances. Very often, these entity and relation instances have to be extracted from multiple documents. We therefore define an information extraction (IE) task as selecting documents and extracting from which entity and relation instances relevant to a user-specified event (aka *domain specific event entity and relation extraction*). We adopt domain specific IE patterns to extract potentially relevant entity and relation instances from documents, and develop a number of document ranking strategies using the extracted instances to address this extraction task. Each ranking strategy (aka *pattern-based document ranking strategy*) assigns a score to each document, which estimates the latter's contribution to the gain in event related instances. We conducted experiments on two document collection datasets constructed using two historical terrorism events. Experiments showed that our proposed pattern-based document ranking strategies performed well on the domain specific event entity and relation extraction task for document collections of various sizes.

1.   INTRODUCTION

1.1   Motivation

Every day, thousands of news articles and reports are published covering a wide spectrum of events ranging from company acquisitions to terrorism attacks [1]. Information relating to events is often hidden in multiple documents from possibly multiple collections. This event related information is an important piece of knowledge about organizations and individuals, and can be used for intelligence analysis.

In the study and tracking of terrorism, terrorists, and terrorist organizations, specialists must periodically peruse a large number of articles in order to gather pieces of information to assemble into a coherent whole. This effort is labor-intensive, and thus frequently involves multiple people coordinating with one another to search and extract information. Invariably, efficiency might not be improved vastly with additional manpower due to duplicated coverage (e.g. multiple specialists reading different articles providing the same information) and communication limitations (e.g. no easy way to consolidate and differentiate between new and existing intelligence information).

To this end, we investigate a special event information extraction task where knowledge about an event is to be gathered from a large document collection. Consider the bombing event that took place in London on July 7, 2005. As shown in Figure 15-1, knowledge about this event can be represented using entity and relation instances in an *entity relation graph*. People, organizations, etc., which are involved in the event can be represented by entity instances appearing as boxes in the figure. Each relation instance then represents the relationship between a pair of entity instances. It is denoted by a directed edge from one entity instance to another entity instance. In order to build the above graph, one will have to select and subsequently analyze the subset of *relevant* documents reporting this event from the document collection. Even after filtering, this relevant subset may still consist of many documents, and reading through all of them will require significant amount of effort and time.

As illustrated by the example, the relevant documents are those that ideally contain different parts of the yet-to-be constructed entity relation graph (see Figure 15-1). Suppose the large document collection has already been indexed by a document retrieval system. To construct the whole entity relation graph, a user will typically use some initial query keywords, e.g. "London bombing July 2005", to search through the system for the relevant documents.

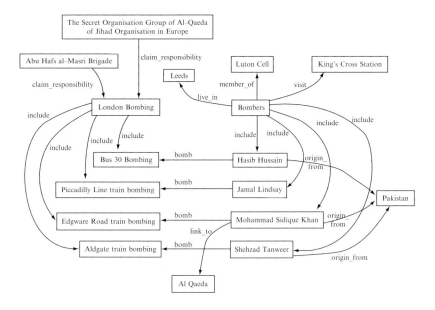

Figure 15-1. Entity Relation Graph about London Bombing

However, it may turn out that only a few of relevant documents can be found using the initial query keywords. Oftentimes, the user has to read through these "hit" documents to extract instances related to the event and also to formulate new query words using those instances. In this process, multiple queries will have to be constructed for the document retrieval system so as to extract the complete set of entity and relation instances.

The above task clearly is not well supported by existing document retrieval systems, which usually assume that each user query (keyword or attribute based) is independent of other queries as they are designed to find documents that contain query terms only [2]. The way a user analyzes the returned documents is however completely beyond the scope of existing IR systems.

Question-Answering (QA) task[1] has been recently introduced by TREC to find answers to questions of different types from a given document collection. However, the QA task does not rank documents by the amount of event relevant instances. QA task also does not provide a relevance feedback mechanism for users to construct answers iteratively while reading as few relevant documents as possible. In other words, QA task focuses on extracting answers while our proposed task allows users to select different documents for constructing the answers.

---

[1] http://trec.nist.gov/data/qa.html

1.2   Domain Specific Event Entity and Relation Extraction

We therefore study information extraction from an analyst's standpoint by treating information extraction as an integral part of a larger task. The task entails finding documents and extracting from them entity and relation instances. We call this the *domain specific event entity and relation extraction task.* A document retrieval system supporting such tasks will therefore have to return documents containing the required instances, and also extract them.

One main objective of the domain specific event entity and relation extraction task is to keep the subset of documents to be read by the analyst as small as possible to minimize his/her effort, thereby improving productivity. However, there are some technical challenges in identifying a subset of documents describing an event and extracting event-related information. They are:

Information about an event often exists across multiple documents. In order not to miss any entity/relation instances about the event, it is necessary to find all documents which contain some instances about the event. However, the same entity/relation instances may be found in multiple documents. Therefore, each selected document should contain minimal amount of overlapping instances with the already found ones. Ideally, we aim to find the smallest subset of documents that can cover all the relevant entity and/or relation instances.

- Document ranking/scoring will have to be vastly revamped from existing document retrieval systems, which simply use query term and document frequencies to compute the relevance score [3]. The document ranking approach for our task should find all relevant documents and assign a higher score to documents containing more related and novel instances. This means that the relevance score of each document (seen and unseen) will change dynamically with each new found entity/relation instance.

- The extraction of entity and relation instances related to an event from documents relies on extraction patterns. The extraction patterns are domain specific, and should help the system identify entity instances and relationships amongst them. We shall focus on creating extraction patterns specifically for the terrorism domain, based on feedback from real-world terrorism experts.

This chapter studies several pattern-based document ranking strategies based on information extraction patterns to address this domain specific entity and relation extraction task. The main objectives and contributions arising from this work are summarized as follows:

- Definition of domain specific event entity and relation extraction task. We formally define the extraction task which incorporates a document ranking strategy to find event related entity and relation instances. The extraction task aims to incrementally select a set of documents relevant to an event, using some document ranking strategies. A set of patterns for extracting domain specific event entity and relation instances from a document are assumed to be given. We also assume that some seed entity instances are given to bootstrap the extraction process. This task has not been studied before and our research therefore establishes the necessary foundation.
- Design of pattern-based document ranking strategies. We describe a few document ranking strategies to identify the smallest possible subset of documents for covering event related instances. Each strategy aims to maximize the novelty of the set of entity and relation instances that can be found in the next document to be extracted. In this way, one can hopefully reduce the number of documents to be examined by the experts.
- Construction of datasets and evaluations of proposed document ranking strategies. Since the extraction task defined in our research is a new direction to this area, there are no suitable datasets available to evaluate our proposed solutions. Therefore, we have created two datasets from two different terrorism events. We have also proposed a set of evaluation metrics to measure the ability of different strategies to find documents and instances. Experimental results showed that our strategies performed well on the proposed extraction task.

2. LITERATURE REVIEW

Information extraction (IE) [4] involves extracting useful text segments from a collection of documents. The focus has been traditionally on building accurate and robust IE systems. However, our work is to examine the IE problem from a different perspective.

2.1 Named Entity Recognition

Finding a set of entity and relation instances of a given event is our research focus, and which is related to named entity recognition. Named Entity Recognition (NER) involves extracting objects of general classes such as person names, locations, and organizations from plain text.

NER has been well studied and remains an essential component of many language processing tasks. Much of the existing named entity recognition research is based on English. Palmer and Day developed statistical methods for finding named entities from newswire articles in multiple languages: Chinese, English, French, Japanese, Portuguese and Spanish [5].

NER can be viewed as a kind of single-slot extraction. Single-slot extraction systems such as AutoSlog [6] and its extensions [7][8][9][10] have been developed and shown to yield high extraction accuracies. With a set of labeled training documents, AutoSlog was able to build a set of single-slot extraction patterns for extracting entities of interest from documents.

Subsequent extensions of AutoSlog [7][8] focused on reducing the effort in labelling training corpus. Ellen presented a system called AutoSlog-TS that used only pre-classified training corpus with relevant and irrelevant documents to create dictionaries of extraction patterns. The AutoSlog-TS system used AutoSlog to find all extraction patterns first from all training documents and then used classified information on the corpus to filter out incorrectly learned patterns.

2.2   Coreference Resolution

Coreference resolution (CR) is a task to determine whether two text expressions appearing in an article refers to the same entity. It is an important IE task that has been well-studied and is an essential component of our system; coreference resolution is performed on our datasets before the domain specific event entity relation extraction starts. In our work, we consider both pronoun and name coreference resolution. We have implemented an auto-coreferenced resolution module and evaluated it against the method proposed in [11] using the MUC-6 metric. Interested readers can refer to [12] for more details.

2.3   Multi-Slot Information Extraction

The goal of multi-slot extraction is to extract several interested entities simultaneously using one extraction pattern. Since these entities are extracted with one pattern, a certain relation among the entities is observed. Therefore, multi-slot information extraction is useful for identifying relations among entities. There have been some research on multi-slot extraction [13][14][15][16][17][18]. Most the prior research on multi-slot extraction was targeted at unstructured (plain) text.

LIEP[16], an IE system, addresses the issue of increasing requirements of hand-craft dictionaries of extraction patterns for most IE system to work. LIEP is able to build dictionaries of multi-slot extraction patterns directly from training texts provided by users. LIEP first generates new patterns from training examples, and then generalizes learned patterns that have same relationship in syntactic structure but are with different constitutes, such as head words and properties. The patterns learnt were shown to perform well compared to a manual approach.

Soderland, in the Crystal project, introduced *Concept Node* (CN) for multi-slot extraction patterns and applied it to any component phrase of a sentence in a document [13]. CN represents an extraction pattern in Crystal. The generation of CN by Crystal requires an induction procedure. Firstly, Crystal creates initial CNs from a training corpus. Crystal then generalizes each pair of CNs according to their syntactic structure. It was shown that CN could be generalized as far as possible without producing errors and it always worked better than human intuitions in creating the rules for extraction. Soderland further modified Crystal to conduct Web IE[14].

In the *Snowball* project, Agichtein and Gravano[19] defined a relation of interest as a tuple, and used a set of pre-defined tuples for training and generating a set of multi-slot extraction patterns. Snowball is a bootstrapping-based pattern generation system that requires very little human-interactions in pattern generation.

2.4 Information Extraction from Multiple Documents

Complete information about an event is always hidden in multiple documents. In this section we review existing research on multiple document extraction [20][21][22][23].

Jade Goldstein et al. [20] presented an approach to create a summary from multiple documents. The summary was built by extracting sentences from different documents. The targets of extraction were sentences, while our work aims to extract entity and relation instances.

Masterson and Kushmerick addressed the problem of extracting entities from multiple documents [21]. In their work, they extended IE techniques to a multi-document extraction task and improved the IE performance by using structural and temporal relationships among documents. They created a template with fixed slots to present the information required, then applied IE on multiple documents to extract entities for the slots. Their research however is still a kind of single slot extraction since it does not concern identifying relationships among entities.

Dennis Reidsma et al. [22] applied IE on multiple documents of multimedia archives. In their work, information extracted from multiple documents were merged and integrated to obtain a more complete summary. The proposed merging algorithm performed alignment, unification and reordering on the extracted information. The merged summary then could be used to enhance the performance of multimedia archive retrieval. However, the IE method proposed was still based on single documents and only the merging algorithm considered multi-document information.

QXtract also dealt with a similar problem [23]. In QXtract, Eugene Agichtein and Luis Gravano developed an automatic query-based technique to retrieve documents useful for the extraction of user-defined relations from large text databases. In their work, they focused on finding a document that was useful to generate queries for a specific relation. The generated query is then used to find more documents and this process repeats itself. This work is quite similar to ours, however there are some key differences:

1. QXtract focuses on learning queries to retrieve relevant documents for extracting a target relation and is not driven by event. Our work is to find all information about a certain event and it may involve multiple relations.
2. QXtract retrieves documents by a search engine and performed IE to provide tuples for generating queries. Our work on the other hand focuses on document selection and uses IE to score documents.
3. Extraction patterns in our work may change adaptively after a document is selected and annotated. The IE system of QXtract is independent of the document retrieval process.

Finn and Kushmerick proposed various active learning selection strategies to incrementally select documents from a large collection for user labeling so as to derive good extraction patterns [24]. In their work, they proposed several document selection strategies to select the most informative documents from a large collection. The focus was to select documents containing predominantly novel information, i.e. documents selected that are textually most dissimilar to each other so as to minimize the effort of human labeling. In contrast, our work focuses on finding documents containing both novel and related information with the help of extraction patterns and extracting event related information from them.

2.5   New Event Detection

There is much research on detecting events and extracting information about events and they are somewhat related to our work.

Harsha et al. [25] presented a method to use *Link Grammar* to discover instances of events and extract them from unstructured documents. Link Grammar represented a certain relation between two constitutions using the syntactic structure in a sentence. Rules of Link Grammar had been used to find specific instances about an event. This is similar to our work as we are also interested on finding instances of entities and relations about an event from text. However, the event defined in [25] was restricted to a specific action only, such as kidnapping or killing. A set of synonymous verbs were used to describe a certain action and it was defined as one event. Moreover, the extraction was limited by a certain syntactic structures supported by Link

Grammar and the event was assumed to exist in a single document only.

Link Detection addresses the problem on detecting stories of the same event, or stories that are linked. A story reporting an airline crash event and another story reporting the subsequent compensation to victims are considered as two linked stories. New Event Detection (NED)[26][27][28] is a document selection task to identify the first story of an event from an time ordered collection of news articles. In NED, the only focus is to find the first story by scoring all articles. In [29], it was shown that link detection and new event detection are asymmetric and they are both related to our work as all these tasks involve finding documents about a certain event. However, the criteria of finding documents in these tasks are different.

The work in [26] and [30] studied several approaches to use TF-IDF similarity metrics to resolve the NED problems. A more recent work [27] presented an enhanced TF-IDF method and integrated normalization techniques, source-specific models to give an improved analysis on NED. A detailed investigation by Giridhar Kumaran and James Allan on NED problem and two modifications were presented in [28]. Text classification models were used to classify articles into specific categories and named-entity techniques were used to create three different document representations for NED task.

NED and our work are similar in finding documents describing a certain event. However, as entity and relation instances of a certain event are usually distributed among multiple documents, the first story does not necessarily contain all the entity and relation instances of an event. The focus of our work is to find as small as possible the subset of documents that contain complete event related information instead of the first story document.

3. DOMAIN SPECIFIC EVENT ENTITY RELATION EXTRACTION TASK WITH DOCUMENT RANKING

3.1 Event Representation using Entity and Relation Instances

In our extraction task, we represent an event by a set of entity and relation instances. The entity instances represent the people, organizations, locations, dates/times and other information involved in the event. The relation instances provide the links between these entity instances so as to represent their inter-relationships. In the extraction task, we assume that an expert user wants to derive all entity and relationship instances for only one event belonging to some domain (e.g., biomedical, terrorism, etc.). To ensure that only relevant instances are extracted, we assume that these entity and relation instances can be grouped under a few entity and relation classes, respectively, appropriate for the domain.

Let E be a set of *entity classes*, i.e. $E = \{E_1, E_2, ..., E_n\}$, and R be a set of *relation classes*, $R = \{R_1, R_2, ..., R_m\}$, and they are known to be relevant to the application domain where the extraction task is to be performed. E and R together define the type of instances to be extracted for a target event. An entity class E_i denotes a set of entity instances of the same type, and each entity instance is usually a noun or noun phrase appearing in the documents. Each relation class R_i represents a semantic relationship from source entity class *SourceEnt(R_i)* to target entity class *TargetEnt(R_i)* and is associated with an *action class A_i*. A_i refers to a set of verbs or verb phrases that relate source entity instances in *SourceEnt(R_i)* to target entity instances in *TargetEnt(R_i)*. Each relation instance is comprised of a source entity instance from *SourceEnt(R_i)*, a target entity instance from *TargetEnt(R_i)*, and an action instance from A_i, i.e., $R_i \subseteq SourceEnt(R_i) \times A_i \times TargetEnt(R_i)$, where *SourceEnt(R_i)*, *TargetEnt(R_i)* $\in E$.

Figure 15-2 illustrates a relation instance of the "Harm" relation class extracted from the following sentence, *"Al-Qaeda Cell had abducted Kim Sun on Jun 17"*. In this example, the source entity instance *"Al-Qaeda Cell"* is from the *"Terrorist Organization"* entity class, the action instance *"abducted"* belongs to the *"Harm"* action class, and the target entity instance *"Kim Sun"* is from the *"Victim"* entity class.

Figure 15-2. A relation instance example of relation class "Harm"

3.2   Domain Specific Event Entity Relation Extraction Task

The domain specific nature of this extraction task allows us to confine the instances to be from a set of entity and relation classes. We assume that these entity and relation classes are known beforehand and a set of extraction patterns are available to extract instances of these classes. Suppose we are given a set of extraction patterns EP, a collection of documents D, and a set of seed entity instances W belonging to an event of interest to a user. Let E and R represent the entity classes and relation classes relevant to the event respectively. We use ε to denote the set of all entity instances contained in E that are relevant to a given event, i.e. $\varepsilon = \bigcup_{i=1}^{n} E_i$, and $\Re$ to denote the set of all relation instances in R relevant to the event, i.e., $\Re = \bigcup_{i=1}^{m} R_i$. W is a small subset of ε to bootstrap the extraction of other instances. To ensure that all instances will be extracted given the seed entity instances W, we require the all event instances ε to be directly or indirectly linked to W through the relation instances in $\Re$. Let r_s denote a relation instance in $\Re$, of which e_s^t and e_s^s are the corresponding source and target entity instances, respectively. Therefore, $r_s = \left(e_s^t, a_s, e_s^s\right)$ is a relation instance in $\Re$ if it satisfies one of the conditions below:

1. $\left(e_s^s \in W\right)$ or $\left(e_s^t \in W\right)$
2. $\exists\ path\ (r_s, r_{s+1}, ... r_{s+m}), r_{s+m} = (e_{s+m}^s, a_{s+m}, e_{s+m}^t)$ and $[(e_{s+m}^s \in W)\ or\ (e_{s+m}^t \in W)]$

In the domain specific event entity relation extraction task, documents for extracting event related instances are selected one at a time. At the beginning, the seed entity instances W are given to identify the relevant documents. Each time a document is selected, it is given to the expert user for manual inspection so as to annotate the event entity and relation instances. Note that manual annotation is conducted to ensure that no instances are missed. This process repeats until all event entity and relation instances are found.

The detailed description of the task is depicted in Algorithm 1. In the extraction task, the extraction patterns EP are used to find the existence of entity and relation instances that could be relevant to the event. The extraction patterns can be for single-slot, or multi-slot extraction. The entity and relation instances extracted from a document d_j using EP are stored in ε_j' and $\Re_j'$ respectively.

In each iteration, a document ranking strategy is used to score every document from D. The expert user then selects a document, presumably from the top scored ones, annotates entity and relation instances and adds them to ε and $\Re$ respectively. The process repeats until all instances are found, or a termination condition is met. For example, the termination condition can be some upper bound on the number of documents extracted, or the number of instances found.

Assuming that the expert user has in mind a set of entity and relation instances to be extracted for an event and these instances exist in a given document collection[2]. We can then define a subset of documents containing

---

the relevant instances as *relevant set* denoted by L. The objective of the domain specific event entity and relation extraction task is to select the smallest subset O of L that covers all relevant instances. We call O the optimal set. Recall that E_j and R_j be the set of entity and relation instances the user wants to extract from document d_j respectively. Then O is an optimal set if and only if it satisfies the following two conditions:

1. $\left(\bigcup_{d_j \in O} R_j = \Re \right)$ and $\left(\bigcup_{d_j \in O} E_j = \varepsilon \right)$

2. $\nexists\ O'\ s.t.\ \left(\bigcup_{d_j \in O} R_j = \Re \right)$ and $\left(\bigcup_{d_j \in O} E_j = \varepsilon \right)$ and $\left(|O'| < |O| \right)$

Algorithm 1 Domain Specific Event Entity and Relation Extraction

input: *EP, D, W*
for each document d_j in D do
    Apply *EP* on d_j to obtain ε'_j, $\Re'_j$ (Extraction Step)
    Compute *score(d_j)* using initial score function (see Section 3.3.1)
end for
repeat
    //User selects a document d_s
    Move d_s from D to S
    //User annotates ε_s and $\Re_s$ in d_s
    Add ε_s and $\Re_s$ to ε and $\Re$ respectively
    for each document d_j in D do
        computer *score(d_j)* based on ε'_j, $\Re'_j$, ε, $\Re$ (using one of the document
        ranking strategies in Section 3.3)
    end for
until termination condition is satisfied
    output: S, ε, $\Re$

Document ranking strategies using different score functions are required in the above extraction task. In general, documents containing more novel and related information about the event of interest should be given higher scores. In Section 3.3, we propose five document ranking strategies, each based on a different score function. Since all these strategies rely on extraction patterns, we call them pattern-based document ranking strategies.

The manner in which extraction patterns are applied in the above entity relation extraction task is another focus of our work. Well-designed extraction patterns can extract entity and relation instances more accurately, which leads to more accurate document ranking. Furthermore, there are some other research issues for the above extraction task:

1. The extraction task is driven by events. User always annotates the document with highest score returned by our proposed score functions of

document ranking strategies. It is important for the score function to give higher scores for documents containing information related to the event of interest. At the same time, we do not want the user to annotate documents containing information already been seen. Therefore, it is challenging to design a good score function.

2. The proposed extraction task has not been studied before. It is necessary to design a set of evaluation metrics to measure the performance of different document ranking strategies on the extraction task. The evaluation metrics must be able to measure how well the extraction task on finding the event-related instances and how accurate the ranking strategies on scoring each document.

3.3   Pattern-based Document Ranking

We have developed several document ranking strategies using different score functions in the proposed event-driven extraction task. In the following, we present the score functions of the proposed document selection strategies. We also describe two existing document ranking strategies based on document content [24], i.e., not using the extraction patterns.

Initial Score Function   This is shown in Equation 15-1 and is used to rank documents based on the given seed entity instances W only in the first iteration when there are no other entity and relation instances already labeled by the user. The first term of the score function

$$\left(\left|\varepsilon_j \cap W\right| + \frac{|W|}{\gamma}\right)\bigg/|W|$$

considers the proportion of W that is extracted. When this term is large, the document will contain more seed entities relevant to the given event. The parameter γ ($>> |W|$) is a smoothing factor that prevents the numerator from becoming zero when $\varepsilon_j \cap W$ is empty. EP_i is a subset of EP that fired on document d_j, and f_k is the number of relation instances extracted by extraction pattern $ep_{j,k}$. The score function therefore favors documents with more seed entities, more extraction patterns fired and more relation instances extracted.

$$score(d_j) = \frac{\left|\varepsilon_j \cap W\right| + \dfrac{|W|}{\gamma}}{|W|} \cdot \log_2\left(|EP_j|\right) \sum_{k=1}^{|EP_j|} f_k$$

Equation 15-1: Initial Score Function

DiffCompare   This strategy examines the amount of overlap between relation instances extracted from the current document d_j with the accumulated relation instance set $\mathfrak{R}$. We only consider relation instances here. This is because our assumption that entity instances annotated are usually linked to previously found entity instances via relation instances in each iteration. The score will be determined by the overlap between relation instances as well as the intersection between the extracted entity instances ε_j' and W. This is to assign higher score for documents having direct links to the seed set. Contributions from the two factors are linearly weighted by $\alpha \in [0, 1]$. Equation 15-2 shows the score function:

$$score(d_j) = \alpha.\frac{\left|\mathfrak{R}_j' - \mathfrak{R}\right|}{\max_{d_l \in D}\left|\mathfrak{R}_l'\right|} + (1-\alpha).\frac{\left|\varepsilon_j' \cap W\right|}{|W|}$$

Equation 15-2: DiffCompare

CombineCompare   This strategy combines the amount of intersection and dissimilarity between relation instances extracted from d_i with instances in $\mathfrak{R}$. A modifier $\beta \in [0, 1]$ is used to adjust the relative importance of overlapping relation instances compared with novel relation instances (i.e., relevant relation instances that have not been extracted so far). When the former is more important, $\beta > 0.5$. When $\beta = 0.5$, both are treated equally important. Equation 15-3 gives the score function of this strategy. Note that when $\beta = 0$, this is equivalent to DiffCompare.

$$score(d_j) = \alpha.\frac{\beta\left|\mathfrak{R}_j' \cap \mathfrak{R}\right| + (1-\beta).\left(\left|\mathfrak{R}_j' - \mathfrak{R}\right|\right)}{\max_{d_l \in D}\left|\mathfrak{R}_l'\right|} + (1-\alpha).\frac{\left|\varepsilon_j' \cap W\right|}{|W|}$$

Equation 15-3: Combine Compare

PartialMatch   I In this document ranking strategy, we want to select documents with relation instances linked to those entity instances that have already been found. This requires a partial match between the former and latter. Note that all entity instances in the event are connected directly or indirectly by relation instances. This applies even in the midst of extraction task. Hence, we need to conduct partial match between relation instances extracted using EP and the relation instances found so far.

Given two relation instances $r_s = \left(e_s', a_s, e_s^s\right)$ and $r_t = \left(e_t', a_t, e_t^s\right)$, the partial match of r_s and r_t denoted by PartialMatch(r_s, r_t) is defined by:

$$PartialMatch(r_s, r_t) = \begin{cases} 0 & if \quad e_s^s \neq e_t^s \wedge e_s^t \neq e_t^t \\ 0 & if \quad e_s^s = e_t^s \wedge e_s^t = e_t^t \wedge (a_s \in A_p, a_t \in A_q, p = q \\ 1 & otherwise \end{cases}$$

With *PartialMatch* measuring the novelty of instances, we now define its score function in Equation 15-4:

$$score(d_j) = \alpha . \frac{\sum_{k=1}^{M_j} \sum_{h=1}^{|\Re|} PartialMatch(r_{j,k}^{'}, r_h)}{|\Re_j^{'}| . |\Re| + 1} + (1 - \alpha) . \frac{|\varepsilon_j^{'} \cap W|}{|W|}$$

Equation 15-4: Partial Match

where M_j is the number of relation instances extracted from d_j using *EP*; $r_{j,k}^{'}$ is the kth relation instance from $\Re_j^{'}$; and r_h is the hth instance in $\Re$.

PartialMatch Plus (+) PartialMatch Plus (+) is an online extension of PartialMatch I, which uses newly extracted instances $\varepsilon_j^{'}$ from each document *j* to enlarge the set of extraction patterns *EP* (see Section 4.3).

PartialMatch II In PartialMatch I, we consider the relation instances of a document linked to those instances found and also the amount of entity instances intersected with the seeds. In PartialMatch II, we want to also consider entity instances which have been annotated by the user. Therefore, we extend the PartialMatch I document ranking strategy to also consider the amount of entity instances observed in E, and we call this strategy PartialMatch II

With the *PartialMatch* function defined, we now derive the score function for the PartialMatch II strategy in Equation 15-5:

$$score(d_j) = \alpha . \frac{\sum_{k=1}^{M_j} \sum_{h=1}^{|\Re|} PartialMatch(r_{j,k}^{'}, r_h)}{|\Re_j^{'}| . |\Re| + 1}$$

$$+ (1 - \alpha) . \left(\lambda . \frac{|\varepsilon_j^{'} \cap \varepsilon|}{|\varepsilon|} + (1 - \lambda) . \frac{|\varepsilon_j^{'} \cap W'|}{|W'|} \right)$$

Equation 15-5: Partial Match II

where λ is a factor to control the importance between seeds and extracted entity instances set; W' = W $- \varepsilon$ represents the seeds which are not extracted by user and not included into the extracted entity instance set.

Comparison and Discussion   Among the five aforementioned pattern-based document ranking strategies, initial score strategy is the only one that does not depend on a pre-selected set of documents or annotated instances. It depends solely on the entity/relation instances extracted by the extraction patterns on the candidate documents. In contrast, the other strategies require a pre-existing set of selected documents or annotated instances in order to give a score on a candidate document.

DiffCompare, CombineCompare and PartialMatch (I and II) all take into account of the entity and relation instances accumulated from previous selections. DiffCompare only needs to compute the difference between extracted relation instances and annotated instances as well as the intersection between seeds and extracted entity instances. Therefore, it is the most efficient strategy among all the strategies. It works well for information distributed in different documents with few overlaps.

CombineCompare is fairly efficient, as it only needs to calculate the intersection and disjunction of two relation instance sets. Compared to DiffCompare, it has one additional user-adjustable parameter β, which makes it more robust and flexible.

PartialMatch (I and II) requires more computations as it compares every pair of relation instances. If there are M relation instances in the resultant set, and N relation instances are extracted from document d_j , the computational complexity of $score(d_j)$ is $O(MN)$. Moreover, it is good for selecting documents containing both related and novel information.

3.4   Content-based Document Ranking Strategies

Finn and Kushmerick developed content-based document ranking strategies for identifying the documents to be manually labeled so as to learn the extraction patterns. Although the nature of the problem is different, the document ranking strategies presented in [24] are related to our work. Among the strategies are *COMPARE* and *EXTRACTCOMPARE* which have been shown to give good performance [24].

COMPARE favors documents that are content-wise least similar to the pool of already selected documents. The score is measured using Equation 15-6.

$$score(d_j) = \sum_{d_k \in s} \frac{\left|T_j \cup T_k\right|}{\left|T_j \cap T_k\right| + 1}$$

Equation 15-6

where *S* is the set of already selected documents; T_j and T_k are sets of terms from d_j and d_k respectively.

EXTRACTCOMPARE gives preference to the document with content most dissimilar to the current set of extracted entities from the already selected document pool. This strategy applies extraction rules only to those already selected documents in *S*, but evaluates a candidate document purely based on its content similarity. Therefore, we consider it a content-based strategy. Equation 15-7 gives the score function:

$$score(d_j) = \sum_{d_k \in s} \frac{\left| \varepsilon_k^i \cup T_j \right|}{\left| \varepsilon_k^i \cap T_j \right| + 1}$$

Equation 15-7

where ε_k^i is the set of entity instances extracted from document *k*.

In our experiments (see Section 4.4), we have implemented COMPARE and EXTRACTCOMPARE strategies with one minor modification. Instead of randomly selecting a document as the first document as in [24], we select the highest scored document according to the initial score function. We feel that this modification gives a fairer comparison between the two content-based strategies and our proposed pattern-based strategies.

4. CASE STUDIES

We now present the experiments evaluating the performance of different document ranking strategies on the domain specific event entity and relation extraction task. We first give a detailed description of the experiment setup, including the construction of datasets, choice of information extraction system components, construction of extraction patterns and performance metrics. This is followed by experimental results.

4.1 Datasets

We used two datasets, one covering Korean Hostage Kim-Sun's beheading event (KSB) in Iraq, June 2004 and the other covering the Australian Embassy bombing event (AEB) in Jakarta, September 2004. They are known as the KSB-100 and AEB-100 datasets respectively. Documents of these datasets were downloaded from an online news website and the documents have been converted to plain text. More than 10 thousands documents downloaded during the week after each of the two terrorism events occurred.

KSB-100 dataset has 100 documents, of which 34 are relevant and 66 irrelevant. The 34 relevant documents were selected by an expert familiar with the beheading event. The 66 irrelevant documents were selected from the ten thousands documents downloaded during the week after the event occurred.

These irrelevant documents were intentionally selected among those describing some other criminal events, such as murders and kidnaps. We use the word *"kill", "murder", "kidnap",* and the synonyms obtained using WordNet[3] to select these irrelevant documents with the help of some search engines. In other words, both relevant and irrelevant documents describe some terrorism and crime related events. This increases the level of difficulty in document ranking. The entity and relation instances about the event were then determined by an expert from the relevant documents as shown in Figure 15-3. In Figure 15-3, the number assigned to each entity/relation instance denotes the number of documents where the entity/relation instance appears. To simulate a user conducting domain specific event entity and relation extraction task, query seed words are then chosen. The query seed words used in the extraction task for this dataset are *"Kim Sun", "Al-Qaeda Cell"* and *"Beheading of Kim Sun".* The seeds were chosen randomly from the entity relation graph of KSB-100.

AEB-100 dataset has 100 documents consisting of 34 relevant documents and 66 irrelevant documents. The 34 relevant documents were selected in a same manner as for KSB-100 dataset by an expert familiar with the event. The 66 irrelevant documents are the same as those used in KSB-100 dataset. Figure 15-4 shows the entity relation graph of AEB-100. The query seed words for AEB-100 are: *"Australian Embassy", "Australian Embassy Bombing", "Suicide Bombers" and "Elisabeth Musu".* Among the seeds of AEB-100, Elisabeth Musu was chosen to ensure the seeds are connected to all other instances in the entity relation graph.

---

[3] WordNet[31] is an English lexical database.

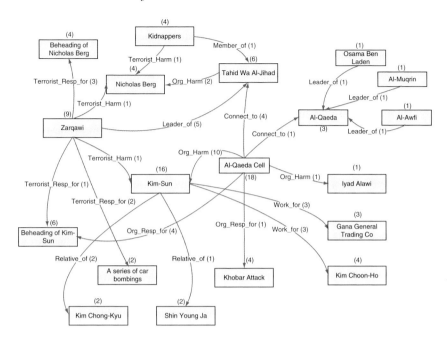

Figure 15-3. Entity Relation Graph of KSB event.

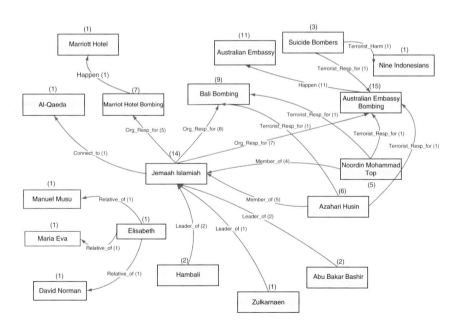

Figure 15-4. Entity Relation Graph of AEB event

In the terrorism domain, we have adopted seven *entity classes* and ten *relation classes*. The entity classes include *Victim, Terrorist, Terrorist Org, Event, Location, Employer,* and *Relative*. The relation classes are *Terrorist_Harm* [4] , *Org_Harm* [5] , *Connect_to, Terrorist_Resp_for* [6] , *Org_Resp_for*[7] *Member_of, Leader_of, Happen, Work_for,* and *Relative_of*. Each relation class is defined for a pair of source and target entity classes as shown in Table 15-1. Table 15-2 shows more detailed information about the three datasets.

Table 15-1. relation classes with their source and target entity classes

<Relation>	(<SrcEnt>,<TgtEnt>)	<Relation>	(<SrcEnt>,<TgtEnt>)
Terrorist_Harm	(Terrorist, Victim)	*Org_Harm*	(Terrorist Org, Victim)
Connect_to	(Terrorist Org, Terrorist Org)	*Terrorist_Resp_for*	(Terrorist, Event)

Table 15-2. Detailed Information of the three datasets.

	$|\varepsilon|$	$|\Re|$	# of relevant docs	# of optimal docs	Total # of docs
KSB-100	18	22	34	9	100
AEB-100	19	20	34	9	100

4.2   Information Extraction System Components

As shown in Algorithm 1, our experiments require a set of extraction patterns and some IE system components in the extraction step. These components have been chosen based on their availabilities. In general, our proposed document ranking strategies are independent of the IE system components used, and the latter can be treated as a "black box".

In our experiments, we use Crystal [13] and BBN's IdentiFinder [32] for extracting entity and relation instances. Crystal can learn a set of single-slot and multi-slot extraction patterns from a training text corpus. The extraction pattern generated is called concept node in Crystal. Crystal is part of the Badger information extraction software suite created by the Center for Intelligent Information Retrieval at the University of Massachusetts [33]. IdentiFinder is a well-known named entity extraction system and we used it to extract entity instances.

---

[4] This represents a terrorist harming some victim.

[5] This represents a terrorist organization harming some victim.

[6] This represents the terrorist responsible for an event.

[7] This represents the terrorist organization responsible for an event.

The objective of domain entity and relation extraction system components is to determine the domain specific entity instances and inter-relationships among them as opposed to general named entity recognition. Moreover, we would like to determine the semantic classes for these entity and relation instances.

Extraction of Entity Instances We adopted IdentiFinder and implemented two other entity extraction modules to extract the entity instances from each document.

1. IdentiFinder

   IdentiFinder was used to extract person names, organization names and locations from each document. It however could not assign domain specific semantic classes to the extracted entity instances. This was because IdentiFinder could only extract general types of named entities. However, since our proposed document ranking strategies do not incorporate entity classes into the score function, it was fine to apply IdentiFinder to extract entity instances without assigning their corresponding domain specific semantic classes in our experiments.

2. Known Directory of Terrorists and Organizations

   In our work, we gathered 21 terrorist names from the FBI website[8] and 54 terrorist organization names from the ICT website[9]. These well-known terrorists and terrorist organizations were added to our extracted entity instances set if they were found in a document.

3. Crystal Single-Slot Extraction Patterns

   A set of single-slot extraction patterns based on some common linguistic structures was used to extract the domain specific entity instances of the defined entity classes. The linguistic structures include <Subject> <Verb> <Object>, <Subject> <Verb> <Prepositional Phrase>, <Verb> <Object> <Prepositional Phrase>, and <Subject> <Prepositional Phrase>. Each part of the linguistic structure was treated as a slot in the extraction pattern. By leaving one slot as a variable without constraining it to some entity instances or action instances, we obtained multiple single-slot extraction patterns. For example, <Subject(Terrorist)> <Verb("belong")> <Object("Al-Qaeda Cell")> is a single-slot extraction pattern that is used to extract instances of entity class *Terrorist*, in which the slot <Subject(Terrorist)> is a variable and the other two slots are constrained by the action instance "belong" and the entity instance "Al-Qaeda Cell" respectively.

---

[8] http://www.fbi.gov/mostwant/terrorists/fugitives.htm

[9] http://www.ict.org.il

The list of terrorist names and terrorist organization names were used to obtain some single-slot extraction patterns in our experiments.

Extraction of Relation Instances   In   order   to   extract   relation instances, we used some multi-slot extraction patterns. By constraining only one slot of some linguistic structures and leaving at least 2 slots as variables, we   obtained   some   multi-slot   extraction   patterns.   For   example, <Subject(Terrorist)> <Verb("belong")> <Object(Terrorist Org)> is a multi-slot extraction pattern that can extract an instance of the *Member Of* relation. The entity class variables (i.e., *Terrorist* and *Terrorist Org*) in parentheses represent entities to be extracted to form a relation. To generalize the multi-slot extraction pattern, we used WordNet[31] to obtain other action instances with similar meaning. For example, "belong" was replaced by "is member of", "part of", etc., to obtain other extraction patterns.

We manually created the set of multi-slot extraction patterns based on Crystal Concept Node format. There were 41 different multi-slot extraction patterns created in this experiment. Readers can refer to [12] for some examples of extraction patterns used in our work.

4.3   Evaluation Settings

Our experiments evaluated all five document ranking strategies, namely: DiffCompare,   CombineCompare,   PartialMatch   I,   PartialMatch   II   and PartialMatch+. We assumed the user always select the document with the highest score assigned by each strategy during the extraction task. It is possible that multiple documents will be assigned the same highest score by some   document   ranking   strategies.   We   therefore   propose   two   steps   to resolve this. The first step is to sort the documents with the same score by their initial scores and the one with highest initial score will be selected. If identical scores are still observed after the first step, random selection will be performed among the documents.

In all the experiments, we set $\alpha = 0.6$ to give more weight to relation instances instead of entity instances as some entity instances are already part of relation instances. For CombineCompare, we set $\beta = 0.8$ as it gave the best   performance   among   different β values   we   experimented.   For PartialMatch II, we set $\alpha = 0.5$ to give equal importance to both seeds and user extracted entity instances. We ran through the extraction task over 100 iterations. To have a more detailed analysis of the performance of different strategies, we zoomed into the first 45 iterations of the extraction task in the experiment.

Ideal Document Ranking Strategy   We introduce an ideal document ranking strategy here to compare it with our proposed document ranking strategies. The ideal strategy selects for each iteration a document that gives the largest gain in performance (according to the chosen performance metric) and the selected document must be a relevant document. Here, the ideal strategy assumes that instances in the entity relation graph are known. Therefore, the score formula for ideal document ranking strategy is defined as follows:

$$score(d_i) = M(d_i)$$

where M refers to the improvement of the performance metric brought by the document d_i. Refer to Section 4.3 for the set of performance metrics to be measured.

Note that the ideal document ranking strategy is not feasible in practice as we do not know the entity/relation instances to be extracted from each document beforehand.

Plus(+) Document Ranking Strategy Plus(+) is an enhancement that can be applied to any of the proposed pattern-based strategies (i.e., DiffCompare, CombineCompare, PartialMatch I and II). The idea is to incrementally increase the number of single-slot extraction patterns by instantiating some slots of some extraction patterns with new entity instances. For example, <Subject(Terrorist)> <hVerb("belong")> <Object("Al-Qaeda Cell")> is a single-slot extraction pattern that can extract an instance of the *Terrorist* entity class. Suppose a new entity instance "Tawhid Wa Al-Jihad" of entity class *Terrorist Org* is manually extracted (labeled) by a user. By instantiating the "Object" slot with this newly found entity instance, we obtain a new single-slot extraction pattern, which is <Subject(Terrorist)> <Verb("belong")> <Object("Tawhid Wa Al-Jihad")>. The new single-slot extraction pattern may extract more relation instances. Once some entity instances of the *Terrorist* class are extracted by the pattern, some new relation instances representing the connections between those entity instances and "Tawhid Wa Al-Jihad" may also be extracted.

The Plus-based methods apply a new set of extraction patterns in every iteration. Thus, this strategy requires additional computational efforts. So far, we have enhanced PartialMatch I with Plus and named it PartialMatch plus(+).

Performance Metrics We propose a set of performance metrics defined below and they were derived after every document was selected. These performance metrics focus on how much relevant instances the selected documents contain, how accurate the relevant documents or optimal documents are selected.

1. Evaluation on Extracted Entity and Relation Instances

Suppose we have all relevant entity instances in set ε_r and all relevant relation instances in set $\Re_r$. To evaluate on the resultant instance sets obtained in extraction task i.e., ε and $\Re$, the recall measure is defined as follows:

$$\operatorname{Recall}_{average} = \tfrac{1}{2}\left(\operatorname{Recall}_{entity} + \operatorname{Recall}_{relation}\right)$$

where $\operatorname{Recall}_{entity} = \dfrac{\left|\varepsilon_r \cap \varepsilon\right|}{\varepsilon_r}$ and $\operatorname{Recall}_{relation} = \dfrac{\left|\Re_r \cap \Re\right|}{\Re_r}$

2. Evaluation on Document Ranking

Let L be the set of all relevant documents and S denote the set of selected documents. The precision and recall measures with respect to the relevant documents are defined as follows:

$$\operatorname{Recall}_{rel\_doc} = \frac{\left|S \cap L\right|}{\left|L\right|}$$

$$\operatorname{Precision}_{rel\_doc} = \frac{\left|S \cap L\right|}{\left|S\right|}$$

Suppose there are v different optimal sets among all relevant documents as the optimal set is not always unique. Let O denote the set of all optimal sets, i.e., $O = \{O_1, O_2, ..., O_v\}$. We have $|O_1| = |O_2| = ... = |O_v|$. Therefore, the recall and precision with respect to optimal set are defined as follows:

$$\operatorname{Recall}_{opt\_doc} = \frac{\max_{O_i \in O}\left|O_i \cap S\right|}{\left|O_1\right|}$$

$$\operatorname{Precision}_{opt\_doc} = \frac{\max_{O_i \in O}\left|O_i \cap S\right|}{\left|S\right|}$$

Since $Precision_{rel\_doc}$ and $Precision_{opt\_doc}$ can be directly derived from $Recall_{rel\_doc}$ and $Recall_{opt\_doc}$ respectively for each iteration, we therefore decided not to use them in the subsequent evaluations.

4.4   Experimental Results

In this section, we show the experimental results of six document ranking strategies on the two auto-coreferenced[10] datasets AEB-100 and KSB-100. Results on a manually coreferenced set has been reported previously[34].

---

[10] Coreference resolution was performed completely by a computer program using some heuristics and algorithms.

We also present some experimental results using difference choices of seeds on the auto-coreferenced datasets in both KSB-100 and AEB-100.

Datasets with Auto-Coreference Resolution In this section, we present the experimental results of different document ranking strategies on the KSB-100 and AEB-100 datasets with auto-coreference resolution. We used the same seeds as in the manually-coreferenced experiments [34], so as to obtain a fair comparison.

KSB-100: Figure 15-5 shows the $Recall_{average}$ of KSB-100 dataset.

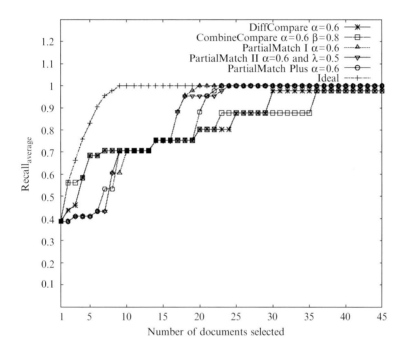

Figure 15-5. Performance on Extracted Instances (auto-co referenced KSB-100).

PartialMatch I achieved perfect recall with the smallest number of iterations (20th) for this dataset. PartialMatch+ was next and gave perfect recall at the 23rd iteration. PartialMatch II performed slightly worse than PartialMatch+ and achieved perfect recall at the 24th iteration. DiffCompare was better than CombineCompare, but none of them could achieve perfect recall in the first 45 iterations. Figure 15-6 shows PartialMatch+ outperformed other strategies on selecting the relevant documents, and Figure 15-7 shows PartialMatch I found the optimal document set earlier than the other strategies.

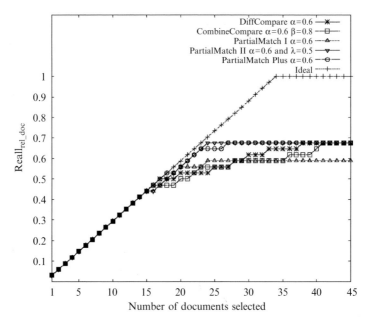

Figure 15-6. Document ranking recall (auto-co referenced KSB-100) with respect to relevant document

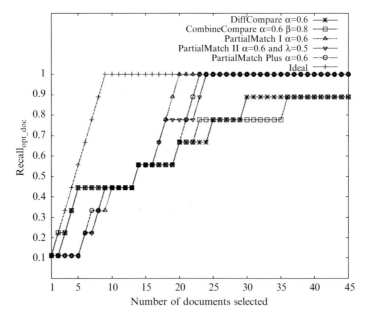

Figure 15-7. Document ranking recall (auto-coreferenced KSB-100) with respect to optimal set

AEB-100: Figure 15-8 shows the Recall$_{average}$ for AEB-100 dataset. We observed that PartialMatch I, PartialMatch II and PartialMatch+ performed consistently better than CombineCompare and DiffCompare in the first 25 iterations. Only at the 43th iteration and beyond did CombineCompare and DiffCompare performed better than the rest and achieved perfect Recall$_{average}$.

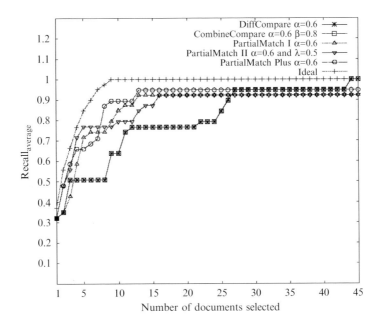

Figure 15-8. Performance on Extracted Instances (auto-coreferenced AEB-100)

Figures 15-9 and 15-10 show that PartialMatch I, PartialMatch II, and PartialMatch+ outperformed DiffCompare and CombineCompare in the first 25 iterations on both *Recall$_{rel\_doc}$* and *Recall$_{opt\_doc}$*, which were similar to our previous observations on the manually-coreferenced experiments.

We conclude from the results on datasets with auto-coreference resolution that auto-coreference resolution affected the performance of different document ranking strategies adversely compared to the manually-coreferenced results reported in [34]. This was due to wrongly coreferenced objects suggested by our auto-coreferencing algorithm. However, the relative performances of different document ranking strategies remained the same. For the auto-coreferenced AEB-100 dataset, DiffCompare achieved perfect *Recall$_{average}$* at the 44th iteration.

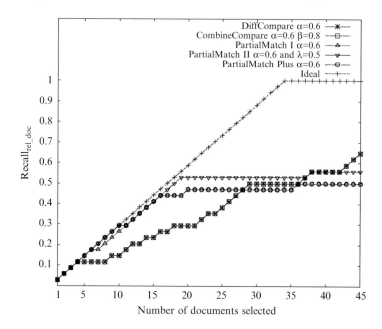

Figure 15-9. Document ranking recall (auto-coreferenced AEB-100) with respect to relevant documents

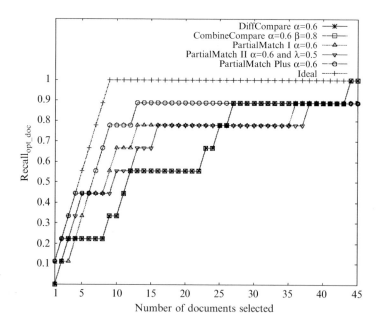

Figure 15-10. Document ranking recall (auto-coreferenced AEB-100) with respect to the optimal set

Table 15-3 shows a summary on different datasets with the best performance strategies in different evaluations. The number shown in brackets indicates the number of iterations required for the document ranking strategy to achieve perfect recall with the particular evaluation metric. Since none of the document ranking strategies could achieve perfect $Recall_{rel\_doc}$ for all datasets in the first 45 iterations, the percentage of $Recall_{rel\_doc}$ found by individual strategy within the first 45 iterations are shown in brackets.

Table 15-3. Summary of winning strategies on different datasets.

	Manual Coreference Resolution		Auto Coreference Resolution	
Metrics	KSB-100	AEB-100	KSB-100	AEB-100
$Recall_{average}$	PartialMatch I	Partial Match I	PartialMatch I	DiffCompare
	(19)	(14)	(20)	(44)
$Recall_{rel\_doc}$	PartialMatch II	PartialMatch+	PartialMatch+	DiffCompare
	(68%)	(61%)	(68%)	(62%)
$Recall_{opt\_doc}$	PartialMatch I	PartialMatch I	PartialMatch I	DiffCompare
	(19)	(14)	(20)	(44)

Choice of Seeds   In the following, we show the experimental results of five document ranking strategies with different choices of seeds. We chose the following seeds in the experiments:

- Randomly picked 2 most frequent entity instances as seeds (MF2)
- Randomly picked 3 most frequent entity instances as seeds (MF3)
- Randomly picked 4 most frequent entity instances as seeds (MF4)
- Randomly picked 2 least frequent entity instances as seeds (LF2)
- Randomly picked 3 least frequent entity instances as seeds (LF3)
- Randomly picked 4 least frequent entity instances as seeds (LF4)

We expected that with the most frequent entity instances as seeds, the different strategies should be able to take fewer iterations to extract all the instances and find all the optimal documents than using the least frequent entity instances as seeds.

Figures 15-11 to 15-13 show the performance of different ranking strategies on the KSB-100 dataset with MF2. PartialMatch I was the best performer, achieving perfect $Recall_{average}$ at the 20th iteration, and it also found the optimal set of documents. PartialMatch+ and PartialMatch II outperformed all other strategies on selecting the relevant documents. DiffCompare and CombineCompare gave the worst performance over all evaluations. Similar observations can be drawn for MF3 and MF4 on the KSB-100 dataset, and their results are not shown.

Figures 15-14 to 15-16 show the performance with LF2 as seeds. PartialMatch II achieved perfect $Recall_{average}$ at the 25th iteration, while other document ranking strategies could not achieve perfect recall within the first 45 iterations. However, we noticed that the performance of DiffCompare, CombineCompare, PartialMatch I, and PartialMatch+ were quite close to the perfect recall (above 95%) at the 45th iteration. PartialMatch II outperformed the other strategies on selecting the relevant documents, followed by PartialMatch+. It also outperformed the other strategies on finding the optimal documents. PartialMatch II considers both accumulated user annotated entity instances and seeds, therefore it is more likely to pick up those documents containing the entity instances but not seeds. Again, as the results of the five document ranking strategies using LF3 and LF4 on KSB-100 were similar to the results of LF2, we have left out their figures.

The performances of the five document ranking strategies on AEB-100 with different choices of seeds were found to be similar to those on the KSB-100. We conclude that using difference choices of seeds with the similar frequency will not affect the performance of the document ranking strategies very much. However, using the least frequent entity instances as seeds adversely affected the performance of different strategies compared to those using the most frequent entity instances as seeds.

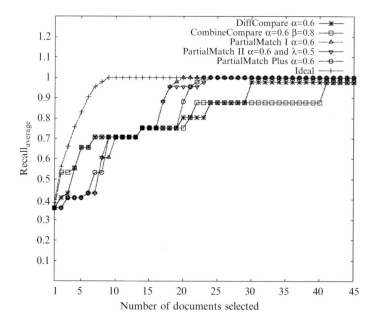

Figure 15-11. Performance on Extracted Instances (auto-coreferened KSB-100 with MF2)

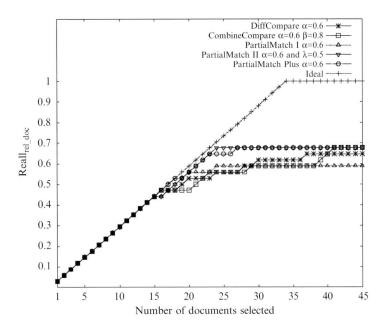

Figure 15-12. Performance on Extracted Instances (auto-co referenced KSB-100 with MF2).

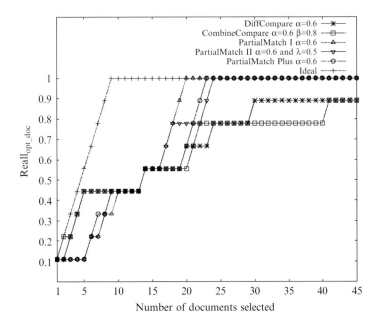

Figure 15-13. Document ranking recall (auto-co referenced KSB-100 with MF2) with respect to the optimal set.

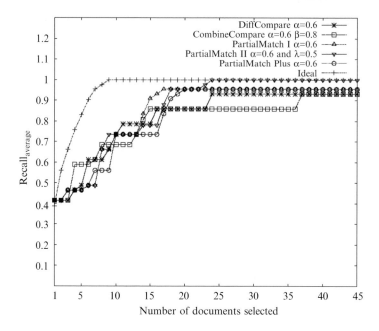

Figure 15-14. Performance on Extracted Instances (auto-co referenced KSB-100 with LF2).

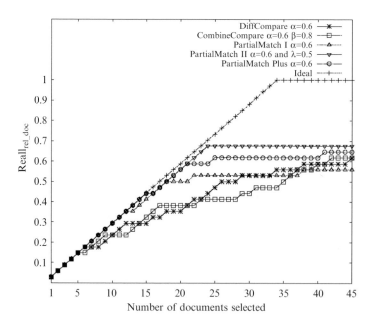

Figure 15-15. Document ranking recall (auto-co referenced KSB-100 with LF2) with respect to relevant documents.

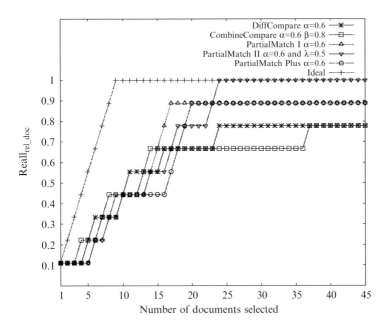

Figure 15-16. Document ranking recall (auto-co referenced KSB-100 with LF2) with respect to the optimal set.

Comparisons between Pattern-based vs Content-based Document Ranking Strategies COMPARE and EXTRACTCOMPARE are two document ranking strategies based on document content described in [24] (see section 3.4). Originally they were developed for identifying documents to be manually labeled by an expert so as to learn some extraction patterns from them. Since PartialMatch I usually performs better than the other four document ranking strategies, we now try to use these two content-based document ranking strategies for the extraction task and compare them with PartialMatch I.

As shown in Figure 15-17, PartialMatch I outperformed COMPARE and EXTRACTCOMPARE in *Recall_average*. PartialMatch I achieved perfect recall on the 14th iteration. In contrast, EXTRACTCOMPARE could only achieve 57% *Recall_average* in the first 45 iterations, followed by COMPARE at 48% *Recall_average*.

Figures 15-18 and 15-19 show that COMPARE and EXTRACTCOMPARE could find only half the number of relevant and optimal documents compared to PartialMatch I in the first 45 iterations. We therefore conclude that PartialMatch I outperforms the two content-based strategies on the proposed domain specific event entity' and relation extraction task. We obtained the same finding for the KSB-100 dataset.

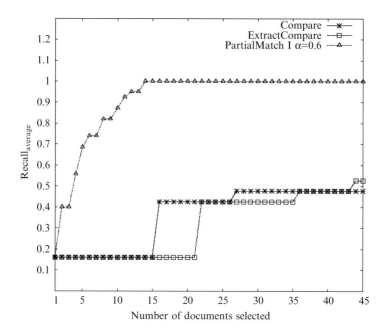

Figure 15-17. Performance evaluation with respect to extracted instances

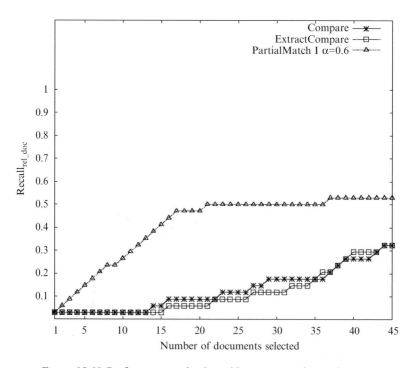

Figure 15-18. Performance evaluation with respect to relevant documents

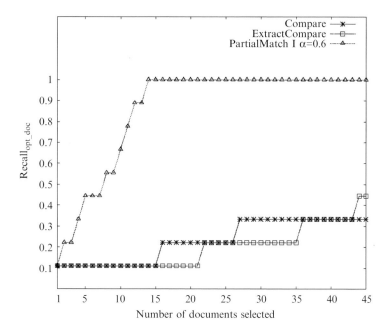

Figure 15-19. Performance evaluation with respect to optimal documents

5.   CONCLUSIONS AND DISCUSSION

We have presented a new domain specific event entity and relation extraction task and developed five pattern-based document ranking strategies. Our primary objective is to select as few documents as possible to construct the entity and relation instances related to some event of interest to the user.

We have defined performance metrics to measure the performance of different document ranking strategies. We also constructed two datasets about two recent terrorism events for experimental evaluations. The results conclude that PartialMatch I was likely to perform better than the other pattern-based document ranking strategies and was better than some existing content-based document ranking strategies on both KSB-100 and AEB-100 datasets.

For future work, we propose the following two directions:
1. Enhancement on the proposed document ranking strategies
   We have shown that our proposed strategies work well on the event entity and relation extraction task and maintain good performance on large document collection. Nevertheless, more investigations are required to further improve their performance. Currently, PartialMatch I gave the best performance on selecting the optimal documents and finding instances from small document collection. PartialMatch+ delivered a

better performance than the other strategies on selecting the relevant documents and also performed well on the large dataset. It will be therefore interesting to explore a combination of strategies to give a better performance in document ranking.

2. Enhancement of Extraction Techniques

We also plan to investigate the impact of IE system components on the extraction task performance. Currently, the performance of our proposed strategies is highly dependent on the performance of IE. Although we have adapted several entity extraction system components, such as IdentiFinder, crystal single-slot extraction patterns, and applying a known dictionary of Terrorists and Organizations, quite a few useful instances in the documents were still missed. Therefore an improved IE system component would contribute to more accurate event entity relation extraction.

6.   ACKNOWLEDGEMENTS

This research was supported in part by a grant from the University Research Council URC RG10/05.

REFERENCES

1. bombsecurity.com: Extremists online, http://www.bombsecurity.com/extremists.html (2006)
2. Apache: Lucene search engine. http://jakarta.apache.org/lucene (2006)
3. Baeza-Yates, R., Ribeiro-Neto, B.: Modern Information Retrieval. Addison Wesley (1999)
4. Techner, K.: A literature survey on information extraction and text summarization. Computational Linguistics Program (1997)
5. Palmer, D.D., Day, D.S.: A statistical profile of the named entity task. In: Proceedings of the Fifth ACL Conference for Applied Natural Language Processing. (1997)
6. Riloff, E.: Automatically constructing a dictionary form information extraction tasks. In: Proceedings of the Eleventh National Conference on Artificial Intelligence. (1993)
7. Riloff, E., Shoen, J.: Automatically acquiring conceptual patterns without an annotated corpus. In: Proceedings of the Third Workshop on Very Large Corpora. (1995)
8. Riloff, E.: Automatically generating extraction patterns from untagged text. In: Proceedings of the Thirteenth National Conference on Artificial Intelligence. (1996)
9. Riloff, E., Jones, R.: Learning dictionaries for information extraction by multi-level bootstrapping. In: Proceedings of the Sixteenth National Conference on Artificial Intelligence. (1999)
10. Thelen, M., Riloff, E.: A bootstrapping method for learning semantic lexicons using extraction pattern contexts. In: Proceedings of the 2002 Conference on Empirical Methods in Natural Language Processing. (2002)
11. Guo, Z., Jian, S.: A high-performance coreference resolution system using a multi-agent

strategy. In: Proceedings of 20th International Conference on Computational Linguistics. (2004)

12. Sun, Z.: Domain specific event information extraction on large text collections. Master's thesis, Nanyang Technological University, School of Computer Engineering (2006)

13. Soderland, S., Fisher, D., Aseltine, J., Lehnert, W.: Crystal: Inducing a conceptual dictionary. In: Proceedings of the Fourteenth International Joint Conference on Artificial Intelligence. (1995)

14. Soderland, S.: Learning to extract text-based information from the world wide web. In: Proceedings of the Third International Conference on Knowledge Discovery and Data Mining. (1997)

15. Krupka, G.: Description of the SRA system as used for MUC. In: Proceedings of the Sixth Message Understanding Conference. (1995)

16. Huffman, S.: Learning information extraction patterns from examples. In: Proceedings of IJCAI-95Workshop on new approaches to learning for natural language processing. (1995)

17. Kim, J., Moldavan, D.: Acquisition of linquistic patterns for knowledge-based information extraction. In: IEEE Transactions on Knowledge and Data Engineering. (1995)

18. Muslea, I.: Extraction patterns for information extraction tasks: A survey. In: Proceedings of AAAI99 Workshop on Machine Learning for Information Extraction. (1999)

19. Agichtein, E., Gravano, L.: Snowball: Extracting relations from large plain-text collections. In: Proceedings of the Fifth ACM International Conference on Digital Libraries. (2000)

20. Goldstein, J., Mittal, V.O., Carbonell, J.G., Callan, J.P.: Creating and evaluating multi-document sentence extract summaries. In: CIKM. (2000) 165–172 21.

21. Masterson, D., Kushmerick, N.: Information extraction from multi-document threads. In: Proceedings of ATEM. (2003)

22. Reidsma, D., Kuper, J., Declerck, T., Saggion, H., Cunningham, H.: Cross document ontology based information extraction for multimedia retrieval. In: Supplementary proceedings of the ICCS03. (2003)

23. Agichtein, E., Gravano, L.: Querying text database for efficient information extraction. In: Proceedings of the 2002 Conference on the 19th IEEE International Conference on Data Engineering. (2003)

24. Finn, A., Kushmerick, N.: Active learning selection strategies for information extraction. In: Proceedings of ATEM. (2003)

25. Madhyastha, H.V., Balakrishnan, N., Ramakrishnan, K.R.: Event information extraction using link grammar. In: Proceedings of the 13th International WorkShop on Research Issues in Data Engineering: Multi-lingual Information Management. (2003)

26. Allan, J., Papka, R., Lavrenko, V.: On-line new event detection and tracking. In: SIGIR '98: Proceedings of the 21st annual international ACM SIGIR conference on Research and development in information retrieval, ACM Press (1998) 37–45

27. Brants, T., Chen, F.: A system for new event detection. In: SIGIR '03: Proceedings of the 26th annual international ACM SIGIR conference on Research and development in informaion retrieval, ACM Press (2003) 330–337

28. Kumaran, G., Allan, J.: Text classification and named entities for new event detection. In: SIGIR '04: Proceedings of the 27th annual international conference on Research and development in information retrieval, ACM Press (2004) 297–304

29. Chen, F.R., Farahat, A.O., Brants, T.: Story link detection and new event detection are asymmetric. In: Proceedings of Human Language Technology Conference (HLT-NAACL 2003). (2003)

30. Yang, Y., Carbonell, J., Brown, R., Pierce, T., Archibald, B.T., Liu, X.: Learning approaches for detecting and tracking news events. In: IEEE Intelligent Systems, 14(4):32–43. (1999)
31. Fellbaum, C.: Wordnet: An electronic lexical database. MIT Press (1998)
32. Bikel, D.M., Schwartz, R.L., Weischedel, R.M.: An algorithm that learns whats in a name. Machine Learning 34(1-3) (1999) 211–231
33. Various: Badger information extraction (ie) software. http://www.nlp.cs.umass.edu/software/badger.html (2006)
34. Sun, Z., Lim, E.P., Chang, K., Ong, T.K., Gunaratna, R.K.: Event-driven document selection for terrorism information extraction. In Kantor, P., Muresan, G., Roberts, F., D., D., eds.: IEEE International Conference on Intelligence and Security. Lecture Notes in Computer Science, Berlin Heidelberg, Springer Verlag (2005) 37–48

SUGGESTED READINGS

- For more details about this work, refer to Sun's thesis [12].
- See Muslea's work [18] for a comprehensive survey of IE tasks.
- Read more on Riloff's AutoSlog IE software [9].

ONLINE RESOURCES

- FBI list of terrorists,
  http://www.fbi.gov/mostwant/terrorists/fugitives.htm
- ICT list of terrorist organizations,   http://www.ict.org.il
- Web Hamas, http://www.bombsecurity.com/extremists.html
- BADGER IE software suite (open source),
  http://www-nlp.cs.umass.edu/software/badger.html
- Lucene Search Engine (open source),
  http://jakarta.apache.org/lucene

DISCUSSION QUESTIONS

1. How should the α parameter in PartialMatch be selected? Should it be static or dynamic?
2. Does the selection of seed words affect the quality of extracted entities and relations?
3. What type of seed words are desirable?
4. How would the system benefit multiple analysts collaborating to track a single terrorism event in real time? What modifications or additions would be useful?
5. What are the changes required to apply the system to a language such as Arabic?

16

DATA DISTORTION METHODS AND METRICS IN A TERRORIST ANALYSIS SYSTEM

Shuting Xu[1] and Jun Zhang[2]

[1] Department of Computer Information Systems, Virginia State University, Petersburg, Virginia, U.S.A. (sxu@vsu.edu); [2] Department of Computer Science, University of Kentucky, Lexington, Kentucky, U.S.A. (jzhang@cs.uky.edu)

CHAPTER OVERVIEW

Preserving privacy is a major concern in the application of data mining techniques to datasets containing personal, sensitive, or confidential information. Data distortion is a critical component to preserving privacy in security-related data mining applications, such as in data mining-based terrorist analysis systems. A sparsified Singular Value Decomposition (SVD) method for data distortion is introduced in this chapter. A few metrics to measure the difference between the distorted dataset and the original dataset and the degree of the privacy protection are also explained in detail. The experimental results using synthetic and real world datasets show that the sparsified SVD method works well in preserving privacy as well as maintaining utility of the datasets.

1.   INTRODUCTION

With the widespread availability of modern computing technology, the advance of fast data collection techniques, and the affordability of vast volume of data storage devices, data of various kinds are collected at an unprecedented speed and scale. The need for understanding and making use of the collected data sparks renewed interest in studying and developing data mining techniques, i.e., the use of computer-aided statistical techniques to "comb" through large amount of data for automatic and semi-automatic exploration and pattern discovery. Today, data is one of the most important corporate assets of companies, governments, and research institutions (Estvill-Castro 1999) and is used for various private and public interest.

The use of data mining technologies in counterterrorism and homeland security has been flourishing since the U.S. Government encouraged the use of such technologies (Taipale 2003). However, government access to and use of personal information in commercial databases raise concerns about the protection of privacy and due process (Dempsey 2004). Recent privacy criticism from libertarians on DARPA's[1] Terrorism Information Awareness Program led to the defunding of DARPA's Information Awareness Office. Thus, it is necessary that data mining technologies designed for counterterrorism and security purpose have sufficient privacy awareness to protect the privacy of innocent people. Unfortunately, most existing data mining technologies are not very efficient in terms of privacy protections, as they were originally developed mainly for commercial applications, in which different organizations collect and own their databases, and mine their databases for specific commercial purposes. In the cases of security and counterterrorism, data mining may mean a totally different thing. Government may potentially have access to any databases and may extract any information from these databases. This potentially unlimited access to data and information raises the fear of possible abuse.

Data can be collected at a centralized location or collected at different locations, but integrated at a centralized location (data warehousing). Alternatively, data can be collected and stored at distributed locations. Different data storage patterns may have different privacy concerns. If the data storage is centralized, the major privacy concern is to shield the exact values of the attributes from the data analysts. Thus, data distortion is a technique that is usually considered in such a situation (Agrawal and Aggarwal 2001; Liew 1985). On the other hand, in a distributed database situation, the major privacy concern is to maintain the independence of the distributed data ownership and to prevent the exchange of exact values of the

---

[1] DARPA stands for Defense Advanced Research Projects Agency, affiliated with the Department of Defense of the United States (Tether 2003).

attributes between different parties of the distributed database ownership. This concern is related to the issue of data mining in a distributed environment (Agrawal et al. 2003; Gilburd et al. 2004). This chapter deals with the first situation, i.e., we study data distortion techniques for a centralized database.

We introduce a class of methods for privacy protection in data processing that may be used in some terrorist analysis systems and other data mining applications. We assume that the vector-space model (Frankes 1992) is used to build the population datasets for analysis. A dataset can be represented by a matrix A. Each row of the matrix represents an object, and each column of the matrix represents an attribute. In modeling populations with individual persons, the dataset matrix is usually sparse, as many of the attributes are not taken by most of the objects simultaneously. The objects can be individual persons of the general population. The attributes can be a person's name, address, age, home address, credit card numbers, etc. Thus, information contained in such datasets is highly confidential. The confidentiality of the personal information should not be compromised in the process of data mining applications.

In order to preserve data privacy, we assume that no one except the data owner or authorized users have the right to access the original data. The analysts will only see the distorted dataset matrix $\bar{A}$, not the original dataset A. The distorted dataset matrix does not have an obvious meaning for the individual attributes. The matrix $\bar{A}$ cannot be used to reconstruct the original matrix A, without knowing the error part $E = A - \bar{A}$. In this way, the analysts, who will run the data mining algorithms on the distorted dataset matrix $\bar{A}$, will not be able to know the original attributes or the distribution of the attributes, unless appropriate permission is granted by higher level officials to do so. Thus, data mining techniques applied on the distorted datasets will maintain the inherent property of privacy protection.

In this chapter, we will discuss several data distortion methods that can be used in protecting privacy in some terrorist analysis systems. We propose a sparsified Singular Value Decomposition (SVD) method for data distortion. There are some publications about using SVD-related methods in counterterrorism data mining techniques, such as in detecting local correlation (Skillicorn 2003), social network analysis (Skillicorn 2004), novel information discovery (Skillicorn and Vats 2004) and information extraction (Sun 2003), etc. However, to the best of our knowledge, there has been no work on using SVD-related methods in data distortion. We also propose some metrics to measure the difference between the distorted dataset and the original dataset and the degree of privacy protection. Our experimental results using both synthetic and real world datasets will show that the sparsified SVD method is very efficient in keeping both data privacy and data utility.

2.   TERRORIST ANALYSIS SYSTEM

A simplified model terrorist analysis system can be consisted of two parts, the data manipulation part and the data analysis part. As illustrated in Figure 16-1, we assume that only the data owner or authorized users can manipulate the original data. After the data distortion process, the original dataset is transformed into a completely different data matrix and is provided to the analysts. All actions in the data analysis part are operated on the distorted data matrix. For example, the analysts can apply data mining techniques such as classification, relationship analysis, or clustering, on the distorted data. As the data analysts have no access to the original database without the authorization of the data owner, the privacy contained in the original data is protected. *k*-anonymity protection (Sweeney 2002) and its variance have been used in similar scenarios, but they do not work for data distortion.

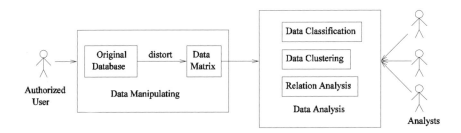

Figure 16-1.

3.   DATA DISTORTION

Data distortion is one of the most important parts in the proposed model terrorist analysis system. The desired distortion methods must preserve privacy, and at the same time, must keep the utility of the data after the distortion (Verykios et al. 2004). Some data distortion methods based on random value have been proposed and applied in (Agrawal and Srikant 2000; Datta et al. 2003; Liew et al. 1985). We will review two of the commonly used random value data distortion methods, as well as propose a class of SVD-based methods for data distortion in this section.

3.1 Uniformly distributed noise

In this method, the original data matrix A is added by a uniformly distributed noise matrix N_u (Agrawal and Srikant 2000). N_u is of the same size as A, and its elements are random numbers chosen from the continuous uniform distribution on the interval from C_1 to C_2. The distorted matrix $\bar{A}_u$ is: $\bar{A}_u = A + N_u$.

3.2 Normally distributed noise

Similarly as the previous method, here the original data matrix A is added by a normally distributed noise matrix N_n, which has the same size as A (Agrawal and Srikant 2000). The elements of N_n are random numbers chosen from the normal distribution with parameters mean μ and standard deviation σ. The distorted matrix $\bar{A}_n$ is: $\bar{A}_n = A + N_n$.

3.3 Singular Value Decomposition

Singular Value Decomposition (SVD) (Golub and Loan 1996) is a popular method in data mining and information retrieval (Deerwester 1990), since it has a mathematical feature to find a rank-κ approximation of a matrix with minimal change to that matrix for a given value of κ (Eckart and Young 1936). It is usually used to reduce the dimensionality of the original dataset. Here we use it as a data distortion method.

Let A be a matrix of dimension $n \times m$ representing the original dataset. The rows of the matrix correspond to data objects and the columns to attributes. The singular value decomposition of the matrix A is (Golub and Loan 1996)

$$A = U\Sigma V^T$$

Equation 16-1

where U is an $n \times n$ orthonormal matrix having the left singular vectors of A as its columns and Σ is an $n \times m$ diagonal matrix whose nonnegative diagonal entries are the singular values in a descending order.

$$\Sigma = diag[\sigma_1, \sigma_2, \cdots, \sigma_S], S = \min\{m, n\}$$

Equation 16-2

The number of nonzero entries in the main diagonal of Σ is equal to the rank of the matrix A. V^T is an $m \times m$ orthonormal matrix having the right singular vectors of A as its rows. These three matrices reflect a breakdown of original relationship into linearly independent vectors.

Due to the arrangement of the singular values in the matrix Σ (in a descending order), the SVD transformation has the property that the maximal variation among the objects is captured in the first dimension, as $\sigma_1 > \sigma_i$, for $i > 2$. Similarly much of the remaining variations are captured in the second dimension, and so on. Thus, a transformed matrix with a much lower dimension can be constructed to represent the original matrix faithfully.

We can create a rank-κ approximation A_k to the matrix A by defining,

$$A_k = U_k \Sigma_k V_k^{T}$$

Equation 16-3

where U_k contains the first κ columns of U, Σ_k contains the κ largest nonzero singular values of A, and V_k^{T} contains the first κ rows of V^{T}.

The rank of the matrix A_k is κ. With κ being usually small, the dimensionality of the dataset has been reduced dramatically from $min\{m,n\}$ to κ (assuming all attributes are linearly independent). It has been proven that A_k is the best κ dimensional approximation of A in the sense of the Frobenius norm (Eckart and Young 1936; Mirsky 1960).

Rank reduction was first proposed by Deerwest as a method for removing the noise of a text collection (Deerwester 1990). The removed part $E_k = A - A_k$ can be considered as the noise in the original matrix A. Thus, in many cases, mining on the reduced dataset A_k may yield better results than mining on the original dataset A. When used for privacy preserving, the distorted dataset A_k can provide protection for data privacy, at the same time it may keep the utility of the original data as it can faithfully represent the original data.

The good choice of the rank of SVD could capture the main structure of a data collection and ignore the irrelevant noise. Large ranks will still retain some noise, but too small ranks will lose the structure and meaning of the collection. How to choose the rank that provides optimal performance of data mining algorithms for any given datasets remains an open question and is normally decided via empirical tests (Berry et al. 1999). In this chapter, we take a close look at the effect of rank of SVD on the accuracy of a binary classification.

SVD computation incurs a significant cost. It is indicated that the cost of computing the SVD of a sparse matrix A using a Lanczos-type procedure could be expressed as (Berry et al. 1999):

$$Total \cos t = I \times \cos t(A^T Ax) + k \times \cos t(Ax)$$

Equation 16-4

where I is the number of iteration required by a Lanczos-type procedure to approximate the eigensystem of $A^T A$, x is a vector and κ is the number of computed singular values in the sparse matrix A.

The dominant computation cost of Lanczos method is related to the size and complexity of sparse matrix multiplication of A and A^T.

3.4 Sparsified Single Value Decomposition (SSVD)

We propose to use sparsified SVD as a new data distortion method.

After reducing the rank of the SVD matrices, we set some small size entries to zero. We refer to this operation as the dropping operation. Given a certain threshold value ε, for any u_{ij} in U_k, if $|u_{ij}| < \varepsilon$, then set $u_{ij} = 0$. The same operation is conducted on V_k^T.

Let $\overline{U}_k$ and $\overline{V}_k$ denote the new matrices created after conducting dropping on U_k and V_k^T respectively, and the new version of the distorted matrix A_k is

$$\overline{A}_k = \overline{U}_k \Sigma_k \overline{V}_k^T$$

Equation 16-5

The sparsified SVD method is equivalent to further distorting the matrix A_k. Denote $E_\varepsilon = A_k - \overline{A}_k$, we have

$$A = \overline{A}_k + E_k + E_E$$

Equation 16- 6

The data provided to the analysts is $\overline{A}_k$ which is twice distorted in the sparsified SVD method.

After dropping the small entries in U_k and V_k^T, the sparsified SVD method will only keep the important features of the original matrix A, thus it can maintain the utility of A. At the same time, the data is twice distorted, which makes it even harder to reconstruct or estimate the value of entries in A. If A is large, the sparsity of $\overline{A}_k$ can help reduce the memory cost and the computational cost. Therefore we believe the sparsified SVD method can work as a good data distortion method.

The SVD sparsification concept was proposed by Gao and Zhang in (Gao and Zhang 2003) for reducing the storage cost and enhancing the performance of SVD in text retrieval applications. Several sparsification strategies were proposed and experimented in (Gao and Zhang 2003). The one that we used in this chapter is the single threshold strategy.

4.   DATA DISTORTION MEASURES

Some data privacy metrics have been proposed in literature (Agrawal and Aggarwal 2001; Agrawal and Srikant 2000). However, the metric used in (Agrawal and Srikant 2000) has been proved to be incomplete (Agrawal and Aggarwal 2001), and the one used in (Agrawal and Aggarwal 2001) needs to know the density function of each attribute *a priori*, which may be difficult to obtain for the real world datasets. We propose some data distortion measures to assess the degree of data distortion which only depend on the original matrix A and its distorted counterpart, $\bar{A}$.

4.1   Value Difference (VD)

After a data matrix is distorted, the value of its elements changes. The value difference (*VD*) of the datasets is represented by the relative value difference in the Frobenius norm. Thus *VD* is the ratio of the Frobenius norm of the difference of A from $\bar{A}$ to the Frobenius norm of A:

$$VD = \frac{\left\| A - \overline{A} \right\|_F}{\left\| A \right\|_F}$$

Equation 16-7

For example, for the following dataset A_e, its distorted data matrix $\bar{A}_e$ is obtained by applying the Sparsified SVD with $k = 2$ and $\varepsilon = 0.001$. The *VD* value computed for this distortion is 0.3136.

$$A_e = \begin{bmatrix} 1 & 2.5 & 5 & 0.3 \\ 2 & 3.9 & 2 & 1.1 \\ 4 & 1.8 & 8 & 0.5 \\ 1 & 3.3 & 6 & 1.2 \end{bmatrix}, \quad \overline{A}_e = \begin{bmatrix} 1.7 & 0.8 & -5.3 & -0.1 \\ 0.2 & 2.8 & -3.8 & -0.8 \\ 3.6 & -0.7 & -8.3 & 0.5 \\ 1.9 & 1.4 & -6.5 & -0.2 \end{bmatrix}$$

4.2   Rank Difference

After a data distortion, the rank of the magnitude of the data elements changes, too. We use several metrics to measure the rank difference of the data elements.

4.2.1 Rank Position (RP)

RP is used to denote the average change of rank for all the attributes. After the elements of an attribute are distorted, the rank of the magnitude of each element changes. Assume a dataset A has n data objects and m attributes. $Rank^i_j$ denotes the rank (in ascending order) of the jth element in attribute i, and $\overline{Rank}^i_j$ denotes the rank (in ascending order) of the distorted element A_{ji}. Then RP is defined as:

$$RP = \frac{\sum_{i=1}^{m} \sum_{j=1}^{n} \left| Rank^i_j - \overline{Rank}^i_j \right|}{m \times n}$$

Equation 16-8

If two elements have the same value, we define the element with the smaller row index to have the higher rank. In dataset A_e, the rank vector for the first attribute can be represented as $Rank^1 = [1\ 3\ 4\ 2]^T$. After the distortion, $\overline{Rank}^1 = [2\ 1\ 4\ 3]^T$. The total change of rank for this attribute is 4. We can calculate the total change of rank for the other attributes and get RP = 1.25.

4.2.2 Rank Keeping (RK)

RK represents the percentage of elements that keep their ranks of value in each column after the distortion. It is computed as:

$$RK = \frac{\sum_{i=1}^{m} \sum_{j=1}^{n} Rk^j_j}{m \times n}$$

Equation 16- 9

where Rk^i_j indicates whether an element keeps its rank during the data distortion process:

$$Rk^i_j = \begin{cases} 1, & if\ \ Rank^i_j = \overline{Rank}^i_j \\ 0, & otherwise \end{cases}$$

Equation 16- 10

For example, the rank vector of the second attribute in A_e is $[2\ 4\ 1\ 3]^T$, and after the distortion, it is still $[2\ 4\ 1\ 3]^T$. Thus all the elements keep their original rank. RK for this example is 0.3125.

4.2.3   Change of Rank of Features (CP)

One may infer the content of one feature from its relative value difference compared with the other attributes. Thus it is desirable that the order of the average value of each attribute varies after the data distortion. Here we use the metric CP to define the change of rank of the average value of the attributes:

$$CP = \frac{\sum_{i=1}^{m}\left|RAV_i - \overline{RAV}_i\right|}{m}$$

Equation 16- 11

where RAV_i is the rank (in ascending order) of the average value of attribute i, while $\overline{RAV}_i$ denotes its rank (in ascending order) after the distortion. For instance, the rank vector of all attributes in matrix A_e is: $[2\ 3\ 4\ 1]^{\mathrm{T}}$. The rank vector for the distorted matrix $\bar{A}_e$ is: $[4\ 3\ 1\ 2]^{\mathrm{T}}$. Then the total change of rank is 6, so CP is equal to 1.5.

4.2.4   Keeping of Rank of Features (CK)

CK is defined to measure the percentage of the features that keep their ranks of average value after the distortion. So it is calculated as:

$$CK = \frac{\sum_{i=1}^{m} Ck^i}{m}$$

Equation 16- 12

where Ck^i is computed as:

$$Ck^i = \begin{cases} 1, & if\ RAV_i = \overline{RAV}_i \\ 0, & otherwise \end{cases}$$

Equation 16- 13

In the previous example, $CK = 0.25$.

The value of RP and CP is proportional to the level of the distortion. On the contrary, the value of RK and CK is inversely related to the level of distortion.

5.   UTILITY MEASURE

The data utility measures assess whether a dataset keeps the performance of data mining techniques after the data distortion, e.g., whether the distorted data can maintain the accuracy of the data mining techniques such as classification, clustering, etc. In this paper, we choose the accuracy in Support Vector Machine (SVM) classification as the data utility measure.

SVM is based on structural risk minimization theory (Vapnik 1998). It has been successfully applied to many applications like face identification, text categorization, bioinformatics, etc. (Burges 1998; Campbell 2002; Li et al. 2000).

In SVM classification, the goal is to find a hyperplane that separates the examples with maximum margin. Given l examples (x_1, y_1), ..., (x_l, y_l), with $x_i \in R_n$ and $y_i \in \{-1, 1\}$ for all i, SVM classification can be stated as a quadratic programming problem:

$$\text{minimize} \quad \frac{1}{2} \| w \|^2 + C \sum_{i=1}^{l} \xi_i$$

Equation 16- 14

$$\text{subject to} \quad \begin{cases} y_i (< w, x_i > + b) \geq 1 - \xi_i \\ \xi_i \geq 0 \\ C > 0 \end{cases}$$

Equation 16- 15

where C is a user-selected regularization parameter, and ξ_i is a slack variable accounting for errors. After solving the quadratic programming problem, we can get the following decision function:

$$f(x) = \sum_{i=1}^{l} \alpha_i y_i < x_i, x > + b$$

Equation 16- 16

where $0 \leq \alpha_i \leq C$.

For the nonlinear case, we apply a mapping $\Phi : X \rightarrow F$ to map the input space into some feature space F. Here we use a kernel function,

$K(x,x_i) =< \Phi(x),\Phi(x_i)>$, which is a symmetric function and satisfies the Mercer's condition. We substitute $K(x, x_i)$ for the dot product, which maps the input space into some reproduced kernel feature space. Then Eq. (16-16) can be rewritten as:

$$f(x) = \sum_{i=1}^{l} \alpha_i y_i K(x_i,x) + b$$

Equation 16- 17

6.   EXPERIMENTS AND RESULTS

We conduct some experiments to test the performance of the data distortion methods: SVD, sparsified SVD (SSVD), adding uniformly distributed noise (UD) and adding normally distributed (ND) noise.

6.1   Synthetic dataset

First, we compare the performance of the four data distortion methods using a synthetic dataset. The dataset is a 2000 by 100 matrix (Org), whose entries are randomly generated numbers within the interval [1, 10] obeying a uniform distribution. We classify the dataset into two classes using a randomly chosen rule: If

$$\left|\sin(Org(i,1)) - Org(i,88)\right| * \left|\cos(Org(i,45))\right| * Org(i,78) > 15$$

Equation 16- 18

then record i is assigned to class 1, otherwise, it is assigned to class -1. We use SVM classification (Joachims 1999) to construct the classifier and a 5-fold cross validation to obtain the classification results. The uniformly distributed noise is generated from the interval [0, 0.8]. The normally distributed noise is generated with $\mu = 0$ and $\sigma = 0.46$. The parameters of UD and ND are chosen so that the *VD* value of UD, ND, and SVD is approximately equal. That is, we will compare these methods under the condition that they change approximately the same percentage of value after the data distortion. For SVD and SSVD, the rank k is chosen to be 85, and in SSVD, the dropping threshold value ε is 0.001. The parameters k and ε are chosen so that SVD and SSVD can obtain the highest classification accuracy.

Table 16-1. Comparison of distortion methods for the synthetic dataset

Data	VD	RP	RK	CP	CK	Accuracy
Org	-	-	-	-	-	76%
UD	0.0760	662.8	0.0058	0	1	76%
ND	0.0763	661.6	0.0067	0	1	76%
SVD	0.0766	664.0	0.0047	8.5	0.82	76%
SSVD	0.7269	666.6	0.0005	33.2	0.02	76%

Table 16-1 shows the value of the privacy measures and the utility measure of applying the data distortion methods. In this experiment, both UD and ND keep the rank of the average value of each attribute. Thus they do not work well for providing privacy protection. Both SVD and SSVD are better in keeping the privacy for the matrix elements and the attributes. SSVD is even better than SVD. It has the highest value in *RP*, and its *RK* value is the smallest, which means fewest elements keep their rank of magnitude after the distortion. Its *CP* value is almost four times higher than that of SVD. The *CK* value for SSVD is 0.02, which means nearly all the attributes change their rank in average value after the distortion. For SVD, only about 20% of the attributes change their ranks. The Accuracy column in Table 16-1 shows the percentage of the correctly classified data records. Here all the distorted methods obtain almost the same accuracy as using the original data.

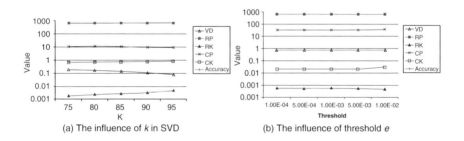

(a) The influence of *k* in SVD (b) The influence of threshold *e*

Figure 16-2. The influence of the parameters in the SVD-based methods.

Figure 16-2 illustrates the influence of the parameters in the SVD-based methods. With the increase of *k* in SVD, *VD* and *CP* decrease while *RK*, *CK* and Accuracy increase. But with the increase of ε in SSVD ($k = 85$), there is no observable trend of change in data distortion or utility measures. It implies that the performance of SSVD is relatively stable within the chosen range of the threshold value ε.

6.2   Real world dataset

To build a real world dataset, we download some information about 100 terrorists from a terrorist analysis web site (www.trackingthethreat.com). We selected 42 attributes (m = 42), such as their nationality, different sibling relationships, pilot training, locations of temporary residency, wedding attendance, meeting attendance, etc. The original matrix is of dimension 100 × 42.

To test the real world dataset, the uniformly distributed noise is chosen from the interval [0, 0.09]. The normally distributed noise is generated with $\mu = 0$ and $\sigma = 0.05$. The rank k for SVD and SSVD is chosen to be 25. The dropping threshold value ε in SSVD is 0.001. Like dealing with synthetic dataset, we use SVM classification to construct the classifiers and a 5-fold cross validation to obtain the classification results.

Table 16-2. Comparison of distortion methods for classification 1 (Bin Laden association)

Data	VD	RP	RK	CP	CK	Accuracy
Org	-	-	-	-	-	67%
UD	0.0566	0	1	11.4	0.15	67%
ND	0.0537	31.9	0.0298	12.2	0.27	66%
SVD	0.0525	31.2	0.0251	12.2	0.12	70%
SSVD	1.0422	37.5	0.0066	13.1	0.05	69%

In Table 16-2, we classify the terrorists into two groups, those are directly related with Bin Laden and those are not. There are 19 terrorists in the dataset who have direct relationships with Bin Laden, for example, the persons who reported to him, who had met him, who were associates of him, and so on. The accuracy of classifying the original dataset is 67%. The UD and ND methods keep this accuracy, while using SVD the accuracy rises to 70%. The accuracy obtained by using SSVD is 69%, also improves a little bit from UD and ND. Thus SVD and SSVD are a little better in keeping data utility.

In order to be fair in comparing the privacy metrics, we also make the VD value of UD, ND and SVD to be almost the same. For privacy protection, UD does not perform well. It does not change any rank of the elements in attributes, and has the lowest *CP* and a high *CK* values. ND is better than UD but is significantly worse than SVD in *CK* measure. The *CK* value obtained by using ND is 0.27, while SVD reduces it more than a half to 0.12. Among the four distortion methods, SSVD is the best to preserve privacy in this experiment. It has the highest *RP* and the lowest *RK* values, which means it is the best in keeping the privacy of the rank of the individual elements. It also has the best *CP* and *CK* values, which means it also exceeds other methods in changing the rank of the magnitude of attributes.

Table 16-3. Comparison of distortion methods for classification 2 (Al Qaeda association)

Data	VD	RP	RK	CP	CK	Accuracy
Org	-	-	-	-	-	67%
UD	0.0575	31.9	0.0166	9.5	0.07	66%
ND	0.0566	34.1	0.0390	12.0	0.07	64%
SVD	0.0525	31.2	0.0251	12.2	0.12	70%
SSVD	1.3829	35.0	0.0090	11.5	0.02	65%

Table 16-3 shows the results of performing another classification on the real world dataset. This time the terrorists are grouped according to whether they have relationship with the terrorist organization Al Qaeda. There are 17 terrorists in the dataset who were members or leaders in Al Qaeda. The previous target attribute about whether a person has relationship with Bin Laden is inserted into the data matrix and the attribute about whether a person has relationship with Al Qaeda is taken out as the target attribute. Thus the original data matrix for privacy analysis is a little different from the one used in the previous classification task. All the distorted matrices are generated from the new original matrix.

Again, we keep the VD value to be very similar for UD, ND and SVD. SVD has the best classification result, it improves the accuracy (70%) over using the original dataset (67%). The other three methods decrease the accuracy slightly. For privacy protection, SSVD works best in keeping the privacy of each element. It has the highest *RP* value but lowest *RK* value. Its *CP* value is slightly lower than those of ND and SVD, but its *CK* value is more than three times lower than that of ND, and six times lower than that of SVD. SVD is not outstanding in preserving privacy in this experiment. ND exceeds it in *RP* and *CK* values. In this example, SSVD is still the best in keeping the privacy of data.

7. CONCLUSIONS AND DISCUSSIONS

We proposed to use the sparsified SVD method for data distortion in a simplified model terrorist analysis system. The experimental results show that, among the fourth data distortion methods we compared, SSVD is the best in preserving data privacy. It is also efficient in keeping data utility. SVD works well, too. Both are better than the standard data distortion methods which add noise straightforwardly to the database. We believe that the SVD-based methods can be used in data mining techniques for data distortion purpose in order to protect privacy and other sensitive information contained and visible in the original datasets. Further research can be done to find out the relationships between the data distortion measures proposed in this paper and other well-known privacy measures. Other SVD sparsification strategies (Gao and Zhang 2003) can also be tested in the data distortion applications. It should be pointed out that the application of the proposed SVD-based data distortion methods is not limited to the terrorist analysis systems. Many data analysis processes in which there is a need for data distortion may benefit from the proposed SVD-based data distortion methods.

The computation of SVD for large scale dataset matrices can be expensive (Berry 1992; Gao and Zhang 2005). Fortunately, for the current and many other applications in data mining and information retrieval, we need only compute SVD corresponding to the first few largest singular values. The data distortion and SVD computation are considered as a data preprocessing and preparation procedure, a reasonable amount of computational cost in this phase may be tolerable. On the other hand, we can employ clustered SVD strategies (Gao and Zhang 2005) to reduce the computational cost substantially when the datasets are large. In many privacy preserving data mining applications, it is possible that values of only certain attributes in the database have to be distorted. The SVD can be applied to the submatrix consisting of these attributes only. The distorted data can be incorporated into the entire database for the data mining purposes.

REFERENCES

Agrawal D, Aggarwal CC (2001) On the design and quantification of privacy preserving data mining algorithms. In: Proceedings of the 20th ACM SIGACT-SIGMOD-SIGART Symposium on Principles of Database Systems, Santa Barbara, California

Agrawal R, Srikant R (2000) Privacy-preserving data mining. In: Proceedings of the 2000 ACM SIGMOD International Conference on Management of Data, Dallas, Texas

Agrawal R, Evfimievski A, Srikant R (2003) Information sharing across private databases. In: Proceedings of the 2003 ACM SIGMOD International Conference on Management of Data, San Diego, CA, pp 86 - 97

Berry MW (1992) Large scale singular value decompositions. Int J Supercomput Applic High Perf Comput, 6:13 - 49

Berry MW, Drmac Z, Jessup ER (1999) Matrix, vector space, and information retrieval. SIAM Rev, 41:335 - 362.

Burges C (1998) A Tutorial on Support Vector Machine for Pattern Recognition. Kluwer Academic Publishers

Campbell C (2002) Kernel methods: A survey of current techniques. Neurocomputing, 48:63 - 84.

Datta S, Kargupta H, Sivakumar K (2003) Homeland defense, privacy-sensitive data mining, and random value distortion. In: Proceedings of the 2003 Workshop on Data Mining for Counter Terrorism and Security, San Francisco, CA

Deerwester S, Dumais S, Furnas G, Landauer T, Harsgman R (1990) Indexing by latent semantic analysis. J Amer Soc Infor Sci, 41:391 - 407

Dempsey JX, Rosenzweig P (2004) Technologies that can protect privacy as information is shared to combat terrorism. Legal Memorandum #11, The Heritage Foundation, May 26, 2004. Available at www.heritage.org/Research/HomelandDefense/lm11.cfm

Eckart C, Young G (1936) The approximation of one matrix by another of low rank, Psychometrika, 1(1936): 211-218

Estvill-Castro V, Brankovic L, Dowe DL (1999) Privacy in data mining. Australian Computer Society, NSW Branch, Australia. Available at www.acs.org.au/nsw/articles/1999082.html

Frankes W, Baeza-Yates R (1992) Information Retrieval: Data Structures and Algorithms. Prentice-Hall, Englewood Cliffs, NJ

Gao J, Zhang J (2003) Sparsification strategies in latent semantic indexing. In: Berry MW, Pottenger WM (eds), Proceedings of the 2003 Text Mining Workshop, San Francisco, CA, pp. 93 - 103

Gao J, Zhang J (2005) Clustered SVD strategies in latent semantic indexing. Information Processing and Management, 41(5):1051--1063

Gilburd B, Schuster A, Wolff R (2004) K-TTP: a new privacy model for large-scale distributed environments. In: Proceedings of the 10th ACM SIGKDD International Conference on Knowledge Discovery and Data Mining, Seattle, WA

Golub GH, Loan CF van (1996) Matrix Computations, John Hopkins Univ, 3rd edn

Joachims T (1999) Making large-scale SVM learning practical, Schölkopf B, Burges C, Smola A (eds), Advances in Kernel Methods - Support Vector Learning, MIT-Press

Liew CK, Choi UJ, Liew CJ (1985) A data distortion by probability distribution. ACM Transactions on Database Systems, 10:395--411

Li Y, Gong S, Liddell H (2000) Support vector regression and classification based multiview face detection and recognition. In: Proc of the IEEE International Conference on Automatic Face and Gesture Recognition (FGR'00), Grenoble, France

Mirsky L (1960) Symmetric gauge functions and unitarily invariant norms, Quart. J Math, 11:50-59

Skillicorn DB (2003) Clusters within clusters: SVD and counterterrorism. In: Proceedings of 2003 Workshop on Data Mining for Counter Terrorism and Security, San Francisco, CA

Skillicorn DB (2004) Social network analysis via matrix decompositions: applications to al Qaeda. Technical Report, School of Computing, Queen's University, Canada

Skillicorn DB, Vats N (2004) Novel information discovery for intelligence and counterterrorism. Technical Report 2004-488, School of Computing, Queen's University, Canada

Sun A, Naing M, Lim EP, Lam W (2003) Using support vector machines for terrorism information extraction. Lecture Notes in Computer Science, Vol. 2665, pp. 1 - 12

Sweeney L (2002) K-anonymity: A model for protecting privacy. International Journal on Uncertainty, Fuzziness and Knowledge-based Systems, 10:557 - 570

Taipale KA (2003) Data mining and domestic security: connecting the dots to make sense of data. Columbia Sci & Tech Law Rev, 5:1 - 83

Tether T (2003) Statement before the Subcommittee on Technology, Information Policy, Intergovernmental Relations and the Census, Committee on Government Reform, U.S. House of Representatives, Available at:
www.fas.gov/irp/congress/2003_hr/050603tether.html

Vapnik VN (1998) Statistical Learning Theory. John Wiley & Sons, New York

Verykios VS, Bertino E, Fovino IN, Provenza LP, Saygin Y, Theodoridis Y (2004) State-of-the-art in privacy preserving data mining. SIGMOD, 33:50 - 57

SUGGESTED READINGS

- For privacy-preserving data mining, please read Agrawal and Aggarwal 2001, and Agrawal and Srikant 2000.
- For Singular Value Decomposition, please read Golub and Loan 1996.
- For Sparsified Singular Value Decomposition, please read Gao and Zhang 2003.
- For Support Vector Machine, please read Vapnik 1998.

ONLINE RESOURCES

- Terrorist analysis web site:
  http://www.trackingthethreat.com
- An implementation of Support Vector Machines:
  http://svmlight.joachims.org

DISCUSSION QUESTIONS

1. Why is data distortion is used terrorist analysis systems?
2. Describe a data distortion method in detail.
3. List desired properties for data privacy metrics.
4. What are the advantages and disadvantages of the data distortion measures used in this chapter?
5. List the advantages and disadvantages of the SVD-based data distortion methods.

17

CONTENT-BASED DETECTION OF TERRORISTS BROWSING THE WEB USING AN ADVANCED TERROR DETECTION SYSTEM (ATDS)

Yuval Elovici[1], Bracha Shapira[1], Mark Last[1], Omer Zaafrany[1], Menahem Friedman[1], Moti Schneider[2], and Abraham Kandel[3]

[1] *Department of Information Systems Engineering, Ben-Gurion University of the Negev, Beer-Sheva, Israel (elovici@inter.net.il, and {bshapira, mlast, zaafrany, and fmenahem} @bgu.ac.il);* [2]*School of Computer Science, Netanya Academic College, Netanya, Israel (motis@netanya.ac.il);* [3]*Department of Computer Science and Engineering,University of South Florida, Tampa, Florida, U.S.A., (kandel@csee.usf.edu)*

CHAPTER OVERVIEW

Many terror-related groups use the Web as a convenient, anonymous communication infrastructure. This infrastructure enables exchange of information and propagation of ideas to active and potential terrorists. The Terrorist Detection System (TDS) is aimed at tracking down suspected terrorists by analyzing the content of information they access. In this chapter we present an advanced version of TDS (ATDS), where the detection algorithm was enhanced to improve the detection and reduce the false alarms. ATDS was implemented and evaluated in a network environment of 38 users comparing it to the performance of the basic TDS. Behavior of suspected terrorists was simulated by accessing known terror-related sites. The evaluation included also sensitivity analysis aimed at calibrating the settings of ATDS parameters to optimize its performance. The evaluation results suggest that ATDS outperformed TDS significantly and was able to reach very high detection rates when optimally tuned.

1.   INTRODUCTION

Terrorist are using the Internet infrastructure to exchange information and recruit new members and supporters [10, 9]. The Internet was intensively used by the members of the infamous "Hamburg Cell" that was largely responsible for the preparation of the September 11 attacks against the United States [19]. This is one reason for the major effort made by law enforcement agencies around the world in gathering information from the Web about terror-related activities. It is believed that the detection of terrorists might prevent further terrorist attacks [9].

One way to detect terrorist activities on the Web is to eavesdrop on all traffic of Web sites associated with terrorist organizations in order to detect the accessing users based on their IP address. Unfortunately it is difficult to monitor terrorist sites (such as "Azzam Publications" [19]) since they do not use fixed IP addresses and URLs. The geographical locations of Web servers hosting those sites also change frequently in order to prevent successful eavesdropping. In addition, it is very difficult to connect the IP of the user that access the monitored terror-related site to his or her real identity. To overcome this problem, law enforcement agencies are trying to detect terrorists by monitoring all ISPs traffic [11], though privacy issues raised still prevent relevant laws from being enforced.

The Terrorist Detection System (TDS) is aimed at tracking down suspected terrorists by analyzing the content of information they access [2]. TDS is deployed in a "closed" environment such as LAN or within a defined organization. Thus, once detecting a suspicious user by his / her IP, it is possible to connect the IP of the user and his or her real identity. TDS operates in two modes: a training mode and a detection mode. During the training mode TDS is provided with Web pages accessed by a typical group of users in the operated environment and computes their typical interests. During the detection mode TDS performs real-time monitoring of the traffic emanating from the monitored group of users, analyzes the content of the Web pages accessed, and generates an alarm if a user is accessing information which is not within the typical interests of the group.

In this chapter we present ATDS, the advanced version of the basic TDS. The main difference between TDS and ATDS is the detection algorithm that considers the history of users accesses for detection of *constant atypical behavior* to determine whether a user is suspicious for accessing terror-related (non-typical) contents. The ATDS detection algorithm is more accurate than TDS and includes additional parameters that can be calibrated by its operator.

The reminder of the chapter is organized as follows. In Section 2, a brief related work on detecting terrorist activities on the web is presented. In

Section 3 the content-based methodology for anomaly detection on the Web, which is the basis of ATDS, followed by ATDS implementation details is portrayed. The experiments conducted to evaluate the feasibility and the performance of ATDS are discussed in Section 4. Section 5 concludes the chapter.

2. RELATED WORK

Currently, since the September 11th attack, many IT-related studies are trying to contribute to the vast homeland security efforts. One of the six critical mission areas defined by the National Strategy for Homeland Security [20,21] deals with Intelligence and Gathering terror-related information: "IT researchers can help build new intelligence gathering and analysis capabilities for an intelligence and warning system that can detect future terrorist activities" [23]. The research described in this chapter fits into this mission as it deals with online identification of potential terrorists that seek or access terror-related content on the Web. In this section, we review studies aiming at identifying terror-related activities on the Web and explain the uniqueness of our approach.

ATDS is aiming at detecting suspicious users on the Web by their IP while they surf in order to prevent them from future terror-related activities. This is done by monitoring defined environments on the Web (such as organizations, campuses, or users of a certain ISP). Other efforts to identify suspicious users on the Web include the work by Abbasi and Chen [30] that used authorship analysis to identify Arabic Web content. This effort is aimed at automatically identifying content submitted by already known terrorists by comparing writing style features of content (i.e., lexical, syntactical, structural, and content-specific features) using statistical and machine learning approaches. Our approach attempts at identifying new recruited terrorists or terrorists that are not known to the system in advance.

Another study by Provos [28] tried to identify terrorists on the Web by detecting users that try to hide their identity using stenography. He developed a method to discover steganographic messages assuming that terrorists use it while communicating with each other. However, the assumption was not yet confirmed as an analysis of two million images downloaded from eBay auctions and one million images obtained from a USENET archive was not able to find a single hidden message. It is hard to tell whether the assumption is incorrect, or the proposed method of detecting steganography is ineffective.

Other studies are aimed at gathering and analyzing terror-related content (not the terrorists) being published and transferred on the Web (sites, emails, chats, forms and other Web infrastructure), in order to learn about terrorist networks, characterize their behavior and dynamic evolution and hopefully prevent a planned attack [21,22]. One known major effort of this kind is the DarkWeb terrorism research [31] conducted at the University of Arizona, in the Artificial Intelligence Lab at the MIS department. This project intends to develop and evaluate scalable techniques for collecting and analyzing terrorism information. An ongoing effort yielded 500,000 terror-related Web pages created by 94 US domestic groups, 300,000 Web pages created by 41 Arabic-speaking groups, and 100,000 Web pages created by Spanish-speaking groups. This huge and growing collection is being analyzed using statistical analysis, cluster analysis, and visualization. Another recent research trend is to use Social Network Analysis (SNA) to identify relationships between human groups on the Internet. SNA enables identification of central players, gatekeepers, and outliers in terrorist groups [24, 21].

Some earlier studies [26, 27] used web-navigation mining techniques to analyze web-navigation data. They perform unsupervised clustering on user navigation data on the Web to identify groups of users, resulting with clusters that were hard to interpret by humans.

Wu, et al, [32] presented the principal clusters analysis approach, used for analyzing millions of user navigations on the Web. This technique identifies prominent navigation clusters on different topics. The method can potentially be used to identify terror-related navigations in order to collect terror related data for analysis. Furthermore, it can determine useful starting points (information items) for exploring a topic, as well as key documents to explore a topic in greater detail and to detect trends by observing navigation prominence over time.

The motivation of ATDS was to identify new potential terrorists, not yet suspected by the law enforcement authorities, using the on-line behavior of those people. ATDS uses intrusion detection inspired methodology to detect potential terrorists, by defining the potential terrorists as non-typical users whose abnormal activities can be detected by the system. While in anomaly-based intrusion detection systems, the activities to be identified as normal or abnormal include behavior in the network environment [29] ATDS analyzes the content accessed by the user to differentiate between typical and suspicious users. Similar explicit content analysis was recently used for detection of insider threats by analyzing the content of communication that was compared to "normal" content [25].

3.   ADVANCED TERRORIST DETECTION SYSTEM

ATDS detection is inspired by anomaly detection principles. Anomaly detection relies on models of the typical behavior of users or applications and interprets deviations from this `normal' behavior as evidence of malicious activity [16-18]. The underlying intuitive assumption of ATDS is that the content of users browsing reflects their interests. This assumption is the basis of many personalization models, algorithms, and systems [15] that generate user "profiles" from the content of pages they browse. A stronger assumption is that users that have similar interests can be identified by the content of their browsing activities and be represented as an identified group of users (referred to also as stereotypes). Individual user profiles may be related to one or more stereotypes by the similarity of their profile to the stereotypic profile.

ATDS (an extension of TDS [2, 5]) uses the content of web pages browsed by a specific group of users as an input for detecting abnormal activities. In this study, we refer only to the *textual* content of web pages only, excluding images, music, and other complex data types.

The basic idea of TDS is to maintain information about the interests of "normal" users in a certain environment (such as a campus), and detect users whose interests are dissimilar to the typical interests of the group under a defined threshold of similarity.

ATDS has two modes of operation, the learning mode and the detection mode:

1. **The learning mode** – during which the Web traffic of a group of users is recorded and transformed to an efficient representation for further analysis. The commonly used vector-space model is used for representation of the collected pages [14], i.e. each page is transformed to a vector of weighted terms representing the relative importance of the terms to the page. The learning mode is applied in the environments where the detection is later applied in order to learn the "normal" content of users' accesses in the environment. The set of collected pages is being mined (using cluster analysis) for derivation and representation of user groups' profiles, i.e., typical common areas of interest of groups of users.

2. **The detection mode** is aimed at detecting abnormal (non-typical) users. Users whose interests are constantly and significantly dissimilar to the typical content accessed by users are detected. The detection process includes transformation of the content of pages accessed by a user to a vector representation that is then compared to the vector representation of the group profiles. One parameter of the detection algorithm that has to be calibrated is the minimum number of suspicious accesses required to issue a suspicious user alert. The detection is performed on-line and should therefore be efficient and scalable. In the following sub-sections, we briefly describe the learning and the detection modes. The reader is referred to [2,5,6] for additional details

3.1   The Learning Mode

The learning mode presented in Figure 17-1 results in a Data-Base of representations of the interests of the monitored group of users. During the detection mode, pages accessed by online users are compared to this Data-Base to detect suspicious accesses to content.

The learning process consists of the *Filter, Vectors-Generator* and the *Clusters-Generator* modules. Each page that is collected as training data is sent to the *Filter* for filtering out non-textual pages and for omitting images and tags related to the content format from the textual pages. The HTTP filter component checks whether the packet belongs to an existing HTTP session and opens a new HTTP session if the packet does not belong to an existing one. The HTTP filter tries to identify the kind of the content type (text, video, audio etc) and discards all HTTP sessions having non-textual content. After the last packet of a textual HTTP session is received, all the packets from that session are moved to the HTML reconstruction.

The filtered pages are sent to the *Vectors- Generator* component that converts each reconstructed HTML page to a weighted terms vector. The vector entries represent terms and their values reflecting the importance of the terms to the page. The weight of a term in a document is determined by the relative frequency of the term on the page, and by other factors such as the term position in the document. For each IP address, the system maintains a sub-queue of web page accesses performed from that IP. This is called the "IP profile" rather than a user profile since it is possible for several users to use the same IP address. If an alarm is issued, the cooperation of the ISP is required to identify the user that used the IP at the time of suspicious activity. It is therefore not efficient to keep long histories for a sub-queue, as it might result in a mixture of several user profiles. The size of the sub-queue for each IP, i.e., the number of accessed pages kept for each IP, which is used by the detection algorithm as the IP history, was one of the parameters examined during the evaluation as described later in the chapter. The vectors are stored for the clustering process that follows.

The *Clusters-Generator* module (Figure 17-1) receives the vectors from the *Vectors-Generator* and performs cluster analysis on them. A typical cluster analysis process receives as input a set of objects with a set of attributes and generates clusters (groups) of objects, so that objects within a cluster have high similarity and objects between clusters are dissimilar. The objects in this model are the pages, and their attributes are the terms. The *n* clusters generated by the *Cluster-Generator* represent the *n* groups of users having common areas of interest. The optimal *n* for a given system is determined empirically by the results of the clustering algorithm. For each cluster, the *Group-Representor* component computes a central vector (centroid), denoted by Cv_i for the cluster *i*. In our model, each centroid represents common areas of interest of the group of users that are related to the cluster. The learning mode is a batch process and should be activated periodically to update the representation of the group, (for more technical details of the software components, the reader is referred to [33]).

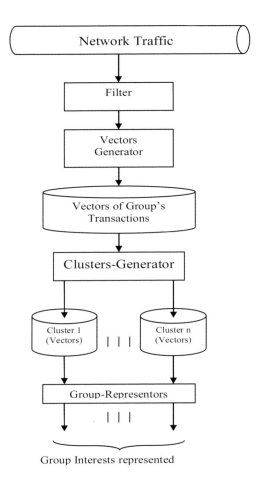

Figure 17-1. ATDS Learning Mode

3.2   The Detection Mode

During the detection mode, a group of computers in a certain environment is monitored to detect non-typical users. The Web-pages accessed by the users of a monitored group are collected online and compared to the set of pre-defined group profiles – the cluster centroids (generated during the learning mode). The detection process aims at monitoring all the network traffic and reconstructing HTML web pages from on-wire packets capturing. A software tool (OHT- Online HTML Tracer) was developed to monitor the network traffic. HTTP packets which contain textual contents of HTML pages are being located and used for HTML page reconstruction. In this approach, the content of the collected information is identical to the content viewed by the user. The detector consists of the *Sniffer, Filter*, the *Vector –Generator* and the *Detector* which is the main component. The *Sniffer* captures the pages that users, (identified by their IPs), access at the network layer, and sends each page to the *Filter* for further processing. The *Filter* and the *Vector-Generator* in the detection mode have the same functionality as in the learning mode. The Detector receives the vectors (and their respective IPs) and decides whether to issue an alarm. The *Detector* measures the distance between each vector and each of the centroids representing an area of interest to the user. While in TDS the detection algorithm considers only one vector of the last user access, in ATDS, the detection is based on the user's access history. The detection algorithm in ATDS can be calibrated with certain parameters to fine-tune the detection.

Some of the parameters are:
1. The dissimilarity threshold,
2. The minimum number of abnormal accesses by the same user that would issue an alarm
3. The maximal time frame of suspicious accesses by the same IP that cause the issuing of an alarm.

The detection algorithm issues an alarm when all the parameters are satisfied. The alarm consists of the suspicious IPs along with the data that caused the issuing of the alarm. The similarity between the vectors accessed by users and the centroids is measured by the cosine of the angle between them. An access is considered abnormal if the similarity between the access vector and the nearest centroid is lower than the threshold denoted by *tr*. The following is the cosine equation used:

$$Min\left(\frac{\sum_{i=1}^{m}(tCv_{i1} \cdot tAv_{i})}{\sqrt{\sum_{i=1}^{m}tCv_{i1}^{2} \cdot \sum_{i=1}^{m}tAv_{i}^{2}}}, ..., \frac{\sum_{i=1}^{m}(tCv_{in} \cdot tAv_{i})}{\sqrt{\sum_{i=1}^{m}tCv_{in}^{2} \cdot \sum_{i=1}^{m}tAv_{i}^{2}}}\right) < tr$$

Equation 17- 1

where Cv_{i} is the *i*-th centroid vector, Av - the access vector, tCv_{i1} - the *i*-th   term in the vector Cv_{1}, tAv_{i} - the *i*-th   term in the vector Av, and m – the number of unique terms in each vector.

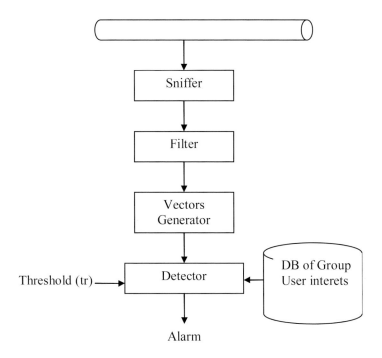

Figure 17-2. ATDS Detection Mode

3.3 ATDS Implementation

ATDS is implemented using four components:
1. Online-HTML Tracer (OHT) – including the Sniffer and the Filter.
2. Vector Generator.
3. The Cluster Generator.
4. Detector.

On-Line-HTML Tracer. The On-Line HTML Tracer consists of the Sniffer and the Filter modules. The Sniffer is implemented using the WinPickup software tool [7]. The packets intercepted by the Sniffer are sent to the Filter module that scans the content of each intercepted packet and filters out packets with non-textual HTML pages. The remaining packets are reconstructed into HTML pages and sent to the Vector Generator.

Vector Generator. The Vector Generator component is implemented using the Extractor software tool [3] that receives an HTML page and generates a vector of up to 30 weighted key phrases scored by their importance to the page.

Cluster Generator. The Cluster Generator is based on the Vcluster program from the Cluto Clustering Tool [13] using the 'k-way' clustering algorithm (a version of k-means). The similarity between the objects is computed using the cosine measure [14]. The Cluster Generator applies clustering to all the vectors in the DB and generates a centroid vector for each of the clusters. The output is a set of centroids representing the areas of interests of the 'normal' users, or the "normal user behavior".

Detector.   The Detector receives as input a newly captured page already represented as a vector along with its IP address. The Detector operates a similarity check (performed by the Similarity Checker) measuring the cosine similarity between the new incoming vector and the set of clusters representing the normal user's profile. If the similarity is above the predefined threshold, the new incoming vector is classified as normal. Only when none of the clusters is found as similar to the incoming vector, it is labeled as abnormal. The vector and its classification (normal or abnormal) are recorded into the queue of the specific IP Address in the Vector Sub-Queues data structure. The next step is performed by the Anomaly Finder which scans the sub-queue of a certain IP Address and counts the vectors classified as abnormal in the queue, if the number is above the alarm threshold, the Detector generates an alarm implying that the user at the specific IP is accessing abnormal information. In this chapter, we describe experiments that examine the effect of tuning the queue size and the alarm threshold on detection quality.

4.   EVALUATION

To evaluate the feasibility and the performance of the model, it was implemented as ATDS. Following are some details on ATDS implementation:

ATDS was implemented using Microsoft Visual C++ and designed in a modular architecture. The computational resources and the complexity of the methodology required a careful design to enable real-time on-line sniffing.

The system was deployed on an Intel Pentium 4 2.4 GHz server with 512 MB RAM. The server was installed in the computation center of Ben-Gurion University (BGU) and was configured to monitor 38 stations in teaching labs of the Department of Information System Engineering (ISE) at BGU. The stations consisted of Pentium 4, 2.4GHz with 512MB of RAM, 1Gbps fast Ethernet Intel adapter and Windows XP professional operating system. The access to those stations is allowed only to students of the one department (Information Systems Engineering).

4.1 Data preparation for the simulations

We prepared a repository (Web pages) for the learning mode of the model and another repository for the detection mode which included accesses to normal and abnormal (terror-related) content to represent "normal" and "abnormal" users.

For the learning mode we collected 170,000 students' accesses to the Web in the teaching labs of one department during one month. The students were aware and agreed to have their accesses collected anonymously. After exclusion of non-English pages (ATDS currently does not handle them) the "normal" collection included 13,300 pages. We then ran the Filtering and Vector Generator processes on the 13,300 pages and received a 13,300 × 38,776 matrix (i.e., 38,776 distinct terms representing the 13,300 pages).

For the detection mode, we have collected 582 terror-related pages to simulate abnormal accesses. We applied Filtering and Vector Generation to these pages resulting with a set of vectors representing terror related sites. We also randomly selected 582 vectors from the normal matrix for the simulation of normal users accessing only normal pages and abnormal users (terrorists) accessing a mix of normal and terror-related pages.

4.2 Evaluation objectives and measures

We evaluated ATDS performance using ROC (Receiver Operator Characteristic) curves and the following evaluation measures (based on [12]):

True Positive (TP) (also known as Detection Rate, Completeness, or hit rate) is the percentage of alarms in case of abnormal (positive) activity.

$$Tp = \frac{postive\_corrected\_classified}{total\_number\_of\_positives}$$

Equation 17- 2

False Positive (FP) is the percentage of false alarms when normal (negative) activity is taking place.

$$Fp = \frac{negative\_incorrecct\_ly\_classified}{total\_number\_of\_negatives}$$

Equation 17- 3

ROC graphs graphically represent the tradeoff between the TP and FP rates for every possible cutoff. Equivalently, a ROC curve represents the tradeoff between sensitivity and specificity. In a ROC graph the X axis represents the FP rate while the Y axis represents the TP alarm rate. A point on the graph represents the FP/TP for a specific similarity threshold.

The experiments intended to evaluate the following:

- Feasibility of the model, i.e., whether the system is able to perform on-line sniffing and accurate Web pages reconstruction.
- The effect of the following system's parameters on the system's performance, (i.e., on the values of TP and FP):
- The size of the sub queue for each IP, i.e., the number of accessed pages kept for each IP used by the detection algorithm as the IP history.
- Alarm thresholds values – the threshold of the ratio between the number of accesses detected as abnormal and the total number of accesses in the user queue for which an alarm is issued.
- Number of clusters representing the normal profile of the monitored users.

4.3   The Experiment

The experiments included three simulation runs:

The **first** related to the **evaluation** of the feasibility of the system and more specifically the monitoring ability of the OHT component, which is crucial to the feasibility of ATDS. During the **second and the third** simulations we tested the feasibility of ATDS as well as the effect of the system's parameters on FP and TP. This was done by running simulations while assigning a range of values of the system's parameters, as described below.

Simulation No. 1 aimed at the evaluation of OHT ability to monitor and intercept **all** HTML pages accessed by users in the experimental environment. Therefore, we ran one simulation measuring the percent of lost HTML pages during the capturing and reconstruction processes. We simulated heavy traffic to and from the Web, while monitoring the traffic, and compared the number of captured pages with the number of pages that were received by the user. All 38 computers were connected to a network switch configured to send all the packets to the network communication port of the system. We developed an emulator of the users' access to the Web that was installed on each of the stations. We used simulations and not real users since their traffic would be too slow to check the limits of OHT.

The simulations consisted of 13 iterations of accesses to a given list of 100 URLs including textual HTML files. All iterations were performed simultaneously by all 38 stations in the lab. Thus, if ideally performed, every iteration would result in 3,800 reconstructed HTML pages. We measured the time between successful accesses to the Web in each iteration to test the frequency of accesses the system was able to handle. A maximal time gap for the iterations was set to a fixed value, while the actual time gap between accesses within iterations varied randomly in a range between zero and the maximal time gap. The first iteration was set to a maximal time gap of 60 seconds and the time gaps decreased in steps of five seconds on the following iterations. Results are shown in Table 17-1, presenting the number of HTML that OHT captured for each maximal time gap, and the percent of the captured pages referred to as "Success Rate".

Table 17-1. Captured HTML Success Rate

Delay between accesses	Captured HTML pages	Success Rate
15-60	3800	100%
10	3798	99.9%
5	3800	100%
0	3796	99.8%

OHT managed to capture almost all HTML pages accessed from the 38 stations with a very high success rate (100% for most time gaps) i.e., OHT, feasibility was proven.

Simulation No. 2. In order to examine the feasibility of the suggested methodology (not only OHT) and the effect of the number of clusters on TP and FP rates, we simulated the learning mode by applying k-mean clustering to group the vectors that represented the typical user's behavior. In this simulation we used the basic TDS detection algorithm. We used its results to calibrate the number of clusters for ATDS. Also, this simulation became the baseline for comparing the performance of ATDS (operated in simulation no. 3) to the performance of the basic TDS. We then simulated "normal" users by accessing typical pages and "abnormal" users by accessing terror-related sites. We applied the simple TDS detection algorithm to detect the abnormal (potential terrorist) users. In this simulation we wanted to test the effect of the number of clusters generated in the learning mode on the detection performance measured by TP and FP presented as ROC graphs. We ran this simulation three times each with a different number of clusters: 50, 100, and 200.

Figure 17-3 describes some results of the simulation showing the TP and FP rates for an abnormal user accessing abnormal pages and a normal user accessing only normal pages. Each curve presents a different number of clusters generated during the learning mode. As can be seen from the graph, 50 clusters and 200 clusters yielded very similar results while the 100 clusters classifier obtained better performance for most ranges of TP and FP. Specifically for TP < 0.84 and FP < 0.4 we will prefer the 100 clusters classifier. Even though it is impossible to generalize about the ideal number of clusters from these simulations, it is possible to conclude that the number of clusters affects the system's performance; therefore a sensitivity analysis (such as this simulation) is required to find the optimal number of clusters for a given system. In addition, these simulations confirmed the system's feasibility, since even when a simple detection algorithm is applied that is not configured to optimize performance we were able to obtain reasonable results (FP and TP).

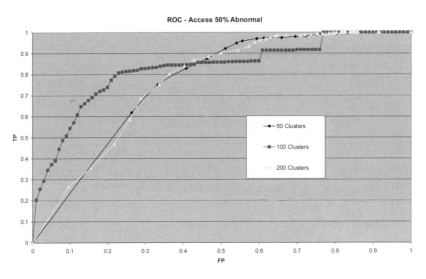

Figure 17-3. TP and FP as a function of the number of clusters

Simulation No. 3.   The ATDS enhanced detection algorithm aimed at applying continuous detection and issue an alarm based on consistent accesses to abnormal pages. Another parameter is the alarm threshold that defines the rate of suspected vectors in a user's queue that should exceed a threshold in order for the alarm to be issued. This simulation evaluated the effect of the queue size and the alarm threshold on the detection quality measured by TP and FP; we therefore ran several simulations applying the detection algorithm with different values of these parameters. We examined the queue size with the values: 2, 8, 16 and 32, and the alarm thresholds with the values of 50% and 100%. Since these simulations might be affected by the order of incoming vectors that might alter the number of suspected pages in a user's access queue and the rate of the abnormal pages in the queue (alarm threshold) we repeated the detection ten times to cancel the effect. We present the results averaged over the ten repeated simulations. As in simulation no. 2, an abnormal user was simulated by accesses to abnormal (terrorist) pages. The graphs on Figures 17-4 and 17-5 show the effect of the alarm threshold, and those on Figures 17-6 and 17-7 show the effect of the queue size.

It can be seen from figures 17-4 through 17-7 that the detection performance improves with the increase of the queue size for both values of the alarm threshold. Also, the graphs show that for this data 100% alarm threshold is better than 50%. Actually the system reached an almost ideal detection for queue size =32 and alarm threshold 100% (see Figure 17-7). This result of superiority of the 100% alarm threshold over 50% cannot be generalized since it might depend on the data. However, the results suggest that with sensitivity tuning of the advanced detection algorithm's parameters it is possible to optimize the system's performance.

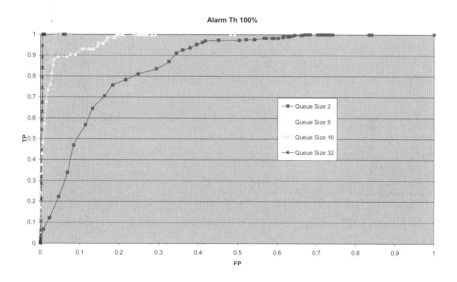

Figure 17-4. TP and FP for 100% alarm threshold

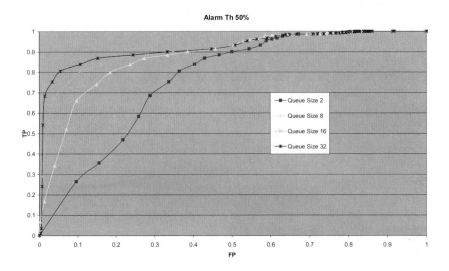

Figure 17-5. TP and FP for 50% alarm threshold.

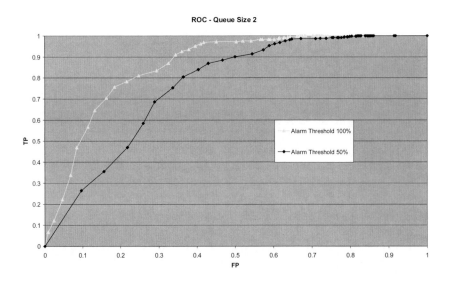

Figure 17-6. TP and FP positive for queue size 2

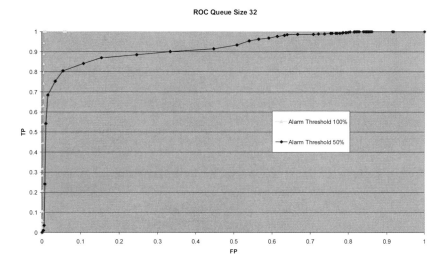

Figure 17-7. TP and FP as for queue size 32

5. CONCLUSIONS AND DISCUSSION

ATDS is aimed at tracking down suspected terrorists by analyzing the content of information they access. ATDS is an extension of the Content-Based Anomaly Detection on the Web suggested by [2,5]. In this chapter we presented ATDS evaluation that confirmed its feasibility and the contribution of the advanced detection algorithm to the detection performance.

An important contribution of ATDS lies in the unique environment of its application. The detection component is planned to run in a real-time wide-area network environment and should be capable of online monitoring of many users. Therefore, a crucial design requirement was high performance which called for enhancement of the algorithms involved, especially the high performance and scalability of the mining algorithm. ATDS is an example of a successful application of data mining and machine learning techniques to the international cyber-war effort against terror.

As for future research issues, we plan to evaluate the system simulating a more realistic model of the terrorist user, i.e., a random mixture of accesses to normal and abnormal pages. In addition, we are developing a cross-lingual version of the system as many terror-related sites use languages other than English (e.g., Arabic). We are also planning to analyze non-textual content on pages, such as logos, pictures, colors and any other non-textual features that may identify normal or abnormal content. We have also developed (but not yet implemented) an opposite (profile-based) method that collects and learns the typical content of terror-related web pages and detects users viewing similar content rather than detecting users by content, which is dissimilar to the normal content. Integration of the behavior-based and the profile-based methods is expected to reduce the false positive rate of the detection system.

6. ACKNOWLEDGEMENTS

This work was partially supported by the Fulbright Foundation that has awarded Prof. Abraham Kandel the Fulbright Senior Specialists Grant at Ben-Gurion University of the Negev in November-December 2005.

REFERENCES

1. Birnhack M., D. and Elkin-Koren, N. Fighting Terror On-Line: The Legal Ramifications of September 11, Internal Report, The Law and Technology Center, Haifa University. (http://law.haifa.ac.il/faculty/lec_papers/terror_info.pdf) (2003)
2. Elovici,Y., Shapira, B., Last, M., Kandell, A., and Zaafrany, O: Using Data Mining Techniques for Detecting Terror-Related Activities on the Web, J of Information Warfare, 3 (1), (2004), 17-28.
3. Extractor DBI Technologies (2003) http://www.dbi-tech.com
4. Fielding, R. Gettys, J. and Mogul, J. "RFC2616: Hypertext Transfer Protocol – HTTP/1.1" Network Working Group, (1999).
5. Last, M. Elovici, Y. Shapira, B. Zaafrany, O, and Kandel, A.: Using Data Mining for Detecting Terror-Related Activities on the Web, ECIW Proceedings (2003), 271-280.
6. Last, M. Elovici, Y. Shapira, B. Zaafrany, O., and Kandel, A.: Content-Based Methodology for Anomaly Detection on the Web, Advances in Web Intelligence, E. Menasalvas et al. (Eds), Springer-Verlag, Lecture Notes in Artificial Intelligence, 2663, (2003), 113–123.
7. Winpcap version 3.0 (2004) http://winpcap.polito.it/
8. Wooster, R., Williams, S. and Brooks, P.: HTTPDUMP: a network HTTP packet snooper. Working paper available at http://cs.vt.edu/~chitra/work.html (1996)
9. Kelley, J.: Terror Groups behind Web encryption", USA Today, http://www.apfn.org/apfn/WTC_why.htm (2002)
10. Lemos, R.: What are the real risks of cyberterrorism?, ZDNet, http://zdnet.com/2100-1105-955293.html (2002)
11. Ingram, M.: Internet privacy threatened following terrorist attacks on US, http://www.wsws.org/articles/2001/sep2001/isps24.shtml (2001)
12. Sequeira, K. and Zaki, M.: ADMIT: Anomaly-based Data Mining for Intrusions, Proceedings of SIGKDD 02, (2002), 386-395
13. Karypis, G.: CLUTO - A Clustering Toolkit, Release 2.0, University of Minnesota, http://www.users.cs.umn.edu/~karypis/cluto/download.html (2002)
14. Salton, G., and Buckley, C.: Term-Weighting Approaches in Automatic Text Retrieval, Information Processing and Management, 24(5), (1988), 513-523.

15. Mobasher, M., Cooley, R., and Srivastava, J. :Automatic personalization based on Web usage mining *Communications of the ACM,* 43 (8), (2002), 142-151.

16. Ghosh, A.K., Wanken, J., and Charron, F.: Detecting Anomalous and Unknown Intrusions Against Programs. In Proceedings of ACSAC'98, December (1998)

17. Tan, K., and Maxion, R.: "Why 6?" Defning the Operational Limits of Stide, an Anomaly-Based Intrusion Detector. Proceedings of the IEEE Symposium on Security and Privacy (2002), 188 -202.

18. Lane,V, and Brodley, C.E.: Temporal sequence learning and data reduction for anomaly detection. In Proceedings of the 5th ACM conference on Computer and Communications Security, (1998), 150-158.

19. Corbin, J. "Al-Qaeda: In Search of the Terror Network that Threatens the World", Thunder's Mouth Press / Nation Books, New York, (2002).

20. Chen, H. "Intelligence and security informatics: information systems perspective", Decision Support Systems: Special Issue on Intelligence and Security Informatics, 41(3), (Mar. 2006), 555-559.

21. Chen, H., Qin, J., Reid, E., Chung, W., Zhou, Y., Xi, W., Lai, G., Elhourani, T., Bonillas, A., Wang, F.-Y., and Sageman M., "The dark web portal: Collecting and analyzing the presence of domestic and international terrorist groups on the web," in Proc. 7th IEEE Int. Conf. Intelligent Transportation Systems, Washington, DC, (Oct. 2004), 106–111.

22. Gerstenfeld, P.B., Grant, D.R., and Chiang, C., "Hate Online: A Content Analysis of Extremist Internet Sites," Analysis of Social Issues and Public Policy, 3(1), (2003), 29–44.

23. Office of Homeland Security, The White House, National strategy for homeland security, (July 2002).

24. Zhou1 Y., Reid, E., Qin, J., Chen H., and Lai, G., "U.S. Domestic Extremist Groups on the Web: Link and Content Analysis", IEEE intelligent systems, 20(5), (2005), 44-51.

25. Symonenko, S., Liddy, E.D., Yilmazel, O., DelZoppo, R., Brown, E., and Downey, M, "Using SVM Approach to classify anomalous content within the organization - Semantic Analysis for Monitoring Insider Threats". In Proceedings of 2nd Symposium on Intelligence and Security Informatics. Tucson, Arizona, (2004).

26. Perkowitz, M., Etzioni, O., "Towards adaptive web sites", Artificial Intelligence, 118, (2000), 245– 275.

27. Shahabi, C., Zarkesh, A., Adibi, J., and Shah, V., "Knowledge discovery from users web-page navigation", Proc. of the IEEE 7th International Workshop on Research Issues in Data Engineering, (1997), 20–30.

28. Provos, N., Honeyman, P., "Detecting Steganographic Content on the Internet", ISOC NDSS'02, (2002).

29. Leckie T., and Yasinsac, A., "Metadata for Anomaly-Based Security Protocol Attack Deduction", IEEE Transactions on Knowledge and Data Engineering, 16(9), (September 2004),1157-1168.

30. Abbasi, A., and Chen. H., "Applying Authorship Analysis to Extremist-Group Web Forum Messages", Published by the IEEE Computer Society, (September, 2005), 67-75.

31. Reid, E., Qin, J., Chung, W., Xu, J., Zhou, Y., Schumaker, R., Sageman, M., & Chen, H. "Terrorism Knowledge Discovery Project: A Knowledge Discovery Approach to Addressing the Threats of Terrorism," in Proc. of the 2nd. Symposium on Intelligence and Security Informatics , Tucson, AZ, (2004), 125-145.

32. Wu, H., Gordon, M., Demaagd, K., & Fan, w. "Mining web navigations for intelligence" Decision Support Systems, 41(3), (2006), 574-591.

33. Zaafrany, O., Shapira, B., Last, M., Elovici, Y., Kandel., A., "OHT- Online-HTML

Tracer for Detecting Terrorist Activities on the Web". Proceedings of the 3rd European Conference on Information Warfare and Security (ECIW 2004), University of London, UK, June 28-29, pp. 371-378, 2004.

SUGGESTED READINGS

M. Last and A. Kandel (Editors), Fighting Terror in Cyberspace, World Scientific, Series in Machine Perception and Artificial Intelligence, 65, 2005.

ONLINE RESOURCES

- International Conference on Fighting Terror in Cyberspace
  http://www.ise.bgu.ac.il/ftc/
- International Policy Institute for Counter-Terrorism, Interdisciplinary Center, Herzliya, Israel
  http://www.ict.org.il/
- Prism - Project for the Research of Islamist Movements
  http://www.e-prism.org/pages/1/index.htm
- SITE Institute - The Search for International Terrorist Entities.
  http://www.siteinstitute.org/
- IDSS - Institute Of Defense and Strategic Studies - Nanyang Technological University, Singapore
  http://www.ntu.edu.sg/idss/
- MEMRI (The Middle East Media Research Institute)
  http://www.memri.org/
- The Intelligence and Terrorism Information Center
  http://www.terrorism-info.org.il

DISCUSSION QUESTIONS

1. Describe how terrorist organizations use the web (use the content of the chapter and the online resources).
2. List the parameters that control the operation of ATDS and explain their effect on ATDS performance measures (TP and FP).
3. Suggest how ATDS can be employed to detect terrorist supporters in various environments.
4. Discuss the privacy issues that may arise from ATDS deployment in a university campus, and explain how they are being handled.
5. Assume ATDS monitoring Internet traffic of terrorist supporters. Suggest methods (if any) for these supporters to avoid their detection by ATDS.

18

TEXT MINING THE BIOMEDICAL LITERATURE FOR IDENTIFICATION OF POTENTIAL VIRUS/BACTERIUM AS BIO-TERRORISM WEAPONS

Xiaohua Hu[1], Xiaodan Zhang[1], Daniel Wu[1], Xiaohua Zhou[1], and Peter Rumm[2]
[1]College of Information Science and Technology, Drexel University, Philadelphia, Pennsylvania, U.S.A. ({thu, xzhang@cis.drexel.edu; {daniel.wu, xiaohuazhou}@drexel.edu); [2]School of Public Health, Drexel University, Philadelphia,Pennsylvania, U.S.A. (r26@drexel.edu)

CHAPTER OVERVIEW

There are some viruses and bacteria that have been identified as bioterrorism weapons. However, there are a lot other viruses and bacteria that can be potential bioterrorism weapons. A system that can automatically suggest potential bioterrorism weapons will help laypeople to discover these suspicious viruses and bacteria. In this paper we apply instance-based learning & text mining approach to identify candidate viruses and bacteria as potential bio-terrorism weapons from biomedical literature. We first take text mining approach to identify topical terms of existed viruses (bacteria) from PubMed separately. Then, we apply a text mining method bridge these terms as instances with the remaining viruses (bacteria) and thus to discover how much these terms describe the remaining viruses (bacteria). In the end, we build an algorithm to rank all remaining viruses (bacteria). We suspect that the higher the ranking of the virus (bacterium) is, the more suspicious they will be potential bio-terrorism weapon. Our findings are intended as a guide to the virus and bacterium literature to support further studies that might then lead to appropriate defense and public health measures.

1.   INTRODUCTION

Terrorist attack concerns many people in the world. Biological agent is one of five categories of terrorist weapons. For certain biological agents, the potential for devastating casualties is very high. The anthrax mail attack in October, 2001 terrorism caused 23 cases of anthrax-related illness and 5 deaths. Due to the widespread availability of agents, widespread knowledge of production methodologies, and potential dissemination devices, bioterrorism can be very cute for now and future. Because it is very difficult for laypeople diagnose and recognize most of the diseases caused by biological weapons, we need surveillance systems to keep an eye on potential uses of such biological weapons [1]. In this paper, we propose an instance based learning method to discover biological agents as potential Bioterrorism Weapons (BW). Before discovering potential BW, it's reasonable to study the characteristics of biological agents identified by human experts as BW. Some human experts have generalized some criteria for identifying virus and bacteria. The more detail is in section 3. However, it's hard for human being to map all the viruses and bacteria one by one to these criteria. Moreover, the list is compiled manually, requiring extensive specialized human resources and time. Because the biological agents such as viruses are evolving through mutations, biological or chemical change, some biological substances have the potential to turn into deadly virus through chemical/genetic/biological reaction, there should be an automatic approach to keep track of existing suspicious viruses and to discover new viruses as potential weapons. We expect that it would be very useful to identify those biological substances and take precaution actions or measurements. For better studying the characteristics of existed biological agents as BW, we use a text mining approach to extract topical MeSH terms from them. This is an exhaustive approach, so we believe that the topical MeSH terms we extract are very representative of the particular BW collection. Then, we use this discovered terms to build a term biological agent matrix from which we check how much these terms can be topical terms for the remaining biological agents. Later, we use the combination of these terms to rank each remaining biological agent. In the end, we get a top ranked term list that can be used as key words for human experts to examine the remaining biological agents. The most important is that we generate a biological agent as potential BW ranked by the extracted terms from the existed biological agents. We suspect that the higher rank the biological agent, the more it can become potential BW. The rest of the paper is organized as follows. Section 2 briefly discusses the relevant works. Section 3 describes the background information of virus and bacteria as biological agent. Section 4 discusses our method in detail. The experimental results are presented in Section 5.

Potential significance for public health and homeland security are discussed in Section 6.

2.   RELATED WORKS

The problem of mining implicit knowledge/information from biomedical literature was exemplified by Dr. Swanson's pioneering work on Raynaud disease/fish-oil discovery in 1986 [9]. Back then, the Raynaud disease had no known cause or cure, and the goal of his literature-based discovery was to uncover novel suggestions for how Raynaud disease might be caused, and how it might be treated. He found from biomedical literature that Raynaud disease is a peripheral circulatory disorder aggravated by high platelet aggregation, high blood viscosity and vasoconstriction. In another separate set of literature on fish oils, he found out the ingestion of fish oil can reduce these phenomena. But no single article from both sets in the biomedical literature mentions Raynaud and fish oil together in 1986. Putting these two separate literatures together, Swanson hypothesized that fish oil may be beneficial to people suffering from Raynaud disease [9] [10]. This novel hypothesis was later clinically confirmed by DiGiacomo in 1989 [2]. Later on [11] Dr. Swanson extended his methods to search literature for potential virus. But the biggest limitation of his methods is that, only 3 properties/criteria of a virus are used as search key word and the semantic information is ignored in the search procedure. In this paper, we present a novel biomedical literature mining algorithms based on this philosophy with significant extensions. Our objective is to extend the existing known virus list compiled by CDC to other viruses that might have similar characteristics. We hypothesize, therefore, that viruses that have been researched with respect to the characteristics possessed by existing viruses are leading candidates for extending the virus lists. Our findings are intended as a guide to the virus literature to support further studies that might then lead to appropriate defense and public health measures. In our former work [5], we let human experts to define the key words that help find viruses that can be potential biological weapons. In this paper, we will provide a text data mining approach to target the terms that help identify potential weapons and to rank the viruses according these terms.

3.   BACKGROUND OF VIRUS AND BACTERIUM

Before initiating suspicious viruses and bacteria mining systems, we should identify what biological agents could be used as biological weapons.

3.1   Virus

Geissler [3] identified and summarized 13 criteria (shown in Table 18-1) to identify biological warfare agents as viruses. Based on the criteria, he compiled 21 viruses. Table 18-2 lists the 21 virus names in MeSH terms. The viruses in Table 18-2 meet some of the criteria described in Table 18-1.

Table 18-1. Geissler's 13 Criteria for Viruses

1	The agent should consistently produce a given effect: death or disease.
2	The concentration of the agent needed to cause death or disease the infective dose should be low.
3	The agent should be highly contagious.
4	The agent should have a short and predictable incubation time from exposure to onset of the disease symptoms.
5	The target population should have little or no natural or acquired immunity or resistance to the agent.
6	Prophylaxis against the agent should not be available to the target population.
7	The agent should be difficult to identify in the target population, and little or no treatment for the disease caused by the agent should be available.
8	The aggressor should have means to protect his own forces and population against the agent clandestinely.
9	The agent should be amenable to economical mass production.
10	The agent should be reasonably robust and stable under production and storage conditions, in munitions and during transportation. Storage methods should be available that prevent gross decline of the agent's activity.
11	The agent should be capable of efficient dissemination. If it cannot be delivered via an aerosol, living vectors (e.g. fleas, mosquitoes or ticks) should be available for dispersal in some form of infected substrate.
12	The agent should be stable during dissemination. If it is to be delivered via an aerosol, it must survive and remain stable in air until it reaches the target population.
13	After delivery, the agent should have low persistence, surviving only for a short time, thereby allowing a prompt occupation of the attacked area by the aggressor's troops

Table 18-2. Geissler's 21 Viruses

Hemorrhagic Fever Virus, Crimean-Congo	Encephalitis Virus, Eastern Equine
Lymphocytic choriomeningitis virus	Encephalitis Virus, Japanese
Encephalitis Virus, Venezuelan Equine	Encephalitis Viruses, Tick-Borne
Encephalitis Virus, Western Equine	Encephalitis Virus, St. Louis

Arenaviruses, New World	Chikungunya virus	Hepatitis A virus
Marburg-like Viruses	Dengue Virus	Orthomyxoviridae
Rift Valley fever virus	Ebola-like Viruses	Junin virus
Yellow fever virus	Hantaan virus	Lassa virus
		Variola virus

Based on the criteria, government agencies such as CDC and the Department of Homeland Security compile and monitor viruses which are known to be dangerous in bio-terrorism.

3.2 Bacterium

There are known some bacteria (by the time we examine, there are 13) that cause deadly disease. For example, anthrax is an acute infectious disease caused by the spore-forming bacterium Bacillus anthracis. Anthrax most commonly occurs in wild and domestic lower vertebrates (cattle, sheep, goats, camels, antelopes, and other herbivores), but it can also occur in humans when they are exposed to infected animals or to tissue from infected animals or when anthrax spores are used as a bioterrorist weapon. Q fever is a zoonotic disease caused by Coxiella burnetii, a species of bacteria that is distributed globally. Coxiella burnetii is a highly infectious agent that is rather resistant to heat and drying. It can become airborne and inhaled by humans. A single C. burnetii organism may cause disease in a susceptible person. This agent could be developed for use in biological warfare and is considered a potential terrorist threat. For other deadly diseases caused by bacteria, please refer Table 18-3.

Table 18-3. Bacteria used in biological warfare

Bacteria name	Disease caused
Bacillus anthracis	Anthrax
Clostridium botulinum	Botulism
Brucella melitensis, Brucella abortus, Brucella suis	Brucellosis
Vibrio cholerae	Cholera
Yersinia pestis	Plague
Francisella tularensis	Tularemia
Burkholderia mallei, Burkholderia pseudomallei	Glanders
Coxiella burnetti	Q fever
Salmonella	Salmonellosis, typhoid fever

4. METHOD

MedMeSH Summarizer [6] summarizes a group of genes by filtering the biomedical literature and assigning relevant keywords describing the functionality of a group of genes. Each Gene cluster contains N genes, while each gene has a set of terms associated with it. A co-occurrence matrix is thus built, using the number of citations associated with the gene and containing the mesh term. Based on this matrix and some statistical information, overall relevance rankings were made for all the terms describing the topic of certain cluster of genes. There are 487 viruses known to us in PubMed database. We found it is quite reasonable to take the 21 viruses (biological weapons) as a cluster of viruses and apply the method discussed above to discover and thereby rank the terms that describes these viruses. We then take the remaining 466 viruses as another cluster and then build a matrix of terms (from 21 known viruses) by viruses (466 viruses) and thus rank all the 466 viruses through a ranking formula. We suspect that the higher the virus rank, the more likely the virus will be bio-terrorism weapon. Similarly, there are 630 bacteria defined in PubMed database. As mention above, we apply the same methodology to the existed 13 bacteria and the remaining 617 bacteria. For clear statements, we only take virus as an example to introduce our algorithm. However, we will introduce the experiment results of both virus and bacteria.

- **Virus Cluster:**

  Let $V = \{V_1, V_2, ..., V_N\}$ be the given cluster containing N viruses, where V_j will be used to denote the Jth virus in the cluster.

- **MeSH Term List:**

  Let $\Omega = \Omega_1 \cup \Omega_2 \cup ... \cup \Omega_N$, where Ω_j is the set of MeSH terms associated with the virus $V_j (j = 1,2,..., N)$ (after MeSH stop word filtering). Moreover, let $\Omega = \{T_1, T_2, ..., T_N\}$, where $T_i (i = 1,2,..., M)$ denote the MeSH terms associated with the virus in the cluster.

- **Matrix:**

$$Let\ F = ((F_{ij}))_{M \times N}$$

Equation 18- 1

be the co-occurrence matrix, where F_{ij} = Number of citations that are associated with the virus V_j by the PubMed database and contain the MeSH term $T_i (i = 1,2,..., M; j = 1,2,..., N)$.

- **Normalization by Virus Relevance**:

There are two contradicting requirements for normalization: dominant viruses in cluster should not highly skew results in their favor; some weight should be given to the fact that the virus is well studied. To achieve this normalized frequency of the MeSH term, T_i for virus V_j is computed as

$$\tilde{f}_{ij} = F_{ij} / (\sum_{i=1}^{M} F_{ij})^{\alpha} \; (0 \leq \alpha \leq 1)$$

Equation 18-2

Based on experiment results of MedMeSH Summarizer, the default value of α in our system is also 0.67. Now each MeSH term $T_i \in \Omega$, is characterized by the MeSH feature vector $\tilde{f}_i = (\tilde{f}_{i1}, \tilde{f}_{i2}, ..., \tilde{f}_{iN})$, where $\tilde{f}_{ij} (i = 1,2,..., M; j = 1,2,..., N)$ are the normalized frequencies described above.

Overall Relevance Ranking:
1. **Cluster Topics (Major):** These are MeSH terms that are "commonly" associated with almost all viruses in the cluster and hence likely to have a high total frequency of occurrence. For this, the MeSH terms are ranked by the mean of their virus distribution feature vectors as follows:
   - Compute

$$\mu_j = (\sum_{j=1}^{N} \tilde{f}_{ij}) / N (i = 1,..., M).$$

   - Ranking Criterion R1: Rank the MeSH terms by decreasing order of the means μ_j.
2. **Cluster Topics (Minor):** These are MeSH terms which had moderate-to-low total frequency but still appear with most of the genes. This type of terms is expected to have moderate mean and low variance. For this, the MeSH terms are ranked by the ratio of mean/standard deviation of their MeSH feature vectors as follows:
   - Compute

$$\sigma_i = \sqrt{(\sum_{j=1}^{N} (\tilde{f}_{ij} - \mu_i)^2) / N}, (i = 1,..., M).$$

   - Ranking Criterion R2: Rank the MeSH terms by decreasing order of the ratios

$$\mu_j / \sigma_i \text{ 's.}$$

3. Particular Topics:

These are MeSH terms that were not related to the whole cluster but were strongly associated with a subgroup of the cluster. This type of terms is expected to have high variance and moderate-to-low mean. For this, the MeSH terms are ranked by the ratio of variance/mean of their MeSH feature vectors as follows:

- Ranking Criterion $R3$: Rank the MeSH terms by decreasing order of the ratios

$$\sigma_i^2 / \mu_j \text{ 's.}$$

4. Each MeSH term in Ω is ranked based on each of the above three criteria. The terms were then given an overall relevance rank R where:

$$R = wR_1 + \frac{1-w}{2} R_2 + \frac{1-2}{2} R_3$$

Equation 18- 3

5. The weight parameter in Equation 18-3 has been assigned so that the major topics are given weight w being the most important set of terms in providing a summary of the cluster. The remaining weight $1 - w$ is divided equally between the minor topics and the particular topics. The default weights in the system are: $w = 0.50$ for the first ranking criterion and 0.25 each for the second and third criteria.

- **Procedure of algorithm**
1. Submit query "virus name [MeSH]" to the pubmed and download Mesh term after applying stop word list for each biological agent. We download documents of 21 known viruses. (MeSH term is the subjective terms presented by human experts for each document) We take each virus as a category. Our stop word list is composed of MeSH terms extracted from PubMed documents (1994-2004) by their overall usage. For example, some MeSH terms are used very frequently such as "English Abstract", "Government Supported", "Non Government Supported" and so on, and these terms have nothing to do with our viruses and bacterium mining.
2. Build a matrix **F** (Equation 18-1) of terms by viruses (21 viruses) and then normalize it through Equation 18-2.

3. Rank all the terms according to Equation 18-3 and pick top k terms.
4. Download the documents of the remaining 466 viruses. And use terms above to build a matrix **F** of terms by viruses (466 viruses) (Equation 18-1). Normalize the matrix by Equation 18-2.
5. Let the rank value of term be $R_i (i = 1,2,...,M)$. R_i is the rank value of term in the term **by** viruses (466 viruses) matrix. Eq.

$$R^V = \sum_{i=1}^{M} \tilde{f}_{ij} \times R_i (i = 1,2,...,M; j = 1,2,...,N)$$

Equation 18- 4

is used to rank each remaining virus marked as **Rank1**. We also rank virus using R_i from term by viruses (21 viruses) matrix marked as **Rank2**.

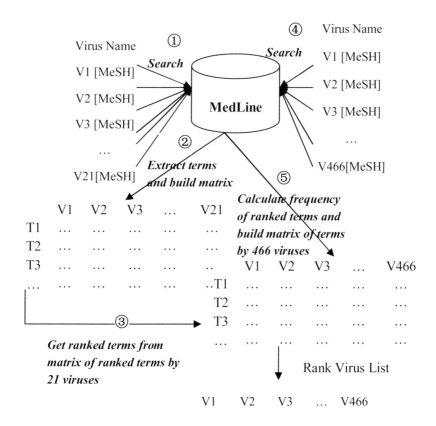

Figure 18-1. The Data Flow Diagram

5.   EXPERIMENTAL RESULTS

We apply our method to two data sets: viruses and bacteria. Section 5.1 lists the experiment results of virus, while section 5.2 is for bacteria. Table 18-6 to 18-9 displays the top ranked topical terms and suspicious viruses by R^V criteria (rank1 and rank2 respectively). Accordingly, Table 18-12 to 18-15 show the top ranked topical terms and bacteria by R^V criteria (rank1 and rank2 respectively). From the results, there is a big match between viruses/bacteria names and their associated diseases and topical terms. Take bacteria as an example, 12 out of 13 known bacteria names were ranked within top 50 terms in Table 18-12. Moreover, most of disease names caused by the 13 bacteria were also matched in the table. For the potential significance of suspicious viruses/bacteria that we detected, please refer to section 6.

5.1   Experiment Results of Suspicious Viruses Mining

Table 18-4. The search keywords (21 Virus names) and the according number of Documents downloaded

Search Keywords	# of Doc.
"Chikungunya virus"[MeSH]	397
"Hemorrhagic Fever Virus, Crimean-Congo"[MeSH]	202
"Encephalitis Virus, Eastern Equine"[MeSH]	292
…	…
Total	31080

Table 18-5. The search keywords (466 Virus names) and the according   number of Documents downloaded

Search Keywords	# of Doc.
"Abelson murine leukemia virus"[MeSH]	416
"Dependovirus"[MeSH]	1874
"Adenoviridae"[MeSH]	20178
…	…
Search Keywords	# of Doc.

Table 18-6. Top ranked topical terms by rank1

Rank1	Top 1-25 terms	Weight		Top 26-50 terms	Weight
1	blood-borne pathogens	1.47	26	infectious anemia virus, equine	1.03
2	transmissible gastroenteritis virus	1.45	27	classical swine fever virus	1.02
3	hepatitis e virus	1.42	28	needlestick injuries	1.01

Rank1	Top 1-25 terms	Weight		Top 26-50 terms	Weight
4	herpesvirus 1, equid	1.4	29	visna-maedi virus	1.01
5	influenza a virus, porcine	1.37	30	rhinovirus	1
6	hepatitis e	1.34	31	african swine fever virus	1
7	muromegalovirus	1.32	32	ectromelia virus	0.98
8	bacteriophage mu	1.32	33	lactate dehydrogenase-elevating virus	0.96
9	rauscher virus	1.24	34	borna disease	0.96
10	mycobacterium	1.2	35	hepatitis a virus, human	0.94
11	staphylococcus aureus	1.17	36	staphylococcal infections	0.94
12	bacillus phages	1.16	37	encephalitis virus, california	0.94
13	rift valley fever virus	1.15	38	mammary tumor virus, mouse	0.92
14	hemorrhagic fever, ebola	1.11	39	murine hepatitis virus	0.9
15	viruses, unclassified	1.11	40	bluetongue virus	0.87
16	herpesvirus 1, cercopithecine	1.11	41	bacteriophage phi x 174	0.86
17	endogenous retroviruses	1.1	42	immunodeficiency virus, feline	0.86
18	mengovirus	1.1	43	arboviruses	0.86
19	salmonella phages	1.1	44	staphylococcus	0.86
20	rift valley fever	1.07	45	mice minute virus	0.85
21	influenzavirus c	1.07	46	phlebovirus	0.84
22	sarcoma virus, woolly monkey	1.06	47	transfusion-transmitted virus	0.84
23	hepatitis delta virus	1.06	48	norwalk virus	0.84
24	ebola-like viruses	1.05	49	monkeypox virus	0.83
25	maus elberfeld virus	1.04	50	molluscum contagiosum virus	0.82

Table 18-7. Top ranked viruses by rank1

Rank1	Top 1-25 viruses	weight		Top 26-50 viruses	weight
1	Blood-Borne Pathogens	45.77	26	Hepatitis Delta Virus	17.52
2	Filoviridae	32.31	27	Rubulavirus	16.94
3	Phlebovirus	28.73	28	Herpesvirus 1, Equid	16.94
4	Hepatitis E virus	28.13	29	Salmonella Phages	16.75
5	Hepatovirus	27.31	30	Visna-maedi virus	16.62

Rank1	Top 1-25 viruses	weight		Top 26-50 viruses	weight
6	Bunyaviridae	22.48	31	Togaviridae	16.61
7	Hantavirus	22.37	32	Encephalomyocardi tis virus	16.47
8	Staphylococcus Phages	22.13	33	Alphavirus	16.32
9	Influenza A Virus, Porcine	21.96	34	Distemper Virus, Canine	16.19
10	Arenaviridae	21.55	35	Rhinovirus	16.13
11	Hepatitis A Virus, Human	21.53	36	Rubella virus	16.08
12	Orthobunyavirus	21.52	37	Mammary Tumor Virus, Mouse	16.03
13	Arboviruses	21.52	38	Herpesvirus 3, Human	15.91
14	Arenavirus	21.3	39	Rubivirus	15.86
15	Viruses, Unclassified	20.62	40	Classical swine fever virus	15.85
16	Encephalitis Virus, California	20.49	41	Picornaviridae	15.71
17	Arenaviruses, Old World	20.05	42	Lyssavirus	15.61
18	Herpesvirus 1, Suid	18.67	43	Mycobacteriophage s	15.55
19	Rauscher Virus	18.65	44	Muromegalovirus	15.49
20	Transmissible gastroenteritis virus	18.58	45	Poliovirus	15.44
21	Encephalitis Viruses	18.2	46	Norwalk virus	15.42
22	Influenzavirus A	18.05	47	Parainfluenza Virus 3, Human	15.4
23	Influenza A virus	17.92	48	Orbivirus	15.39
24	Flavivirus	17.87	49	Norovirus	15.38
25	Mumps virus	17.59	50	Rabies virus	15.36

Table 18-8. Top ranked topical terms by rank2

Rank2	Top 1-25 terms	Weight		Top 26-50 terms	Weight
1	variola virus	2.06	26	yellow fever	1.27
2	lymphocytic choriomeningitis virus	1.84	27	hepatitis antibodies	1.27
3	arenaviruses, new world	1.78	28	dengue virus	1.26
4	hepatitis a virus, human	1.73	29	hepatitis a antibodies	1.26
5	hepatitis a	1.72	30	viral hepatitis	1.26

Rank2	Top 1-25 terms	Weight		Top 26-50 terms	Weight
				vaccines	
6	chikungunya virus	1.68	31	influenza a virus	1.25
7	encephalitis viruses, tick-borne	1.64	32	encephalitis virus, western equine	1.2
8	smallpox	1.63	33	lassa virus	1.2
9	encephalitis, tick-borne	1.63	34	encephalomyelitis, venezuelan equine	1.19
10	hepatitis a virus	1.62	35	influenza, avian	1.19
11	yellow fever virus	1.6	36	hemorrhagic fever with renal syndrome	1.18
12	encephalitis virus, japanese	1.57	37	hemorrhagic fever virus, crimean-congo	1.17
13	influenza	1.54	38	hemorrhagic fever, crimean	1.16
14	encephalitis virus, venezuelan equine	1.52	39	influenza b virus	1.14
15	hantaan virus	1.49	40	dengue	1.12
16	ebola-like viruses	1.47	41	encephalitis virus, eastern equine	1.11
17	hemorrhagic fever, american	1.47	42	ixodes	1.11
18	lymphocytic choriomeningitis	1.45	43	cd8-positive t-lymphocytes	1.1
19	rift valley fever virus	1.44	44	Encephalitis virus,st louis	1.07
20	hepatitis a vaccines	1.4	45	influenza vaccines	1.06
21	encephalitis, japanese	1.38	46	dengue hemorrhagic fever	1.03
22	rift valley fever	1.37	47	influenza a virus, human	1
23	smallpox vaccine	1.37	48	lassa fever	0.93

Rank2	Top 1-25 terms	Weight		Top 26-50 terms	Weight
24	hemorrhagic fever, ebola	1.27	49	neuraminidase	0.9
25	influenza a virus, avian	1.27	50	arenaviridae	0.9

Table 18-9. Top ranked viruses by rank2

Rank2	Top 1-25 viruses	weight		Top 26-50 viruses	weight
1	Hepatovirus	62.38	26	Hepatitis E virus	33.34
2	Arenaviridae	60.56	27	Influenza A Virus, Porcine	33.29
3	Arenavirus	59.56	28	Poxviridae	32.56
4	Arenaviruses, Old World	58.77	29	Encephalitis Virus, California	32.18
5	Filoviridae	56.96	30	Flaviviridae	32.03
6	Flavivirus	51.46	31	Viruses, Unclassified	31.56
7	Encephalitis Viruses	49.86	32	Picornaviridae	31.03
8	Hepatitis A Virus, Human	47.99	33	Vaccinia virus	30.01
9	Blood-Borne Pathogens	47.3	34	Vesiculovirus	29.7
10	Influenza A virus	46.95	35	West Nile virus	29.66
11	Influenzavirus A	46.81	36	Vesicular stomatitis-Indiana virus	29.59
12	Phlebovirus	45.73	37	Poliovirus	29
13	Arboviruses	42.59	38	Norovirus	28.94
14	Bunyaviridae	39.7	39	Polioviruses	28.92
15	Alphavirus	39.1	40	Gross Virus	28.55
16	Hantavirus	38.68	41	Adenoviridae	28.54
17	Influenza A Virus, Human	38.3	42	Nairovirus	28.4
18	Togaviridae	37.31	43	Respirovirus	28.07
19	Orthopoxvirus	36.58	44	Semliki forest virus	27.87
20	Encephalitis Viruses, Japanese	36.21	45	Norwalk virus	27.56
21	Influenzavirus B	35	46	Caliciviridae	27.5
22	Influenza A Virus, Avian	34.68	47	Enterovirus	27.37

Rank2	Top 1-25 viruses	weight		Top 26-50 viruses	weight
23	Chordopoxvirinae	33.4	48	Parainfluenza Virus 3, Human	26.84
24	Orthobunyavirus	33.39	49	Sindbis Virus	26.83
25	Influenza B virus	33.37	50	Encephalomyocarditis virus	26.37

5.2 Experiment Results of Suspicious Bacteria Mining

Table 18-10. The search keywords (13 bacteria names) and the according number of downloaded

Search Keywords	# of Doc.
"Bacillus anthracis" [major]	1153
"Clostridium botulinum" [major]	1191
"Brucella melitensis" [major]	391
"Brucella abortus" [major]	1415
"Brucella suis" [major]	18
"Vibrio cholerae" [major]	3503
"Yersinia pestis" [major]	1323
"Francisella tularensis" [major]	621
"Burkholderia mallei" [major]	19
"Burkholderia pseudomallei" [major]	443
"Coxiella burnetti" (No major topic)	172
"Salmonella" [major]	21677
"Shigella dysenteriae" [major]	687
Total	32613

Table 18-11. The search keywords (617 bacteria name) and the according number of documents downloaded

Search Keywords	# of Doc.
"Acetobacter"[major]	279
Acetobacteraceae" [major]	543
"Acetobacterium"[major]	4
…	…

Table 18-12. Top ranked topical terms by rank1

1	erysipelothrix	1.69	26	leuconostoc
2	sarcina	1.65	27	leptospira interrogans serovar canicola
3	campylobacter fetus	1.6	28	bacillus megaterium
4	yersinia pseudotuberculosis	1.5	29	nocardia asteroides

5	photobacterium	1.49	30	proteus vulgaris
6	providencia	1.49	31	yersinia pseudotuberculosis infections
7	haemophilus ducreyi	1.43	32	micromonospora
8	brevibacterium	1.4	33	chlorobi
9	coxiella burnetii	1.4	34	actinobacillus pleuropneumoniae
10	erysipelothrix infections	1.36	35	rhizobium leguminosarum
11	q fever	1.34	36	mycobacterium paratuberculosis
12	streptococcus suis	1.33	37	corynebacterium pyogenes
13	clostridium tetani	1.33	38	saccharopolyspora
14	chromobacterium	1.32	39	mannheimia haemolytica
15	vibrio parahaemolyticus	1.29	40	campylobacter coli
16	erwinia	1.28	41	plesiomonas
17	bacillus stearothermophilus	1.27	42	yersinia enterocolitica
18	chancroid	1.27	43	thermus thermophilus
19	spheroplasts	1.26	44	acetobacter
20	anabaena	1.26	45	haemophilus influenzae type b
21	streptococcus bovis	1.23	46	corynebacterium diphtheriae
22	l forms	1.23	47	swine erysipelas
23	pediococcus	1.21	48	mycobacterium leprae
24	spirochaeta	1.19	49	mycobacterium smegmatis
25	mycoplasma mycoides	1.18	50	peptococcus

Table 18-13. Top ranked bacterium by rank1

Rank1	Top 1-25 Bacterium	Rank Value		Top 26-50 Bacterium	Rank value
1	Clostridium tetani	38.8	26	Mycobacterium avium	18.69
2	Erysipelothrix	36.96	27	Treponema pallidum	18.58
3	Coxiellaceae	31.57	28	Vibrionaceae	18.43
4	Sarcina	31.27	29	Vibrio	18.41
5	Yersinia pseudotuberculosis	28.16	30	Clostridium difficile	18.26
6	Atypical Bacterial Forms	26.41	31	Bacillus stearothermophilus	18.18
7	Corynebacterium diphtheriae	26.22	32	Escherichia coli O157	18.01
8	Photobacterium	26.13	33	Erwinia	18.01
9	Brucella	24.9	34	Propionibacterium acnes	17.9
10	Haemophilus ducreyi	24.69	35	Lactobacillus casei	17.88
11	Brucellaceae	23.68	36	Chromobacterium	17.83
12	Campylobacter fetus	22.74	37	Bordetella pertussis	17.79
13	Yersinia enterocolitica	21.95	38	Lactobacillus acidophilus	17.67
14	Bacillus thuringiensis	21.24	39	Mannheimia haemolytica	17.65
15	Pediococcus	21.2	40	Nocardia	17.63

Rank1	Top 1-25 Bacterium	Rank Value		Top 26-50 Bacterium	Rank value
16	Mycobacterium bovis	20.36	41	Bordetella	17.52
17	Proteus vulgaris	20.23	42	Mannheimia	17.48
18	Haemophilus influenzae type b	19.89	43	Leuconostoc	17.2
19	Nocardia asteroides	19.88	44	Citrobacter	17.19
20	Bacillus megaterium	19.69	45	Clostridium perfringens	17.11
21	Clostridium	19.59	46	Pasteurella multocida	17.05
22	Providencia	19.56	47	Mycobacterium leprae	16.96
23	Vibrio parahaemolyticus	19.53	48	Bartonellaceae	16.89
24	Brevibacterium	19.36	49	Bartonella	16.87
25	Burkholderiaceae	19.11	50	Rhizobium radiobacter	16.86

Table 18-14. Top ranked topical terms by rank2

Rank2	Top 1-25 terms	weight		Top 26-50 terms	Weight
1	vibrio cholerae	3.69	26	salmonella enteritidis	1.72
2	brucella abortus	3.36	27	brucella vaccine	1.65
3	clostridium botulinum	3.19	28	brucellosis	1.65
4	bacillus anthracis	3.01	29	cholera vaccines	1.63
5	yersinia pestis	3.01	30	fleas	1.5
6	shigella dysenteriae	2.81	31	shigella sonnei	1.42
7	cholera	2.72	32	complement fixation tests	1.36
8	botulinum toxins	2.42	33	spores, bacterial	1.31
9	salmonella typhimurium	2.4	34	shigella flexneri	1.28
10	anthrax	2.38	35	salmonella food poisoning	1.28
11	francisella tularensis	2.32	36	shiga toxins	1.27
12	plague	2.27	37	mutagens	1.27
13	botulism	2.13	38	brucella	1.2
14	dysentery, bacillary	2.1	39	food microbiology	1.2
15	brucellosis, bovine	2.1	40	shigella boydii	1.2
16	cholera toxin	2.09	41	escherichia coli o157	1.18
17	burkholderia	2.09	42	fimbriae	1.18

Rank2	Top 1-25 terms	weight		Top 26-50 terms	Weight
	pseudomallei			proteins	
18	tularemia	2.03	43	drug resistance, bacterial	1.16
19	salmonella	2.01	44	drug resistance, multiple, bacterial	1.15
20	salmonella infections, animal	1.99	45	anthrax vaccines	1.15
21	salmonella enterica	1.95	46	bioterrorism	1.15
22	salmonella infections	1.9	47	plague vaccine	1.12
23	melioidosis	1.86	48	bursa of fabricius	1.12
24	mutagenicity tests	1.73	49	neurotoxins	1.12
25	brucella melitensis	1.72	50	colony count, microbial	1.11

Table 18-15. Top ranked bacterium by rank2

Rank2	Top 1-25 Bacterium	Weight		Top 26-50 Bacterium	weight
1	Brucella	82.21	26	Endospore-Forming Bacteria	49.17
2	Brucellaceae	79.08	27	Gram-Positive Endospore-Forming Rods	49.05
3	Clostridium tetani	71.33	28	Bacillaceae	48.31
4	Vibrio	70.21	29	Vibrio parahaemolyticus	48.27
5	Vibrionaceae	67.1	30	Photobacterium	47.9
6	Clostridium	61.73	31	Campylobacter	46.71
7	Escherichia coli O157	59.79	32	Proteobacteria	46
8	Sarcina	58.5	33	Bacillus thuringiensis	45.65

Rank2	Top 1-25 Bacterium	Weight		Top 26-50 Bacterium	weight
9	Yersinia pseudotuber culosis	57.81	34	Bacteria	45.51
10	Enterobacter iaceae	57.76	35	Gram- Negative Bacteria	45.46
11	Spores, Bacterial	57.54	36	Lactobacillu s acidophilus	45.33
12	Listeria	56.71	37	Erysipelothri x	44.73
13	Listeria monocytoge nes	55.04	38	Escherichia	44.56
14	Burkholderia ceae	54.79	39	Campylobac ter jejuni	44.51
15	Mycobacteri um bovis	54.7	40	Escherichia coli	44.51
16	Gram- Negative Facultatively Anaerobic Rods	53.79	41	Lactobacillu s casei	44.31
17	Clostridium perfringens	53.58	42	Alphaproteo bacteria	44.13
18	Atypical Bacterial Forms	53.31	43	Pasteurella multocida	43.25
19	Bacillus cereus	50.56	44	Corynebacte rium diphtheriae	43.21
20	Gammaprote obacteria	50.55	45	Mannheimia haemolytica	43.11
21	Probiotics	50.51	46	Propionibact erium	43.01
22	Yersinia enterocolitic a	50.3	47	Mannheimia	42.87
23	Gram- Positive Endospore- Forming Bacteria	49.81	48	Bifidobacteri um	42.7
24	Propionibact erium acnes	49.6	49	Micrococcus	42.48
25	Coxiellaceae	49.22	50	Propionibact eriaceae	42.35

6.   POTENTIAL SIGNIFICANCE FOR PUBLIC HEALTH AND HOMELAND SECURITY

This work is critical to public health and homeland security. Our nation is spending alone this year just in disbursements to states, territory and local health over a billion dollars to prepare for terrorism including such efforts as building public health capacity, disease surveillance and laboratory notification [4]. However, without the ability to prioritize these resources which have improved public health capacity and laboratory capacity we cannot further improve both national and international preparedness efforts [7]. In 1999 the Department of Defense was involved in building a directory of known emerging infectious diseases and laboratory tests worldwide and identified approximately 40 high threat agents for bio-terrorism including many of the hemorrhagic viruses [8]. However since that time we have had the emergence of SARS, Avian Flu virus and many other threats to the public health. We must be prepared and without continued work such as this to identify additional threats, the preparedness efforts may fall short.

7.   ACKNOWLEDGEMENTS

This work is supported partially by the NSF Career grant IIS 0448023 and NSF 0514679 and PA Dept of Health Tobacco Formula Grants.

REFERENCES

1.   Büchen-Osmond C. Taxonomy and Classification of Viruses. In: Manual of Clinical Microbiology, ASM Press, Washington DC, 8th ed, Vol 2, p. 1217-1226, 2003

2.   DiGiacome, R.A, Kremer, J.M. and Shah, D.M. Fish oil dietary supplementation is patients with Raynaud's phenomenon: A double-blind, controlled, prospective study, American Journal of Medicine, 158-164m, 8, 1989.

3.   Geissler, E. (Ed.), Biological and toxin weapons today, Oxford, UK: SIPRI (1986)

4.   Guidance on cooperative agreements from the U.S. Department of Health and Human Services, Centers for Disease Control and Prevention and the Human Resource Service Administration.   Accessible at www.bt.cdc.gov

5.   Hu X., I. Yoo. P. Rumm, M. Atwood., Mining Candidate Viruses as Potential Bio-Terrorism Weapons from Biomedical Literature, in 2005 IEEE International Conference on Intelligence and Security Informatics (IEEE ISI-2005), Atlanta, Georgia, May 19-20, 2005

6.   Hu X., Zhang X., Yoo, I., Atwood M., Rumm, P., A Text Mining Approach for Identifying Candidate Viruses as Potential Bio-terrorism Weapons, GESTS International Transaction on Compute Science and Engineering, Vol. 9, NO 1., July 2005

7.   P. Kankar, S. Adak, A. Sarkar, K. Murari, K. and G. Sharma. "MedMeSH Summarizer:

Text Mining for Gene Clusters", in the Proceedings of the Second SIAM International Conference on Data Mining, Arlington, VA, 2002

8. Rumm P.D. Bioterrorism preparedness: potential threats remain. Am J Public Health. 2005 Mar;95(3):372 (comment on previous article)

9. Rumm P, Gaydos J, Mansfield J and Kelley P, A Department of Defense (DOD) Virtual Public Health Laboratory Directory, *Mil Med*, 2000;Jul,165-Supp. 2):73.

10. Swanson, DR., Fish-oil, Raynaud's Syndrome, and undiscovered public knowledge. Perspectives in Biology and Medicine 30(1), 7-18, 1986

11. Swanson, DR., Undiscovered public knowledge. Libr. Q. 56(2), pp. 103-118 1986

12. Swanson, DR, Smalheiser NR, & Bookstein A. Information discovery from complementary literatures: categorizing viruses as potential weapons. JASIST 52(10): 797-812 , 2001

SUGGESTED READINGS

- Hu X., I. Yoo. P. Rumm, M. Atwood., Mining Candidate Viruses as Potential Bio-Terrorism Weapons from Biomedical Literature, in 2005 *IEEE International Conference on Intelligence and Security Informatics* (IEEE ISI-2005), Atlanta, Georgia, May 19-20, 2005.

- Hu X., Zhang X., Yoo, I., Atwood M., Rumm, P., A Text Mining Approach for Identifying Candidate Viruses as Potential Bio-terrorism Weapons, *GESTS International Transaction on Compute Science and Engineering,* Vol. 9, No. 1, July 2005.

- Swanson, D.R., Undiscovered public knowledge. *Libr. Q.* 56(2), pp. 103-118, 1986.

ONLINE RESOURCES

- Taxonomy and Classification of Viruses:
  http://www.ncbi.nlm.nih.gov/ICTVdb/MCM8.pdf
- Guidance on cooperative agreements from the U.S. Department of Health and Human Services, Centers for Disease Control and Prevention and the Human Resource Service Administration. Accessible at
  http://www.bt.cdc.gov/
- PUBMED:
  http://www.ncbi.nlm.nih.gov/entrez/query.fcgi?db=books

DISCUSSION QUESTIONS

1. In our presented problem, we summarize all existed viruses/bacteria as a whole and try to identify topical terms crossing all different

viruses/bacteria related documents. What other techniques might help to summarize existing viruses/bacteria? How do you balance those terms against viruses/bacteria that have very few documents?

2. Given the weight of topical terms, what other techniques do you think can help target the most suspicious virus/bacteria?

3. Can the terms used to describe disease symptoms caused by viruses/bacteria help identify potential viruses/bacteria? How can these terms be extracted?

4. Describe three other problems that can be solved using the method presented in this chapter.

19

LEVERAGING ONE-CLASS SVM AND SEMANTIC ANALYSIS TO DETECT ANOMALOUS CONTENT

Ozgur Yilmazel[1], Svetlana Symonenko[1], Niranjan Balasubramanian[1], and Elizabeth D. Liddy[1]

[1]*Center for Natural Language Processing, School of Information Studies, Syracuse University, Syracuse, New York, ({oyilmaz, ssymonen, nbalasub, liddy}@syr.edu)*

CHAPTER OVERVIEW

Experiments were conducted to test several hypotheses on methods for improving document categorization for the malicious insider threat problem within the Intelligence Community. Bag-of-words (BOW) representations of documents were compared to Natural Language Processing (NLP) based representations in both the typical and one-class categorization problems using the Support Vector Machine algorithm. Results from our Semantic Anomaly Monitoring (SAM) system show that the NLP features significantly improved classifier performance over the BOW approach both in terms of precision and recall, while using many fewer features. The one-class algorithm using NLP features demonstrated robustness when tested on new domains.

1.   INTRODUCTION

Malicious insider activities pose serious threats to the intelligence community (IC) when they go undetected. A malicious insider is someone who, while a valid user of IC systems, performs unauthorized malicious acts, including sharing of information with groups unfriendly to the organization. The goal of our research was to develop solutions for efficiently detecting such unwanted behaviors. While the IC is the main focus of our development efforts described herein, targeting potential insider threats has been recognized as essential security practice in many other sectors such as banking and securities, utilities, and communications. Additionally, with the recent proliferation of Internet-based technologies enabling a wide range of activities, including covert ones, organizations of every kind and scale are becoming concerned with the problem of timely detection of abnormal cyber behavior of their employees

The approach described in this chapter addresses the problem of improving security within the IC by leveraging Natural Language Processing (NLP) and Machine Learning (ML) technologies. We developed a system that monitors insiders' workflow documents and raises alerts if the content of the documents shifts away from the expected scope, given the insider's assignments. The information accessed by analysts can be described in terms of specific topics of interest (TOIs) and geo-political areas of interest (AOIs), where the task assigned to an analyst dictates the scope of their TOI/AOI. The system uses one-class categorization, a Machine Learning technique, to model the expected behavior of an analyst. Unlike typical categorization systems which differentiate between two classes of documents, a one-class categorization system can identify documents that do not belong to a certain class, without prior knowledge of the potential domain of interest to the malicious insider. In addition, the system uses NLP technologies to improve the effectiveness and efficiency of the categorization task and to produce higher level conceptual profiles of texts.

It is important to note that the system is not intended to replace human supervisors, but rather to assist them by reducing the data to manually analyze to only the detected 'anomalies'. In addition to monitoring insiders' communications, semantic analysis can be run *ex-post-facto* if an information assurance engineer were to grow suspicious of an individual. Alternatively, it can help with forensic analysis of large collections of documents by separating them into semantic-driven categories. This could be applied to a wide range of applications, such as semantic factoring of the contents of a confiscated hard-drive.

2.   OVERVIEW OF RELATED WORK

Until recently, the problem of detecting malicious insider activity was mainly approached from the standpoint of cyber threat and cyber security, with *systems* as the main object of potential attacks . Semantic-based methods were applied to describe the role-based access policy of an organization (Anderson, 1999; Upadhyaya et al., 2001). Over time, the integrity of information itself has received growing attention as an important factor in national security. Linguistic knowledge has been utilized to develop boundary control rules, protecting the intellectual property and the integrity of shared information (Liddy, 2001). Raskin et al., (2001) advocated the use of knowledge resources, such as ontologies and lexicons, borrowed from the field of Natural Language Processing, for a number of information security tasks and, in particular, to scan texts for indicators of possible intellectual property leakage. Aleman-Meza et al., (2005) attempted to apply an ontology to assess relevance of a document to the legitimate scope of an analyst's interests. The Annual Symposia on Intelligence and Security Informatics (ISI), which have become a venue for cutting edge research in the field, demonstrate increased appreciation of textual information.

One approach to the problem of detecting malicious insider communications addresses behavioral aspects, such as deception, communicated through linguistic cues. Examples of such studies include an ongoing project at the University of Arizona that applies linguistic knowledge to recognize deception indicators in synchronous computer-mediated communication (Burgoon et al., 2003; Twitchell et al., 2005; Twitchell et al., 2004). Also, Zhou et al. (2003) conducted a longitudinal study of linguistic cues of deception in email messages. Newman et al., (2003) used transcripts of focused group discussion, where some participants were instructed to convey certain beliefs in order to identify distinct linguistic styles, or profiles, of deception communicated through such "markers" as use of fewer self-references, other-references, and exclusive words and more extensive use of "negative emotion" and "motion" words.

Another approach to the problem of detecting shift of topic in an insider's communication originates from the conceptually similar task of identifying novel topics in a stream of news, which has been a focus of the federally-funded Topic Detection and Tracking (TDT) program. This line of research is distinguished by extensive application of machine learning and data mining algorithms, in particular, classification and clustering (Allan, 2002). For an extensive review of the research efforts and accomplishments in application of statistical learning approach to the task of novelty detection in data of various kinds, including textual, the reader is also referred to (Markou & Singh, 2003).

As the TDT research program demonstrates particularly well, the recent accumulation of vast electronic collections of texts has spurred interest in the application of data mining and machine learning techniques to characterize the content of such large textual datasets. In particular, machine learning based classification algorithms have been widely used for the task of text categorization (Sebastiani, 2002). A typical machine learning approach to the text categorization task involves observing pre-categorized training documents, approximating a categorization function (a "classifier") defined in terms of the features (usually words in the training dataset), and evaluating the classifier's performance on a collection of test documents. The implicit assumption in a machine learning approach is that the observed words are independent and hence form the dimensions of a document vector in a feature space, over which the categorization function is defined. Text categorization problems often use thousands of features and hence some feature selection methodologies may be used to reduce the dimensionality of the feature space.

The most commonly used document representation has been the "bag-of-words" (BOW), where, essentially, every unique term from the document, with the possible exception of designated stopwords, becomes a feature in the feature space (Dumais et al., 1998). It has been shown that knowledge of the statistical distribution of terms in texts is sufficient to achieve high categorization performance. However, in situations where the available training data is limited (as is frequently true in real-life applications), categorization performance on BOW sets suffers. To address this issue, our investigation has focused on the use of NLP techniques for feature selection. Natural Language Processing covers a range of computational techniques for analyzing and representing natural texts at various levels of linguistic analysis, similar to the way humans utilize their knowledge of semantics, syntax, discourse, etc., in order to understand texts (Liddy, 2003). Gabrilovich and Markovitch (2005) showed empirically that augmenting BOW representations with features generated using an ontology, such as the Open Directory, improves categorization results. In the TDT line of research, it has been shown that the more effective classification and clustering models utilize not only words, but also features abstracted from texts, such as named entities (Kumaran & Allan, 2004) or concepts (Allan et al., 2000), using a subject ontology, which can be derived from the text itself or from an external ontology (Hotho et al., 2003). Yilmazel (2006) demonstrated that NLP-driven feature selection achieves similar or superior performance compared to BOW, while using many fewer features.

In the information security domain, machine learning techniques have become an increasingly popular approach to the task of detecting text-based indicators of anomalous and, potentially, malicious insider activity. Stolfo et al. (2003) ran n-gram analysis of email texts to identify patterns typical of particular user groups in order to recognize deviation from patterns. Sreenath et al. (2003) employed latent semantic analysis to reconstruct users' original queries from their online browsing paths and applied this technique to detecting malicious (terrorist) trends. Zheng et al. (2003) used machine learning algorithms for the task of recognizing the authorship of email messages. Bengel et al. (2004) applied classification algorithms to the task of chat topic detection. Yilmazel et al. (2005) investigated the effect of NLP-enhanced document representation on the performance of Support Vector Machine (SVM) classifiers.

Traditionally, the categorization problem is described with at least two classes of data, conventionally called "positive" and "negative". In reality, however, this is not always the case. A recent line of text categorization research concerns itself with situations where providing 'negative' examples for training is not feasible, for example, in intrusion detection, adaptive information filtering, and spam filtering. The problem is addressed by applying a one-class categorization algorithm that is trained on positive examples only and then tested on data that contains both positive and negative examples. Conceptually, the classifier's task is to acquire all possible knowledge about one class and then apply it to identify examples that do *not* belong to this class. A number of traditional classification algorithms have been adapted to fit the one-class categorization problem, including Naïve Bayes (Denis et al., 2002; Schneider, 2004), neural networks (Manevitz & Yousef, 2001), K-Nearest Neighbor (k-NN) (Datta, 1997), and SVM . One-class SVM has been shown to outperform other algorithms on the one-class text categorization task .

The one-class categorization approach is especially appropriate to the insider threat context, where it is not possible to predict potential topics of interest to malicious insiders. Rather, as in one of our recent projects described in greater detail in the next section, the effectiveness of the one-class classifier is evaluated on various sets of features selected to represent documents. In particular, we compared the BOW representation with different combinations of linguistic features generated using NLP techniques.

3.   CASE STUDY: ONE-CLASS CATEGORIZATION APPROACH TO THE PROBLEM OF IDENTIFYING ANOMALOUS CONTENT

In this section we describe a proto-typical operational scenario for the IC; our approach for monitoring potential malicious insiders; and the performance of our system on a collection of workflow documents from the intelligence community.   The system monitors insiders' workflow documents, alerting the system assurance administrator if the content of the documents shifts away from what is expected, given the insiders' individual assignments. It is known from Subject Matter Experts (SMEs) from the IC that analysts operate within a mission-based context, focused mainly on specific TOIs and AOIs. The information accessed by analysts ranges from news articles to analysts' reports, official documents, emails, and possibly other information sources. In addition, analysts' queries to these information sources reflect the role and the task assigned to an analyst, which in turn dictates the subject scope of documents in terms of their TOI/AOI.

To illustrate the "insider-gone-bad" problem, consider the following "Threat Scenario" developed for the project, based on a review of known malicious insider cases and consultations with the IC. An analyst with appropriate security clearance works on assignments dealing with the Biological Weapons Program (TOI) in Iraq (AOI). For some reason, the analyst begins collecting information on ballistic missiles in North Korea. Since this topic is beyond his assigned task, these actions are covert, interspersed with his 'normal', 'on-topic' communications. Now and then he would query a database and retrieve documents on North Korea's missiles; occasionally, he would send a question to another analyst from the North Korea shop and receive documents via email in order to pass the information to his external partners. He would copy data to a CD or print documents out. As these actions involve such textual artifacts as documents, database queries, and emails, analysis of their semantic content should be indicative of which topics are being pursued by the analyst. Further comparison of these observed topics to what is *expected*, given the analyst's task, would reveal whether they are beyond the expected scope of their assigned work.

3.1   Description of selected techniques

3.1.1   Text categorization system

The task of identifying whether a document is within or beyond the scope of the insider's interests in terms of their assigned TOI and AOI was conceptualized as a categorization problem, where each document is assigned to either the 'on-topic' or 'off-topic' category.

In a traditional categorization system both 'positive' and 'negative' examples are available for training. Figure 19-1 illustrates the components of such a system. A collection of documents, which have been manually labeled as 'positive' or 'negative', is split into training and test sets of documents. The training documents are processed at some selected level of sophistication to obtain features which are then used by a learning algorithm, such as SVM, to approximate a categorization function. This categorization function is then applied to test documents to obtain labels. The system-assigned labels are then evaluated for their accuracy using measures such as precision and recall (Sebastiani, 2002).

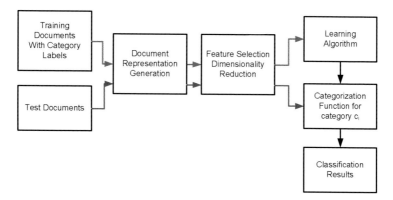

Figure 19-1. Outline of a traditional categorization system

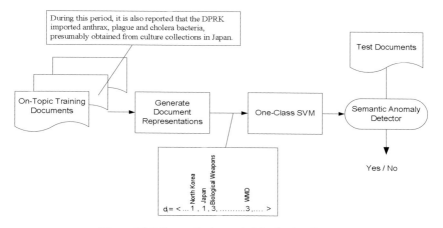

Figure 19-2. Semantic Anomaly Monitoring System

Given the context of our project, we assume that analysts' 'normal' document flow includes only 'on-topic' examples. Since only the 'on-topic' (positive) class of documents is known in advance and it is difficult to predict topics of interest to a malicious insider, a one-class categorization approach was chosen. With this approach, categorization models of expected topics are built from the semantic content of 'on-topic' documents. Next, the models (learning algorithms) are applied to categorize new documents as either 'on-' or 'off-topic' based on their semantic similarity to this 'on-topic' model. That is, the algorithm either assigns a document to the 'on-topic' class or fails to assign it and then raises an alert. Figure 19-2 depicts the Semantic Anomaly Monitoring (SAM) system built for this project. An important component of the system is feature generation using NLP technologies.

3.1.2   NLP-driven document representations

The effectiveness of any categorization solution is dependent on how well the categories are modeled, as well as on their generalizability to new documents. We hypothesized that leveraging a one-class SVM with NLP-driven feature generation would outperform the traditional BOW representation, particularly in the case of limited training data, by using fewer, more discriminative features. Intuitively, in the context of identifying 'off-topic' documents in the IC domain, one can expect features related to AOI and TOI to be more important than other general features. An NLP system can identify features such as entities (nouns and noun phrases), named entities (proper names), and their semantic categories (such as PERSON, ORGANIZATION, COUNTRY, etc.). Furthermore, such systems can map these features into higher-level concepts, using external knowledge sources. Particularly, features that are indicative of TOI and AOI can be identified by incorporating relevant external knowledge sources.

In our example (Figure 19-2), the input sentence,

"During this period, it is also reported that the DPRK imported anthrax, plague and cholera bacteria, presumably obtained from culture collections in Japan",

is boiled down to two AOI concepts (North Korea and Japan) and two TOI concepts (Biological Weapons and WMD), which become features in a document vector. The NLP-driven approach allows for different combinations and granularity levels for feature generation. Resulting document vectors become input for the One-Class SVM algorithm.

The NLP analysis is performed by TextTagger™, a text processing system developed at the Center for Natural Language Processing (CNLP). The system employs a part-of-speech tagger and a sequence of rule-based shallow parsing phases that use lexico-semantic and syntactic clues to identify and categorize entities, named entities, and events, as well as relations among them. Next, individual topics and locations are mapped to appropriate categories in knowledge bases. The choice of knowledge bases was driven by the context of our project – the IC with its focus on TOI and AOI. Concept inference for TOI is supported by an ontology developed for the Center for Nonproliferation Studies' (CNS) collection of documents from the nonproliferation of weapons of mass destruction (WMD) domain.

The process of TOI inference begins when the system recognizes that a term from a document exists in the knowledge base. It then augments the term extraction by all classes it belongs to. The system also utilizes information about the entity, found in the "gloss"-like ontology attributes, to enhance the term extraction with related terms[1]. For the conceptual organization of AOI, we utilize the SPAWAR Gazetteer, which combines resources of four publicly available gazetteers: NGA (NIMA); USGS; CIA World Factbook; and TIPSTER. Given that analysts usually operate on the country-level of AOI, the inference for geographical concepts is set to the 'Country' level, but other levels of granularity are possible. The entity and event extractions are output as frames, with relation extractions as frame slots. Figure 19-3 shows sample extractions for the named entity 'Bavarian Liberation Army' with inferred AOI ('Country') and TOI ('CNS_Superclasses').

Authorities suspect the Bavarian Liberation Army, an extreme right-wing organization, may be responsible.

Bavarian Liberation Army
Country=Austria
CNS_Superclasses=Terrorist-Group

Figure 19-3. A sample extraction and concept inference

The NLP-extracted features are then used to generate document vectors for the machine learning algorithms. By utilizing such higher level conceptual features, the categorization system can produce document vectors that are well separated in the feature space.

3.2 Categorization Experiments

This section describes in greater detail the experiments conducted using the Semantic Anomaly Monitoring system, presents experimental results, and concludes with a discussion of advantages and challenges of the chosen approach.

3.2.1 Experimentation Dataset

Experiments were run on a subset of the larger Insider Threat collection created for the project. Its core comes from the CNS collection and covers

---

[1] Thus simulating analysts' utilizing background knowledge to produce useful associations

such topics as WMD and Terrorism, and such genres as newswires, articles, analytic reports, international treaties, emails, and so on. Training and Testing document sets were drawn from the collection based on the project scenarios, one of which was described earlier in this section. These scenarios are synthetic datasets that represent the insiders' workflow through atomic actions (e.g. 'search database', 'open document'), some of which are associated with documents. The scenarios span a period of six months each and include a baseline case (with no malicious activity) and six threat cases. The scenarios cover the workflow of hundreds of insiders with different work roles and tasks.

3.2.2   Classification System

For the categorization experiments, we used an SVM classifier not only because it has been shown to outperform kNN, Naïve Bayes, and other classifiers on the Reuters' Collection (Manevitz & Yousef, 2002), but also because it can handle one-class categorization problems as well. Experiments were run in LibSVM (Hsu et al.), modified to handle file names in the feature vectors and to compute a confusion matrix for evaluation.

We experimented with the following feature sets:
1. Bag-of-words representation (BOW): each unique word in the document is used as a feature in the document vector.
2. Categorized entities (CAT): only words identified as entities or named entities constitute features in the document vector.
3. TOI/AOI extractions (TOI/AOI): document vector includes only terms assigned as TOI/AOI indicators
4. TOI/AOI extractions + important categories (TOI/AOI_cat): document vector uses TOI/AOI features (as in 3) plus all entities and named entities categorized as geographical or domain-relevant concepts (e.g. 'WMD', 'missile', 'terrorism')

We applied stemming, a stop-word filter, and lower case conversion in all of the representations. The associated value for each term in the document representation is the frequency of the term in that document. In course of experiments, we have tried linear and RBF kernels in SVM, as well as tuning the gamma and C values. The best results reported herein were achieved with the linear kernel SVM with default parameters.

Classifier performance was assessed using standard metrics of precision and recall and a weighted F-score, calculated for each class. In the following formulas for precision on the ON-topic (Equation 19-1) and recall of the OFF-topic (Equation 19-2) classes, TrueON are documents correctly classified as ON-topic; FalseON are OFF-topic documents assigned to the ON-topic class; TrueOFF are correctly detected OFF-topic documents, and

FalseOFF are ON-topic documents misclassified into the OFF-topic class

$$\Pr ecision(ON) = \frac{TrueON}{TruON + FalseON}$$

Equation 19- 1

$$\mathrm{Re}\,call(OFF) = \frac{TrueOFF}{TrueOFF + FalseON}$$

Equation 19- 2

In mainstream text categorization research, the performance focus is usually on the 'positive' class, so the scores (precision, recall, F-measure) are often reported for this class only. The context of our project, however, gives much greater importance to detecting the 'negative' (i.e. potentially malicious) cases, while keeping the rate of 'false alarms' (FalseOFF) down. This provided a rather uncommon task for training the classifier: to aim not only for higher precision on ON-topic, but also for greater recall of OFF-topic. Therefore, in evaluating the classifier, we focused on the scores for the OFF-topic class and used the F-measure that weighs Recall 10 times as important as Precision (Equation 19-3).

$$F - score = \frac{11 * \Pr ecisionOFF * \mathrm{Re}\,callOFF}{10 * \Pr ecisionOFF + \mathrm{Re}\,callOFF}$$

Equation 19- 3

3.2.3   Experiment 1

For the first set of experiments, we focused on the above described scenario where an analyst from the Iraq/Biological Weapon shop becomes interested in information on missiles and North Korea. The documents were retrieved in a manner simulating the analysts' work: manually constructed task-specific queries (Table 19-1) were run against the Insider Threat collection. These queries were also included in the training and test datasets, in order to represent this kind of analysts' typical information workflow.

Table 19-1. Sample queries

Topic	Query
'Biological weapons program in Iraq'	("UNMOVIC" AND "inspect*" AND "biolog*" AND "Iraq*")
'Missile program in North Korea'	("missile*" AND "test*" AND " North Korea*")

Both data sets included 'noise' (i. e. webpages on topics of general interest) as it is realistic to assume that, in the course of their workday, analysts may use the Web for personal reasons as well.

Documents retrieved by the 'North Korea' queries were labeled as OFF-topic given that the analyst was from the biological weapons in Iraq shop. All other documents were labeled as ON-topic, since, for the purposes of the project, it will suffice if the classifier distinguishes the 'off-topic' documents from the rest. The training set contained only ON-topic documents, whereas the test set also included OFF-topic documents. Table 19-2 shows the content and the volume of the training and test datasets used. The relatively small share of OFF-topic documents in the test set (only 8.4%), though realistic given the context of the project, represented yet another challenge, as classification algorithms tend to favor more populated classes. \

Table 19-2. Training and Test datasets, Experiment 1

	Training	**Test**	
	ON (Iraq/Bio)	ON (Iraq/Bio)	OFF (NK/Missile)
Documents	3194	3191	181
Queries	222	222	132
Total Class	*3416*	*3413*	*313*
Total Set	**3416**		**3726**

In Experiment 1 we obtained high precision on 'ON-topic' and recall of OFF-topic examples (Table 19-3), thus, meeting the goals set. Up to 84% recall of 'OFF-topic' examples is especially impressive, considering that the classifier had no prior knowledge of what constitutes 'OFF-topic'. The "cost" of such a high recall of the 'OFF-topic', however, was the modest recall of the 'ON-topic'. In other words, the one-class SVM errs in favor of the previously unknown 'negative' class, thus, causing 'false alarms'.

Table 19-3. Experiment 1 results

	Features	**Prec** **ON**	Rec ON	F ON	Prec OFF	**Rec** **OFF**	F OFF
BOW	12286	**93.39**	28.57	30.49	9.10	**77.96**	46.19
CAT	5272	**93.17**	32.38	34.42	9.13	**74.12**	45.00
AOI/ TOI	289	**95.73**	**31.56**	**33.61**	**10.19**	**84.66**	**50.87**
AOI/TOI_cat	1189	**95.32**	28.66	30.61	9.81	**84.67**	49.99

The results also demonstrate that, similar to what was observed in experiments with the regular binary SVM classifier (Yilmazel et al., 2005), NLP-driven document representation improves the classifier performance over the baseline (BOW), while utilizing many fewer features. In particular, categorization using only AOI/TOI features achieves 6% improvement in

Recall (OFF) and 4 % improvement on the weighted F-measure (OFF) over the baseline (BOW), with forty-two times fewer features.

3.2.4 Experiment 2

In binary classification tasks, "domain change" often presents a challenge. Models learned may "overfit" the original (training) domains and, thus, perform poorly on new (test) domains. One-class categorization systems should be robust to domain change in the negative class, since negative examples are not used in training. The second set of experiments aimed to assess how the one-class SVM would perform on different 'OFF-topic' domains. We used the same training set and the ON-topic part of the test set. For the OFF-topic portion of the test set, the documents were retrieved from the Insider Threat dataset with queries on the topic of 'China/Nuclear weapons' (Table 19-4):

Table 19-4. Training and Test datasets, Experiment 2

	Training	**Test**	
			OFF
	ON (Iraq/Bio)	ON (Iraq/Bio)	(China/Nuclear)
Documents	3194	3191	181
Queries	222	222	129
Total Class	*3416*	*3413*	*310*
Total Set	**3416**		**3723**

Experimental results (Table 19-5) support the trend observed in the prior experiments. One-class categorization on the NLP-enhanced document representations achieves superior performance compared to the baseline (BOW). In addition, the domain change for the 'off-topic' documents does not seem to impact the classifier performance to a significant extent, which had been the case with the regular SVM. Such robustness is quite reasonable, since the one-class SVM is not biased (via training) towards a particular kind of 'negative' data.

Table 19-5. Experiment 2 results

	Features	**Prec ON**	Rec ON	F ON	Prec OFF	**Rec OFF**	F OFF
BOW	12286	**90.11**	28.57	30.46	7.69	**65.48**	38.90
CAT	**5272**	**95.51**	**32.38**	**34.45**	**10.05**	**83.23**	**50.08**
AOI/TOI	289	**91.58**	31.56	33.56	8.28	**68.06**	41.09
AOI/TOI_cat	1189	**92.35**	28.66	30.58	8.6	**73.87**	43.71

For the second set of experiments, the document representation that has all the categorized terms outperforms all the other representations. Different performance of a classifier on different data sets is not unusual and commonly related to the sets' particular characteristics, which the classifier may or may not fit well. In our case, we can hypothesize that ontologies used to generate AOI/TOI features had better coverage of Iraq/Bio topics, as opposed to China/Nuclear ones. As a result, category-based set (CAT) provided better representation of China/Nuclear texts, than the AOI/TOI-based one. Supporting this hypothesis is the fact that augmenting AOI/TOI features with important categories (AOI/TOI_cat set, Table 19-5) contributed to better results, compared to the ones achieved on AOI/TOI set, though still inferior to the performance on the CAT set. Overall, the results show that the one-class SVM performs impressively well, especially, on recall of the OFF-topic class. Another important point is that the algorithm appears to be robust in handling different subject domains of 'negative' examples. The results also demonstrate that the use of NLP-driven document representations achieves consistently better performance in categorization while using many fewer features than the commonly used bag-of-words representation.

4.   CONCLUSIONS AND DISCUSSION

The experiments described herein show that leveraging one-class SVM with NLP-extracted features for document representation improves categorization effective-ness and efficiency. The one-class approach fits particularly well these situations where it is not feasible to provide 'atypical' examples.

It appears worthy to note that in our experiments, linear kernel SVM, on the overall, outperformed the RBF kernel based one. The RBF kernel tries to capture long-range dependencies between dimensions, which can be effective when applied to bag-of-words representations. But since NLP already accomplishes this by extracting semantically strong features, any further generalizations on these features is actually hurting the classification performance. Our results suggest that NLP driven document representations improve generalizability of a linear SVM classifier, so that complex kernels are not needed.

Overall, the research reported herein holds potential for providing the IC and other security-conscious organizations with the analytic tools to recognize anoma-lous insider activity; as well as to build content profiles of vast document collec-tions when applied in a broader context.

In future research we will seek to evaluate the impact of different combinations of linguistic features, extractions from text, and concepts inferred from external knowledge bases on categorization accuracy. While it has been feasible to utilize AOI and TOI for the Insider Threat application within the IC, other sectors are likely to have different key facets of content that would be important in classification decisions. In addition, further exploration of the one-class classifier in other domains and on other genres will stress test the robustness of the approach and our SAM technology in a broader set of subject domains for the 'off-topic' class.

REFERENCES

Aleman-Meza, B., Burns, P., Eavenson, M., Palaniswami, D., & Sheth, A. P. (2005). *An Ontological Approach to the Document Access Problem of Insider Threat.* Intelligence and Security Informatics, IEEE International Conference on Intelligence and Security Informatics, ISI 2005, Atlanta, GA.

Allan, J. (2002). *Topic Detection and Tracking: Event-based Information Organization* (1st ed. Vol. 12): Springer.

Anderson, R. *Research and Development Initiatives Focused on Preventing, Detecting, and Responding to Insider Misuse of Critical Defense Information Systems: Results of a Three-Day Workshop.* (1999) http://www.rand.org/publications/CF/CF151/CF151.pdf

Bengel, J., Gauch, S., Mittur, E., & Vijayaraghavan, R. (2004). *ChatTrack: Chat Room Topic Detection Using Classification.* Second NSF/NIJ Symposium on Intelligence and Security Informatics (ISI2004).

Burgoon, J., Blair, J., Qin, T., & Nunamaker, J., Jr. (2003). *Detecting Deception Through Linguistic Analysis.* First NSF/NIJ Symposium on Intelligence and Security Informatics, Tucson, Arizona.

CNLP *Center for Natural Language Processing (CNLP).* www.cnlp.org

CNS *Center for Nonproliferation Studies (CNS).* http://cns.miis.edu/

Datta, P. (1997). *Characteristic Concept Representations.* University of California, Irvine, Irvine, CA.

Denis, F., Gilleron, R., & Tommasi, M. (2002). *Text classification from positive and unlabeled examples.* Conference on Information Processing and Management of Uncertainty in Knowledge-Based Systems (IPMU 2002).

Dumais, S., John, P., Heckerman, D., & Sahami, M. (1998). *Inductive Learning Algorithms and Representations for Text Categorization.* Seventh International Conference on Information and Knowledge Management, Bethesda, Maryland, United States.

Gabrilovich, E., & Markovitch, S. (2005). *Feature Generation for Text Categorization Using World Knowledge.* 19th International Joint Conference on Artificial Intelligence, Edinburgh, Scotland, UK.

Hsu, C.-W., Chang, C.-C., & Lin, C.-J. A Practical Guide to Support Vector Classification.

Kumaran, G., & Allan, J. (2004). Text Classification and Named Entities for New Event Detection.

LibSVM *LibSVM.* http://www.csie.ntu.edu.tw/~cjlin/libsvm/

Liddy, E. D. (2001). Information Security and Sharing. *Online Magazine.*

Liddy, E. D. (2003). Natural Language Processing. In *Encyclopedia of Library and Information Science* (2nd ed.). New York: Marcel Decker, Inc.

Manevitz, L. M., & Yousef, M. (2001). *Document classification via neural networks trained exclusively with positive examples*: Department of Computer Science. University of Haifa.

Manevitz, L. M., & Yousef, M. (2002). One-class SVMs for Document Classification. *The Journal of Machine Learning Research, 2*, 139-154.

Markou, M., & Singh, S. (2003). Novelty Detection: A Review Part 1: Statistical Approaches. *Signal Processing, 83*(12), 2481 - 2497.

Newman, M. L., Pennebaker, J. W., Berry, D. S., & Richards, J. M. (2003). Predicting Deception from Linguistic Styles. *Personality and Social Psychology Bulletin, 29*, 665--675.

Raskin, V., Hempelmann, C., Triezenberg, K., & Nirenburg, S. (2001). *Ontology in Information Security: a Useful Theoretical Foundation and Methodological Tool.* 2001 Workshop on New Security Paradigms.

Schneider, K.-M. (2004). Learning to Filter Junk E-Mail from Positive and Unlabeled Examples.

Sebastiani, F. (2002). Machine Learning in Automated Text Categorization. *ACM Computing Surveys, 34*(1), 1-47.

Shanahan, J. G., & Roma, N. (2003). *Boosting SupportVector Machines for Text Classification Through Parameter-Free Threshold Relaxation.* The 12th International Conference on Information and Knowledge Management, New Orleans, LA, USA.

Sreenath, D. V., Grosky, W. I., & Fotouhi, F. (2003). *Emergent Semantics from Users' Browsing Paths.* First NSF/NIJ Symposium on Intelligence and Security Informatics, Tucson, AZ, USA.

Stolfo, S., Hershkop, S., Wang, K., Nimeskern, O., & Hu, C. (2003). *Behavior Profiling of Email.* First NSF/NIJ Symposium on Intelligence and Security Informatics., Tucson, AZ, USA.

Twitchell, D. P., Forsgren, N., Wiers, K., Burgoon, J. K., & Nunamaker, J. F. (2005). *Detecting Deception in Synchronous Computer-Mediated Communication Using Speech Act Profiling.* Intelligence and Security Informatics, IEEE International Conference on Intelligence and Security Informatics, ISI 2005, Atlanta, GA.

Twitchell, D. P., Nunamaker Jr., J. F., & Burgoon, J. K. (2004). *Using Speech Act Profiling for Deception Detection.* Second NSF/NIJ Symposium on Intelligence and Security Informatics (ISI2004), Tucson, AZ.

Upadhyaya, S., Chinchani, R., & Kwiat, K. (2001). *An Analytical Framework for Reasoning About Intrusions.* 20th IEEE Symposium on Reliable Distributed Systems.

Yilmazel, O. (2006). *Empirical Selection of NLP-Driven Document Representations For Text Categorization.* Syracuse University, Syracuse.

Yilmazel, O., Symonenko, S., Liddy, E. D., & Balasubramanian, N. (2005). *Improved Document Representation for Classification Tasks For The Intelligence Community (Forthcoming).* AAAI, CA.

Yu, H., Han, J., & Chen-Chuan Chang, K. (2004). PEBL: Web Page Classification without Negative Examples. *IEEE Transactions on Knowledge and Data Engineering, 16*(1).

Zheng, R., Yi, O., Zan, H., & Hsinchun, C. (2003). *Authorship Analysis in Cybercrime Investigation.* First NSF/NIJ Symposium on Intelligence and Security Informatics, Tucson, AZ, USA.

Zhou, L., Burgoon, J. K., & Twitchell, D. P. (2003). *A Longitudinal Analysis of Language Behavior of Deception in E-mail.* First NSF/NIJ Symposium on Intelligence and Security Informatics., Tucson, AZ, USA.

ACKNOWLEDGEMENT

This work was supported by the Advanced Research and Development Activity (ARDA).

SUGGESTED READINGS

Categorization:
- Sebastiani, F. 2002. Machine Learning in Automated Text Categorization. *ACM Computing Surveys, 34*(1): 1-47.

One-class SVM:
- Scholkopf, B., J. C. Platt, J. Shawe-Taylor, A. J. Smola and R. C. Williamson
  (1999). Estimating the Support of a High-Dimensional Distribution, Microsoft Research.

NLP:
- Liddy, E. D. 2003. Natural Language Processing. In *Encyclopedia of Library and Information Science* (2nd ed.). New York: Marcel Decker, Inc.

ONLINE RESOURCES

- CNS collection:
  http://cns.miis.edu/

Open-source NLP applications:
- GATE:
  http://gate.ac.uk/
- LingPipe:
  http://www.alias-i.com/lingpipe/
- LibSVM:
  http://www.csie.ntu.edu.tw/~cjlin/libsvm/

DISCUSSION QUESTIONS

1. How could the Semantic Anomaly Monitoring (SAM) system be modified to handle topic shift in the On-topic documents?
2. In Experiment 1 and 2, different representations achieved the best performance indicating the impact of domain change in the Off-topic documents. When the Off-topic data is unknown in advance, what

methods can be used to select the representation that would produce optimal results?

3. What other problems are amenable to the one-class categorization approach?

4. What other domains can benefit from this approach to the anomaly detection problem?

20

INDIVIDUAL AND COLLECTIVE ANALYSIS OF ANOMALIES IN MESSAGE TRAFFIC

David B. Skillicorn
Professor, School of Computing, Queen's University, Kingston, Canada
(skill@cs.queensu.ca)

CHAPTER OVERVIEW

We consider four properties by which intercepted messages can be selected for deeper analysis: their external properties, their content, their authorship, and the mental state of their authors. We argue that, rather than trying to differentiate directly between 'good' messages and 'bad' messages, it is better to use a two-pronged approach, where a simple detection scheme triggers a reaction in authors of 'bad' messages. This reaction is easier to detect than the original difference. We also suggest that differentiation is more effective when it is done for sets of messages, rather than on a message by message basis.

1.   INTRODUCTION

Many governments intercept message traffic in a widespread way as part of their efforts to understand existing and potential threats.   Historically, such interception was directed towards enemies. With the development of models of 4th generation or asymmetric warfare, and with the experience of the September 11th attacks and, even more so, the July 2005 attacks in London, it has come to be appreciated that enemies are not necessarily outside. As a result, interception programs increasingly include 'domestic' message traffic, although the tradeoffs between security and civil liberties implicit in this decision are still the subject of volatile discussion.

Similar kinds of interception can occur within organizations, either as part of a general managerial effort to prevent, discourage, or deal with issues such as intimidation, sexual harassment, or fraud; or in response to legislative requirements such as Sarbanes-Oxley which makes management responsible for "adequate internal control structures and procedures for financial reporting". This may take the form of analyzing email within the organization, either in real-time, or forensically in response to an incident.

In both of these settings, the volume of messages to be analyzed is so large that direct human processing is infeasible.   Analysis requires automated tools that are capable of selecting those messages most likely to be of interest for the problem being addressed. If this is done effectively, the set of selected messages can then be analyzed by downstream processes that might be too expensive or ineffective to deploy on the entire message set (for example, human analysis).

This initial selection process does not have to be perfect. Because selected messages will be subjected to further analysis, it is critical that its false negative rate be extremely low, so that few, if any, relevant messages are discarded. A high false-positive rate is an annoying, but not critical, deficiency.

We address analysis techniques for message selection, making two particular arguments:

1. Finding the boundary between relevant messages and ones that can be ignored (i.e., between 'bad' messages and 'good' messages) is usually difficult, because the differences are small. Better separation of bad and good messages can be achieved by using a two-pronged approach. First, deploy a visible, but weak, detection system for bad messages. Then deploy a second, more subtle, system that looks for *reaction to the first system*. Those who are communicating innocently tend not to be aware of the first detection system, and if they are, tend not to react to it. Those who wish their messages not to be noticed *must* react to the first detection

system, and their reactions often discriminate them better from innocent traffic.

The first system works best if its existence is well-known, but the precise details of its workings are not known. An element of randomization may be useful to ensure this latter property. Even if those who want to conceal their communications know about the two-pronged approach, they still cannot afford to ignore it. If they do, their communication could be selected on the basis of the first system alone.

For example, it is widely believed that government interception systems use a watch list of words and select messages that contain them for further scrutiny. Such a list, once in use by the German government, is given in the European Union Report on the Echelon system [3]. A terrorist who wants to send an email or make a cell phone call must be aware that words like 'nuclear' and 'bomb' should not be used. But it is far from obvious how long such a watch list might be, and whether words such as 'ammonium nitrate' or 'Strasbourg cathedral' are on it (although they plausibly could be).

2. Although most analysis tools and system treat each message independently, there is much additional information available by analyzing sets of messages at a time.

One model for analyzing message traffic is to treat it as a prediction problem—for each message, predict whether it is innocent, or possibly suspicious, with the second class selected for further analysis. However, messages are not usually isolated utterances, but part of conversations, and this wider structure can be exploited to make better decisions.

For example, given the existence of a watch list, a terrorist might replace a word that is probably on the watch list with another, innocuous, word—for example, replace 'bomb' by 'football'. In a single message, it might be quite difficult to detect the existence of this substitution. However, the reply to this message is overwhelmingly likely to use the same substitute word (otherwise the group has to remember that when *he* says 'football' he means 'bomb', but when *she* says 'telephone' she means 'bomb', and the conversation quickly becomes unintelligible). In a set of messages collected over some short time period, then, there are likely to be multiple messages containing the same substitution, and this may make it easier to detect the existence of any of them.

The bottom line is that those who want to hide the existence and content of their communication in a background of innocent messages must do something to make this happen. In many ways, their actions make it easier, rather than harder, to detect and select their messages. Forcing them to act will, in general, make it easier to detect their messages.

2.   ANALYSIS OF SINGLE MESSAGES

Given a single message, there are four kinds of information that we can learn from it:

1. Characteristics of (the outside of) the message, such as its sender and receiver, when it was sent, and how long it is.
2. The content of the message—what it is about.
3. Properties of the author of the message (who it is, what his or her first language is).
4. What was the author's mental and emotional state of mind (does the content express what the author really thinks, or is the content designed for a particular audience).

For each of these properties, we will consider simple detection mechanisms, countermeasures that senders can take to evade these simple detection mechanisms, and whether there are secondary detection mechanisms that can take advantage of the evasions.

2.1   Detecting Message Characteristics

A simple way to select messages of interest based on their characteristic is to keep lists of endpoints (senders, receivers, IP addresses, web sites) of interest, and use these as selection criteria.

Selecting such messages can provide useful information, even if the content is not accessible, perhaps because it has been encrypted. For example, the volume of traffic among a set of endpoints may point to the imminence of an attack.

Unfortunately, countermeasures to such selection techniques are relatively easy. For example, email addresses can be set up anonymously and with very little work, so the apparent senders and receivers of an email are easy to obscure. IP addresses can be obscured using anonymizing servers or Crowd systems [12]. The identity of cell phones can be obscured by replacing their SIM cards, and a lively industry in stolen SIM cards exists in most countries. Web sites make it easy to upload and download content, perhaps even concealed content using techniques such as steganography. In the asynchronous technologies such as email, it is straightforward to obscure times, although the interleaving of messages forming a conversation is usually maintained. For synchronous technologies such as cell phones, the use of answering machines can blur timings, although again the interleaving of messages in a conversation must be maintained. The only property that cannot be obscured is the total volume of messages (so-called 'chatter') which may be detectable even with obscuring because it originates from one geographical area, or passes along one intermediate channel (although mixed with other, normal traffic).

The problem of detecting single messages for which the endpoint markers have been obscured does not seem to have been addressed in the research literature. When short-term email addresses are used, it is conceivable that some level of detection is possible by observing an increase frequency of messages from 'new' email addresses originating in certain places. However, opportunities to detect this seem better in the context of multiple messages—we will return to this later. Detecting other kinds of endpoint obscuring seems even more difficult.

2.2   Detecting Message Content

As mentioned above, the obvious way to select messages based on content is to use a watch list of words of interest. Even this is not entirely trivial because it is probably necessary to impose a lower threshold, so that messages that contain, say, only a single word from the watch list are not selected, and an upper threshold, so that messages that contain large numbers of watch list words are not selected either (since such messages are usually designed to be selected).

Those who want to evade selection of their messages will want to replace words that they suspect are on the watch list with more innocuous words. The kind of word they might choose as a replacement depends on their model for how detection is done. If they (naively) imagine that humans are involved in analysis at an early stage, they might choose words that 'make sense' in context. For example, al Qaeda was, for a time, using the word 'wedding' as a replacement for 'attack'. Such a substitution makes sense in many contexts: both weddings and attacks take place at a particular time and a particular place, and require travel arrangements that assemble a particular group there. Hence messages that contain this substitution will probably appear to 'make sense'.

If they imagine that the analysis is automatic, then there is no need to choose words that make sense; instead they will want to choose words that are like the words they replace in more surface ways, such as frequency.

There are three different strategies for replacement that might be used in different settings. These are:

1. Replace the word by a randomly chosen word. This might typically be what happens when communication is being generated in real-time or near-real-time, and there has been no time to agree upon an organized pattern for replacements. The problem for the sender in this setting is that it is hard to choose a replacement word with the right surface

properties, for example frequency, since most people have little intuition about such properties.

2. Replace the word by a word of similar frequency chosen using a simple algorithm. This assumes that the sender and receiver have access to a frequency-ranked list of words. Such lists are readily available on the Web, for example at www.wordcount.org/main.php. A simple replacement rule might be to replace a revealing word with the word five places down from it in the frequency-ranked list. This, of course, produces semantic nonsense: for example, the sentence "the bomb has been planted in the mosque" becomes "the sand has been planted in the aspirin". The advantage of this scheme is that it does not require prior agreement about which words should be replaced; each sender is free to make his or her own judgment.

3. Replace the word by a word of similar frequency chosen in advance, that is creating a codebook of carefully chosen replacements known to all. This again requires access to a frequency-ranked list of words, but only once.

4. The important differences between this strategy and the previous one are that it opens up more choices for replacement words, which could be chosen to be the same parts of speech as the words they replace; and that the ranking of each word and its replacement need not always be separated by the same gap, sometimes being the next ranked word, sometimes the word two ranks below and so on. On the other hand, the words to be avoided must be decided in advance, and each sender must have access to the codebook, if only by memory. This may be problematic in stressful or fluid situations.

All of these substitution strategies turn out to be reliably detectable in text because of the changes in the local, contextual structure of the sentences that they create.

Fong, Skillicorn and Roussinov [4] designed a set of measures that consider different properties of sentences that might change when a substitution has been made. These measures use frequency oracles such as Google or Yahoo to determine the frequencies of words, bags of words, and (quoted) sentence fragments, from which the measure scores are derived. The measure scores are:

• The *Sentence Oddity* (SO) which is defined for a sentence and a particular target word (a possible substitution) as

$$SO = \frac{\text{frequency of bag of words, target word removed}}{\text{frequency of entire bag of words}}$$

The intuition is that, when a contextually appropriate word is removed from a sentence, the frequency of the rest of the sentence should not increase much; whereas if the word was contextually inappropriate, the frequency of the rest of the sentence might be much greater. Hence a large value for this measure signals the presence of a possible substitution.

- The *Enhanced Sentence Oddity* (ESO) is a related measure in which the numerator explicitly excludes the target word.

  It is defined for a sentence and target word as:

$$ESO = \frac{\text{frequency of bag of words, target word excluded}}{\text{frequency of entire bag of words}}$$

Again a large value signals a possible substitution.

- The *Left k-gram* measures the frequency of a phrase (a quoted string) beginning from the closest non-stop word to the left of the target word and extending up to and including the target word. A small value signals a possible substitution.

  Somewhat surprisingly, many short phrases do not occur even in the largest indexes and repositories [14]. The left k-gram measure is a compromise between the considering as much of the left context of the target word as possible, and still getting usable frequency information.

- The *Right k-gram* measures the frequency of the quoted string beginning from the target word and extending to the right, up to and including the next non-stop word. This measure considers the right context of the target word which, in English, is quite different to its left context.

- The *Average k-gram* is simply the average of the left and right k-grams.

- The maximum, minimum, and average *Hypernym Oddity* (HO) measures what happens to the frequency of a sentence when the target word is replaced by one of its hypernyms. The hypernym of a word, usually a noun, is the word or locution that represents the next level of generality in taxonomy. For example, the hypernym of 'dog' is 'canine'.

  When a word is contextually appropriate, its hypernym tends to be a rather technical word, so the frequency of the sentence with the hypernym tends to be lower than the original sentence. However, when the word is contextually inappropriate, its hypernym tends to be more general, and therefore contextually appropriate in more situations, so the frequency of the sentences with the hypernym tends to be higher than that of the original sentence. The hypernym oddity of a sentence with respect to a target word is:

$$HO = f_H - f$$

where f_H is the frequency of the sentence with the target word replaced by its hypernym (as a bag of words), while f is the frequency of the initial sentence (as a bag of words). This measure will be large and positive for sentences containing a substitution, and close to zero or negative for sentences without a substitution. Since a word may have several hypernyms, because of different senses in which it can be used, the maximum, minimum and average hypernym oddities can be defined over such possibilities.

Hypernyms are semantic properties of words, but hypernyms for many words can be obtained from Wordnet (wordnet.princeton.edu), and so this measure can be computed automatically.

- The *Pointwise Mutual Information* (PMI) measures how well a word fits into its context by measuring the likelihoods of one piece given the other. The basic definition of pointwise mutual information is:

$$PMI = \frac{p(\text{word})\ p(\text{adjacent region})}{p(\text{word} + \text{adjacent region})}$$

where $p()$ is a probability, and + indicates concatenation in either direction, depending whether an adjacent region that precedes or follows the target word is being considered. The probabilities can be approximated as inverse frequencies, and the reciprocal of the resulting expression is used so that large PMI values suggest the presence of a substitution. The practical definition of the pointwise mutual information is:

$$PMI = \frac{f(\text{word})\ f(\text{adjacent region})}{f(\text{word} + \text{adjacent region})}$$

where $f()$ is the oracle frequency for the argument string. The adjacent regions are grown out independently in both directions from the target word until the frequency of the adjacent region as a quoted string drops to zero. The maximum of the PMI scores over the possible adjacent regions is typically the best measure for detecting the presence of a substitution.

These four families of measures are, individually, quite weak at detecting substitutions. However, they make prediction errors on different sentences, so an ensemble predictor that combines the predictions of each measure into a single prediction is much more effective.   When the measures are combined using a decision tree, the prediction accuracy for single sentences exceeds 90% with a false positive rate around 10%. This can be mapped to a per-message prediction using different thresholds for the number of sentences per message that must be predicted to contain a substitution in order for the entire message to be predicted to contain a substitution, further reducing the false positive rate. It is, of course, likely that a message that is written to conceal its content will contain more than one substitution.

This form of detector does not seem to be very sensitive to how similar the frequencies of the original and replacement word are. Hence, on a single message basis, it makes little difference whether the substitution is of a random word, a word with a fixed different rank, or a word with a carefully chosen different rank.

2.3   Detecting Message Authorship

A message whose endpoints have been obscured, and whose content has been obfuscated by word substitution may still be selected for further analysis based on who wrote it. This requires a robust way to detect authorship, using the unconscious variations in the way each person writes.

For example, a terrorist leader may have issued public statements, making visible an authorship signature that can be applied to other, more covert, communications.

Authorship detection has a long history [2, 5], and is usually based on stylistic, semantic or lexical markers in text. However, robust authorship detection has typically required large amounts of text, while an email or phone call may only provide a few hundred words or less. Chen and Abbasi, in another chapter in this volume, show how authorship detection can be done using such short messages. They slide a window across the available text and map the resulting data into a set of two-dimensional semantic spaces that capture various stylistic properties. The images of the windows in the semantic space create a trajectory which defines a signature for each author.

In related work, Koppel *et al.* [10] show that it possible to discover the native language of an author writing in English. This may be used as another criterion for message selection, especially as a preprocessing step for authorship detection.

2.4   Detecting Mental State

Discovering the content of a message may not be enough to assess its significance. For example, a message that seems to threaten a major attack could be written by someone who does not have the resources to mount it, but wishes that they could; as a kind of catharsis. The message may have a content that is carefully crafted to appeal to a particular audience, but no foundation in reality. The message may even be a joke, or disinformation designed to be intercepted.

It would be useful to be able to assess the mental state of the author that is *why* he or she wrote the message, as well as the apparent content. This can be done at present with respect to one dimension: how deceptive the message is.

Pennebaker [11] empirically developed measures of how word usage changes when authors are arguing for a position they believe in versus when they are arguing for a position that they do not believe in. The differences are not in the content words that convey the sense of what is written; rather, the differences appear in the small words that do not usually receive attention, either cognitively or linguistically. Pennebaker suggested that deception is characterized by four patterns of change in word frequency:

1. Reduced use of first-person pronouns, perhaps as a way of distancing the author from the deception;
2. Reduced use of exception words (but, or, except), perhaps because the cognitive load of creating the deception is too large to allow for fancy touches, or because of an awareness of the need to be consistent if questioned;
3. Increased use of negative emotion words, perhaps because of negative feelings, inadequately suppressed, about the process or consequences of deception; and
4. Increased use of action verbs, perhaps as a way of keeping the story moving, and perhaps only as a consequence of a reduction in other, more-subtle, kinds of verbs.

The Pennebaker model was applied to the Enron email dataset [8, 9] a large collection of emails made public as a side-effect of the investigation of the company and its officers. The dataset contains emails to and from Enron employees who never imagined that their writing would be made public. As a result, it is an appropriate surrogate for intercepted messages.

The Pennebaker deception model reliably selected a small number of emails that could be characterized as deceptive [9]. However, it also selected messages with lower levels of deceptiveness, down to emails that were negotiations, where an element of deception, in a sense, is expected. This more-general category of emails that Pennebaker's model can be characterized as containing elements of 'spin', that is they are texts that express views that are not wholeheartedly those of their authors, Spin is a much broader concept than deception.

The Pennebaker deception model is based on a set of 88 words. A deception score can be computed on a per-message basis by summing the frequencies of each of these words (with a sense reversal for those words for which a *reduced* count is the marker of deception). This score provides a way to select messages that contain elements of deception, but further analysis would be required to select those messages that are outright deceptive.

2.5   Summary

We have outlined four analysis techniques that can be applied to individual messages, and the results used to select messages of interest for further scrutiny.

For external characteristics of messages, simple countermeasures to obscure the obvious properties exist. It is not clear that, when these countermeasures are applied, much can be done to select suspicious messages on a per-message basis.

For the content of messages, the situation is rather different. The watch list approach is a simple selection technique, but countermeasures such as substitution are straightforward. However, in this case substitution creates its own signature that is detectable with relatively high accuracy. Choosing the words for a watch list is a difficult process, and runs the risk of missing words that later turn out to be important. A watch list, any watch list, however, forces substitutions of all the words that an author imagines *could* be on the list, and this tends to make such messages detectable in another way.

For determining authorship of messages, techniques are so new that it is not easy to come up with countermeasures to obscure authorship, or to see whether such obscuring itself creates a detectable signature. Recent work in de-identification of text may be relevant here [6].

For concealing mental and emotional state, countermeasures are bound to be difficult because the channels that convey this information are almost completely subconscious. Knowing how the deception model works and that it is being deployed are not necessarily enough to allow authors to modify their text to make it seem less deceptive.

Overall, selection techniques for messages of potential interest are weak, and countermeasures that can be used by senders are often straightforward to use. However, we have shown that, in some cases, the reaction to the awareness of analysis tools itself produces signatures that can make messages more detectable rather than less. We will now consider how the availability of sets of messages changes the problem of detecting bad messages.

3.   ANALYSIS OF MULTIPLE MESSAGES

We now consider ways in which a set of messages can be used to improve selection techniques, and our understanding of them. This does not add any onerous requirements, since an interception program is likely to collect large numbers of messages. Considering them in groups is no more difficult than considering them one by one.

We assume throughout that countermeasures that message senders have available to them, discussed in the previous section, have been applied. Therefore we are considering both the effects of reaction to visible selection mechanisms, and the extra information implicit in having access to multiple messages.

3.1   Detecting Message Characteristics

Suppose we have a collection of messages, and the external characteristics of those messages whose senders do not want us to select them have been obscured by the techniques discussed above, for example, by using temporary identifiers for senders and receivers.

Most of the messages in the collection will be ordinary ones, that is to say they will represent conversations among subsets of the individuals about particular subjects. We use conversation in a quite general sense. For example, the cell phone calls between a pair of individuals during the course of, say, a day or a few days will tend to form a conversation. Similarly, the exchange of emails between two individuals over a period of hours to a few days can be considered a conversation.

If each sender and receiver mentioned in the message collection is considered as a node or vertex, then each message can be considered as a directed edge linking the sender's node to the receiver's node. Ordinary conversations create a set of links between their participants, perhaps even forming a clique if the set of messages is rich enough.

Conversations whose endpoints have been obscured create an entirely different pattern. The nodes that they create are unusual nodes in the graph, since they only ever communicate with a few other nodes. Cell phones are purchased for communication, so it is very rare that they are only used for one or two calls over their lifetimes, but such sparse use is exactly characteristic of covert usage. In a graph created from the cell phone usage of a large number of calls, suspicious calls may appear as pairs of nodes with no other connections other than to each other.

The same pattern will occur with email addresses—ordinary email addresses are created to send or receive large numbers of messages; one that only sends or receives one or two is unusual. The whole machinery of link analysis can be brought to bear on such a graph, to search for outlying, sparsely connected nodes and edges [7]. These parts of the graph are most likely to contain the kind of messages that need to be selected. This problem has been extensively investigated in the context of cell phone fraud [1]. This approach can also be used to predict when a new node is an alias for an older node, because their call environment (whom they call, and who calls them) is similar.

Of course, unless the collection of messages is really large, and represents traffic over an extended period of time, there will be some innocent messages that happen to appear in the graph as a single message between nodes that communicate with no other nodes. The false positive rate may be high. The false negative rate is likely to be low since a covert endpoint exists to interact with only a few messages. Collecting a set of messages and carrying out the analysis on the whole set allows good messages to be detected and removed based on the characteristic structure and richness of their connection environments. Once again, the attempts of those originating bad messages to make them harder to detect in fact creates a signature that distinguishes them.

3.2 Detecting Message Content

We have seen that substitutions in individual messages can be detected with high reliability. Given a collection of messages, other techniques can be used to look for groups of messages with common, or overlapping, substitutions.

Given a collection of messages, we can form two matrices that capture their word usage. The first is a message-word matrix, whose rows correspond to messages, whose columns correspond to words, and whose ijth entry records the frequency of word j in message i. Such matrices are commonly used in information retrieval.

The second matrix is a message-rank matrix. Its rows correspond to messages, its rows correspond to ranks of words in messages, and its ijth entry is the global rank in the dataset of the word that appears as the jth ranked word in message i.

The relationships among the messages, and among the words or word ranks, can be explored using two matrix decompositions, each of which separates the data into more accessible forms.

Singular Value Decomposition (SVD) decomposes a data matrix A into a product

$$A = USV^t$$

where the superscript indicates transposition, $U U^t = I$, $V V^t = I$ and S is a diagonal matrix whose diagonal elements (the singular values) are non-increasing. If A is n × m then U is n × m, S is m × m, and V^t is m × m.

An SVD transforms the data to a new basis described by the rows of V^t so that the maximum variation in the data is captured in the first dimension, as much as possible of what remains in the 2nd dimension, and so on. This means that the SVD can be truncated at some k $\ll$ m so that

$$A \approx U_k S_k V_k^t$$

where U_k is n × k, S_k is k × k, and V_k^t is k × m.

Independent Component Analysis (ICA) decomposes a data matrix A into a product

$$A = WH$$

where W is $n \times k$ and H is $k \times m$, for some choice of k. ICA decomposes the data into components that are statistically independent.

A collection of messages consists of conversations, plus some individual messages. A conversation tends to be about something, so we expect that the messages that make up a conversation will be partially correlated, based on the words that are used. Such correlations can be detected by matrix decompositions.

Of course, our goal is to detect conversations that are made up of messages that contain substitutions. Will such conversations look different from ordinary conversations? If the word substitutions replace words by new words whose frequency is substantially lower in English, then the answer is yes. Conversations about rare subjects are naturally rare, so when a conversation about a common subject appears to be about a rare subject, then the whole conversation starts to look unusual.

We illustrate with a simple, artificial dataset. Suppose that we generate a message-word matrix with 1000 rows (messages) and 400 words. We assume that the columns of the matrix have been sorted into decreasing natural frequency of the words. The entries of the matrix are generated so that the *ij*th entry is sampled from a Poisson distribution with mean $f * 1/j + 1$, where f controls the overall frequencies, and $1/j$ ensures that frequencies decrease in later columns in a Zipf-like way. With $f = 3$, this generates a matrix that is about 4% sparse, with each message containing about 20 distinct words. This is a reasonable approximation to typical emails from which stopwords have been removed. The first 200 columns of this matrix represent common words that tend to appear in almost all messages. Their presence does not provide useful correlation information, so we ignore these columns in the analysis.

We can construct the equivalent message-rank matrix from the message-word matrix. If a particular message contains, as its first three most common words, w_1, w_2, and w_3, then the first three columns of the message-rank matrix contain the values $r(w_1)$, $r(w_2)$, and $r(w_3)$ where $r()$ is the natural rank of its argument word in English. The size of the resulting message-rank matrix is 1000 by 26. (Notice that this makes the message-rank matrix much easier to work with, because it is so much smaller.)

We can now add rows that mimic messages containing substitutions to these matrices, and use SVD and ICA to see how detectable such added rows are. We add 10 extra rows (rows numbered 1001 to 1010) by generating their entries using the Poisson distribution above, and then replacing a block of entries in columns 301—306 by a uniformly random set of 0s and 1s. These entries represent the words that are used in these messages as replacements. The probability of a 1 in column 301 in the ordinary part of the matrix is about 1%, whereas the probability of occurrence in the added block is 50% so this represents replacement of a common word. Each added message has an overlap of 2 or 3 words with other added messages, representing the common subject matter of the conversation.

Figure 20-1 shows a plot of the first three columns of the U matrix from the SVD. Recall that these dimensions capture the most significant variation in the data. The messages from the added group are marked with (red) circles. They separate clearly from the other messages in the first and second dimensions.

Figure 20-2 shows a plot of the first three columns of the W matrix from the ICA. The messages from the added group are marked with (red) circles, and again are well separated from the other messages.

Fortunately, both unusual frequency and correlation are required for such groups to be detectable. Otherwise, this approach would detect conversations about ordinary topics, or individual messages with unusual word use, which would make it much less useful.

To explore whether correlation among ordinary frequency words (ordinary conversations) is detectable, we generate a new set of 10 added rows, by generating a block of 5 rows by 6 columns, but filled with appropriate Poisson-generated frequency entries, and then add the block to rows 1001-1005, and again to rows 1006-1010.

Figure 20-3 shows that, using SVD, the points corresponding to rows 1001-1010 are not separated from the main mass of points. Figure 20-4 shows that, using ICA, there is no separation of the points corresponding to rows 1001-1010 either.

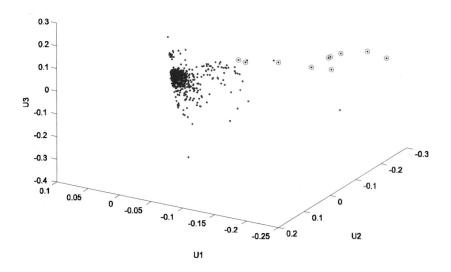

Figure 20-1. The 3-dimensional plot of messages for a dataset containing correlated unusual word usage

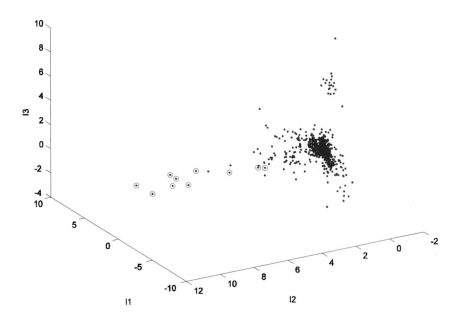

Figure 20-2. The 3-dimensional plot from ICA of a dataset containing correlated unusual word usage

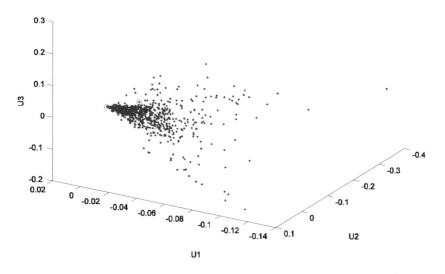

Figure 20-3. 3-dimensional plot from SVD for a dataset with correlation but typical frequencies

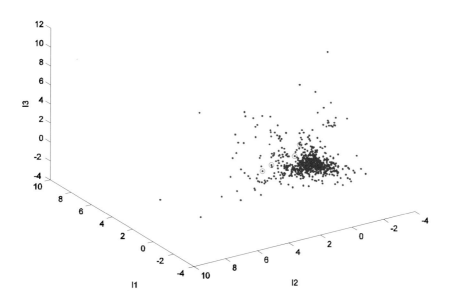

Figure 20-4. 3-dimensional plot from ICA for a dataset with correlation but typical frequencies

To explore whether messages containing unusual (rare) words are detectable, we generate 10 independent vectors of length 6 with a uniform distribution of 0s and 1s, and then overlay these on the added messages in rows 1001-1010, but in non-overlapping columns starting from column 280.

Figure 20-5 shows that, using SVD, the points corresponding to the added messages are distributed all over the plot, although they do tend to be far from the origin because of their unusual word usage. Similarly, ICA (Figure 20-6) fails to see this set of added messages as unusual.

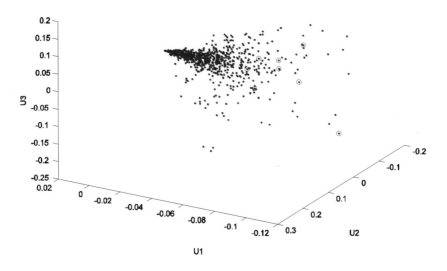

Figure 20-5. 3-dimensional plot from SVD for a dataset with unusual word frequencies but not correlation

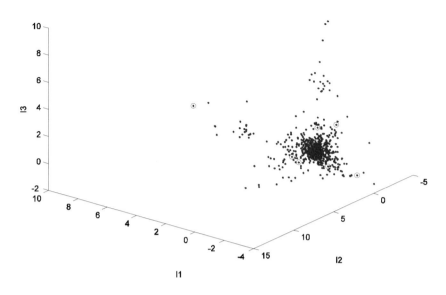

Figure 20-6. 3-dimensional plot from ICA for a dataset with unusual word frequencies but not correlation

Applying both SVD and ICA to a message-word matrix picks out correlated word usage of words with the 'wrong' frequency, but does not pick out either correlated word usage (ordinary conversations) or words with the 'wrong' frequency independently.

We now consider the strategy of replacing words by words with a fixed shift in the global frequency ranking, for example, rules like "always replace a word at rank *i* by the word at rank *i+j*", where *j* is either fixed, or different for each author. We mimic this by once again adding 10 rows to the dataset, copies of row 1, but shifted by 1,2,3 and so on places to the right, to represent using words with ranks below those of the actual words.

Figure 20-7 shows an SVD plot of the message-word matrix. As expected, the added messages are not particularly distinctive. Figure 20-8 shows the SVD plot of the message-rank version of the matrix. Now the relationship between these messages (and their relationship to message 1) is much clearer. In the message-rank matrix, the rows corresponding to these messages have a similar profile, so that they are visibly correlated. As messages are shifted to the right, they contain less frequent words, so that their average word rank increases, moving them farther from the origin.

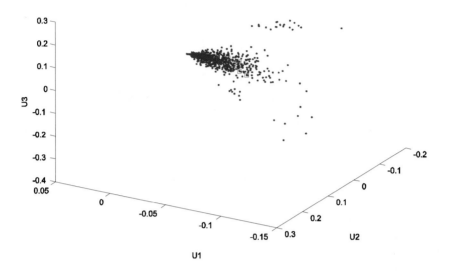

Figure 20-7. SVD plot of message-word matrix with words of similar frequency substituted (copies shifted by increasing amounts marked by (red) boxes; original message marked by (red) diamond)

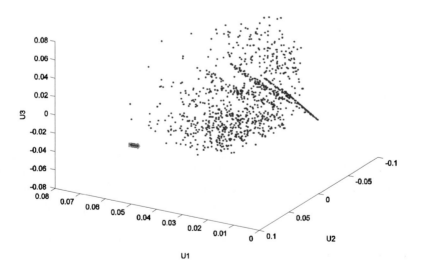

Figure 20-8. SVD plot of message-rank matrix with words of similar frequency substituted (copies shifted by increasing amounts marked by (red) boxes; original message marked by (red) diamond)

Both the message-word and message-rank matrices, and the SVD and ICA decompositions use the correlation information available in a set of messages to make better discriminations about messages that should be selected for further analysis [13].

3.3 Detecting Message Authorship

Successful authorship detection is relatively new, and techniques for detecting it more easily, given a set of messages, are not known. Of course, a set of messages is more likely to contain more than one example of a message by the same author, but we don't know which ones they are. The problem reduces to clustering based on authorship markers. What such a clustering would produce is an interesting question.

3.4 Detecting Mental State

The Pennebaker model allows individual messages to be scored, based on the frequencies of marker words. However, the model suggests that deception is signaled by decreases in the frequencies of certain kinds of words, and increases in the frequencies of other kinds of words. This invites the question: increase/decrease with respect to what? Such a simple scoring method also creates the possibility of manipulating the score by inserting, more or less randomly, word types that the deception model expects to find decreased, and being parsimonious in the use of word types that the deception model expects to increase. This may not be easy in practice, since language production mechanisms are largely subconscious, so the result of too much manipulation may be stilted sentences.

Taking a set of messages and considering them as a whole allows both a principled way to create a baseline score, and a defense against straightforward manipulation of frequencies.

The following process applies the Pennebaker model to a dataset of multiple messages:

- Build a matrix whose rows correspond to messages, whose columns correspond to words from the Pennebaker model, and whose *ij*th entry is the count of the *j*th word in the *i*th message. This matrix will be quite sparse, because most marker words do not appear in any given message.
- Normalize the matrix by computing the mean of the non-zero entries in each column, and subtracting this mean from the non-zero entries. This ignores the zero entries, but ensures that the non-zero entries are mean-centered.
- Negate the values in the columns corresponding to first-person pronouns

and exception words. This means that *decreases* in word frequency in messages becomes increases in the values of this attribute. Note that, both here and in the previous step, the presence of innocent messages is what creates a baseline against which deceptive messages can be evaluated. The presence of innocent messages also means that those who write deceptively cannot reverse engineer their messages to appear innocent, since they don't know what set of particular innocent messages they will be compared to.

- Carry out an SVD of the resulting matrix. The resulting U matrix (especially its early columns) captures the relationships among documents, while the V matrix captures the relationship among words of the model.
- Choose an appropriate number of dimensions (by looking at how quickly the magnitudes of the singular values decrease) and project the rows of U, considered as vectors in this number of dimensions, onto the vector from the origin passing through $(1,1, \ldots , 1)$. The distance from the origin of the projection of each row onto this vector (positive or negative) gives the new deception score.

Messages with a positive deception score can be considered to be deceptive; those with a negative deception score can be considered not to be deceptive. The magnitude of the score provides an estimate of how deceptive each message is relative to the entire set. We might expect that, in a typical setting, almost all messages would have deception scores close to 0, with a few having much higher (positive) scores.

One of the improvements that the new deception score has over the direct Pennebaker score can be seen by considering the following. Suppose a particular column of the matrix has random frequencies inserted in it. These random entries all contribute to the Pennebaker score, so that these insertions will change the ranking of messages by Pennebaker score substantially—a message with a large inserted value will suddenly seem more deceptive. However, the SVD will correctly detect that the entries for this column are uncorrelated with anything else, discount its effect, and give a ranking that is unchanged from what it would have been before the insertions. Hence the new, collective, deception score is resistant both to words that are in the model, but play very little roles; and to attempts by authors to manipulate deception scores directly by, say, adding exclusive words at random to decrease the Pennebaker deception score.

Once again, analyzing a collection of messages allows us to do better selection of suspicious messages.

3.5   Summary

We have seen that most techniques that look for bad messages on a message by message basis can be defeated or weakened by relatively simple countermeasures. However, even in this case, countermeasures to avoid selection because of the use of certain words fail because the substitutions designed to avoid these words are themselves detectable.

When analysis is done on sets of messages, rather than on a per-message basis, the use of countermeasures becomes even more obvious. Concealing endpoints by using short-term identifiers (email addresses, IP addresses, SIM cards) makes messages obvious because the edges they create tend to be isolated, whereas ordinary messages create edges that connect their senders and receivers into a web of neighbors.

Concealing message content by word replacement can also generate a detectable structure among messages that share common replacements. Although there are a number of possible ways to generate such substitutions, all create some kind of correlation which can be detected by appropriate matrix decomposition. This goes beyond message by message detection of substitution because it allows related bad messages to be connected together, revealing the presence and structure of conversations on the basis of their common evasion strategy.

4. CONCLUSIONS

We consider the problem of detecting bad messages among a large set of intercepted messages. We argue that two important properties are required to do well:

Detection should be two-pronged, with a first simple but visible technique, and a second-string technique that looks for reactions to the first technique. Innocent messages tend to ignore the first technique, while those who wish to conceal their messages cannot afford to.

We have showed how the attempt not to use words that may be on a watch list creates a signature of substituted words that is reasonably detectable.

Detection is more effective when it is applied to sets of messages, rather than on a message by message basis. The countermeasures that can be used to defend against message by message analysis tend to create signatures that are visible in sets of messages.

For example, using short-term endpoints creates unusual nodes and edges in a graph derived from a set of messages. Using the same, or related, substitutions to replace words that should not appear creates correlations among messages that make individual bad messages easier to detect, but also reveals connections between related messages that would otherwise not be visible. Looking for evidence of deception is more robust in the presence of a set of messages, as the innocent messages provide a baseline against which deception model scores can be judged, and also make it hard to manipulate word frequencies, even if the characteristics of the model are known.

Systems that are to be deployed to look for bad messages in large sets of intercepted messages, whether those intercepted by governments, or those gathered by organizations, should be aware of these important properties which can improve performance and resistance to reverse engineering.

5.   ACKNOWLEDGEMENTS

This research was supported by the Natural Science and Engineering Research Council of Canada.

REFERENCES

C.Cortes, D. Pregibon, and C. Volinsky. Computational methods for dynamic graphs. *Journal of Computational and Graphical Statistics*, 12:950--970, 2003.

O. de Vel, A. Anderson, M. Corney, and G. Mohay. Mining {E-mail} content for author identification forensics. *SIGMOD Record*, 30(4):55--64, December 2001.

European Parliament Temporary Committee on the ECHELON Interception System. Final report on the existence of a global system for the interception of private and commercial communications (ECHELON interception system), 2001.

SW. Fong, D.B. Skillicorn, and D. Roussinov. Detecting word substitutions in text. *IEEE Transactions on Knowledge and Data Engineering*, to appear, 2007.

G. Fung. The disputed Federalist papers: SVM and feature selection via concave minimization. In *Proceedings of the 2003 Conference on Diversity in Computing*, pages 42--46, Atlanta, Georgia, USA, 2003.

D. Gupta, M. Saul, and J. Gilbertson. Evaluation of a deidentification {(De-Id)} software engine to share pathology reports and clinical documents for research. *American Journal of Clinical Pathology*, 121(2):176--186, February 2004.

R.D. Horn, J.D. Birdwell, and L.W. Leedy. Link discovery tool. In *ONDCP/CTAC International Symposium*, August 1997.

P.S. Keila and D.B. Skillicorn. Detecting unusual email communication. In *CASCON 2005*, pages 238--246, 2005.

P.S. Keila and D.B. Skillicorn. Structure in the Enron email dataset. *Computational and Mathematical Organization Theory*, 11(3):183--199, 2005.

M. Koppel, J. Schler, and K. Zigdon. Automatically determining an anonymous author's native language. In *Intelligence and Security Informatics, IEEE International Conference on Intelligence and Security Informatics*, ISI 2005, Atlanta, GA, USA, May 19-20, pages 209--217. Springer-Verlag Lecture Notes in Computer Science LNCS 3495, 2005.

M.L. Newman, J.W. Pennebaker, D.S. Berry, and J.M. Richards. Lying words: Predicting deception from linguistic style. *Personality and Social Psychology Bulletin*, 29:665--675, 2003.

M. K. Reiter and A. D. Rubin. Crowds: Anonymity for web transactions. *ACM Transactions on Information and System Security*, 1(1):66--92, November 1998.

D.B. Skillicorn. Beyond keyword filtering for message and conversation detection. In *IEEE International Conference on Intelligence and Security Informatics (ISI2005)*, pages 231--243. Springer-Verlag Lecture Notes in Computer Science LNCS 3495, May 2005.

X. Zhu and R. Rosenfeld. Improving trigram language modeling with the world wide web. In *Proceedings of International Conference on Acoustics, Speech, and Signal Processing, 2001.*, pages 533--536, 2001.

SUGGESTED READINGS

- Newman, M.L., Pennebaker, J.W., Berry, D.S., and Richards, J.M. (2003). Lying words: Predicting deception from linguistic style. Personality and Social Psychology Bulletin, 29, 665-675. This paper outlines Pennebaker's model of deception and how it was constructed empirically.
- Campbell, R.S., and Pennebaker, J.W. (2003). The secret life of pronouns: Flexibility in writing style and physical health. Psychological Science, 14, 60-65. This paper shows how much information about a person's internal state can be gleaned from their use of `small' words.
- DePaulo, B.M., Lindsay, J.J., Malone, B.E., Muhlenbruck, L., Charlton, K., and Cooper, H. (2003). Cues to deception. Psychological Bulletin, 129, 74-118. This paper summarizes a large amount of research on deception, not just in text but in other modalities as well.

DISCUSSION QUESTIONS

1. What are some other law-enforcement or intelligence settings where a two-pronged approach is used? Does it work the same way as the two-pronged approach described here?
2. Honey traps are mechanisms that encourage criminals and terrorists to reveal how that work and think by presenting them with apparent opportunities that are actually crafted to learn about them without letting them cause any damage. Can you think of any ways in which honey traps can be used in the kinds of problems addressed here?
3. Are there ways in which authorship can be more reliably determined given a set of messages, even though we don't know which messages are by which author. Is there a clustering technique that will work well for this problem?
4. Most graph analysis algorithms look at the central structure of the graph. We have indicated that suspicious messages are more likely to be found in small, outlying pieces of graph. Should link analysis algorithms be modified to attack the kinds of problems that arise here?

21

ADDRESSING INSIDER THREAT THROUGH COST-SENSITIVE DOCUMENT CLASSIFICATION

Young-Woo[1] Seo and Katia Sycara[2]

[1]*Research Programmer, Robotics Institute, Carnegie Mellon University, Pittsburgh, Pennsylvania, U.S.A. (ywseo@cs.cmu.edu);* [2]*Professor, Robotics Institute, Carnegie Mellon University, Pittsburgh, Pennsylvania, U.S.A. (katia@cs.cmu.edu)*

CHAPTER OVERVIEW

Most organizations use computerized security systems to manage and protect their confidential information. While security is mostly concerned with prevention of attacks from outsiders, security breaches by insiders have recently gained increasing attention from the security community. In this chapter, we describe a cost-sensitive document classification scheme which forms the basis for determining the legitimacy of confidential access by insiders. Our scheme enforces compliance with the "need to know" security principle, namely that the requests for access are authorized only if the content of the requested information is relevant to the requester's current information analysis project. First, we formulate such content-based authorization, i.e., whether to accept or reject access requests as a binary classification problem. Second, we implement this problem in a cost-sensitive learning framework in which the cost caused by incorrect decision is different according to the relative importance of the error types; false positive and false negative. In particular, the cost for a false positive (i.e., accepting a security violating request) is considered more expensive than that of false negative (i.e., rejecting a valid request). The former is a serious security problem because confidential information, which should not be revealed, can be accessed. We experimentally compared various cost-sensitive classifiers with conventional error-minimizing classifiers. Our results indicate that costing using logistic regression showed the best performance, in terms of the smallest cost paid, the lowest false positive rate, and the relatively low false negative rate.

1.   INTRODUCTION

Most organizations use computerized security systems for managing and protecting their confidential information and restricting unauthorized access. Robust fire-walls are in place to control the access from outside whereas a fine-grained access control list with a sophisticated encryption could be imposed to restrict internal access. However, sometimes, malicious insiders may want to gain access to confidential information which they should not be able to see. Illegitimate access to confidential information by insiders poses a great risk to an organization. The issue of protecting confidential information from illegitimate access from insiders is a very challenging problem since insiders have (or could easily get) information authorization. Since malicious insiders are well aware of where the valuable information resides and which cause damaging effects, the results of illegitimate confidential access are far more costly. To make matters worse, illegitimate access is difficult to effectively prohibit or detect because malevolent actions are done by already trusted persons. In addition, some areas of confidential information are "grey areas", i.e. it is not clear whether access to this information may harm the organization. Moreover, it is difficult to know whether illegitimate access by an insider is intentionally malicious or just a mistake guided by curiosity. Finally, organizations need to balance the need for protecting information from illegitimate access from insiders versus inhibiting people to do their job by not allowing them access to information they may need. Therefore, sophisticated techniques that enforce the "need to know" principle are required.

In this chapter, we present a new approach for controlling confidential access by insiders. This is also called the "insider threat" problem. One of the common ways to deal with the insider threat problem is to control access to confidential information based on the need-to-know principle; The requests for access are authorized only if the content of the requested information is relevant to the requester's current information analysis project. For instance, if an information analyst's current project concerns the development of nuclear weapon by Iran, it would be illegitimate for the analyst to have access to documents on other aspects, e.g., feminist activities in Iran. However, since it is not clear what analysis topics, and hence, which queries may be relevant for some particular analysis topic, documents on these different aspects of Iranian politics and welfare are not necessarily a priori separated in different secured data bases. Therefore, the issue of allowing access on a need-to-know basis on particular confidential documents is very challenging.

A variety of ways could be used to address the insider threat problem.

Requests to access confidential information may occur, for example, when an employee is assigned to a new project and needs to access background knowledge. The project manager could either hand select only those documents of confidential information that he will let the employee see, or completely bar access to the entire collection rather than exposing information that should not be exposed. However this approach is quite inflexible. It does not allow easy adjustment to frequent changes of a user's task assignment. Project assignments for an employee may be changed quite often and hence the employee needs to access confidential information related to the newly assigned project. Alternatively, since the organization wants to make sure that the employee accesses only pertinent information, a set of access control lists (ACL) may be compiled manually to control those requests. Each item of confidential information is associated with an ACL, which ensures a corresponding level of security and can be accessed by anyone who has been authorized. However this approach has a crucial security weakness. Since, for the purpose of indexing and security, confidential information is grouped into containers on some basis (e.g. by country that the information pertains to), a user who is authorized to access a segment of confidential information in a container is actually able to access the entire container.

In this chapter, we describe a flexible and reliable solution for addressing these problems. The proposed solution takes advantage of machine learning classification algorithms for the authorization of requests for confidential information. Instead of relying on coarse-grained ACLs and hand-selected information, our method automatically extracts the relevant content of requested confidential information and compares it with the content of the requester's particular current project. If the comparison determines that the content of the requester's project is similar enough to the requested access, then permission is granted. If not, permission could be denied or the employee's supervisor could be notified [Seo et al., 2004]. Instead of conventional error-minimizing classification, we utilize a cost-sensitive classification. In domains where there is differential cost for misclassification of examples, an error-minimizing approach may not give results that reflect the requirements of the domain. Experimental results show that this cost-sensitive approach is more effective than competing classification approaches [Seo and Sycara, 2006].

The rest of the chapter is organized as follows. Section 2 discusses related work, section 3 presents an overview of the system architecture. Section 4 presents the classification algorithm. Section 5 presents the experimental results and section 6 concludes.

2.   RELATED WORK

Content-based management of text document access control has been proposed by Weippl and Ibrahim [Weippl and Ibrahim, 2001]. They applied a self-organized map (SOM) to cluster a given collection of text documents into groups with similar content, thus allowing human security administrators to impose dynamic access control to identified text document groups. However Weippl and Ibrahim did not address the potential problems that occur when the security policy for individual documents of a cluster does not match with the security policy for that cluster. Giuri and Iglio [Giuri and Iglio, 1997] addressed the issue of determining a user's access to confidential information. Their approach is based on the content of the information and the role of the user. For example, they propose subdividing medical records into several different categories (e.g., pediatrics), and allow access to only relevant physicians (e.g., pediatricians). Since they do not mention automatic techniques in their paper, one is left with the suspicion that they manually categorize content and roles. Moreover, they do not discuss the situation when a document may be classified under many different categories that may present the need for different user roles to access it. For example, another medical specialty (e.g. orthopedics) may need to access a pediatric document (e.g. document on childhood arthritis). What would then be the access policy? In the intelligence analysis security domain, the cases of multiple classifications of documents into different topics are the ones that are most problematic and must be dealt with. Aleman-Meza and his colleagues proposed an ontological approach to deal with the legitimate document access problem of insider threat [Aleman-Meza et al., 2005]. An attempt to access a document is regarded as legitimate if the job assignment of a requester (e.g., an intelligence analyst) has a semantic association with the documents that are requested for access. This approach is quite similar to ours in that they enforce the need-to-know principle by using a predefined ontology. A well-defined ontology might be useful to determine the semantic associations between the existing documents and the analysts' assignments, but regular updates are required to accommodate the change of the document collections and the topics of assignments. Symonenko and his colleagues propose a hybrid approach that combines role-based access monitoring, social network analysis, and semantic analysis of insiders' communications, in order to detect inappropriate information exchange [Symonenko et al., 2004]. Lee and his colleagues [Lee et al., 2002] introduced a cost-sensitive framework for the intrusion detection domain and analyzed cost factors in detail. In particular, they identified the major cost factors (e.g., costs for development, operation, damages and responding to intrusion) and then applied a rule induction learning technique (i.e., RIPPER) to this cost model, in order to maximize security while minimizing costs. However their cost model needs to be changed manually if a system's cost factors are changed.

3. OVERVIEW

Figure 21-1 presents the overview of our implemented system [Seo et al., 2004].

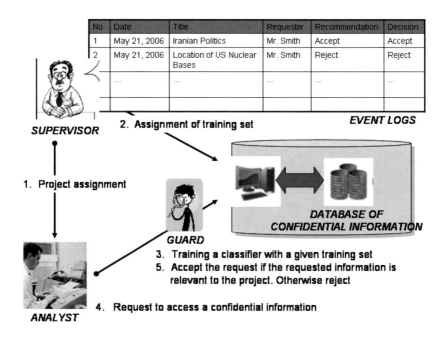

No	Date	Title	Requester	Recommendation	Decision
1	May 21, 2006	Iranian Politics	Mr. Smith	Accept	Accept
2	May 21, 2006	Location of US Nuclear Bases	Mr. Smith	Reject	Reject
...	...	...	...	...	...

2. Assignment of training set   **EVENT LOGS**

SUPERVISOR

1. Project assignment

DATABASE OF CONFIDENTIAL INFORMATION

GUARD

3. Training a classifier with a given training set
5. Accept the request if the requested information is relevant to the project. Otherwise reject

4. Request to access a confidential information

ANALYST

Figure 21-1. The architecture of our intelligent agent system for managing confidential access

Suppose a user has been assigned to do intelligence analysis on a particular topic. Let us call the set of documents that are strictly relevant to the user's topic, *T*. The secure database of documents that the user has authorization to access, however includes documents that are not only relevant to his topic, i.e. documents in the set *T*, but also documents that are not strictly relevant. Let us call the contents of the overall secure database *D*. The set *D* includes *T*. Therefore, the problem is to restrict the user's access to documents in *T* and prohibit his access to documents in *D-T*. (- means set complement).

We have developed an agent, called *guard* that operates in the background of the user's computer. The overall system operates as follows.

1. Given an analysis topic for a particular user, the guard agent gets trained on a set of documents T that are relevant to the user's topic. These relevant documents could be hand picked by the user's supervisor. It is of course important to ensure that the training set does not require laborious selection of a large set of relevant documents.

2. Given a user request for access to a particular document in the secure database set D, the guard agent automatically classifies the requested document as similar to documents in class T, or not.

3. If the requested document has been classified as similar to documents in class T, then the guard agent permits access; if not, there are two alternatives: (a) either the guard agent denies access to the requested document and notifies the user's supervisor, or (b) the guard agent permits access, but notes the suspected illegitimacy of the request, and notifies the user's supervisor. Which one of these two different policies to address suspicious requests an organization wants to use may depend on how tolerant of suspicious requests it wants to be. Our cost sensitive classification approach fits in directly with possible sensitivity of organizations to suspicious requests.

Our approach utilizes conventional classification methods for enforcing the need-to-know principle. By doing this, our method allows the supervisor a means of specifying subsets of per-user and per-task access control policies, and a way to automatically enforce them through the guard agent. Since the proposed system learns, or adapts to, the supervisor's decision criteria based on a small number of supervisor-provided examples, and generalizes from such examples, the supervisor need not identify all relevant information. Through our proposed system, it becomes possible for the supervisor to define, assign, and enforce a security policy for a particular subset of confidential information.

Our approach is quite flexible and adaptive to changes of project assignment because only an updated description of newly assigned projects is necessary to re-train the classifiers. By contrast, ACL-based approaches require recompilation of all changing relevant information. Therefore, our approach is much less expensive than ACL-based or other approaches, both computationally, and also in terms of human time and effort. Furthermore, in the case of either acceptance or rejection, the suspicious request can be logged for security audits and alarms.

Our approach has an additional advantage: it captures the differential cost sensitivity of the secure access domain, through cost sensitive classification. Cost sensitive classification, unlike conventional error minimization classification approaches, takes into consideration the differential cost of misclassification of different events (in our case, events are document requests). For example, suppose that there are 100 medical cases that are comprised of 5 cancer cases and 95 flu cases. Without considering the cost for misclassification (e.g., compensation for misdiagnosis), an error-minimizing classifier would simply achieve the lower error rate by ignoring the minority class, even though the actual consequences of misdiagnosis of cancer is far worse than that of flu. Thus, it is undesirable to use an error-minimizing classification method, which treats all misclassification costs equally, for cost-sensitive domains because error-minimizing methods classify every example as belonging to the most probable class. In addition, the cost minimization approach fits very naturally into the secure access domain, since, different cost parameters can be set by the organization to reflect organizational policies with respect to tolerance of suspicious requests, e.g. whether to deny every suspicious request or to monitor suspicious requests and only take punitive action after a number of repetitions.

4. CLASSIFICATION FOR CONFIDENTIAL AUTHORIZATION

A classification method refers to a decision rule that assigns one of (or more than one) predefined classes (or class labels) to a set of given examples (testing examples). The goal of a classification method is to find the optimal decision boundary from given data collection (often called training examples). The optimal decision boundary is a decision criterion and allows a classifier to produce the best performance [Duda et al., 2001].

Let us consider a hypothetical example in figure 2 which shows two classes with overlapping boundaries due to their intrinsic randomness. In this example, the class-conditional density for each class is a normal distribution, that is,

$$f_0(x \mid class = 0) \sim N(\mu_0, \sigma_0^2) \text{ and } f_1(x \mid class = 1) \sim N(\mu_1, \sigma_1^2) \text{ (i.e.,}$$
$$\mu_0 = 0.35, \sigma_0 = 0.1448, \mu_1 = 0.7, \sigma_1 = 0.1736).$$

Given an overlapped boundary condition (e.g., the sub-figure at the middle of figure 1), a classifier can generate four possible classification outcomes for a given example; a: true positive (an example actually belongs to class 1 and is classified as class 1), b: false positive (an example belongs to class 0, but is classified as class 1), c: false negative (an example belongs to class 1, but is classified as class 0), and d: true negative (an example belongs to class 0 and is classified as class 0). Table 21-1 captures this information as well as the cost (λ_{ij}) involved in those four outcomes.

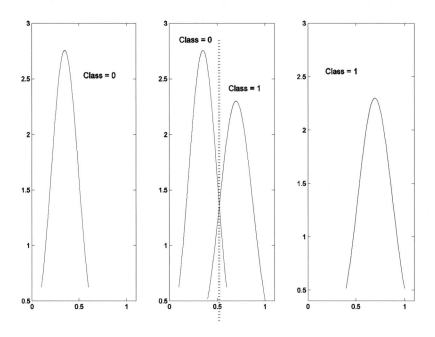

Figure 21-2. The figure at left shows the distribution of examples belonging to class 0 and the figure at right shows that of examples belonging to class 1. If one puts those two distributions together, the areas of two classes overlap because of their intrinsic randomness. The optimal decision boundary for a binary classification is the dotted vertical line (in red) of the figure at the center.

Table 21-1. A 2-by-2 contingency table representing four possible classification outcomes and their associated costs. λ_{ij} is the cost for classifying an example belonging to j as i.

	True class = 1	True class = 0
Output class = 1	a (λ_{11})	b (λ_{10})
Output class = 0	c (λ_{01})	d (λ_{00})

In the insider threat domain, the cost refers to any cost for recovering from the consequences of a careless release of confidential information. This might include monetary cost or social cost of restoring discredited reputation.

Let us consider first the case where there is no cost for misclassification. Under equal cost for misclassification, the optimal decision boundary is the dashed vertical line in the figure 2 that lies in the center of two class distributions. An example randomly generated will be assigned to class 1 if its value is greater than 0.52 (the actual value of the optimal decision boundary in figure 2 is 0.52). Otherwise it is assigned to class 0. This type of classification is called an *error-minimizing classification.*

Error minimizing classification works well for many domains. However, there are many domains, e.g. medical, or security, where costs of misclassification are not equal for different categories. Let us consider the case that there are text documents belonging to "class 0" and "class 1," and all of them are confidential information of which careless release may have a damaging effect. An employee is newly assigned to a project for which records are labeled as "class 1." He is authorized to access only documents in "class 1" because he needs to know background knowledge of the project. Since in general a zero cost is assigned to the correct classification[1], the costs for two types of error should be considered carefully for providing a reliable confidential access control; false negative (λ_{01}) – reject the valid request (e.g., reject the request that the employee asks to access a "class 1" document); false positive (λ_{10}) -- accept the invalid request (e.g., accept the request that the employee asks to access a "class 0" document). Particularly, a false negative causes the employee to be inconvenienced because he is not able to access need-to-know information. However, not approving valid requests does not cause a serious problem from the security perspective. On the contrary, a false positive is a serious problem because confidential information, which should not be revealed, can be accessed.

Therefore, for a need-to-know basis confidential authorization, the cost for false positive (i.e., the damaging effect) is much higher than that of false negative. Where then would the optimal decision boundary be for the case of unequal misclassification cost? The decision boundary for uniform-cost must be re-located, in order to minimize the cost for misclassifications. For example, if the cost of false positive is higher than that of false negative, the dashed vertical line in the figure 2 should be moved toward the right. However a tradeoff must be considered because choosing one of the extremes will not consider the error. In particular, the classifier could reduce the false negative close to zero if the dashed vertical line moves to the left, but with higher false positive. If either of extremes is not the solution, the optimal decision line should be chosen somewhere between extremes by considering the tradeoff.

Approaches for Cost-Sensitive Classification

In domains with unequal misclassification costs, the goal of cost-sensitive learning is to find the boundary between the regions that divide optimally the example space. Obviously the misclassification cost,

---

[1] We assume that the classification system recommends the supervisor to authorize an employee's request if the requested document is classified by the system as "class 1."

particularly a cost table (e.g., table 1), is the dominant factor for the optimal boundaries. That is, the region where class j must be predicted will expand at the expense of the regions of other classes if misclassifying examples of class j is more expensive relative to misclassifying other classes, even though the class probabilities remain unchanged.

There have been two major approaches for cost-sensitive learning. The first one is a *glass-box* approach that converts particular error-minimizing classifiers into cost-sensitive ones by modifying their classification rules [Drummond and Holte, 2000], [Fan et al., 1999]. The second one is a *black-box* approach that makes arbitrary error-minimizing classifiers cost-sensitive without altering classification rules [Domingos, 1999], [Zadrozny et al., 2002].

In this paper, we utilize two methods in the black-box approach; *costing* [Zadrozny et al., 2002] and *metacost* [Domingos, 1999]. A black-box approach makes use of sampling techniques that change the original example (or data) distribution by incorporating the relative misclassification cost of each instance, according to a given cost matrix. This changes the proportion of a certain class (e.g., confidential documents that are "need-to-know" to perform a given project). The costing and metacost methods make any cost-insensitive classifiers perform cost minimization on the newly generated distribution.

> **Costing** (cost proportionate rejection sampling with aggregation) is a wrapper for cost-sensitive learning. This method trains a set of error-minimizing classifiers by a distribution, which is the original distribution with the relative cost of each example, and outputs a final classifier by taking the average over all learned classifiers [Zadrozny et al., 2002]. Costing is comprised of two processes: rejection sampling and bagging. Rejection sampling (often called acceptance-rejection sampling) has been used to generate independently and identically distributed samples that are used as a proxy distribution to achieve simulation from the target distribution. Rejection sampling for the costing assigns each example in the original distribution with a relative cost[2] and draws a random number r from a uniform distribution, $U(0,1)$. The example will be kept if $r > \dfrac{c}{Z}$. Otherwise it is discarded and the sampling is continued until certain criteria are satisfied. The accepted examples are regarded as a realization

---

[2] $\hat{x}_i = \dfrac{c}{Z} \times x_i$, where c is a cost assigned to an example, x_i, and Z is a normalization factor, satisfying $\max_{c \in S} c$

of the altered distribution, $\hat{D} = \{S_1', S_2', ..., S_k'\}$ With the newly generated distribution, $\hat{D}$, cost trains k different classifiers, $h_i \equiv Learn(S_i')$, and predicts the label of a test example x by combining those hypotheses,

$$h(x) = sign\left(\sum_{i=1}^{k} h_i(x)\right)$$

Metacost is another black-box method for converting an error-minimizing classifier into cost-sensitive classifier by re-sampling [Domingos, 1999]. The underlying assumption is that an error-minimizing classifier could learn the optimal decision boundary based on the cost matrix if each training example is relabeled with the cost. Metacost's learning process is also comprised of two processes: bagging for re-labeling and retraining the classifiers with cost. In particular, it generates a set of samples with replacement from the training set and estimates the class of each instance by taking the average of votes over all the trained classifiers. Then Metacost re-labels each training example with the estimated optimal class and re-trains the classifier to the relabeled training set.

5.   EXPERIMENTS

Our experimental domain is confidential access control based on the need-to-know principle. We model the decision of rejecting or accepting the user's access request as a binary classification problem. In particular, our system classifies the content of the requested information as positive or negative with respect to the content of the requester's project and authorizes the request if the requested information is classified as positive with respect to the requester's project. Otherwise the request is rejected. In our experiments, we choose three different error-minimizing classification methods, linear discriminant analysis (LDA), logistic regression (LR), and support vector machines (SVMs), because of their relative good performance, particularly in text classification [Joachims, 1998], [Schutze et al., 1995], [Torkkola, 2001].

The purpose of the experiments is two-fold; (1) to find a good classification method that minimizes the cost and the false positive rate while holding the false negative rate reasonably low, (2) to test our research hypothesis that the cost-sensitive learning methods reduce the total cost for misclassification in comparison with error-minimizing classifiers.

5.1   Experimental Setting

Three performance metrics were primarily used to measure the usefulness of classifiers; false negative rate, defined as,

$$fn = \frac{c}{a+c}\left(= P(output = 0 \mid true = 1) = \frac{P(output = 0, true = 1)}{P(true = 1)} \right)$$

by using the values in the table 1, false positive rate,

$$fp = \frac{b}{b+d}$$

and cost of misclassification. These metrics are better matched to our purpose than conventional measures based on precision-recall because we are interested primarily in reducing the error and the cost. Moreover, the above two error measures are not sensitive to changes of class frequency whereas the precision and recall measures are sensitive to the frequencies of the target classes [Fawcett, 2003].

Since there are no publicly available datasets that are comprised of confidential information, we choose the Reuters-21578 document collections for experiments. This data set, which consists of world news stories from 1987, has become a benchmark in text classification evaluations. It has been partially labeled by human experts with respect to a list of categories. Since our task is a binary classification task where each document must be assigned either positive or negative value, we discarded documents that are assigned no topic or multiple topics. Moreover, classes with fewer than 10 documents are discarded. The resulting data set is comprised of 9,854 documents as a training set and 4,274 documents as a test set with 67 categories.

The experimental setting is as follows. All the documents are regarded as confidential. At each trial, one category is chosen and documents belonging to the selected category are regarded as confidential information that the requester needs to know. Conversely the rest of test documents are confidential information that should not be revealed. A false positive occurs when a method classifies a document as positive that should have not been revealed (i.e., the document actually belongs to the negative class) whereas a false negative occurs when the method classifies a request as negative that should have been accepted. For both errors, the system pays the cost for misclassification.

According to the class assignment – not the original Reuters-21578 category label, but the artificially assigned class label, such as need-to-know confidential or otherwise (simply, positive or negative) – each of the documents in both the training and testing sets is assigned a cost, ensuring that the misclassification cost of a need-to-know confidential information is higher than that of the remaining confidential documents (i.e., $\lambda_{10} > \lambda_{01} > \lambda_{00} = \lambda_{11}$). Since the Reuters-21578 document collection does not have cost information, we devised a heuristic for cost assignment. There is a cost involved in incorrect classification. Moreover, a higher cost is assigned to a false positive than a false negative. Particularly, the cost for misclassifying a confidential document is computed by:

$$cost(d_i) = \begin{cases} \left[s, s + |c_j|\right] & \text{if } d_i \in c_j \text{ and } c_j = \text{positive} \\ \left[0, \dfrac{\sum\limits_{d_i \in c_j} cost(d_i)}{|\text{ number of negative documents }|}\right] & \text{otherwise} \end{cases}$$

where,

$$s = \ln\left(\frac{N}{|c_j|}\right) \times 100$$

N is the total number of documents and $|c_j|$ is the number of documents belonging to the jth category. The total cost for misclassification is added to the cost of confidential documents (i.e., positive class) misclassified if a classifier is not able to predict any of the positive documents, in order to prevent the case that a low cost is simply achieved by ignoring the class with a low frequency. For example, suppose that there are 15 out of 10,000 documents belonging to the positive class. The cost assignment ensures that the total cost for misclassifying those 15 examples should be either equal to or higher than that of the remaining documents.[3]

---

[3] For this case, the cost for false positive is

$$650.229 \left(= \left(\frac{10000}{15}\right) \times 100\right)$$

and the sum of the cost for false positive is 9753.4. The cost of misclassification of a negative document is

$$0.9768 \left(= \frac{9751.1835}{9985}\right)$$ and the cost sums to 9753.348.

5.2   Experimental Results

In our experiments we chose five out of the 67 selected categories of the Reuters-21578 dataset. The chosen five categories were considered as representative according to their category frequencies: small ("livestock" and "corn"), medium ("interest"), and large ("acq" and "earn"). 70% of the documents in a category were used as "training" and the remaining 30% documents were used for "testing", respectively. Nine different classifiers were tested: LDA, LR, and SVMs, and the combination of those three classifiers with two methods for cost-sensitive learning: metacost and costing.

A binary classifier was trained for each of the selected categories by considering the category as positive (i.e., documents that an employee needs to know) with the rest of the data as negative examples. We made use of the LIBSVM[4] and tested three different kernels, such as linear, polynomial, and Gaussian. The Gaussian kernel (i.e., width = 1 / max feature dimension) was chosen due to its best performance and the different cost factors were assigned[5] for $C=10 \sim 100$. Those values are chosen optimally by 10-fold cross validation.

As mentioned earlier, the experimental results were primarily analyzed by "false positive," "false negative," and "cost." The experimental procedure was as follows: first, pick one of five selected categories; second, assign the cost to each of documents according to its importance using the heuristic described in the previous section; third, train each of nine classifiers by training examples with cost; fourth compute three performance measures (i.e., false positive, false negative, and cost for incorrect classification).

---

[4] http://www.csie.ntu.edu.tw/~cjlin/libsvm/

[5] The cost of constraint violation is set to 100 if there are relatively small numbers of positive examples available. Otherwise it is set to about 10.

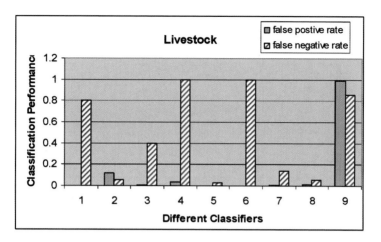

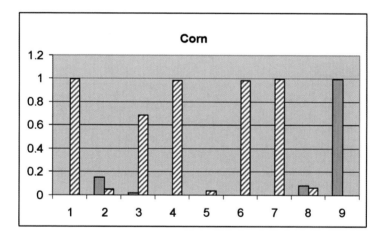

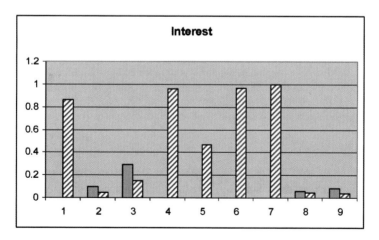

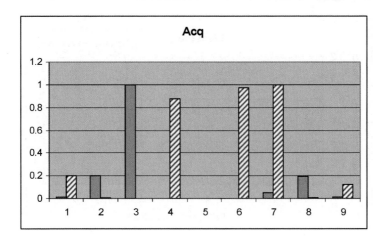

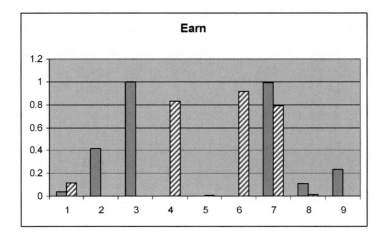

Figure 21-3. Pairs of false positive (diagonally crossed bar) and false negative (empty bar) for five categories by nine different classifiers, which are numbered from the left to the right at the x-axis: 1: SVM, 2: SVM with costing, 3: SVM with metacost, 4: LR, 5: LR with costing, 6: LR with metacost, 7: LDA, 8: LDA with costing, and 9: LDA with metacost, respectively. From the top left, the results for "livestock," "corn," "interest," "acq," and "earn" are presented. The y-axis represents false positive rate and the false negative rate in the range of 0.0 to 1.0.

Figure 21-3 shows pairs of false positive and false negative for the five selected categories that resulted from classification by nine different classifiers. The x-axis represents the nine different classifiers and the y-axis represents the misclassification rate in the range of 0.0 to 1.0. Except for the "interest" category, LR with costing showed the best results that minimize false positive while holding false negative relatively low. In particular, for the "livestock" category, LR trained by only 18% training data (i.e., 1,781 out of 9,854 documents) resulted in 0% false positive and 2.8% false negative rate. For the costing, we carried out five different sampling trials for each category (i.e., 1, 3, 5, 10, and 15) and represented the trial with the best performance. For the "livestock" category, a newly generated distribution by 10 rejection sampling trials was used to achieve this result. Each re-sampled set has only about 178 documents. LDA with the costing showed the smallest error for the "interest" category that is comprised of 5.6% false positives and 4.5% false negatives. We believe that the rejection sampling generated a set of good representative samples of the original data collection so that two discriminative classifiers (i.e., LR and LDA) could converge to the optimal (performance) asymptote quickly, even with a small number of examples [Ng and Jordan, 2001].

Table 21-2. The costs for misclassification by nine different classifiers are presented. The values in bold face are the best for corresponding category.

Methods	Livestock (114)	Corn (253)	Interest (513)	Acq (2448)	Earn (3987)
SVM	13967	66453	54065	83141	108108
SVM (w/costing)	4035 ± 30	8851 ± 52	9058 ± 159	40009 ± 252	96007 ± 331
SVM (w/mc)	7147 ± 50	23596 ± 64	32011 ± 321	194165 ± 451	228612 ± 453
LR	35809	32759	60031	349080	710631
LR (w/costing)	**484 ± 11**	**1333 ± 44**	29614 ± 110	**606 ± 145**	**2521 ± 191**
LR (w/mc)	34980 ± 35	32759 ± 79	60374 ± 154	386859 ± 1185	788819 ± 263
LDA	2638	66453	124733	591300	908690
LDA (w/costing)	1461 ± 28	6092 ± 89	**7301 ± 152**	39354 ± 205	41478 ± 159
LDA (w/mc)	40079 ± 57	45778 ± 71	8955 ± 157	51789 ± 285	54084 ± 244
Base line cost	42625	79084	139113	591357	1090498

Table 21-2 replicates the trend that the best classifier is a logistic regression with costing, in terms of the total cost for misclassification, which is the sum of the cost for false positive and false negative. The number in parenthesis next to the topic name in table 2 is the total number of text documents belonging to that category. For example, there are 114 text documents belonging to the "livestock" category. The results reported for the costing and the metacost are the average of 5 different runs. The bottom line entitled "base line cost" is the total cost for a category if a classifier classifies all the testing examples incorrectly (e.g., the misclassification cost of a classifier for "livestock" will be 42,625 if the classifier classifies all incorrectly). For the "earn" category, LR with the costing caused only 0.002 out of the total cost (2,521 out of 1,090,498). For the remaining categories, the best-performer paid only less than 0.05 out of the total cost.

From the comparison with error-minimizing classifiers, the costing proved its effectiveness in that it requires relatively small amount of training data for a better performance. For the "corn" category, LR with the costing, which only used 10% of the training data (i.e., 986 out of 9,854 documents) showed the best result in terms of the smallest loss (1,333 out of 79,084), zero false positive, and lower false negative rate (0.039). The LR classifier was trained by a sample set by three rejection sampling trials that is comprised of 458 positive and 528 negative examples. The expected cost is 1.1% of the total cost caused by incorrect confidential access control (i.e., misclassification). From the false positive perspective (zero false alarm), there is no leaking of confidential information. 39% false negative rate means that there would be 39 out of 1,000 valid requests to the confidential information that are mistakenly rejected. This inconveniences employees because they have to access particular information for their projects, but the system does not authorize their access requests. This trend holds good for the remaining four categories.

6.   CONCLUSION

In confidential access control based on the need-to-know principle, a false positive occurs when the system accepts a request that should not have been accepted whereas a false negative occurs when the system rejects a request that should have been accepted. For both errors, the system pays the cost for misclassification. From the security perspective, it is more tolerable to have an authorization process with a high false negative rather than one with a high false positive rate because the latter is a serious security problem since confidential information, which should not be revealed, can be accessed.

In this chapter we present approaches to cost-sensitive classification for confidential access. We model the binary decision whether to reject or accept a document access request in a cost-sensitive learning framework, where the cost caused by incorrect classification for the request is different according to the relative importance of two types of error: false positive and false negative. In addition, we invented a cost assignment method that ensures that the cost of a false positive decision (i.e., accept an invalid request) is higher than that of the false negative one (i.e., reject a valid request). Finally we tested three different error-minimizing classification methods and their combination with two cost-sensitive wrappers.

From the comparison of the cost-sensitive learning methods with the error-minimizing classification methods, we found that the costing with a logistic regression showed the best performance. In particular, it requires far less training data for much better results, in terms of the smallest cost paid, the lowest false positive rate, and the relatively low false negative rate. The smallest cost implies that it is expected to pay 1.1% of the total cost caused by incorrect confidential access control. The nearly zero false positive rate means that there is no leaking of confidential information.

The classification algorithms were implemented in a guard agent that performed the automated classification and denied or permitted user access based on the classification of the request. Besides demonstrating cost-sensitivity and good computational performance compared to other methods, our approach has three important benefits for the domain of insider threat. First, the required training set is small. The benefit of smaller training data is two-fold; (a) obviously it takes less time to train the classifier; (b) it enables a human administrator to conveniently identify arbitrary subsets of confidential information, in order to train the initial classifier. In other words, through our proposed methods, it becomes easier for a human administrator to define, assign, and enforce an effective access control for a particular subset of confidential information. Second, our method allows an organization to flexibly set different costs for misclassification to reflect the organization's tolerance for suspicious confidential access requests. Third, the implementation is flexible, allowing either monitoring of suspicious requests or outright denying those requests and notifying the user's supervisors or security administrators. In addition, the system saves every suspicious request for audit trailing and alarms.

Although our approach demonstrates promising results, we believe that such an automated content-based approach should be used as a complementary tool for a human administrator, not as a primary tool for confidential access authorization.

Since no actual classified data are available, our experiments utilized a well-known dataset in a simulated confidential authorization scenario that primarily generates a dichotomous decision space. In particular, text documents belonging to one of the selected categories are regarded as positive to need-to-know confidential and the remaining documents are regarded as negative. Since an unclear (or overlapped) boundary between two classes is one of the reasons that allows most of security leaks (or classification errors), our experiments focused on discovering the classification method that is capable of identifying the boundary (i.e., minimizing error metrics). These unclear boundaries between positive and negative examples are primarily caused by the usage of the same feature space (i.e., word set). In particular, documents under "livestock" and "corn" categories use a number of the same word features (e.g., tone, import, export, price, trader, report, and so on) to describe their contents because they are notionally belonging to the same category called "commodity" (same as "acq", "earn", and "interest" are "economic") [Ankolekar et al., 2003].

Therefore the actual contents of documents used in experiments may or may not be the same as the true nature of confidential documents. Nevertheless, we believe our study is valuable to practitioners for two reasons. First, our approach is general and does not depend on any particular characteristics or structure of the data set. Second, we believe that our approach would work well for actual classified documents in practice because our methods were able to show promising results, for example good performance for the case of unclear boundary between positive and negative examples (e.g., "livestock" as positive and "corn" as negative class). However, it would be good for the organization that may want to apply the method in practice to conduct additional validation experiments with the actual data they would like to use. Such validations are necessary and are a general practice whenever research prototype methods are applied to real world situations.

7. ACKNOWLEDGMENTS

This work was supported in part by a grant form ARDA through a subcontract of Computer Technology Associates, BAA-03-02-CMU, and in part by AFOSR contract number F49640-01-1-0542 to Carnegie Mellon University.

REFERENCES

Aleman-Meza, B., Burns, P., Eavenson, M., Palaniswami, D., and Sheth, A., An ontological approach to the document access problem of insiders threat, In *Proceedings of IEEE International Conference on Intelligence and Security Informatics* (ISI-05), pp. 486-491, 2005.

Ankolekar, A., Seo, Y.-W., and Sycara, K. Investigating semantic knowledge for text learning, In *Proceedings of SIGIR-2003 Workshop on Semantic Web*, pp. 9-17, 2003.

Domingos, P., Metacost: A general method for making classifiers cost-sensitive, In *Proceedings of International Conference on Knowledge Discovery and Data Mininig*, pp. 154-164, 1999.

Drummond, C. and Holte, R.C., Exploiting the cost (in)sensitivity of decision tree splitting criteria, In *Proceedings of International Conference on Machine Learning* (ICML-00), pp.

239-246, 2000.

Duda, R.O., Hart, P.E., Stork, D.G., *Pattern Classification*, Wiley-Interscience, 2001.

Elkan, C., The foundations of cost-sensitive learning, In *Proceedings of International Joint Conference on Artificial Intelligence* (IJCAI-01), pp. 973-978, 2001

Fan, W., Stolfo, S.J., Zhang, J., and Chan, P.K., Adacost: Misclassification cost-sensitive boosting, In *Proceedings of International Conference on Machine Learning* (ICML-99), pp. 97-105, 1999.

Fawcett, T., ROC graphs: Notes and practical considerations for researchers, HP Lab Palo Alto, *HPL-2003-4*, 2003.

Giuri, L. and Iglio, P., Role templates for content-based access control, In *Proceedings of ACM Workshop on Role Based Access Control*, pp. 153-159, 1997.

Lee, W., Miller, M., Stolfo, S., Jallad, K., Park, C., Zadok, E., and Prabhakar, V., Toward cost-sensitive modeling for intrusion detection, *ACM Journal of Computer Society*, Vol. 10, No. 1-2, pp. 5-22, 2002.

Joachims, T., Text categorization with support vector machines: Learning with many relevant features, In *Proceedings of European Conference on Machine Learning* (ECML-98), 1998.

Ng, A.Y. and Jordan, M.I., On discriminative vs. generative classifiers: A comparison of logistic regression and naïve Bayes, In *Proceedings of Neural Information Processing Systems* (NIPS-01), pp. 841-848, 2001.

Seo, Y.-W., Giampapa, J., and Sycara, K., A multi-agent system for enforcing need-to-know security policies, In *Proceedings of International Conference on Autonomous Agents and Multi-Agent Systems* (AAMAS) *Workshop on Agent Oriented Information Systems* (AOIS-04), pp. 163-179, 2004.

Seo, Y.-W. and Sycara, K., Cost-sensitive access control for illegitimate confidential access by insiders, In *Proceedings of IEEE Intelligence and Security Informatics* (ISI-06), pp. 117-128, 2006.

Schutze, H., Hull, D.A., Pedersen, J.O., A comparison of classifiers and document representations for the routing problem, In *Proceedings of International ACM Conference on Research and Development in Information Retrieval* (SIGIR-95), pp 229-237, 1995.

Symonenko, S., Liddy, E.D., and Yilmazel, O., Semantic analysis for monitoring insider threats, In *Proceedings of Symposium on Intelligence and Security Informatics*, 2004.

Torkkola, T., Linear discriminant analysis in document classification, In *IEEE Workshop on TextMining*, 2001.

Weippl, E. and Ibrahim, K., Content-based management of document access control, In *Proceedings of the 14th International Conference on Applications of Prolog*, 2001.

Zadrozny, B., Langford, J., and Abe, N., A simple method for cost-sensitive learning, Technical report, *IBM Tech Report*, 2002.

SUGGESTED READINGS

- For more information about (error-minimizing) classification and technical details on pattern classification, see Duda et al., 2001, and Mitchell, 1997: Mitchell, T.T., *Machine Learning*, McGraw-Hill, 1997.
- For more information about text classification, see Joachims, 1998, Ng and Jordan, 2001, Schutze et al., 1995, Torkkola, 2001, and Chapter 16, "Text Categorization," in Manning and Schutze, 1999: Manning, C.D.

and Schutze, H., *Foundations of Statistical Natural Language Processing*, MIT Press, 1999.
- For more information about cost-sensitive classification, see Domingos, 1999, Elkan, 2001, Fan et al., 1999, and Zadrozny et al., 2002.

ONLINE RESOURCES

- A companion site of the book "Foundations of Statistical Natural Language Processing", http://www-nlp.stanford.edu/fsnlp/
- Dawn Cappelli, Andrew Moore, and Timothy Shimeall, Common sense guide to prevention and detection of insider threats, US-CERT (a government organization), http://www.us-cert.gov/reading_room/prevent_detect_insiderthreat0504.pdf
- Insider Threat Study by National Threat Assessment Center, http://www.secretservice.gov/ntac_its.shtml
- Eric D. Shaw, Keven G. Ruby, and Jerrold M. Post, The insider threat to information systems, http://www.dss.mil/training/csg/security/Treason/Infosys.htm
- Defending Against Insider-Threat Conference, http://www.homelanddefensejournal.com/conf_insider.htm

DISCUSSION QUESTIONS

1. This chapter presents a way to address illegitimate information access by malicious insiders. Can you think of additional ways to address this problem?
2. What are some additional aspects of insider threat?
3. Can you think of ways of addressing those additional insider threat aspects identified in 2 above?
4. Can you think of additional domains (besides security and medicine) and additional applications where cost sensitive classification is important?

22

USING WEB MINING AND SOCIAL NETWORK ANALYSIS TO STUDY THE EMERGENCE OF CYBER COMMUNITIES IN BLOGS

Michael Chau[1] and Jennifer Xu[2]

[1]*School of Business, The University of Hong Kong, Pokfulam, Hong Kong (mchau@business.hku.hk);* [2]*Department of Computer Information Systems, Bentley College, Waltham, Massachusetts, U.S.A. (jxu@bentley.edu)*

CHAPTER OVERVIEW

Blogs have become increasingly popular in recent years. Bloggers can express their opinions and emotions more freely and easily than before.Many communities have emerged in the blogosphere, including racist and hate groups that are trying to share their ideology, express their views, or recruit new group members. It is imperative to analyze these cyber communities in order to monitor for activities that are potentially harmful to society. Web mining and social network analysis techniques, which have been widely used to analyze the content and structure of Web sites of hate groups on the Internet, have not been applied to the study of hate groups in blogs. In this research, we present a framework, which consists of components of blog spider, information extraction, network analysis, and visualization, to address this problem (Chau & Xu, 2007). We applied this framework to identify and analyze a selected set of 28 anti-Blacks hate groups on Xanga, one of the most popular blog hosting sites. Our analysis results revealed some interesting demographical and topological characteristics in these groups, and identified at least two large communities on top of the smaller ones. We suggest that our framework can be generalized and applied to blog analysis in other domains.

1.   INTRODUCTION

Blog is a Web-based publication that allows users to add content easily and periodically, normally in reverse chronological order. Blogs have become increasingly popular in recent years, partly due to the availability of easy-to-use blogging tools and free blog hosting sites, such as www.blogger.com, www.xanga.com, and www.livejournal.com. These tools also support the linking to other pages or the posting of comments to blogs (Blood, 2004). Instead of having a few people in control of the discussion (like in traditional Internet forums), blogs basically allow anyone to express their ideas and thoughts freely in one's own blog space.

There are many communities in the blogosphere. These could be support communities such as those for technical support or educational support (Nardi *et al.*, 2004), or groups of bloggers who already knew each other in other context, such as a group for a high school or a company. Moreover, there are also communities formed by people who share common interests or opinions. Many free blog hosting sites have the function to allow bloggers to link to each other to form explicit groups. Similar to other Web-based media such as Web sites, discussion forums, or chat rooms where hate groups are present (Anti-Defamation League, 2001; CNN, 1999; Glaser *et al.*, 2002), there are also hate groups in blogs that are formed by bloggers who are racists or extremists. The consequences of the formation of such groups on the Internet cannot be underestimated. Hate groups or White supremacist groups like the Ku Klux Klan have started to use the Internet to spread their beliefs, recruit new members, or even advocate hate crimes with considerable success (Anti-Defamation League, 2001). The Web has allowed these groups to reach much further into society than ever before. Young people, the major group of bloggers, are more likely to be affected and even "brainwashed" by ideas propagated through the Web as a global medium. Hatred and extremism ideas could easily be embedded into their minds to make them become members of these hate groups or even conduct hate crimes.

To investigate the cyber activities of hate groups in blogs, it is important to devise an efficient and effective way to identify these groups, extract the information of their members, and explore their relationships. In recent years, advanced techniques such as text mining, Web mining, and social network analysis have been widely used for cyber crime and terrorism analysis (e.g., Chen *et al.* 2004). For example, network analysis techniques have been used to study the relationships between extremist Web sites on the Internet (Zhou *et al.*, 2005). However, the application of these techniques to blog analysis on the Web is a new area and no prior research has been published. We suggest that these techniques could be used to help identify and analyze hate groups on the Web, particularly in blogs. In this chapter, we present a semi-automated framework that combines blog spidering and social network analysis techniques to facilitate such analysis (Chau & Xu, 2007).

The rest of the chapter is organized as follows. In Section 2 we review the research background of hate group analysis and related research in text mining, Web mining, and social network analysis. We pose our research questions in Section 3, and a semi-automated framework for hate group analysis in blogs is presented in Section 4. In Section 5 we present a case study that we have performed on a popular blog hosting site based on the proposed framework and discuss our analysis findings. Lastly, we conclude our research in Section 6 and suggest some directions for future work.

2. RESEARCH BACKGROUND

In this section we will review the background of hate groups on the Web and in blogs. We also review relevant techniques in Web mining and social network analysis that have been applied in analyzing Web contents.

2.1 Cyberhate and Blogs

Hate crimes have been one of the long-standing problems in the United States because of various historical, cultural, and political reasons. It is reported that 60% of hate criminals are youths (Levin & McDevitt, 1993), who are, perhaps unfortunately, also one of the largest groups of Internet users. Hate groups have been increasingly using the Internet to express their ideas, spread their beliefs, and recruit new members (Lee & Leets, 2002). Glaser *et al*. (2002) suggest that racists often express their views more freely on the Internet. The Hate Directory (Franklin, 2005) compiles a list of hundreds of Web sites, files archives, newsgroups, and other Internet resources related to hate and racism. Several studies have investigated Web sites that are related to racism or White supremacy (e.g., Lee & Leets (2002); Gerstenfeld *et al*. (2003)). Burris *et al*. (2000) systematically analyzed the networks of Web sites maintained by white supremacist groups and found that this network had a decentralized structure. Zhou *et al*. (2005) used software to automate the analysis of the content of hate group Web sites and the linkage among them. They found that one of the major objectives of these Web sites was to share ideology. Online communities such as White Supremacists and Neo-Nazis were identified among these sites.

In recent years, hate groups have emerged in blogs, where highly-narrative messages are popular. Blogs, also known as weblogs, have become increasingly popular since 2000. Weblog was first introduced in 1997 and in those early days, blogs were used mainly to designate pages where links to other useful resources were periodically "logged" and posted. At that time blogs were mostly maintained by hand (Blood, 2004). After easy-to-use blogging software became widely available in 1999 and early 2000, the nature of blogs has changed and many blogs are more like personal Web sites that contain various types of content (not limited to links) posted in reverse-chronological order. Bloggers often make a record of their lives and express their opinions, feelings, and emotions through writing blogs (Nardi *et al.*, 2004). Many bloggers consider blogging as an outlet for their thoughts and emotions. Besides personal blogs, there are also blogs created by companies. For example, ice.com, an online jewelry seller, has launched three blogs and reported that thousands of people linked to their Web site from these blogs (Hof, 2005).

One of the most important features in blogs is the ability for any reader to write a comment on a blog entry. On most blog hosting sites, it is very easy to write a comment, in a way quite similar to replying to a previous message in traditional discussion forums. The ability to comment on blogs has facilitated the interaction between bloggers and their readers. On some controversial issues, like those related to racism, it is not uncommon to find a blog entry with thousands of comments where people dispute back and forth on the matter.

Any individual can create an account on a blog hosting site and start writing their blogs in minutes. According to Alexa (2005), Blogger (www.blogger.com) and Xanga (www.xanga.com) are the two most popular blog hosts. Both blog hosts are free to use and have their own characteristics. For example, Xanga supports subscriptions and groups (as blogrings) while Blogger has a nice search capability supported by Google. A screenshot of the first page of Xanga is shown in Figure 22-1. Users can log in their accounts from this page and edit their blogs. Alternatively, users can create new accounts or browse the blogs of other users.

Cyber communities have also been formed in blogs. Communities in blogs can be categorized as explicit communities or implicit communities, like other cyber communities on the Web (Kumar *et al.*, 1999). Explicit communities in blogs are the groups, or blogrings, that bloggers have explicitly formed and joined. Most blog hosting sites allow bloggers to form a new group or join any existing groups. On the other hand, implicit communities are not explicitly defined as groups or blogrings by bloggers. Instead, these communities are identified by the interactions among bloggers, such as subscription, linking, or commenting. For example, a blogger may subscribe to another blog, meaning that the subscriber can get updates when the subscribed blog has been updated. A blogger can also post a link and add a comment to another blog, which are perhaps the most traditional activities among bloggers. These interactions signify some kind of connection between two bloggers. Similar to the analysis of hyperlinks among Web pages to identify communities (Chau *et al.*, 2005; Chau *et al.*, 2007), the analysis of these types of connections between bloggers could also identify cyber communities and their relationships.

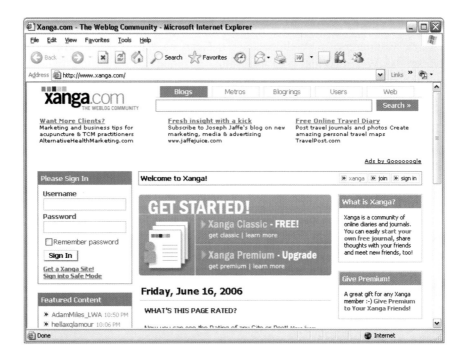

Figure 22-1. The hompage of Xanga

2.2 Web Mining and Social Network Analysis

In recent years, Web mining techniques have been widely adopted from data mining, text mining, and information retrieval research and applied to various domains. Web mining research can be classified into three categories: Web content mining, Web structure mining, and Web usage mining (Kosala & Blockeel, 2000; Chen & Chau, 2004). Web content mining refers to the discovery of useful information from Web contents, including text, images, audio, video, etc. Web content mining research includes resource discovery from the Web, document categorization and clustering, and information extraction from Web pages. Wcb structure mining studies the model underlying the link structures of the Web. It usually involves the analysis of in-links and out-links information of Web pages, and has been used for search engine result ranking and other Web applications. Google's PageRank (Brin & Page, 1998) and HITS (Kleinberg, 1998) are the two most widely used algorithms. Web usage mining focuses on using data mining techniques to analyze search logs or other activity logs to find interesting patterns. One of the main applications of Web usage mining is its use to learn user profiles.

In Web mining research, Web spiders have been widely used to traverse the Web and collect Web pages for further analysis. Spiders, also known as crawlers, wanderers, or Webbots, are defined as "software programs that traverse the World Wide Web information space by following hypertext links and retrieving Web documents by standard HTTP protocol" (Cheong, 1996). Since the early days of the Web, spiders have been widely used to build the underlying databases of search engines, to perform personal search, to archive particular Web sites or even the whole Web, or to collect Web statistics. Chau and Chen (2003) provide a review of Web spider research.

Various methods have been proposed in Web structure mining research to identify Web communities (Gibson *et al.*, 1998; Kumar *et al.*, 1999). Many of these methods are rooted in the HITS algorithm (Kleinberg, 1998). Kumar *et al.* (1999) propose a trawling approach to find a set of core pages containing both authoritative and hub pages for a specific topic. The core is a directed bipartite subgraph whose node set is divided into two sets with all hub pages in one set and authoritative pages in the other. The core and the other related pages constitute a Web community (Gibson *et al.*, 1998). Treating the Web as a large graph, the problem of community identification can also be formulated as a minimum-cut problem, which finds clusters of roughly equal sizes while minimizing the number of links between clusters (Flake *et al.*, 2000; Flake *et al.*, 2002). Realizing that the minimum-cut problem is equivalent to the maximum-flow problem, Flake *et al.* (2000) formulate the Web community identification problem as an *s-t* maximum flow problem, which can be solved using efficient polynomial time methods. Hierarchical clustering methods have also been proposed to partition networks, especially unweighted networks such as the Web in which hyperlinks do not have associated weights (e.g., Radicchi *et al.*, 2004).

On the other hand, a recent movement in statistical analysis of network topology (Albert & Barabási, 2002) has brought new insights and research methodology to the study of network structure. Networks, regardless of their contents, are classified into three categories: *random network* (Bollobás, 1985), *small-world network* (Watts & Strogatz, 1998), and *scale-free network* (Barabási & Alert, 1999). In a random network the probability that two randomly selected nodes are connected is a constant p. As a result, each node has roughly the same number of links. In addition, communities are not likely to exist in random networks. Small-world networks, in contrast, have a significantly high tendency to form groups and communities. Most empirical networks including social networks, biological networks, and the Web have been found to be nonrandom networks. In addition, many of these networks are also scale-free networks (Barabási & Alert, 1999), in which a large percentage of nodes have just a few links, while a small percentage of the nodes have a large number of links. Thus, nodes in scale-free networks are not homogenous in terms of their links, and some nodes become hubs or leaders that play important roles in the functioning of the network. The Web has been found to have both small-world and scale-free properties (Albert & Barabási, 2002). Researchers have been employing social network analysis methods to analyze the structure of the Web (Kumar *et al.*, 2002).

Social network analysis (SNA) is a sociological methodology for analyzing patterns of relationships and interactions between social actors in order to discover the underlying social structure (Wasserman & Faust, 1994). Not only the attributes of social actors, such as their age, gender, socioeconomic status, and education, but also the properties of relationships between social actors, such as the nature, intensity, and frequency of the relationships, are believed to have important implications to the social structure. SNA methods have been employed to study organizational behavior, inter-organizational relations, citation patterns, computer mediated communication, and many other areas.

Recently, SNA has also been used in the intelligence and security domain to analyze criminal and terrorist networks (Krebs, 2001; Xu & Chen, 2004; 2005). When used to mine a network, SNA can help reveal the structural patterns such as the central nodes which act as hubs, leaders, or gatekeepers, the densely-knit communities or groups in which nodes have frequent interactions with each other, and the patterns of interactions between the communities and groups. These patterns often have important implications. For example, the central nodes often play a key role by issuing commands or bridging different communities. The removal of central nodes can disrupt a network more effectively than peripheral nodes (Albert *et al.*, 2000).

3. RESEARCH QUESTIONS

We believe that it is an important and timely issue to identify the hate groups in blogs and analyze their relationships. Web mining and network analysis techniques have been used to analyze Web content such as Web pages and hyperlinks; however, we have not been able to identify any prior research on blogs in this aspect in the literature. Based on our review, we pose the following research questions: (1) Can we use a semi-automatic framework to identify hate groups in blogs? (2) What is the pattern of interaction between bloggers in hate groups? (3) Can social network analysis techniques be used to analyze the groups and their relationships in blogs?

4.   A FRAMEWORK FOR BLOG COLLECTION AND ANALYSIS

In this section, we present a semi-automated framework for identifying groups and analyzing their relationships in blogs (Chau & Xu, 2007). The framework is diagrammed in Figure 22-2. Our framework consists of four main modules, namely Blog Spider, Information Extraction, Network Analysis, and Visualization. The Blog Spider module downloads blog pages from the Web. These pages are then processed by the Information Extraction module. Data about these bloggers and their relationships are extracted and passed to the Network Analysis module for further analysis. Finally the Visualization module presents the analysis results to users in a graphical display. In the following, we describe each module in more detail.

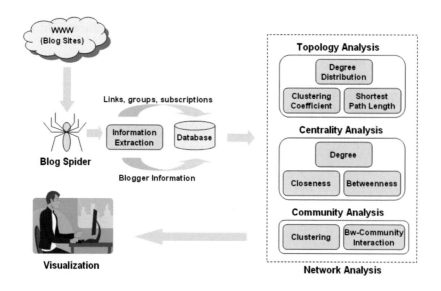

Figure 22-2. A semi-automated framework for blog link analysis

4.1   Blog Spider

A blog spider program is first needed to download the relevant pages from the blogs of interest. Similar to general Web fetching, the spider can connect to blog hosting sites using standard HTTP protocol. After a blogring description page or a blog page is fetched, URLs are extracted and stored into a queue. However, instead of following all extracted links, the blog spider should only follow links that are of interest, e.g., links to a group's members, other bloggers, comment links, and so on. Links to other external resources are often less useful in blog analysis. In addition, the spider can use RSS and get notification when the blog is updated. However, this is only necessary when monitoring or incremental analysis is desired.

4.2 Information Extraction

After the blog pages have been downloaded, information extraction can be performed. This includes information related to the blog or the blogger, such as user profiles and dates of creation. This can also include linkage information between two bloggers, such as linkage, commenting, or subscription. Because different blogs may have different formats, it is not a trivial task to extract the user profiles, links, comments, and other useful information from blogs. Even blogs hosted on the same hosting site could have considerably different formats as they can be easily customized by each blogger. Pattern matching or entity extraction techniques can be applied. The information extracted can be stored into database for further analysis. Links extracted can be passed back to the blog spider for further fetching.

4.3 Network Analysis

Network analysis is a major component in our framework. In this module we propose three types of analysis: *topological analysis*, *centrality analysis*, and *community analysis*.

The goal of topological analysis is to ensure that the network extracted based on links between bloggers is not random and it is meaningful to perform the centrality and community analysis. We use three statistics that are widely used in topological studies to categorize the extracted network (Albert & Barabási, 2002): *average shortest path length*, *clustering coefficient*, and *degree distribution*. Average path length is the mean of the all-pair shortest path lengths in a network. It measures the efficiency of communication between nodes in a network. Clustering coefficient indicates how likely nodes in a network form groups or communities. The degree distribution, $p(k)$, is the probability that a node has exactly k links. Another measure related to average path length is the network's global efficiency, which is defined as the average of the inverses of shortest path lengths over all pairs of nodes in a network (Crucitti *et al.*, 2003).

Centrality analysis follows the topological analysis if the extracted network is shown to be a nonrandom network in which node degrees may vary greatly. The goal of centrality analysis is to identify the key nodes in a network. Three traditional centrality measures can be used: *degree, betweenness,* and *closeness* (Freeman, 1979). Degree measures how active a particular node is. It is defined as the number of direct links a node has. "Popular" nodes with high degree scores are the leaders, experts, or hubs in a network. In the intelligence and security context, the removal of these key nodes in a criminal or terrorist network is often an effective disruptive strategy (Sparrow, 1991). Betweenness measures the extent to which a particular node lies between other nodes in a network. The betweenness of a node is defined as the number of geodesics (shortest paths between two nodes) passing through it. Nodes with high betweenness scores often serve as gatekeepers and brokers between different communities. They are important communication channels through which information, goods, and other resources are transmitted or exchanged (Wasserman & Faust, 1994). Closeness is the sum of the length of geodesics between a particular node and all the other nodes in a network. A node with low closeness may find it very difficult to communicate with other nodes in the network. Such nodes are thus more "peripheral" and can become outliers in the network (Sparrow, 1991; Xu & Chen, 2005).

Community analysis is to identify social groups in a network. In SNA a subset of nodes is considered a community or a social group if nodes in this group have stronger or denser links with nodes within the group than with nodes outside of the group (Wasserman & Faust, 1994). An unweighted network can be partitioned into groups by maximizing within-group link density while minimizing between-group link density. In this case, groups are densely-knit subsets of the network. Note that community and groups here do not refer to the explicit groups (blogrings). They refer to a subset of nodes which form implicit clusters through various relationships, even if these nodes do not belong to the same explicit group.

After a network is partitioned into groups, the between-group relationships become composites of links between individual nodes. In SNA, a method called *blockmodeling* is often used to reveal the patterns of interactions between groups (White *et al.*, 1976). Given groups in a network, blockmodel analysis determines the presence or absence of a relationship between two groups based on the link density (Wasserman & Faust, 1994). When the density of the links between the two groups is greater than a predefined threshold value, a between-group relationship is present, indicating that the two groups interact with each other constantly and thus have a strong relationship. By this means, blockmodeling summarizes individual relational details into relationships between groups so that the overall structure of the network becomes more prominent.

4.4   Visualization

The extracted network and analysis results can be visualized using various types of network layout methods. Two examples are *multidimensional scaling* (MDS) and *graph layout* approaches. MDS is the most commonly used method for social network visualization (Freeman, 2000). It is a statistical method that projects higher-dimensional data onto a lower-dimensional display. It seeks to provide a visual representation of proximities (dissimilarities) among nodes so that nodes that are more similar to each other are closer on the display and nodes that are less similar to each other are further apart (Kruskal & Wish, 1978). Various graph layout algorithms, such as the force-directed method, have been developed particularly for drawing aesthetically pleasing network presentations (Fruchterman & Reingold, 1991).

5.   A CASE STUDY ON XANGA

5.1   Focus and Methods

We applied our framework to perform a case study on hate groups in blogs (Chau & Xu, 2007). We chose to study the hate groups against Blacks because of two reasons. First, the nature of hate groups and hate crimes is often dependent on the target "hated" group. By focusing on a type of hate groups it is possible to identify relationships that are more prominent. Second, among different hate crimes, anti-Black hate crimes have been one of the most widely studied. This allows us to compare our results with previous research in the literature.

We limited our study to blogs on Xanga (www.xanga.com). We chose Xanga over Blogger because Xanga has more prominent features to support subscriptions and groups (as blogrings). These features are useful for the identification of hate groups in the blogs and the relationships between bloggers. Also, it has been suggested that apparently more hate blogs exist in Xanga than in Blogger (Franklin, 2005).

After choosing our focus, we identified a set of hate groups in Xanga. We used the search feature in Xanga to semi-automate the task. First, a set of terms related to Black-hatred, such as "KKK", "niggers", "white pride", were identified. We used these terms to search in Xanga for groups (blogrings) that have any of these words in their group name or description. We then checked these groups and filtered out those not related to anti-Black. Groups with only one single member, which were often formed by one blogger but no one else had joined afterwards, were also removed from our list. This resulted in a set of 40 groups. While most of these groups showed some beliefs of racism or White supremacies, we tried to further narrow these down to groups that demonstrated explicit hatred, so as to make sure that our analysis focused on "hate groups".   So, we then manually checked these groups and only included those that explicitly mentioned hatred (e.g., "I hate black people", "hate the black race") or used offensive languages (e.g., "nigger beaters", four-letter words) towards the Blacks in their group name or description. Finally we had a list of 28 groups. The list of the 28 groups is provided in the Appendix.

Spiders were used to automatically download the description page and member list of each of these groups. A total of 820 bloggers were identified from these 28 groups. The spiders then further downloaded the blogs of each of these bloggers. The extraction program was then executed to extract the information from each blogger, including user id, real name, date of creation, date of birth, city, state, and country. One should note that these data were self-reported; they could be fraud or even missing.

The extraction program also analyzed the relationship between these bloggers. In this study, two types of relationships were extracted: (1) Group co-membership: two bloggers belong to the same group (blogring). This is an undirected relationship with an integer weight (based on the number of groups shared by the two bloggers). As using all co-membership links would result in a very large network that corresponds to the original blogring information, we only included links whose weights are at least 2. (2) Subscription: blogger A subscribes to blogger B. This is a directed, binary relationship.

5.2   Analysis

After collecting the blogs and extracting information from them, we performed demographical and network analysis on the data set in order to reveal the characteristics of these groups and study whether any patterns exist. Visualization was also applied to present the results. We discuss the details of our analysis in the following subsections.

5.2.1   Demographical Analysis

We provide a brief summary of the demographical information of the bloggers of interest and the growth patterns of the blog space of hate groups. As in many other Internet-based media such as forums and chat rooms, the real identities of bloggers are unknown. Thus, the self-reported demographical information of bloggers is also subject to the problems of anonymity. However, since blogs are often personal online diaries many bloggers still choose to release partial information about their demographics such as gender and country. Six hundred and fifty-nine bloggers out of the 820 in our data set have explicitly indicated their gender. Sixty three percent of them are male and 37% female. These bloggers are from various countries, with 81.9% from the United States and the remaining 18.1% from other 45 countries. It can be seen that hate groups are dominated by male bloggers from the United States. However, one should note that this finding is based on the problematic source of demographic information.

We also analyzed the growth of the hate group blogs over the years since their inception at Xanga in 2002. Unlike demographical information, the exact time when a blogger registered on Xanga is recorded by the server and thus is generally not subject to fraud. We found that the number of "hate" bloggers increased steadily between 2003 and the third quarter of 2004. The number has fluctuated since the forth quarter of 2004. This may be because some bloggers who have recently registered have not joined those popular blogrings or have not formed large communities. As a result, some of them were not included in the data set after we filtered the raw data. The finding suggests that as blogs become popular in general, hate groups have also been gaining popularity in blog space over years. Such a trend should not be underestimated because the ideas, beliefs, and opinions advocated by racists and extremists may pose potential threats to the society.

5.2.2 Topological Analysis

When analyzing the topology of the network, we ignored the weight of co-membership relationship and the direction of subscription. We connected two nodes if they belonged to at least two common groups or one subscribed to the other. So, there could only be at most one link between a pair of nodes. The resulting network was an unweighted, undirected network consisting of 1193 links. This network was not a connected graph in that it consisted of several disjoint components, between which no link existed. The largest connected component, often called a giant component in graph theory (Bollobás, 1985), contained 273 nodes connected by 1115 links. This giant component was a rather dense graph with an average node degree of 8.2.

Table 22-1. The topological properties of the giant component (number in the parentheses are standard deviations)

	Average Shortest Path Length	Global Efficiency	Clustering Coefficient
Giant Component	3.62	0.33	0.37
Random Counterpart	2.89 (0.03)	0.37 (0.00)	0.03 (0.00)

We performed topological analysis for the giant component. Table 22-1 provides the statistics of the average shortest path length, global efficiency, and clustering coefficient. To compare the giant component with its random graph counterpart, we generated 30 random networks consisting of the same number of nodes (273) and links (1115) with the giant component. The resulting statistics are also reported in Table 22-1. It shows that the giant component is less efficient than its random graph counterpart. On average, a node in the giant component must take 0.75 more steps than in the random graph to reach another arbitrary node. Accordingly, the global efficiency of the giant component is also relatively low. However, the giant component has a significantly higher clustering coefficient, which is 31 times more than its random graph counterpart. This implies that the giant component is a small-world, in which densely-knit communities are very likely to exist.

The degree distribution of the giant component also seems to follow a power-law distribution, meaning the network has a scale-free structure (see Figure 22-3). The most distinctive feature of a power-law distribution curve is its long tail for large degrees (k), which is significant different from a bell-shaped Poisson distribution. The long tail indicates that a small number of nodes in the network have a large number of links and they are the key nodes to identify. A pure power-law distribution, $p(k) \sim k^{-\gamma}$, appears as a straight line in logarithmic scale.

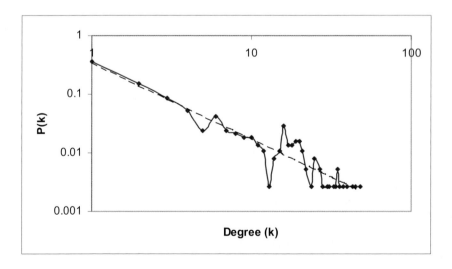

Figure 22-3. The scatter plot of the degree distribution of the giant component in logarithmic scale. The dashed straight line is the fitted power-law degree distribution, $p(k) \sim k^{-\gamma}$, with $\gamma = 1.29$.

5.2.3   SNA and Visualization

We performed centrality and community analysis using a prototype system we developed (Xu & Chen, 2005). The system has a graphical user interface to facilitate the interaction between users and the system (see Figure 22-4). The user interface visualizes the network and presents the results of social network analysis. In the visualization, each node represents a blogger. A straight line connecting two nodes indicates that either the two corresponding are co-members in more than one blogring, or one blogger subscribes to the other.

The layout of the network is determined using the MDS method. In order to position nodes which are likely to belong to the same community close to each other on the display, we assigned each link an "edge clustering coefficient", which measures the likelihood of two incident nodes of the link to form a cluster (Radicchi *et al.*, 2004).

The community analysis can be performed by adjusting the "level of abstraction" slider at the bottom of the panel. At the lowest level of abstraction, each individual node and link are presented. As the abstraction level increases, the system employs hierarchical clustering method to gradually merge nodes, which are connected by links of high edge clustering coefficients. When the highest abstraction level is reached, the whole giant component becomes a big community.

At any level of abstraction, a circle represents a community. The size of the circle is proportional to the number of bloggers in the community. Straight lines connecting circles represent between-group relationships, which are extracted using blockmodel analysis. The thickness of a line is proportional to the density of the links between the two corresponding communities.

Figure 22-4 presents the giant component at its lowest abstraction level. The bloggers who have the highest degree and betweenness scores are highlighted and labeled with their usernames. These bloggers are those who may participate in multiple blogrings or have many subscription relationships with other bloggers. It is interesting to see from this figure that in addition to joining explicit groups (blogrings), bloggers have also formed implicit communities through co-membership and subscription. Three circles of nodes are apparently communities in which bloggers share many common memberships.

Because the communities can be analyzed at different levels, a big community may consist of smaller communities. Our analysis found two communities at the 70% abstraction level (not shown in Figure 22-4). We drew two dashed circles in Figure 22-4 to roughly represent the two communities. It shows that the bigger community consists of two smaller circles of nodes, which may also be communities. In addition, a blogger who ranks the highest in degree in the community would likely be the leader of the community. Also, bloggers with a high in-degree would be those who can disseminate their ideas and opinions through their blogs easily to many subscribers. These "leader" bloggers are the ones who should be substantially monitored by authorities which hope to regulate the activities of hate groups in blogs.

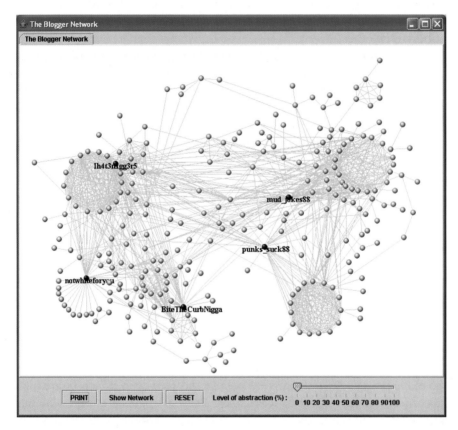

Figure 22-4. The prototype system for SNA and visualization, showing the giant component with both co-membership and subscription links. The highlighted nodes are those who have large degree or betweenness scores.

6.   CONCLUSION AND FUTURE DIRECTIONS

In this chapter, we have discussed the problems of the emergence of hate groups and racism in blogs. We have presented a semi-automated framework for blog analysis, and applied this framework to investigate the characteristic and structural relationships among the hate groups in blogs. We believe that this research is important to the security of society. By disseminating both explicit and implicit hatred messages through blogs, racists can easily target youths with a ubiquitous coverage – basically anyone who has access to the Internet – that was never possible in the past. Youths are often easily influenced by these messages and could eventually become terrorists and pose a threat to our society (Blazak, 2001). Our study has provided a framework that could facilitate the analysis of law enforcement and social workers in studying and monitoring such activities.

While the framework has been studied in the context of hate group analysis, we have tried to keep the framework general such that it is not specific to such analysis. We believe that the framework can also be applied to other content and network analysis research that involves blog mining, which we believe would be an increasingly important field for various applications. These applications include not only other security informatics research but also applications in other domains such as marketing analysis and business intelligence analysis (Chau *et al.*, 2005).

We are extending our study in two major directions. First, the current study only investigated the hate group activities on one single blog site, Xanga. Although Xanga has been reported to have the most number of blogs associated with hate groups (Franklin, 2005), a further study that includes other popular sites such as Blogger would be more comprehensive. Second, only two types of relationships, namely co-membership and subscription, were considered in the present study. It would be interesting to expand our study to include other types of relationships, such as commenting and hyperlinking, in the network analysis. Inclusion of these relationships could reveal other implicit linkages among the bloggers.

7. ACKNOWLEDGEMENTS

This research has been supported in part by a grant from the University of Hong Kong Seed Funding for Basic Research, "Searching and Analyzing Blogs for Competitive Advantages," 10206775 (PI: M. Chau), January 2006 – December 2007. We would like to thank Porsche Lam and Boby Shiu of the University of Hong Kong for their participation and support in this project.

REFERENCES

Albert, R. & Barabási, A.-L. (2002). Statistical Mechanics of Complex Networks. Reviews of Modern Physics 74(1), 47-97.

Albert, R., Jeong, H., Barabási, A.-L. (2000). Error and Attack Tolerance of Complex Networks. Nature 406, 378-382.

Alexa (2005). Top English Language Sites. [Online] Retrieved from http://www.alexa.com/site/ds/top_sites?ts_mode=lang&lang=en on October 7, 2005.

Anti-Defamation League (2001). Poisoning the Web: Hatred Online. [Online] Retrieved from http://www.adl.org/poisoning_web/poisoning_toc.asp on October 7, 2005.

Barabási, A.-L., Albert, R., & Jeong, H. (1999). Mean-Field Theory for Scale-Free Random Networks. Physica A 272, 173-187.

Blazak, R. (2001). White Boys to Terrorist Men: Target Recruitment of Nazi Skinheads. American Behavioral Scientist 44(6), 982-1000.

Blood, R. (2004). How Blogging Software Reshapes the Online Community. Communications of the ACM 47(12), 53-55.

Bollobás, B. (1985). Random Graphs. London, Academic.

Brin, S. & Page, L. (1998). The Anatomy of a Large-Scale Hypertextual Web Search Engine. Proceedings of the 7th WWW Conference, Brisbane, Australia, April 1998.

Burris, V., Smith, E., & Strahm, A. (2000). White Supremacist Networks on the Internet. Sociological Focus 33(2), 215-235.

Chau, M. & Chen, H. (2003). Personalized and Focused Web Spiders, in N. Zhong, J. Liu, & Y. Yao (Eds), Web Intelligence, Springer-Verlag, 197-217.

Chau, M., Shiu, B., Chan, I., & Chen, H. (2005). Automated Identification of Web Communities for Business Intelligence Analysis, in Proceedings of the Fourth Workshop on E-Business (WEB 2005), Las Vegas, USA, December, 2005.

Chau, M., Shiu, B., Chan, I., & Chen, H. (2007). Redips: Backlink Search and Analysis on the Web for Business Intelligence, Journal of the American Society for Information Science and Technology 58(3), 351-365.

Chau, M. & Xu, J. (2007). Mining Communities and Their Relationships in Blogs: A Study of Online Hate Groups, International Journal of Human-Computer Studies 65(1), 57-70.

Chen, H. and Chau, M. (2004). Web Mining: Machine Learning for Web Applications, Annual Review of Information Science and Technology 38, 289-329, 2004.

Chen, H., Chung, W., Xu. J., Wang, G., Qin, Y., & Chau, M. (2004). Crime Data Mining: A General Framework and Some Examples. IEEE Computer 37(4), 50-56.

Cheong, F. C. (1996). Internet Agents: Spiders, Wanderers, Brokers, and Bots. Indianapolis, Indiana, USA: New Riders Publishing.

CNN (1999). Hate Group Web Sites on the Rise, CNN News [Online] Retrieved from http://edition.cnn.com/US/9902/23/hate.group.report/index.html on October 7, 2005.

Crucitti, P., Latora, V., Marchiori, M., & Rapisarda A. (2003). Efficiency of Scale-Free Networks: Error and Attack Tolerance. Physica A 320, 622-642.

Flake, G. W., Lawrence, S., & Giles, C. L. (2000). Efficient Identification of Web Communities. In Proceedings of the 6th International Conference on Knowledge Discovery and Data Mining (ACM SIGKDD 2000), Boston, MA.

Flake, G. W., Lawrence, S., Giles, C. L., & Coetzee, F. M. (2002). Self-Organization and Identification of Web Communities. IEEE Computer 35(3), 66-71.

Franklin, R. A. (2005). The Hate Directory [Online] Retrieved from http://www.bcpl.net/~rfrankli/hatedir.htm on October 7, 2005.

Freeman, L. C. (1979). Centrality in Social Networks: Conceptual Clarification. Social Networks 1, 215-240.

Freeman, L. C. (2000). Visualizing Social Networks. Journal of Social Structure 1(1).

Fruchterman, T. M. J. & Reingold, E. M. (1991). Graph Drawing by Force-Directed Placement. Software-Practice & Experience 21(11), 1129-1164.

Gerstenfeld, P. B., Grant, D. R., & Chiang, C. P. (2003). Hate Online: A Content Analysis of Extremist Internet Sites. Analyses of Social Issues and Public Policy 3, 29-44.

Gibson, D., J. Kleinberg, & Raghavan, P. (1998). Inferring Web Communities from Link Topology. In Proceedings of the 9th ACM Conference on Hypertext and Hypermedia, Pittsburgh, PA.

Girvan, M. & Newman, M. E. J. (2002). Community Structure in Social and Biological Networks. Proceedings of the National Academy of Science of the United States of America 99, 7821-7826.

Glaser, J., Dixit, J., & Green, D. P. (2002). Studying Hate Crime with the Internet: What Makes Racists Advocate Racial Violence? Journal of Social Issues 58(1), 177-193.

Hof, R. (2005). Blogs on Ice: Signs of a Business Model? Business Week Online – The Tech Beat, June 2, 2005. [Online] Retrieved from http://www.businessweek.com/the_thread/techbeat/archives/2005/06/
blogs_on_ice_si.html on October 7, 2005.

Kleinberg, J. (1998). Authoritative Sources in a Hyperlinked Environment, in Proceedings of the 9th ACM-SIAM Symposium on Discrete Algorithms, San Francisco, California, USA, Jan 1998, pp. 668-677.

Kosala, R. & Blockeel, H. (2000). Web Mining Research: A Survey. ACM SIGKDD Explorations 2(1), 1-15.

Krebs, V. E. (2001). Mapping Networks of Terrorist Cells. Connections 24(3), 43-52.

Krupka, G. R. & Hausman, K. (1998). IsoQuest Inc.: Description of the NetOwlTM extractor system as used for MUC-7, in Proceedings of the Seventh Message Understanding Conference, April 1998.

Kruskal, J. B. & Wish, M. (1978). Multidimensional Scaling. Beverly Hills, CA, Sage Publications.

Kumar, R., Raghavan, P., Rajagopalan, S., & Tomkins, A. (1999). Trawling the Web for Emerging Cyber-Communities. Computer Networks 31(11-16), 1481-1493.

Kumar, R., Raghavan, P., Rajagopalan, S., & Tomkins, A. (2002). The Web and Social Networks. IEEE Computer 35(11), 32-36.

Lee, E., & Leets, L. (2002). Persuasive Storytelling by Hate Groups Online: Examining Its Effects on Adolescents. American Behavioral Scientist 45, 927-957.

Levin, J., & McDevitt, J. (1993). Hate crimes: The Rising Tide of Bigotry and Bloodshed. New York: Plenum.

Nardi, B. A., Schiano, D. J., Gumbrecht, M., & Swartz, L. (2004). Why We Blog. Communications of the ACM 47(12), 41-46

Radicchi, F., Castellano, C., Cecconi, F., Loreto, V., & Parisi, D. (2004). Defining and Identifying Communities in Networks. Proceedings of the National Academy of Science of the United States of America, 101, 2658-2663.

Sparrow, M. K. (1991). The Application of Network Analysis to Criminal Intelligence: An Assessment of the Prospects. Social Networks 13, 251-274.

Wasserman, S. & Faust, K. (1994). Social Network Analysis: Methods and Applications. Cambridge, Cambridge University Press.

Watts, D. J. & Strogatz, S. H. (1998). Collective Dynamics of 'Small-World' Networks. Nature 393, 440-442.

White, H. C., Boorman, S. A., & Breiger, R. L. (1976). Social Structure from Multiple Networks: I. Blockmodels of Roles and Positions. American Journal of Sociology 81, 730-780.

Xu, J. J. & Chen, H. (2004). Fighting Organized Crime: Using Shortest-Path Algorithms to Identify Associations in Criminal Networks. Decision Support Systems 38(3), 473-487.

Xu, J. J. & Chen, H. (2005). CrimeNet Explorer: A Framework for Criminal Network Knowledge Discovery. ACM Transactions on Information Systems 23(2), 201-226.

Zhou, Y., Reid, E., Qin, J., Chen, H., & Lai, G. (2005). US Domestic Extremist Groups on the Web: Link and Content Analysis. IEEE Intelligent Systems 20(5), 44-51.

APPENDIX

The list of the 28 groups analyzed in this study:

Group Name	Xanga Group ID*
! ! ! !Hatred 4 SoCiEtY! ! ! !	709048
! White Power !	76863
** WHITE POWER NATION **	1298240
~I Hate negros~	1470409
::White::Power::	261285
`*~NEGRO HATERS~*`	325247
aLL NiGgErS sTiNk	107296
Angry and White	258062
are u racist? hate queers and niggers? me too.	191887
Black Haters and Negro Hangers	1401428
Dj aNDIE	794267
Honor+The+Ku+Klux+Klan	323614
I HATE BLACK PEOPLE	525845
I hate G-Unit	916827
□□□□□I HATE N1GGERS□□□□□	1733297
I HATE THE FREAKIN PORCH MONKEYS	1066584
K.K.K. MEMBERS	1447382
KKK WE GONNA KILL THE NIGGERS!!!	250810
KKK white is right	84971
Ku Klux Klan_White Knights Of America	1014877
N I G G E R S L A Y E R	1184100
nigger beaters	58711
niggerzsmellfunny	317512
the "i like to beat negros and mexicans" blog rin	387326
The KKK (Ku Klux Klan)	164821

THE REAL KU KLUX KLAN	1315712
WHITE f**kin PRIDE	240012
White-power	1244436

*   The home page of each group can be found at:
http://www.xanga.com/groups/group.aspx?id=[Xanga Group Id]

SUGGESTED READINGS

- Burris, V., Smith, E., & Strahm, A. (2000). White Supremacist Networks on the Internet. Sociological Focus 33(2), 215-235.
- Chen, H. and Chau, M. (2004). Web Mining: Machine Learning for Web Applications. Annual Review of Information Science and Technology 38, 289-329, 2004.
- Freeman, L. C. (2000). Visualizing Social Networks. Journal of Social Structure 1(1).
- Kumar, R., Raghavan, P., Rajagopalan, S., & Tomkins, A. (2002). The Web and Social Networks. IEEE Computer 35(11), 32-36.
- Lee, E., & Leets, L. (2002). Persuasive Storytelling by Hate Groups Online: Examining Its Effects on Adolescents. American Behavioral Scientist 45, 927-957.
- Xu, J. J. & Chen, H. (2004). Fighting Organized Crime: Using Shortest-Path Algorithms to Identify Associations in Criminal Networks. Decision Support Systems 38(3), 473-487.

ONLINE RESOURCES

- The Hate Directory: http://www.bcpl.net/~rfrankli/hatedir.htm
- The Xanga blog hosting site: http://www.xanga.com
- The Google blog search engine: http://blogsearch.google.com/

DISCUSSION QUESTIONS

1. Discuss whether and how online hate groups can lead to hate crimes or even terrorist attacks. Suggest some preventive measures.
2. Have you encountered racist or supremacist messages on the Web? What were your reactions towards those messages? Is it possible to ban these messages by law?
3. Discuss how to apply the Web mining and social network analysis techniques presented in this chapter to address other problems in terrorism

informatics.
4. New technologies, such as the Web and the blogosphere, have changed the way that supremacists and terrorists recruit new members, spread their ideas, and plan their actions. Discuss how new technologies, besides those discussed in this chapter, can also be used to tackle these issues.

23

AUTOMATIC EXTRACTION OF DECEPTIVE BEHAVIORAL CUES FROM VIDEO

Thomas O. Meservy, Matthew L. Jensen, W. John Kruse, Judee K. Burgoon, and Jay F. Nunamaker Jr.
Management Information Systems Department, University of Arizona, Tucson, Arizona, U.S.A. ({tmeservy, mjensen, jkruse, jburgoon, jnunamaker}@cmi.arizona.edu)

CHAPTER OVERVIEW

This chapter provides an overview of an initial investigation into a novel approach for deriving indicators of deception from video-taped interactions. The team utilized two-dimensional spatial inputs extracted from video to construct a set of discrete and inter-relational features. The features for thirty-eight video interactions were then analyzed using discriminant analysis. Additionally, features were used to build a multivariate regression model. Through this exploratory research, the team established the validity of the approach and identified a number of promising features and future research directions.

1.   INTRODUCTION

Deception and its detection have been a source of fascination for centuries, with literally thousands of publications on the topic testifying to its importance in the conduct of human affairs. Deception detection accuracy from manually coded behavioral indicators has typically hovered around 50-50, or chance, even among trained professionals (Levine et al. 2005). Researchers and practitioners have pursued a host of deception detection techniques, from determining trustworthiness from the shape of one's head and ears, to the use of physiologically-based instruments such as the polygraph and voice stress analyzer, to reliance on behavioral cues as potentially telltale cues to deception. Some of these methods are more reliable than others; however, no single cue has proven to be an accurate indicator of deception.

The most promising avenues for distinguishing deceit from truth lie in tools and techniques that utilize constellations of cues. Moreover, because deception indicators are subtle, dynamic, and transitory, they often elude humans' conscious awareness. If computer-based detection tools can be developed to augment human detection capabilities by discerning features of behavior and by tracking these elusive and fleeting cues over a course of time, accuracy in discerning both truthful and deceptive information and communications should be improved.

This chapter outlines initial attempts at identifying and validating a set of behavioral indicators automatically extracted from video.

2.   LITERATURE REVIEW

A primary goal of deception detection research is to identify which behaviors are correlated with deception and to identify behavioral cues that are consistent across contexts. Decades of research have yielded numerous insights into the nature of deception and factors influencing its detection. However, a limited number of consistent cues have been identified. In this section we first discuss the nature of deception and what cues might be exhibited when a person deceives and then we briefly explain some existing methods that have been developed to measure deceptive cues. For ease of comparison, these methods have been classified as physiological methods, verbal methods, and nonverbal methods.

2.1   Evidence of Deception

Deception has been defined in numerous ways (Masip et al. 2004), however, for our discussion we adopt Buller and Burgoon's definition: deception is "the intent to deceive a target by controlling information to alter the target's beliefs or understanding in a way that the deceiver knows is false" (Buller and Burgoon 1994). Thus, according to this definition, for deception to exist someone must have the intent to mislead another individual. Theories of deception can be roughly dichotomized into nonstrategic and strategic theories of deception. The majority of deception theory focuses on "nonrational, uncontrollable, and low-awareness cognitive processes that trigger nonstrategic cues indicative of deception" (Buller and Burgoon 1994). The process of deceiving can impact an individual's emotions and/or an individual's thought processes, which in turn may create outwardly detectable behavior. However, a long stream of research also suggests that individuals strategically and voluntarily adapt behavioral patterns in response to the receiver's perceived acceptance of previous messages (Buller and Burgoon 1996). By understanding cues that may be triggered in both the nonstrategic and strategic processes of deception, we are better prepared to investigate appropriate methods of deception detection.

2.1.1   Nonstrategic Theory of Deception

The process of deceiving can cause a variety of emotions (Vrij 2000). An individual may feel guilty about telling a lie or may fear being caught. In some cases, individuals feel excitement about being able to fool or trick someone else. These emotions may be manifested in observable, detectable behavior. For example, guilt might result in a decrease of involvement or a shying away from a conversation. Fear might result in heightened arousal, including increased blood flow, heavier breathing, and a rise in vocal pitch. Excitement might be manifested in increased smiling or laughing. In each case, the individual may exhibit outward behavior based on changes in physiological state or emotions felt. If deceivers can appropriately monitor these messages and if they have control over particular communication channels, "they may be able to suppress external manifestations of internal arousal states" (Buller and Burgoon 1994).

Deception may also impact the amount and type of thinking involved in an interaction. Creating a plausible lie often requires an individual to manage and weave together multiple streams of information into a coherent story (Zuckerman et al. 1981). Past research suggests that the mental processes for retrieving an actual event are different than fabricating an imagined event (Schacter et al. 1998). Individuals may portray different outward behaviors when a real event is recalled compared to when an imagined one is created. For example, speech dysfluencies, such as ums, ahs and other pauses may be indicative of increased cognitive load when manufacturing an answer. Additionally, some researchers have noted an increase in the amount of time it takes for an individual to respond to a question (response latency) and also an increase in the blinking of the eyes (DePaulo et al. 2003).

2.1.2   Strategic Theory of Deception

Humans are thoughtful, strategic creatures who closely monitor interpersonal interactions and voluntarily adapt behavioral patterns based on perceived acceptance of previously transmitted messages. During a deceptive interchange, deceivers often take into account the verbal and nonverbal messages of the receiver and adjust their strategies of communication. In addition to the receiver's behavior, deceivers also monitor their own behavior and adjust their communication strategy.

Interpersonal Deception Theory (IDT) (Buller and Burgoon 1996) is the leading theory of deception that views deception as strategic communication. IDT models deception as a strategic interaction between participants. Both the deceiver and the receiver approach an interaction with a number of preconceived factors that will influence the interaction. These factors might include expectations, goals, familiarity, suspicion, and so forth. During the course of the interaction, the deceiver and receiver may alter strategies as their respective effectiveness is observed. During the interaction, both parties will likely unintentionally reveal behavioral signals of their respective deception or suspicion.

A variant of this idea is what DePaulo calls a "self-presentational" or "impression-management" perspective on deception. Deceivers deliberately attempt to manage impressions of the interactions in which they are involved. This process of self-regulation consumes additional mental resources (Maruven and Baumeister 2000). When conveying false impressions, deceivers are likely to experience a sense of deliberateness and often act "unnatural" (DePaulo et al. 2003). These actions often come across as planned, rehearsed, or lacking in spontaneity.

Table 23-1. Deception theories, sample cues, and deception detection methods

	Nonstrategic Theories		Strategic Theories
	Arousal and Emotions	Cognitive Effort and Memory	Interpersonal Deception Theory
Short Description	Deception evokes emotions (fear, delight, etc.) that trigger physiological changes or other	Deception impacts the amount and type of thinking involved in an interaction.	Deception is a dynamic interaction in which the deceiver and receiver adjust their actions based

	Nonstrategic Theories		Strategic Theories
	outward behavior that may be observed		on observed behavior.
Sample Possible Cues / States	Increased heart rate Higher pitch Faster tempo False smiles	Response latency Speech disfluencies Fewer details Briefer messages	Overcontrol Guarded position More word quantity Planned or rehearsed behavior Increasing involvement over time
Primary Detection Methods	Physiological Nonverbal	Verbal Nonverbal	Verbal Nonverbal

2.2 Deception Detection Methods

Deception detection methods can be divided into groups based on the types of cues they attempt to capture—physiological methods, verbal methods, and nonverbal methods. Physiological methods capture arousal-based and emotion-based cues. Verbal methods typically capture cognitive-effort-based, memory-based cues and strategic communication-based cues. Various nonverbal methods attempt to capture cues from all of the discussed categories. Table 23-1 provides an overview of deception perspectives, sample cues, and deception detection methods.

2.2.1 Physiological Methods

Perhaps out of all the approaches to deception detection, the most well-known is the polygraph or the "lie-detector." The polygraph relies on cardiac, electrodermal, and pneumo-respiratory measures to infer deception. It is believed that such physiological measures are directly linked to conditions brought on by deception (Vrij 2000). There are two main methods of deception detection that use the polygraph: the Control Question Test (CQT) and the Guilty Knowledge Test (GKT). The CQT uses a series of irrelevant control questions for comparison to crime-specific questions to ferret out possible deception. However, it has often been criticized as subjective, non-scientific, and unreliable (Ben-Shakhar and Elaad 2003). The GKT determines whether an interviewee has knowledge about a crime that would only be known by the perpetrator. A series of crime-related objects or pictures may be shown to the interviewee and the interviewee's reaction is recorded. The GKT enjoys a more objective, scientific footing

(Ben-Shakhar and Elaad 2003); however, specific and confidential details about a crime must be known for it to be used.

Another rising method of deception detection is the analysis of brain activity. Improvements in functional magnetic resonance imaging (fMRI) have allowed the monitoring of brain activity during an interview. Some researchers have noticed differences between the brain activity of truth-tellers and deceivers (Ganis et al. 2003; Johnson et al. 2004). Near infrared spectroscopy (NIRS) (Villringer 1993) is an alternative, noninvasive method which uses optical technology to measure neuronal, metabolic, and hemodynamic changes. NIRS shows promise in differentiating truth from lies based on physiological changes in deceivers (Izzetoglu et al. 2003).

Most physiological methods of deception detection require the use of invasive sensors attached to the body. Thus, cooperation from the interviewee is required.

2.2.2   Verbal Methods

Two methods of verbal analysis are Criterion-Based Content Analysis (CBCA) and Reality Monitoring (RM). CBCA is based on the Undeutsch-Hypothesis which states that "a statement derived from a memory of an actual experience differs in content and quality from a statement based on invention or fantasy" (Vrij 2000). CBCA takes place during a structured interview where the interviewer scores responses according to predefined criteria such as logical structure, unusual or superfluous details, and self-deprecation or pardoning the perpetrator. RM also uses a scoring mechanism to judge potential deception, based on the supposition that truthful responses will contain more perceptual, contextual, and affective information than deceptive responses.

CBCA and RM require trained interviewers to conduct interviews and trained coders to score the interviews. Although these verbal analysis methods offer more flexibility than the physiological methods, the training required is extensive and results are not immediate.

2.2.3   Nonverbal Methods

Computerized voice stress analysis (CVSA) has been proposed as a method to automatically detect deception. Signals that accompany psychological stress are identified from multiple cues in the voice. Accuracy of CVSA is comparable to the polygraph (Tippett 1994). However, CVSA works best in a controlled environment with little background noise.

Observation of behavioral cues is also used as a method of deception detection. Numerous studies have shown that deceivers act differently than truth-tellers (Ekman and Friesen 1969; Zuckerman and Driver 1985; DePaulo et al. 2003). Among the differences are lack of head movement (Buller et al. 1994) and lack of illustrating gestures which accompany speech (Vrij et al. 2000). Many people suspect deceivers act differently than truth-tellers; however, most people are mistaken in their beliefs about which cues are associated with deception. Even trained professionals are fooled by over reliance on misleading cues (Vrij 2000). Additionally, the cognitive load of simultaneously tracking behavior and maintaining an interview can be too heavy for a single interviewer to manage.

2.3   Theory for Behavioral Analysis

To avoid the problems associated with the current methods for identifying deceit, we propose a new method of deception detection which builds upon existing nonverbal methods. This method involves automated extraction and identification of behavioral cues which are associated with deception.

Interpersonal Deception Theory (Buller and Burgoon 1996) provides the foundation for our method of deception detection. The intention of our method is to automatically identify these indicators of deception. Our method focuses on deriving cues from the head and hands inasmuch as certain movements of the head and hands have been consistently correlated with deception.

3.   RESEARCH METHOD AND EXAMPLES

The research approach that we use to categorize nonverbal behavior into deceptive/truthful classes is commonly used in pattern classification— (1) raw data are split into discrete units, (2) general metrics are extracted from the discrete units, (3) features are extracted and inferred from these metrics, and (4) selected features are used to classify each unit (Duda et al. 2001). The input to this process is nonverbal behavior of an individual captured as video frames and the output is a classification or level of deception or truth.

3.1   Identification of Head and Hands in Video

First, video streams are segmented into discrete, logical units. In an interview setting, these units might typically be responses by the interviewee to a specific question or topic.

General metrics are extracted from the video using a method called "blob analysis." We utilize a refined method of blob analysis developed by the Computational Biomedicine Imaging and Modeling Center (CBIM) at Rutgers University (Ganis et al. 2003). This method uses color analysis, eigenspace-based shape segmentation and Kalman filters to track head and hand positions throughout the video segment. Lu et al (Lu et al. 2005) explain this process in detail. While we choose to use blob analysis to track the head and the hands, other tracking methods could also be employed.

Metrics—including position, size, and angles—are produced by the software and are utilized when generating additional meaningful features. Figure 23-1 shows a video frame that has been subjected to blob analysis.

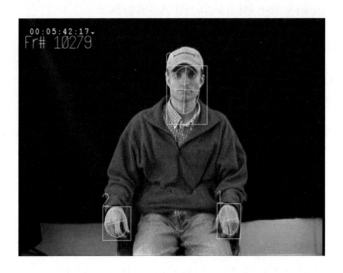

Figure 23-1. Video frame after blob analysis

3.2   Feature Extraction

A number of features can be extracted or inferred from the relatively simple metrics produced in the previous phase. Many of these features attempt to capture some of the key elements that researchers would look for when trying to detect deception (e.g. behavioral over control). However, a number of additional features that typically aren't used by humans (e.g., distance of movement per frame) are extracted because of their potential discriminatory power in an automated environment.

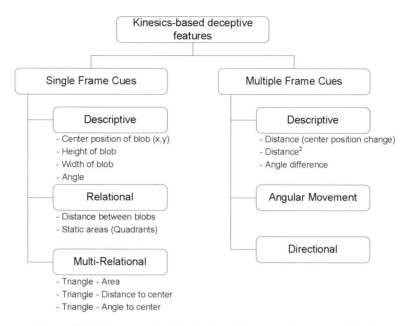

Figure 23-2. Taxonomy for kinesics-based deceptive features in video data

The movement-based or kinesics-based deceptive features that are extracted from video can be sub-divided into single frame features and multiple frame features. Single frame features, as the name implies, are calculated using information from a single video frame. These features can be further categorized as descriptive, relational, or multi-relational features. Multiple frame features require information from two or more frames. Multiple frame features can be classified as descriptive, angular movement, or directional features. Figure 23-2 illustrates a taxonomy of these kinesics-based features.

3.3   Single Frame Features

The features in the descriptive category of single frame features are actually provided as the output of blob analysis. These features include the center position of each blob (x, y), the height (h) and width (w) of each blob, and the angle of the major axis (θ). Figure 23-3 illustrates these features as they relate to a single blob.

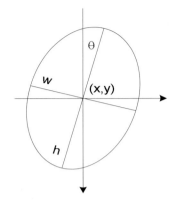

Figure 23-3. Single frame descriptive features

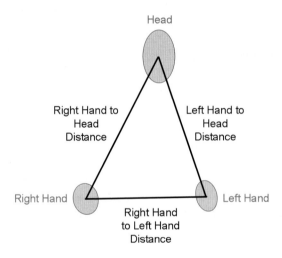

Figure 23-4. Blob distance features

The relational category of single frame features contains features that represent relationships between two objects—either a blob to another blob or a blob to a reference point or area. In the former case, the distance between two blobs of interest is calculated using a simple Euclidean distance formula. Figure 23-4 demonstrates some single frame relational features; specifically distance features. The distance between the head, the right hand, and the left hand allows us to know when they are touching (distance is zero) or how far apart they are. This may hint at gestures that are indicative of nervousness (such as preening, scratching, rubbing, etc), but only between the objects identified.

Features that track a blob in comparison to other regions are also part of the relational category. Quadrants derived from the head position and head width have been used in other experiments (Burgoon et al. 2005). We extract quadrant information in a similar manner, creating one region for the area above the shoulders (quadrant 1) and three areas below (quadrants 2-4). Quadrant 3 is derived based on the width of the head. Quadrants 2 and 4 occupy any additional area to the left and right, respectively. Figure 23-5 maps the quadrants onto the sample video frame. This feature allows us to understand how often each blob is in each quadrant. It was hypothesized that the hands of deceivers, who are more closed in their posture, would spend more time in quadrant 3 than truth tellers (Burgoon et al. 2005).

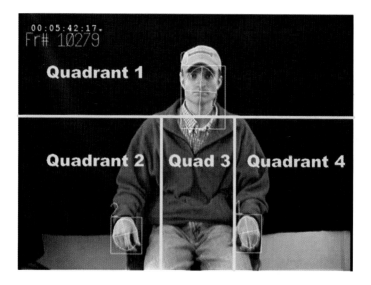

Figure 23-5. Quadrant features

The multi-relational category contains features that involve information from 3 or more blobs or objects. The features of interest in our approach include calculating the area of the triangle between the 3 blobs, the distance from each blob to the center point of the triangle, and the angle of each blob in relation to the center of the triangle.

The area of the triangle is calculated using the center points from the head and hands in Equation 23-1.

$$\frac{\left|\left(\left(x_{head}*y_{left}-x_{left}*y_{head}\right)+\left(x_{right}*y_{head}-x_{head}*y_{right}\right)+\left(x_{left}*y_{right}-x_{right}*y_{left}\right)\right)\right|}{2}$$

Equation 23-1

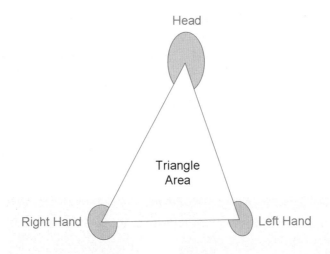

Figure 23-6. Triangle Area Feature

Figure 23-6 depicts the triangle area feature. This feature can show the openness of the individual's posture. Additionally, we get a feel for when the hands touch the head or each other (the triangle area is zero). However, we have to rely on other features to determine which blobs are involved.

The distance from each blob to the center of triangle uses a simple Euclidean distance formula. The formula uses the center point coordinates from one of the blobs and the center point of the triangle. Figure 23-7 illustrates this feature. This feature captures the relationship of one blob to the two other blobs in a single metric and may provide insight into posture of an individual.

A blob's angle relative to the center of the triangle is also classified into the multi-relational category of single frame features. The center point of a blob and the triangle center are used when calculating the angle. This angle, initially in radians, is converted to degrees. Figure 23-8 illustrates the triangle center angle feature for a right hand blob. This feature can discriminate when one hand is up but not the other or when the body is asymmetric (both hands to the left or right of the head).

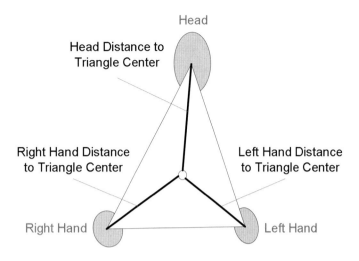

Figure 23-7. Distance to triangle center

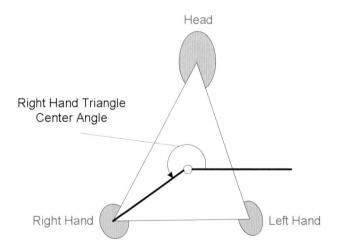

Figure 23-8. Tri. center angle features

3.4   Multiple Frame Features

The features in the descriptive category of multiple frame features are calculated using the descriptive single frame features. The distance feature tracks how much a single blob has moved from one frame to another. Figure 23-9 illustrates this concept for a right-hand blob between frame one (dashed border) and frame two (solid border). Once again this distance is calculated using a simple Euclidean distance formula. Since we calculate this metric for each frame, which represents approximately 1/30th of a second, we can also view this metric as a representation of speed of movement. This gives us insight into how much an individual moves her or his head and hands over time.

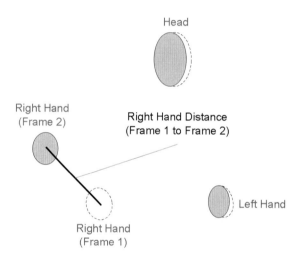

Figure 23-9. Multiple frame distance feature

Another feature in the multiple frame descriptive category is angle difference. To calculate this feature we simply subtract the last frame's angle for a specific blob from the current frame's angle for that same blob. Whether this feature is positive or negative captures not only the rotation of the major axis, but also the direction of rotation. It was hypothesized that the angle differences for the head may be useful, but not for the hands. By naïve observation it was noticed that the shape of the hand blobs and the major axis frequently change when the hands are pivoted at the wrist.

The angular movement category of multiple frame features contains features that attempt to capture arced movement of a blob over a period of time.

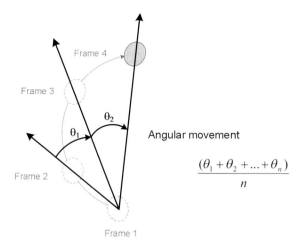

Figure 23-10. Angular movement feature

Figure 23-10 illustrates how this is calculated for a series of frames. The first frame serves as a reference point and vectors are calculated using the first frame as the origination point and other frames as destination points. Polar coordinate angles are calculated for each vector. The angular movement feature consists of the average change in vector angles. Our calculations utilize 5 frames when calculating this feature. This feature was designed to capture patterns that are representative of certain types of illustrator gestures.

The multiple frame directional category of features contains information about the direction that a blob has moved. A vector is created using the center points of the same blob in two different frames and a polar coordinate angle is extracted and converted to degrees. This feature can further be split into binary-value classifications (e.g. up, up-left, down-left, right, etc). It is hypothesized that these values will be particularly useful when using time-series analysis and it is anticipated that they will capture information associated with illustrator and adaptor gestures.

3.5 Analysis of Summarized Features

In order for these extracted features to be analyzed by specific statistical methods, such as discriminant analysis and multiple regression, they need to be summarized over the length of a segmented video clip. Simple descriptive statistics (means and variances) are calculated for all of the features for each video segment. We anticipated that the variance of some features would be more telling than the feature itself. For example, by calculating the variance of the triangle area, we can quickly see how much overall change in hand and head position occurred during the length of the clip.

4.   EXPERIMENTS AND RESULTS

The features described above were used to identify deception in a Mock Theft experiment.

4.1   Description of Mock Theft Experiment

The purpose of the Mock Theft experiment (Burgoon et al. 2003; Burgoon et al. 2003) was to reveal cues that can be used in deception detection. In this experiment, a wallet was left unattended in a classroom and some participants played the role of a thief who took the wallet. Other participants either observed the theft or were unaware of the theft. All the participants were interviewed by untrained and trained interviewers via chat, audio-only, and face-to-face channels and these interactions where recorded. The participants in the experiment were undergraduate students in a large mid-western university.

The face-to-face interactions from the Mock Theft experiment where used in this study.   There were a total of 42 possible face-to-face interactions that could be included in the study. Four were not used because of problematic video capture or because the participant did not follow instructions.   Each interaction was composed of a number of question-answer exchanges. In this study only the theft narrative was included in the analysis. Of the 38 responses, 16 were truthful and 22 were deceptive.

4.2   Discriminant Analysis

Initially, we used discriminant analysis to evaluate the features that were extracted from the video segments. Due to the exploratory nature of this research, we decided to do a stepwise discriminant analysis. Initially, with stringent entrance and exit criteria few features were selected and classification results were little better than chance.   However, using less stringent exit and entrance criteria (p-in .20 and p-out .30) a larger number of variables were included in the model, the model was even more significant, and classification accuracy increased substantially. While many of the features included in the final model are directly supported by current deception theory, some of the features need to be examined in more detail to understand why they discriminate truth from deception. Table 23-2 displays the features included in the final discriminant analysis model.

Table 23-2. Features included in discriminant analysis model

Category	Feature
Single frame descriptive	Average head x
	Average triangle center x
	Variance of the right hand height
	Variance of the right hand angle
Single frame relational features	Average time the right hand was in quadrant 2
	Average time the right hand was in quadrant 4
Single frame multi-relational	Average of the left hand triangle center angle
	Variance of the left hand triangle center angle
Multiple frame descriptive	Average right hand angle difference
	Variance of the head angle difference
Angular movement features	Average head angular movement sum
	Average of the left hand angular movement sum
	Variance of the left hand angular movement sum
	Variance of the head angular movement sum

The results of the discriminant analysis are shown in Table 23-3. The deceptive and truthful participants were classified with an accuracy rate of 95.2% percent. However, when using hold-one out cross validation, the accuracy falls to 88.1% percent. This preliminary result appears promising in its discriminatory ability as the overall model is highly significant (p< .001).

Table 23-3. Discriminant analysis accuracy results

		Predicted	
	Actual	Truthful	Deceptive
Original	Truthful	94.7	5.3
	Deceptive	4.3	95.7

4.3 Regression Model

As part of the mock theft experiment, participants were asked to rate the level of honesty (a number from 1 to 10) that they displayed during the narrative portion of the experiment. We built a multivariate regression model with honesty level as the dependent variable.

We used the same starting features as we did in the discriminant analysis and then used forward stepwise regression (p-in .10; p-out .20) to create a predictive model of honesty. The resulting model had an R^2 of .775, an adjusted R^2 of .600. Predictors for this model are displayed in Table 23-4.

Table 23-4. Discriminant analysis accuracy results

Category	Feature
Single frame descriptive	Average triangle x
	Variance of the right hand angle
Single frame multi-relational	Average angle of the head to triangle center
	Variance of the distance between the left hand and the triangle center
	Average distance between the head and the triangle center
Multiple frame descriptive	Average of the squared distance the head moved between frames
	Variance of the change in right hand angle between frames

As a whole, the model had a significance of p=.0000355. The ANOVA table for the overall model is shown in Table 23-5.

Table 23-5. Regression ANOVA

	Sum of Squares	Df	Mean Square	F	Significance
Regression	417.366	7	59.624	7.074	.0000355
Residual	278.146	33	8.429		
Total	695.512	40			

While the regression model shows promise for the task of classifying the level of honesty of an individual under similar circumstances, the main purpose of applying the statistical methods was to help understand the contributions of the extracted features and validate our hypothesis about their usefulness. Additional testing and refinement of the models need to occur to validate the predictive ability. However, we believe the utility of these novel features and the method of deception detection described in this chapter is supported by this and other preliminary studies (Jensen et al. 2005; Meservy et al. 2005; Meservy et al. 2006).

5.   CONCLUSION

The automated extraction of behavioral cues associated with deception exceeds typical human performance and overcomes many of the weaknesses that hinder other methods of deception detection. It is noninvasive and can be used without cooperation from the interviewee. This method allows flexibility, could provide prompt feedback, and does not require specially trained interviewers. This method does not require the same controlled setting as many of the other deception detection methods mandate and capitalizes on numerous nonverbal indicators of deception identified throughout the deception literature.

6. ACKNOWLEDGEMENTS

Portions of this research were supported by funding from the U. S. Air Force Office of Scientific Research under the U. S. Department of Defense University Research Initiative (Grant #F49620-01-1-0394) and Department of Homeland Security - Science and Technology Directorate under cooperative agreement NBCG20300030001. The views, opinions, and/or findings in this report are those of the authors and should not be construed as an official U.S. Government position, policy, or decision.

A previous version of this chapter was presented at the 2005 IEEE International Conference on Intelligence and Security Informatics held in Atlanta, Georgia and is published in its proceedings.

REFERENCES

Ben-Shakhar, G. and E. Elaad (2003). "The Validity of Psychophysiological Detection of Information with the Guilty Knowledge Test: A Meta-Analytic Review." *Journal of Applied Psychology* 88(1): 131-151.

Buller, D., J. Burgoon, et al. (1994). "Interpersonal Deception: VII. Behavioral Profiles of Falsification, Equivocation and Concealment." *Journal of Language and Social Psychology* 13(4): 366-395.

Buller, D. B. and J. K. Burgoon (1994). Deception: Strategic and nonstrategic communication. *Strategic interpersonal communication*. J. A. Daly and J. M. Wiemann. Hillsdale, NJ, Erlbaum: 191-223.

Buller, D. B. and J. K. Burgoon (1996). "Interpersonal Deception Theory." *Communication Theory* 6: 203-242.

Burgoon, J. K., M. Adkins, et al. (2005). *An Approach for Intent Identification by Building on Deception Detection*. Hawaii International Conference on System Science (HICSS'05), Hawaii.

Burgoon, J. K., J. P. Blair, et al. (2003). *Effects of Communication Modality on Arousal, Cognitive Complexity, Behavioral Control and Deception Detection During Deceptive Episodes*. Annual Meeting of the National Communication Association, Miami Beach, Florida.

Burgoon, J. K., J. P. Blair, et al. (2003). Detecting Deception through Linguistic Analysis. NSF/NIJ Symposium on Intelligence and Security Informatics.

DePaulo, B., J. Lindsay, et al. (2003). "Cues To Deception." *Psychological Bulletin* 129(1): 74-118.

Duda, R. O., P. E. Hart, et al. (2001). *Pattern Classification*. New York, Wiley.

Ekman, P. and W. V. Friesen (1969). "Nonverbal Leakage and Clues to Deception." *Psychiatry* 32: 88-105.

Ganis, G., S. M. Kosslyn, et al. (2003). "Neural Correlates of Different Types of Deception: An fMRI Investigation." *Cerebral Cortex* 13(8): 830-836.

Izzetoglu, K., G. Yurtsever, et al. (2003). *NIR spectroscopy measurements of cognitive load elicited by GKT and target categorization.*

Jensen, M. L., T. O. Meservy, et al. (2005). Identification of Deceptive Behavioral Cues Extracted from Video. International IEEE Conference on Intelligent Transportation Systems, Vienna, Austria.

Johnson, R., J. Barnhardt, et al. (2004). "The contribution of executive processes to deceptive responding." *Neuropsychologia* 42: 878-901.

Levine, T. R., T. H. Feeley, et al. (2005). "Testing the Effects of Nonverbal Behavior Training on Accuracy in Deception Detection with the Inclusion of a Bogus Training Control Group." *Western Journal of Communication* 69(3): 203-217.

Lu, S., G. Tsechpenakis, et al. (2005). Blob Analysis of the Head and Hands: A Method for Deception Detection. Hawaii International Conference on System Science (HICSS'05), Hawaii.

Maruven, M. and R. F. Baumeister (2000). "Self-Regulation and Depletion of Limited Resources: Does Self-Control Resemble a Muscle." *Psyhcological Bulletin* 126(2): 247.

Masip, J., E. Garrido, et al. (2004). "Defining deception." *Anales de Psicología* 20(1): 147-171.

Meservy, T., M. L. Jensen, et al. (2005). "Deception Detection through Automatic, Unobtrusive Analysis of Nonverbal Behavior." *IEEE Intelligent Systems* (September/October).

Meservy, T. O., M. L. Jensen, et al. (2006). *Detecting Deception in a Security Screening Scenario*. Thirty-Ninth Annual Hawaii International Conference on System Sciences (CD/ROM), Kauai, Hawaii, IEEE Computer Society Press.

Schacter, D. L., K. A. Norman, et al. (1998). "The cognitive neuroscience of constructive memory." *Annual Review of Psychology* 49(30): 289.

Tippett, R. G. (1994). "A Comparison Between Decision Accuracy Rates Obtained Using the Polygraph Instrument and the Computer Voice Stress Analyzer in the Absence of Jeopardy." Retrieved September, 2003, from:
http://campus.umr.edu/police/cvsa/compar1.htm.

Villringer, A. (1993). "Near infrared spectroscopy (NIRS): a new tool to study hemodynamic changes during activation of brain function in human adults." *Neuroscience Letters* 154: 101.

Vrij, A. (2000). *Detecting Lies and Deceit: The Psychology of Lying and the Implications for Professional Practice*. West Sussex, John Wily & Sons Ltd.

Vrij, A., K. Edward, et al. (2000). "Detecting Deceit via Analysis of Verbal and Nonverbal Behavior." *Journal of Nonverbal Behavior* 24(4): 239 - 263.

Zuckerman, M., B. M. DePaulo, et al. (1981). Verbal and nonverbal communication of deception. *Advances in Experimental Social Psychology*. L. Berkowitz. New York, Academic: 1-59.

Zuckerman, M. and R. E. Driver (1985). Telling Lies: Verbal and Nonverbal Correlates of Deception. *Nonverbal Communication: An Integrated Perspective*. A. W. Siegman and S. Feldstein. Hillsdale, NJ, Erlbaum: 129-147.

SUGGESTED READINGS

Deception
- Buller, D. B. and J. K. Burgoon (1996). "Interpersonal Deception Theory." <u>Communication Theory</u> **6**: 203-242.
  An explanation of Interpersonal Deception Theory that views deception as a strategic interaction between deceiver and receiver. During the course of the interaction, the deceiver and receiver may alter strategies as their effectiveness is observed.
- Vrij, A. (2000). Detecting Lies and Deceit: The Psychology of Lying and the Implications for Professional Practice. West Sussex, John Wily & Sons Ltd.
  An excellent review of the practical aspects of deception detection methods in real-world environments
- DePaulo, B., J. Lindsay, et al. (2003). "Cues To Deception." *Psychological Bulletin* 129(1): 74-118.
  A comprehensive meta-analysis of deceptive research and indicators of deception.

Blob Analysis used for Deception Detection
- Lu, S., G. Tsechpenakis, et al. (2005). Blob Analysis of the Head and Hands: A Method for Deception Detection. Hawaii International Conference on System Science (HICSS'05), Hawaii.
  An in-depth, mathematical explanation of blob analysis.
- Meservy, T., M. L. Jensen, et al. (2005). "Deception Detection through Automatic, Unobtrusive Analysis of Nonverbal Behavior." *IEEE Intelligent Systems* (September/October).
  An overview of our approach of deception detection and a comparison of various classification methods including discriminant analysis, alternating decision trees, neural networks, and support-vector machines.

ONLINE RESOURCES

- Center for the Management of Information (CMI)
  http://www.cmi.arizona.edu
  A research center at the University of Arizona that conducts numerous innovative experimental, field, and systems research programs including the Automatic Detection of Deception and Intent. CMI and its partners have developed a number of deception corpuses for various environments and contexts.
- Center for BioImaging and Modeling (CBIM)
  http://cbim.rutgers.edu/
  A research center at Rutgers University conducts novel research in the

areas of Computational BioMedicine, Computer Vision and Computer Graphics. CBIM developed the head and hand tracking software we use in our method of deception detection.

- Open Source Computer Vision Library (OpenCV)
  http://www.intel.com/technology/computing/opencv/index.htm
  An extensive and well-accepted computer vision library that includes modules for gesture recognition and motion tracking.
- Department of Defense Polygraph Institute
  http://www.dodpi.army.mil/
  US Department of defense institute that does polygraph research and trains federal polygraphers.

DISCUSSION QUESTIONS

1. How common is deception? In your daily life? In different cultures?
2. When deception occurs, how often are behavioral indicators of deception emitted? Are they the same in different contexts? What factors would affect the emmision of deceptive indicators?
3. What are the benefits and drawbacks of using a constellation of cues to detect deception?
4. Which indicators of deception (listed in this chapter and the other references) can be automatically extracted? Which computational methods are most appropriate for each indicator of deception? Why?
5. How would you categorize behavioral methods of deception detection? (Invasiveness, cost, accuracy, and operational expertise needed, etc.)
6. What are the benefits and limitations of the proposed method in comparison to other existing methods of deception detection? In what situations would this method be most applicable?

24

SITUATIONAL AWARENESS TECHNOLOGIES FOR DISASTER RESPONSE

Naveen Ashish[1], Ronald Eguchi[2], Rajesh Hegde[3], Charles Huyck[2], Dmitri Kalashnikov[1], Sharad Mehrotra[1], Padhraic Smyth[1], and Nalini Venkatasubramanian[1]

[1]*Donald Bren School of Information and Computer Sciences, University of California, Irvine, California, U.S.A. ({ashish, dvk, sharad, smyth, nalini} @ics.uci.edu);* [2]*Image Cat, Inc., Long Beach, California, U.S.A. (chk@imagecatinc.com);* [3]*Department of Electrical and Computer Engineering, University of California, San Diego, California, U.S.A. (rhegde@ucsd.edu)*

CHAPTER OVERVIEW

This chapter highlights some of the key information technology challenges being addressed in the RESCUE project, a National Science Foundation (NSF) funded 5-year effort, with a particular focus on *situational awareness* technologies. A key premise of the project is that the critical decision making required in disaster situations relies heavily on the availability, accuracy, and timeliness of information that can be made available to the decision makers. A major thrust within RESCUE is focusing on developing next generation situational awareness technologies. Our approach in building situational awareness systems is to build information systems that consider situations and events as fundamental entities, and our research is focused on the key technical challenges in the extraction and synthesis, management, and analysis of such situational information. This chapter focuses on our research accomplishments in each of these areas and also provides an overview of technology transition activities.

1.   INTRODUCTION

Responding to natural or man-made disasters, in a timely and effective manner, can reduce deaths and injuries, contain or prevent secondary disasters, and reduce the resulting economic losses and social disruption. During a crisis, responding organizations confront grave uncertainties in making critical decisions. They need to gather situational information (e.g., state of the civil, transportation and information infrastructures), together with information about available resources (e.g., medical facilities, rescue and law enforcement units). There is a strong correlation between the accuracy, timeliness, and reliability of the information available to the decision-makers, and the quality of their decisions. Dramatic improvements in the speed and accuracy at which information about the crisis flows through the disaster response networks has the potential to revolutionize crisis response, saving human lives and property.

This chapter highlights some of the key information technology challenges being addressed in the Project RESCUE[1] [1], with a particular focus on *situational awareness* technologies. Appreciating the IT challenges in improving crisis response requires a thorough understanding of how communication and control networks form among responding organizations, and how the response process is organized. Since the crisis domain might be new to a large number of readers, we begin by first briefly summarizing the crisis response process. This is done to set the stage for a discussion of the challenges being addressed by RESCUE and particularly the situational awareness thrust within it.

1.1   The Crisis Response Process

Organized crisis response activities include measures undertaken to protect life and property immediately before (for disasters where there is at least some warning period), during, and immediately after disaster impact. Such activities may span a few hours to days or even months, depending upon the magnitude of the event. Depending upon the scale of the disaster, crisis response may be a large-scale, multi-organizational operation involving many layers of government, public authorities (such as state-

[1] The work reported in this paper is part of the RESCUE Project (http://www.itr-rescue.org) whose goal is to radically transform the ability of organizations to gather, manage, analyze and disseminate information when responding to man-made and natural catastrophes. The 'Responding to Crises and Unexpected Events' (RESCUE) Project is funded in part by National Science Foundation (NSF) through its large ITR program under contract numbers 0331707 and 0331690.

managed utility companies), commercial entities, volunteer organizations, media organizations, and the public. In a crisis, these entities work together as a virtual organization to save lives, preserve infrastructure and community resources, and reestablish normalcy within the community. Depending upon the magnitude of the crisis, the operation of this virtual organization can span multiple levels. Field level operations such as evacuation, traffic management, triage, and provision of medical services are usually under the control of an on-site incident commander that reports back to a central Emergency Operations Center (EOC). In a large disaster, the management of area-wide resources requires a broader participation of government and industry. In large urban areas such as Los Angeles and New York, it is not uncommon for each city within a county to have its own EOC where representatives from fire, police, utility companies, Red Cross, and many other organizations participate in the response. Furthermore, each agency represented in the City EOC also has its own emergency operations center, usually in another location. In addition to these government-run centers, private industry (large businesses, NGO's, etc.) may also set up response centers that feed and receive information from government EOCs. While small disasters may be handled at the local level, the resources of local governments can become overwhelmed by the demands of larger events; in these cases, higher levels of the government become active participants in the response effort. Such a large-scale response may involve hundreds of autonomous organizations with different tasks and priorities. For example, a county-wide disaster in the Los Angeles Area may mobilize emergency offices of State, County, and up to 88 different municipal authorities, along with a variety of other organizations (including fire departments, health services agencies, and NGOs such as the Red Cross), Each of these organizations may themselves represent a large consortium; for example, the health services organizations may consist of a variety of hospitals, triaging services, clinics, etc.

The Response Cycle: Irrespective of the nature and scale of the crisis and the organizations involved, crisis response activities can be viewed (at an abstract level) as consisting of four interrelated phases:

- *Damage assessment:* In this phase, disaster-related losses are identified on both incident-level and regional scales, and their magnitudes are assessed. Severely impacted areas, disruptions to critical infrastructure, situations where secondary hazards may develop if initial damage is not mitigated (e.g., earthquake-induced hazardous materials releases or dam failures), and other problems of high urgency are identified, and estimates of the time needed to restore disrupted systems are developed.
- *Needs assessment:* In this phase, incidents requiring some level of response are identified. For example, building collapses where victims

are trapped may require search, rescue and medical resources, release of hazardous materials may require large-scale evacuation, etc. Operationally, these incidents are assigned a measure of urgency/priority, typically based on immediate threats to life safety.

- *Prioritization of Response Measures:* In this phase, incidents requiring response are matched with available resources. If the total demand is greater than the system's capacity to respond – as is invariably the case in large-scale disasters – decision-makers must establish priorities for response. Decision-makers must have an accurate assessment of the disaster situation and available resources in order to establish priorities.
- *Organizational Response:* In this phase, emergency resources are deployed and organizational decisions are disseminated to crisis-workers and the population at large. Ideally, response activities take place in accordance with pre-disaster planning. Decision-support systems are used to track key incidents and the progress of responding units, to optimize response activities, and to act as a mechanism for queuing ongoing incidents.

Each aspect of the above process is part of an ongoing cycle, in which assessments, decisions, and interventions at one point in time produce implications for subsequent response activities. As the response proceeds and as more accurate information becomes available, new problems are identified, decisions are reassessed, and response activities may be reprioritized and sometimes even reversed. For this process to proceed effectively, government leaders, response personnel, and other actors must communicate rapidly with one another during each phase. The quality of the resulting decisions and the speed with which the process transitions through the four phases depends upon the timeliness and accuracy of information available to response workers.

1.2   IT Challenges and RESCUE

In the RESCUE Project, our focus is to radically transform the speed and accuracy with which information flows through disaster response networks, networks that connect multitudes of response organizations as well as the general public. We are working to develop information technology solutions that dynamically capture and store crisis-relevant data as it is generated, analyze this data in real-time, interpret it, and disseminate the resulting information to decision makers in the forms most appropriate for their various tasks. Challenges in realizing such IT solutions arise due to the scale and complexity of the problem domain, the diversity of data and data sources, the state of the communication and information infrastructures through which the information flows, and the diversity and dynamic nature of the responding organizations.

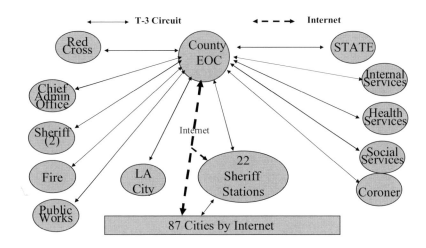

Figure 24-1. LA County Disaster Network

Diversity of Information Sources: Information relevant to decision making may be dispersed across a hierarchy of storage, communication, and processing units – from sensors (in-situ sensors, satellite imagery, remote sensing) where data is generated to heterogeneous databases belonging to autonomous organizations. Critical information may span various modalities – e.g., field-observations communicated via voice conversations among emergency workers, video data transmitted from cameras embedded in civil infrastructures, dispersed at crisis site, or carried by first responders, sensor data streams, or textual and relational information in databases. In some cases, information may even be embedded in the relationships among persons themselves; for instance, the migration and patterns of those fleeing an incident site may provide valuable clues as to the nature and exact location of the incident.

Diversity of Information Users: Information may need to be shared across diverse, loosely coupled, emergent multi-organizational networks in which different entities play different roles in response activities, have different needs and urgencies, have different cultures, and may have vastly different capabilities with respect to technology utilization. These organizations may or may not have policies in place regarding data sharing and collaboration. Furthermore, these organizational networks must rapidly reconfigure to adapt to the changing communication and control demands present during crisis events. Finally, different people/organizations have different needs and urgency levels regarding the same information. For example, while a field worker might require detailed information about the specific location of hazardous materials in a burning building, the monitoring and response team at a nearby command center may only need to know the number of hazardous-material locations in the vicinity of the catastrophe.

State of the Infrastructure: Information must be transferred across highly distributed, mobile infrastructure consisting of heterogeneous communication channels and systems that are prone to failures and vulnerable to attacks during a crisis. To address the above challenges in building an information infrastructure that provides reliable, timely, and integrated information, we are developing technology at two levels.

At the *systems* level our goal is to develop robust communications and systems infrastructure to ensure connectivity and availability of reliable and efficient pipeline for information flow between different organizations and entities. For instance the *Robust Networking project* within RESCUE is focused on developing systems that provide computing, bi-directional communication, and higher layer services at a crisis site. The crisis site may lack electric power, fixed communication networks may be unpredictable, and responders might bring in heterogeneous mutually conflicting communication technologies. The goal is to develop a system that can operate under such extreme conditions by consolidating and enhancing available systems and seamlessly extending new capabilities to all end users and devices as communication services get incrementally restored. The *Information Dissemination project* (part of RESCUE) is exploring how customized warnings, alerts, advisories, and messages can be disseminated to the public at large under extreme situations when the infrastructure is failing and under surge demands. The approach developed exploits peer-based techniques to achieve fast, reliable, and scalable dissemination.

At the *informatics* level, the RESCUE project is exploring capabilities for information collection, sharing, fusion, and analysis. For instance, in the *situational awareness project* our objective is to design and develop technologies that can create actionable situational awareness from the avalanche of heterogeneous multi-modal data streams (audio, speech, text, video, etc.) including human-generated input (e.g., first responders' communications, field reports, etc.) during or after a disaster. In the *Information sharing* project we are developing a flexible, customizable, dynamic, robust, scalable, policy-driven architecture that ensures seamless information sharing amongst all entities involved in response with minimal manual human intervention and automated enforcement of information-sharing policies.

Finally, privacy concerns in infusing technology into real-world processes and activities arise for a variety of reasons, including unexpected usage and/or misuse for purposes for which the technology was not originally intended. These concerns are further exacerbated by the natural ability of modern information technology to record and make persistent information about entities (individuals, organizations, groups) and their interactions with technologies – information that can be exploited in the future against the interests of those entities. Such concerns, if unaddressed, constitute barriers to technology adoption or worse, result in adopted technology being misused to the detriment of the society. Another of our objectives thus is to understand privacy concerns in adopting technology from the social and cultural perspective, and design socio-technological solutions to alleviate such concerns. The challenge guiding our research is whether Information Technologies can be designed with "knobs" that can be used to control disclosure of information amongst entities (individuals, organizations, government) with the objective of empowering technology adopters to fit the technology into existing (and possibly dynamically evolving) societal and cultural expectations with respect to privacy.

In this section we have introduced the RESCUE project and provided a brief overview of the various research thrusts centered on the IT challenges in improving disaster response. The following sections will focus on the situational awareness project, including our objectives, approach, research in various areas and also technology transition into artifacts.

2. SITUATIONAL AWARENESS

2.1 Response and Situational Awareness

Each of the different sub-phases of response, as described in the introduction, as well as phases of a disaster cycle are decision-centric in which individuals and organizations make critical decisions that have implications on life and property. The quality of such decisions depends upon a variety of factors including social and cultural factors, level of expertise knowledge, and training, the established practice, etc. Among the most critical factors (of central interest to us in the situational awareness project) is the awareness of the situation (past, present, and future) and implications of actions or inactions. The situational information broadly consists of information about people (their vulnerabilities, location, demographics), resources (food, water, shelter) and progression of the event and activities (plume spread, storm track, evacuation progress). Our objective in the situational awareness project is to significantly enhance the situational awareness of decision-makers thereby improving their ability to make correct decisions. Specifically our goal is to develop advanced information processing and management technologies to turn the *available* information into *actionable* information for people and decision systems.

2.2   A Situational Awareness Driven Application

As a motivating example, we present a real world application and process that we believe could benefit significantly (in terms of efficacy and timeliness) from advanced situational awareness technologies. *Damage assessment* is an important task, immediately following a major disaster such as a hurricane or earthquake. An accurate and timely estimate of damage in the impacted and surrounding areas can help in several important decisions, such as resource allocation in response. The information, using which such assessments can be made, is collected in a variety of different ways: through use of aerial or satellite imagery; ground or field coverage; simulating the effects of the disaster through sophisticated loss or impact modeling tools – these tools are common for most hazards (e.g., hurricane, flooding, and earthquake); and finally use of information that becomes available on the internet – this may include blogs, internet surveys (e.g., the "did you feel it" system operated by the U.S. Geological Survey for earthquake events), reports by government or non-profit organizations.

The typical *modalities* for post-disaster information can include the following: aerial photos, field-based photos, satellite imagery (low, moderate and high-resolution optical data; radar or synthetic aperture radar data; lidar), video (with possibly audio commentaries), written reports, simulation results, etc.   Data sources for much of this information come from government agencies (NOAA, USGS, FEMA, NASA, and local and state emergency response organizations); non-profit organizations, such as the Red Cross; industry (companies affiliated with or providing data to the insurance industry), and the public (e.g., through the internet)

All the above, raw, information today needs to be collected from the different sources above and then processed and integrated, mostly manually. Ultimately this information must be analyzed to convey the following kinds of information: a) areas of greatest impact, measured in terms on expected losses, lives lost, and social disruption; b) areas needing immediately response, either because of developing incidents, e.g., fire-following earthquake, or flooding after a storm; and c) areas that may be impacted by impeding disasters, e.g., level breaks because of excessive storm surge.

The above problem is precisely of the nature that our situational awareness technologies aim to address i.e., if we can employ such technologies to make the information processing pipeline from raw disparate information to the end damage assessment analyses above, more automated, efficient, and timely. We now describe the technologies we are developing that can make such an assessment analysis application feasible.

2.3   Our Approach

Our approach to building situational awareness systems is an *event-centric* one i.e., one that is centered around events as fundamental units of information. The motivation comes from our observation that situations (including disaster situations) are fundamentally comprised of events at various levels. For instance the out break of a fire, recovery of victims, dispatch of responders, collapse of a bridge are all events in a situation. It is information about such events that feeds into the analysis tools of the kinds described above. In very general terms an event is an occurrence of something of interest of a certain type, at a certain place and at/over a certain period of time. It is a semantic, *domain independent* concept which may have associated with it a set of different entities that play different roles and that may bear relationships to other events and/or to other entities in the real world. Events, in our view, provide a natural abstraction for modeling, representing, and reasoning about situations.

We have identified the following three key technical components in building situational awareness systems centered around events.

1. **Event Extraction, Interpretation, & Synthesis** - Multi-modal extraction, fusion and assimilation technology that enables the *extraction and synthesis* of higher level situational information from low level (signal) inputs. For instance in the damage assessment application above, we need automated capabilities to process the various pieces of information, such as images, audio and video feeds, text feeds, etc. and also integrated and fuse information coming from multiple disparate sources.

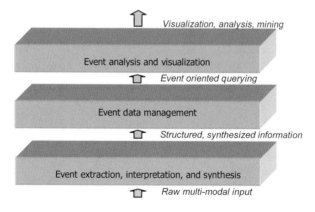

Figure 24-2. Situational Awareness System Tiers

2. **Event Data Management** – Technologies that support *modeling, storing, querying and indexing,* situational information. In the damage

assessment application for example, we need data management capabilities for storage and structured querying of the information collected, processed and integrated in the ingest phase. The information obtained about the unfolding situation and status should be queryable in a structured manner.

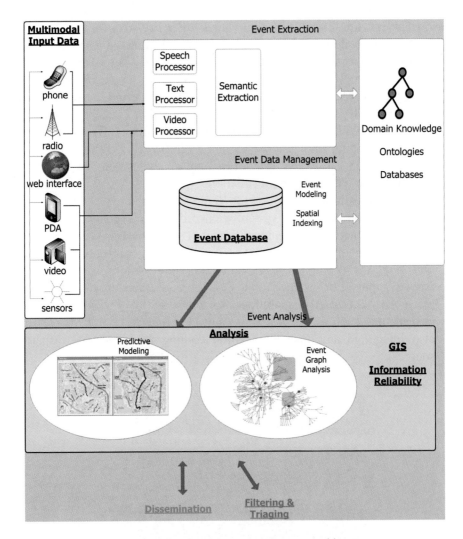

Figure 24-3. Situational Awareness System: Architecture

3. **Event Analysis and Visualization** – An environment that supports *end user analysis and visualization* tools over the situational information. The end goal is to obtain information useful for decision making, for instance assessments of damage, predicted areas still in danger, estimates of

evacuation times etc. This aspect of situational awareness technologies is concerned with such analysis tools (model based simulations, estimation tools etc as an example) that perform such analysis over the collected information now in a situational database.

Event information thus flows through the three tiers described above. Events are first extracted from raw information, then stored and indexed in an event database, and finally end user analysis and visualization capabilities are provided over these extracted and stored events. An important point we wish to emphasize is that events in our view are independent of the media that they may be captured in and extracted from. The event is a higher level semantic concept corresponding to a real-world occurrence and abstracted from the media it is captured in.

We now describe our work and progress related to the three tiers.

3.   EVENT EXTRACTION

Event extraction is concerned with the extraction of high level events from raw streams, we are interested in event extraction from streams of all modalities i.e., text, audio, and video. Recall that we mentioned that human generated information is a key and often major source of information during disasters. A lot of such human generated information is available in forms such as audio (for instance phone calls, radio conversations between responders or responders and victims, etc.) or text (for instance operations command whiteboards, scribed text notes, etc.). In many instances the audio information can be converted to text, via a speech recognizer, for analysis. Analysis of text, particularly the extraction of events from text is thus a prime focus of our work in event extraction. In text extraction we have developed a system and platform for semantic extraction from text which starts from extraction of information from raw reports and documents and goes all the way to high quality extracted information. In audio-visual event extraction we have developed techniques for extraction of information by exploiting simultaneous audio and video streams, a multi-microphone based approach for robust speech recognition, and also an approach to video stream fusion from multiple sources and visual event detection.

3.1   Semantic Extraction from Text

Event information is presented in text streams in many forms. At real-time for instance, we may have textual information streaming in from a scribe at the disaster making observations and notes as the situation unfolds, or we may have transcribed (audio) conversations between say first responders and operations commanders. Examples of such scribed notes and transcribed conversations are shown in Figure 24-4.

```
ST1:   Sampling team still inside.

COM1: Decon teams head out now.

RESP1: Victim 1 shifted to hospital.

RESP1: Sampling team, please provide status.

ST1:   Sampling team task completed, returning to
base.
```

Figure 24-4. Transcribed (Responder) Conversations

There are interesting events described in the example text segment in Figure 24-4, for instance we have a report of the event of the Decon teams having left, the Sampling team having completed its task, etc. Then we also have information in text reports that become available *post* the disaster. For instance a large number of online news reports, postings in blogs, and message boards become available following a disaster. From the awareness perspective we would be interested in tasks such as extraction of facts from such reports (for instance extracting all reports of donation pledges for the affected victims) for further analysis.

We are developing a next generation extraction platform, called XAR (Figure 24-5), that performs all tasks in the extraction of information and events from text, starting with raw reports or documents and providing extracted information of high quality and reliability at the end. A key feature of XAR is that the architecture provides for exploiting many "off-the-shelf" and powerful text and language processing systems and tools that have recently become available to the research community; for instance text analysis tools such as GATE [9], and semantic (natural language) parsers such as Shalmaneser [10] and the Stanford Parser [11]. The XAR system allows for building new extraction applications by specifying a 'schema' for the infor mation or event to be extracted along with any *semantic* information that can be provided about the event (such as properties about the different event attributes or 'slots'). The user may also further provide some processing rules which are essentially logical (Horn Clause based) deductive rules that state what event slot should be filled with what kind of entities. As an example one may define a schema for a donation pledge event to consist of the slots donor, and donor amount. Then we have a rule which states that for instance containing the verb "pledged", any entity in the sentence which is a country or a relief organization and which appears before the verb pledged, is a value of the donor slot. The system employs the text processors provided to first identify such significant entities in the text and also their features (such as whether it is a country, its relative position in the sentence, etc.) Then, inductive rules are used for the extraction of the detailed information in the event. Such event extraction actually involves several phases such as first classifying which documents or reports could contain the event to be extracted in the first place, then identifying sentences (or groups thereof) that contain the event or are relevant to it, finally slot values are extracted from the sentences; these phases are illustrated in Figure 24-5 below. We have designed XAR to be able to exploit the semantic information (about the event to be extracted) to the maximum extent. This serves to a) Make the extraction rules simpler and b) Handle extraction cases that cannot be handled by pure linguistic analysis.

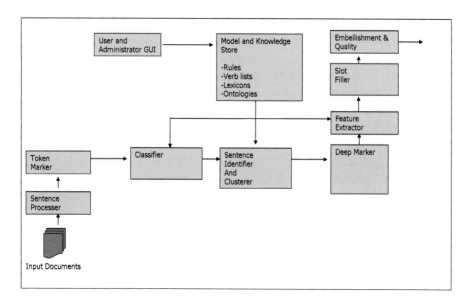

Figure 24-5. XAR Event Extraction System

Strictly speaking the above kinds of capabilities serve to extricate information i.e., extract no more than the explicitly stated information in text. This leaves us with limitations, for instance, from the text in Figure 24-4 we can (at best) extract that the location that the victim has been moved to is "the hospital" but not be able to specify which hospital. This is a problem of disambiguation. In many cases, including extraction problems, it is possible to disambiguate such extracted entities. For instance in the above example we may have further contextual information that helps us infer that "the hospital" referred to is most likely the "UCI Hospital". XAR includes the capability of improving the quality of extracted information by disambiguation. The disambiguation problem is one which we have originally investigated in the data management context, it arises because objects/entities, such as people, organizations, etc, in real world datasets are often referred to using object descriptions, e.g. person name, which might not serve as unique identifiers of those objects, leading to ambiguity. To solve this problem we have proposed a new domain-independent named-entity disambiguation framework [3,4]. The strength of the framework comes from its ability to analyze inter-object relationships, which the traditional techniques cannot do. The proposed approach views the underlying dataset as a graph of entities, represented as nodes, interconnected via relationships, represented as edges. To decide if two object representations co-refer, or refer to the same real-world entity, the approach analyzes all the relationships that exist between the two object representations by discovering all paths that exist in the graph between the two nodes corresponding to the two object representations. Therefore, the framework analyzes both: the direct relationships that exist among objects, that correspond to the direct edges among the objects, as well as indirect relationships among objects that correspond to paths of length more than one. The proposed disambiguation framework is capable of solving two common types of disambiguation challenges. These types are known under a variety of names in different research communities, we will refer to them as (fuzzy) lookup and (fuzzy) grouping. In the settings of the lookup problem the list of all possible objects in the dataset, along with their descriptions, is provided and the goal is for each reference to pinpoint the exact right object it refers to [3,4,22]. In grouping, there is no such list available and the goal is to simply correctly group references that co-refer [3]. Thus, lookup is a classification problem and grouping is a clustering problem.

To solve the lookup problem, the framework discovers the paths that exist among object and it them employs, what is called, a connection strength model to weigh those paths. The outcome of that process is a Nonlinear Programming Problem that needs to be resolved. While it can be solved using a mathematical solver software, we proposed a simple iterative methods that scales better to large problem sizes. Once the problem is solved, the outcome is interpreted to produce the desired mapping of references to objects [4,22]. The framework solves the grouping problem by also measuring the connections strength and attribute similarity among objects. It then combines those measures and employs either merging or correlation clustering algorithm to produce the desired groups of references [3].

3.2 Audio-Visual Event Extraction

This area of research focuses on developing robust technologies for extraction of information from all modalities and exploiting multimodality and contextual knowledge for the extraction of situational information. We are developing approaches for both extraction of information from independent single modality streams as well as extraction and fusion of information from multi-modal information streams about a situation. The research areas spanned by this effort on signal interpretation and analysis based on multiple modalities are Robust speech recognition, Speech enhancement, Auditory stream segregation, Audio Visual event detection and modeling, and cross integration areas like emotion detection from speech signals in enhanced QoS for emergency networks.

Speech Enhancement using multi microphone speech processing: We have developed techniques for more accurate identification and separation of audio information sources. This is done using a multi-microphone approach. We have developed a robust broadband adaptive *beamforming* algorithm (for identifying a particular audio signal source), which combines the robustness of the delay and sum (DS) beamforming in the look direction uncertainty with the high interference rejection capability of the conventional adaptive beamforming algorithm [6,7]. Such a broadband adaptive beamforming algorithm is robust to spatially spread sources. A handheld two-microphone array system has been prototyped and deployed in various RESCUE drills.

Video-based event detection for enhanced situational awareness: Work in this area is centered around *homography*, which in computer vision denotes a linear projective transformation that relates two different views of a scene [8]. This is a novel approach to track people and vehicles in crowded scenes using multiple cameras. Camera calibration is not needed in this approach to extract the world coordinates of objects. Object representation and tracking in the homography domain are independent of detailed appearances of the objects, and are an efficient and robust method for handling visual events. Semantic understanding of visual events is achieved by spatio-temporal analysis of the objects in the multiple homography representations.

4. EVENT DATA MANAGEMENT

Event data management is concerned with providing data management or "database like" capabilities for events. Our aim is to provide a data management system that treats events as first-class objects and provides storage, querying, retrieval, and indexing capabilities for the events. We are working on several issues in this regard. The first is the issue of event modeling where we have developed a semantic data model for events. Amongst the various attributes we associate with events, there is an important notion of uncertainty of information. Specifically spatial or location uncertainty is something that we have explored in depth. Below we described the work in event modeling as well as in handling spatial uncertainty in events.

4.1   Event Modeling

A semantic data model E, for events is described in [12]. There are some key notions related to events and the event centric approach to situational awareness. For instance a *report* is the fundamental information source containing event information. A report could be of any modality, for instance an (audio) phone call reporting the event, information in text reports such as text alerts or news stories, or audio-visual information from say a live TV coverage of a situation. A report is defined then as a physical atomic unit that describes one or more events. An *event* is an instance of an event type in space and time. So an instance of a bridge having collapsed is an example of an event. A situation comprises of a number of events. Events are extracted from reports. An *entity* is an object that occupies space and exists for an extended period of time. Events generally have entities, such as people, objects (such as say cars or planes), etc. associated with them. For instance a vehicle overturning event will have the particular vehicle overturned as one of the entities associated with that event. A *milieu* is the spatial, temporal or spatio-temporal context in which an event, an object or report is situated. Continuing with the bridge collapsing event example, the time and place where the incident occurred are milieus associated with the event.

Note that we have deliberately separated the notion of an event from a specific media, an event may certainly be related to a media (that it is captured in and extracted from) however the event itself is an event per se and not a "text event" or an "audio event". We now describe the spatial uncertainty work.

4.2   Spatial Awareness and Indexing

When reasoning about events and situations, *location* is a key attribute for understanding. To deal with the spatial aspects of events, we have proposed an approach to model and represent (potentially uncertain) event locations described by human reporters in the form of free text [13]. In addition, we have analyzed several types of spatial queries of interest in the context of awareness applications.

As a motivating example, consider the excerpts from two real reports filed by *Port Authority Police Department* (PAPD) Officers who participated in the events of September 11th, 2001:

"... the PAPD Mobile Command Post was located on West St. north of WTC and there was equipment being staged there ..."

"... a PAPD Command Truck parked on the west side of Broadway St. and north of Vesey St. ..."

These two reports refer to the same location of the same command post -- a point-location in the New York, Manhattan area. However, neither the reports specify the exact location of the events, nor do they mention the same street names. We would like to represent such reports in a way that it enables efficient evaluation of spatial queries and analyses. For instance, the representation must enable us to retrieve events in a given geographical region (e.g., around World Trade Center). Likewise, it should enable us to determine similarity between reports based on their spatial properties; e.g., we should be able to determine that the above reports might refer to the same location. Our goal is to represent uncertain locations specified in reports to allow for effective execution of analytical queries. Clearly, merely storing location in the database as free text is not sufficient either to answer spatial queries or to disambiguate reports based on spatial locations. For example, spatial query such as "retrieve events near WTC", based on keywords alone, can only retrieve the first report mentioned earlier. To support spatial analyses on free text reports, we need to project the spatial properties of the event described in the report onto the domain. We do so by modeling uncertain event locations as random variables that have certain probability density functions (*pdfs*) associated with them. We have developed techniques to map free text onto the corresponding pdf defined over the domain. When the exact address of the event is available, there are many ready solutions that can allow to map it into the corresponding point inside the domain. We instead focus on another relatively frequent case where people report event locations based on certain *landmarks*. Landmarks correspond to significant spatial objects such as buildings, streets, intersections, regions, cities, areas, etc. embedded in the space in which the events or situation are immersed. Spatial location of events specified in those reports can be mapped into *spatial expressions* (s-expressions) that are, in turn, composed of a set of *spatial descriptors* (s-descriptors) (such as *near*, *behind, infrontof*, etc) described relative to landmarks. Usually, the set of landmarks, the ontology of spatial descriptors, and the precise interpretations of both are domain and context dependent. Table 24-1 shows excerpts of free text referring to event locations and the corresponding spatial expressions.

Table 24-1. Examples of s-expressions

free text	s-expression
'near WTC'	near(WTC)
'on West St., north of WTC'	on(West St.) $\wedge$ north(WTC)

These expressions use WTC and West St. as landmarks. While the locations of landmarks are precise, spatial expressions are inherently uncertain: they usually do not provide enough information to identify the exact point-locations of the events. Our approach to representing uncertain locations described in free text consists of a two-step process. First, a location specified as a free-text is mapped into the corresponding s-expression, which in turn is mapped to its corresponding pdf representation. Given such a model, we have also developed techniques to represent, store and index pdfs to support spatial analysis and efficient query execution over the pdf representations [15,16]. This allows to have complex representations of (location) uncertainty but at the same time support complex queries over such representations efficiently.

5.   EVENT ANALYSIS AND VISUALIZATION

Analysis and visualization is concerned with providing intuitive and (possibly) visual analysis and querying capabilities for end users of situational information. It is reasonable to expect that end users of such systems, such as EOC managers or field commanders would finally like to see patterns and trends in the information collected and get intuitive and visual views of the information (say overlayed over maps etc.). In this regard we have developed tools such as a graph based query algebra and language over events which enables us to query and analyze events in a graphical manner. We have also developed techniques and systems in the area of predictive modeling, that we have applied to tasks such as people estimation and route prediction. We describe these below.

5.1   Semantic Graph Query and Analysis

A large collection of text reports are generated during a disaster. In its original form, this data is of limited use since the user can apply only keyword based search. Although event/entity extraction can be employed to extract events, related entities and inter-event relationships to produce a more structured data, the extracted semi-structured data still does not fit the traditional tabular representation and hence most existing exploratory and analytical tools can not be readily applied (in most cases). Our *semantic graph query and analysis* research aims at developing techniques tailored to analyzing such data.

Once events and entities, their attributes and their relationships are extracted from various textual sources, they need to be represented using a generic data model that is amenable for more sophisticated query and analysis. Semantic graphs which capture data at the lowest semantic granule provide such a common representation. The nodes in such a graph correspond to uniquely identified events, entities, their attribute values and source reports. The edges correspond to a variety of semantic relationships among the nodes. In addition to extracted data, semantic graphs are also used to represent domain knowledge in the form of taxonomies and ontologies which can be used in the query and analysis of the data. This ability of semantic graphs to symmetrically represent both extracted data and domain knowledge makes them ideal for a variety of disaster report analysis tasks. For instance, Figure 24-6 provides an illustration of the use of graphs for analyzing news reports (of a disaster). We have nodes (of different colors) representing entities such as news stories, news sources, news topics etc. and the graph edges depict relationships amongst them. The graphical representation is more intuitive and powerful for end users, for instance one can visually see correlations between news stories and sources and news topics, correlations with and over certain periods of time etc.

Below we discuss three ways in which our research is extending current technology to enable query and analysis on semantic graphs.

(1) Query Algebra: We have developed a query algebra, called *Graph Analytic Language* (GAL), which offers a number of features to enable analysis of semantic graphs including graph-aware aggregation and grouping, well-defined integration of graph and set-based operations, operators to interface with ontology inference engines as well as a variety of bulk operators [17]. These operators enable us to pose analytical queries similar in spirit to OLAP queries (for example, over events at multiple levels of composition/ resolution).

(2) Exploratory Analysis Operators: We have developed a number of exploratory analysis operators (and their implementation algorithms), that enable the identification of taxonomy concepts that best *summarize* a set of reports, or best *differentiate* or *associate* a pair of report collections, for example from two disaster incidents [17,18].

(3) Semantic Relationship Analysis: We have developed a version of the OLAP cube operator (called Multi-Relational Iceberg-Cubes) that enables the user to detect entity attribute values that characterize prominent semantic relationships among them [17].

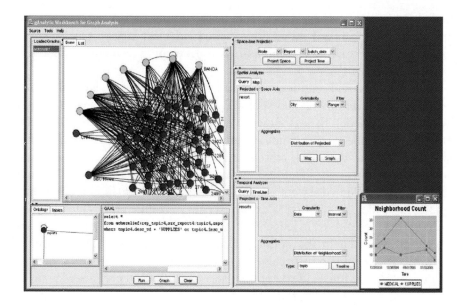

Figure 24-6. Graph Analysis of Events

5.2   Predictive Modeling

Another key aspect of analysis, particularly in disasters, is the ability to predict and estimate certain things. For instance, an estimation of the current location and number of people in a disaster area and a prediction of the future movement of those people could provide critical information to EOC (Emergency Operations Command) personnel responsible for rescue and evacuation, and also to members of the public looking for the best way to navigate to their desired destination. We are using statistical models and bayesian techniques to extract information about human behavior from a variety of "human detection" sensors such as loop sensors counting cars on a freeway, people counters at doors to buildings and GPS devices on cell-phones or cars. Our aim is to enable the creation of a "People Forecast" similar to a weather forecast that, instead of giving current weather conditions and a prediction of the weather throughout the rest of the day, gives an easily interpretable picture of the current condition of the population (such as the location and density of people in an area, indications of unusual behavior or unusual events taking place) and also a prediction of where people will be moving in the near future. We are working on two

projects, one dealing with situational analysis and estimation of current conditions and the other dealing with predicting future movement of people.
.

5.3   Situational Assessment/Current conditions

Occupancy analysis in real time is a difficult problem that has not been approached in a systematic way to our knowledge. Current approaches to large scale estimation of the number of people in a given area often use dated census information, perhaps with some simple adjustment for daytime versus nighttime predictions. No current approaches appear to use real-time measurements of human activity such as freeway traffic information given by loop sensors on highways to influence their predictions. While occupancy analysis remains a difficult problem, we have identified smaller sub-problems that also give useful information, and we have had some success in extracting interesting and useful information.

The first problem we identified is detecting unusual activity or events from sensors that measure human activity in some form such as people counters or freeway sensors.

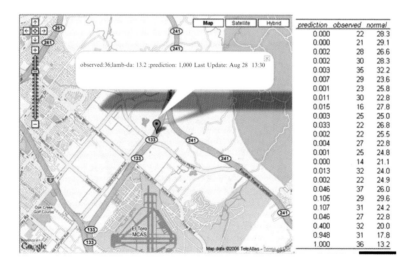

prediction	observed	normal
0.000	22	28.3
0.000	21	29.1
0.002	28	26.6
0.002	30	28.3
0.003	35	32.2
0.007	29	23.6
0.001	23	25.8
0.011	30	22.8
0.015	16	27.8
0.003	25	25.0
0.033	22	26.8
0.002	22	25.5
0.004	27	22.8
0.001	25	24.8
0.000	14	21.1
0.013	32	24.0
0.002	22	24.9
0.046	37	26.0
0.105	29	29.6
0.107	31	24.2
0.046	27	22.8
0.400	32	20.0
0.948	31	17.8
1.000	36	13.2

Figure 24-7. Anomalous Event Detection

Our algorithm learns (unsupervised) normal traffic patterns and detects "event" activity defined as short bursty periods of unusually high or low traffic in real time using a time varying Poisson process model. The output of the inference algorithm is a probability that an event is taking place at any given time, along with an estimate of the extra number of people or cars or whatever you are counting that are attributed to that event   Also, we are creating software for a real time event detection system for freeway traffic in southern California. Users will be able to log on to a website that will display a map of the area of interest that shows current event activity and a history of event activity (see screen-shot below). As an example of how this could be used in an EOC center, imagine evacuation planning during a bomb threat to downtown LA; the real-time event detection system is brought up, events at off-ramps in the past 3 hours is selected, and all off ramps near Dodgers stadium indicate the presence of an event, furthermore an extra 20,000 cars are predicted to have used those off ramps above the normal traffic; this gives a quick indication that something is going on in Dodgers stadium as well as an idea of the popularity of the event.

Our second project deals with modeling car travel activities of individuals using GPS data. In particular, we have developed a probabilistic model that answers the following questions about individuals:

1. Given the current time, where the individual is most likely to be (e.g. his home, office or traveling).
2. Given the current time, where the individual is most likely to go (e.g. pick up his kids from the day-car center, grocery shopping etc).
3. Given that the person is traveling, which route the individual is most likely to take to the destination.

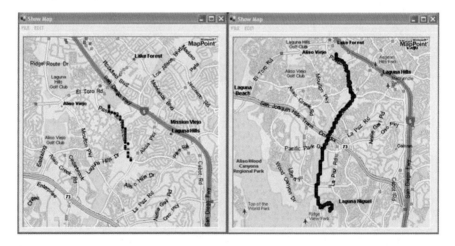

Figure 24-8. Route Prediction

Our probabilistic model [19,20,21] is accurate almost 84% of the time in predicting the most likely destination/location of a typical individual and thus could provide valuable information to first responders and transportation planners in planning evacuation. Our hope is that even if a small sample of the traveling public agreed to collect their travel data and make that data publicly available, transportation management systems could significantly improve their operational efficiency. We also envision our probabilistic model to be used in devices like "*personal traffic assistants*" that run on the mobile devices which could help travelers re-plan their travel when the routes they typically use are impacted by failures in the system arising from accidents, terrorist attacks and natural disasters such as earthquakes.

In Figure 24-8, we show a typical execution of our system. On the left is the person's current location derived from the GPS device on his car/cell-phone and on the right is the route the person is most likely to take based on his past history (predicted by our model).

6.   ARTIFACTS

In addition to research, a key aspect of all RESCUE projects, including situational awareness, is the development of representative *artifacts* that are essentially practical demonstrations of our technology capabilities, and driven by first responder needs. In situational awareness we are pursuing the development of two such artifacts at the conceptual level. One is a conception of an "information dashboard" which is essentially an integrated dashboard of processed, integrated, multi-modal information that can be used for decision making and the other is a real-time multi-modal reconnaissance system that can be employed in real-time data collection and extraction. Here we describe our work on the situational dashboard.

6.1   The Situational Dashboard

This artifact is aimed at facilitating awareness from multi-modal data and enabling end-users to apply situational information in decision-making and analysis. The situational dashboard provides integrated and fused information from multiple sources and provides analysis, querying, triaging and filtering functionality. Such a system can provide, say, an EOC with an awareness of events as they unfold. Emergency managers can use the information processed for planning, analysis and logistics tasks. For instance, information about traffic conditions and also the location of people or vehicles can be used for analysis such as evacuation and route planning. Clusters of information can be used for damage and impact assessment. It can be used to dispatch search and rescue and support logistical needs.

We are developing different actual manifestations of the dashboard concept. These include a set of disaster information portals that provide integrated online access to a variety of useful information, to both citizens as well as responders in a crisis. In conjunction with the City of Ontario, CA, we are developing a web-based portal (Figure 24-9) for dissemination of information to that community. This information includes real-time details of incidents and response, as well as the status of public infrastructure, such as roadways. During large-scale events the information to be shared can include general announcements, maps, emergency shelter information, family reunification assistance, management of donations and volunteer resources, etc. Other capabilities we have developed include the ability for users to perform searches for the whereabouts of displaced family and friends, traffic flow monitoring and identification of anomalous events, and an automated system by which local businesses and organizations can sign up to receive customized information during an incident via a number of modalities including web, phone, or SMS.

Figure 24-9. Ontario Disaster Portal Interface

The other portal instantiation is a Hurricane Portal for large scale disaster. During such disasters it can be difficult for first responders groups as well as the public to extract a good level of situational awareness from the vast amount of information which is quickly generated by media as well as individuals. The RESCUE Hurricane Portal aims to vastly improve access to information of use to these groups, especially during the first several days after a hurricane makes landfall. The initial portal is focused on developing tools to help users find pertinent data from the Web, eyewitnesses, and computer simulations, and aiding in transforming the found data into information which is actionable for the purpose of minimizing negative impact of the event to people and property. A key capability in this application is the development of multi-dimensional, *faceted* web search, analysis, and visualization capabilities which are customized to the disaster management subject domain.

We are aiming to release test versions of both these portals in the coming months, also we are taking active and regular guidance from responders and emergency response organization personnel affiliated with RESCUE in the development.

7.   CONCLUSION

We described above our work in many areas towards a situational awareness system for disaster response. From the application perspective, our interactions with the first-responder community as well as our field work with the emergency organizations have led us to identify the key challenges in situational awareness. First, sometimes the information is almost entirely missing or so uncertain that it is impossible to meaningfully ascertain the situation. This is usually the case in the immediate aftermath of the disaster. An approach to improve situational awareness in such a case is better preparedness – e.g., deploying sensing equipment that can provide an early synopsis of the damage, etc. maintaining accurate information about resources, vulnerabilities, etc. so that accurate predictions can be made even in the absence of field level data. Second, situational information often arrives across multiple modalities at different times in an uncorrelated fashion from diverse sources. While there is an avalanche of data, much of it is underutilized since there do not exist any tools that support seamless access to useful actionable information in a timely fashion. The situational awareness technologies we have described in all the tiers i.e., event extraction, event data management and event analysis are aimed at addressing exactly this problem of converting available data to actionable information. Third, much of the information is human generated (e.g., by first responders, citizen journalists, etc.). While such information has the advantage of human interpretation, it could also suffer from cognitive bias and misinterpretation by humans. Technologies to leverage such human-generated information in a robust timely manner do not exist. Furthermore, even if such tools existed, the impact of taking actions based on such information is unclear. Also such information is usually "report-centric". To make the information useful for decision making there is a need to make the information "situation-centric" through processing. The event-centric approach that we are developing to situational awareness serves to convert the report-centric information to information at the event and situation level of abstraction. Finally, information required to gain situational awareness often resides across different organizational boundaries with restrictions on their availability and policies for sharing. Tools for seamless sharing of information across information silos do not exist. We are addressing this problem as part of the policy based information sharing project described in the introduction.

The applicability of our research thus goes to the core of the advancements required for next-generation situational awareness systems in disaster response; our hope is to be able to advance the state-of-the-art in situational awareness technology as well as impact first responders in emergency organizations.

8.   ACKNOWLEDGEMENTS

We have described the work of several researchers and students working on the situational awareness technologies project in RESCUE. We wish to acknowledge these members who have made key contributions to the research as well as to the writing of this chapter. These include Rina Dechter, Ron Eguchi, Vibhav Gogate, Jon Hutchins, Charles Huyck, Yiming Ma, Sangho Park, Bhaskar Rao, Dawit Seid, Shankar Shivappa, Mohan Trivedi and Wenyi Zhang.

REFERENCES

[1]   Sharad Mehrotra, Carter Butts, Dmitri Kalashnikov, Nalini Venkatasubramanian, Ramesh Rao, Ganz Chockalingam, Ron Eguchi, Beverly Adams and Charles Huyck. Project Rescue: Challenges in Responding to the Unexpected. IS&T/SPIE 16th Annual Symposium on Electronic Imaging. January 18–22 2004, San Jose, California, USA, 2003-12.

[2]   Dmitri Kalashnikov, Dawit Seid, Yiming Ma, Naveen Ashish, Sharad Mehrotra and Nalini Venkatasubramanian. Event Based Approach to Situational Awareness. Calit2 Report, UC Irvine.

[3]   Zhaoqi Chen, Dmitri V. Kalashnikov, Sharad Mehrotra: Exploiting relationships for object consolidation. IQIS 2005: 47-58.

[4]   Dmitri V. Kalashnikov, Sharad Mehrotra, Zhaoqi Chen: Exploiting Relationships for Domain-Independent Data Cleaning. SDM 2005.

[5]   Reynold Cheng, Dmitri V. Kalashnikov, and Sunil Prabhakar. Evaluating probabilistic queries over imprecise data. In Proc. of ACM SIGMOD Int'l Conf. on Management of Data (ACM SIGMOD), June 9-12, 2003.

[6]   Wenyi Zhang and Bhaskar Rao. Robust Broadband Beamformer with Diagonally Loaded Contraint Matrix and its Application to Speech Recognition, IEEE International Conference on Acoustics, Speech, and Signal Processing, ICASSP-2006, Toulose, France.

[7]   Wenyi Zhang and Bhaskar Rao. Robust Adaptive Beamformer with Feasibility Constraint on the Steering Vector, European Signal Processing Conference, EUSPCO-2006, Italy.

[8]   S. Park, M. M. Trivedi. A Track-based Human Movement Analysis and Privacy Protection System Adaptive to Environmental Contexts. Proc. IEEE International Conference on Advanced Video and Signal based Surveillance, Sep 2005.

[9]   H. Cunningham, D. Maynard, K. Bontcheva, V. Tablan. GATE: A Framework and Graphical Development Environment for Robust NLP Tools and Applications. Proceedings of the 40th Anniversary Meeting of the Association for Computational Linguistics (ACL'02). Philadelphia, July 2002.

[10] K. Erk and S. Pado. Shalmaneser - a flexible toolbox for semantic role assignment. Proceedings of LREC-06, Genoa.

[11] Dan Klein and Christopher D. Manning. Fast Exact Inference with a Factored Model for Natural Language Parsing. In Advances in Neural Information Processing Systems 15 (NIPS 2002), December 2002.

[12] Bo Gong, Utz Westermann, Srikanth Agaram and Ramesh Jain. Event Discovery in Multimedia Reconnaissance Data Using Event Clustering. AAAI Workshop on Event Extraction and Synthesis, Boston MA, July 2006.

[13] Dmitri V. Kalashnikov, Yiming Ma, Sharad Mehrotra, Ram Hariharan, Nalini Venkatasubramanian, and Naveen Ashish. SAT: Spatial Awareness from Textual Input. In Proc. of Int'l Conf. on Extending Database Technology (EDBT), demo publication, March 26–30, 2006.

[14] S. Mehrotra, C. Butts, D. Kalashnikov, N. Venkatasubramanian, K. Altintas, et al. CAMAS: A Citizen Awareness System for Crisis Mitigation. In Proc. of ACM SIGMOD Int'l Conf. on Management of Data (ACM SIGMOD), demo publication, June 13-18, 2004.

[15] Dmitri V. Kalashnikov, Yiming Ma, Sharad Mehrotra, and Ram Hariharan. Index for Fast Retrieval of Uncertain Spatial Point Data. In Proc. of Int'l Symposium on Advances in Geographic Information Systems (ACM GIS), November 10-11, 2006.

[16] Dmitri V. Kalashnikov, Yiming Ma, Sharad Mehrotra, and Ram Hariharan. Modeling and Querying Uncertain Spatial Information for Situational Awareness Applications. In Proc. of Int'l Symposium on Advances in Geographic Information Systems (ACM GIS), November 10-11, 2006.

[17] Dawit Seid and Sharad Mehrotra. Algebraic Support and Optimization for Semantic Queries. RESCUE technical report, 2006.

[18] Dawit Yimam Seid and Sharad Mehrotra. Efficient Relationship Pattern Mining Using Multi-Relational Iceberg-Cubes. ICDM, 2004, pp. 515-518.

[19] Vibhav Gogate, Rina Dechter, Bozhena Bidyuk, Craig Rindt and James Marca. Modeling Transportation Routines using Hybrid Dynamic Mixed Networks. In Uncertainty in Artificial Intelligence 2005.

[20] Vibhav Gogate and Rina Dechter. Approximate Inference Algorithms for Hybrid Bayesian Networks with Discrete Constraints. In Uncertainty in Artificial Intelligence 2005.

[21] Vibhav Gogate, Rina Dechter, Bozhena Bidyuk, Craig Rindt, and James Marca. Model-ing Travel and Activity Routines using Hybrid Dynamic Mixed Networks. In 85th annual meeting of the Transportation Research Board, 2006.

[22] Dmitri V. Kalashnikov, Sharad Mehrotra. Domain-independent data cleaning via analysis of entity-relationship graph. ACM Transactions on Database Systems 31(2): 716-767 (2006).

ONLINE RESOURCES

- RESCUE Project, http://www.itr-rescue.org/
- Federal Emergency Management Agency (FEMA), http://www.fema.gov
- Community Emergency Response Team, Los Angeles, California, http://www.cert-la.com/index.shtml
- New York State, State Emergency Management Office (SEMO), http://www.semo.state.ny.us/
- American Red Cross, http://www.redcross.org/

QUESTIONS FOR DISCUSSION

1. What are the limitations of the relational data model for representing situations and events ?
2. How can semantics and knowledge play a role in situational information systems; in all the three SA system aspects, namely signal analysis and synthesis, situational data management, and analysis ?
3. What should be the capabilities for a next-generation data management system that can store, manage, and reason with situational information?

AUTHOR INDEX

SUBJECT INDEX

Printed in the United States of America